OXFORD HISTORY

General Editors

LORD BULLOCK AND SIR WILLIAM DEAKIN

The Shock of America

Ever since the end of the nineteenth century, America has been a force for change in the world. How Europeans have come to terms over the decades with this dynamic power in their midst, and what these terms were, is the story at the heart of this text. Masses of Europeans have been enthralled by the real or imaginary prospects coming out of the USA. Important minorities were deeply upset by them. Sometime the roles were reversed or just all shook up. But no-one could be indifferent for long. Inspiration, provocation, myth, menace, model: all these categories and more have been deployed to try to cope with the Americans. Every European conception of identity, modernity, and sovereignty has been changed by this encounter.

The Shock of America combines political, economic, and cultural themes. It demonstrates that American mass culture has always been a distinctive and incisive form of American power, provoking the most intense responses for, against, and everything in between. The plan of the narrative is based on the view that this characteristic American influence was present most conspicuously during and after Europe's three greatest upheavals of the contemporary era: the Great War, World War II, and the Cold War. The story concludes with the emotional upsurge in Europe which greeted the arrival of Barack Obama on the world scene, suggesting that in spite of all the disappointments and frictions of the years, the US might still retain its privileged place as a source of innovations for the future across the Western world.

David W. Ellwood is Senior Adjunct Professor at the Johns Hopkins University, SAIS Europe, Bologna, Italy. He was an Associate Professor at the University of Bologna, 1991–2012. The fundamental theme of his research—the function of American power in contemporary European history—has shifted over the years to emphasise cultural power, particularly that of the American cinema industry. He was President of the International Association of Media and History 1999–2004 and a Fellow of the Rothermere America Institute, Oxford, in 2006.

OXFORD HISTORY OF MODERN EUROPE

THE TRIUMPH OF THE DARK
EUROPEAN INTERNATIONAL HISTORY 1933–1939
ZARA STEINER

THE LIGHTS THAT FAILED
EUROPEAN INTERNATIONAL HISTORY 1919–1933
ZARA STEINER

IRELAND
THE POLITICS OF ENMITY 1789–2006
PAUL BEW

BULGARIA
R. J. CRAMPTON

A PEOPLE APART
A POLITICAL HISTORY OF THE JEWS
IN EUROPE 1789–1939
DAVID VITAL

THE RUSSIAN EMPIRE 1801–1917
HUGH SETON-WATSON

THE STRUGGLE FOR MASTERY IN EUROPE 1848–1918
A. J. P. TAYLOR

**THE TRANSFORMATION OF EUROPEAN
POLITICS 1763–1848**
PAUL W. SCHROEDER

THE LOW COUNTRIES 1780–1940
E. H. KOSSMANN

GERMANY 1866–1945
GORDON A. CRAIG

The Shock of America

Europe and the Challenge of the Century

DAVID W. ELLWOOD

OXFORD

UNIVERSITY PRESS

OXFORD
UNIVERSITY PRESS

Great Clarendon Street, Oxford, OX2 6DP,
United Kingdom

Oxford University Press is a department of the University of Oxford.
It furthers the University's objective of excellence in research, scholarship,
and education by publishing worldwide. Oxford is a registered trade mark of
Oxford University Press in the UK and in certain other countries

© David W. Ellwood 2012

The moral rights of the author have been asserted

First published 2012
First published in paperback 2016

Published in the United States of America by Oxford University Press
198 Madison Avenue, New York, NY 10016, United States of America

British Library Cataloguing in Publication Data
Data available

Library of Congress Cataloging in Publication Data
Data available

ISBN 978–0–19–822879–0 (Hbk.)
ISBN 978–0–19–877883–7 (Pbk.)

Contents

List of Illustrations

We have made every effort to contact all copyright holders but if in any case we have been unsuccessful, please get in touch with us directly.

Introduction

This book sets out to tell the story of America's role as a model of modernity in contemporary European history. Challenge, inspiration, provocation, menace, America has presented itself for well over a hundred years as a force for change that could never be ignored, always demanded a response. To Europeans, the society of the United States has meant many things, but among them has always been an impression of the future, or at least one powerful version of it.

By gaining a hold on Europe's imagination in this way, wittingly or otherwise, American symbols and stories, images, products, and people acquired a form of power that sooner or later penetrated every debate on the Old World's prospects. The presence in their world of so many elements from America's ways of life brought Europeans repeatedly up against the cultural dimensions of American power and the power dimensions of American culture. How they dealt with this reality, how they related it to their own debates about the way that change should work, the resources they mobilized to fashion their answers, all these processes lie at the heart of what follows.

America and the modernization of Europe? What modernization? That is the question; that is the point of a mass of struggles over ideas and propositions, policies and laws, standards and products, aspirations and expectations, which flared up repeatedly in Europe from the end of the nineteenth century, all through the twentieth and into the twenty-first. In 1924 the Anglo-American novelist Mary Borden explained why it was so necessary to keep an eye on the Americans. They should be watched, she wrote,

> ... by everyone interested in the future of mankind, for the scaffolding of the world of the future is reared against the sky of America, and a rough map of it is spread over that continent and its voice is pounding and screaming out the news of what is to come to pass on the earth.[1]

Renewed arguments about 'Americanization' across the century reflected an awareness that the ability of the Americans to project their ways of life

---

[1] See Chapter 2, n. 10.

abroad, or at the very least to render them so easily accessible, expressed powers more difficult to deal with than the variety bought by their dollars or manipulated by their national security state after World War II. On the far side of the Atlantic, creative energies were at work considerably more dynamic and appealing—especially to the broad mass of the people—than those that took Europe from crisis to crisis. What American society displayed repeatedly was its capacity to create, produce, and distribute desirable visions of progress on an unrivalled, industrial scale. This was a power potential almost wholly lacking in the Old World most of the time, and one that brought back to traditional elites their original, nineteenth-century worries about industrial and commercial capitalism, but now with a new intensity and a specific place in mind.

The pressure to adapt, adopt, or reject was felt even in the most marginal corners of the Old World. Ireland in 1940 was one such place. Yet it produced a writer, Sean O'Faolain, and a phrase that, in the simplest fashion, summed up the situation of every society when it turned to face America as embodiment of the future:

> Our problem is to find a formula of life as between the old traditions and the new world rushing into us from every side.[2]

Later commentators in Europe saw it as a place that instinctively fell back on its 'traditions', even inventing new ones if necessary, to defend its peoples from the shock of change. The Americans instead liked to present themselves as a people who felt aroused by change's energy and drama, loving to go out and invent the future, and so dominate it.[3] But the keenest European minds knew they had to find ways to bridge these two great impulses of contemporary life, to look for that form of living balance between 'tradition' and 'modernity' that would most enjoy consensus, growth, and success.

This book is one version among the many possible of the story of this search, of the choices and mediations it involved, the controversies it provoked, the self-interrogations it generated in every class, society, and generation caught up in its constraints. Because of America's supreme role in its contemporary development, creative culture in all its forms—old and new, high and low, popular and 'mass'—was the key ground where this search went on.[4] That is why culture has come to matter more over the years of

---

[2] See Chapter 6, pp. 265–6.

[3] Cf. Andreas Fickers and Jonathan Bignell, 'Conclusion', in Bignell and Fickers (eds), *A European Television History* (Oxford, 2008), 232. The example cited here is the contrast between the presentation of the new medium of television at the Paris World's Fair of 1937 and the New York version of 1939–40; see Chapter 5, pp. 207–8.

[4] Cf. Akira Iriye, *Cultural Internationalism and World Order* (Baltimore, 1997), 9–12. Like Iriye I embrace 'the generally accepted definition of culture as "structures of meaning", including "memory, ideology, emotions, life styles, scholarly and artistic works, and other

post-industrial society, and why identity politics are so common today. Force is not the only kind of power. Nothing like culture adds value—and values—to power. The key cultural power is the one that most successfully defines the content, direction, and pace of change for the rest, and so presents itself as the leading model of modernity in any given era. This was the challenge of America. As we shall see, in many ways it still is.[5]

* * *

The text is structured in three parts, a separation based on the proposition that America's influence as a decisive force for or against innovation was present most conspicuously—and so can be understood most easily—after Europe's three greatest military-political conflicts of the contemporary era: the Great War, World War II, and the Cold War. Each of them America considered a victory, each of them left Europeans reeling. All three of the phases threw up its own challenge and response pattern across the Atlantic, a motion that became ever more complex as ideas circulated, as the waves reverberated on both sides of the ocean, and as each adapted to the other's reactions. In each of the eras, American innovations—cultural, technical, economic, political—set agendas, created unmissable precedents, expressed an energizing faith in the future, redefined the dominant definitions of progress in the West. Every time, these energies caught the Europeans severely off balance, with traditional elites anxiously trying to re-establish their legitimacy and authority in the confusion. After the two World Wars, the reasons were obvious; after the end of the Cold War, the Old World had to be reunited, redefined, and relaunched in a context of 'globalization' and American triumphalism.

The Oxford English Dictionary defines the noun 'challenge' as 'an invitation to participate in a competition'. Webster's talks of 'a bold and defiant summons', provocative, inciting, arousing. The suggestion here

---

symbols"' (ibid. 3), but insist on the special role played in America's world presence by the function of its cultural, or 'creative', industries. On the concept of 'creative industries' in the American context, Frédéric Martel, *Mainstream: Enquête sur cette culture qui plaît à tout le monde* (Paris, 2010), 11, 155, 421.

[5] In days gone by, 'ideology' could also fulfil the function of legitimizing and rationalizing power, in the name of some universal vision of change, as explained by the Italian Marxist Antonio Gramsci in the 1930s; cf. Benedetto Fontana, 'Political Space and Hegemonic Power in Gramsci', *Journal of Power* (December 2010), 356. Other thinkers between the wars, perhaps influenced by Woodrow Wilson's world view, preferred to dwell on the role of 'morality', as in E. H. Carr, *The Twenty Years' Crisis, 1919–1939*, reprint of second edition of 1946, largely unaltered from original of 1939 (London, 1974), chs 7, 9, 13, 14: 'Every effective demand for change, like every other effective political force, is compounded of power and morality' (p. 209). Since the end of the Cold War, elements of ideology, morality, culture have been melded together in the concept of 'soft power', in an effort to fashion a new, user-friendly tool able to magnetize support for US foreign policy; discussion in Chapter 10, pp. 458–61.

then is that in the three post-war phases, although taking a variety of different forms, the American invitation was particularly vigorous and explicit, could not be ignored by any other society that believed in its obligation to *stay modern*, i.e. to keep up with, if not actually define, the leading standards of innovation as expressed by the most forceful people of the time.[6]

The first part of the text begins in 1898, the year of America's victory over the old European empire of Spain. This exceptional geopolitical event has been chosen as the starting point because it brings together a series of impressions then gathering in Europe about the significance of America's growth in the world, and it opens the way to a far more conscious reflection on the likely meanings for Europe's future of the new powers of the United States, in all their commercial, cultural, and political variations. The first systematic writings over the alleged transforming power of America's influences—'Americanization'—date back to this time, and the first divisions over its imagined consequences. Subsequently, in the Great War, the power of the American state was mobilized to save a part of European civilization, while the whole of the Old World discovered America's capacity to invent new ways to project its power: Woodrow Wilson and his messages were only the most prominent among them.

But it is in the first post-war period that the old European powers and their societies are obliged to make the most intense effort of reckoning around the potential meanings of America in their future. Among the supreme impulses of modernity that hit Europe after 1919—mass democracy, mass production, and mass communication—the latter two came with unmistakable American features. This was a reality profoundly upsetting to cultural authorities anxiously engaged in trying to re-establish their positions in society in the wake of the great catastrophe. Their sense of shock carried over well beyond the crash of 1929, producing a wave of

---

[6] 'The United States was often seen to be quintessentially modern', declares a 2008 American encyclopedia definition of 'modernity', i.e. the supreme inheritor and developer of European ideas of the individual, the rational, and the democratic, tireless creator of contemporary theories of 'modernization' which always referred to more or less conscious processes of economic, political, technological, and cultural innovation as lived in America; cf. entries on 'Modernity' and 'Modernization' in Peter N. Stearns (ed.), *Oxford Encyclopedia of the Modern World*, v (New York, 2008). In *Mandarins of the Future: Modernization Theory in Cold War America* (Baltimore, 2003), Nils Gilman shows how the urge to theorize modernization from the 1950s on corresponded to a need to seek confirmation at home of America's historical experience, even as it was being turned into a prescription for others. For Western influences in Asia's contemporary 'March to Modernity', Kishore Mahbubani, *The New Asia Hemisphere: The Irresistible Shift of Global Power to the East* (New York, 2008), pp. 14–23 and ch. 1 in general. For the 'set of promissory notes' of modernity that Europe has offered to the world, Björn Wittrock, 'Modernity: One, None or Many? European Origins and Modernity as a Global Condition', *Daedalus* (Winter 2000), 31–59; transnational comparisons in this special edition of *Daedalus* dedicated to 'Multiple Modernities'.

French and German denunciations. But the popular masses and the commercial spirits embraced the films, music, and dances the US sent over, as intensely as the 'cultivated minds' denounced them.

The interwar period is of course the age of the totalitarian regimes, and the account goes on to examine how each of the three most important of them engaged with the American myths, models, and practices of change of their time. The American slump confirmed the totalitarians in their predictions of the inevitable end of capitalism, and Roosevelt's New Deal had no attraction for them whatsoever. But in spite of the noisy isolationism all around him, the President and his endeavours made a great impression in the rest of Western Europe, on centre-left opinion in particular. This was especially the case when the decade of the depression ended with the great San Francisco and New York World's Fairs of 1939–40. Just when Europe was plunging into the near-death experience of Hitler's war, here was the US jubilantly proclaiming that it had already found the path to the future, a highway that was technological, private, consumerist, democratic, and vastly enjoyable.

The second part of the text demonstrates how World War II and its aftermath turned out to be the pivotal experience in Europe's exposure to the American modernizing challenge. At a time when the pre-war Europeans thought that they had begun to domesticate the transatlantic model of progress, the American governing class decided suddenly and without warning that the new outbreak in Europe was a call from destiny. To stop all this from ever happening again, defeat isolationism, and realize the nation's true potential, the United States must consciously mobilize and organize to project the nation's expanding power in all its forms throughout the globe.

Called upon a second time to save the Old World from its self-destructive tendencies, Roosevelt's Washington decided that this time round, Woodrow Wilson's vision would be made to stick. It would be reconfigured, institutionalized, propagandized within and without the US in such a way as to ensure that no one could misunderstand the universal meaning of the message, or the seriousness with which the US intended to impose its diagnosis of the cause of two world wars and three totalitarianisms, *and its cures*. The new 'superpower'—a word of 1944—believed it knew whence came Europe's impulse to plunge the world into war, dragging America in as well sooner or later, and was determined to uproot that malignancy once and for all.

But the start of the Cold War meant that new means had to be invented to project American diagnoses and resources as quickly as possible into specific situations. The Marshall Plan was one such invention. It represented at the same time the highest expression of the urge to turn

America's perceived successes into recipes for others, and an emergency weapon against the Communism that—in Washington's eyes—inevitably flourished in the post-war misery. How the Marshall Plan message expanded into the all-enabling concept of 'growth', and the political consequences of this epochal development, is analysed in Chapter 9, dedicated to the 1950s, which completes the second part of the book.

The third part of the text fast-forwards the analysis, taking it to the years that separate the end of the Cold War from the years 2008–9, the moment of the election of President Barack Obama, and the greatest financial crash since 1929. The 1990s are presented as a decade resembling in some important ways the 1920s. The 'globalization' concept expands the 'interdependence' notion of the earlier era. Great new cultural innovations emanating from America echo around the world, even as the US government and public display very little interest in the repercussions of the nation's many forms of power abroad. The technological innovations of the film and the telephone era are matched by those based on the Internet, and the myth of Hollywood morphs into that of Silicon Valley.

The all-or-nothing ideological thrust of the War and Cold War years, of a very explicitly political, State-oriented nature, is much diminished and discredited by this time. Instead there is a pressing American invitation to economic competition, based on a widespread governing-class consensus in favour of deregulation, liberalization, and the ideology of the free market. The dynamics of a globalization based on these standards soon produce critical voices, and here the historical role of Europe in supplying precedents looms large. For example, the attempts by Communist China to limit the penetration of Hollywood films in the early 2000s strikingly mirror the behaviour of conservative European governments of the 1920s and 1930s.

The 1990s paid tribute to the swelling cultural dimension of the American presence with the invention of the concept of 'soft power', a device for bringing others willingly to share American perceptions, values, and objectives, as well as all the symbols and experiences. But soft power was pushed well to the margins of official action after the attacks on the Twin Towers and Washington of 2001, and the subsequent declaration of the 'war on terror', culminating in the attack on Iraq of 2003. 'Hard' power was back with a vengeance. In reality it had never gone away.

But the backlash that the Iraq war's unwinding produced in sectors of opinion across the world—strongly reminiscent of the Vietnam War era—demonstrated that the US could ill afford to neglect the kind of legitimacy its successes as myth and model of modernity had brought it before. The explosion of hostility to whatever the US appeared to be or do in these years was generally termed 'anti-Americanism', a confusing label that blurred many a distinction. While some Americans worried over the kind of 'empire' their nation might have become, Europeans noted the continuing flow of novelties—from Google to eBay, from Wikipedia to Amazon, etc.—which kept the United States in the forefront of innovation in that marketplace where technology met the dreams of popular culture, where fantasies turned into the real thing.

The United States appeared to be on top of the world at the end of the twentieth century, and whatever the worries of the experts, the nation's general sense of optimism seemed unbounded. But the elation of the turn of the millennium was much tarnished by the end of the succeeding decade, and not only in the eyes of the Europeans. The mechanism that for so long had turned America's successes into formulas for others to grasp, backfired very badly when the combined effects of limitless credit creation and globalization exploded in the financial crisis of 2007 and after. Only when the unprecedented figure of Barack Obama succeeded in being elected to the White House did Europeans find themselves united—along with much of the rest of the world—in rediscovering how much faith they had invested over the years in American democracy's ability to reinvent itself, and so provide a resource of hope for all the West. But by this time, Europe's weight in the world looked much diminished, a direct product of the refusal of the leading European nations to contemplate a future of ever-closer partnership between them, whatever the cost.

* * * *

Because this is a *political* history of the consequences in Europe of some of America's practices of modernity, the text does not offer a detailed study in symbols, metaphors, perceptions, or discourse, all handled to great effect by other scholars. What matters is the functioning of a mass of relationships, the evolution of America's place in so many of those processes that made contemporary Europe what it is today, the endlessly shifting balance of cultural power and innovation between the two sides of the Atlantic. Sometimes it was the explicitly political novelties that caused the controversy, all the way from Woodrow Wilson via Ronald Reagan and George W. Bush Jr to Barack Obama. Often economic and technological developments forced the Europeans to think again, from Fordism and the Marshall plan down to the 'Washington Consensus' and the 'digitalize or die' message of the hi-tech boosters. Always there was stimulating and original cinema, artful music, seductive stars, experiences, messages. So the emphasis in telling this story shifts constantly, to try to reflect where the most provocative form of the challenge came from at any given time.

The building materials of the study are the works that contemporary witnesses and later thinkers have produced, in the context of each society's efforts to define its place in the great competition of modernity. These can be political or philosophical tracts, speeches, memoirs, newspaper articles, novels, films, television programmes, photographs, cartoons. There is official documentation from the public realm, semi-official material from protagonists or experts, and a mass of private, individual productions from every nation, class, generation, and gender. Widely used are the academic studies of each period, and of course those that have come later. Many an obscure collection of essays finds a new meaning in life here.

Over the last twenty-five years or so a rich transatlantic debate has sprung up among historians and social scientists around the issues dealt with in these pages. In particular the terrible twins 'Americanization' and 'anti-Americanism' have been repeatedly deconstructed and reconstructed, as concepts, discourse, and historical phenomena, as well as deathless sources of political controversy. Classic studies have illuminated key aspects of the interdependence of America and Europe in their experience of modernization. Over decades, Rob Kroes's work has illuminated the 'rules of transformation' which have governed on the one hand America's ruthless, demystifying manipulation of its European cultural heritage, and on the other contemporary Europe's terms of reconciliation with some of the results. Richard Pells—in *Not Like Us: How Europeans have loved, hated and transformed American culture since World War II* (1997)— has set out to explain to his fellow Americans why the output of their cultural industries has provoked over time such a variety of strong reactions across Europe.

Three key studies have shown the American challenge at work in specific settings. In *Coca-Colonization and the Cold War* (1994), Reinhold Wagnleitner explains how the Austrian experience of liberation and occupation after World War II offers a prism through which the emergence of an American will to ideological power emerged, and was applied to an unprecedented task of nation-building. Richard Kuisel's *Seducing the French: The Dilemma of Americanization* (1993) and his *The French Way: How France Embraced and Rejected American Values and Power* (2012) are indispensable keys to understanding why France has for long been the nation carrying on the most intense and wide-ranging debates over American power in all its forms. With an ideological form of self-identification second in strength only to the American version, suggests Kuisel, it was perhaps inevitable that from France would come the most distinguished book anywhere on 'anti-Americanism', Philippe Roger's *L'ennemi américain: Généalogie de l'anti-americanisme français* (2002). For Germany, Volker Berghahn has been tireless in explaining the function of America in the consolidation of that artificial nation's sense of itself, and was among the first to suggest that Europeans tried to take over from America's models just what was useful to them and nothing more.[7] Offering a truly transatlantic perspective, Victoria de Grazia's work has contributed much to our understanding of the force of certain key American cultural models, nowhere more than in her monumental *Irresistible Empire: America's Advance through Twentieth-Century Europe* (2005), a text that marries contemporary work on the rise of consumerism in the West to the long-running debates on the alleged 'Americanization' of Western Europe since the start of the twentieth century. Like so many of these discussions, de Grazia concludes by showing just how effective Europeans of all generations and genders have been in 'selectively appropriating' (Rob Kroes) whatever it was that the United States cared to send over.

The intention in this book is to offer a different, broader perspective; one that tells of a contest between civilizations, a competition in cultural power that often took on very explicit political and economic forms, and ended by becoming a lasting, character-forming element of every nation's experience of modernity. The evidence presented here suggests that the result has been to reinforce the ancient cultural divisions that have kept the Europeans apart, encouraging them to 'cling to their idiosyncrasies', as Stanley Hoffmann put it, even as so many features of their outward circumstances and systems of living seemed to converge.[8] The great split in Europe over attitudes to the Iraq war of 2003 was one of those moments that revealed deep differences over the meaning of each nation's legacy of its dealings with 'America' in all its forms. The contrast between French and British lines of thought and action on that occasion was so strong as to suggest that the heritage of emotion and experience of America that divides them is far more powerful than any transitory arrangement they might make to share life in the EU, the UN, the IMF, or anywhere else. The pages that follow explain why this is so.

In reality of course, American power in all its manifestations has usually interacted with the processes of change happening on the ground in Europe (as elsewhere), in a completely disorderly manner, one that often created friction and 'anti-Americanism'. Everywhere, says an Italian commentator, local protagonists of adaptation adjusted as best they could 'to opportuni-

---

[7] Cf. Berghahn, 'Conceptualizing the American Impact on Germany: West German Society and the Problem of Americanization', paper presented at the German Historical Institute conference at Washington DC (March 1999), <http://www.ghi-dc.org/conpot-web/westernpapers/berghahn.pdf>, still accessible from the Wayback Machine Web archive: <http://wayback.archive.org>.

[8] In 1964 Hoffmann wrote: 'the more European societies become alike in their social structures and economic makeup, the more each national society seems to heighten its idiosyncrasies', in Hoffmann, *The European Sisyphus: Essays on Europe 1964–1994* (Boulder, Colo., 1995), 18.

ties and difficulties flowing out of technological changes that were not solely or uniquely American, and would probably have taken place—albeit with different shape and timing—even without US influence'.[9] Meanwhile every group, generation, locality, productive, or cultural sector set out to negotiate its own accommodation with whatever America was offering, just as they did with all the other sources of innovation in any given era. But choose they must, with whatever cultural will and resources they could muster, *if* they wished to stay in the race to be up-to-date, set in motion by the leading power of the twentieth century.[10]

We start at the turn of the nineteenth into the twentieth century, years that were much more tumultuous than ours, full of wars, racism, and imperial clashes. But as an era that still fervently believed in the dominant notions of progress of the day, it was also more energetic and bright, full of anticipations and promise. Were the winds blowing in from the Atlantic responsible for stimulating European appetites for the future at the end of the old century? Or would the civilizing missions that the great colonial empires proclaimed still hold sway? What follows then is the story of a special sort of power confrontation: not over whose armies or industries would best define the West's road forward into the world of the new century, but whose hopes and expectations, narratives, symbols, and ideas.

Note on the Second Edition: I have taken advantage of this new edition to correct errors and text defects in the original, as well as to add a list of new books (in English) which take the arguments on and provide new evidence. Key films discussed in the text are now indexed. I am grateful to all the reviewers who greeted the first edition so warmly, and to the History team at Oxford University Press for suggesting this new version. They brought it to fruition with their usual expertise and friendliness.

Turin
December 2015

---

[9] See Chapter 11, n. 18.

[10] The discussion concentrates on the experiences of France, Britain, Germany, and Italy. Another perspective would be acquired if this rather narrow notion of 'Europe' was expanded to embrace the lands of the former Habsburg, Ottoman, and Soviet empires, not to mention nations on the edge: Greece, Portugal, Spain, et al. Certain big stories have escaped the net. Feminism, environmentalism, and the politics of technology are the most obvious cases. Women's history in particular still awaits the chronicler who will explain the functioning of so many American inspirations and precedents in what happened here in Europe (and elsewhere in the world). The worlds of business, sport, science, applied arts such as architecture, the communications media, all have a politics of modernization in them, which means some form of American challenge sooner or later.

PART I

1898–1941

Prologue

The Historical Setting at the Beginning: America and Europe in the 1890s

'It is both a glorious and a frightening time': the phrase was written to characterize the 1990s in the West;[1] it could just as easily have been written about the 1890s. 'Imperialism in the air', said a leading London intellectual Beatrice Webb, commenting on Queen Victoria's great jubilee celebrations of 1897; 'all classes drunk with sightseeing and hysterical loyalty.'[2] In February 1898 *The Economist* newspaper wrote: 'The European world is in an unusual and most aggressive temper.'[3] In July *The War of the Worlds* appeared, a futuristic invasion fantasy written with scientific accuracy by the young Herbert George Wells. It was a best-seller of the decade, destined to echo through all the three phases of this study.[4]

There was plenty to excite war fever in that year 1898, in Britain as well as in 'Europe'. To assert Imperial control over the headwaters of the Nile, Lord Kitchener's army massacred 11,000 Muslims in southern Sudan with a first generation of machine guns. It faced down the French at Fashoda, in the same area. These were two truly war-like moments. In southern Africa the British plenipotentiary, Lord Milner, was manoeuvring hard to create another at the expense of the Afrikaans residents of the Transvaal; his efforts would be rewarded with the start of the Boer War in the following year. Her Majesty's army in India meanwhile was

---

[1] See Chapter 10, n. 136.
[2] Cit. in James Joll, *Europe Since 1870: An International History* (London, 1976), 84.
[3] Edition of 26 February 1898.
[4] Germany was thought to be the force invading Britain in some readings of Wells's sources. Wells's son notes his father's reflections on the fate of native peoples exposed to European violence in these years in places such as Tasmania, the Congo, and southern Africa; cf. David C. Smith, *H. G. Wells: Desperately Mortal: A Biography* (New Haven, Conn., 1986), 64–7; Anthony West, *H. G. Wells: Aspects of a Life* (London, 1984), 233. The novel was recast as a radio show in 1936—notoriously staged and read by Orson Welles—as a Hollywood product in 1952, and again as a film in Stephen Spielberg's production of 2005.

contemplating a fresh push into Afghanistan, in the endless confrontation with Russia over central Asia and India's frontiers. Battling for influence and markets in China, the British stole a march on the other European powers, as well as on Japan and the US, by taking out a 100-year lease on Hong Kong. Looking back in 1905 the Liberal Foreign Secretary of the world's greatest power told President Theodore Roosevelt:

> Before the Boer war (1899–1902), we were spoiling for a fight. We were ready to fight France about Siam, Germany about the Kruger telegram (the Kaiser's pro-Boer intervention in Britain's troubles in south Africa), and Russia about anything. Any government here, during the last ten years of the last century, could have had war by lifting a finger. The people would have shouted for it. They had a craving for excitement and a rush of blood to the head.[5]

There were large portions of the German nation who apparently felt the same. The Kruger telegram had been 'written from the soul of the German people', said a liberal newspaper. In 1898 Bismarck died, but not before leaving for posterity his judgement that the decisive factor in contemporary history was 'the fact that the North Americans speak English'. In spite of his reputation as the 'Iron Chancellor', this was as clear an illustration of the 'soft power' principle at work in international affairs as might be imagined.[6]

Notoriously, Bismarck's successors preferred the hard version. The German parliament passed the first of its laws providing for a new battle fleet in 1898. About the same time one of Bismarck's successors as Chancellor told the impetuous and truculent new Kaiser that he might become the '*arbiter mundi*': arbiter of the world's destiny. In the name of *Weltpolitik*—a global political strategy based on Darwinian fantasies— this new Germany was pushing into China and reaching out to the Ottoman Empire in 1898. It had already provoked a quite new diplomatic understanding between France and Russia, and—'oblivious to the impact of [its] policies' (Henry Kissinger)—set in motion a revolution in British foreign policy. After eighty years, antagonist number one in the inevitable war of the future might not after all be the Russia of the Tsars. Instead it began to look more and more like Wilhelmine Germany.[7]

---

[5] Cit. in Bernard Porter, *The Lion's Share: A Short History of British Imperialism, 1850–1970* (London, 1975), 128; full contextualization ibid. ch. 4.

[6] Kruger telegram remark cit. in Henry Kissinger, *Diplomacy* (London, 1994), 185; Bismarck cit. in Kathleen Burk, *Old World, New World: The Story of Britain and America* (London, 2007), 380.

[7] A. J. P. Taylor, *The Struggle for Mastery in Europe, 1848–1918* (1954 edn repr., Oxford, 1977), 365–6, 372–3; Kissinger, *Diplomacy*, 184–6; Paul Kennedy, 'British and German Reactions to the Rise of American Power', in R. J. Bullen et al. (eds), *Ideas into Politics: Aspects of European History, 1880–1950* (Exeter, 1984), 19–21.

The list of imagined British enemies did not include America, and yet for a while in the mid- 1890s warlike feelings could be seen on all sides in that boiling nation, sentiments of violent hostility directed against the young Republic's most traditional enemy—Great Britain. The spasm was provoked by a dispute over frontiers in an obscure corner of Latin America, the border between Venezuela and British Guyana. But the eruptions and posturing it provoked reflected the new sense of national strength pervading the American people, and the will to turn it into defiance. A republic whose final shape had only come into focus over the previous thirty-five years, 'without purpose or plan' in the world up to this point, discovered now that its Western frontier expansion was over. So it sought 'fresh outlets for [its] expansionist energies', with economic, strategic, and psychological impulses all mixed up.[8] The US government took up the Venezuelan cause in the name of the Monroe Doctrine, and stimulated by a violent popular and press wave of Anglophobia, forced the mighty British government to submit to arbitration. 'It was truly a turning point', writes Katherine Burk. With far greater problems to handle in Europe and her empire, the British decided that conciliation must henceforth be the central theme of their policy towards the swelling United States.[9]

The Americans had already begun building a modern steel-and-steam navy at the time, and they had also produced a wide-ranging geopolitical doctrine to go with it in the shape of Captain Mahan's *The Influence of Sea-Power upon History, 1660–1783*, of 1890, influential itself far beyond the bounds of the United States: for example, it fed into the German decision in favour of a new naval force.[10] Meanwhile, in 1892–3, the representatives of the powers at Washington had been raised from legation to Embassy status; Congress was about to do the same to the nation's delegations abroad.

These early years of the nineties decade saw severe economic depression in America, but once through them the economy started to grow again with extraordinary speed. 'The United States seemed to have *all* the economic advantages which some of the other powers possessed *in part*, but *none* of their disadvantages', judges Paul Kennedy. '...In industry *and* agriculture *and* communications there was both efficiency and size.'[11]

    [8] Maldwyn A. Jones, *The Limits of Liberty: American History, 1607–1980* (Oxford, 1983), 397.
    [9] Burk, *Old World, New World*, 410–11.
    [10] Great influence in England described in R. H. Heindel, *The American Impact on Great Britain, 1898–1914* (1940 edn repr., New York, 1968), 117–19.
    [11] Paul Kennedy, *The Rise and Fall of the Great Powers: Economic Change and Military Conflict, 1500 to 2000* (New York, 1987), 243 (emphases in original).

Business began to fret over outlets for its ever-expanding industrial and agricultural production. Export markets had to be found for 70 per cent of the cotton crop, 40 per cent of the wheat, 50 per cent of copper production, 15 per cent of iron and steel.[12] Faced with the threat of a trade war with Germany (in particular), instinctive protectionist impulses found themselves obliged to move towards managed trade deals with foreign nations. 'Diplomacy is the management of international business', a Republican leader was quoted as saying in 1897. In such a context, President McKinley's priority was clear. His 'greatest ambition', he declared, 'was to round out his career by gaining supremacy in world markets'.[13]

In spite of waves of unemployment that provoked riots, strikes, and a mass march on Washington in 1894, the immigrants flooded in: 3.7 million in the course of the decade. The overall population grew by 13.3 million. Over four thousand of them were millionaires, including the famous tycoons—Morgan, Rockefeller, Vanderbilt, Carnegie, Harriman, and others. Their giant operations and mergers, the outrageous world of the 'yellow press' with its emphasis on speed and scandal, the thrusting commercial interests pushing for the 'Open Door' in China, all contributed to the optimism and confidence that ushered out the old century. At the same time, technological progress meant that 'an endless stream of exciting discoveries offered concrete evidence of the abundant life ahead', as a witness of the time recalled. The first motor car built for sale was brought forth in 1898.[14] A Senator called Chauncey Depew would proclaim:

> There is not a man here who does not feel 400 per cent bigger in 1900 than he did in 1896, bigger intellectually, bigger hopefully, bigger patriotically, bigger in the breast from the fact that he is a citizen of a country that has become a world power for peace, for civilization and for the expansion of its industries and the products of its labor.[15]

Even such a traditional great aristocrat as the British Prime Minister Lord Salisbury was starting to think—in 1895—that the world would soon be divided between 'living' and 'dying' powers, reflecting the growing waves of thinking that saw the nation as a living organism, all deriving from the vulgarization of Charles Darwin's lessons of these years.[16] What today would be called racism was not just fashionable, it was bidding to become a leading ideology of the future, turbo-charging the nationalism of the era by supply-

---

[12] Cited in Walter LaFeber, Richard Plenberg, and Nancy Woloch, *The American Century: A History of the United States Since the 1890s* (6th edn, Armonk, NY, 2008), 23.
[13] Ibid.; McKinley cit. in Lloyd C. Gardner, *Imperial America: American Foreign Policy since 1898* (New York, 1976), 25.
[14] Walter Lord, *The Good Years: From 1900 to the First World War* (New York, 1960), 4.
[15] Ibid. 1.
[16] Kennedy, *Rise and Fall*, 195; Jones, *Limits of Liberty*, 307, 308.

ing imperialism with the force of popular sentiment. 'Imperialist fervour reached a peak in 1898', writes Robert Gildea.[17] The Germans, French, and Italians all spurred the race for colonies in these years, but the Americans too wanted their place in the world to get bigger. As well as the former Spanish empire, Hawaii was annexed in 1898. The commentator James Bates Clark said: 'A certain manly quality in our people gives assurance that we have the personal material out of which a millennium will grow.'[18]

But the man who turned a 'civilizational' view of the world's competitions into an American policy principle was the vigorous Assistant Secretary of the Navy, Theodore A. Roosevelt. 1898 would be his kind of year, the Cuban war of that year his kind of war. When he entered the White House in 1901, he would become 'the first modern president in foreign affairs', says Frank Nincovich, 'because he was the first to deal with the implications of modernity'. Roosevelt himself had this to say: 'We are all peering into the future to try to forecast the action of the great dumb forces set in motion by the stupendous industrial revolution which has taken place in this century.'[19]

Great dumb forces? With organized populism on the march in America, and socialisms, suffrage movements, and trade unions of every hue rising all over Europe? With the rights of women on national political agendas everywhere? With local nationalisms spreading from the Hapsburg and German empires to Spain, from Brittany to Ireland? With anarchists in the grip of a revolutionary theory of violence that drove them to assassinate heads of government and state, including—in 1898—the Empress of Austria? If ever there was a time when the masses stepped on to the stage of history, as left-wing visionaries of all sorts liked to declare ever after, the 1890s were that time.

The established authorities and their spokesmen took fright. In 1892 the French philosopher Gustave Le Bon had published *The Crowd*, inaugurating a long wave of denunciations of the danger of 'the masses', seen to be in the grip of uncontrollable, infantile emotions, impervious to reason and wholly destructive. Would this mob be the inheritors of the democratizing trend of the era?[20] Even such a deeply conservative force as

---

[17] R. Gildea, *Barriers and Borders: Europe 1800–1914* (2nd edn, London, 1996), 340.

[18] Lord, *Good Years*, 5.

[19] F. Nincovich, *Modernity and Power: A History of the Domino Theory in the Twentieth Century* (Chicago, 1994), 2. What these implications were, and how Roosevelt dealt with them, is treated in Chapter 1.

[20] Gustave Le Bon's *The Crowd: A Study of the Popular Mind* (original French edn, Paris, 1892; London, 1896) had made a great impression with its depictions of a new, frightening kind of mentality in which all individuality was submerged by the emotions of the mass. The study was based on Le Bon's experiences during the revolutionary upheaval of the Paris Commune of 1870–1.

the Vatican could see that movement was all around. In a famed encyclical of 1890 on 'Capital and Labour', the Pope and his Cardinals had written in their opening paragraph of the 'spirit of revolutionary change' sweeping through all the mechanisms of industrial society:

> The elements of the conflict now raging are unmistakable, in the vast expansion of industrial pursuits and the marvellous discoveries of science; in the changed relations between masters and workmen; in the enormous fortunes of some few individuals, and the utter poverty of the masses; the increased self reliance and closer mutual combination of the working classes; as also, finally, in the prevailing moral degeneracy. The momentous gravity of the state of things now obtaining fills every mind with painful apprehension...[21]

The remedies, said the encyclical, were to be found in the Church, its gospels and Christian morality, and, of course, in the principle of private property. But the relatively weak impact of these propositions meant that by 1898 the Church would be thoroughly embroiled in what was called its 'Americanist Controversy'. This swelled up after an American Archbishop told the Curia, in a most outspoken manner, that only in America would 'the Church' and 'the age' be able to solve 'the problem of their reconciliation'.[22] What happened next is described in Chapter 1.

Meanwhile, many of those unwilling to trust Rome's sources of consolation attacked the very idea of modernity, filling the 1890s atmosphere with a lamentful *fin de siècle* refrain which long echoed in Europe. *Modernism*, said the Parisian critic René Doumic, was simply the all-conquering 'mania for modernity' of the age, saturating the air, 'our readings and our conversations...it's in fashion and the shape of hats'. Its greatest threat was to the freedom of the individual spirit, and 'the matrix of ourselves'. The only way it could be engaged and dominated was with tradition: 'that's what tradition is for.' It was the 'basic pre-condition for any sort of broadness of view and independence of judgment'.[23] And where inherited, familiar traditions were not up to the job, new ones might be invented. At no time was this mechanism more over-worked than at the end of the nineteenth century, says Eric Hobsbawm, as the old hierarchies

---

[21] Cit. in Joll, *Europe Since 1870*, 47; full text of encyclical *Rerum Novarum* at: <http://www.vatican.va/holy_father/leo_xiii/encyclicals/documents/hf_l-xiii_enc_15051891_rerum-novarum_en.html>.

[22] William R. Hutchinson, 'American Dreams and European Responses, from the 1840s to the 1920s', in Norbert Finzsch and Herman Wellenreuther (eds), *Visions of the Future in Germany and America* (Oxford, 2001), 49–68, cits at p. 54.

[23] R. Dounic, 'La Manie de la Modernité', in *Revue des Deux Mondes* (1 March 1898), 205–9.

of custom and order faced all the changes mass politics brought, or threatened to bring.[24] The appeal to traditions real and imagined was a secular article of faith that would reappear in some form or other in every decade of Europe's American century.

Reflections of the defensive sort from writers and critics opened up yet another enduring pattern of contrasts across all the leading societies of the age, since the gloom of the intellectuals was not matched by the daily experience of the classes blessed with the wealth and the health to appreciate all the technical novelties of the 1890s. The cinema, the radio, x-rays, and the electron were all invented or discovered in Europe in these years. And each of them depended on the great force destined to supersede the grimy age of coal and steam: *electricity*. Where the mature potential of the electrical current was shown off most effectively was at the massive international expositions held in Europe and America in these years—vast outpourings of energy and confidence in the future, and at the same time 'promissory notes' of modernity and identity which every level of society could understand.[25] Paris's fair of 1889 enjoyed attendances of over 28 million, Chicago in 1893 played host to more than 27 million, in 1900 50 million bought tickets for the Universal Exposition, once more in the capital of France.

The 1889 show in Paris had featured the extraordinary Eiffel Tower, built for the occasion and illuminated all the way to the top. In Chicago Westinghouse's incandescent lighting system lit up the whole great fairground, while General Electric offered the Edison Tower of Light 'a seventy-eight foot shaft glowing with thousands of colored flashing lights'.[26] In 1900 the greatest pavilion at the Universal Exposition in Paris would be the one dedicated to electricity, where the victory of light over darkness, of science over ignorance, and progress over misery and disease would be officially hailed in the name of the 'victorious march of the human spirit'.[27]

While supposedly evoking great, formative events from the past—Paris in 1889 was held on the anniversary of the Revolution of 100 years before, the Chicago event dedicated to Columbus's 'discovery' of America—here

---

[24] Eric Hobsbawm, 'Introduction', in Hobsbawm and Terence Ranger (eds), *The Invention of Tradition* (1984 edn repr., 2007), 4; cf. Hobsbawm, 'Mass-producing traditions: Europe, 1870–1914', ibid. 263–307.

[25] On the concept of promissory notes, Wittrock, *Modernity: One, None or Many?*, 37–8; cf. Introduction, n. 6.

[26] Emily Rosenberg, *Spreading the American Dream: American Economic and Cultural Expansion, 1890–1945* (New York, 1982), 5.

[27] Emilio Gentile, '1900: Inizio secolo', in Gentile et al. (eds), *Novecento italiano* (Rome, 2008), 4–6; phrase from ministerial inaugural speech. Filmed glimpses of the Paris exposition at: <http://www.youtube.com/watch?v=KQxTzKQ1R5A>.

were visions of worlds to come, placed in open competition with each other. It was the 'continuation of war by other means', writes Wolfram Kaiser.[28] Not just technology and industry, but civilizations were put on display in great games of symbolism, anticipating the age of ideology. The British had projected their conceptions of free trade at the Crystal Palace in 1851, now the Americans and the French competed in Republicanism, Universalism, and Science. The Paris events expressed the power of the organizing State; Chicago's were put on by big business and expected to make money. All of them celebrated the nation as a form of progressive utopia. The Pledge of Allegiance came out of the Chicago commemoration, amidst a blizzard of organized flag-waving. Here was the invention of tradition on the grandest of scales. The traveller and diarist Henry Adams claimed that the fair offered 'the first expression of American thought as a unity'.[29]

Enlightenment and entertainment, culture and commerce, all fought each other for the attention of the masses in Paris and Chicago, masses that were imagined to be white, flourishing and family oriented, even as women's rights and trade union movements asserted their claims with their own stands.[30] But the fairs were equally important for attracting and impressing foreign powers. A French writer commenting on the Columbian spectacle said: 'Chicago, the enormous town we see expanding, the gigantic plant which grows before our eyes seems now in this wonderful new country to be in advance of the age. But is this not more or less true of all America?' Chicago celebrated 'the international launch of America', writes Jon Savage, meaning 'its industry, its culture and its perception as a way of life to rival Europe'.[31]

Japan, soon to be at war with China and to annex Taiwan, appeared at Chicago and talked officially about its 'formal introduction to the West'. 'Immobility is death', the Japanese emperor is supposed to have said, endorsing his nation's outward turn and openness to Western-style modernity,

---

[28] W. Kaiser, 'The Great Derby Race: Strategies of Cultural Representation at Nineteenth-Century World Exhibitions', in Jessica C. E. Gienow-Hecht and Frank Schumacher (eds), *Culture and International History* (New York, 2003), 47.

[29] The birth of the Pledge and its relation to the Chicago event are explained in Robert W. Rydell and Rob Kroes, *Buffalo Bill in Bologna: The Americanization of the World, 1869–1922* (Chicago, 2005), 55–63; Adams cit. in Jon Savage, *Teenage: The Creation of Youth Culture* (London, 2007), 50.

[30] Kaiser, 'Great Derby Race', 46, Rydell and Kroes, *Buffalo Bill in Bologna*, 64–5; Rydell and Kroes make clear that African-American attempts to do the same were very badly treated, though not as badly as the non-white peoples involved in the various 'ethnographic' displays.

[31] Cit. in Rosenberg, *Spreading the American Dream*, 3; full discussion of Chicago show in Robert W. Rydell, *All the World's a Fair: Visions of Empire at American International Expositions, 1876–1916* (Chicago, 1984), ch. 2; Savage, *Teenage*, 50.

and, implicitly, his contempt for China's feeble backwardness.[32] Movement, improvement, and progress, these were the great dogmas of the era, feeding the popular and commercial upswell of enthusiasm on both sides of the Atlantic for the turn of the century: 'The adjective "new" was everywhere', says Emilio Gentile, 'in the arts, in literature, in science, technology and medicine, in fashion. New means modern, modernity is novelty and the new sense of life and the world.' After its remarkable victory over the old Catholic empire of Spain in 1898, to Europeans nothing in the world looked newer than the United States of America, to Americans nothing looked *younger*.[33]

---

[32] Japan's rise described in Philip D. Curtin, *The World and the West: The European Challenge and the Overseas Response in the Age of Empire* (Cambridge, 2002), 161–72; cf. Kaiser, 'Great Derby Race', 47, 48.

[33] Gentile, '1900: Inizio il secolo', 7; on birth of American cult of national youthfulness at this time, Savage, *Teenage*, pp. xv, 70–3. In a well-known jibe, Oscar Wilde asserted that this was their oldest tradition.

1

How the American Century Started

1898: A 'TURNING POINT IN THE WORLD'S EVOLUTION'

Is it right to begin with George Bernard Shaw? This is the stage direction that the great revolutionist offered to introduce a principal character in his 1899 production, *Captain Brassbound's Conversion*:

> Captain Hamlin Kearney is a robustly built western American, with the keen, squeezed wind-swept eyes and obstinately enduring mouth of his profession. A curious ethnological specimen, with all the nations of the old world at war in his veins, he is developing artificially in the direction of sleekness and culture under the restraints of an overwhelming dread of European criticism, and climatically in the direction of the indigenous north American, who is already in possession of his hair, his cheek-bones, and the manlier instincts in him which the sea has rescued from civilization. The world, pondering on the great part of its own future which is in his hands, contemplates him with wonder as to what the devil he will evolve into in another century or two... [1]

It was appropriate that Shaw should participate in this fashion in the great debate on America's future in the world sparked off by the remarkable United States victory over the Spanish Empire in the previous year. As a great debunker of the general assumption in his country of adoption that Britain ruled the world—quite rightly, with its navies and its principles— he of all people could appreciate the many ironies latent in the American discovery of imperialism. Captain Kearney discovers that the US Navy's new reputation strikes fear into Moroccan sultans, but wavers before the intrigues of a clever lady from Britain's old ruling class. [2]

---

[1] Bodley Head edition (London, 1971), 393; in *Man and Superman* of 1904, Shaw presented an even longer and more heavily ironic sketch of an American character he had created, Hector Malone.

[2] Captain Kearney's ship the 'Santiago', named after the great American naval victory of the previous year, so presumably new, is equipped with the most modern machine guns. These serve to deliver an aristocratic British couple from the clutches of a Moorish chieftain, and then dignify the Captain's role as peace-broker in an imperial family quarrel. This aspect of the play is neglected by Shaw's biographers, e.g. Michael Holroyd, *Bernard Shaw*, ii: *1898–1918* (London, 1991), 31.

In the name of this class, over-stretched and perhaps a little tired, Rudyard Kipling joined his welcome of the imperial turn in American history with a warning. In 1891 he had journeyed through the US, met an American he would marry, and added his words to the immense pile of traveller's tales left by the closing century. He had written of the good sense of the (Asian) Indian way of life when compared to the 'grotesque ferocity' he found in Chicago, and thought the republic defenceless and complacent. But in commenting on the war, he felt that with their new protectorates in the Caribbean and the Pacific, the Americans had arrived at a further stage of maturity, one in which they might begin to do their bit in sharing 'the white man's burden'.[3] *Noblesse* had begun to *oblige*, everyone agreed. As a French observer put it: '[America's] strength gives it a right, that right becomes a claim, and that claim turns into a duty to have a say in all questions that until recently were resolved by agreements among European powers alone.'[4]

In Britain there was widespread excitement at the prospect opened up by the Spanish war. The episode 'acted as a cathartic for race sentiment', judged the American historian R. H. Heindel forty years later in his great survey of 'The American Impact on Great Britain' in those years; 'the weary Titan contemplated a new ally.'[5] Enthusiastic journalists asked, 'Why Not a British Celebration of the Fourth of July?', and that year the Lord Mayor's Day procession in London featured a float illustrating the theme that 'Blood is Thicker than Water'.[6] The Prime Minister Salisbury noted that this was 'the first year in which the mighty force of the American Republic has been introduced among the nations whose instruments, to a certain extent, are war...'.[7] Leading French observers too thought

---

[3] R. Kipling, *American Notes* (1st edn, 1891; 1899 edn repr., New York, 1974), 102, 126; on 'The White Man's Burden', Denis Judd, 'Diamonds are Forever? Kipling's Imperialism', *History Today* (June 1997).

[4] The French political scientist Emile Boutmy cit. in Jacques Portes, *Fascinations and Misgivings: The United States in French Opinion, 1870–1914* (Cambridge, 2000), 404.

[5] Heindel, *American Impact on Great Britain*, 51; Heindel's vivid fresco of every variety of American personality, idea, product, debate present in British life in the years of its title was based on 17,000 miles of travel in Britain, talks with thousands of British citizens, including over 800 formal, high-level interviews, and contacts with a vast range of relevant official organizations on both sides of the Atlantic. It remains unique.

[6] Journalist W. T. Stead cited in Murney Gerlach, *British Liberalism and the United States: Political and Social Thought in the Late Victorian Age* (Basingstoke, 2000), 246; float and Salisbury cit. in Heindel, *American Impact on Great Britain*, 74, who provided a full survey of Press and official reaction to American policy in the war; ibid. ch. 4.

[7] The US Ambassador to London noted that at the closing ceremony of the British army's manoeuvres on Salisbury Plain in September, the United States flag was the only foreign one present along with those of the British state; *Foreign Relations of the United States, 1898* (Washington DC, 1901), 380.

that 'the prestige of victory' was 'an indispensable precondition for her industrial and commercial expansion'.[8]

Elsewhere in Europe other sentiments prevailed. By the time the Spanish–American war came round it had already become fashionable in certain European chancelleries and press circles to speak of an 'American peril'. The earliest German survey of relations between the Second Reich and the US, published in 1935, presents a former foreign minister of France who was reported to have asked: 'Are we to be confronted by an American peril...before which the Old World is to go down in irretrievable defeat?' Unrestrained competition in beef, grain, and sugar had been upsetting powerful Prussian landowners for years, and in late 1897 an economist from the German Navy Ministry 'ranked the American economic threat above that of England'.[9] In Italy too economists warned of the Darwinian 'struggle for life' that America's expansion was setting off. The aged Austrian emperor was reported to have denounced, by the mouth of his foreign minister, 'this disastrous war of competition which we meet with at every step', and called for comprehensive and joint European resistance. There was even talk of setting up a federal customs union of Europe for the purpose.[10] In the event, no coalition of Old World nations came forward to rescue Spain's dilapidated empire in its hour of need. Yet as the century turned the fears grew. The former foreign minister of Italy, Admiral Canevaro, invited fellow Europeans 'to consider the possibility and the necessity of uniting against America, as the future of civilisation would require them to do'. The Kaiser and the Tsar were reported to have shared a similar degree of high alarm in a 1903 meeting. In Paris it dominated talk 'in the press, at meetings, in Parliament', according to a 1905 witness.[11]

---

[8] Cit. in Ernest R. May, *Imperial Democracy: The Emergence of America as a Great Power* (New York, 1961), 230–1; a wide range of responses to the war is examined in Sylvia L. Hilton and Steve J. S. Ickringill (eds), *European Perceptions of the Spanish–American War of 1898* (Bern, 1999).

[9] May, *Imperial Democracy*, 5; cf. Séverine Antigone Marin, ' "L'américanisation du monde"? Etude des peurs allemandes face au danger américain, 1897–1907', paper presented at the Roubaix conference (September 2001); Markus M. Hugo, ' "Uncle Sam I Cannot Stand, for Spain I have no Sympathy": An Analysis of Discourse about the Spanish–American War in Imperial Germany, 1898–1909', in Hilton and Ickringill (eds), *European Perceptions*.

[10] For Austrian reactions to the war, Nicole Slupetzky, 'Austria and the Spanish–American War' in Hilton and Ickringill (eds), *European Perceptions*; on the general incomprehension of the Hapsburg elites faced with the rise of America, Reinhold Wagnleitner, *Coca-Colonization and the Cold War: The Cultural Mission of the United States in Austria after the Second World War* (Chapel Hill, NC, 1994), 39.

[11] W. T. Stead, 'The Americanisation of the World or the Trend of the Twentieth Century', *Review of Reviews*, (London, 1902), 73; May, *Imperial Democracy*, 5–6, 181–7, 202; cf. Portes, *Fascinations and Misgivings*, 377, 399–403; David Strauss, *Menace in the West: The Rise of French Anti-Americanism* (Westport, Conn., 1978), 42.

SPECTRE, MYTH OR MODEL?

The events of 1898 transformed European interest in the potential force of America in the affairs of the world, and obliged leaders and opinion-makers in and out of power to ponder the likely consequences for their nations at home and abroad.[12] Lenin considered the conflict 'the first war for a redistribution of the world already distributed'. In contrast, an Irish nationalist leader believed that:

> America had established a very important precedent—that of interfering with arms on behalf of an oppressed nationality. Yesterday it was Crete, today it was Cuba, and tomorrow many people thought it would be an island very much nearer to home.[13]

Indeed this dream of liberation was precisely what upset the most distinguished Briton of all. Queen Victoria did not share the general euphoria among her citizens, deploring the principle the Americans had cited to defend their action: 'No doubt Cuba was dreadfully governed... [but] they might as well say we governed Ireland badly and they ought to take possession of it and free it.'[14]

But such preoccupations arrived at a time when a fundamental shift in West European attitudes to all that the United States stood for and did was already under way. 'Until the middle of the nineteenth century, America had been discussed as a place or country', reports the political philosopher James Ceaser. A steady build up of stereotypes, prejudices, and imagery, mostly culled from travellers tales, dwarfed a small number of more serious studies, of which the most celebrated was de Tocqueville's great reflection on the future of republican democracy of 1835–40.[15] However by the second half of the nineteenth century, continues Ceaser:

---

[12] The agonizing post-war reckoning in Spain—especially over the modernizing challenge the defeat implied—is the subject of Sebastian Balfour, *The End of the Spanish Empire* (Oxford, 1997), ch. 2; cf. Laura Rodriguez, ' "El Desastre": Spain in Defeat, 1898', *History Today* (December 1998).

[13] Lenin cit. in Ludmila N. Popkova, 'Russian Press Coverage of American Intervention in the Spanish-Cuban War', in Hilton and Ickringill (eds), *European Perceptions*, 124; nationalist cited in Steve J. S. Ickringill, 'Silence and Celebration: Ulster, William McKinley and the Spanish–American War', in ibid., p.97; in reality the US was not involved in the question of Crete, which in 1898—under the combined auspices of France, Britain, Russia, and Italy—saw the final expulsion of the Turks from the island and the installation of a Greek prince as ruler.

[14] Cit. in Walter L. Arnstein, 'Queen Victoria and the United States', in Fred M. Leventhal and Roland Quinault (eds), *Anglo-American Attitudes: From Revolution to Partnership* (Aldershot, 2000), 100–1.

[15] Cf. C. Vann Woodward, *The Old World's New World* (New York, 1991), pp. xv–xviii, 79.

[America] was also being seen as a process or a worldview capable of being separated from its physical home and transferred elsewhere. America was entering the realm of the spirit.[16]

Something of this discovery coloured the greatest survey of American institutions, habits, and ideas produced by the later decades. This was James Bryce's three-volume study of *The American Commonwealth* of 1888, the work of an aristocratic Liberal ex-Cabinet Minister. At the very beginning of his two thousand pages, Bryce noted how 'thoughtful Europeans' had begun to realize, 'whether with satisfaction or regret, the enormous and daily-increasing influence of the United States', and what he saw as the splendid part they would play 'in the development of civilization'. He talked of how American social and political experiments were 'constantly' referred to in Europe 'both as patterns and warnings', and explained how only a true understanding of that nation—which he proposed to offer—could make sense of such debates.[17]

But Bryce's great effort, although of lasting significance, dwelt on politics, and his keen optimism on the potential development of the transatlantic form of popular democracy seemed more and more out of place to visitors who could see at first hand the corruption of the party system, the workings of the political machines in the big cities, the unbounded influence of the trusts and all the other 'anarchical and predatory tendencies' (*The Times*) produced by the country's tumultuous shift to great city industrialization.[18] The huge political significance of the American revolution, and the founding of the new republic that had so coloured opinion on the results in the first half of the nineteenth century, was now giving way to an ever-growing concern with the novelties behind America's rise to economic predominance, and their implications for the prospects of the rest of the industrial world.

No longer 'a remote barometer to be watched for what to expect', or hope or fear, the land of the future was quickly becoming 'a force to be resisted as an intruding influence'.[19] Here were phenomena that could

---

[16] James W. Ceaser, *Reconstructing America: The Symbol of America in Modern Thought* (New Haven, Conn., 1997), 163.

[17] On Bryce, Heindel, *American Impact on Great Britain*, 2, 238–40, 292, 312; Vann Woodward, *Old World's New World*, 79; full contextualization in Henry Tulloch, *James Bryce's 'American Commonwealth'. The Anglo-American Background* (London, 1988); cf. James Startt, 'James Bryce and the Promise of the American Press', in Joel H. Wiener and Mark Hampton (eds), *Anglo-American Media Interactions, 1850–2000* (London, 2007), 94–100.

[18] The word 'Americanization' had become common in British politics in the 1860s and 1870s, according to Murney Gerlach, when Conservatives began to use it as an 'evil expletive' to denounce the influence in Britain of the model of caucus politics originating in the US; *British Liberalism*, 189; details in Henry Pelling, *America and the British Left: From Bright to Bevan* (London, 1956), ch. 3, 'The Liberal Party "Americanized"'.

[19] Vann Woodward, *Old World's New World*, 80.

impinge directly and soon on Europe's own economic and social preferences, and in ways that existing mechanisms of choice and control might
not necessarily be able to master. The world everywhere was already discovering that America's preferred instruments of conquest were not war at
all. Instead they were industry, business, inventions, entertainments, and
a new kind of man and woman. Everywhere original means of thinking
and reflection became necessary to come to terms with a force or challenge whose permanence no one doubted any longer. The Yale historian
Vann Woodward wrote:

> The future intruded in the shape of missionaries, evangelists, salesmen, ad-
> vertisements and movies. It took the form of new brides in the oldest of
> families, new faces in the highest society. It also appeared at lower social
> levels in strange attitudes and ideas, new ways of thinking, new styles of
> living, and alien values. Europeans began to hear these innovations from the
> mouths of their own children and with increasing apprehension and
> dismay.[20]

It was quite common for thoughtful people to travel across the Atlantic
'to recover a little faith in the future of civilisation', as the French political
commentator Paul Bourget did in the early 1890s.[21] But the kind of reflection that spread from 1898 onwards was more urgent and challenging:
the future the Americans were building might be much closer than anyone
had hitherto thought possible. Conceivably it could even start to arrive on
terms defined by them and not by Europeans. If so, 'unfamiliar accom-
modations' would have to be made.[22]

Fifty years earlier it had been possible for a Thomas Carlyle to say
loftily that he found nothing and no one to admire in America—it
was neither 'a model republic or a model anything'. He had been told
that they had an 'unspeakable' quantity of cotton, dollars, industry,
and resources, 'but I can by no means worship the like of these'.[23] Yet
within a year the first Great Exhibition had been staged in London,
and such had been the success of the new industrial products from
across the Atlantic—Colt revolvers, farm implements, sewing machines, and others—that the British had quickly begun to send delegations of manufacturers to America to study the new 'systems' of
industrial production emerging there, inaugurating in this way a

[20] Ibid.
[21] P. Bourget, *Outre-Mer (Notes sur l'Amérique)* (Paris, 1895), 328–30; on Bourget and
his output, May, *Imperial Democracy*, 192–3.
[22] Charles Jennings, *Them and Us: The American Invasion of British High Society* (Stroud,
2007), 23.
[23] 'No. I: The Present Time (1 February 1850)', in *Latter-Day Pamphlets* (London, n.d.),
17–18.

century-long tradition which half the world would eventually come to share.[24]

As long as Gladstone was alive, Liberal opinion in Britain would remain inspired by his vision of a shared Anglo-American destiny, and the conviction that America was 'the one country in which Popular Government existed successfully'. In power in the early 1890s, Liberals accordingly sought to construct a new official outlook and adapt British foreign policy.[25] But James Bryce's opus turned out to be the last of the great nineteenth-century readings of the outcome of the republican political experiment born from a rib of the British Empire. And there were few indications in that work of a need for Britain to import its lessons, much less reproduce its contemporary methods, which even Bryce could only deplore.[26]

Across the Channel no great French political scientist turned his attention to the United States in the forty years before the First World War, says Jacques Portes, although there were innumerable lesser studies and reflections by journalists, writers, and witnesses of all sorts.[27] Yet it was becoming more and more obvious that crucial parts of Europe's future might well be found in that society and its contemporary evolution. The impressions of French commentators suggested they were to be glimpsed for instance, not in its institutions but 'in the fast-paced rhythm of sprawling cities, in the speed of the trams, in the apparent freedom of women, and in the charm of the comforts that coddled the lives of the privileged'. The result was the appearance of an endless variety of 'fragmentary models' each involving its own form of perceived impact and response.[28]

The Vatican, for example, took exception to the variety of freewheeling Catholicism that seemed to be emerging forcefully in the United States. In 1899 a Belgian aristocrat expressed some of its sentiments in a violent attack against what these circles were beginning to call 'Americanism':

[24] James M. Macpherson, *Battle Cry of Freedom: The Civil War Era* (New York, 1988), 16.

[25] Gerlach, *British Liberalism*, 56–7, 166; cf. Bradford Perkins, *The Great Rapprochement: England and the United States, 1895–1914* (New York, 1968); Burk, *Old World, New World*, 381–2.

[26] Cf. Heindel, *American Impact on Great Britain*, 2; Pelling, *America and the British Left*, ch. 4, esp. pp. 54–5; Startt, 'James Bryce', 101–2.

[27] Portes, *Fascinations and Misgivings*, 435–6; for intellectual fascination with America in this period, Elizabeth Fordham, 'From Whitman to Wilson: French Attitudes toward America around the Time of the Great War', in Luisa Passerini (ed.), *Across the Atlantic: Cultural Exchanges between Europe and the United States* (Brussels, 2000), 124–6.

[28] Portes, *Fascinations and Misgivings*, 435–6; on the rise of the American woman as a distinguishing social phenomenon in British views of the United States, Heindel, *American Impact on Great Britain*, 343–4: 'she emerged in British pages as a "type" before the American male ever achieved his identity.'

Americanism is not only a movement towards heresy; it is an *invasion of barbarism*... it is an attack by a new power against society, against Christian society...; it is money against honour, coarse brutality against delicacy,... machinery against philosophy...[29]

The Curia quickly produced a pastoral letter that warned its flock across the Atlantic of the dangers of the new practice. Here, in more measured terms, the danger was seen as an impossible but insidious attempt to reconcile Liberal, rationalist principles of social tolerance and democracy with the ageless faith of the Popes.[30] The episode, together with the fate handed out to an ancient, fellow-Catholic power in the 1898 war, tended to swing intellectual opinion in the rest of Italy against Protestant-bred America in these years. Attitudes of 'condescending scorn and hostile diffidence' began to appear, according to an early historical survey in that country, leading to a radical rejection of the modernity supposedly embodied in America, a denunciation of its alleged social and aesthetic mediocrity, which was seen as an inevitable product of the urge to turn social development into a technical problem. It was easy to see an antique form of anti-Americanism in all this, said a later Italian historian, but the nationalistic impulse to set up a contrast between 'Latin' and 'American' outlooks on life, understood as the product of two distinct civilizations, was destined to leave a profound mark on future attitudes in this part of Europe.[31]

Meanwhile at the popular level, even as Italian emigration to the United States peaked, with very contrasting images returning of what the new masses found on their arrival, American idioms were beginning to penetrate the everyday language of the English-speaking peoples.[32] Western comics began their long career, Buffalo Bill arrived as elsewhere in the Old

---

[29] Cit. in May, *Imperial Democracy*, 184–5 (italics in this citation); there was great concern that the mass of new Italian emigrants were losing their Catholic faith when exposed to life in America; cf. Daniela Saresella, 'La scoperta cattolica dell'America', in Agostino Giovagnoli and Giorgio Del Zanna (eds), *Il mondo vista dall'Italia* (Milan, 2004), 408–10.

[30] Ceaser, *Reconstructing America*, 163–5; Portes, *Fascinations and Misgivings*, 293–307; Daniela Rossini, 'The American Peril: Italian Catholics and the Spanish–American War, 1898', in Hilton and Ickringill (eds), *European Perceptions*; the Encyclical had little effect, reports Saresella, and a more general anti-modernist Encylical arrived soon after; 'La scoperta cattolica dell'America', 411.

[31] Pier Paolo D'Attore, 'Sogno americano e mito sovietico nell'Italia contemporanea', in D'Attorre (ed.), *Nemici per la pelle: Sogno americano e mito sovietico nell'Italia contemporanea* (Milan, 1991), 17; cf. Strauss, *Menace in the West*, ch. 3; Rossini points out that American Catholicism identified strongly with the 'civilizing' and modernizing mission that the Cuban adventure proclaimed; 'American Peril', 179.

[32] Heindel, *American Impact on Great Britain*, 309–10, offers a discussion of the arrival of American linguistic uses and idioms in Britain, and a list of words, with the inevitable criticisms.

World to wild enthusiasm, and Alcott's *Little Women* topped the fiction list of the day. A different mythology propagated by a new kind of commercial culture began to spread, and it was one that only rarely coincided with the phenomena the intellectual critics were talking about when they expressed their judgements on whatever America was supposed to represent.[33]

A German author, Emil Dubois Reymond, was one of the first to notice this difference and take it seriously. At a time when emigration from Germany to the US was also rising quickly, Reymond explained part of the attraction. The possibility of becoming an American—one's personal 'Americanization'—was not so seductive because of what America's principles or institutions might offer. Instead it was a response to the awakening among working people of 'a deep-felt desire for political, economic and cultural democratization'.[34] But if emigration was one thing, exposing one's national heritage to the risk of importing this stimulus looked quite different. German thinkers since Goethe and Hegel had been willing to acknowledge that America offered some sort of key to the future, but few were happy at the prospect. From the 1870s on the leading spirits began to imagine a dreadful scenario in which German civilization itself came under pressure from what America was coming to represent: its 'mammonism, materialism, mechanization and mass society', as the distinguished historian Fritz Stern recalled years later. Not content with turning Germans into its own citizens on American soil, it threatened to turn them into Americans on German soil: 'Americanization' would come to challenge the very soul of the most noble culture in central Europe.[35]

This sort of judgement had been anticipated by Friedrich Nietzsche. In 1882 the most renowned philosopher of his day had written:

[33] Over two million Italians moved to the US in the decade 1900–1910, the highest number of any ethnic group, Alexander DeConde, *Half Bitter, Half Sweet: An Excursion into Italian–American History* (New York, 1971), ch. 5 (figs. at p. 77); on popular culture, D'Attorre, 'Sogno americano e mito sovietico nell'Italia contemporanea', 18; cf. Daniela Rossini, *Il mito americano nell'Italia della Grande guerra* (Bari, 2000), 24–8.

[34] Cit. in Ceaser, *Reconstructing America*, 163; the process of becoming an American was by no means painless; for a vivid evocation of the existential difficulties suffered by poor Italian emigrants as they passed from a rural, largely feudal world to the American universe of movement, experimentation, and individuality, Thomas Belmonte, 'The Contradictions of Italian–American identity: An Anthropologist's Personal View', in Pellegrino D'Acierno (ed.), *The Italian–American Heritage: A Companion to Literature and Arts* (New York, 1999), 15–16.

[35] Ceaser, *Reconstructing America*, 165–7, 171; cf. Peter Bergmann, 'The Specter of *Amerikanisierung*, 1880–1940', in Mike-Frank G. Epitropoulos and Victor Roudometof (eds), *American Culture in Europe: Interdisciplinary Perspectives* (Westport, Conn., 1998), 68–9; traces of similar British worries cit. in Heindel, *American Impact on Great Britain*, 45.

The breathless haste with which the [the Americans] work—the distinctive vice of the new world—is already beginning ferociously to infect old Europe and is spreading a spiritual emptiness over the continent.[36]

Nietzsche denounced the obsession with production and productivity he saw dominant in the American way of life, the urge to ever more intense and competitive work, what today we would call the 'present-mindedness' of everyone. And worse, this attack on the heritage of every cultural standard worth respecting was spreading across the Atlantic: 'The faith of the Americans today is more and more becoming the faith of the European as well.'[37]

Nietszche went on to inspire a significant generation of revolutionary conservative thought, writes James Ceaser, one that created a symbolic America whose evolution followed a distinct pattern of its own, separated at a distance from the actual behaviour of that nation in any particular sphere of life. But because this tradition was taken up and elaborated by thinkers of the prestige of Oswald Spengler and Martin Heidegger as an element in their great and influential critiques of all the forms of contemporary modernity, the marks it left must be taken with utmost seriousness.

Metaphysics meant much in the redefinition and exaltation of national identity that took place in the Wilhelmine years, and it was German philosophers of the first order who saw most clearly that the rising American challenge involved an effort—perhaps even an all-out struggle—to find ways to strike a balance between the technological modernity that in their view drove America's will-to-power, and what was considered best in the way of life that German society had inherited from the past.[38] In 1904 Max Weber talked of the 'steel-hard casing' that, most fully developed in America, was arising round those advanced nations where the power of technical development had taken on a near uncontrollable dynamic of its own. In the same year, a lesser writer, Paul Dehn, consolidated the German practice of using explicitly the term 'Americanization', and then reflecting in moral as well as historical terms on its meaning:

Americanization in an economic sense means the modernization of the methods of industry, exchange and agriculture as well as all the other areas

---

[36] Cit. in Ceaser, *Reconstructing America*, 173.

[37] Ibid. In the twentieth century panorama of European experience, Germany's encounter with American models of modernity was 'exceptionally fraught', writes Victoria de Grazia, a leading historian of these confrontations; in Pamela E. Swett et al. (eds), *Selling Modernity: Advertising in Twentieth-Century Germany* (Durham, NC, 2007), p. xv.

[38] Cf. 'Introduction', ibid. 4–5; the authors talk of a German 'obsession with America' that became focused and explicit when presented with such challenges as consumer advertising.

of practical life. Americanization in its widest sense, including the societal and the political, means the uninterrupted, exclusive and relentless striving after gain, riches, and influence.[39]

This sort of anguished cry, audible from the top to the bottom of Europe, says Vann Woodward—'the more advanced [the country] the earlier and louder'[40]—was a new way of coping with modernity in its unfolding. During the nineteenth century all sorts of metaphors about America had been invented by outside observers in an effort to come to terms with the development of the restless experiment across the Atlantic. Now America itself *became a metaphor*, called upon to take the imaginative strain of a whole series of processes identified with the latest phases of industrialization, democratization, and deepening economic interdependence.[41]

Yet the quickening transatlantic relationship in politics, business, and mass culture was also an ever-swelling fact of life. Use of the word 'Americanization' was not just about creating a new critical language for fending off the undesirable effects of progress, or a self-serving alibi, enabling intellectual whingers and moralizers to shift the blame to another nation for the novelties in contemporary life they found distasteful, as so many American commentators have complained.[42] It reflected also a response to an unprecedented material challenge, a reaction to a radical, one-sided change in the value of those currencies of power that European nations had traditionally esteemed the most, and thought their own. As David Landes has written, for centuries Europe had been the 'prime mover of development and modernity', the definer of all the dominant notions of

---

[39] Weber discussed in Jan-Werner Müller, *Contesting Democracy: Political Ideas in Twentieth Century Europe* (New Haven, Conn., 2011), 26–32; Dehn cit. in Ceaser, *Reconstructing America*, 163. At the time Dehn was a leading voice in a widespread middle-class movement against the arrival of department stores in Germany, writes the historian Kevin Repp. The protest was not economic but aesthetic, the defence of a certain idea of taste and *Kultur*; Repp, 'Marketing, Modernity, and "The German People's Soul": Advertising and its Enemies in Late Imperial Germany', in Swett et al. (eds), *Selling Modernity*, 34.

[40] Was the French poet Charles Baudelaire the first? His denunciation, in an 1855 essay entitled 'On the Modern Idea of Progress as Applied to the Fine Arts', is discussed in Marshall Berman, *All That is Solid Melts into Air: The Experience of Modernity* (2nd edn, New York, 1988), 138–9; a comparable British complaint came from the poet and critic Matthew Arnold in 1861, in a debate on popular education, cit. in Pelling, *America and the British Left*, 3.

[41] Vann Woodward, *Old World's New World*, 35–6, 82; the imaginative creation of America by European witnesses (and others) has attracted the attention of many scholars, e.g. Peter Conrad, *Imagining America* (London, 1980), esp. ch. 1; Rob Kroes, *If You've Seen One You've Seen the Mall: Europeans and American Mass Culture* (Urbana and Chicago, 1996), esp. ch. 1; Rob Kroes et al. (eds), *Cultural Transmissions and Receptions: American Mass Culture in Europe* (Amsterdam, 1993), contributions in Part I.

[42] Vann Woodward, *Old World's New World*, 36; Heindel, *American Impact on Great Britain*, 12–13; Richard Pells, *Not Like Us: How Europeans Have Loved, Hated and Transformed American Culture since World War II* (New York, 1997), 97.

progress.[43] It was no easy prospect to be forced to cede this position in a matter of years to an upstart nation of which little was known and even less appreciated. This moment truly was, as Woodrow Wilson said in 1902, a 'turning point in the world's evolution'.[44]

All sorts of questions ensued from these novelties, but one of them looked particularly urgent after 1898. Just how much would America's presence in all its new forms effectively impinge on the patterns of development that each of the separate national traditions in the Old World was preparing to offer to the twentieth century? In other words, how much would the new power of America begin to condition the unthinking freedom national societies had hitherto possessed in deciding whatever they might want to be? In no nation was this test more eagerly anticipated than Great Britain, heart of a world empire then at the very height of its might and prestige.

LAND OF GLORY AND HOPE

The overwhelming force of the American question in Britain's future was one of William Ewart Gladstone's favourite preoccupations in later life:

> Not what matter of producer, but what manner of man is the American of the future to be? How is the majestic figure, who is to become the largest and most powerful on the stage of the world's history, to make use of his power? Will it be instinct with moral life in proportion to its material strength?[45]

In the 1880s and early 1890s the Liberal leader had been a key figure in arguments about Britain and the US, writes Gerlach, debating Darwinism and religion, divorce and population control, trusts and tycoons, all the while insisting that '[we] are not to make the United States our model'. But with the death of the Grand Old Man in 1898, his age came to an end, and with it his particular brand of Liberalism.[46] Yet it was from this tradition that there came the first significant British reflection on the workings of the new kinds of American inspiration and influence in European life. This was the long essay published in 1902 by the prominent journalist W. T. Stead in his *Review of Reviews*, and entitled: 'The

---

[43] Landes ref. and discussion in Nick Cullather, 'Development? It's History', *Diplomatic History* (Fall 2000), 646.

[44] Woodrow Wilson, 'The Ideals of America', *Atlantic Monthly* (December 1902).

[45] Gerlach, *British Liberalism*, 137, cf. Stead, 'Americanisation of the World', 163.

[46] Gerlach, *British Liberalism*, 246; Gladstone cit. in Heindel, *American Impact on Great Britain*, 353.

Americanisation of the World or the Trend of the Twentieth Century', an effort rediscovered at the end of that century as the 'Americanisation' challenge seemed to be coming round again with renewed force. Stead's professional inclinations led him to concentrate on documenting and denouncing the ever-increasing presence of American products, methods, and people, even religions, in British society.[47] Perhaps because of this approach, the key questions of modernity and sovereignty looked more urgent and explicit in the British case: how could the Empire keep its character and world status, and at the same time continue to compete on a basis of equality?

Pessimists thought the game was already up. A Russian correspondent was quoted by Stead as likening Britain's relationship to the US with Austria's to Germany:

> The British have lost all pride in their relations to the United States. They admit that they cannot successfully resist the republic. They no longer trust their strength, but place their reliance on the racial, literary and social ties which attract the Americans to England. . . . Losing her maritime, commercial and even financial primacy, England can bear with more resignation the passing of this primacy to a nation akin to her in language, civilisation and even blood.[48]

Andrew Carnegie, the expatriate steel tycoon, wished to tell the country via his friend Stead that it had no future in manufacturing, and was inviting it to take comfort from the fact that 'you will become more and more popular as the garden and pleasure ground of the race, which will always regard Great Britain as its ancestral home'.[49] At a time when 15,000 rich Americans were said to live in London, many of them heiresses busy as elsewhere in Europe saving ancient families from extinction, this was not

---

[47] On Stead's place in British political life at the time, Pelling, *America and the British Left*, p. 69, n. 3, on his place in Press life, Heindel, *American Impact on Great Britain*, 21, 27. In 1898 he had published *Satan's Invisible World Displayed, or Despairing Democracy: A study of Greater New York*, whose purpose, said Heindel, was 'to show the Britons what would happen if they lost their municipal pride', Heindel, *American Impact on Great Britain*, 251; European intellectual comparisons and context in Rydell and Kroes, *Buffalo Bill in Bologna*, 149–50.

[48] Stead, 'Americanisation of the World', 13, footnote. The 'civilizational' view of the world, meaning the difference between those peoples to be considered 'civilized' and the rest, was very common in these years; cf. Iriye, *Cultural Internationalism*, 20–1.

[49] Stead, 'Americanisation of the World', 138; it might be argued that this prediction came true in the images conveyed by the large number of British films and television programmes that met success in America from the 1970s onwards; cf. D. L. LeMahieu, 'America and the Representation of British History in Film and Television', in Leventhal and Quinault (eds), *Anglo-American Attitudes*. Carnegie 'probably received more press space than any other American during the pre-War years', reckoned Heindel, *American Impact on Great Britain*, 363, his widespread activities and discourses on behalf of peace, republicanism, popular education, and democracy are reported ibid. 361–3.

just an idle sociological speculation.[50] But Stead took the significance of the matrimonial connection too literally. He believed that it opened the way to the next chapter of Anglo-Saxon hegemony in world history: the union of the English-speaking race.[51]

Stead had been one of those most aroused by the Spanish–American war of 1898, an event that much of British opinion saw as America finally facing up to the challenge of imperial rivalries. But the rejoicing in London at this spectacle was based on the conviction that the new American power in the world would immediately be available for the benefit of the Mother Country: 'she tried to make American expansion a counterweight to European competition and a reinsurance of the [world] status quo satisfactory to Great Britain', said Heindel later. It was logical that of all the enthusiasts for Anglo-Saxonism as the key to world peace, none should have been more energetic than Joseph Chamberlain, proponent of British Empire federation and a man once identified by Gladstone as the most American statesman in England.

The war fever was greatly stimulated of course by contemporary notions of the workings of Darwinistic principles in international life, and schemes flourished on all sides for friendship clubs, alliances, and unions.[52] The Prime Minister and foremost Tory of the early years of the twentieth century, A. J. Balfour, supported the vision, as of course did all the leading Liberals, but it was the imperial adventurer Cecil Rhodes who provided it with money and the famous (on-going) Oxford scholarships.[53] And for the first time, there were significant American supporters. People like the aristocratic Senator Henry Cabot Lodge, however, were moved not so much by culture and sentiment as by the feeling that the white Anglo-Saxon heritage that had fostered the American Union was about to be overwhelmed by the immigrant hordes.[54]

---

[50] Early discussion of the phenomenon and its social consequences, Heindel, *American Impact on Great Britain*, ch. 14, literary consequences ibid. 347–9; general survey in Jennings, *Them and Us*; for literary treatments, Edith Wharton, *The Buccaneers* (1st edn, New York, 1938); Thomas Mann's *His Royal Highness*, first published in 1909, is particularly eloquent on the effects that a great magnate's fortune might have on the affairs of an impoverished little German state, when his daughter marries the brother of the hereditary prince; 1916 London edition (reprinted 1997), pp. 299–300.

[51] The crustiest members of the British aristocracy feared miscegenation and the spread of 'vulgar commercialism' among their ranks; Jennings, *Them and Us*, 82.

[52] Cf. Norman Rose, *The Cliveden Set: Portrait of an Exclusive Fraternity* (London, 2000), 2–3, 45, 214–15; Gerlach, *British Liberalism*, 246; 'surprisingly little was heard of a brotherhood of democracies', noted Heindel, *American Impact on Great Britain*, 238.

[53] Cf. Kennedy, 'British and German Reactions', 19–21; on Rhodes's vision, cf. Clifford Sharp, in *The Great Victorians* (London, 1932), 435–6, on the impact of the Rhodes scholarships on Oxford up to 1939, Heindel, *American Impact on Great Britain*, 274–5.

[54] Cf. J. N. Larned, 'England's Economic and Political Crisis', *Atlantic Monthly* (March 1898); John R. Dos Passos, *The Anglo-Saxon Century and the Unification of the English-*

There was much loose talk and illusion in these developments, which Heindel attributed to a British wish to 'project the United States upon an Old World background'.[55] But two consequences would be of lasting significance. One was the birth in Continental Europe of the daunting prospect of a common Anglo-Saxon front, one whose potential for adding power to both British and American purposes seemed unlimited (it had been foreshadowed in British neutrality in the Spanish–American conflict, enough to dissuade would-be coalitionists on the Continent[56]). Kaiser Wilhelm raged about the 'Anglo-American Society for International Theft and Warmongering'. More calmly, a French sociologist began the long national tradition of considering the British and the Americans as a united geo-cultural bloc, addressing a book-length investigation to the question, 'What does Anglo-Saxon Superiority Mean?'[57] And his answer too would endure. Either one imitated the rivals' method of progress or one would be forced to submit to their influence; one studied them and learned their lessons, or eventually one's own race would succumb, as so many before in the competitive history of civilizations.[58]

For certain of the British, the other inheritance of the moment of high, pro-American enthusiasm after 1898 lay precisely in that vision: the bonding of the Anglo-Saxon peoples. After all between 1891 and 1900, 72 per cent of the nation's emigrants had chosen the US as their destination of preference, not the colonies. In 1899 as much as one half of

---

Speaking People (New York, 1903). Dos Passos was the father of one of the leading American authors of the interwar period, John Dos Passos. Stuart B. Anderson, *Race and Rapprochement: Anglo-Saxonism and Anglo-American Relations, 1895–1904* (East Brunswick, 1981); Paul A. Kramer, 'Empires, Exceptions and Anglo-Saxons: Race and Rule between the British and United States Empires, 1880–1910', *Journal of American History* (March 2002), 1315–53.

[55] *American Impact on Great Britain*, 125–32.

[56] A committee of European Ambassadors had approached McKinley with an offer of mediation. 'Despite its seeming inconsequence', writes May, 'this joint *démarche* represented Europe's one united response to the emergence of America as a power', *Imperial Democracy*, 181. Rebuffed by the President, a second attempt broke down as foreign ministries contemplated the ambiguities of their domestic public opinion on America and the potential economic costs; ibid. 218–19; cf. Introduction to Hilton and Ickringill (eds), *European Perceptions*.

[57] Wilhelm II cit. in Perkins, *Great Rapprochement*, 52; Edmond Demolins, *A Quoi tient la superiorité des Anglo Saxons?* (Paris, n.d. [*c*.1900]); Demolins pointed to the interaction of social and technological innovation as the key to America's progress, and admired its culture of individualism and social mobility, ibid. 342–3, 366. But a French reviewer of W. T. Stead's discussion of Americanization talked of a 'detestable internationalism' and regretted that foreign ideas could not be kept out of the country any more than foreign goods, A. Léger cit. in Portes, *Fascinations and Misgivings*, p. 401, n. 22.

[58] Portes, *Fascinations and Misgivings*, 367, 394; cf. Strauss, *Menace in the West*, 50; on French and Italian academic efforts to learn these lessons, May, *Imperial Democracy*, 182–3; for comparable German discussions, Hugo, 'Uncle Sam', 87–9, for Austria, Slupetzky, 'Austria and the Spanish–American War', 190.

Britain's overseas income may have come from the American economic expansion; of America's exports 56 per cent went to Great Britain or her empire.[59] W. T. Stead, who believed that the Americanization of the world was but 'its Anglicising at one remove', suggested that:

> ...the Briton, instead of chafing against this inevitable supersession, should cheerfully acquiesce in the decree of Destiny, and stand in betimes with the conquering American.[60]

Even as experienced a figure as James Bryce endorsed the race vision, talking of a community of blood, tongue, habits, thoughts, and feelings that was democratically based and so might carry on beyond the already intense mutual economic dependence, towards some form of common citizenship and mutual diplomatic protection.[61] Only partly disillusioned by the events of World War I and Versailles—which included Woodrow Wilson's outspoken rejection of any such linkage[62]—this impulse would reappear again in the 1930s and in World War II under Winston Churchill's powerful patronage. Thanks to his glories it would attain a permanent status in the mythology of Anglo-American relations.[63]

THE ECONOMIST'S EXPECTATIONS

There would of course be no such union, no formal alliance, not even a joint newspaper.[64] But the British were able to present another kind of visiting card in their effort to make the most of their connection with the

[59] Heindel, *American Impact on Great Britain*, 45, 179; export figure cited in Alastair Burnet, *America 1843–1993: 150 Years of Reporting the American Connection* (London, 1993), 67.

[60] Stead, 'Americanisation of the World', 9; for discussion of the diplomatic evolution of this outlook, conducted under the sign of appeasement, and its effects in turning suspicion into friendliness in US foreign policy in the years after 1898, Edward P. Crapol, 'From Anglophobia to Fragile Rapprochement: Anglo-American Relations in the Early Twentieth Century', in Hans-Jürgen Schröder (ed.), *Confrontation and Cooperation: Germany and the United States in the Era of World War I, 1900–1924* (Providence and Oxford, 1993).

[61] J. Bryce, 'The Essential Unity of Britain and America', *Atlantic Monthly* (July 1898); for a sceptical American comment, Carl Schurz, 'The Anglo-American Friendship', ibid. (October 1898). The idea of a common citizenship was again propounded by the British constitutionalist Dicey, in the same number of the monthly; for Henry James's notions on the subject—which imagined an English-led 'melting together' of the Anglo-Saxon races—Heindel, *American Impact on Great Britain*, 303–4.

[62] Conversation between Wilson and King George V cit. in David Dimbleby and David Reynolds, *An Ocean Apart: The Relationship Between Britain and America in the Twentieth Century* (London, 1988), 64. This book is much more original and detailed than its background would suggest, appearing as it did to accompany a BBC television documentary of the same name.

[63] 1930s version cit. in Carr, *Twenty Years' Crisis*, 233; WWII evolution in Chapter 6.

[64] British efforts in this direction failed, but the first Euro-American newspaper had already come into being, the *New York Herald*, established in Paris in 1887.

new success story, and to express their devotion to a certain vision of America as model. In 1843 *The Economist* had been founded, a weekly journal whose purpose, according to a memorial edition, had been to act as 'an independent supporter of the free trade cause' articulated by leading thinkers of the day like the industrialist Richard Cobden and the Liberal parliamentarian John Bright. As early as 1836 Cobden had warned his countrymen that America's 'commercial and naval ascendancy' already threatened to thrust Britain into the second rank of nations. In his view the effects of their 'quicker mechanical genius' were already apparent. Unless the country abandoned the Empire and all its expensive defences, stuck exclusively to its commercial interests by free trade, and invested massively in popular education—all things the Americans were already doing, claimed Cobden—then it would surely be overtaken.[65]

In the United States the free-traders and *The Economist* saw the nation most likely to embody all their beliefs and hopes. The paper 'was fascinated by America and the Americans from the beginning', wrote Alastair Burnet, a former editor, in a 1990s survey celebrating a hundred and fifty years of continuous publication. 'It was captivated by the potential of the country, the energy of the people, their intellectual vigour and by the very difference between their society and manners and British ways.'[66] When the prospect of war between Spain and the US began to appear, *The Economist* decided to ignore recent Anglo-American frictions and see the US as 'a separate but not a foreign nation', peopled by 'kinsmen', to whom Britain had recently been drawn 'in a remarkable way'. Seen from this perspective, the war looked likely to change America's view of the world, and her status in it, in ways that could only benefit the Mother Country. The Americans would understand that the Atlantic under British control would act as their best external defence, while they might well act together in the Pacific, where they both wanted 'peace, order, and freedom to trade anywhere at will...'. As long as Germany presented the British with nothing but rivalry and provocation, the strategic conclusion was obvious: 'The friendship of America is worth much more to us than that of Germany.' Henceforth, this would always be the case, and whenever accommodation by Britain to American aspirations seemed necessary, the weekly was likely to approve of the necessary steps. Looking back, Burnet

---

[65] Richard Cobden, 'A Manchester Manufacturer', *England, Ireland and America* (6th edn, Edinburgh, 1836). Unlike his contemporary De Tocqueville, Cobden showed no interest whatsoever in America's political experiment, declaring that 'democracy forms no element in the materials of English character', ibid. 34; yet Cobden was attacked by conservatives as an agent of political Americanization: Jennings, *Them and Us*, 22.

[66] Burnet, *America 1843–1993*, 1.

commented: 'Britain was determined to appease the United States, and did so repeatedly, to the paper's satisfaction.'[67]

While 'the American peril' remained in any event no more than a growth in markets and exports, *The Economist* was not likely to object. Many years were to pass before the newspaper began positively to urge its countrymen to emulate American ways of production and consumption on every plausible occasion. But even *The Economist* could not hide the fact that the US did not live up to its own promise of ever-freer markets, even when urging the 'Open Door' on everyone else, as the Secretary of State did in 1899. Clever travellers such as John Muirhead, author of the first *Baedeker* travel guide to the United States and his own 1902 survey of 'the land of contrasts', was astonished by the freedom of trade within the huge extent of the country, and thought it 'the most wonderful market on the globe', a proof that 'Brother Jonathan, the rampant Protectionist', was in fact 'the greatest Cobdenite of them all!'[68] But it was impossible to hide the fact that imports faced tariffs of anything from 10 to 70 per cent, that many Americans felt they owed their prosperity to such shelters, and that politicians competed as to who could be most effective in keeping them up.[69]

Liberal opinion, led by Gladstone, had of course long denounced this great offense to the cause of freedom.[70] *The Economist* too would fight endlessly against what it called 'the most rigid tariff in the civilised world', denouncing it as a betrayal of its first, most fundamental, principle of faith; and when, after the end of hostilities against Spain, the post-war settlement proposed by the US Congress was seen to include the annexation of Hawaii and the semi-possession of the Philippines and Puerto Rico, as well as Cuba, its other most profound instinct was aroused. Imperialism, it cried, was 'not in harmony with the spirit or the letter of American institutions. That is a plain matter of fact as to which dispute is impossible.' The great shift would bring an endless series of miseries, the paper predicted, plunging the US into European power politics, legitimizing a new round of colonization in South America, expanding the Federal government and its taxes, creating a new, non-productive military and imperial class. The crudest forms of nationalism were blinding the Americans as to the true nature of their place in the world:

[67] Ibid. 63–6, 74; cf. Burk, *Old World, New World*, 432–3.
[68] J. F. Muirhead, *America the Land of Contrasts*, (1902 edn repr., New York, 1970), 12–13.
[69] Cf. Kipling, *American Notes*, 101; contemporary views and politics of Anglo-American tariff disputes in Heindel, *American Impact on Great Britain*, 152–60; on the context of American attitudes, Anthony Howe, 'Free Trade and the International Order: The Anglo-American Tradition, 1846–1946', in Leventhal and Quinault (eds), *Anglo-American Attitudes*, 146–52.
[70] Gerlach, *British Liberalism*, 133–6.

Free trade economists distinguish a trade empire from a territorial empire, and hold that annexation is by no means essential to secure markets. But the American people have never been guided by Free-trade principles, and some of them seem to be sharing the notion now raging here and all over Europe, that to acquire markets you must annex.

Of course the US needed new markets for its ever more serious problem of over-production—hence the American push towards China—but that was no reason, concluded the newspaper, to overturn the fundamentals of structure and policy inherited from the Founding Fathers.[71]

THE POWER OF THE NEW AMERICA

By November 1899 the US had become, in the eyes of *The Economist*, 'a mighty nation whose action is watched by all eyes, whose alliance is sought by all Governments, whose movements, however slight, promote or derange all combinations'.[72] The war had unleashed a huge boom in manufacturing, distributing, and consuming, and the surge in America's exports was plain for all to see: a rhythm of 25 per cent per annum expansion was being quoted.[73] The US Government reported in 1900 that the leading players in world trade were Great Britain with 18.3 per cent of it, Germany with 10.8 per cent, and America itself with 9.7 per cent, but it was the latter power that had come from nowhere most quickly and promised to overtake them all, with its new stakes in Asia and Oceania.[74] While the bulk of US exports remained agricultural products, oil, and coal, the fastest growing sector was manufacturing, and the results could be seen on an occasion like the Paris exhibition of 1900, where American exhibitors were double those from Britain.[75] In Berlin a delegation from the American Mechanical and Civil Engineers Association arrived in July

---

[71] *The Economist*, 9 July 1898; Bryce also saw the results of the Spanish–American war in these terms (letter to T. Roosevelt cit. in Heindel, *American Impact on Great Britain*, 53), as did *The Manchester Guardian*, ibid. 85.

[72] *The Economist*, 11 November 1899.

[73] Ibid. 7 January 1899.

[74] Ibid. 2 June and 16 June 1900; only weeks after the US Navy had eliminated Spanish power in the Philippines, business interests pressed Congress for a commercial mission to China. Their reasoning was very blunt: the output of their manufactures had clearly overtaken the capacity of the domestic market to absorb them, and with a new base in the Pacific, 'we can and will take a huge slice of the commerce of Asia. That is what we want'; docs cit. in Lester H. Brune (ed.), *Chronological History of U.S. Foreign Relations*, i (New York, 2003), 279–80. The celebrated 'Open Door' notes of Secretary of State John Hay formally declared an interest in equal opportunity for all in the China trade, and in the maintenance of China's territorial integrity for this purpose.

[75] Heindel, *American Impact on Great Britain*, 183.

of the same year. The Chicago Exposition had already convinced leading German firms of the effectiveness of the American system of standardization and interchangeable parts, and now the visitors were able to see US-made machines and appliances everywhere. An English manufacturer had even sent men to Germany to copy some of these machine tools, it was reported, as British manufacturers had been unwilling to adapt their output to his needs.[76]

The German capital was in the throes of building department stores, transforming its old guild-based corporations into a new American-style Chamber of Commerce, and opening an amusement park based on the Coney Island model. So it was no coincidence that the journalist Stead would single out Hamburg and Berlin, 'with their feverish concentrated energy', as the most Americanized cities in Europe in his well-known tract. There were obvious ironies in these developments:

> The centre of resistance to American principles in Europe lies at Berlin, and the leader against and great protagonist of Americanisation is the Kaiser of Germany. There is something pathetic in the heroic pose of the German Emperor resisting the American flood...all the while the water is percolating through the sand on which he is standing, undermining the very foundations upon which his feet are planted, so that he himself is driven to Americanise, even when he is resisting Americanisation...[77]

The construction of new department stores in Berlin was where this paradox was most obvious, writes Kevin Repp, producing an unmistakable contrast between 'unreflective' and 'reflective' Americanism in their design. Oskar Tietz's huge glass-and-steel construction showed off the first of these impulses. It opened in 1900 amidst a blizzard of publicity stunts prepared with the aid of American advertising experts, and attracted widespread ridicule. In contrast Alfred Messel's design for the Wertheim store, completed in 1907, was thought by local critics to have been the first successfully to 'Gothicize the Renaissance', a so produce 'a *spontaneous expression of national traditions*'.[78] The art critic Karl Scheffler praised 'the bold American spirit that haunts Berlin' as the spur for Messel's talent, which had then gone on to produce an architectural modernity wonderfully pleasing to the conservative upper-middle-class souls of the city.[79]

---

[76] *The Economist*, 21 July 1900; on the Chicago fair and its impact, Rosenberg, *Spreading the American Dream*, 3–9.

[77] Stead, 'Americanisation of the World', 65–7; the amusement park model and other pre-World War I American influences in Germany are discussed in Deniz Göktürk, 'How Modern Is It? Moving Images of America in Early German Cinema', in D. W. Ellwood and R. Kroes (eds), *Hollywood in Europe: Experiences of a Cultural Hegemony* (Amsterdam, 1994).

[78] Repp, 'Marketing, Modernity', pp. 30–9, cit. at p. 37 (emphasis in original).

[79] Ibid. 36–7.

Fig. 1. The 'American invasion of Europe' as seen by a Chicago cartoonist in 1907.

(Library of Congress)

Everywhere could be seen a new 'infiltration of capital and business spirit into European economic life', said a pioneering historical study on the subject.[80] With the arrival of the first wave of US investments in Europe, led by the big money, oil, and tobacco trusts, came complaints of unfair competition and the impulse to raise barriers, just as the Americans were doing to them. Because of its accessible language, and the openness and size of its empire, Britain was the key destination of the new US trade and investment push, a development that accelerated after 1898. By 1900 seventy-five companies were present with subsidiaries or joint ventures, and another seventy would take stakes by 1914. Famous names such as Singer sewing machines, H. J. Heinz processed foods, and F. W. Woolworths with its 'penny markets' would be among them, as would Gordon Selfridge with his department store, opened in 1909. Selfridge from Chicago was a man who said he wanted to combine 'American "zip" and "go" with English poise'.[81] There were challenges too in shoes, bicycles, textiles, and cars. Henry Ford opened his first overseas car-building opera-

---

[80] Haldvan Koht, *The American Spirit in Europe: A Survey of Transatlantic Influences* (Oslo, 1949), 208–9; for the American context, Rosenberg, *Spreading the American Dream*, 15–28.

[81] For origins of Woolworth's in Britain, Heindel, *American Impact on Great Britain*, 190; Selfridge cit. ibid. 192.

tion outside Manchester, in 1908. Commentators saw that their entire technology was more advanced. The Americans were doing with electricity what the British had done with steam at the start of the last century, thought Stead.[82]

It was the speed and intensity of this thrust that took the British by surprise. At a time of increasing nervousness about the long-term prospects for Britain's prodigious world position, there was great resentment of the American 'invasion' (even *The Economist* used the term in 1900). Where was it all leading? What changes must be made to accommodate it? Would the tyranny of the great American trusts now be reproduced here? Vast business battles broke out over specific industries, over control of the new London underground train system, and the strategically crucial transatlantic shipping sector. Titanic figures risen from nowhere suddenly loomed into view, the banker J. P. Morgan, the property speculator Charles Tyson Yerkes, and the tobacco tycoon James Buchanan Duke.[83] 'Buck' Duke from New York explicitly set out to capture the British and continental cigarette markets by buying every local business within his reach, setting off a furious 'tobacco war' with his activities. Eventually a division of the world into smoking spheres of influence brought forth the joint company 'British American Tobacco' (BAT) in 1902.[84]

'These take-over battles of 1901–2 provoked a response of near panic in Britain', writes David Reynolds in his fresco of Anglo-American relations in these years. The *Daily Express* cried 'Wake Up, England!', while a journalistic fantasy in the *Daily Mail* warned of a situation in which every aspect of daily life was determined or coloured by the presence of American products:

> …we have almost got to this. The average citizen wakes in the morning at the sound of an American alarum clock; rises from his New England sheets, and shaves with his New York soap, and a Yankee safety razor. He pulls on a pair of Boston boots over his socks from West Carolina, fastens his Connecticut braces, slips his Waterbury watch into his pocket and sits down to breakfast. … Rising from his breakfast table the citizen rushes out, catches an electric tram made in New York, to Shepherds Bush, where he gets into

[82] J. H. Dunning, *American Investment in British Manufacturing Industry* (London, 1958), 18–36 (Dunning notes that Britain was the only country to treat foreign capitalists in the same way as residents, ibid. 32); Stead, 'Americanisation of the World', 137; Rosenberg, *Spreading the American Dream*, 25–8.

[83] Under the heading 'Morganizing', the *St James's Gazette* denounced the absorption of English shipping lines by the New York magnate and insisted the matter be brought before Parliament; *International Herald Tribune*, 23 April 1902 (reprinted 23 April 2002).

[84] Dimbleby and Reynolds, *An Ocean Apart*, 35–7; Pelling, *America and the British Left*, 68–9.

a Yankee elevator, which takes him on to the American-fitted railway to the city. At his office of course everything is American ... [85]

In the ranks of socialists, radicals, and trade unionists, the alarm concerned not just the direct threat to the livelihood of British workers, but the increasing tendency on the part of employers to use American examples when demanding greater freedom in the organization of factory life. In the engineering strike of 1897 the employers talked explicitly of their need to compete with American products made without the supervision of trade unions. As Henry Pelling pointed out in a classic account of the development of views of the United States on the British left, the rise of the trusts and the violence of American labour relations in these years made US precedents very worrying for British workplace organizers. Yet close-up examination of the operations of American factories soon revealed that American growth was not simply down to monopoly, exploitation, and repression. At a National Cash Register factory in Ohio a visiting delegation was struck by a large notice announcing that: 'Improved Machinery Makes Men Dearer, Their Products Cheaper.' The discovery that both sides of industry were devoted to high wages and increasing efficiency by way of new technology and organization, struck British visitors as full of lessons for their future.[86]

In the eyes of British employers though, the American experience taught how to use machinery to substitute individual workers, and how to manipulate the law to blunt the organized power of labour unions. No one had any intention of paying high wages if it could possibly be avoided. It was easy to agree across manufacturing that 'the existing state of America reflected the future state of Britain', as Pelling wrote. But in the specific area of industrial organization the spread of this conviction tended to exacerbate division and conflict. While the employers enlisted the news media of the day and Parliament to press their case, the trade unions attempted to redress the balance of power between employers and workers by organizing a new committee to represent labour interests at the national level, in the House of Commons itself. The politics of the American challenge in this area was one of the factors that led from that committee to the birth, in 1903, of the modern Labour Party.[87]

[85] F. A. McKenzie, *The American Invaders* (London, 1902), cit. in Dimbleby and Reynolds, *An Ocean Apart*, 37–8; both *The Express* and *The Mail* were deeply influenced themselves by American practices, people, and news; Heindel, *American Impact on Great Britain*, 18–20; Heindel offers his own long lists of American social practices, products, and fashions adopted in Britain in these years, ibid. 191, 350–2.

[86] Pelling, *America and the British Left*, 70, *passim*; on the German experience of this discovery, Marin, 'L'américanisation du monde'.

[87] Pelling, *America and the British Left*, 80–8; on the impact of scientific management theories, American factory practice and trade unionism in Britain, Heindel, *American Impact on Great Britain*, 195–205.

Still the economic pressure was on and something would have to be done about it: here all sides could agree. The sheer numbers of the American expansion began to be documented with concern. The trade gap between Britain and the US had grown from £68 million to £108 million between 1890 and 1903 alone; the US overtook Britain as Germany's leading source of imports in the 1890s, and was poised to do the same in France, the Netherlands, Italy, and Japan, while also expanding rapidly in Asia and Latin America. But as one expert pointed out, the danger was not simply the competition; it was the sense of losing economic sovereignty, of 'being drawn deeply into the organization of trade and production now proceeding outwards from the United States'.[88] In launching its attack on the existing pattern of world trade, why should the US stop at Puerto Rico and not take over the whole of the British Caribbean sphere? With the Panama Canal project now under way, how could her economic and political hegemony in the Pacific be anything but a matter of time?[89] How would the undefendable Canadian border keep out the Americanizing and republicanizing thrust of US trade and journalistic imperialism? Canada indeed might find herself proceeding from a commercial union to a political union overnight. Seeing all this, the Irish, with their Irish–American cousins aroused, wouldn't wait a minute to be assimilated.[90]

A NEW MEDIUM, A NEW MESSAGE

'Our growth [said Heindel] led to a severe British self-analysis which had spiritual as well as technical significance. Prosperity and competition, which perhaps are essential to cultural diffusion in an industrial civilization, enhanced the value of American experience.'[91]

One of the most startling features of the new America now began to rise into general view. This was its apparent ability to turn any variety of

[88] Heindel, *American Impact on Great Britain*, pp. 139, 141, 161–3, and ch. 7 in general.

[89] Under the Anglo-American Hay-Pauncefote Treaty of 1901, Britain had voluntarily renounced hitherto recognized rights to participate in the construction and fortification of any canal across the isthmus of Panama; cf. Burk, *Old World, New World*, 425–8.

[90] Cf. Robert E. Hannigan, 'Continentalism and *Mitteleuropa* as Points of Departure for a Comparison of American and German Foreign Relations in the Early Twentieth Century', in Schröder (ed.), *Confrontation and Cooperation*, 75–8; on British fears of the influence of US periodicals in Canada, Heindel, *American Impact on Great Britain*, 26, of general American influence in Empire, ibid. 163–70; on Ireland, Stead, 'Americanisation of the World', 25–6; Steve J. S. Ickringill, 'Silence and Celebration: Ulster, William McKinley and the Spanish–American War', in Hilton and Ickringill (eds), *European Perceptions*.

[91] Heindel, *American Impact on Great Britain*, 211.

the nation's collective experience into a form of entertainment and then to project it outwards on a commercial basis, to make money, into any receptive part of the world. From the start of the twentieth century the evolution of contemporary culture in Europe at all levels was to be ever more strongly coloured by this impulse, a reflection of what would eventually prove America's most distinctive currency of power. The spectacles of the era 'affirmed that the American genius was in showmanship, spectacle, accumulation, and the instant realization of pleasure', writes Jon Savage; it was 'a new kind of imaginative vision elevated into a national principle that would bond all these disparate peoples together'. Under American skies there truly would be no business like show business: 'America's vitalist dream economy', intense, popular, empowering, and made for export from the start.[92]

After the Spanish–American war broke out the London stage played host to three American theatre companies. Within months of the war's ending the Barnum and Bailey circus company's London branch had put on a water spectacular dramatizing the US Navy's victory at Santiago.[93] From the turn of the century came new producers, new types of musical show, and a tendency—as Bernard Shaw understood—to turn the staging of melodramas and farcical comedies from an art into an industry. With varying degrees of success, the Americans exported in this way female characters and choruses of a like never seen before, idioms, music, moral codes, and myths, remoulding conscious and unconscious desires. 'The glories of the romantic West were constantly offered to the London public' in the first decade of the new century, Heindel reported, 'as if taste were being stimulated by the new-born cinema.'[94]

But it was Buffalo Bill's 'Wild West' show that had opened the way to fame and fortune for this commercial fantasy, with his all-conquering London shows of 1887, 1892, and 1902. The second of these featured a command performance for Queen Victoria where Royal heads from all over Europe, present for her Golden Jubilee, were invited to share the excitement. There was also an invitation to the leading performers to appear on the lawns in front of Windsor Castle. When the aged monarch

[92] Savage, *Teenage*, 54, 115.
[93] For the impact of *The Belle of New York* in London in 1898, Heindel, *American Impact on Great Britain*, 327–8; cf. Richard D. Fulton, 'Sensational War Reporting and the Quality Press in Late Victorian Britain and America', in Wiener and Hampton (eds), *Anglo-American Media Interactions*, 28.
[94] Savage, *Teenage*, 54; on show business Heindel, *American Impact on Great Britain*, 323–30; on the 'flood of American films' that arrived from 1907 onwards, and speculations on their influence, ibid. 334–8.

came out, she immediately conquered the hearts of the visiting show-people by bowing before the American flag.[95]

The enterprising operation of frontier all-rounder William 'Buffalo Bill' Cody has attracted significant scholarly attention in recent years, since it is seen as the precursor of those entertainment industries of the twentieth century that eventually took on a life of their own far from their American origins, achieving global resonance.[96] But the ideological content of Cody's message was no less significant at the time. Buffalo Bill understood intuitively that the new possibilities of mass entertainment provided access to hearts and minds as well as the senses. Taking fun seriously was not just sound commercial sense; it was also a new expression of American identity and intention. Starting out as 'America's National Entertainment', a dramatization of episodes that had occurred in the exploration and conquest of the Frontier, the show was advertised in Europe as the 'Drama of Civilizations'.

Ideological, moral, and didactic, the 'Drama' evolved over the years into an irresistible spectacle of adventure and violence, teaching explicitly, in the words of a programme essay, that 'the bullet is the pioneer of civilization...without the rifle ball we of America would not be today in the possession of a free and united country, and mighty in our strength'.[97] At the same time Cody was an early master of the notion that the medium is the message, making sure that almost all the action was non-verbal (meaning that illiteracy was no bar to participation in the show and foreign language speakers might watch it), involving authentic Indians from past battles as a sign of reconciliation, and employing the latest technologies in lighting, advertising, and transport.

Historians have calculated that the show was seen in its over thirty years of travelling by some fifty million people, in more than a thousand cities in twelve countries.[98] Every level of society from crowned heads downwards went to see it, and its message of triumph for the new white civilization of the United States over the 'lesser breeds' (Kipling) of its day, found resonances everywhere that the Darwinian outlook on culture and

[95] Arnstein, 'Queen Victoria', 99; John G. Blair, 'First Steps toward Globalization: Nineteenth-Century Exports of American Entertainment Forms', in Reinhold Wagnleitner and Elaine Tyler May (eds), *'Here, There and Everywhere': The Foreign Politics of American Popular Culture* (Hanover, NH and London, 2000), 25.

[96] Cf. Rydell and Kroes, *Buffalo Bill in Bologna*, 105–7; Savage, *Teenage*, ch. 9.

[97] Richard Slotkin, 'Buffalo Bill's "Wild West" and the Mythologization of the American Empire', in Amy Kaplan and Donald E. Pease (eds), *Cultures of United States Imperialism* (Durham, NC and London, 1993), 14.

[98] Sarah J. Blackstone cit. in Blair, 'First Steps toward Globalization', 23; for the French experience, Jacques Portes, *De la scène à l'écran: Naissance de la culture de masse aux Etats-Unis* (Paris, 1997), 63–4.

races had taken hold.[99] To American politicians the message was heaven sent. So much was demonstrated in the birth of the most successful myth of the Spanish–American War: that of the 'Rough Riders', the barely trained, volunteer cavalry who had stormed Spanish defences outside the Cuban capital, and whose name was taken straight from Cody's pageant. Their leader in Cuba had been the Assistant Secretary of the Navy Theodore Roosevelt, and his highly personalized success in the war had transformed his political prospects. In an exchange of letters with Cody, 'Colonel' Roosevelt acknowledged his pride in sharing the name with 'those free fearless equestrians, now marshalled under the leadership of the greatest horseman of them all'.[100]

Cody had already begun applying his 'Rough Rider' badge to the cavalry units from European armies who took part in his show under the label of the 'Rough Riders of the World'. Later, a 'Congress of Rough Riders of the World' emerged, whose displays came to include non-white horsemen from tribes recently 'emancipated' by the imperial nations. In the grand finale of his show, Buffalo Bill would ride at the head of this cavalry procession, pronouncing himself 'King of all the Rough Riders of the World'. After the Spanish–American War, Cody replaced his 'Custer's Last Fight' reconstruction with one featuring 'The Battle of San Juan Hill' as led by Theodore Roosevelt, and made sure with a huge poster show that his patrons understood what the 'object lesson' of all America's recent history signified. As Richard Slotkin has explained, when the 'Wild West' show had begun, it represented a commemoration of a disappearing past. This had now been deliberately merged into a celebration of the impending imperial future. America's message of progress would be refreshed and universalized in this way, becoming the victory of Christian civilization over paganism. The scope of 'Manifest Destiny' was ready to be redefined again.[101]

Buffalo Bill was not America's first cultural export, but he was by far the most significant in his era, opening the way to a new sense of the possibilities of 'Americanization', not just its drawbacks. Here was a cultural

---

[99] But European youth identified more closely and romantically with the Indians, claims Jon Savage, judging from the 'Western' popular novels and cartoon strips that began to flourish from this time; *Teenage*, 114.

[100] Slotkin, 'Buffalo Bill's "Wild West"', 28.

[101] Ibid.; cf. Joy S. Kasson, *Buffalo Bill's Wild West: Celebrity, Memory and Popular History* (New York, 2000); 'Manifest Destiny' was a phrase originally invented by a New York editor in 1845 to express the notion that Providence itself had designated the citizens of the United States to take control of the North American continent; it would subsequently take on romantic, idealistic, even ideological meanings—linked to the spread of democracy and freedom—according to changing national circumstances; cf. Anders Stephanson, *Manifest Destiny: American Expansionism and the Empire of Right* (New York, 1995).

product that could be adapted, dismantled, and reassembled, as survivors of the recent Boer battles in South Africa did with their own touring military spectacle in America itself, and as Cody's imitators attempted in countries like Germany and Austria.[102] On display too was a vivid sense of America's emerging leadership potential among the nations of the advanced world, its understanding of the concept of the 'survival of the fittest', and its sense of a duty to bring peoples such as the Red Indians up to the levels where they might join the advancing ranks, 'whose steps march cheerily to the tune of honest toil, industrious peace, and placid fireside prosperity', as another programme tract put it. And there was a glory too for a new style of American hero: Theodore Roosevelt. Cody's historical arguments were paralleled in Roosevelt's manifesto for American imperialism, 'Expansion and Peace' of 1899. This explained 'that "peace" can only be imposed on the "barbarian races" of the world by the armed force of a superior race'. Cody, who fancied himself a frontier Napoleon, showed the world how this task could be done in the idioms of America, the language of democracy, prestige, and show business.[103]

THE STRENUOUS LIFE*

In 1900 Brooks Adams, noble scion of a celebrated political dynasty from Boston, wrote a much-discussed essay that predicted the eventual emergence of two economic superpowers, the US and Russia, with the American economic empire centred on Manila and embracing the entire Far East.[104] Seen from Europe the most significant aspect of Adams's book, *America's Economic Supremacy*, was its insistence that the US would and should *substitute* the European empires, especially the British, whose position in manufactures, exports, and agriculture was already known to be tottering. Whether this transition was to be peaceful or otherwise, Adams

[102] Cf. Blair, 'First Steps toward Globalization', 26–7; on French reaction to the Wild West show, divided more than elsewhere by class and education, Portes, *Fascinations and Misgivings*, 420–1.

[103] Slotkin, 'Buffalo Bill's "Wild West"', 24; in a 1898 Wild West poster 'Art Perpetuating Fame', Cody had himself portrayed on horseback alongside Napoleon, also mounted. Both are 'Men on Horseback', men of destiny, but the American is superior because his figure is youthful, peaceful, and democratic, rather than tyrannical and militaristic; ibid. 29.

* *The Strenuous Life* was the title Roosevelt gave to a collection of his essays and speeches (New York, 1901).

[104] New York, 1900; reprinted New York, 1947; Adams had come to prominence as the author of *The Law of Civilization and Decay* of 1895, a treatise designed to show how civilizations followed distinct patterns of commercial growth and decline; cf. John Lamberton Harper, *American Visions of Europe: Franklin D. Roosevelt, George F. Kennan and Dean G. Acheson* (Cambridge, 1994), 25.

did not care to predict. But only slightly later Adams seemed to think that a general clash was more likely to happen, 'as the present policy of the United States is to force a struggle for subsistence, of singular intensity, upon Europe...'.

... The European sees in America a competitor who, while refusing to buy, throws her wares on every market, and who, while she drives the peasant from his land, reduces the profits of industry which support the wage-earners of the town.[105]

A distinguished British economist, Sydney Brooks, took up the argument in a forceful reply to Adams. 'At present all is bewilderment and speculation.... America's plunge into *Weltpolitik*, the American swoop upon industrial Europe, the first strokes of the new American finance, have been too dramatic and too recent to allow men's thoughts to settle.' Brooks tried hard to convey something of the 'feverish' response, the 'angry uncertainty' set off in the Old World by the revolution in America's status, with its 'intensely irritating consciousness of success' and its formidable, erratic ways. He was prepared to concede that Europe's plight might be due in part to 'a certain mental and manual backwardness and an artificial valuation of the non-productive side of life among the conquered...'. But above all he saw a Republic that had put into production and innovation the immense human resources that the Continental Europeans were devoting to armies and navies. The Russian Tsar had already drawn the consequences, said Brooks, launching a call for a grand conference on disarmament.[106]

Meanwhile, said the English commentator, '[t]he United States has no friend in Europe'. To a 'despairing envy of her prosperity and success' was coupled a disagreeable new sense of impotence: commercial, diplomatic, and moral. 'Cultured Europeans intensely resent the bearing of Americans; they hate the American form of swagger, which is not personal like the British, but national.' Diplomats found the same: arrogance and overweening hypocrisy. But at least they did not have to deal with the consequences of 'of a country so crudely and completely immersed in materialism', said Brooks. Little wonder that 'anti-Americanism' was on the march, with a wave of lesser incidents aggravating the big differences over trade, China, and above all Latin America. There lay an entire continent over which the United States had hung a great 'hands-off' sign, the

---

[105] B. Adams, 'Reciprocity or the Alternative', *Atlantic Monthly* (August 1901).

[106] This was a reference to the celebrated Hague Peace Conference of 1899, which was followed by a second in 1906; but the force of the American question in forming the Tsar's plan is doubtful says May, *Imperial Democracy*, 235–6; cf. Popkova, 'Russian Press Coverage', 132.

Monroe Doctrine, 'the most domineering mandate issued to the world since the days of Imperial Rome'. Germany and Russia were said to be particularly aroused, each for its own geopolitical reasons, but in Continental Europe as a whole feeling was running high, reported Brooks:

> In newspapers, in clubs, in society, even in the street, the dislike of America, the desire, if it were only safe, to give her some savage snub, is unmistakeable.[107]

It was into this inflamed atmosphere that Vice President Theodore Roosevelt stepped when President McKinley was assassinated in September 1901. Unlike his recent predecessors, Roosevelt was a serious thinker on America's future in the world, as well as a man of action, ('Democracies always like a man', said *The Economist*[108]). His force of personality was legendary, bringing back an era when the prestige and vision of the man in the White House in themselves had constituted an extra power asset for the United States.[109] But this was probably the only feature Roosevelt shared with his slightly later successor Woodrow Wilson.

The President would proclaim a 'new nationalism' for the US, but it was strictly conventional in European terms, a Buffalo version of 'Bismarckian bluntness', said Sydney Brooks.[110] For Roosevelt the power of nations was strictly biological, Malthusian, and Darwinian. It was not ideological in any of the senses that became conventional after 1917. Peoples should 'fight well and breed well'; the weak and antiquated must make way for the nations of the future, which were the products of endeavour, true manhood, and righteousness. With the aid of the military man, the merchant, and the missionary, civilization must advance forcefully in the face of barbarism (though even Roosevelt admitted he couldn't always tell which was which in his terms, when mediating in the Russo-Japanese war). So the British Empire should be supported in Asia and Africa, even if England herself was beginning to decay. The Germans were a source of great suspicion: expansive, envious, and in thrall to the Kaiser's personality with its 'violent and wholly irrational zig-zags'.[111] France was

---

[107] S. Brooks, 'Europe and America', *Atlantic Monthly* (November 1901); for a comparable, but less outspoken, French view from the distinguished economist P. Leroy-Beaulieu, 'Les Etats-Unis Puissance coloniale', *Revue des Deux Mondes* (1 January 1902); for Russian worries, Popkova, 'Russian Press Coverage', 128–31.

[108] Cit. in Burnet, *America 1843–1993*, 73.

[109] Impact in Britain described in Heindel, *American Impact on Great Britain*, 267.

[110] Brooks was referring to Roosevelt's speech 'The Two America's' delivered at the Buffalo Pan-American Exposition in May 1901; reproduced in *The Strenuous Life: Essays and Addresses* (New York, 1901).

[111] The German government under the Kaiser's lead went to considerable lengths to counter these impressions, using cultural policy in particular in this phase; on the rise and decline of this tactic, Frank Trommler, 'Inventing the Enemy: German–American Cultural Relations, 1900–1917', in Schröder (ed.), *Confrontation and Cooperation*, 100–12.

a 'stationary' land, not likely to spread commercially or industrially. Meanwhile only a strong and growing navy, backed by a people united and convinced of its righteousness, could deter the potential trouble-makers: Germany above all, later perhaps Russia and Japan.[112]

But no matter how loud the 'cry against Americanization' sounded in European ears, the westerly Atlantic winds made it inaudible in America. Although Roosevelt was aware of the immediate, intense resentments caused in Europe by US tariff policies, even adapting his inaugural speech after reading the Adams article mentioned above, he never felt strong enough to do other than tiptoe around tariff reform.[113] Of the issues mentioned in all the other Old World writing on 'the American peril' and 'the American invasion', there is no trace in his public pronouncements or in his correspondence. England's situation interested him more than any other, but still only in general geopolitical terms. He had one or two influential friends there and felt that 1898 had brought a genuine change towards 'real and practical friendliness' to the US; Britain was the only European nation that might be counted on in a fight. But he had no time for Anglo-Saxonism, and believed that England's attitude too was based on respect for force and success and nothing else.[114]

Roosevelt's major efforts by far were dedicated to the challenges of deciding just what kind of industrial nation the US wanted to be, focus of the era's great political battles between capital and labour, between city and country. But as President his innovations in the world relations of the great powers did leave profound and enduring traces. He made clear that America was not interested in territorial aggrandizement, trying to contain US involvement in the Philippines and granting Cuba a form of protected independence. There was endorsement for the 'Open Door' approach to China and other such zones of interest to European imperialism, meaning they should be conceived as markets available to all, not as possessions to be carved up. This emphasis was particularly distinctive and American, and not only in the context of an era that would see the US turn from being a debtor to a creditor nation. The consequences of it for the evolution

---

[112] Roosevelt, *The Strenuous Life*; *The New Nationalism* (1910 edn repr., Englewood Cliffs, NJ, 1961); *The Letters of Theodore Roosevelt*, ed. Elting E. Morison, iii, iv (Cambridge, Mass., 1951); *A Compilation of the Messages and Papers of the Presidents*, xvii (Washington DC, Bureau of National Literature, n.d.); for extensive discussions of German–America political and economic relations in this period, essays in Schröder (ed.), *Confrontation and Cooperation*, Part I.

[113] Letter to Brooks Adams, 27 September 1901, in *Letters of Theodore Roosevelt*, iii. 152–3; on Roosevelt and tariff reform, Burnet, *America 1843–1993*, 71–3; Henry F. Pringle, *Theodore Roosevelt: A Biography* (New York, 1931), 64.

[114] Letter to A. Hamilton Lee, 18 March 1901, *Letters of Theodore Roosevelt*, iii. 20–1; Letter to Finley Peter Dunne, 23 November 1904, ibid. iv. 1040–1.

of the nation's power presence across the globe turned out to be permanent. As the political commentator John Judis has written:

> [It] committed America to seeking to transform the world through the export of its goods and values rather than through creating a formal empire.[115]

Whether Roosevelt was fully aware of these implications of the Open Door approach is not entirely clear. In his own distinctive language and practice, the Colonel of the Rough Riders certainly built a new definition of the national interest, both political and economic.[116] In asserting it, Roosevelt sent an American ambassador to exert influence on a European great power negotiation for the first time ('to keep matters on an even keel'), mediated successfully in the Russo-Japanese war (winning the Nobel Peace Prize for his efforts), and accelerated decisively the great Panama Canal project (sponsoring violence to take over a piece of Columbia for the purpose). His own demonstration of the link between the medium and the message came with the dispatch of America's new battle fleet on a round-the-world cruise in 1907, an unprecedented naval feat by any power. This was not meant as a menace to anyone, said Roosevelt, but 'as the strongest kind of provocation to friendliness'.[117] After winning a crushing victory in the 1904 Presidential elections, he appeared to a famous contemporary admirer from abroad, H. G. Wells, as 'the mind and will of contemporary America'. Ending in Washington DC an intense exploration of just what this will consisted of, and its implications for the world's future, Wells thought that Theodore Roosevelt confirmed all of his conclusions.[118]

H. G. WELLS'S AMERICA

Science educator, novelist, would-be political reformer, Herbert George Wells was the most celebrated and prolific seer of his day, the best-known living English writer in Europe, the original inventor of time-travelling

---

[115] J. B. Judis, *Grand Illusion: Critics and Champions of the American Century* (New York, 1992), 9.

[116] Emily Rosenberg talks of the ever more conscious development of a 'promotional state' in these years, *Spreading the American Dream*, ch. 3.

[117] Kissinger, *Diplomacy*, 38–41; the European negotiation was the Algeciras conference of 1906 on Morocco, cf. Pringle, *Theodore Roosevelt*; on the meaning of the fleet's voyage, speech by T.R. of 2 September 1910, in *TR: An Autobiography* (1913 edn repr., New York, 1920), 110–12; reactions in Britain and Japan cit. in Heindel, *American Impact on Great Britain*, 114; on the long-term ambiguities of Roosevelt's international behaviour, Ninkovich, *Modernity and Power*, 16–17; William E. Leuchtenberg, Introduction, in Roosevelt, *New Nationalism*.

[118] H. G. Wells, *The Future in America* (1906 edn repr., London, 1987), 185.

and futurology. As a man with a 'prophetic habit of mind', and a belief that 'there is no being but becoming', it was inevitable that Wells should sooner or later make the transatlantic crossing. America 'is [the Englishman's] inheritance,' he wrote, 'his reserved accumulating investment. In that sense indeed, America belongs to the whole Western world, all Europe owns her promise...'[119] So his 1906 account of *The Future in America* was not a typical traveller's tale. Instead it stands out, amidst a profusion of reflections across the industrial world on the possibilities opened up by the new century, as one of those that came closest to identifying the problems in America's present most likely to challenge the future of Western civilization. It also offered a lucid discussion of the solutions to them that the creative American spirits of the day were contemplating.

> Now, my picture of America is...one of a gigantic process of growth, of economic coming and going, spaced out over vast distances and involving millions of hastening men; I see America as towns and urgency and greatnesses beyond, I suppose, any precedent that has ever been in the world.[120]

Wells believed that in travelling to America he might get nearer to the decisive front in 'the coming war of thought against chaos'. In this phase of his political evolution the author of *The First Men in the Moon* was more interested in the meaning of the era's social and ideological confrontations than in technology or time, convinced that out of the material confusion and human misery produced by the Victorian revolution in industry there must of necessity come a new and better age. This would be one that discovered how to dedicate all the science and rationality now available to the organization of human coexistence. America was irresistible because in no other land was the tension so great between the 'moblike rush of individualistic undertakings' and the promise of a 'planned and ordered progress'. There might be found the clues of how the nineteenth-century experience of industrialization—'coaly and mechanical'—could finally be superseded, replaced by electricity, knowledge, and rational public management.[121]

Meanwhile explosive tension dominated the relations between all the various components of America's social existence: industrial, racial, cultural. Wells witnessed on one side the 'smoky, vast, undisciplined growth'

---

[119] H. G. Wells, *The Future in America*, 13; on the context of Wells's trip in his career, David C. Smith, *H. G. Wells: Desperately Mortal: A Biography* (New Haven, Conn., 1986), ch. 4, esp. pp. 103–5; on his own later view of its significance in terms of his thinking on universal reform schemes, *Experiment in Autobiography*, ii: *1898–1918* (1934 edn repr., London, 1966), ch. 9, 'The Idea of a Planned World'.

[120] Wells, *Future in America*, 185.   [121] Ibid. 162, 38, 64.

of Chicago, supreme example of that 'dark disorder' produced by the nation's furious expansion. In contrast he saw the enormous potential resource represented by millions of immigrants made literate and brought to participate fully in national life (a privilege of course denied at the time to the 'black and coloured' masses, to whose fate Wells dedicated an eloquent chapter). If education could be truly democratized, then America and Europe with her would see a new phase of hope in the age-long struggle between 'intelligence' and 'instinct, individual passion, prejudice and ignorance'. With its extraordinary new university system, and commitment to the sciences, both natural and social, America might yet lead the way to a more rational future. But for this vision to be fulfilled, its educated leaders must keep their promise to supply the mind and nervous system for a new and progressive machinery of State, to be constructed from scratch. In Harvard and Yale renewed, in young universities such as Cornell and Stanford, the citadels of a new civilization might emerge, thought Wells. There would be found the rallying points for a fresh collective will dedicated to fighting 'mercantilism, materialism and Philistinism', those huge biases—the devils in the American-world drama—that haunted the whole of the nation's recent development.[122]

Wells had nothing but scorn for American political institutions, and showed no interest in its imperial adventures. The promise of its trade and business expansion in the world left him cold. Graft, child labour, and the abasement of the black population he found everywhere, provoking in his mind disgust and contempt. He also had direct, extraordinary experience of the instant, all-destroying hysterias that the mass newspapers of the day were capable of whipping up.[123] The overwhelming, thoughtless obsession with 'getting and losing' left him thoroughly dismayed: there specifically he saw the magnified version of a trend already on display in commercial England. Wells, the social prophet, was unique in linking this push to the class structure of American society. Just as in Britain, an overblown, triumphant middle class of purblind individualists had become convinced it could do without an organized sense of collective enterprise, rejecting out of hand the need for the thinking, ordering intelligence of an effective public system.[124]

Wells ignored the accumulated baggage of stereotypes, myths, and cultural references left by all the distinguished travellers of the nineteenth century, and took no notice of the 'American invasion' talk current at home and in Europe. That seemed mostly to concern trade and money,

---

[122] Ibid. 43, 155, 163–6.   [123] Ibid. ch. 10.
[124] Ibid. 54–5; Professor Portes notes that French thinkers did *not* at this stage construct an analysis of America as a middle class universe; *Fascinations and Misgivings*, 338.

issues he did not care for. Like every other visitor, Wells did of course project his own concerns on to the American body politic, but in making this most obvious of imaginative efforts, the writer of 'The Discovery of the Future' was explicit in his aims and sought to be systematic in his methods.[125] What Wells went to find in America was neither model nor metaphor, but an *inspiration*; a source of energy and ideas that could be used to reinforce his own great dreams for the reform of post-Victorian Britain, tired, bloated, and chaotic.[126] In America's best men he was delighted to find 'a spirit of criticism and constructive effort, of a scope and quality the world has never seen before'. To Wells its university leaders, its social scientists and investigators, the President himself, all appeared to share an impulse to self-examination and reform which could provide a galvanizing stimulus, a drive towards the reorganization for all those societies that had blindly embraced the scheme of progress via spontaneous industrial development and social alienation.

And for a Fabian socialist like the Wells of 1906, even if an unorthodox one, that meant looking for the creation of a new kind of State under a new kind of leader. It was a feat without precedent, but one 'that any people which aspires to lead the future is bound, I think, to attempt'. In Teddy Roosevelt, Wells believed he had found the inspirational man for the job.[127] He was destined to be disappointed, but not until Wells's faith in human progress was completely shattered, in the last years of his life, did he finally abandon his belief that America's role in its unfolding would be a noble and distinctive one.

ROOSEVELT'S EUROPE

In the 1908 elections Roosevelt left the Presidential battle in the hands of a follower, took a break from America's political turmoil, and went to hunt big game in Africa. Yet within two years he was being welcomed to Europe as a world hero, by far the most famous American of his era and the first to tour the capitals and heads of State of all the major powers. 'As cowboy, Rough Rider and hunter he seemed to the people of Europe, to typify the slightly mad national characteristics of the republic across the sea', said an early American biographer.[128] In Oxford he confirmed the

---

[125] On the cultural and literary significance of his results, Conrad, *Imagining America*, ch. 5, 'Futuristic America: H. G. Wells'; on the context of his reflections within the European socialist movement of the time, R. Laurence Moore, *European Socialists and the American Promised Land* (New York, 1970), 163–5, 192.

[126] Cf. H. G. Wells, *The New Machiavelli* (London, 1910).

[127] Wells, *Future in America*, 163, 89, 98; *Experiment in Autobiography*, 755–9.

[128] Pringle, *Theodore Roosevelt*, 511.

stereotype by lecturing unconvincingly on 'Biological Analogies in History'. London was another matter: there he lectured the British government on the need for a firm hand in Egypt. No foreign dignitary had ever presumed so much, said observers.[129] In Paris he was honoured with official receptions by the President of the Republic, the Institut de France, and the Sorbonne. The Kaiser's welcome was exceptional. The former President was given the privilege—the first private citizen ever to receive it—of reviewing German troops alongside the Emperor himself. On the back of a photograph of the occasion, depicting himself and Roosevelt on horseback, William II wrote: 'When we shake hands, we shake the world.'[130]

But whether he was conscious of it or not, the Europe Roosevelt toured had changed in its attitudes and behaviour to American power over the decade. His quite unprecedented reception was in a sense a symptom of that evolution, a sign of a more mature and balanced recognition of the meaning of America's progress. The US had not gone on to devour other parts of Europe's empires, neither had it succumbed to class war or disintegration under the weight of the immigrants: all fates conjured up by European doomsayers over the years. Now the ex-President's arrival provoked a different sort of European unity, not as threatened in 1903 by the Kaiser, against US economic power (the issue was once more trade and tariffs), but in favour of a more positive, outgoing view of the transatlantic future. French historians, for example, can point to a long era of *rapprochement* between the two countries at the official level which, with hindsight, could be traced as far back as 1898. Statues and busts were inaugurated, professors exchanged, 'travel and official missions became increasingly frequent'. German researchers have found a similar pattern, though organized more self-consciously, under more explicit political priorities, those of trying to conciliate the Americans. Even pacifying trade treaties had eventually been signed.[131]

The implications of the 'Open Door' demands were ignored in France, as it became clear that, unlike Great Britain, America did not in fact depend on the outside world for its prosperity or sense of national purpose.

---

[129] 'We dislike his intrusion and regard his lecture as an example of things that should have been left unsaid', said *The Economist*, demanding to know whether there was not 'more order in Egypt than in Montana?'; edition of 27 August 1910.

[130] On Paris, J. B. Duroselle, *France and the United States: From the Beginnings to the Present* (Chicago, 1978); on Berlin Pringle, *Theodore Roosevelt*, 511–21; the trip included conversations with the Emperor in Vienna, representing the US at the State funeral of Edward VII, and controversy over a failed audience with the Pope. There were also celebrations in Italy, Belgium, Sweden, Norway, and Denmark.

[131] Portes, *Fascinations and Misgivings*, 6; Trommler, 'Inventing the Enemy', 105; Marin, 'L'américanisation du monde'.

US imperialism was a matter of business opportunity, nothing more. As a French Socialist observer had put it as early as 1899:

> ...all it has attested is that the uniform economic system of the major powers of the day has spread among them a uniform civilization, marred by the same flaws everywhere.[132]

Yet even within this uniformity there could be seen emerging new imbalances in the traffic in models and influence. In 1910 *The Economist* reported that Wall Street was now becoming an important influence in the movements of the Paris and Berlin bourses.[133] The opposite was certainly not true. The same paper also reported the example of the long term effects of the 'invasion' of Germany by a specific American product, in this case shoes. Under the pressure of competition, leading German shoe manufacturers were starting to adopt US methods and styles. Large American-type shoe stores had opened in Berlin, Frankfurt, and elsewhere, reported an American Consul, and US managers and foremen had been brought over to reproduce their operations for the benefit of German companies.[134] This again was a one-way flow.

The French fought back by leading the exploitation of the new film medium they had pioneered. By 1907 the leading production and distribution company in the world was a French one, Pathé, and it was French companies that introduced to the US market cartoons, the regular newsreel, and the narrative told in weekly installments, or 'serial'. With no legal regulations or precedents, markets were open for all, and it was European producers who rushed ahead, capturing up to 70 per cent of the US market for short films in 1908. The powerful inventor and entrepreneur Thomas Edison, built up a trust to fight off the invader. He told the magazine *Variety* in 1908: 'the French are somewhat in advance of us. But they will not long maintain their supremacy....Americans in any department of effort are never content to stay in second place.' Comprehensive trade and cultural wars dominated the transatlantic movie scene from that time onwards, but with Italian, British, and Danish producers just as

---

[132] Portes, *Fascinations and Misgivings*, 401–2.

[133] *The Economist*, 27 August 1910, 12 November 1910. In the same weeks, the London *Standard* appointed a special correspondent in New York whose sole task was to supply a daily financial cable from Wall Street. The *Standard*'s editor explained: 'In this day it no longer is possible to cover financial news of the world in bits. There is too much interdependency, and modern facilities have brought about too close relationship [*sic*] between nations, to permit that any more'; story reprinted in *International Herald Tribune*, 15 September 2010.

[134] *The Economist*, 21 May 1910; on the commercial work of American consuls in Germany, Marin, 'L'américanisation du monde'; on Britain, R. A. Church, 'The Effect of the American Export Invasion on the British Boot and Shoe Industry, 1885–1914', *Journal of Economic History* (June 1968).

important in the early years as the Americans, there was as yet no sense of a domination by any one creative or organizational centre. Just before the Americans clamped down, a prominent French commentator was able to write that 'the cinematograph is an international institution, which provides the identical satisfactions in all latitudes'.[135]

In Germany the Kaiser and his government continued to worry about the American geopolitical peril, conservative agrarian interests went on denouncing trade iniquities, and intellectuals began to complain of the spread of a new 'low' culture from the US via the cinema. But German businessmen were busy constructing their own version of the world the Americans were making.[136] They made a great splash at the St Louis Exposition of 1904, playing up the German–American heritage, including the immigrant communities, and linking their sense of economic pride to their idea of German cultural identity. This was one result of the 'second discovery of America', led under the Emperor's auspices by the German economist Max Goldberger. Based on a new vision of that country's revolution in technological efficiency, his book was called *The Land of Unlimited Possibilities*. It was among the first in Europe to discuss the implications of the work on scientific industrial organization produced by the American engineer F. W. Taylor, a development of great importance for the future of European manufacturing.[137]

This German experience was typical of a more general trend. Haldvan Koht recorded how attitudes among the leading business personalities had evolved in the period:

> Soon they understood that efficient machinery and closely knit sales organizations were what made it possible to offer cheap goods. Discovering that business was a science demanding scientific study, they began to establish both technical schools and business schools after American patterns, and American merchandizing methods were adopted one after the other. Efficiency became the slogan of economic life in Europe as in America.[138]

---

[135] David Puttnam, *The Undeclared War: The Struggle for the Control of the World's Film Industry* (London, 1997), ch. 3, Edison quote at p. 48; detailed picture in Gerben Bakker, 'America's Master: The Decline and Fall of the European Film Industry in the United States (1907–1920)', in Passerini (ed.), *Across the Atlantic*, 216–19; quote from André Tardieu in Portes, *Fascinations and Misgivings*, p. 421, n. 12.

[136] Trommler, 'Inventing the Enemy', 120; cf. Ragnhild Fiebig-von Hase, 'The United States and Germany in the World Arena, 1900–1917', in Schröder (ed.), *Confrontation and Cooperation*, 42–3; on the spread of US films in Germany pre-WWI, Göktürk, 'How Modern Is It?'.

[137] For St Louis exposition, Goldberger, and general context, Marin, 'L'américanisation du monde', Bergmann, 'Specter of *Amerikanisierung*'; on Taylor's limited impact in Britain at this stage, Pelling, *America and the British Left*, 94–7.

[138] Koht, *American Spirit*, 208–9; cf. Heindel, *American Impact on Great Britain*, 284; on the origins of business schools in Europe, C. Engwall and V. Zamagni (eds), *Management*

But the results were to transform divisions between the European nations and the US into divisions within them. In 1910, says Trommler, these first consequences were on view of that 'competition in modernity' that would characterize first transatlantic, then global relations through all the rest of the twentieth century.[139]

EUROPEANS AND THE AMERICAN WAY OF WAR

After the old Europe of the great, imperial powers decided to commit slow and bloody suicide from August 1914 onwards, Americans counted their blessings. The US Ambassador in London, Walter Hines Page, wrote to President Wilson's guide, counsellor, and friend, Colonel House, of 'the *magnificent* spectacle our country presents! We escape murder, we escape brutalization; we will have to settle it; we gain in every way.' Teddy Roosevelt thought events demonstrated the worth of the Monroe Doctrine. Without it European colonies in the area would have dragged the Americas in from the start. As it was, no one was clamouring for US intervention.[140] These attitudes, coupled with Wilson's insistence on the most complete neutrality—political, philosophical, and commercial—pleased no one among the combatants. French historians register them as 'deeply disconcerting' for their people; their British colleagues talk of 'vacillation, moral insensitivity or even craven cowardice' as accusations against the US common among opinion in the United Kingdom.[141]

But it soon emerged that the members of the Entente, particularly Britain and France, would become dependent on the force and outlook of the United States in ways they had not foreseen. The longer the war went on, the more the resources of the Americans—financial, industrial, psychological—became indispensable to the very survival of the Allied war effort, and this of course placed the land of the future in an ever more powerful political position. It was the logic of events that made sure that these currencies of power were convertible, but as time went on it was the Americans who inevitably came to dictate the exchange rates. As their consciousness of this position took root, in the mind of Woodrow Wilson

Education in Historical Perspective (Manchester, 1998). The researchers in this text, from various European countries and the US, make clear the very limited influence of American patterns at this stage, cf. Introduction, 10–15.

[139] Trommler, 'Inventing the Enemy', 122.
[140] Pringle, *Theodore Roosevelt*, 578; emphasis in original.
[141] Duroselle, *France and the United States*, 85; Dimbleby and Reynolds, *An Ocean Apart*, 43.

the sensation spread that with this power would come a new kind of world-transforming responsibility.

What Wilson developed was an original conviction that to the republic's material power should be added an explicit moral mission in the world. 'Manifest Destiny' would be redefined again, offering the benefits of America's historical beliefs and experience in such a way that they might become a means for the salvation of all of suffering humanity. In this way a start might be made in eliminating the perceived causes of the great catastrophe, and in the end the world might, in Wilson's famous words, be 'made safe for democracy'.

Woodrow Wilson's great project has been the object of innumerable reflections since, as Henry Kissinger wrote without pleasure, it 'would become the dominant intellectual school of American foreign policy'. Teddy Roosevelt, judged the former Secretary of State, had understood much better the workings of the international system of the era, but it was Wilson who 'grasped the mainsprings of American motivation, perhaps the principal one being that America did not see itself as a nation like any other ... '.

... Whatever the realities and the lessons of power, the American people's abiding conviction has been that its exceptional character resides in the practice and propagation of freedom.[142]

Wilson himself said:

We set this Nation up to make men free, and we did not confine our conception and purpose to America, and now we will make men everywhere free. If we did not do that, all the fame of America would be gone, and all her power would be dissipated.[143]

Far from dissipating America's power, the Great War transformed its force, its reach, and its scope. For the first time, if only temporarily, the US *became a European power*, and it did so with means and languages that changed the very significance of the word 'power'. It was one thing for His Majesty's Government to discover that 'America is now in position to dictate to us on matters that affect Britain more than America', as the Cabinet told the King in 1916.[144] These 'matters' were the traditional preoccupations of ministers, diplomats, and soldiers. But then there came the gradual realization that Wilson's America understood the whole meaning and purpose of the war in terms quite different to those heard hitherto, and intended to impose in its own way its very distinctive vision of international life, after the conflict was over. Moreover US direct

---

[142] Kissinger, *Diplomacy*, 44.   [143] Cit. ibid. 50.
[144] *An Ocean Apart*, BBC1, September 1988, episode 1.

participation, when it eventually arrived in 1917, would take place with means of intervention never seen before, using private-sector people, original systems of organization, and the languages of the new mass media.

The net result was that whatever the pledges about the universal worth of the freedom America was offering, even on the same, victorious side some people came out of the great struggle much freer than others. They were well aware of it. With the British Empire on its knees financially by 1917, Wilson wrote:

> England and France have not the same views with regard to peace that we have by any means. When the war is over we can force them to our way of thinking, because by that time they will, among other things, be financially in our hands.[145]

Among those most acutely aware of the changes the war was bringing about was the rising Bolshevik faction in Imperial Russia, whose day was about to dawn. Their leading lights, including Lenin, had made considerable efforts to apply the tools of Marxist analysis to the New World economic system. The economist Bukharin's analysis in *The World Economy and Imperialism* of 1916, stated clearly and at length the effects the war was having on America's world role:

> The war has placed the United States in a quite exceptional condition. With the end of Russian grain exports the demand for America agricultural products has increased. At the same time at the door of the Americans has arrived a monstrous demand for war materials from the belligerent nations. And finally the world has looked to them to supply its needs for credit.[146]

Bukharin noted too that the United States pan-American strategy had been aided by the fact that Canada, Argentina, Panama, and others had turned from London to New York for their credit supplies, and predicted that reconstruction financing would transform America's world financial status, including the size of her reserves, and would enable her to assume hegemony over areas previously dependent on Europe. Equipped with ample statistical analyses, Bukharin's vision was remarkable at the time for the accuracy of its predictions and the rigour of its exposition. The author

---

[145] Cit. in K. Burk, 'War and Anglo-American Financial Relations in the Twentieth Century', in Leventhal and Quinault (eds), *Anglo-American Attitudes*, 247; Burk notes that by 1916, 40% of all British war expenditure was being spent in the US and Canada, and that Britain was 'also financing or guaranteeing…the purchases of France, Russia, Belgium, Italy, Rumania and Greece. In due course the burden almost bankrupted Britain'; ibid. 246.

[146] N. Bukharin, *L'economia mondiale e l'imperialismo*, translation of 1916 edition (Rome, 1966), 296.

did not go so far as to label the new US role vis-à-vis Europe as 'imperialistic', since he insisted, in strict Marxian logic, that true imperialism occurred only when a power imposed abroad its own mode of production. Instead, for Bukharin, it was the dramatic change of roles in the old inter-imperial struggle that characterized the new era.

MOBILIZING FOR MODERNITY

Europeans everywhere were bewildered by the speed with which after so much hesitation the Americans prepared for battle, and then exhilarated by the 'health, vitality and hope' the hundreds of thousands of 'doughboys' brought with them across the Atlantic. A French officer recalled: 'We all had the same impression that we were about to see a wonderful transfusion of blood. Life was coming in floods to reanimate the dying body of France.' One of Britain's most telling witnesses, the writer Vera Brittain, talked of the 'fearless swagger of their proud strength', and saluted the arrival of 'our deliverers at last'. Hope finally surged that the war could be ended and won.[147]

As Jon Savage has written, these Americans brought with them a vast array of psychic and material assets: 'in its combination of industrial might, cultural vitality and physical confidence, America embodied the future to many Europeans, all the more so because the November 1918 armistice revealed a terrifying vacuum within the combatant countries.'[148] But the Europeans were completely unprepared for the endless variety of instruments the Americans deployed to extend US influence in every direction. The Western Front had looked on with wonder at the revolution in government organization that produced a huge, lavishly financed army in a matter of months. Now the 'promotional state' repeatedly startled allies and enemies alike in its ability to mobilize the energies of civil America, communicate the nation's purposes abroad, and build a world fit for business expansion as soon as the fighting ended.

The French film entrepreneur Léon Gaumont lamented: 'This war was made for America.' The film industries of the combatant nations collapsed one by one within months of the war's outbreak, and American output was pulled in to fill the vacuum. Then, from 1916 onwards, came a change, reports David Puttnam, a film producer turned industry historian. The studios began actively to organize their overseas markets, expand them, produce and distribute in them, now consciously reaching for global domination by taking over all the old imperial spheres as well. A well-known

---

[147] Savage, *Teenage*, 176.   [148] Ibid.

Californian producer recalled: 'Our industry was slowly starting but expanded leaps and bounds during the European setback, and by the end of the war we were so far ahead technically and had such a grip on foreign audiences that our gross revenues put us in an impregnable position.'[149]

But it was the new connection between the Californian producers—moving to their expanded, sunlit base at Hollywood to cope with the vast surge in demand—and the Federal government in Washington DC that transformed movie production into an unprecedented currency of American power. Barely an industry, its pioneers knew that it still had to win respectability as a recognized national institution. Wilson for his part came to understand that 'it was increasingly associated in the eyes of the world with the modernity of the United States'. When the producers and the presidency finally came together, a new capacity for communicating the meaning of the land of the future appeared on the world's cinema screens. Launching the first Films Division of the Committee on Public Information in September 1917, Wilson said:

> The film has come to rank as the very highest medium for the dissemination of public intelligence, and since it speaks a universal language, it lends itself importantly to the presentation of America's plans and purposes.[150]

The Committee on Public Information was run by a journalist from Denver named George Creel, one of the many enterprising types the war threw up who knew instinctively how a private citizen could transform himself temporarily into a public servant. The title of his memoir of the Committee says much about Creel's attitudes to his official efforts: *How We Advertised America: The First Telling of the Amazing Story of the Committee on Public Information that Carried the Gospel of Americanism to Every Corner of the Globe*.[151] 'The full scope of the Creel Committee's work is simply staggering to contemplate', write Rydell and Kroes. On the film front alone, aided by high-level volunteers from the studios and companies such as Eastman Kodak, the Committee was distributing documentaries, comedy shorts, and commercial films on a huge scale throughout the Allied countries including Russia, and even into neutral areas such as Scandinavia, Spain, Holland, and German-dominated Switzerland. By

---

[149] Puttnam, *Undeclared War*, 86–7.

[150] Ibid. 89, 91; a satirical view of this period in the history of Washington and of Hollywood is provided by Gore Vidal's historical novel, *Hollywood* (London, 1989).

[151] New York, 1920; survey and analysis of the Committee's work in Rydell and Kroes, *Buffalo Bill in Bologna*, 134–40; cf. Nicholas J. Cull, *The Cold War and the United States Information Agency: American Propaganda and Public Diplomacy, 1945–1989* (Cambridge, 2008), 6–9.

the end of the war China, Japan, and the whole of Latin America were within its reach, transmitting values and opening markets.[152]

It was the limitless pragmatism of attitudes towards the division between the public and the private spheres that guaranteed the Committee's dynamism and its ever-expanding scope, as in so many other areas of Washington's war effort. The American machinery of government, it turned out, could be redesigned and reconstructed as needs might be. Universal Pictures or Eastman Kodak were not nationalized for the duration as in Europe, but lent their men, their products, and their energies to the US Government on a temporary, flexible basis. The same method was applied to trade unions such as the powerful American Federation of Labor, to philanthropic organizations like the American Red Cross, and missionary movements led by the Young Men's Christian Association (YMCA). And they quickly learned to work together in the field, where anyone, it seemed, was entitled to put on stripes and help push the new media and their messages. It was the YMCA and the Red Cross that took the officially approved films into Siberia, as the Bolshevik Revolution pushed them ever eastwards.[153]

MYTHMAKING IN WARTIME—THE ITALIAN EXPERIENCE

From Italy has come the most detailed study so far of the origins and fate of the myths that built up around America thanks to the efforts of these organizations. As the Rome historian Daniela Rossini has shown, a vast gulf of political and mental incomprehension separated the Italian and American associates in the war, which their respective leaders did not care to look into.[154] Italy was a case that showed how useless was a view of the world based on anything resembling Roosevelt's old distinction between 'civilized' and 'barbarian' peoples. The war had demonstrated to Wilson that in crisis, the most civilized of nations were perfectly capable of choosing barbarism rather than compromise their vaunted, antiquated war

---

[152] Rydell and Kroes, *Buffalo Bill in Bologna*, 134; details of film operations in Kristin Thompson, *Exporting Entertainment: America in the World Film Market, 1907–1934* (London, 1985), ch. 3.

[153] Rosenberg, *Spreading the American Dream*, ch. 4; Thompson, *Exporting Entertainment*, 98; details in Norman E. Saul, *The United States and Russia, 1914–1921* (Kansas City, 2001), ch. 3; this recounts the rise and fall of various efforts by American missions, diplomats and business figures to capitalize on the Russian fascination with *Amerikanikizm* of the time.

[154] Rossini, *Il mito americano*; on the Italian studies of Wilson's famous Inquiry project under Colonel House, their limits and their impact, ibid. 171–4, 208–9.

aims. Now was the moment for America with its 'information and education' machine to show the ignoble and backward ruling classes of a country like Italy the meaning of modernity in war, how to mobilize consensus, promote democracy, and provide peoples with a vision of a future truly worth fighting for—a future of security and abundance *for them*.

The frightened and insecure rulers of Italy were indeed deeply uninterested in all of this, and unlike other members of the Entente, did not even pretend to democratize the meaning or methods of their war effort as the struggle became more and more 'total'.[155] Nevertheless, as one of the lands where the spectre of Bolshevism spread fastest after the October Revolution of 1917, the government and its allies quickly fastened on to Wilson's popular appeal to bolster their own positions and revitalize the popular will to fight after recent disasters. Helped by the US propaganda agencies, the Red Cross, and the YMCA, national and local committees were set up to spread America's image and Wilson's word. The point, suggest witnesses of the time, was not to build a mass consensus for Wilson's vision, considered too difficult and abstract, but firstly to bolster continuing Italian participation in the war, and secondly to open the way to a direct contact between America and the country's popular masses.

In spite of the almost complete absence of US soldiers in Italy—except on a 'pretend' basis[156]—and the limited role of the country in the war, the American propaganda machine made a quite extraordinary effort up and down the peninsula. No means of communication was left unused as the Committee on Public Information sought to build dialogue with as many of the Italian people as it could reach, products of a still largely rural society where illiteracy remained around 25 per cent, but where the emigrant link loomed large in every peasant family. For the first and only time, popular celebrations of the Fourth of July were organized in large and small towns alike.[157] Millions saw the Committee's photo exhibitions and its theatre and film shows: around 500 films were shown, put on by 350 specialized operators. Through the YMCA an enormous supply of writing materials, sweets, cigarettes, and magazines was organized for the benefit of the soldiers. YMCA and American Red Cross 'comfort stations', hospitals, ambulances, gyms, gifts, entertainments, and English lessons left an unforgettable trail of generosity and goodwill. In the summer of 1918,

[155] Rossini, *Il mito americano*; on the Italian studies of Wilson's famous Inquiry project under Colonel House, their limits and their impact, 54–5, 86.

[156] The one regiment detached to Italy, vastly welcomed, in practice spent its time marching from area to area, often changing its uniforms in secret along the way to give the impression of much greater numbers than in fact existed. It was sent into 'action' on the last day of the war, against an Austrian unit that had already signalled it would not fight, ibid. 110–13.

[157] W. T. Stead and friends wished the day to become a standing celebration of Anglo-American solidarity, Heindel, *American Impact on Great Britain*, 37.

3,600 poor families a month were receiving direct financial assistance from the American Red Cross, if they were known to have a breadwinner in uniform.[158]

Everywhere the new messengers of salvation encountered the living legends of America inherited from the popular experience of emigration. In Turin the youthful revolutionary Antonio Gramsci wrote that Wilson had made himself the human symbol of the America of riches, work and fortune, for that mass of peasants and workers who still saw in emigration the solution to all their problems. The poorer and remoter the country village, the stronger seemed to be the attachment to this myth, which often took on mystical, pseudo-religious connotations.[159] Essay contests, debates, soldier's letters, and trench newspapers bear witness to the popular response that rose up from all sides as a result of such intense American activity. A local army command newspaper wrote:

> Our ally does miracles. They looked like people only interested in buying and selling, completely obsessed with getting rich, and yet they have shown themselves to be champions. They have joined the battle with no other ambition than to guarantee the victory of the rule of Law. Devoid of hatred unless against the new tyrants of the world, they did not settle for spending their accumulated wealth, but chose to spill on the earth of France their radiant blood. They fight and they win...[160]

In a land such as Italy, deeply split on the worth of participating in the war, lines were drawn up in this way for a new kind of political confrontation. A commentator of the era talked of a million bayonets in search of an idea. For a brief moment Wilson seemed to provide one. For the disaffected workers of the north, in uniform or out of it, Lenin provided another. Ancient divisions of party, faith, and class seemed to be turning into a contrast between all-embracing world outlooks imported from abroad. The modern age of *ideology* was born, in a distinctive, Italian version.

THE WILSON EFFECT

Wilson believed that he spoke for 'the silent mass of mankind', and the overwhelming enthusiasm on display everywhere he or his name went in Europe confirmed the weight of the hopes now placed in America's

---

[158] Ibid. ch. 4.

[159] Ibid. 99–100; in one Sardinian village the distribution of Red Cross aid had to be suspended to allow a spontaneous religious procession in their honour to take place. In the hand of the Virgin's statue, a Stars and Stripes flag had been placed; loc. cit.

[160] Cit. ibid. 101.

deliverance. A young member of a huge crowd gathered under the balcony of Buckingham Palace to witness his appearance alongside the King and Queen recalled:

> Everybody cheered and clapped. He spoke optimistically. The world was going to be safe for Democracy and there would be no more wars, which pleased everybody. We were all very young and believed all we were told.[161]

In spite of the complete absence in the President's programmatic Fourteen Points of any reference to the topic of wealth creation, *The Economist* anticipated a Wilsonian peace 'in which mankind may be united into one great throbbing hive of industry, in which the best workers will win battles by turning out the best stuff, and the world's output and consumption of goods may be quickened to an extent undreamed of'.[162]

H. G. Wells was another keen admirer of the American head of state. Inventor on the conflict's first day of the prophesy about 'the war that will end war', Wells was long a believer in the old Liberal notion of a permanent World Council to preserve peace and promote disarmament. So he greeted Wilson's vision of a League of Nations with outspoken admiration. In 1915 he offered an apology to the United States. Having expected nothing but 'levity' and 'irresponsibility', he saw a new collective will forming, one with a firm sense of responsibility for the welfare of mankind. All that was lacking was 'a man of force and genius' to provide the needed leadership. Wilson's emergence, and his determination to establish a new form of world government based on the rule of international law, brought Wells joy unbounded. Here was 'the one man who has risen to the greatness of this great occasion, the man who is, in default of any rival, rapidly becoming the leader of the world towards peace...'.[163] The brilliant young economist John Maynard Keynes recalled later how Wilson upon his departure from Washington had 'enjoyed a prestige and moral influence throughout the world unequalled in history'. With his control of money, materials, and men, the American President had the power to transform the prospects of civilization: 'Never has a philosopher held such weapons wherewith to bind the princes of this world.... With what curiosity, anxiety, and hope we sought a glimpse of the features and

---

[161] Cit. in Dimbleby and Reynolds, *An Ocean Apart*, 63.

[162] Cit. in Burnet, *America 1843–1993*, 93; Point III of the Fourteen Points contained a declaration of principle in favour of non-discriminatory trade, but Wilson made clear this was intended to remove those economic frictions that fed political antagonism: tariff barriers, preferences, protectionisms. The Fourteen Points are visible at: <http://www.firstworldwar.com/source/fourteenpoints.htm>

[163] H. G. Wells, *The Peace of the World* (London, n.d. [1915]); *In the Fourth Year: Anticipations of a World Peace* (London, 1918), cit. at p. 130; for context, Smith, *H. G. Wells*, 232–42.

bearing of the man of destiny who, coming from the West, was to bring healing to the wounds of the ancient parent of his civilisation and lay for us the foundations of the future.'[164]

In France Wilson's heroic status transcended the bitter party battles of the time, providing, as the cultural historian Elizabeth Fordham writes, 'a mystical moment in French thought', one that seemed to match up to the horrors and desperation of the closing stages of France's war. The political groups tried to outdo each other in exaltation, with the socialists promoting a Parliamentary motion to the effect that Wilson had earned the gratitude not just of France but of all mankind. Poets and novelists had imagined a Wilsonian peace that 'provided a means of imagining a bridge between the past and the future in terms other than those dictated by the butchery of the present' (Fordham), at least as long as the US stayed out of the war. Now in early 1919, keeping at least a part of this faith, almost all the most prominent intellectuals of the day, left and right, queued to celebrate in an intensely spiritual fashion this 'citizen of the world', this 'apostle of peace'. Forgotten was the wave of popular exasperation caused by the behaviour of some of the almost two million American soldiers in France, with their rough, careless ways and inflationary spending power.[165]

Then, in one the greatest falls from grace of the contemporary era, only months after his triumphal arrival in Europe, Wilson and his legend parted company. By the time the Versailles conference ended we can see that from Keynes to Lenin, Wilson's European peers had come to consider him a ridiculous figure, incapable of dealing on the same level as razor-sharp power brokers such as Lloyd George and Clemenceau. For Keynes, he had 'no plan, no scheme, no constructive ideas whatever for clothing with the flesh of life the commandments he had thundered from the White House'. Lenin poured scorn on the President's 'sanctimonious piffle' and pronounced his ideology bankrupt. His greatest French eulogist, the poet Romain Rolland, deplored 'the flagrant violation of Wilsonian principles by Wilson himself'.[166] The Italian disillusion was particularly bitter, as Wilson sought to dismiss most of their territorial claims out

---

[164] *The Collected Writings of John Maynard Keynes*, ii: *The Economic Consequences of the Peace* (1919 edn repr., London 1971), 23–4.

[165] Duroselle, *France and the United States*, 106–8; Fordham, 'From Whitman to Wilson', 128–38; for an American literary reflection on the confrontation between soldiery and people, Willa Cather, *One of Ours* (1922 edn repr., New York, 1971), 275, *passim*.

[166] *The Economist*'s epitaph said: 'Having failed to achieve peace without victory, he soon became a stalking horse for his European colleagues in their not unsuccessful endeavours to achieve victory without peace', edition of 9 February 1924; Keynes, *Collected Writings*, ii. 25–34; Harold Nicolson, *Peace-making 1919* (New York, 1923); V. I. Lenin, *On the United States of America* (Moscow, 1967), Report on the International Situation, 19 July 1920; Rolland cit. in Fordham, 'From Whitman to Wilson', 138.

of hand. The populist agitator Benito Mussolini emerged now as the man who knew best what the bayonets wanted after this humiliation: an ideology of their own, homegrown and nationalistic.[167] But no European leader could deny that Wilson still possessed—at least potentially—the force, the opportunity, and the methods to overthrow the traditional balance-of-power approach to relations between states, if only because of the leverage that could come from the immense debts of the combatants. Alone among the Powers, Lenin noted in 1920, America could act with complete financial independence in world politics.[168] Europe had already ceased to be the centre of the world in January 1918, judged A. J. P. Taylor, at that moment when Wilson had launched his platform for the modernization of politics between nations in the Fourteen Points. This was his measured response not just to the deeply worrying challenge of Bolshevism, but to the general clamour for a new sort of peace, permanent and 'secured by some other means than the Balance of Power' (Taylor). By the time he arrived at the Versailles peace conference, Wilson believed he was God's instrument, chosen by Him to bring the providential benefits of America's values and progress to the salvation of the devastated empires of old Europe.[169] But as its propaganda campaign demonstrated, the experience of war had developed in the US a remarkable ability to invent new ways to project its power abroad, and these were strictly secular.

Wilson's personal vision had derived its messianic quality not from any supernatural power of its expounder, but from its colossal ambition: nothing less than a wish to extend American experiences and institutions universally, and thereby offer responses to the presumed causes of international war *and* the class war. The eminent commentator Walter Lippmann, a junior Wilson advisor at the time, declared later that 'the Wilsonian ideology [was] American fundamentalism made into a universal doctrine'. To replace the jungle of the international power struggle, there would be collective security guaranteed by an assembly of nations, and an international court of justice. As in America, in other words, the law should serve wherever possible to substitute politics in conflict resolution.[170]

---

[167] For Mussolini's entirely opportunistic attitude to Wilson, R. Vivarelli, *Il dopoguerra in Italia e l'avvento del Fascismo (1918–1922)* (Naples, 1967), i. 244–9.

[168] Lenin, *On the United States of America*, report of 27 November 1918, address of 22 November 1919, report of 19 July 1920.

[169] Taylor, *Struggle for Mastery*, 567–8; Lloyd C. Gardner, 'The United States, the German Peril and a Revolutionary World: The Inconsistencies of World Order and National Self-Determination', in Schröder (ed.), *Confrontation and Cooperation*.

[170] Walter Lippmann, *Isolation and Alliances: An American Speaks to the British* (New York, 1952); Robert Boyce, *The Great Interwar Crisis and the Collapse of Globalization* (London, 2009), 45.

Meanwhile, behind these lofty visions, there stood a readiness among Wilson's associates to use food as a political weapon. They did not hesitate to buy up factories and industries in prostrate countries such as Poland. From the White House came the impulse to unite the US Navy with corporate interests in order to build a global communications system to give access to public opinion everywhere, and trump the British. 'With the control of world public opinion, trade and dominion would follow', reflected a BBC television documentary later, describing the Anglo-American battle in the sector that ensued.[171] These were the sort of realities that would define Europe's encounter with the force of American modernity throughout the 1920s, long after Wilson and his legend had been eclipsed. And they were the first answers to all those new questions of 1898 on what sort of power the US would set out to be in the world of the twentieth century.

---

[171] David Dimbleby, opening of *An Ocean Apart*, BBC1, episode 2. The sequence describes the founding of the Radio Corporation of America (RCA), and the role of Owen Young, a director of General Electric and future inventor of the 1928 plan for the financial salvation of Germany; details of the Anglo-American struggle over communications in Rosenberg, *Spreading the American Dream*, 88–97; subsequent evolution of competition in Boyce, *Great Interwar Crisis*, 180–2.

2

The Roaring Twenties in Europe

AT THE CROSS-ROADS OF DEMOCRACY

It was not just the centre of world politics and finance that shifted to America as a result of World War I. So too had the 'the prewar form of modernism, with its positive urge', suggests the cultural historian Modris Eksteins, and 'Europe recognised this'.[1] Just as the results of the Spanish–American conflict had set in motion in the Iberian nation a tortuous process of redefinition of that society's identity and place in the modern world—producing the 'Regeneration' movement of the 1920s[2]—so too on a much larger scale, the upheaval of the world war forced its European protagonists, winners and losers alike, to reflect on all the possible reasons for their current situation, on their prospects, expectations, and fears. In crucial sections of society a sense spread that only a dramatic alteration in the schemes of living pursued hitherto would restore the possibility of hope, of some sort of faith in the future. It was the youth, the young men who had survived the war, who were most affected. Jon Savage writes: 'Nineteen-nineteen heralded the arrival of adolescence as a powerful social and political force within Europe. As a positive, if abstract, principle, youth embodied the headlong flight into the future.'[3]

But other generations strongly preferred to look backwards in time for comfort and compensation. This fracture between the old and the young was one of the factors producing the 'crisis of classical modernism' identified by German historians, and it touched all the survivors to varying degrees after the war. But only those strong in character and culture could

---

[1] M. Eksteins, *Rites of Spring: The Great War and the Birth of the Modern Age* (London, 1989), 267.

[2] On the 'Regeneration' movement, Sebastian Balfour, 'The Loss of Empire, Regenerationism, and the Forging of a Myth of National Identity', in Helen Graham and Jo Labanyi (eds), *Spanish Cultural Studies: An Introduction* (Oxford, 1995). It was this current that produced one of Europe's best-known commentators on contemporary developments, Ortega y Gasset; see below.

[3] Savage, *Teenage*, 183, 236.

match the depth of their reflections to the intensity of this crisis, without sliding into irrationality and extremism.[4]

Everywhere there emerged the centrality of America—whether loved or loathed—as the crucial term of comparison when the topic was building the future in any form. In Joseph Roth's 1924 novel *Hotel Savoy*, a war-weary town on the eastern edge of Europe was the backdrop for a meeting between a returning Austrian prisoner of war and an eccentric old Croat comrade-in-arms, Zwonimir. Together they recalled feeling the endlessness of the war: 'In ten years' time [the Croatian had predicted], no fruit will grow in any country in the world, only in America.' It was Zwonimir's habit to call any piece of fortune 'America'—a decent billet, a strong position, a good officer. An emigrant from the town, the son of old Blumenfeld, grown rich in America, was back as Bloomfield and all were looking to him for salvation. 'It's remarkable', said the narrator to his friend, 'do you notice how people are altering because...Bloomfield is here? Everyone suddenly has ideas for business, in this hotel and in this town. Everyone wants to earn money.' But Bloomfield had returned only to honour his roots. Terrified by the threat of typhus and Red revolution, he would soon depart, leaving only a scattering of charity. The ex-prisoners move on too, dreaming of reaching New York. The narrator concludes: 'I think to myself: America; that is what Zwonimir would have said, just America.'[5]

But there quickly spread in Europe the conviction that it was America as a nation that was fleeing before the chaos left by the war. The urge to repudiate the peace treaty, demand payment for all the war debts, and pass laws against immigration: all this looked like closure, rejection, panic—especially after it had become clear to Americans too that the Bolsheviks had won their struggle to survive, and intended to fulfil the Leninist promise to export the Revolution far and wide. After a visit in late 1920 to a starving Germany, the Cambridge essayist Lowes Dickinson urged the Americans not to give up:

> ...Europe is still mad with war passions. Europe can think of no remedy but more killing. If Europe is to be saved, it must be by America. Perhaps America might do it yet. Will she not at least try?[6]

Eventually, after 1923, something like the Bloomfield effect did begin to happen, as American products and symbols, dollars, investors, and tourists started to spill into Europe from the swelling prosperity across the

---

[4] Cf. ibid. 184–96.
[5] Joseph Roth, *Hotel Savoy*, translation of 1924 edition (London, 1986), cits at pp. 63, 103, 123.
[6] G. Lowes Dickinson, 'SOS—Europe to America', *Atlantic Monthly* (March 1921).

Atlantic.[7] A German historian has best expressed—not without a hint of ironic exaggeration—what became of the earlier desire for salvation, how it would subsequently evolve in this decade into a much broader sense of America's meaning for the discredited Old World, something like a new 'Americanism':

> …Americanism developed in the 1920s [in]to a truly European umbrella term that could refer to anything that was "modern" and could even remotely be linked to materialism, efficiency, size, mechanization, standardization, automation, technocracy, uniformity, pragmatism, reform consciousness, naive optimism, spontaneity, generosity, openness, advertising, democracy, or influence exercised upon the masses.[8]

This new America presented itself to Europeans explicitly as a political, economic, and cultural *competitor*, unprecedented in its ubiquity and dynamism. 'It is obvious that the next Power to make a bid for world empire will be America', proclaimed the philosopher Bertrand Russell in 1923. '[T]he prodigal returns, not to repent but to dream and demonstrate and sell', wrote the *Chicago Daily News* journalist Mowrer in 1928, in a remarkable survey of the competitor's challenging effects.[9] European societies were obliged, whether they liked it or not, to reckon with a new kind of presence at work in their destiny. The Anglo-American novelist, Mary Borden, explained why it was so necessary to keep an eye on the Americans. They should be watched, she wrote,

> …by everyone interested in the future of mankind, for the scaffolding of the world of the future is reared against the sky of America, and a rough map of it is spread over that continent and its voice is pounding and screaming out the news of what is to come to pass on the earth.[10]

H. G. Wells scandalized his friends on the Left by proclaiming: 'I shall look to America rather than Moscow for the first instalments of the real revolution.'[11]

[7] Figures in Boyce, *Great Interwar Crisis*, 80, 178–9.

[8] Philipp Gassert, ' "Without Concessions to Marxist or Communist Thought": Fordism in Germany, 1923–1939', in David E. Barclay and Elisabeth Glaser-Schmidt (eds), *Transatlantic Images and Perceptions: Germany and America since 1776* (Cambridge, 1997), 220; this list is based on a very similar one proposed by Frank Costigliola, *Awkward Dominion: American Political, Economic, and Cultural Relations with Europe, 1919–1933* (Ithaca, 1984), 167; another is in Pells, *Not Like Us*, 11.

[9] Bertrand Russell and Dora Russell, *The Prospects of Industrial Civilisation* (London, 1923), 88; Edgar Ansel Mowrer, *This American World*, with a preface by T. S. Eliot (London, 1928), 77. Mowrer was Berlin correspondent of the Chicago newspaper from 1923 to 1933; his early career and 1928 book discussed in Morrell Heald, *Transatlantic Vistas: American Journalists in Europe, 1900–1940* (Kent, O., 1988), 156–7, 207–10.

[10] Borden cit. in Eksteins, *Rites of Spring*, 269; for the German equivalent of this prognosis, Mary Nolan, *Visions of Modernity: American Business and the Modernization of Germany* (New York, 1994), 9.

[11] Cit. in West, *H. G. Wells*, 125–6; the book is a form of biography written by the son of Wells and the writer Rebecca West.

It was a time when the prevailing meaning of the condition of being 'modern' was radically altered. Everywhere new senses of modernity's demystifying, rationalizing power emerged. *Mass democracy, mass production, and mass communications:* these were the victorious products of the second industrial revolution, and their triumph, everyone agreed, had been accelerated by the war. The definitive encounter of these three characterizing social forces of the twentieth century at a single cross-roads in time gave the 1920s something of their peculiar historical significance. Patterns of conflict and compromise emerged that all the traditional societies would display at some point, usually involving prolonged phases of painful adaptation. And two of these challenges, 'Fordism' and industrial-scale entertainment, emanated from the tremendous economic and technical development America had known by way of the Great War. 'America's mass was the crucible of 'massification', writes David Reynolds, 'And that mass was mobilized through the multiplier effect of modern technology.'[12] Or as a leading commentator of the time in France asked his readers:

> Of all the existing civilisations, which one possesses sufficient moral and physical vigour to adapt itself to mass needs, in order to impose itself on the rest of the world?... Is it Europe or America?[13]

In an epoch when traditional elites and historical institutions in Europe faced the greatest difficulty in re-establishing their authority and legitimacy in the wake of the catastrophe, the triple assertion of the new modernity with its unmistakable American features was more than many could cope with.

The democratic inspiration and its fate

For a short, triumphant time it appeared that Woodrow Wilson's heritage was to be an outburst of democratic development across Europe. The Czech nationalist Declaration of Independence of October 1918 proclaimed: 'We accept the American principles as laid down by President Wilson: the principles of liberated mankind—of the actual equality of nations—and of governments deriving their just power from the consent

---

[12] D. Reynolds, 'American Globalism: Mass, Motion and the Multiplier Effect', in A. G. Hopkins (ed.), *Globalization in World History* (London, 2002), 252; on the centrality of youth in this dynamic of change, Savage, *Teenage*, ch. 16.

[13] Michael Ermarth cit. in Nolan, *Visions of Modernity*, 10; Lucien Romier, *Who Will Be Master, Europe or America?* (London, 1929), 32; for Romier and his context, Richard Kuisel, *Ernest Mercier, French Technocrat* (Berkeley, 1967), 64–5; Roxanne Panchisi, *Future Tense: The Culture of Anticipation in France Between the Wars* (Ithaca, 2009), ch. 4, 'The Future is a Foreign Country'.

of the governed.'[14] An American political historian whose family was Czech in origin recalled in the late 1950s how:

> Before World War II the western traveller arriving by the Orient Express in Prague, Czechoslovakia, would detrain at the Wilson Station. Coming out of the station, he would face the Wilson Square and the Wilson Park, with a statue of President Woodrow Wilson in its center. There were innumerable Wilson avenues, Wilson Squares, and Wilson statues in Belgrade, Bucharest, Warsaw, Prague and the other cities of the new national states of East Central Europe, all testifying to the fact that the Yugoslavs, Rumanians, Poles, and Czechoslovaks regarded President Wilson as one of their liberators and heroes.[15]

This was democracy as self-determination, and it accompanied the promise of democracy as republicanism, democracy as the League of Nations, democracy as parliamentarism and popular sovereignty, as constitutionalism and legitimacy, as universal suffrage and equality, as the end of monarchy, feudalism, and privilege entrenched. Democracy under the Wilsonian spell seemed to have fused the strongest of the nineteenth-century European currents of Liberalism and nationalism and made them modern and real. Obviously it was America's continuing duty to defend this vision, whose fulfilment had been its only declared war aim. As Wilson himself put it in his outgoing Presidential message to the US Congress: 'It is surely the manifest destiny of the United States to lead in the attempt to make this spirit prevail.... The United States is of necessity the sample democracy in the world, and the triumph of democracy depends upon its success.'[16]

The parabola of democracy's rise and fall in Europe between the wars has now been traced in detail by historians, revisited particularly after the end of the Cold War as a third effort was made to produce self-supporting government by consent in those nations most afflicted by the international conflicts of the century.[17] But the role of America in Europe's interwar fate remains ambiguous. For some European historians it was

---

[14] Cit. in Mark Mazower, *Dark Continent: Europe's Twentieth Century* (London, 1999), 4.

[15] This is the opening paragraph of Victor S. Mamatey, *The United States and East Central Europe 1914–1918: A Study in Wilsonian Diplomacy and Propaganda* (Princeton, 1957); on the survival of democracy in Czechoslovakia and the limits of the American contribution, Tony Smith, *America's Mission: The United States and the Worldwide Struggle for Democracy in the Twentieth Century* (Princeton, 1994), 100–2, 108.

[16] Woodrow Wilson, *War and Peace: Presidential Messages, Addresses and Public Papers (1917–1924)*, ed. Ray Stannard Baker and William E. Dodd (New York, 1927), 513–15, address of 7 December 1920.

[17] Mazower, *Dark Continent*, ch. 1; Carl Levy and Mark Roseman (eds), *Three Postwar Eras in Comparison: Western Europe 1918–1945–1989* (London, 2002); John Garrard, Vera Tolz, and Ralph White (eds), *European Democratization since 1800* (London, 2000).

always perfectly possible to write the story with no reference at all to the US after Wilson's defeats of 1919–20, and the victory of militant political 'isolationism' across the Atlantic. Lenin had survived after all, while America's prophet had been disowned and humiliated by his own people.[18] But historians in the US itself, searching for the roots of their nation's contemporary situation in the world, discovered countless forms of American presence in the Europe of the 1920s. They provided vivid analyses that showed just how much American energy and capital had in fact been devoted to the causes of recovery, democracy, and capitalism in the Old World in these years.[19]

Using the idea of 'stabilization' as an analytical guide, these works highlighted the efforts made by the protagonists of American action at the time—not statesmen but financiers, industrialists, opinion-makers, and the unique figure of Herbert Hoover—to convince opinion on both sides of the Atlantic that the survival of democracy was linked to the *economic* fate of the continent, to the development of a credible vision of material progress from which all could potentially benefit: democracy as a shared prosperity. Later it would become common wisdom in the West that a properly functioning market system was one of the necessary preconditions for the success of Liberal democracy. But this was not at all clear in the 1920s. To the British Prime Minister Stanley Baldwin, the link worked the other way round and was by no means guaranteed. 'The assertion of the people's rights has never yet provided that people with bread', he said in late 1924 when the postwar democratic wave was already ebbing fast. And even *The Economist*, in reporting Baldwin's speech, emphasized simply the moral duty of the English-speaking peoples to defend the 'peculiar set of institutions' they had developed for themselves and then, through Wilson, offered to the world.[20]

'Hunger does not breed reform', Woodrow Wilson had told Congress in his address announcing the armistice; 'it breeds madness and all the ugly distempers that make an ordered life impossible. . . . Unhappy Russia

---

[18] For example, Mazower, *Dark Continent*; Eric Hobsbawm, *Age of Extremes: The Short Twentieth Century, 1914–1991* (London, 1994); Stefan Berger, 'The Attempt at Democratization under Weimar', in Garrard, Tolz, and White (eds), *European Democratization*, 96–115.

[19] Cf. Emily S. Rosenberg, *Financial Missionaries to the World: The Politics and Culture of Dollar Diplomacy, 1900–1930* (Cambridge, Mass., 1999); Smith, *America's Mission*; Costigliola, *Awkward Dominion*; Nolan, *Visions of Modernity*; Charles S. Maier, *Recasting Bourgeois Europe* (Princeton, 1975); Stephen A. Schuker, 'Origins of American Stabilization Policy in Europe: The Financial Dimension 1918–1924', in Schröder (ed.), *Confrontation and Cooperation*.

[20] *The Economist*, 13 December 1924.

has furnished abundant recent proof of that.' So the moral was clear: 'Nations that have learned the discipline of freedom' should now rule, 'by the sheer power of example and of friendly helpfulness.'[21] Wilson of course was no economist, and shared the disdain heaped by Keynes on the peacemakers of Versailles, who had neglected all the unappealing material realities that in his view were the key elements in restarting the life of the war-torn continent: 'The fundamental economic problem of a Europe starving and disintegrating before their eyes was the one question in which it was impossible to arouse the interest of the Four', he famously wrote afterwards.[22]

But there was one man at the peace conferences who struck Keynes quite differently: an American mining engineer with experience across the world who had turned himself into an expert on the supply of emergency relief to devastated populations. This was Herbert Hoover.

> Mr Hoover was the only man who emerged from the ordeal of Paris with an enhanced reputation. This complex personality, with his habitual air of weary Titan...his eyes steadily fixed on the true and essential facts of the European situation, imported into the councils of Paris, when he took part in them, precisely that atmosphere of reality, knowledge, magnanimity, and disinterestedness which, if they had been found in other quarters also, would have given us the Good Peace.[23]

The magnanimous Hoover

Future President Herbert Hoover was not a professional public figure of any sort when the US intervened in World War I, but had arrived in Europe as a technical expert with a distinguished international career built from scratch. Yet he emerged from the first post-war phase as a hero, a decisive leader in American intervention in Europe in these years, even a Republican hopeful for the White House. Hoover's contribution was to invent another new means for projecting American power into Europe: large-scale humanitarian relief organizations. Starting with an emergency operation for Belgium, he had quickly been called to Washington by Wilson when the government needed to organize food provision after entering the conflict. His Food Administration took charge of production, prices, supply, and distribution, connecting the output of the nation's

---

[21] Wilson, *War and Peace*, i. 300–2; Address of 11 November 1918.
[22] Keynes, *Collected Writings*, ii. 134, 211; on the limited and instrumental nature of Wilson's economic liberalism, Smith, *America's Mission*, 92–3.
[23] Keynes, *Collected Writings*, vol. ii, p. 174, n. 1.

farms to the needs of the armies and the peoples they were 'liberating'. It became a model of effective technical control, and led him to direct the great majority of Allied relief efforts in Europe as soon as the fighting ended.[24]

The Food Administrator quickly set up a large organization based in Paris, divided into missions for the eighteen 'liberated and enemy' countries, plus six more for neutrals, staffed by specialists in all the key problems of currency, finance, railways, coal supplies, and industrial revival. New governments were supplied with American economic advisers, and for a period there was a measure of direct control over the economic mechanisms that enabled life to restart in the countries devastated or impoverished by war. Hoover gave special priority to children, and calculated he was dealing with 10–12 million starving infants overall. These he undertook to feed as an act of American charity, under a separate, well-publicized operation. The others paid with cash, credit, or barter goods for the import of some 27 million tons of food and 840 million pounds of clothing, medical, and miscellaneous supplies from the United States. These quantities represented about 96 per cent of the tonnage and 95 per cent of the financial effort, according to Hoover's arithmetic.[25]

The Food Administrator's temporary but immense empire, with its own telecommunication and passport system, tried to start the rehabilitation of central Europe including Germany and Austria, and compensate for some of the worst, immediate effects of the debts and reparations mess left by Versailles.[26] Whether Allies, 'liberated' friendly peoples, neutrals or ex-enemies, all required food, coal and ships if mass relief programmes were to be effective. 'And relief had to be brought fast if we were to maintain the order and stability upon which peace and freedom of men could be built.'[27] Hoover witnessed how within weeks of the end of the war 'thirteen liberated nations and four enemy nations went through democratic revolutions. They set up national independence, and guarantees of personal liberty under provisional governments.' Yet the seeds of their own destruction had burst through with astonishing rapidity: 'Half a dozen small wars took place among them in the first six months.'[28]

But Hoover's most intense scorn was reserved for the Bolsheviks and all they represented, and he quickly moved to organize his relief campaign in an openly political direction. He later explained:

---

[24] Hoover, *The Memoirs of Herbert Hoover*, i: *Years of Adventure, 1874–1920* (New York, 1952), ch. 31.

[25] Ibid. 295–6, 301–2, 321.

[26] Austrian experience recounted in Wagnleitner, *Coca-Colonization*, 40–1.

[27] Hoover, *Memoirs*, i. 285.   [28] Ibid. 446.

[The Communists] found so receptive an audience in hungry people that Communist revolutions at one time seized a dozen large cities and one whole country—Hungary. We sought diligently to sustain the feeble plants of parliamentary government which had sprung up in all of those countries. A weak government possessed of the weapon of food and supplies for starving people can preserve and strengthen itself more effectively than by arms.[29]

The US food regime's intervention in Russia was particularly controversial. Hoover opposed the Anglo-French intrigues aimed at promoting war against the Bolsheviks and pressed Wilson to minimize US military support for them. His own view was based on direct experience and the conviction that such manoeuvres would only restore autocracy. Instead, he told Wilson, 'a foundation of real social grievance' fed the revolutionary movement. The Bolsheviks were able to gain leverage from 'the not unnatural violence' of masses who had 'learned in grief of tyranny and violence over generations. Our people, who enjoy so great liberty and general comfort, cannot fail to sympathise to some degree with these blind gropings for better social conditions...'[30] Hoover sought to test 'the Bolshevik murderers' to discover whether they were 'a militant force engrossed on world domination' or just a passing menace. He had to be content with support that went to both White and Red Russia as long as the Civil War went on.[31]

After his return to the US, Hoover was called upon by the Soviets themselves to organize another emergency relief drive on behalf of Russia, and succeeded on a basis that included Soviet gold, US official funds, and public charity. Again his methods saved lives: over 9 million by 1923, according to a letter sent afterwards by the man who had originally appealed to him, the writer Maxim Gorky.[32] Along the way he had demonstrated one of the secrets of America's distinctive ability to invent new ways to project its power. This lay in a striking lack of prejudice, ideological, legal, or practical, among the leading groups concerning the boundary between the public and the private spheres of national governance. When official relief budgets began to be cut back in mid-1919, Hoover simply privatized himself and his operation, founding a new humanitarian organization,

---

[29] Hoover, *Memoirs*, 301.
[30] Ibid. 412, letter to Wilson of 28 March 1919.
[31] Details in Costigliola, *Awkward Dominion*, 87–92.
[32] Hoover, *The Memoirs of Herbert Hoover*, ii: *The Cabinet and the Presidency, 1920–1933* (New York, 1952), 23–6; for details, Costigliola, *Awkward Dominion*, 87–92; cf. Lloyd C. Gardner, *Safe for Democracy: The Anglo-American Response to Revolution, 1913–1923* (New York, 1984), which claims that Hoover's long-term aim was 'to have a foothold inside Russia when the inevitable change came', pp. 331, 335–6.

the American Relief Administration European Children's Fund. This organization could appeal to public and private support as appropriate and bypass State Department diplomacy, which in the case of Soviet Russia, refused official recognition. Hoover developed his own role in and beyond government to an extent rarely seen before in American public life. In this way he became, in the historian Frank Costigliola's view, 'the single most important foreign policymaker from 1921 to 1933'.[33]

As such Hoover left a series of important traces in the American attitude towards Europe's democratic modernization. His experience of the war and the Versailles conference reinforced a long-held American official view—traceable at least back to Jefferson—that considered historical Europe a world of nationalistic hates, autocratic miseries, revolutionary disorders, and power politics of the most imperialistic sort, between and within nations. Wilson of course shared many of these convictions. But the President had possessed an unlimited faith in the redemptive example of the history of the United States, and so armed had set out on a 'gigantic crusade to impose American ideas and ideals upon Europe', as Hoover recalled. The result? All but a few of the valorous aspirations Wilson had brought to Paris had been 'variously violated or distorted by the time they came out from under the millstones of the best European diplomatic thought'.

Once back home Hoover campaigned for a version of Wilson's League plan, but modified to strengthen US freedom of action within its framework. He became an outspoken champion of American exceptionalism, and never failed to preach the separateness and superiority of his native land, whose national pride, he felt, must be stiffened 'lest the disintegrating theories of Europe infect more of our own people'. At Paris he had witnessed, he said, a 'collision of civilizations that had grown three hundred years apart'.[34] With Hoover, splits destined to endure opened up among those of America's leading groups who faced the Atlantic and those who faced inwards, and between those convinced that Europe could be saved by America's democratic example and action, and others who feared it could never be. The three great modernizing challenges of the 1920s were, in this latter 'realistic' view, more likely to produce conflict across the ocean rather than harmony, and the US should be prepared to face the consequences. These might include attempts by the Europeans to use superior American power for ends designed by them and not by the US

[33] Costigliola, *Awkward Dominion*, 40; Hoover, *Memoirs*, ii. 40; cf. Rosenberg, *Financial Missionaries*, 117–18.
[34] Ninkovich, *Modernity and Power*, 86; Hoover, *Memoirs*, i. 469; ch. 54, 'Why America Cannot Make Peace in Europe'; after Hoover's 1928 Presidential victory the London *Times* ran a powerful editorial highlighting Hoover's extreme nationalism; reproduced in part in Boyce, *Great Interwar Crisis*, 234.

itself. Even worse was the risk of contamination by European political diseases, such as socialism and fascism.[35]

What America could and could not do for European democracy

Specific US policies in the post-Wilson–Hoover era of course did little to safeguard European liberal democracy as such, and in certain economic circumstances may well have contributed to its undermining, even before the Wall Street crash of 1929.[36] 'United States leaders sought Europe's recovery without American sacrifice', writes Costigliola. 'This matched Europe's hope to solve problems at American expense.' The resulting hiatus over Allied war debts and reparations from former enemies set off chain reactions of political crisis and social tension.[37]

The Americans hoped to promote a gradual process of movement away from the crushing financial provisions of the Versailles treaty, 'without either entangling the United States or unleashing the forces of revolutionary change'. But they preached prosperity for all while imposing the harshest forms of deflation, and pushed for expanded world trade while building ever higher tariff barriers around the US itself.[38] They insisted that private bankers and corporate heads should organize the foreign and economic policies of governments up and down the Old World. In this way local politics need not interfere with the application of strictly business-based solutions to the problems everyone faced. A New York banker explained disarmingly the features of the mechanism:

> The debts of the outside world are the ropes about their necks, by means of which we pull them towards us. Our trade restrictions are pitchforks pressed against their bodies, by means of which we hold them off.[39]

[35] Cf. Ninkovich, *Modernity and Power*, 70–1; 83–5; Boyce, *Great Interwar Crisis*, 231–2.

[36] Emily Rosenberg's study, *Financial Missionaries*, examines the role of US financial missions in a series of national economic crises around the world, including various post-war situations in Europe. Most of these enterprises proved disappointing in methods and results, and this particular form of improvised power projection, semi-private, semi-public, was eventually abandoned; for the crises the US financial adviser provoked in Poland in particular, ibid. 176–83.

[37] Costigliola, *Awkward Dominion*, 100; cf. Schuker, 'Origins of American Stabilization', 386.

[38] In 1922 new tariff legislation placed America's barriers among the highest in the world. They affected 64% of European exports overall, in particular 72% of French external trade and 52% of the British; R. W. D. Boyce, *British Capitalism at the Crossroads, 1919–1932* (Cambridge, 1987), 106, 131.

[39] Cf. Costigliola, *Awkward Dominion*, 114–26 on the 'Dawes plan', a privately organized loan strategy to restructure German finances and reparations payments. The scheme, which in local eyes put Germany under a kind of official receivership, set off a wave of US banking investments in European government bonds, and a resentful round of French and British political adjustments; Benjamin Strong, New York banker cit. in Sherwood Eddy, *The Challenge of Europe* (London, 1933), 273; for a defence of US policy and a strong critique of European official attitudes, Schuker, 'Origins of American Stabilization', 386; for evolution of US official context, Rosenberg, *Financial Missionaries*, chs 4, 6; birth of Dawes plan in Boyce, *Great Interwar Crisis*, 128–9.

By the mid-1920s the consequences of America's first experience as a European power were becoming clear, and were analysed strikingly by the Bolshevik hero Leon Trotsky in two important speeches, in 1924 and 1926. For the first time, said the creator of the Red Army in 1924, it seemed appropriate to apply the term 'imperialism' to America's use of her power in Europe: 'If in the past it was European capitalism that revolutionized the backward sections of the world, today it is American capitalism that revolutionizes overmature Europe.' What did America's new-found hegemony in Europe mean?

> [It] means that Europe will be permitted to rise again but within limits set in advance, with certain restricted sections of the world market allotted to it. American capitalism is... preparing and is ready to issue instructions to European banks and trusts, to the European bourgeoisie as a whole.... This is its aim. It will divide up the market into sectors; it will regulate the activity of the European financiers and industrialists. If we wish to give a clear precise answer to the question of what American imperialism wants, we must say: *It wants to put capitalist Europe on rations.*[40]

European bourgeoisies might resist this humiliation, even militarily, judged Trotsky, but in the end they would succumb. Even the British: 'The conduct of war requires the Lloyd Georges and the Churchills; the MacDonalds are required for the conduct of retreats without a battle.'[41] Yet the Soviet revolution in its own way needed America very badly, as Trotsky and Lenin both admitted openly. Specifically it wanted American science, technology, and labour efficiency. As Trotsky declared with a flourish, winding up an address on 'The Premises for the Proletarian Revolution':

> If we Americanize our still frail socialist industry, then we can say with tenfold confidence that the future is completely and decisively working in our favour. Americanized Bolshevism will crush and conquer imperialist Americanism.[42]

[40] L. Trotsky, *Europe and America: Two Speeches on Imperialism* (New York, 1971), 17 (emphasis in original); for Bolshevik context, Moore, *European Socialists*, 171, 178, 182–8; German versions of this analysis, from Left and Right, in Dan Diner, *America in the Eyes of the Germans: An essay on Anti-Americanism* (Princeton, 1996), 65–6; French versions in Strauss, *Menace in the West*, ch. 6.

[41] Trotsky, *Europe and America*, 29 (Ramsay MacDonald had become the first Labour Prime Minister in 1924); Moore, *European Socialists*, 183–5.

[42] Cit. in *Antonio Gramsci: Selections from Political Writings (1921–1926)*, ed. tr. Quintin Hoare (London, 1978), pp. 492–3, n. 168; Trotsky's speech on 'Europe and America' of 1926 looked at the consolidation of the processes he saw emerging in 1924, particularly the substitution of industrial for public capital in American loans, the political consequences of support for European currencies, and the British role as 'chief tax collector for America in a province called Europe'. On the very significant impact of Taylorism in Soviet Russia—at least on the theoretical level—Judith A. Merkle, *Management and Ideology: The Legacy of the International Scientific Management Movement* (Berkeley, 1980), pp. 115–21 and ch. 4 in general.

Within a few years the limits of the disjointed, transient American attempts to save first Germany and Poland, and then the rest, became clear. European democracy was not stabilized either politically or economically, and neither Wilson and Hoover nor their banker successors were able to leverage European political developments through financial compulsion as they—and Trotsky—had imagined.[43] When forced to choose between the stability provided by new authoritarian regimes and democratic principles, American interests had little difficulty in coming to terms with the former. Mussolini's Italy was a prime beneficiary of this trend.[44] For their part, the defenders of liberal democracy in Europe rarely looked to the example of US political institutions or methods, especially after Prohibition was declared in 1920, and large-scale immigration blocked off by Congress in the laws of 1921 and 1924.[45] 'To most German commentators, the American political system was irrelevant to American economic success, and thus was not discussed at length', writes Mary Nolan in her great history of the debate on 'Americanismus' in Weimar Germany.[46]

Instead it was the burgeoning functions of production, distribution, and consumption in jazz age America that attracted the most avid attention, in Germany as all over impoverished Europe. While local institutions were struggling to decide how or even whether to incorporate the newly enfranchised working classes and women into traditional political communities, an extraordinary new series of American experiences all promised to *supersede* such class-based projects, rooted in bourgeois continuity. Here was an actually functioning society, apparently able to combine the most reliable features of parliamentary democracy with an economic mechanism that made sure the system delivered on its promise of prosperity for the majority.[47] Before the First World War, progressive politics in America had already begun to redefine prevailing notions of citizenship in economic terms, imagining a democracy based ever more squarely on consumption rights as much as on laws and voting. Some visionaries even foresaw how tensions would emerge between the claims

[43] Kathleen Burk sees a failure of American political will as much as of organization or awareness: K. Burk, 'Money and Power: America and Europe in the 20th century', *History Today* (March 1993), 37.
[44] Schuker, 'Origins of American Stabilization', 402, and succeeding discussions; on Italy, John P. Diggins, *Mussolini and Fascism: The View from America* (Princeton, 1972), chs 4, 7, 11; Gian Giacomo Migone, *Gli Stati Uniti e il fascismo: Alle origini dell'egemonia americana in Italia* (Milan, 1980).
[45] For a discussion of the impact of these laws in France, Strauss, *Menace in the West*, 160–6.
[46] Nolan, *Visions of Modernity*, 108; for detailed discussion, Peter Krüger, 'Germany and the United States, 1914–1933: The Mutual Perception of Their Political Systems', in Barclay and Glaser-Schmidt (eds), *Transatlantic Images*, 181–7.
[47] Cf. Romier, *Who Will Be Master, Europe or America?*, 124–9.

of public and private consumption, and in an era of burgeoning arguments about socialism, imagined an enlightened capitalism that would provide economic well-being for all through the perpetual increase of material output. The huge surge in national wealth set off by the war industries soon confirmed the progressive era's 'discovery of abundance' in America's genetic inheritance.[48]

In the 1920s this enhanced form of national identity was assiduously cultivated by the swelling world of business, with its partners in scientific management and production. Professional economists talked of a 'fundamental contrast between the European and American systems', i.e. 'the contrast of poverty with abundance, of low standards of living with high standards of living'.[49] Thanks to the flood of cinema products and stars emanating from the US film industry's new industrial base in Hollywood, California, even European societies embroiled in civil war and hyperinflation, such as Weimar Germany, could see the difference. Abundance was a message, 'peculiarly able to preach its own gospel without words', reflected a later critic.[50]

Not everyone had eyes and ears to take it in. The editor of one of Germany's leading liberal newspapers, the *Frankfurter Zeitung*, doubted whether Europe could ever reach the levels of frenzied selling and buying visible in the booming America of 1928: 'Our destiny is meagerness and narrowness', he sadly concluded.[51] Further down the social ladder however, many others were beginning to wonder how they might get a share of the bounties on display.

A popular egalitarian spirit could be seen at work in America's ways of doing things, which started to generate in the European folk imagination a distinctive and stimulating sense of desire. In a 1980s British television documentary, a Glasgow office worker recalled the picture of America

[48] Christopher Lasch, *The True and Only Heaven: Progress and its Critics* (New York, 1991), 68; Kathleen M. Donohue, *Freedom from Want: American Liberalism and the Idea of the Consumer* (Baltimore, 2003), p. 95 and chs 3–4 in general; Alexis de Tocqueville's more abstract considerations on the subject of plenty in America pointed in the same direction: *Democracy in America*, tr. of 1835/1840 editions by Harvey C. Mansfield and Delba Winthrop (Chicago, 2000), 267–74.

[49] Quotation from John R. Commons in Daniel M. Fox, *The Discovery of Abundance: Simon N. Patten and the Transformation of Social Theory* (Ithaca, 1967), 168; the debate on the wider implications of abundance for the future of American democracy—traced in Donohue, *Freedom from Want*, chs 4–5—reached a culmination with the publication of *People of Plenty: Economic Abundance and the American Character*, by the social historian David M. Potter (Chicago, 1954); cf. Donohue, *Freedom from Want*, 277.

[50] Potter, *People of Plenty*, 134; cf. Romier, *Who Will Be Master, Europe or America?*, 224–6; on youth as the special focus of new consumer markets, Savage, *Teenage*, 199–200.

[51] Arthur Feiler, *America Seen Through German Eyes* (New York, 1928), 2.

imported into his youth by the California-made films that flooded grey, unhappy Britain after the war:

> I saw life in America as a classless society, where you could rise to become anything.... In this promised land the skies were always blue, blue all the time with a few white clouds. And we saw all the long avenues with the palm trees lining on either side, and houses, big houses set back from the road with lovely lawns in front, and the porch where people could sit out in the summertime and sip their mint juleps or whatever they did.... I thought that must be what Pasadena's like, a form of life that was far beyond anything we knew...a land of unlimited opportunity where we could really become something different from what we were.[52]

FORDISM IN EUROPE: GERMAN AND BRITISH EXPERIENCES

Of all the components of the triptych of post-war modernity, it was the promise of America's new mass-production-for-mass-consumption system that attracted most attention in the era of reconstruction. Like democracy, capitalism and industrial technique had all been imported into the US from Europe, noted the *Chicago Daily News* correspondent Edgar Mowrer in his 1928 reflection on America's new influences in the Old World. 'But their offspring, industrialism,... can best flourish in a country classless enough to accept standardized products and lavish enough to keep the machines running full time.' That was what made the American experience of the assembly line so special: 'Where the producers' mentality is substantially one with the consumers', the industrial system can be developed almost without limit.' Now its lesson was galvanizing the thoughts of leaders and masses alike on the other side of the Atlantic. 'Its material benefits loom so luscious that it would take more abnegation than impoverished Europe possesses to refuse them.' Mowrer saw in his Europe 'a tendency that is almost a determination to remodel itself along American lines'.[53]

Mary Nolan notes that in the Weimar republic alone in the 1920s 'over fifty books on American technology, economic prosperity and mass consumption' appeared. There was an unparalleled stream of specialized commentators and journalists, a large-scale student exchange programme, and in 1929 the World Advertising Conference came to Berlin. Henry Ford's

---

[52] *An Ocean Apart*, BBC TV, episode 2; also Dimbleby and Reynolds, *An Ocean Apart*, 108.
[53] Mowrer, *This American World*, 131–2, 45.

image and his biography attracted intense, magnifying attention. All this became part of a passionate and wide-ranging debate in Germany on how the lessons of US economic progress could be adapted to serve national recovery after the desperate and revolutionary years of 1918–23, followed by the American financial rescue of 1924. Nolan writes:

> Far from being a comprehensive solution to Germany's economic problems, the new Mark and renegotiated reparations merely created a respite. Many Germans were now eager to define that amorphous term 'rationalization,' which kept cropping up in debates on economic reform. They desperately sought efficient, modern models for individual aspects of production and management and for the country's economic life as a whole. America was the logical place to turn.[54]

A future for Germany?

Among the most prominent contemporary explorers of the American model—and one of the few to enjoy the privilege of an English translation—was the well-connected government adviser and economics professor Moritz Bonn. Active in politics and diplomacy (he was a member of the German delegation at Versailles and Rapallo), Bonn had taught frequently at leading American universities before the First World War, and returned to a research institute at Williams College, Massachusetts between 1924 and 1926.[55] His 1931 volume entitled *Prosperity: Myth and Reality in American Economic Life* provided a vivid account of the rise and fall of the American way of doing things in the 1920s as he saw it. It also denounced Weimar's 'infatuation' with this myth, its futile impulse to attempt a sort of 'tragic mimicry'.

Bonn was convinced that the American universe was a naturally expansionist one, but he offered a then-novel explanation of the success of the making-and-getting system made famous by Ford. With the end of first the frontier and then immigration, industry in that country was forced to 'find new ways of creating customers'. In other words, production as an end in itself no longer sufficed to keep the factories turning over. New and more 'refined demands' had to be gratified or provoked, in such a way as to 'pull the consumers into the foreground and push back producers' industries'.[56]

---

[54] Nolan, *Visions of Modernity*, 22; cf. Axel R. Schäfer, 'The Study of Americanisation after German Reunification: Institutional Transfer, Popular Culture and the East', *Contemporary European History*, 12/1 (February 2003), 132–3.

[55] Cf. M. J. Bonn, *Wandering Scholar* (London, 1949).

[56] *Prosperity: Myth and Reality in American Economic Life* (London, 1931), 31.

This was where Ford's revolution had come in: 'It was democratisation of the motor-car by Ford, by dint of systematic cheapening, that transformed the direction and the rhythm of American life.' The entire population had taken to the road, 'dashing about in every direction', transforming the national geography and creating a host of new service industries; in fact 'the commercialised exchange of services plays an ever-increasing part in people's lives'. In spite of its obvious capacity to satisfy all basic needs in return for an ever smaller portion of work, the system had chosen instead to 'strain after an increase of consumption at a more and more feverish rate'. This was the work of 'standardised giant industries and distributing institutions', which expressed 'the fanaticism of a levelling democracy' constantly striving to conquer 'the ultimate consumer'. Motor car manufacturers, store proprietors, film stars, and cinema magnates were all bound up in the same crusade, greatly aided now by the transformation of the old installment purchase arrangement into a vast new system of consumer credit, which served to amplify the demand effects of high wages.[57]

Looking back after the onset of its first great crisis, Bonn denounced the German subservience to this dream image. 'In the land of poets and thinkers', he complained, 'a torrent of unbounded admiration streamed through the channels of the book trade.' In the world of production the 'mental colonization' was particularly intense:

> The splendour of the American commercial apparatus dazzled many German industrial leaders, whose mental outlook was purely technical....Organised labour pressed in the same direction, hoping to prevent a lowering of wages by means of a capitalistic rationalisation of industry....German industry but also German thought tied themselves slavishly to American models...

...just as their forefathers had done when England ruled the roost after the first industrial revolution.[58]

Today's historical research has greatly refined this drastic judgement, but has not entirely cancelled it out. Bonn made clear that the period of the 'infatuation' was a short one, coinciding with the 'rationalizing' years of 1924–9, when a happier future for Europe and even Germany seemed possible. But this moment saw the culmination of a vital public debate over Germany's own culture 'and the challenge of modernity it faced', in which America served as a key reference point, the reflecting mirror and

---

[57] *Prosperity: Myth and Reality in American Economic Life* (London, 1931), ch. 1; Belgian writer's reflections on the deplorable effects of the democratization of motoring in America cit. in Kroes, *If You've Seen One*, 24.
[58] Ibid. 8–9.

the measure of success or failure.[59] Every key element of German society built up its own image of the America that mattered to it, and then proceeded to construe this idea to suit its own domestic purposes. The former chancellor Hans Luther told his audience at the World Advertising Conference in Berlin in 1929 that German industry and commerce must learn the new language of advertising as developed in the United States. At the same time he insisted on the need to 'develop the German dialect of this language and to do this with a German sense of intellectuality and art appreciation'.[60]

The fate of Fordism in these processes was instructive. 'All were convinced that Ford and Fordism spoke directly to the German condition', says Mary Nolan, 'even if they disagreed bitterly on what the message was.'[61] There was a more or less imaginary Ford for industrialists, engineers, and managers, another for trade unionists, yet another for economists, and one who became a hero of popular culture, a model capitalist, leader or servant of his people. Adolf Hitler read Ford while imprisoned after his first putsch attempt in 1923, and became a devoted admirer, a development that had a variety of historical repercussions.[62]

Yet in practice German industry in the late 1920s was never 'Fordized'—not even Ford's own plants in the republic copied Detroit—and the full social implementation of the model, with high wages to stimulate high domestic demand, was never even contemplated.[63] Some employers took advantage of mass unemployment to apply scientific models of efficient production, to screw down wages and raise the tempo of work. Meanwhile they maintained as traditional an outlook to profits, products, and customers as they could successfully get away with in the marketplace. Joy in creating a product that embodied the old German values of quality and skill was the official justification for this outlook. In reality

---

[59] Gassert, 'Without Concessions', 220–1; it was not of course the only reference point, a romanticized vision of the German past was at least as important; cf. Jeffrey Herf, *Reactionary Modernism: Technology, culture and politics in Weimar and the Third Reich* (Cambridge, 1986), ch. 2; cf. Stephen Lamb and Anthony Phelan, 'Weimar Culture: The Birth of Modernism', in Rob Burns (ed.), *German Cultural Studies: An Introduction* (Oxford, 1995), 61–2, 68–70, which emphasizes anti-republicanism and anti-socialism in middle class thinking much more than anti-Americanism.

[60] Cit. in Corey Ross, 'Vision of Prosperity: The Americanization of Advertising in Interwar Germany', in Swett et al. (eds), *Selling Modernity*, quote at p. 61.

[61] Nolan, *Visions of Modernity*, 31; there is no evidence in the text that Ford was conscious of speaking to anyone other than his fellow Americans: Henry Ford, *My Life and Work* (New York, 1922).

[62] Nolan, *Visions of Modernity*, 34; Gassert, 'Without Concessions', 223–32; Kurt Möser, 'World War I and the Creation of Desire for Automobiles in Germany', in Susan Strasser et al. (eds), *Getting and Spending: European and American Consumer Societies in the Twentieth Century* (Washington DC, 1998), 212; see Chapter 4.

[63] Möser, 'Creation of Desire', 212–13.

more rational and efficient production offered a quick way of restoring battered profit margins.[64] 'Rationalization' in this view might embrace new forms of social engineering, the explicit fostering of a more intense devotion to work, the community, and the nation, but it emphatically did not look forward to the arrival of a mass-production-for-mass-consumption model of society in Weimar Germany. Large parts of the moderate unions and the mass Social Democrat party tried hard to push for this latter half of the Fordist equation, as did the American advertising agencies that began to arrive in Germany after 1927. But they were all destined to be disappointed. 'Rationalization', concludes Mary Nolan, 'far from being a panacea, produced new economic problems and intensified the political and social crisis of late Weimar.'[65]

But Germany was not the only land to discover that borrowing from the American system of production and consumption was harder than it looked.

America and Britain's first identity crisis

At the end of the 1920s a US journalist published a dramatic account of all the conflicts in course or looming between the two principal economies of the world at that time, and predicted the outcome: that American business would soon comprehensively defeat that of the old Mother Country. This 'record of economic war' was in fact a compendium of the American nation's economic and commercial triumphs, leading to a warning that the British Empire would never be able to withstand the ever-rising competition from the US, as well as from Europe. 'Britain', diagnosed Ludwell Denny, 'is approaching the time when she must decide on a working agreement with the European cartel alliance or with the United States. As yet there is much confusion in the British mind between these alternatives.'[66]

The decade that followed the First World War changed Britain in ways the country was neither prepared to face nor much cared for when they had

---

[64] Nolan, *Visions of Modernity*, 175–8; Mark Rupert, *Producing Hegemony: The Politics of Mass Production and American Global Power* (Cambridge, 1995), 76.

[65] Nolan, *Visions of Modernity*, 11; Gassert, 'Without Concessions', 229; Lamb and Phelan, 'Weimar Culture', 61–2; on the difficulties of applying American advertising techniques in 1920s Germany, Ross, 'Vision of Prosperity', 62–5.

[66] L. Denny, *America Conquers Britain: A Record of Economic War* (New York, 1930), 123; this was a sequel to Denny's *We Fight for Oil* (New York, 1928), a study of one of the most intense and strategically significant battles between American and British business empires in this period; evidence of the confusion Denny refers to in Boyce, *British Capitalism*, 110–12, 241–50.

happened, and tensions with America were among its most characteristic and unwelcome features. These were for the most part grim years in which the heart of the Empire sought to find some sort of headway after the relief of victory had passed, uncertain whether to try simply to rebuild the Old World as it was imagined to have been—the main thrust of economic policy—or recast the nation's standing on some new basis. Brought up sharp at the great post-war crossroads where the three modernizations of democracy, production, and communication met, Britain's finance and commerce-based capitalism struggled to adapt. The challenge, say the specialists Cain and Hopkins, was not simply to organize the exchange of 'tradition' for 'modernity', but to manage 'a selective amalgamation of elements inherited from the past with introductions from the continuously evolving present'.[67] The unspoken question concerned how much sovereignty Britain now really commanded to control these complicated processes of selection and amalgamation.

Today's experts insist that compared to Britain's, America's strength was more potential than real in the 1920s and that US supremacy was not so obvious as a foregone conclusion. Men in the City, Fleet Street, and Whitehall were perfectly conscious that a struggle for financial and commercial primacy had started, and believed that their nation and Empire, never so great in extension and reach, must win through.[68] But of all the strategies proposed at the time there was only one destined to endure: the New World challenger must be beaten at its own game. British industries should take over America's methods and thoroughly modernize themselves with Fordist techniques and attitudes. The 1920s were a time when many enduring patterns of transatlantic action and reaction were created, and this was one of them. A limited and *controlled* adjustment to American patterns was to be attempted, one of the few effective responses possible to the rising challenge of US economic power across an ever-increasing number of sectors and markets.[69]

---

[67] P. J. Cain and A. G. Hopkins, *British Imperialism: Crisis and Deconstruction, 1914–1990* (London, 1993), 298; cf. Boyce, *Great Interwar Crisis*, 85–9, 189–95.

[68] B. J. C. McKercher, *Anglo-American Relations in the 1920s: The Struggle for Supremacy* (London, 1991), 3–4, 8; selections from the American mass-media debate on the various disputes in David A. Richards, 'America Conquers Britain: Anglo-American Conflict in the Popular Media During the 1920s', *Journal of American Culture*, 3/1 (Spring 1980), 95–103; a typical semi-official view in Hubert Douglas Henderson, *The Interwar Years: A Selection from the Writings of Hubert Douglas Henderson* (Oxford, 1955), 61–5 (memo of 21 August 1930); Henderson was editor of *The Nation*, and Secretary of the Government's Economic Advisory Council, 1930–4.

[69] Boyce, *British Capitalism*, p. 101 and ch. 4 in general; a precise Italian parallel is to be found in debates within the Ansaldo heavy engineering group on its strategic future, the same search for a rigorously controlled introduction of US examples, e.g. by combining them with practices from other advanced countries; Fernando Fasce, 'Appunti sull'americanismo all'Ansaldo nel Novecento', *Archivi e imprese*, (July–December 1993), 35–6.

On 27 January 1926 Stanley Baldwin, the British Prime Minster, stood before a large crowd of supporters in the beleaguered, north-eastern engineering town of Sunderland. His message was one of modest optimism and pleaded for a return to cooperation between employers and employees, at a time when the coal industry was racked by the crises that would within months produce the General Strike. But in looking for a better future, Baldwin found hope not in Britain's own industrial tradition, ailing and worn out. Instead, he pointed his audience's attention across the Atlantic Ocean, where he saw a young and vigorous example of economic progress and social harmony on display. Building on a new, postwar political custom of looking to America as the nation's preferred source of inspiration for its revival, the Prime Minister exhorted his audience to 'study and emulate' the experience of the former colony. In particular:

> I venture to think that no trade union leader could do better service to the cause he represents than by investigating closely what the methods are that enable the American workmen to enjoy a better standard of living than any other working people in the world, to produce more, and at the same time to have so much higher wages.[70]

Within days Baldwin's challenge had been picked up. Not indeed by any section of the trade union movement itself, but by one of the leading national newspapers of the epoch, the *Daily Mail*. 'As a matter of public duty', the newspaper offered to organize its own 'mission of inquiry' to the United States, inviting a select group of trade unionists 'drawn from the engineering and kindred industries' to explore American industrial practice at first hand.[71]

Accordingly, a month to the day after Baldwin's speech, eight men ranging from a machine man to a patternmaker, a turner to a blacksmith, set sail on official leave from their various employers, accompanied by a rousing send-off from the highest levels of the newspaper's management and ownership. In a visit of thirty-three days they would travel 12,000 miles, visit thirteen cities, and inspect forty-two industrial plants. Following an elaborate and prestigious programme put on by the *Daily Mail*, distinguished manufacturers, trade unionists, and experts greeted them at every turn, as did President Coolidge himself. The grand final dinner in New York was hosted by the founder, Charles Coffin, and the president of the board of the General Electric Company, Gerard Swope, one of the most prominent American businessmen of his day.[72]

---

[70] Text of speech reproduced in *The Times*, 28 January 1926.

[71] Late nineteenth-century origins of British industrial missions of enquiry to the US in Heindel, *American Impact on Great Britain*, 177, 211–18.

[72] *The Daily Mail Trade Union Mission to the United States*, published by the *Daily Mail* (n.p., n.d. [1926]).

'What we do not understand', the representative of the Amalgamated Engineering Union had told the waiting New York press upon disembarkation, 'is why it is possible for American industries to pay higher wages than we are paid and yet undersell us on the same product in the world market.' Perhaps it was a case of 'your mass production and standardisation against our old theory of good workmanship based on the individual'. Within hours the working men were beginning to find their answers, realities that made them 'tired...bewildered' and 'astonished', in the words of the mission's report. They saw the construction of the largest power plant in the world, an ice company where 100 men produced 1,000 tons of ice daily 'as the directors of machinery instead of the slaves of human muscle', a meter factory where working processes eliminated 50 per cent of the human element and paid twice as much as English wages, workshops with 'fountains of *running* drinking water'. They found working schemes of 'industrial democracy', examples of equal pay between men and women, profit-sharing, holidays with pay, 'strange new inventions, electrically-driven, for the tabulation and making out of bills', and everywhere clues to the secret of high wages and the obvious prosperity of the country.

In Schenectady they encountered 'an air of contentment and a spirit of comradeship between employers and men from the highest to the lowest'; they also saw women workers in fur coats and silk stockings, and working men's homes with 'hardwood floors, a tiled bathroom and a telephone.' In Buffalo, British working-class emigrants were earning four times the rate for the same job as at home; in Detroit a huge trade in second-hand vehicles paid for by hire purchase meant that 40 per cent of workers owned motor cars. In the vast shops of the capital of Fordism, the trade unionists were struck by the endlessly moving production lines and the ingenious use of conveyor belts. It was in Detroit too that the mission came upon an extraordinary new device for controlling the onrush of traffic that swirled around the city and its factories:

[Drivers] obeyed unhesitatingly the signals displayed automatically in a kind of miniature lighthouse at the principal street crossings, moving or halting as the beacon showed red or green.[73]

In general the mission was left in no doubt that high wages were the start of the cycle of prosperity and not the end of it, high wages combined with labour-saving machinery. President Coolidge's Secretary of Labor, J. J. Davis, told the visitors that 'Americans did not favour what was known as a living wage. What he preferred was a "saving wage"—in other words, a

[73] Ibid. 30.

wage that enabled a worker to maintain a high standard of living and at the same time to save for future needs.' In case the word 'productivity' was a new one to their ears, the Pittsburgh *Gazette Times* spelled out to the British visitors exactly what it meant:

> Ever more production at a declining unit of cost is the aim here. The workmen have caught the spirit. They have found it means more money in their pockets, more employment for a greater number of men to produce efficiently. It makes for general prosperity and markets constantly widen.[74]

Reflecting on their experiences before a large gathering of industrialists, the owners of the *Daily Mail* and the President of the Board of Trade brought together to celebrate their return home, the trade unionists made it clear that America had much to teach and Britain, if it chose to do so, much to absorb. Without idealizing conditions in the United States—no unionist could ignore the triumph of the open shop—the unbeatable equation of high wages, high production, and high consumption stood out for all to see. It was clearly the product of ceaseless technological innovation, unlimited worker–employer cooperation, and that characteristic mentality of ever more, ever newer, ever better. Above all, one stark fact cited by the unionists brought home how great was the distance the British would have to cover if they wished to compete economically and socially with the new civilization of the US, in their own market and in the world. They were being beaten by a nation whose workers were paid on average 50 per cent more in real terms than pre-war; at home the figure was 25 to 40 per cent less.[75]

Industrialists travelled, so did journalists, economists, and politicians. And the traffic was two-way. The Rotary movement held its first-ever overseas Congress in Edinburgh in 1921, its 1,347 delegates bringing a new message of how business should serve society. Building the 'businessman's League of Nations' was to be the great aspiration. London saw the first World Advertising Convention in 1924, with two thousand American professionals present. They enjoyed the patronage of the Prince of Wales and Churchill, and the British Advertising Association's President talked of 'the commencement of the effective organization of British advertising'.[76] But it was the experts who worked hardest to preach, to teach,

---

[74] *The Daily Mail Trade Union Mission to the United States,* published by the *Daily Mail* (n.p., n.d. [1926]), 53.

[75] Ibid. 89–90; for the results of a comparable delegation from the Federation of British Industry, Boyce, *British Capitalism*, 102.

[76] Roger Livy, *Rotary International in Great Britain and Ireland* (Plymouth, 1978), 52; cf. *The Scotsman*, 11 June, 14 June 1921, on origins of Rotary in Britain, Heindel, *American Impact on Great Britain*, 189–90; on Advertising Convention, LeMahieu, 'America and the Representation of British History in Film and Television', 161.

and to warn. Compared to the vast German debate on industrial regeneration and Henry Ford, the British effort was feeble. But book after book, as well as a parliamentary enquiry, tried to put across the new 'science of management' and the lessons of productivity, reinvent the conventional criteria for economic progress, and above all emphasize just how big was America's lead.[77] In so doing engineers such as Austin and Lloyd, business journalists such as J. Ellis Barker, and the editor of *The Economist* invented a pattern of attitudes that soon became permanent. These extolled the American example while placing the responsibility for Britain's 'decline' firmly within a specific industrial and class setting inherited from the past. Implicitly the 'gentlemanly capitalists' who remained at the helm, unmoved and unmovable, were assumed to be blameless.[78]

But events quickly showed that both industry and the Treasury were failing in their efforts at controlled modernization on American lines. The *Daily Mail* mission was a straw in the wind, but the wind was the General Strike of 1926. The manufacturers proved unable to rise to the challenge of American competition, and the money men lost out because their efforts to reassert sterling hegemony in Europe and the Dominions with resources underwritten by New York deceived no one across the Atlantic, or in Europe. Instead it was American-run stabilization plans (including, indirectly, Britain's return to gold in 1925), which unleashed a stream of US capital and goods on Europe.[79]

The *Wall Street Journal* spoke of the amazing rate at which American firms, films, and plays were invading London, and of the new building boom promoted by American entrepreneurs for the surging mass of US tourists. There was even talk of a new hotel 'with the unheard of luxury of a bath with every room'.[80] When the Ford Motor Company announced

---

[77] The parliamentary Committee on Industry and Trade was run by the former Prime Minister, A. J. Balfour. For its exhortations to industry to follow the American example, Costigliola, *Awkward Dominion*, 143, Boyce, *British Capitalism*, 104–5; for American reactions to the wave of European interest in their economic success, United States Government, *Recent Economic Changes in the United States: Report of the President's Conference Committee*, i (New York, 1929), 1–6.

[78] Cf. Bertram Austin and W. Francis Lloyd, *The Secret of High Wages* (London, 1926), with foreword by Walter Layton, editor of *The Economist*; J. Ellis Barker, *America's Secret: The Causes of Her Economic Success* (London, 1927); on Barker's view of Ford and Fordism as 'the incarnation of twentieth-century Americanism' ibid. p. 284 and ch. 15 in general; Cain and Hopkins, *British Imperialism*, 68–70.

[79] Detailed contemporary description and analysis in Frank A. Southard, *American Industry in Europe* (Boston, 1931); lively reporting and commentary in Frances P. Miller and H. D. Hill, 'Europe as a Market', *Atlantic Monthly* (September 1930); cf. Boyce, *Great Interwar Crisis*, 149–51.

[80] *Wall Street Journal* cit. in Richards, 'America Conquers Britain', 98; on the tourist wave—which reached 300,000 visitors per annum in 1928—Francis P. Miller and H. D. Hill, 'Europe as a Playground', *Atlantic Monthly* (August 1930).

its huge new plant at Dagenham, east of London, in 1928, its planned output was equal to the total of the British car industry. The effect of all this, say Cain and Hopkins, was to arouse 'fear and hostility...a sense of the imminent Americanisation of the world'.[81] The Communist writer Palme Dutt warned: 'With every year American goods press British goods harder from their markets; and rationalization and modern mass production intensifies the process. the antagonism can be traced...in the whole economic field, in every part of the world, in every leading industry and raw material, even in such varied fields as literature, the cinema...'[82]

These remarks remind us that the impact of 'Fordism' in Europe can only be understood as one element in a general effort to come to terms with the workings of the *combined* political, economic, and cultural forces coming out of the new America. As Frank Costigliola puts it:

> Europeans interpreted every manifestation of American culture, whether it was music, films or automobiles, as the product of a society dominated by technology and the machine. America's technological superiority, moreover, made other aspects of its culture more attractive to Europeans.[83]

ANTI-MODERNISM OR ANTI-AMERICANISM?

By the end of the 1920s then, the debate on Fordism had become embroiled in a much larger reflection on the post-war modernity in all its forms, and the choice of the made-in-America mass-production industries as a special target of discontent had become swept up in a great wave of intellectual anxiety about the survival of Western 'civilization', as traditionally understood, faced with the triple challenges of mass society and now the rising force of totalitarianism. 'Amid the aimless drift of society's disorganisation and the cacophony of demands accompanying the advent of the masses on to the political market-place', writes the Dutch commentator Rob Kroes, 'Americanism as a concept had come to serve the purpose of focusing the diagnosis of Europe's plight.'[84]

---

[81] Barker claimed that in buying and running cars Americans spent a sum annually equal to UK national income, *America's Secret*, 302; on the history and context of Ford's experience at Dagenham, Mira Wilkins and Frank Ernest Hill, *American Business Abroad: Ford on Six Continents* (Detroit, 1964), 142–3, 185–204; Miller and Hill, 'Europe as a Playground', 404; Cain and Hopkins, *British Imperialism*, 72; cf. George Harmon Knoles, *The Jazz Age Revisited: British Criticism of American Civilization During the 1920s* (Stanford, 1955), 134; Boyce, *Great Interwar Crisis*, 179–95.

[82] Cit. in Richards, 'America Conquers Britain', 96; cf. Boyce, *British Capitalism*, pp. 117–18 (esp. n. 84).

[83] Costigliola, *Awkward Dominion*, 19.

[84] Kroes, *If You've Seen One*, 19.

As Kroes and many other writers have shown, the 1920s question of rationalization stood at the heart of criticisms in Europe of what civilization in the United States appeared to stand for, especially in terms of the life of the future.[85] Ever since the end of the previous century, thinkers on both sides of the Atlantic had been trying to explain the massive paradox they perceived between the chaos and wastefulness of competitive capitalism as produced by nineteenth-century industrial progress, and the ineffable rationality of the scientific and technological discoveries on which this progress was based. Total war and the Ford system seemed to have finally bridged the gap. In wartime the power of the State had been used everywhere to rationalize and speed up the output of factories, aided by the new science of industrial efficiency management or 'Taylorism', named after the American production engineer F. W. Taylor, whose moment in Europe had now arrived.[86]

But Ford's innovations took this leap forward out of the hands of the State and applied it to the material enrichment of society as a whole. The promise of the Ford system changed the balance of hopes and expectations between the masses and the classes everywhere it was contemplated. 'Expect more!'—that was the message of Fordism. Or, as a 1929 publication *Selling Mrs Consumer* explained: 'Pay them more, sell them more, prosper more is the equation.'[87] And while the cost of motor cars continued to fall, forcing even the British government to abandon protectionism— 'The Briton must have his cheap automobile, just like the American', cried the *Herald Tribune*[88]—cultivated minds rushed to denounce the

---

[85] For a 1930s survey of the critics, William T. Spoerri, *The Old World and the New: A Synopsis of Current European Views on American Civilization* (Zurich, 1937), esp. ch. 3, 'The Prophets of Doom'; American intellectual sympathizers with these attitudes discussed in Kroes, *If You've Seen One*, 11, 21; French experience discussed in Panchisi, *Future Tense*, 111–15.

[86] On Taylor's impact and its limits, Merkle, *Management and Ideology*, chs on experience in France, Britain, and Germany; Robert Kanigel, *The One Best Way: Frederick Winslow Taylor and the Enigma of Efficiency* (London, 1997), 488, 492–4; for an example of its propagation, Edward A. Filene, 'Mass Production Makes a Better World', *Atlantic Monthly* (May 1929).

[87] Cf. Ford, *My Life and Work*, ch. 10, 'How Cheaply Can Things Be Made?', and ch. 13, 'Why Be Poor?'; Christine Frederick, *Selling Mrs Consumer* (London, 1929), cit. in Christine Hardyment, *From Mangle to Microwave: The Mechanization of Household Work* (Cambridge, 1988), 188.

[88] *International Herald Tribune*, 27 May 1924, reproduced ibid. 27 May 1999; the editorial noted that only one person in seventy owned a car in Britain, while in the US the ratio was one to seven. The price of new cars in Edinburgh in 1921 was as follows: Ruston-Hornsby, £585; Vauxhall (large), £1100; Sunbeam, from £1225; Austin, from £695; Fiat (large), £995; Chevrolet (medium), £330; Ford, from £240, the latter two *including* a 33% import duty inherited from wartime; advertisements in *The Scotsman*, 1 June, 2 June, 21 June 1921.

mechanical standardization they saw spreading out from Fordism to affect all parts of society. The celebrated French poet Paul Valéry was an early denouncer of the efficiency mania. 'The world, which calls by the name of progress its tendency towards a fatal precision', he wrote in 1919, 'marches on from Taylorization to Taylorization.' The British philosopher Bertrand Russell declared in 1923 that the most important fact of the day was 'not the struggle between capitalism and socialism, but the struggle between industrial civilization and humanity.' André Siegfried, the leading light among the large number of French commentators on contemporary America and its effects, wrote in 1927:

> For so much luxury brought within reach of every worker a heavy price is being paid: nothing less than the transformation of millions of workers into automatons. 'Fordism', i.e. the essence of American industry, results in the standardisation of the worker-as-such. Craftsmanship . . . has no more place in the New World, and with it have gone certain conceptions of man that we in Europe do consider as the veritable basis of civilisation.[89]

One of the most striking analyses of the likely impact of the Ford system in Europe was offered from his prison cell by the Italian communist thinker Antonio Gramsci. In the pages that introduced the concept of 'Fordism' into the vocabulary of Marxian diagnoses of contemporary capitalism, Gramsci distinguished between the evolution of the productive machinery as such and the implications for social life that the Ford revolution looked likely to bring about. By a unique combination of force in the factory and persuasion outside it, the company had gradually succeeded in 'making the whole life of the nation revolve around production'. What else was Prohibition but an attempt by the State to prevent the highly paid Ford-style worker from spending his money on drink, and thus reducing his productivity? Why were sexual relations so closely

[89] Valéry cit. in Kanigel, *One Best Way*, 486; Russell and Russell, *Prospects*, 8; André Siegfried cit. in Rob Kroes, 'Between Rejection and Reception: Hollywood in Holland', in Ellwood and Kroes (eds), *Hollywood in Europe*, 22; for a contemporary view of Siegfried and his work, Spoerri, *Old World and the New*, 14–25; historical perspective in Philip Nord, *France's New Deal: From the Thirties to the Postwar Era* (Princeton, 2010), 70–1, Panchisi, *Future Tense*, 118; for the wide French discussion of the significance of Fordism, Paul A. Gagnon, 'French Views of the Second American Revolution', *French Historical Studies* (Fall 1962), 438–43, Panchisi, *Future Tense*, 116. The pioneering motor manufacturer André Citroën was the leading industrial interpreter of Fordism and Taylorism in France, along with Ernest Mercier, the engineer who revolutionized the electrical and oil industries in the 1920s. But as Richard Kuisel shows, the hopes of a man like Mercier were disappointed, mostly by the conservatism of his own social peers, Kuisel, *Ernest Mercier*, 51–61.

policed by American puritanism if not for the same reason? Taylorism and Fordism required the State to supervise the emergence of a new kind of man and women, whose stability and reliability in the workplace could be guaranteed.[90] But Gramsci did not believe that the cheap-product–high-wage system could ever function properly in Europe. The arrival of certain American procedures in the Fiat car factories in Turin had convinced him at first that this was big capitalism's choice for the future, promising to sweep away small and medium industry in Italy. In fact Fiat never became a model for Italian industrial enterprise, partly for the reasons implied by his own thinking. Gramsci believed that such was the weight of the 'parasitical' element in the European social make-up, that the Old World would never succeed in competing with the US on international markets. What the likes of Siegfried called the 'veritable basis of civilisation' were in reality 'a heap of passive sedimentations... [made up] of civil service personnel and intellectuals, of clergy and landowners, piratical commerce and the...army. One could even say that the more historic a nation the more numerous and burdensome are these sedimentations of idle and useless masses living on "their ancestral patrimony", pensioners of economic history...'[91]

But Gramsci's outlook was not typical, even if critics such as himself on the Left were more likely to sympathize with the promise of productivity than those on the Right. Instead what predominated was the old Victorian men-against-machines lament refashioned to suit the challenges of mass production. This could be heard and seen in a variety of memorable forms. Art critics such as Siegfried Kracauer famously saw the new American troupes made up of perfect lines of dancing girls as a form of human assembly line. Artificial products of 'American distraction factories...when they kicked their legs high with mathematical precision, they joyously affirmed the progress of rationalization.'[92] Fritz Lang's movie classic *Metropolis* of 1926 presented a fantasy of urban life that included biplanes

---

[90] A. Gramsci, 'Americanism and Fordism', in David Forgacs (ed.), *A Gramsci Reader* (London, 1988), 277–94; cit. at p. 278; Ford was indeed militantly in favour of Prohibition. *Time* magazine called him 'Prohibition's prime industrial protagonist'; edition of 24 March 1930 visible at: <http://www.time.com/time/magazine/article/0,9171,738875,00 .html>. Yet Ford avoided the question entirely in his best-selling memoir *My Life and Work*, and in his survey of the contemporary world, *Today and Tomorrow* (New York, 1926).

[91] Gramsci, 'Americanism and Fordism', 277–8, Franco De Felice, 'Introduzione', in Antonio Gramsci, *Americanismo e Fordismo* (Turin, 1978) pp. viii–ix, xviii–xix.

[92] S. Kracauer, 'The Little Shop-Girls Go to the Movies', in *The Mass Ornament: Weimar Essays* (Cambridge, Mass., 1995); on Kracauer and his context, Lamb and Phelan, 'Weimar Culture', 93–7; for the French writer Duhamel's similar fixation on legs, Panchisi, *Future Tense*, 127.

darting between skyscrapers, a world run by huge industrial trusts, and human engineering featuring spectacular irradiant energy sources. Meanwhile a mass of automatons worked below ground to keep the brilliant surface life alive with energy and light. In this way, older science fiction nightmares were connected, using the visual language of Expressionism, to fears of a new civilization, not located geographically but with unmistakable American features.[93] French writers of the era achieved a notorious distinction with the force of their invectives on 'machinism' and the 'instrumental man'.[94] After his return from a short, unhappy trip through the United States, the novelist George Duhamel offered, instead of the usual traveller's tale, a diatribe entitled *America the Menace: Scenes from the Life of the Future*. 'As yet no nation has thrown itself into the excesses of industrial civilisation more deliberately than America', wrote Duhamel. American cinema was 'a pastime for slaves', the Ford car symbolized the vulgar triumph of moneyed materialism, their sports stadia offered 'the mysterious pleasures of the herd, the hive, and the ant-hill', their fruit tasted like an 'industrial by-product'; even eating had been turned into a mechanical process with the introduction of the cafeteria fast-food system.[95] In France, by way of contrast, a hundred kinds of cheese flourished:

... all good, wholesome, sound, substantial and pleasing. Every one of them has its history, its affinities, its particular rôle. In that one characteristic fact I recognize and admire the genius of my country; through that one fact I understand why it has produced so many great men in every walk of life.[96]

---

[93] The film studies bibliography on *Metropolis* is extensive; cf. Michael Minden and Holger Bachmann (eds), *Fritz Lang's Metropolis: Cinematic Visions of Technology and Fear* (New York, 2000).

[94] A contemporary Swiss commentary in Spoerri, *Old World and the New*; full contextualization and analysis in Gagnon, 'French Views', Panchisi, *Future Tense*, ch. 4. Both Gagnon and Panchisi (and Strauss, *Menace in the West*, ch. 11) make clear that the reflection on America offered by French writers of the late 1920s was more complex and systematic than their later reputation would suggest; cf. Bernadette Galloux-Fournier, 'Un regard sur l'Amérique: Voyageurs français aux Etats-Unis, 1919–1939', *Revue d'histoire moderne et contemporaine* (April–June 1990), 308–23; on Alexis De Tocqueville as the great precursor in this area, Kroes, *If You've Seen One*, 16–17.

[95] G. Duhamel, *America the Menace: Scenes from the Life of the Future* (London, 1931); cits at pp. xii, xiii, 34, 157, 181; discussion in Galloux-Fournier, 'Un regard sur l'Amérique', 313, 318–19; Panchisi, *Future Tense*, 117–27.

[96] Ibid. 201; Duhamel's book was a best-seller, but the intense debate it set off in French intellectual opinion on America and the future of France was divided and contradictory. For instance, Duhamel was a violent critic of contemporary cinema in all forms, but this attitude alienated those who believed in the medium as a growing part of the national artistic inheritance; Anne-Marie Duranton-Crabol, 'De l'anti-américanisme en France vers 1930: La réception des *Scènes de la vie future*', *Revue d'histoire moderne et contemporaine* (January–March 2001), 120–37.

'There was much in modernity that Modernists despised', reflects Daniel LeMahieu, speaking of England, and high on the list was its American components. But compared to the currents of thought on contemporary American influences prevailing in Paris and Berlin, British commentary was mild and often preferred satire to heavier weapons. Douglas Woodruff, a London *Times* editorialist, went as far as granting 'that the United States held no monopoly of the evils of a business civilization; it had however provided those evils with a very spacious home, and they affected an American style and dress'.[97] But in the course of these years a group of French and German intellectuals dedicated themselves to building an imposing litany of complaints about the alleged American contribution to the degraded state of contemporary existence. This was a repertory that would take on a life of its own, to become over succeeding decades a qualifying component of the outlook known as *anti-Americanism*.[98]

The 'stigmata of this devouring civilisation' were appearing all over Europe, hailed by all but a handful of sceptics, thundered Georges Duhamel. The psychoanalyst Müller-Freienfels denounced the determinism of American psychology, the sensationalism and sentimentalism of its culture, the 'depersonalization' of the soul that accompanied its technocratic civilization wherever it spread. 'The more Europe's cultural leaders witness the inroads of the American system into their world, the more pointed their hostility and sweeping their derogation become', noted the journalist Mowrer in 1928. 'Degeneration through modernity—that was the basic message of anti-Americanism' in Germany, writes Dan Diner, on the basis of a variety of powerful Weimar writings in this sense.[99]

---

[97] LeMahieu, 'America and the Representation of British History in Film and Television', 121; Woodruff cit. in Knoles, *Jazz Age Revisited*, 20; commentary on his satire *Plato's American Dream* (1926) in Spoerri, *Old World and the New*, 220–5; Spoerri points out that along with Hilaire Belloc, G. K. Chesterton, and Eric Linklater, Woodruff exemplified a British impulse to see the America of their day as a source of amusement, rather than the dire threat perceived by comparable French writers: *Old World and the New*, 225.

[98] For French contributions, Richard Kuisel, *Seducing the French: The Dilemma of Americanization* (Berkeley, 1993), 10–14; Gagnon, 'French Views'; Strauss, *Menace in the West*, ch. 4; Galloux-Fournier, 'Un regard sur l'Amérique'; for German comparisons, Diner, *America in the Eyes of the Germans*, 55, *passim*. There were of course plenty of American critics of the new mass society; discussion in Donohue, *Freedom from Want*, 152–3, 170–3.

[99] Duhamel, *America the Menace*, p. xiv; on Müller-Freienfels, Spoerri, *Old World and the New*, 87–96; Mowrer, *This American World*, p. 176 and ch. 5 in general; Diner, *America in the Eyes of the Germans*, 73; a Weimar example is the advertising and propaganda expert Hans Domizlaff, a leading inventor of a German conception of commercial branding and a classic example of German 'reactionary modernism'; for his critiques of American 'fairground' techniques in advertising, Holm Friebe, 'Branding Germany: Hans Domizlaff's *Marchentechnik* and Its Ideological Impact', in Swett et al. (eds), *Selling Modernity*, 90–2.

In the short term, a form of spiritual protectionism was at work, a defence against Europe's loss of authority and command in human evolution since the war. 'The life of the world has become scandalously provisional', wrote one of the most distinguished philosophers of the era, the Spanish thinker Ortega y Gasset, in 1930. His critique of the new way of progress explained that much of the demoralization felt by Europe's cultivated minds was due to this loss of the hitherto unshakeable centrality of their nations and themselves in the ordering of the world. There was no respectable cultural power remotely in sight to take the place of the old rule-giving trinity of France, England, and Germany. America in Ortega's view was still far too young, too connected to its origins to bring a new meaning to the world's life and organization. 'America has not yet suffered; it is an illusion to think that it can possess the virtues of command.'[100]

Like Gramsci's and most French critiques, Ortega's analysis was intended for local consumption; it was part of the dispute over present choices and the future going on within European elites in the decade after the war, and was not aimed directly at American actions or meant to be heard by Americans. Even when on American soil itself, the dozens of French commentators on the US were all in truth dedicated to 'searching for France', says Bernadette Galloux-Fournier.[101]

But different societies showed different emphases. French hostility dwelt on the problem of civilization and the individual, was conservative in inspiration, and long term in its outlook. It set the dominant tone for the decade, not least through its discovery of 'Europe' as a possible antidote—that is, the invention of a unifying space on the Old World side of the Atlantic that, if decently organized, could act in the future as a counterweight to the American presence.[102] The German hostility was in the

[100] Ortega y Gasset, *The Revolt of the Masses* (1932 edn repr., New York, 1957), ch. 14; cits at pp. 181, 139; cf. Mowrer, *This American World*, 185–6; for the French debate on the crisis of 'Europe', Strauss, *Menace in the West*, ch. 5.

[101] 'Un regard sur l'Amérique', 320; there was some open dialogue between the two sides: Waldo Frank's *Our America* of 1919 was prompted by the French publisher Gallimard, and translated immediately; Romier's *Who Will Be Master?* was written for both peoples, as was Mowrer's *This American World*. Eugène Brieux's post-war play *Les Américains chez nous* ('The Americans in Our Midst') also opened in New York (Panchisi, *Future Tense*, 111–13). Gagnon argues that the majority of French writers came to believe that 'the future of the West…lay in the willingness of Frenchmen and Americans to learn from each other', ('French Views', 449), but only a handful of the French commentaries were translated into English. For a sympathetic contemporary treatment of the French 'protectionist' outlook, Earnest Elmo Calkins, 'If Big Business Came to France', *Atlantic Monthly* (April 1929).

[102] The definition of 'Europe' as a space of values, culture, and identity to be rediscovered and revitalized was first of all an intellectual effort, as described in the French case by Panchisi, *Future Tense*, 133–4, Phillipe Roger, *The American Enemy: The History of French Anti-Americanism* (Chicago, 2005), 289–99; under the pressure of the transatlantic security, financial, and trade conflicts of the day, it began by the end of the 1920s to take on an

first instance anti-'imperialist', a response to the alleged effects of specific American policies in Germany. So it was more short term, more explicitly politicized, and often united left and right.[103] But by the end of the decade, anti-Americanism, precisely because it was an 'ism', began to be caught up in the generalized ideological escalation of those years. For a while this trend brought all the grievances together.

Duhamel insisted that he had no grudge against Americans as individuals or as a people; the ruling idea of civilization in that land was the target of his distaste.[104] In an epoch that transformed the most intense nationalisms into would-be ideologies of the future, this kind of distinction became increasingly difficult to sustain. As critics of the time liked to point out, the US brandished its own militant variety of the nation-as-ideology formulation in the language of '100 per cent Americanism' and 'Americanization', this latter being the mental melting and refounding process that turned immigrants of all shapes and origins into true-believing citizens. The editor of the *Frankfurter Zeitung* complained of the endless exaltation of national pride he had found on his trip to the States: 'this incessant spirit of propaganda permeates all American institutions', including the language and the education system, the glue of the nation's social fabric.[105] Meanwhile the gap between rhetoric and reality in American actions and policies, whether at home or abroad, was becoming ever more conspicuous. Older accusations of moral hypocrisy, dating back to Dickens, de Tocqueville, and the European debates on slavery, were now updated and intensified, becoming ideologically charged.[106]

---

explicit political form, culminating in the call by the French foreign minister Briand for 'a kind of federal link' to unite the European nations; Strauss, *Menace in the West*, 213–16; discussion in P. M. R. Stirk, *A History of European Integration since 1914* (London, 1994), 34–8; Boyce, *Great Interwar Crisis*, 172–4, 196–7, 200–1, 247–57; eloquent exposition of this idea of 'Europe' by German Foreign Minister Gustav Streseman, ibid. 196.

[103] Diner, *America in the Eyes of the Germans*, 65–6; Rosenberg, *Financial Missionaries*, 175.

[104] Duhamel, *America the Menace*, p. xv; contemporary comment in Spoerri, *Old World and the New*, 76–87; full contextualization in Roger, *American Enemy*, chs 9, 10.

[105] Feiler, *America Seen Through German Eyes*, 195–6; cf. Romier, *Who Will Be Master, Europe or America?*, 122–3.

[106] The moral and political theme of hypocrisy was explored with the greatest intensity in Weimar Germany: cf. Diner, *America in the Eyes of the Germans*, 58–62 (for British equivalents, Knoles, *Jazz Age Revisited*, 15); another European approach to it can be seen in the enthusiastic reception given in some quarters to US writers who were particularly critical of the evolution of their own society, e.g. H. L. Mencken and Sinclair Lewis; on Mencken, Krüger, 'Germany and the United States', 186, on Lewis, Benjamin Schwarz, 'Sheer Data' (a review of R. Lingeman, *Sinclair Lewis: Rebel from Main Street*, New York, 2001), *Atlantic Monthly*, (February 2002). Lewis's award of the Nobel Prize for Literature in 1930—the first ever American to be so recognized—was seen by his fellow novelists in the US to be a sign of European disdain for their culture. Not everyone shared it: Old World intellectual snobbism towards Lewis's characters was a form of anti-Americanism, wrote Antonio Gramsci, 'comical before it is stupid'; cit. in Gramsci, 'Americanism and Fordism', 296–8; French treatment of native critics of US society in Strauss, *Menace in the West*, ch. 12.

These were all reasons why the forms of criticism that American society and its behaviour attracted in the 1920s did not disappear when circumstances changed and time moved on. They were instead destined to endure, adding a quite new weight and meaning to the heritage of prejudices, stereotypes, negative symbols, and icons left from the nineteenth-century experience of the New World. The nostalgic anti-modernity thrust remained supreme; the characterizing feature of 1920s anti-Americanism. But the anti-imperialist accusation was never far away, colouring not only the German resentment but much of the British language of resistance to America's outwards industrial push, as well as important sections of the French debate.[107] Where the two impulses came together was in opposition to that current in America's economic will-to-power that projected new values, legitimized new expectations, and promised to revolutionize the prevailing standards of modern living for the indigent popular masses, from their humble tin bathtubs upwards.[108]

The novelist George Duhamel condemned, among all the other contemporary excesses, the survival of what he called the old nineteenth-century enthusiasm for 'the future', especially in the minds of 'the people', and he deplored America's contribution to the spread of such attitudes. But in the course of the 1920s the people, by way of the three special modernizing forces of the era—democracy, production, and communication—had begun to expect that a goodly part of the world to come would belong to them.[109] When America sent over its most glamorous and heroic figure from the future, the aviator Charles Augustus Lindbergh, they received him in raptures.

---

[107] For British resistance to American economic expansionism, Dimbleby and Reynolds, *An Ocean Apart*, 98–105; Boyce, *British Capitalism*, ch. 4; a British communist version in W. T. Colyer, *Americanism: A World Menace* (London, 1922), ch. 11; French case in Gagnon, 'French Views', 436, Panchisi, *Future Tense*, 133–4.

[108] By 1929 the Woolworth's retail chain had opened 350 stores up and down Britain. In them a bathtub cost sixpence, compared with two shillings and eleven pence (almost six times as much) in the traditional local hardware store; a personal memory of this confrontation is offered in the BBC documentary *An Ocean Apart*; cf. Dimbleby and Reynolds, *An Ocean Apart*, 105; other examples of the democratization of consumption offered by American selling methods in Miller and Hill, 'Europe as a Market', 406; on American influences in the spread of modern household appliances, Hardyment, *From Mangle to Microwave*, 28–32, 63–4, 87, 142, 172–7; general discussion in Victoria de Grazia, *Irresistible Empire: America's Advance through Twentieth-Century Europe* (Cambridge, Mass., 2005), ch. 3.

[109] Duhamel, *America the Menace*, p. xii; this change in popular expectations is a central theme of Ortega's essay *The Revolt of the Masses* (see in particular, pp. 22–3), and of Romier, *Who Will Be Master, Europe or America?*, 30–1; its appearance as a logical consequence of expanded democracy is treated in Potter, *People of Plenty*, 15–16.

The American myth takes wings

The frenzied welcome that greeted Lindbergh wherever he went in Europe after his dramatic transatlantic flight to Paris in May 1927 left an unprecedented impression on cultivated minds then and ever after. Was this a revolt of the masses such as those Ortega would warn of? The 'right not to be reasonable' on the part of the ever-restless crowd? Or a form of direct action, a violent overthrowing of all the restrictions, rules, and courtesies that made civilized communities possible?[110] In reality, considers Modris Eksteins, the theme of all the celebrations was 'that of a revival of imagination . . . in the midst of a ruined civilization, of a revival of individual will and spirit'.[111]

With extraordinary rapidity, Lindbergh's triumph of daring and perseverance was loaded with symbolic meaning by European observers of all persuasions. The image of the youthful pilot was transformed overnight into that of a Christ-like figure, one who had conquered death, the incarnation of the frontier spirit, hope, romance, 'Dionysian energy and will' (Eksteins). The hero, 'served as a blank screen onto which each person projected his own best images of man', wrote a later biographer.[112] Many dwelt on the aesthetic significance of his feat, talking of its 'incomparable beauty' or celebrating the lone aviator as 'the poet of the blue . . . creator of a new myth'. Others used language from the long-lost days of glory and chivalry, before the murderous juggernaut of total war had been let loose. Modris Eksteins insists that the scale and quality of the reaction is incomprehensible if detached from the war and its aftermath of psychological desolation, the spiritual atmosphere of the wasteland.[113]

In brilliant contrast to the post-war distress, Eksteins goes on, 'Lindbergh was constantly referred to as a symbol of the "high courage and dash of young America," as a representative of America's unrestrained energy.' An unknown 25-year-old from the provinces, but blonde and good-looking, he confirmed the star-making myth of democratic glamour too, needing no military uniform to earn his celebrity. His daring demonstrated that technical progress need not crush the individuality of the heroic temperament, which was one reason why regimes such as Italian Fascism were so enthralled by flying, its pioneers, and all its rituals. Meanwhile if America lacked 'depth' and the European sense of 'historical tragedy'—as the likes of Oswald Spengler insisted in tomes dedicated to

---

[110] Ortega y Gasset, *Revolt of the Masses*, 73, 75.
[111] M. Eksteins, *Rites of Spring*, 267.
[112] A. Scott Berg, *Lindbergh* (New York, 1998), 170.
[113] M. Eksteins, *Rites of Spring*, 263.

'the decline of the west'—who cared, when Lindbergh had found life and victory in the highest of skies?[114]

It was Lindbergh and the celebration of his achievement that demonstrated how the pre-war form of modernism, 'with its positive urge', had moved to America, argues Eksteins. But in recognizing this reality, European opinion of the 1920s did more than create a fresh series of metaphors and myths about American life and values to fit a different era. Lindbergh represented yet another demonstration of America's exceptional capacity to find new ways of fusing medium and message. The medium was the man and the machine—'We', as Lindbergh termed them in his own immediate account of the flight. The message was speed, communication, risk, and a special kind of gamble on the future. For Americans the exploit opened a new chapter in civil aviation history, and the unassuming hero went on to become a catalyst for a fresh impulse in transatlantic diplomacy, a national media protagonist, and later a vocal commentator on international affairs.[115] European enthusiasts in contrast saw in him a reflection of their own potential as transformed by America's vitalizing, galvanizing, enriching power, by the force of its grand modernizing challenges. In the meantime, until this potential could be realized, it was worth remembering that, as the Speaker of the Hungarian Parliament told the US Secretary of State, 'the propelling force carrying Captain Lindbergh across the ocean' was 'the American national ambition'.[116] In the 1920s Europeans had begun to come to terms with what that ambition was made of.

---

[114] On Spengler, Kroes, *If You've Seen One*, 17, 18, 21, 31; on the distinguishing features of Lindbergh's celebrity, Leo Braudy, *The Frenzy of Renown* (New York, 1986), 19–25.

[115] On Lindbergh's post-flight career Berg, *Lindbergh*, chs 9, 13, 14; on French Foreign Minister Briand's use of his triumph to launch a grand international public relations campaign in favour of pacifism—culminating in the so-called Pact of Paris signed with US Secretary of State Frank Kellogg in 1928—Duroselle, *France and the United States*, 130–4; on Lindbergh as a prophet of America's technological and financial lead in globalization, Boyce, *Great Interwar Crisis*, 142–3.

[116] Cit. in Costigliola, *Awkward Dominion*, 181.

3

Modernity and the European Encounter with Hollywood

CINEMA AND IDENTITY POLITICS IN THE 1920S

Nations at the movies

Of all the battles that broke out at the post-war crossroads of mass modernity in Western European societies, the most prolonged was the one for the construction of a satisfactory national identity in the new era. In a country like Britain, suggests Daniel LeMahieu in a classic study, there were two main sides in this struggle: the 'commercial' and the 'cultivated' spirits of the land. What made the conflict between them so difficult in the 1920s was that on every site of their confrontation—language, literature, newspapers, broadcasting, music, and above all, cinema—there was an uninvited guest, one that constantly forced the protagonists to define and redefine what it was they were fighting for. That presence was industrially produced, commercially distributed American mass entertainment, vastly expanded compared to its pre-war life.

As elsewhere in Europe, the post-war decade was an era that created many of the cycles of love and hate linking the various components of British society to whatever America's new cultural industries were selling. As intensely as the popular masses—the young and the commercial spirits—embraced the films, music, and dances the US sent over, so the cultivated elites denounced them and rushed to set up bulwarks against them, such as the British Broadcasting Corporation, born in 1922. The decade saw the first systematic, explicit use of the term 'anti-Americanism', and mass culture—the culture of the crowd, of popular democracy, and commercial modernity—was the force that most often provoked its display.[1] As we have already seen, hostility to whatever idea or practice stood

---

[1] Cf. Daniel L. LeMahieu, *A Culture for Democracy: Mass Communication and the Cultivated Mind in Britain Between the Wars* (Oxford, 1988), ch. 3; on the BBC, ibid. 179–90; for a contemporary American view of this experience, Mowrer, *This American World*, 145–7; theoretical discussion of concepts 'mass' and 'popular' culture in Rydell and Kroes, *Buffalo Bill in Bologna*, 3–6.

Fig. 2. The 1920s Jazz Age in Paris as seen by the French artist Pol Rab. The influence of the black singer and dancer Josephine Baker is clear.

for the United States had never been absent among European elites. But the arrival of jazz, Hollywood, advertising, chorus girls, slang, streamlining, chain stores, and the making–getting–spending philosophies that stood behind them, all this was profoundly upsetting to cultural authorities anxiously engaged in trying to re-establish their positions in society in the wake of the war.[2]

---

[2] On jazz in Europe—its origins, evolution, impact, and varieties of reception—Reinhold Wagnleitner, 'Jazz—The Classical Music of Globalization', in Wagnleitner (ed.), *Satchmo Meets Amadeus* (Innsbruck, 2006).

Sovereignty over culture had always been taken for granted as a distinguishing feature of nationhood, notes the historian Victoria de Grazia. Now it was disrupted on all sides. The result was a 'highly visible effort to devise strategies of resistance' to the penetration of America's cultural industries:

> From the 1920s, European policymakers, intellectuals, and party leaders sought to define what was 'national' about popular culture and to distinguish how European cultural traditions differed from American models in terms of their relationship to the market, the political system, and the forming of social consensus.[3]

A striking demonstration of the perceived dangers was supplied by the new-born Irish Republic. The first national film censor told readers of a Jesuit periodical of the situation he had faced when starting his job:

> Every evening boys and girls, from our educational institutions, crowded the Picture Houses in the cities, while in every little town—and in some remote villages people flocked from shop and farm to the cheapest of all amusements—absorbing ideas of life, which, with few exceptions were vulgar and sensational. Could any people for long preserve a distinct national character in the face of such a bombardment?[4]

But authorities in old-established nations like Britain were no less disturbed, and the way the processes of adaptation functioned in that country at the time supplied crucial precedents for later identity debates. Because the stakes seemed so high and the threat so forceful, policies and positions were defined—or so it was hoped—for decades to come. His Royal Highness, the Prince of Wales, told a 1923 meeting:

> It is well worth the British Nation's while to take the film industry seriously and to develop it to its utmost as a national industry.... It is up to us to see that British film pictures take their place in the theatres of the world and particularly on British screens.[5]

Knoles, *Jazz Age Revisited*, ch. 2; general context in Peter Miles and Malcolm Smith, *Cinema, Literature and Society: Elite and Mass Culture in Inter-War Britain* (London, 1987), 10–11, 81–6; Savage, *Teenage*, 239–42.

[3] Victoria de Grazia, 'Mass Culture and Sovereignty: The American Challenge to European Cinemas, 1920–1960', *Journal of Modern History* (March 1989), 56; cf. John Trumpbour, *Selling Hollywood to the World: U.S. and European Struggles for Mastery of the Global Film Industry, 1920–1950* (Cambridge, 2002), 2; the search for national film identity would feed British government film policy in the 1950s and once again in the 1990s; see Chapters 9 and 10.

[4] Cit. in Kevin Rockett, 'Protecting the Family and the Nation: The official censorship of American cinema in Ireland, 1923–1954', *Historical Journal of Film, Radio and Television*, 20/3 (2000), 283–300; cit. at p. 283.

[5] Cit. in the semi-official report *The Film in National Life* (London, 1932), 41.

Later decades saw the British do their best to attract American patronage and favour for their film industry; by comparison the earlier years demonstrated far more hostility, and a belief by the cultural authorities—educators, bishops, judges, intellectuals, concerned politicians—that the State must act to defend the masses, the Empire, and the best of the national heritage from the corrupting moral and cultural effects of the Hollywood industry.[6] Cinema was *the* battleground, not least because of the size of the audience—3,760 cinemas catered to roughly 20 million spectators per week in 1927[7]—but also because the American market share was so overwhelming: 95 per cent on average at this time. The answer was economic and cultural protectionism. As in most countries in Europe in the late years of the decade, a system of fiscal levers and import quotas was installed, the hope being to restore the balance of cultural power and domesticate the beast, as was happening in the burgeoning worlds of recorded sound, jazz, and dancing. In this way tradition might reassert itself, and Americanization, as LeMahieu asserts, become 'something recognizably British'.[8]

But unlike other societies going through similar tortuous processes of redefinition at this time—Weimar Germany, France, and Italy being prominent examples—the British succeeded in their efforts, says LeMahieu. And later studies showed that there were few lasting signs of the Americanization so feared by the cultural authorities earlier: people were 'not completely taken in'.[9] By bringing forth the BBC, the cultural authorities provided a new form of common ground for all the nation's citizens in the era of electronic communications, and built an institution that would prove a pillar of society in the supreme test of World War II. At the same time an idea of public broadcasting was established that deliberately set out to avoid the chaos and vulgar commercialism thought to prevail in the world of American radio. For decades onwards from this time, says the historian Valeria Camporesi, the 'public discourse' on broadcasting in

---

[6] Richard Maltby and Ruth Vasey, ' "Temporary American Citizens": Cultural Anxieties and Industrial Strategies in the Americanisation of European Cinema', in Andrew Higson and Richard Maltby (eds), *'Film Europe' and 'Film America': Cinema, Commerce, and Cultural Exchange 1920–1939* (Exeter, 1999); Knoles, *Jazz Age Revisited*, 121–2; for a full survey and social contextualization of these issues, Ross McKibbin, *Classes and Cultures: England 1918–1951* (Oxford, 1998), ch. 11, 'The Cinema and the English', 419–56; Miles and Smith, *Cinema, Literature and Society*, 170.

[7] Rachel Low, *The History of the British Film, 1918–1929* (London, 1971), 47.

[8] Puttnam, *Undeclared War*, 151; Trumpbour, *Selling Hollywood*, 119–23; Andrew Higson, *Waving the Flag: Constructing a National Cinema in Britain* (Oxford, 1995), 9–13; Jeffrey Richards, *The Age of the Dream Palace: Cinema and Society in Britain 1930–1939* (2nd edn, London, 2009), 99; LeMahieu, *Culture for Democracy*, 82; for his discussion of the impact and transformation of jazz in 1920s Britain, ibid. 88–98.

[9] McKibbin, *Classes and Cultures*, 456.

Britain returned obsessively to the notion that radio (and later television) must offer a contrasting vision of society to that displayed by their American equivalents.[10]

But the European territory that best demonstrated the kinds of conflict unleashed by the arrival of the new forms of mass entertainment was always Britain's recently semi-detached province, the Irish Free State. Unprotected hitherto by cultural barriers or its own film industry, the country's founding fathers felt particularly vulnerable. The problem, says the Irish film historian Kevin Rockett, was 'the overwhelming viscerality of the cinematic image itself *irrespective of its content*' [*sic*]. Consequently, during the 1920s and 1930s Irish Catholic Bishops blamed the cinema for dwelling obsessively on the habits of the 'divorcing classes' in England and America, and carrying an alien message: that of consumerism, which was responsible for everything from demands for higher wages to emigration. Their response was repression. From the earliest appearance of the cinema in the country, nationalists and Catholics alike created a pattern of intense cultural and moral protectionism, managed by a powerful and highly repressive censorship system that would endure until the 1960s. By the simple procedure of insisting that any film shown should be acceptable to every part of the population, even the youngest—since cinemagoing was presumed to be an experience that should defend and reinforce the family—the censor succeeded in 'infantilizing' the entire cinema audience, says Rockett, and retarding its encounter with all the most problematic issues of contemporary life.[11]

Traditional European elites everywhere feared the 'cosmopolitan eclecticism', innovation, and radiant power of attraction of the characteristic Hollywood film product and its marketing. 'Hireling of our dreams', the French novelist Ferdinand Céline called it in 1932, 'there to be bought like a prostitute for an hour or two of make-believe.' His fellow scribe Duhamel proclaimed: 'The cinema is a pastime for slaves, an amusement for the illiterate, for poor creatures stupefied by work and anxiety.... I

[10] ' "There are no kangaroos in Kent": The American "Model" and the Introduction of Commercial Television in Britain, 1940–1954', in Ellwood and Kroes (eds), *Hollywood in Europe*, 267; comparable German experience discussed in Kaspar Maase, 'From Nightmare to Model? Why German Broadcasting Became Americanized', in Alexander Stephan (ed.), *Americanization and Anti-Americanism: The German Encounter with American Culture after 1945* (New York, 2005), 79–80. The German model, reports Kaase, envisaged a more complex private–public mix than the British version, and took advertising. But the impulse to avoid the reproduction of conditions in America was just as conscious.

[11] K. Rockett, 'Protecting the Nation: The Reception of American Cinema in Ireland 1923–1954', paper presented at the conference *Hollywood and its Spectators* (London, February 1998), published in Melvyn Stokes and Richard Maltby (eds), *Hollywood spectatorship: Changing perceptions of cinema audiences* (London, 2001).

assert that any people subjected for half a century to the actual influence of the America "movie" is on the way to the worst decadence..."[12] And the movies continued to play a special role too as pretext in the contemporary lament over standardization and modernity, a denunciation that would echo through time after the appearance in 1936 of the German social philosopher Walter Benjamin's tract, *The Work of Art in the Age of its Technical Reproducibility*.[13] More typical were the pages written earlier by Holland's greatest twentieth-century historian, Johan Huizinga, a famed specialist on the Middle Ages.

In a book published after a long trip to the US, Huizinga wrote that it would be hard to overestimate the importance of the movies 'as a cultural factor'. The movies, he believed, were 'an extraordinarily democratic component' of contemporary culture, giving rise to 'a solidarity of emotions and interests in the broadest circles...'. But these were among the few self-evident qualities of the medium. In a biting paragraph of denunciation, Huizinga went on to condemn the price paid for this egalitarianism, and the contribution the movies made to the 'mechanization' of taste, sensibilities, and common living visible to him on all sides:

> [The film] creates a necessarily limited and crude code of expression and imagination, and it does so in accordance with a purely commercial attitude. It develops from the already existing low taste a catchy, crudely romantic, sensational, gruesome, and low-comedy taste, and then mechanically delivers such an excess of satisfactions in this taste that it raises it to a cultural norm of the very greatest weight, which is enforced every day in a thousand places. When we accept the art of the cinema as the daily spiritual bread of our time, we acknowledge the enslavement by the machine into which we have fallen.[14]

[12] Céline cit. in Eugen Weber, *The Hollow Years: France in the 1930s* (New York, 1996), 66; Duhamel, *America the Menace*, 34–5, cf. Trumpbour, *Selling Hollywood*, 240; for comparable remarks by Dutch socialists and Calvinists, Kroes, *If You've Seen One*, 89–90.

[13] W. Benjamin, *The Work of Art in the Age of its Technical Reproducibility, and Other Writings*, ed. Michael W. Jennings et al. (Cambridge, Mass., 2008). Film, said Benjamin, 'with its continuous sequence of discontinuous images' is to consumption what the assembly line is to production'. Liquidating the value of tradition in the cultural heritage, and the 'beautiful semblance' of the unique work of art, film's 'technology of reproduction detaches the reproduced object from the sphere of tradition'. The medium's vast potential was wasted by the capitalist exploitation of mass tastes: the 'cult of the audience' was a profoundly counter-revolutionary force; ibid. 21–40, 340.

[14] J. Huizinga, *America: A Dutch Historian's Vision from Afar and Near* (New York, 1928), 113; for comparable French critiques, Strauss, *Menace in the West*, 182–3; for British versions, Vincent Porter, 'The Construction of an anti-Hollywood Film Aesthetic: The Film Criticism of Walter Mycroft', in Alan Burton and Loraine Porter (eds), *Crossing the Pond: Anglo-American Film Relations Before 1930* (Trowbridge, 2002), 72–81; for those of the great American anthropologist Margaret Mead, Savage, *Teenage*, 224–5.

Huizinga saw in the commercial mass media a perfect illustration of his conviction that with his day 'the fatal moment of the modern history of civilization' had arrived, the moment when 'organization becomes mechanization'. With more formal democracy came more standardization, less individuality, more conformity, less liberty, and America—'the most perfect example' of these trends with its militant ideal of rationalization—was Europe's future, unless the cultivated minds decided to rouse themselves to face the threat.[15] So the militant manifesto of the Amsterdam Film league of 1927 declared: 'Once every hundred times we see: film. For the rest we see: movies. The herd, the commercial régime, America, kitsch.'[16]

But observers today are virtually united in their belief that the mechanism that traditionally connected the impact to the fear was not a direct one. Instead, they suggest, the flow of films (and all the rest) has always passed through a sort of two-way mirror, constructed in the European subconscious to reflect an idealized image of the past, present, and future of each society. So it was on this partly reflecting, partly absorbing surface, this 'silver screen in the west'—as C. Vann Woodward termed it—, that the great drama is played out between an America half real, half invented (the proportions shift constantly) and each specific, local variety of civilization.[17]

American cinema and the Modern Girl

The first—and for years the most conspicuous—section of society to be changed by the Hollywood cinema and its effects was women. The American film historians Antonia Lant and Ingrid Perez quote Alma Taylor, one of Britain's first film stars, as among the most effective of early commentators on the consequences of mass feminine film-going. Writing in 1931, Taylor stated her belief that: 'The cinema has contributed to the greatest single triumph of progress of the twentieth century—the emergence of the Modern Girl.' She suggested that the cinema had 'completed Mrs Pankhurst's work by establishing the Modern Girl's right to a good time and evoking her capacity for enjoying one. Women and films have

---

[15] Kroes, 'Between Rejection and Reception', 22, how the film question aroused elite opinion in Holland and affected traditional cultural divisions is the main point of this article; expanded version in Kroes, *If You've Seen One*, ch. 3.

[16] Lary May, *Screening Out the Past: The Birth of Mass Culture and the Motion Picture Industry* (Oxford, 1980); manifesto cit. and discussed in Kroes, 'Between Rejection and Reception', 33.

[17] Vann Woodward, *Old World's New World*, ch. 2; cf. Kroes, 'Between Rejection and Reception', 34.

been closely associated from the commencement of moving pictures. With the invention of the cinema, women secured, for the first time, a form of entertainment which was peculiarly their own.' Heedless of the full implications of what she was saying and the likely reactions to its truth, Taylor concluded: 'Already weakening, the authority of fathers, husbands and brothers over their womankind came definitely to an end with the opening of the cinema.'[18]

And it was Hollywood whence this danger came. In 1927 an article in the mass circulation and conservative *Daily Express* denounced the transformation of British film-goers into beings who 'talk America, think America, and dream America'. Ringing alarm bells in a fashion that would soon become a reflex action, the newspaper declared: 'We have several million people, mostly women, who, to all intent and purpose are temporary American citizens.' In Italy the Fascist regime, dedicated to building an anti-modernist cult of heroic masculinity, set out to organize feminine free time in order to counteract the local success of Hollywood (in 1926 30,000 Italian girls had sent photographs of themselves in bathing costumes to the Fox studio, noted Antonio Gramsci without pleasure[19]). Among their other deplorable tendencies, the movies exalted such degenerate Latin figures as Rudolf Valentino and Ramon Navarro. Fascist critics went on to accuse the cinema of aggravating the demographic crisis by transforming the healthy search for pure love into a sensual experience of voyeurism. 'Not least of all', writes Victoria de Grazia, 'Americanized leisure threatened to transform Italian girls, making them masculine and independent like their American counterparts.'[20]

'Why do women go to the movies?' was a question women writers and observers began to ask systematically in Europe and America alike from the 1920s onwards. The dominant part of the mass audience by all accounts, subject and object of hundreds of mainstream Hollywood films, women were held by the experience of watching these films in a sort of

---

[18] A. Lant and I. Perez, 'The Red Velvet Seat', paper presented at the conference *Hollywood and its Spectators* (London, February 1998); but the American observer of Britain, R. H. Heindel, claimed in 1940 that 'the screen, especially of our prohibition era, left a haunting memory of a glorified American woman, sometimes much divorced and intoxicated', *American Impact on Great Britain*, 338.

[19] *Americanismo e Fordismo*, 76, 84; Gramsci noted that this was a result of a Fascist newspaper's effort to bolster the Italian presence in Hollywood film and so counteract some of its influence in Europe; the only result thought Gramsci would be to encourage a new form of white slave trade (as with beauty contests), and amplify Hollywood's prestige.

[20] Richard Maltby and Ruth Vasey, 'The International Language Problem: European Reaction to Hollywood's Conversion to Sound', in Ellwood and Kroes (eds), *Hollywood in Europe*, 71; V. de Grazia, *How Fascism Ruled Women: Italy, 1922–1945* (Berkeley, 1992), 209.

'social bondage' and then released 'into a dream of potency and freedom', as the American film historian Jeannine Basinger explains in her grand study of how, in its heyday, Hollywood spoke to women. In this view, classical Hollywood movies from the 1920s on were overwhelmingly about 'a kind of yearning... a desire to know what you didn't know, have what you didn't have, and feel what you were afraid to feel'. And yet their attitude to these desires was profoundly 'contradictory, elusive, hypocritical and deceptive'. The direct connection between these impulses and Hollywood cinema was the new conception of *glamour*, which the industry's most special invention, the 'star system', brought with it.[21]

Glamour was the hard-to-define quality that transformed the apparently ordinary individual, by way of the great studios and the cinema screen, into that uniquely American human phenomenon: the film-star. In Basinger's view it involved a physical and aesthetic transformation into something 'beautiful, exotic, enviable and desirable', creating a being who was at the same time accessible and yet exclusive. Other witnesses have spoken of 'average, unknown Americans' whose talents for 'expressing charisma, charm and sex-appeal', off the screen as much as on it, '... could be democratised', made to appear within the reach of young women anywhere.[22]

Beauty contests were the first step up the ladder, and in a country like Britain the mass media of the day made intense efforts to organize the production of the nation's own screen goddesses using this device. Unhappily the winners never knew success, for whatever reason; certainly not in Los Angeles, usually not even at home.[23]

But women everywhere could, if they so chose, console themselves with the new fan clubs, magazines, and star-related goods that arrived in the wake of the movies. To democratize its appeal by way of a product like cosmetics was a prime example of Hollywood's star system at work. This was one of those 'elements of the woman's film that women could actually get their hands on' (Basinger). The impact of Max Factor's company in

---

[21] Jeanine Basinger, *How Hollywood Spoke to Women 1930–1960* (Hanover, NH, 1993), 5, 6, 7, 20; on Hollywood's exploitation of new ideas of young, feminine sexuality, Savage, *Teenage*, 203; on the general history of the concept and reality of 'glamour', Stephen Gundle, *Glamour: A History* (Oxford, 2008).

[22] Basinger, *How Hollywood Spoke*, 115, 140, and the chapter on 'Fashion and Glamour' in general; May, *Screening Out the Past*, 233; Savage, *Teenage*, 228–9.

[23] Jenny Hammerton, 'Screen-Struck: The Lure of Hollywood for British Women in the 1920's', in Burton and Porter (eds), *Crossing the Pond*, 100–5; differences in attitudes to the individual and the community as reflected in the roles assigned to female stars may have been one reason, according to Miles and Smith, *Cinema, Literature and Society*, 172–3: Hollywood's women were expected to be optimistic, individualistic, and sexy, their British counterparts were fatalistic and class conscious.

Britain, after its arrival in 1927, was described by the company's first representative in the *Ocean Apart* television documentary: 'Film-star make-up came as an absolute revolution to this country…with the most wonderful advertising campaign imaginable…a film-star make-up chart for everyone [which] revolutionised make-up….Nothing like this had been done before, and suddenly here it was available for you to go and buy in the shops….The cosmetics of the stars…it was glamour and it was American.'[24]

In 1928 the *Chicago Daily News* journalist Mowrer was happy to report that 'the plucked eyebrow, a typically American contribution to female beauty, [had] fortunately failed to make much headway in Europe'. Ten years later though, things had changed. The British popular novelist, J. B. Priestley, denounced the influence in Dunbury, an imaginary provincial town, of Hollywood's 'outpost' there, the *Elite Picture Theatre*. This was a place…

> …where you may see its tough guys, who knock fellows down so readily and so easily, and its young women with their egg faces and voices like seagulls. Nearly all the girls in the shops round the square try to look like these glamorous beings, with the result that there is hardly a whole young feminine eyebrow left in this part of Dunbury.[25]

Outside the captivated universe of film-goers, the arrival of the glamour-based human fashion system provoked endless suspicion and scorn. Believing that 'films are the mirror of the prevailing society', the caustic German film critic Siegfried Kracauer wrote at the end of the 1920s that 'sensational film hits and life usually correspond to each other because the Little Miss Typists model themselves after the examples they see on the screen'. Kracauer of course did not see a literal, simple emulation, but how in their very unreality, films represented 'the daydreams of society', revealing its secret psychological mechanisms and giving form to its 'otherwise repressed wishes'.[26] After the economic rationalization, the film audience had multiplied, said Kracauer, but its centre of gravity was the 'low-level white-collar workers', particularly the 'little shop-girls', whose sparse moral and mental furniture left them defenceless in front of products made just to please them. The 'wretched' output of the German

---

[24] *An Ocean Apart*, BBC TV, 1983, episode 2; cf. Dimbleby and Reynolds, *An Ocean Apart*, 106.
[25] Mowrer, *This American World*, 140; J. B. Priestley, *Let the People Sing* (London, 1940), 86.
[26] S. Kracauer, 'The Little Shopgirls Go to the Movies'.

industry had become indistinguishable from Hollywood's, said Kracauer, all united in the effort to provide escapism and illusion on an industrial scale.[27]

In time it would become evident that audiences did not simply absorb in passive fashion whatever was offered up by Hollywood (or any other mass medium), as so many of its early critics seemed to assume. Seeing was *not* believing. Instead they took over American cinema and their own using priorities and selection mechanisms that each generation, gender, ethnic, or any other sort of community, with experience, worked out for itself.[28] In his 1987 discussion of the consumption of American cinema in Fascist Italy, James Hay anticipated much later work on European film audiences by demonstrating that Italian film-goers, women as well as men, encoded and decoded the celluloid myths proposed by the American industry in a variety of different ways, revealing sentiments that were uneven and often contradictory. They developed profoundly ambivalent attitudes of fear and admiration when presented with the American dream of modernity as fashioned by Hollywood.[29] In a country like Mussolini's Italy, these were feelings that turned out to be shared by the Fascist regime itself.

The power of a creative industry

> Between the world wars the principal film companies derived an average of 35% of their gross revenue from the foreign field, a larger proportion of revenues than most other America export industries earned abroad.[30]

The collapse of much European film production during the Great War gave the American studios the chance to turn themselves into a large-scale entertainment industry, and, as already seen, they seized it with extraordinary vigour and speed, spilling into the possessions and protectorates of the Old World powers and thence into surrounding lands. In sheer volume terms, the studios multiplied their exports to Europe five times between 1914 and 1920.[31] Although Hollywood's was a globalized view of the world and its commercial possibilities from the very beginning, the

---

[27] 'Film 1928', *The Mass Ornament*, cf. Romier, *Who Will Be Master, Europe or America?*, 90–1 and the whole thrust of his remarkable chapter on 'The Masses and the "Sex Problem"'.

[28] In contrast with many contemporaries, a Berlin pastor, Günther Deln, saw the young people—especially young women—of 1930 as galvanized by the new tools for the construction of selfhood that American or American-style consumer models offered; cit. in Andreas Wirsching, 'From Work to Consumption: Transatlantic Visions of Individuality in Modern Mass Society', *Contemporary European History* (February 2011), 11–13.

[29] J. Hay, *Popular Film Culture in Fascist Italy* (Bloomington, 1987), 72.

[30] Ruth Vasey, *The World According to Hollywood, 1918–1939* (Exeter, 1997), 7.

[31] Details and complexities of this situation in Bakker, 'America's Master', esp. pp. 228–30.

European market remained crucial, and the industry was well aware of its dependence on pleasing patrons in all its customer nations grand and not so grand. Long before the Soviet state had built an official anti-American prejudice, the stars could be seen across Russia 'in the most unexpected places', reports J. D. Parks:

> Gloria Swanson played in tiny Caucusus towns; Tom Mix, Corinne Griffith and Williak Hart starred in Rostov-on-Don. One Moscow theatre devoted itself solely to Clara Kimball Young, while Douglas Fairbanks and Mary Pickford, who travelled to the Soviet Union in 1926 to meet their fans, displayed their screen talents all over the city.[32]

By the middle of the decade over two-thirds of Hollywood's foreign revenues were earned in Europe (including the USSR), and of that figure 30.5 per cent came from the British market alone in 1927. By comparison, France provided 8.5 per cent of total foreign revenues in that year, Germany 5.25 per cent, Central Europe 4.0 per cent, and Italy 3.5 per cent. Only Latin America could begin to compare in significance.[33]

Unlike other production industries, the European film studios never recovered their vitality after the war, and everywhere except Germany succumbed to the scale and dynamism of the Hollywood oligopoly, which controlled production, distribution, and exhibition over an ever-widening horizon.[34] By 1925 the American market share in Britain was, as already seen, 95 per cent, in France and Central Europe it was 70 per cent, in Mussolini's Italy 65 per cent. Even in the Weimar Republic, where a government-supported trust had done much to keep production going, it was 60 per cent.[35] In Stalin's Soviet Union the share was 42 per cent, but much bigger for hits, and an American observer familiar with the scene complained in 1925 that Hollywood's products 'dominate, inundate, glut, overwhelm the Russian motion picture industry today'.[36]

The reasons for this predominance were not hard to trace. Thanks in part to their vast domestic market, the four major studios were able to mobilize financial resources on a scale that increased constantly: from $20,000 per picture in 1914 to $60,000 by 1920 on an infinite upward

---

[32] J. D. Parks, *Culture, Conflict and Coexistence: American–Soviet Cultural Relations, 1917–1958* (Jefferson, NC, 1983), 19.

[33] On global view, Thompson, *Exporting Entertainment*, footnote at p. 117; Vasey, *World According to Hollywood*, 15; full list of revenues ibid. 85.

[34] Bakker, 'America's Master', 230–2.

[35] Full list in Vasey, *World According to Hollywood*, 70.

[36] Market share quoted in Marsha Siefert, 'Allies on Film: US–USSR Filmmakers and *The Battle of Russia*', in M. Siefert (ed.), *Extending the Borders of Russian History* (Budapest, 2003), 374; quote in Parks, *Culture, Conflict*; in fact, says Parks, the official outlook was in favour of further film imports at this stage, in the hope of encouraging two-way trade, co-production, and mutual understanding.

trend. But it was in the power of their integrated production and distribution systems that the secret of their hold lay: '[the] four companies together managed to encircle virtually the entire globe with regional networks', writes the industry historian Ruth Vasey.[37]

Hollywood was well aware that its activities provided more than a harmless evening's entertainment for emotionally starved masses. A memorandum of 1928 was particularly eloquent:

> Motion pictures are the most CONSPICUOUS [*sic*] of all the American exports. They do not lose their identity. They betray their nationality and country of origin. They are easily recognized. They are all-pervasive. They colour the minds of all who see them. They are demonstrably the greatest single factors in the Americanization of the world and as such fairly may be called the most important and significant of America's exported products.
>
> They are such indirect and undesigned propaganda for the purveying of national ideals, modes of life, methods of thought and standards of living as no other country in the world has ever enjoyed.

This reflection came from within the association of Motion Picture Producers and Distributors of America (MPPDA), the trade organization built up from 1922 by the unlikely figure of Will H. Hays, a former Republican Postmaster General. Created to coordinate finance (New York) and production (Los Angeles), and to ensure that the industry and not government ran cinema censorship, the 'Hays Organization' also represented Hollywood's interests in the public arena at home and abroad. During the decade this body and its President built up a formidable reputation in Europe for its effectiveness in the sort of half-public–half-private diplomacy that was making the New York banks such key players in the Old World's fortunes, and which contributed so much to the distinctiveness of American methods of power projection.[38] A leading French critic René Jeanne, in an eloquent 1930 denunciation of the 'American cinema invasion', called the Hays outfit the brains and heart of an entire industry, and the man himself its Interior Minister and Foreign Minister combined. A colleague of Jeanne's had said, 'He's not an industrialist but a statesman, not a businessman but more like a conqueror.'[39]

The MPPDA consolidated its power and reputation most successfully when it persuaded Congress to set up a Motion Picture Section in the US

---

[37] Vasey, *World According to Hollywood*, 15.

[38] Comprehensive discussion of MPPDA ibid. Introduction, ch. 2; cf. Trumpbour, *Selling Hollywood*, ch. 1, which describes the private–public connection in the film sector as a form of corporatism.

[39] René Jeanne, 'L'invasion cinématographique américaine', *Revue des Deux Mondes* (15 February 1930), 870–2.

Department of Commerce, then being transformed to boost American commercial activities throughout the world under the leadership of Herbert Hoover.[40] But it was when the State Department joined the Washington–Hollywood axis that a connection became established that would be crucial in supporting the US film hegemony in Europe and elsewhere in the decades to come. The producers' association described its methods as 'Direct, amicable representation of the American interests, coupled with personal consultation with the foreign interests and government officials concerned'. Its effectiveness in this mission put it at the heart of confrontations about the workings of cinema markets everywhere in Europe.[41]

Given the success of Hollywood's market penetration abroad, admitted the 1928 memo, it was not surprising that overseas nations should be rushing to put up trade and cultural barriers against the American moving picture.[42] Meanwhile, at home, these very same features, presented first of all in terms of sales opportunities for US goods, were used by the MPPDA and its allies in government to promote the industry's reputation in public opinion and gain support from Congress. The Commerce Department apparently was the source of the legend that every foot of film shown abroad sold a dollar's worth of US goods. The State Department argued in 1926 that without the anti-immigrant laws, the movies would have provoked a flood of aspiring US citizens. 'As it is, in vast instances, the desire to come to this country is thwarted, and the longing to emigrate is changed into a desire to imitate.'[43]

As already seen in the examples of Britain and Ireland, the general response to the situation in Europe was to invent official mechanisms for restricting the physical flow of US-made films on to local screens, or at

[40] Thompson, *Exporting Entertainment*, 117–18; Trumpbour, *Selling Hollywood*, 64–5; a 1924 declaration of the government's interest in supporting the US picture industry is reproduced in Higson and Maltby (eds), '*Film Europe' and 'Film America'*, 1; film trade historian Ian Jarvie insists that all this was strictly a business-support policy, the US government as such had no 'film policy' of its own: 'Dollars and Ideology: Will Hays' Economic Foreign Policy 1922–1945', *Film History*, 2 (1988), 212; Hoover's wide-ranging strategy discussed in Rosenberg, *Spreading the American Dream*, 140–3.

[41] Authorized history of MPPDA quoted in Thompson, *Exporting Entertainment*, 111–12; cf. Trumpbour, *Selling Hollywood*, 65–6.

[42] Vasey, *World According to Hollywood*, 43–4; the full document is reproduced in Higson and Maltby (eds), '*Film Europe' and 'Film America'*, 353–79; when acting abroad the industry of course was anxious to avoid any suggestion that it was propagandizing its audiences, Vasey, *World According to Hollywood*, 45.

[43] Commerce Department claim discussed in Vasey, *World According to Hollywood*, 42, endorsed in *The Economist*, 16 August 1930; amplified by Commerce Department and others in late 1930s as cit. in John Eugene Harley, *World-Wide Influences of the Cinema: A Study of Official Censorship and the International Cultural Aspects of Motion Pictures* (Los Angeles, 1940), 245–7; on movies and immigration Maltby and Vasey, 'Temporary American Citizens', pp. 39–41, cit. at p. 41; on the splits and resentments this mechanism caused in British society, as reported in the American press, Richards, *Age of the Dream Palace*, 99.

least tying them to the promotion of the native industry.[44] The politics of protectionism were explained in these terms by an industry representative sent to survey the problem in 1926:

> ...virtually everywhere there is being made an effort to overcome the predominance of the American picture.... One of [the motives] is the intense spirit of nationalism that now pervades all Europe. For patriotic and political reasons, governments of the several countries now seeking to restrict the importation of American pictures desire the establishment of a national picture industry in their own country that will serve as propaganda and that will reflect the life, the customs and the habits of its own people.[45]

Made aware of these considerations by the State Department and the MPPDA, American production was frequently adapted to local sensibilities, at least those expressed by censorship systems run by the State, or in its name. Local censors, say Maltby and Vasey, were always much more sensitive to the Hollywood industry's representation of their own nation in any form than to any image of the US that might be screened (indeed one American observer wrote that 'no foreign censors will cut anything that may slander American life'.[46]) This meant, for example, that the 1924 version of *Peter Pan* would be filmed 'in "a score" of different versions, with Peter running up a different national flag over Captain Hook's pirate ship each time'. French diplomats would be consulted whenever a film depicting the French Foreign Legion or any other feature from the French national heritage was about to appear, and the guardians of values and images on behalf of the British Empire were no less vigilant. The influence of British preoccupations was deeply felt throughout the heyday of the studios, notes Ruth Vasey.[47] But the Chinese, the Mexicans, the Italians could be just as prickly as the upholders of British honour. 'Certain Balkan countries objected to their countrymen being portrayed as spies', recalled Sam Goldwyn, a founder of MGM. 'This was immediately done away with....It has got so lately [*sic*] that the only people who do not object to being ridiculed are the Americans.'[48]

---

[44] A chronology of European quota legislation from 1921 to 1934 is offered by K. Thompson, *Exporting Entertainment*, 211–12; it is reproduced with relevant industry and government documents in Higson and Maltby (eds), *'Film Europe' and 'Film America'*, 346, *passim*.

[45] Cit. in Vasey, *World According to Hollywood*, 40.

[46] Heindel, *American Impact on Great Britain*, 339.

[47] Vasey, *World According to Hollywood*, 144–51; examples of State's monitoring of foreign reactions to American films in Trumpbour, *Selling Hollywood*, 66–71.

[48] Maltby and Vasey, 'Temporary American Citizens', 42; the adaptation of US productions to local tastes abroad is a major theme of Vasey, *World According to Hollywood*; in a review of this book the film industry historian Ian Jarvie describes how the State Department's files were filled up with 'avalanches of protests' from offended governments, all hoping in vain that the US authorities could bring official pressure to bear on the studios to modify their output, *Historical Journal of Film, Radio and Television* (June 1998), 304; Goldwyn cit. in Harley, *World-Wide Influences*, 23.

Until the arrival of sound it seemed possible that certain national film industries might offer serious competition to what was imported from across the Atlantic. In Germany especially the question was widely debated theoretically and practically throughout the 1920s, since the full American onslaught arrived only after 1924, by which time the domestic industry had been thoroughly consolidated by government and financial interests, and audiences had developed a clear preference for the local product, one that turned out to be enduring. Even the most successful US-made films in Germany were often the ones that made use of settings familiar from German productions.[49] For local film-makers the problem was seen as not simply about establishing an authentically 'German' cinema culture, with its own conscious and appreciative public, but to produce titles that would compete internationally and in America itself. The dilemma faced by German cinema, writes Thomas Saunders, was that of any culture threatened by displacement or extinction, namely whether borrowing presented a viable method of preserving independence. To enter into competition with Hollywood implied accepting American terms of reference. It simultaneously stiffened resistance to American methods and mentalities.[50]

Eventually rejecting this option, the German cinema and its supporters in business and government tried by trial and error to strike a balance between restricting the market for foreign films, boosting home-grown production on a large scale, and cooperating with the big US studios. By 1927, said a French report, 75 per cent of German film production was being supported financially by American money.[51] But the key question was once again, as in so many other branches of modern industry, that of selective amalgamation. How was it possible to evolve a 'third way' between pure nationalism—which was unappealing abroad—and homogenization on the American pattern? And at the heart of that challenge stood 'the critical issue of the link between cinema and society', says Saunders. A contemporary critic lamented:

> In America the cinema is immediate because the producers are themselves the public. In Germany they either consider themselves better: literati and

---

[49] Joseph Garncarz, 'Hollywood in Germany: The Role of American Films in Germany, 1925–1990', in Ellwood and Kroes (eds), *Hollywood in Europe*; K. Thompson, 'The Rise and Fall of Film Europe', in Higson and Maltby (eds), *'Film Europe' and 'Film America'*, 57–8; Thomas J. Saunders, *Hollywood in Berlin: American Cinema and Weimar Germany* (Berkeley, 1994), ch. 1.

[50] Saunders, *Hollywood in Berlin*, chs 2, 5; a reflection on the results is offered in the most celebrated discussion of Weimar cinema, Siegfried Kracauer's 'psycho-biography' of the entire society and its films, *From Caligari to Hitler: A Psychological History of the German Film* (1947 edn repr., Princeton, 1974), especially chs 11, 12, and the discussion of G. W. Pabst's *The Love of Jeanne Ney* (1927), 174–5.

[51] Cit. in Andrew Higson and Richard Maltby, ' "Film Europe" and "Film America": An Introduction', in Higson and Maltby (eds), *'Film Europe' and 'Film America'*, 13.

intellectuals; or they are worse: speculators and dealers....In America the film public is there from the beginning. In Germany it has to be created by each film.[52]

France imported 565 US films in 1926, the Americans imported 9 from France, the latter a concession by the MPPDA and the American studios to protectionist pressures building up around the government of the day in Paris. In the following year indeed the Education and Fine Arts Ministry set up an elaborate structure of commissions to supervise the whole industry and fight 'colonization', as the Prime Minister put it. It was this body that decided to regularize France's quota system on a basis of nine metres of foreign films to be released for every metre of French film produced (whether actually screened or not). The ensuing confrontation heralded the opening of a century-long trade dispute over films as trade that embroiled all the Europeans, but which very often saw French governments in the vanguard of the argument.

Basic questions of free trade and commercial law were invoked, threats of retaliation and boycotts flew about involving specific products such as wine, the MPPDA and the State Department were mobilized and official delegations crossed the ocean. Lines of economic and cultural policy were drawn up that would still be in place seventy years later. They divided the unwavering American official position that movies were a commercial product like any other, from the emerging view—most energetically expressed in France—that cultural sovereignty and identity were at stake in how films were made and what they showed. Each of these positions of course concealed significant divisions and conflicts within their respective camps. Observers in the Hays Organization were, when willing, perfectly able to comprehend the worries of the French, while the various players in the French industry could not decide whether they would do better to fight the Americans or make deals with them. Because they were—and always would be—more united, the Americans usually won the endless trade confrontations, with the aid of the hundreds of French cinema owners who could not make a living without a constant supply of US moving pictures. The business versus culture divide, it soon turned out, was just as deep within the European nations as it was between their own authorities and those appointed by Hollywood.[53]

[52] Saunders, *Hollywood in Berlin*, 164–5; on the intense politicization of the German film industry (in an anti-democratic sense) in these years, and the place of the film industry wider Weimar cultural battles, Lamb and Phelan, 'Weimar Culture', 88–93.

[53] These paragraphs are based on Jens Ulff-Møller, 'Hollywood's "Foreign War": The Effect of National Commercial Policy on the Emergence of the American Film Hegemony in France, 1920–29', in Higson and Maltby (eds), *'Film Europe' and 'Film America'*; cf. Vasey, *World According to Hollywood*, 45–6; Trumpbour, *Selling Hollywood*, chs 9, 10.

Antagonists or competitors? Resisting the Hollywood challenge

As the decade of the 1920s wore on, Hollywood's effectiveness as a currency of American power began to provoke forms of counteraction that had not been seen before in the Old World. One reason was that this currency was not convertible. European producers had quickly discovered that since the war their efforts stood almost no chance in the American market, except by good fortune or under the strictest control. They noticed that protectionist walls surrounded almost all of America's industrial output, and soon joined the chorus of complaint this behaviour provoked, refusing to believe that differences of style, technique, or content alone explained the enormous imbalance between imports and exports in movies. 'Anyone who has read contemporary criticism of British films will recognise the Rottweiler-fierce competitiveness with which the US trade press ensured a lack of competition for its product', commented a UK historian many decades later.[54]

At the time, the movie press in countries such as Germany simply denounced the US impulse to claim a 'Monroe declaration for films', and began to demand the creation of a 'European' cinema, a combined response in organization, production, and distribution to the US refusal to tolerate in their own marketplace any standard except their own. Cinema, it turned out, was destined to play its own special role in the pre-history of Western European integration. Nations with small film industries such as Holland never thought of the movie trade other than on a European basis, i.e. as a Continent-wide challenge demanding a Continent-wide response.[55] In a remarkable series of film conferences from 1923 to 1930, interested representatives from the major national film industries faced up the question of whether they wished to be simply a counterweight to the Americans or define themselves *against* the US.

> Film Europe is nothing more than a security pact, a sort of film Locarno against America, which will not grant reciprocity. The more quickly and securely Film Europe is realised, the more quickly and surely Film America will come to terms with Film Europe. Here lies the deeper meaning of European film union and the current intense concentration of European film forces.

So wrote the Director of the leading German production company Terra in 1928.[56] A year later, at the European film congress of 1929, the President of the French exhibitors' association insisted that the purpose of the meeting was to organize the defence of 'our intellectual patrimony, achieved during two thousand years of civilisation', in order to prevent it from 'passing into

---

[54] Bryony Dixon, 'Crossing the Pond: The Special Relationship between Britain and American Film before 1930', in Burton and Porter (eds), *Crossing the Pond*, 5.

[55] Kroes, 'Between Rejection and Reception', 34.

[56] Cit. in Higson and Maltby (eds), *'Film Europe' and 'Film America'*, 1.

other hands, afterwards to be rented back to us by authors of a culture much different to our own'.[57] The most imposing of the conferences was probably the one held under the auspices of the League of Nations and its International Committee on Intellectual Cooperation in Paris in 1926. The League was a body from which the Americans were notoriously absent, and Hollywood interests looked at the imposing gathering with great suspicion. (This was the occasion that had prompted the MMPDA and Congress to set up the Motion Picture Section in the Department of Commerce.[58])

In reality it quickly became clear that the Europeans were too divided to offer a serious source of worry to their transatlantic rivals. The intellectual organizers were soon swamped by trade interests, who were always willing to defend film on artistic and educational grounds, but much more concerned with questions of taxes, markets, deal-making, and supply, and few of these could be settled without the people from the great studios across the ocean. A journalist reported that 'the Europeans waited for the Americans as if they were waiting for a rich uncle'.[59] When the Americans did make their move, in 1928, it was to challenge the League of Nations to live up to another of its founding promises—freer trade—and so declare film import barriers to be illegal. But the League had no enforceable powers on questions of this kind.[60] As the challenge of sound arrived, the Europeans had come to define a consistent cultural approach that insisted that film was a national artistic and educational reality as much as a global commercial product, and attributed to public authorities the defence and promotion of the growing cinema heritage, national or otherwise. But they had come to no workable conclusion on how to develop their industry as a functioning business reality across frontiers, and created no body to match the powerful Washington–MPPDA connection. In so failing they established yet another pattern that would endure in a significant degree down to the present day.

THE HOLLYWOOD SOUND REVOLUTION AND 1930S NATIONALISM

'Patriotism in entertainment selection—some kind of European quirk?'

The arrival of working sound cinema over three years between 1929 and 1932 dramatically raised the stakes in the ongoing struggle between

---

[57] Cit. ibid. 17.   [58] Thompson, 'Rise and Fall of Film Europe', 117.
[59] A. Higson, 'Cultural Policy and Industrial Practice: Film Europe and the International Film Congresses of the 1920's', in Higson and Maltby (eds), *'Film Europe' and 'Film America'*; citation at p. 124.
[60] Ibid. 128.

Hollywood and the European cinema industries for the conquest of the world's movie audiences. Along with many others, Bernard Shaw proclaimed: 'The talkies have nationalised the cinema.' The leading French critic René Jeanne denounced the new form of linguistic protectionism the Americans had invented for themselves.[61] Sound indeed came just when the intensification of nationalistic rivalries between the powers was entering its final, suicidal phase. Every major nation felt obliged to amplify its power presence by cultural means, and the cinema was inevitably enlisted in the general mobilization. This effort developed both external and internal dimensions: abroad to organize better the connection of power to 'influence'; at home to stiffen the national will for all the battles to come. In early 1932 the British, for instance, invented the Empire Service of the BBC, broadcasting initially to Canada. Then in 1933 came imperial preference, and in 1934 the British Council was set up for the purpose of 'showing the world what it owed to Britain', as the King put it in his address for the occasion.[62] Meanwhile the British Film Institute had been created in 1933, the hoped-for outcome of an imposing semi-official report on 'The Film in National Life' of 1932.

Like the French, who had launched a new programme of cultural projection in 1923, the British justified their new institutions for the projection of Britain as responses to the challenge of totalitarian propaganda in the world (Fascist Italy, for instance, had inaugurated the Venice Film Festival in 1932).[63] But the radical reorganization of national film industries that took place after the arrival of sound, under government auspices, demonstrated that a challenge to identities and cultural relationships had arisen within their national borders that had little to do with the totalitarian states as such, and everything to do with the new invention that Hollywood was perfecting. In Finland, Denmark, and elsewhere in Scandinavia, where no fascist threat existed, Social Democratic governments took it upon themselves throughout the 1930s to restrict the reach of Hollywood and promote indigenous film culture. Spain looked forward to capturing Latin American markets, and built large new studios, again under the auspices of the central State. Meanwhile first Fascist Italy and then Nazi Germany promoted similar national film-industry reorganizations to those in the major democracies, even if in direct competition with the market mech-

---

[61] Bernard F. Dukore (ed.), *Bernard Shaw on Cinema* (Carbondale, Ill., 1997), 91–3; R. Jeanne, 'La France et le film parlant', *Revue des Deux Mondes* (1 June 1931) 537.

[62] Ellwood, ' "Showing the World What it Owed to Britain": Foreign policy and "cultural propaganda", 1935–45', in Nicholas Pronay and D. W. Spring (eds), *Propaganda, Politics and Film, 1918–45'* (London, 1982), 50–73.

[63] Nicholas J. Cull, *The Cold War and the United States Information Agency*, 10–11.

anism and so expressed in different terms. The Film Europe movement died away, in spite of last ditch efforts by German interests to preserve it, and the circulation of films between nations in Europe began to dry up.[64] The Americans viewed these trends at first with wry bewilderment. A reviewer in *Variety* concluded that defensiveness over national film identities must be 'some kind of European quirk, that patriotism in entertainment selection'.[65] But as controls on the American presence became ever tighter, causing the studios to boycott or otherwise exit one European market after another, then the irony turned to alarm and full-scale MPPDA political mobilization. At the same time the suburbs of Los Angeles began to fill up with the exiled film talents of central Europe. The US industry's commitment to profits and entertainment, although always the final, defining consideration, now had to contend with the ever more unpleasant pressure of events, and the impulse of some film-makers to give American audiences at least an inkling of what was happening. The resulting compromises rarely brought credit to the industry, at least not until the Second World War had actually broken out in Europe, and not always even then.[66]

The arrival of sound revealed to general surprise the extraordinary potential for political good or evil embedded in the issue of film language. In the experimental days, before dubbing or subtitling had been perfected, audiences in Warsaw and Prague rebelled physically against films with German subtitles; in France large-scale riots broke out on several occasions when films were shown with English sounds coming from them.[67] The Italian government immediately decreed that films shown in their country must be shown only in the national language as dubbed locally, 'thus making it possible to substitute dialogue to make it politically acceptable', says the specialist James Chapman. Spain and Portugal quickly followed suit.[68]

---

[64] On Scandinavia, James Chapman, *Cinemas of the World: Film and Society from 1895 to the Present* (London, 2003), 204; Thompson, 'Rise and Fall of Film Europe', 63–7; cf. René Jeanne, 'La crise cinématographique', *Revue des Deux Mondes* (1 September 1933); this claims that the Danish government thought at one point of taking over the whole cinema industry, not least to save foreign currency; on Spain, ibid. 123–4.

[65] Cit. in Martine Danan, 'Hollywood's Hegemonic Strategies: Overcoming French Nationalism with the Advent of Sound', in Higson and Maltby (eds), *'Film Europe' and 'Film America'*, 233.

[66] H. Mark Glancy, *When Hollywood Loved Britain: The Hollywood 'British' Film, 1939–45* (Manchester, 1999), 47–58.

[67] Ibid. 230; Joseph Garncarz, 'Made in Germany: Multiple Language Versions and the Early German Sound Cinema', in Higson and Maltby (eds), *'Film Europe' and 'Film America'*, 255; Thompson, 'Rise and Fall of Film Europe', 159.

[68] Vasey, *World According to Hollywood*, 91; Chapman, *Cinemas of the World*, 205; Examples from Spain of how censorship through mistranslation functioned to sterilize allegedly

The Paris commentator René Jeanne denounced the governments of the day for not realizing that with the arrival of sound a new process of 'colonization' was under way, and asserted that protecting the language, that 'great national treasure', involved 'a work of national defense'.[69] Jeanne insisted: 'a film speaking French must be more French than a silent', and demanded support to ensure that the nation's cinema, particularly its productions seen by foreigners, should fulfil the medium's destiny of education and morality, promoting 'the lesson they should listen to and the example they should emulate'. But first, said Jeanne, the cultural authorities and intellectual organizations should define exactly what a French film was, from a national point of view. Would this be decided by where it was made? Or by whom it was made? Or with whom? At a time when co-production was already well-established, and the industry often cosmopolitan in its people and organization, these questions were by no means easily answered.[70]

For its part, the government in Paris, which had already engaged in intense diplomatic and trade-policy battles with the MPPDA over film quotas, appeared to take up the challenge very speedily. An Undersecretary from the Ministry of Public Instruction and Fine Arts assured industry representatives in early 1932 that the State recognized just what was at stake in this battle, and would be directly involved in it:

> [The talking film] must be turned to profit... to organize production in France, for... only a film made in France can be representative of French culture.... It is your duty... to collaborate with the French Government in such a manner that the French Cinema Industry may be directed towards the highest and noblest aims and that productions of France may hold their premium place in all the world.[71]

Yet these 'highest and noblest aims' were not to be fulfilled, and the government–industry alliance that made the US film industry so formidable a competitor was never replicated in the French-speaking world. The weak and unstable governments of the period brought no consistent policy to cinema or even to the manipulation of their own quota system,

---

subversive (i.e. erotic) messages in Jo Labanyi, 'Censorship or the Fear of Mass Culture', in Graham and Labanyi (eds), *Spanish Cultural Studies*, 210.

[69] Jeanne, 'L'invasion cinématographique américaine'; cits at pp. 878, 884 (emphasis in original); for aesthetic and political controversies surrounding the arrival of sound in France, Trumpbour, *Selling Hollywood*, 245–6.

[70] Jeanne, 'La France et le film parlant', pp. 533–54; cits at p. 552 (emphasis in original), 554; at a time of rising anti-Semitism, the 'cosmopolitan' nature of the industry attracted many derogatory comments, suggesting it was dominated by Jewish interests and figures, Ian Jarvie, *Hollywood's Overseas Campaign: The North Atlantic Movie Trade, 1920–1950* (Cambridge, 1992), 162; Trumpbour, *Selling Hollywood*, 231–9.

[71] Cit. in Maltby and Vasey, 'Temporary American Citizens', 75.

and the big production companies lacked the scale or business skills to build an industry for the new situation. The most significant of them went bankrupt.[72] While the exhibitors always preferred the American product (at least in the provinces), Hollywood eventually learned how to adapt its output to the ever more fragmented language-based markets it encountered in Europe and the world.

New forms of local production by major American studios, the perfection of dubbing but above all the success of Paramount in 'getting to understand the French mind and making pictures for it'—as *Variety* put it in 1933—all these factors undermined the idea of a national cinema, purpose-built under State supervision. As elsewhere in Europe, there would be no repetition of the total State takeover of radio of ten years before. When a distinctive new French cinema for the sound era did emerge in the mid-1930s, in the hands of directors such as Renoir, Carné, Grémillon, and Duvivier, its prolific success was that of small companies and talented individuals on and off the screen. Theirs was the recognition that sound did provide an opportunity for a new kind of film vernacular to emerge, an extension not a substitute for the mature inherited codes and narratives of popular culture. Of the top twenty box office successes of 1936, 18 were native-born, led by Marcel Pagnol's minor classic *César*, written directly for the screen and not—as in previous episodes of the trilogy it concluded—first for the theatre stage. Only after sound did movie-going in France become a social phenomenon on a scale comparable with Britain and Germany.[73]

The arrival of sound in the Weimar Republic was no less controversial, but it also eventually 'allowed the German cinema to become master in its own house', reports Thomas Saunders. The route, though, was a very different one. By the end of 1931 the German studios had produced 142 sound features, while only 42 Hollywood products went on release in the country in that year (previously each industry had offered roughly 200 products per annum). These were the years of *The Blue Angel* and Marlene Dietrich's emergence, of *Westfront 1918*, of the return of the leading director Erich Pommer and star actors Conrad Veidt and Emil Jannings from Hollywood to Germany, and the prominence of Austrian or German directors even in the films that the American industry did choose to

[72] Trumpbour, *Selling Hollywood*, 258–63; Jens Ulff-Møller, *Hollywood's Film Wars with France: Film Trade Diplomacy and the Emergence of the French Film Quota Policy* (Rochester, 2001), 116–17; de Grazia, 'Mass Culture and Sovereignty', 70–2.

[73] Danan, 'Hollywood's Hegemonic Strategies', 232–42; Thompson, 'Rise and Fall of Film Europe', 165–6, 220 (which shows that Hollywood commanded just under 50% of the French market in the early 1930s); Ulff-Møller, *Hollywood's Film Wars*, p. 129 and p. 133, n. 18; on the expanded cinema audience, Weber, *Hollow Years*, 67, production context in Trumpbour, *Selling Hollywood*, 250–7.

Fig. 3. Marlene Dietrich attends the premiere of her first Hollywood-movie 'Morocco' in London, carrying a boy dressed up as Charlie Chaplin. March 1931.

(Getty Images/Hulton Archive)

release.[74] The critics exulted. Here was the possibility of a new beginning for German and European culture, a chance to relaunch the finest of Germany's stage: musical and poetic traditions in films that would bring to the world's notice the distinctiveness of German 'character' and 'conviction', thereby finally bringing Hollywood's hegemony to an end. If the Americans had believed they could rely on a technological novelty to defend their declining world position, they were wrong: 'For the present they calculate only in dollars. But one day they will have to re-insert the notion of film art into their calculation.'[75]

In reality the German adaptation to sound was by no means an easy one, and forced the industry's financiers, artists, and critics to invent new terms for their relationship with whatever the Americans were producing and their audiences demanding. In the end they kept a hold on a diminishing German public by mixing the ever more intense call of nationalism with their own version of what Hollywood did best: light entertainment. If war films emerged as the most popular genre, musicals came next, followed by a mystical mountain series featuring 'sparkling ice-axes and inflated sentiments', as the critic Kracauer recalled.[76] Nostalgia for authority, especially of the Prussian variety, was ever more apparent, claimed Kracauer, but for those who could still afford to go to

[74] Saunders, *Hollywood in Berlin*, 222–3, 236; Garncarz, 'Hollywood in Germany', 96.
[75] Saunders, *Hollywood in Berlin*, pp. 229–32; cit. at p. 227.
[76] Kracauer, *From Caligari*, 110.

the cinema, escapism and wish-dreaming were just as popular in the midst of Weimar's economic crisis as they were in America's. So 'the German industry created settings and themes as socially and intellectually vacuous as any attributed to Hollywood' (Saunders). In such a context the American presence fell away simply because it had become redundant.[77]

But the initial reaction to the sound challenge had revealed much about the underlying political—as well as the cultural—anxieties that America's unpredictable gift for innovation had provoked throughout the Weimar era. As ever it was the clarity, urgency, and inevitability of the need to choose—Sound or silent? Mass or minority? National or cosmopolitan?— that brought out the underlying resentments. A national newspaper sneered:

> Millions were invested in the play toy, sound film, and when the harmless mental babies enjoyed the noise, when this record player nation was captivated by musical hits, the movie moguls of Hollywood went back unscrupulously with regard to screenplays to the primitive beginnings of 1905...[78]

Sound film, comments Saunders, 'appeared a typically American solution to a chronic state of national cultural backwardness.' Contemporary commentators of right and left complained that it was regressive, mechanical, and industrial, and pushed yet further the abolition of any sort of distinction between business and culture. The market provided the supreme measure of the worth of any product, artistic or otherwise, and for every market disappointment there was supposed to be a technical solution. Thirty years of development of the silent film—from a grubby, low class amusement to a refined medium of national expression—were to be jettisoned overnight for pure reasons of profit, and Hollywood, 'the international surrogate of American civilization', would once more bend an all-too compliant Europe to its will. Only if writers and poets from Germany and Europe rose to the unwonted challenge of sound might there be hope for a new kind of film culture.[79]

But the success of the German film in its own market after an awkward period of transition silenced many of the critics, as did the rising force of nationalist conformism. A war over patents and royalties deriving from the use of German-led or American sound technology was defused by an unsteady private settlement between Germany's cartel and the MPPDA.

[77] Garncarz, 'Hollywood in Germany', 105–6; Saunders, *Hollywood in Berlin*, 238–9; Kracauer, *From Caligari*, 207–8, 263, 267.
[78] Cit. in Saunders, *Hollywood in Berlin*, 227.
[79] Ibid. 226–30.

It divided the world into sound spheres of influence. In one critical season, 1929–30, all the major cinemas in the Republic had been converted to sound with German-built systems, and audiences of every level had been successfully convinced that this was the future of the cinema, with German companies taking a leading hand in it.

The US studios were put on the defensive. They had already learned how useless was the tactic of changing for the German market the endings of major films, such as Chaplin's *The Gold Rush* (1925), or *Love* (1927, with Greta Garbo, based on the Anna Karenina story), so as to render them *sad* instead of *happy*: audiences were not taken in. So it should have been no surprise that the German versions of standard films produced in Europe by US companies, with alternating casts for each language area, never enjoyed favour either. In contrast the German industry successfully remade a number of 1920s silents for the new medium.[80]

But the German studios could not do without their Hollywood connection, and by this time it had become ever harder to define what exactly was a German film. As elsewhere the authorities tried repeatedly to do so in the early sound era, narrowing the definition each time in a vain effort to keep up with swelling trend of militant nationalism.[81] The industrialization of the cinema that resulted from sound, with its need for a new scale of investment in a very short time, played into the hands of UFA: the notorious and dominant trust led by the far-right press baron and financier Alfred Hugenberg, soon to be Minister of Economics in Hitler's first government. UFA was a company dedicated, among other aims, to building an international export market for its movies; even, if possible, in America itself. But this could only be done by adapting the lessons of Hollywood's appeal. UFA brought back to Germany Erich Pommer, a director with limited success in California, but clear about the means of its world domination. He told a Berlin audience in 1932 that insisting on national differences was not enough. While essential up to a point,

> ... [the] idea itself must be capable of being understood all over the world. In the scenario it is absolutely necessary to take into account those great human emotions that are the same for all countries.... That is why, as far as possible, novel yet nonetheless perennial plots are chosen—love and pain, humour and sentiment, art and nature, science and the primitive, in a word all the immortal subjects of the poets of all the ages.[82]

---

[80] Cit. in Saunders, *Hollywood in Berlin,* 228–9; Garncarz, 'Hollywood in Germany', 103, 107.

[81] Saunders, *Hollywood in Berlin,* 233–5.

[82] Article reproduced in Higson and Maltby (eds), *'Film Europe' and 'Film America',* 394–6.

UFA's great international success in this spirit was *The Blue Angel*, produced in separate German, French, and English versions, but directed by an Austrian who spent most of his career in Hollywood—Joseph Von Sternberg—and the launch pad for Marlene Dietrich's American success. 'There was an extremely fine line between a national cinema which enjoyed international recognition and absorption by Hollywood', concludes Saunders.[83] It was a line that even the new regime of the Nazis would be forced to take into account.

Britain and Hollywood after sound: a very special relationship

In 1932 in London the leaders of 'a hundred educational and scientific organisations' came together under the chairmanship of a leading schools official to produce a detailed report on the role the cinema ought to play in the onward progress of the British people. This gathering of the great and the good had no doubt about the situation it wished to encourage. It looked forward…

> …to the time when the film industry in Great Britain has gathered power and is producing films which are an unequivocal expression of British life and thought, deriving character and inspiration from our national inheritance, and have an honoured international currency.[84]

Aiming for a 'constructive and ordered use of the new medium', the committee felt that the entertainment film had lost effective contact with the culture of the country, and cinema as a whole still looked like 'a bastard of the arts'. At a time when cinema audiences had swelled to the point where roughly half the population was going to see films every week, and 200 new cinemas were under construction, often of a size and lavishness that only America could have inspired, a form of 'national planning' was required, said the committee. The challenge was one 'from which the finest intelligences of the country should no longer hold aloof… if the film industry continues to develop without some influence exerted upon it from the point of view of national welfare—we shall continue to get the films we deserve.'[85]

---

[83] On UFA efforts to create an international market using multiple language versions of its products, Garncarz, 'Made in Germany', Saunders, *Hollywood in Berlin*, 249.

[84] The full title of the document was *The Film in National Life: Being the Report of an Enquiry Conducted by the Commission on Educational and Cultural Films into the Service which the Cinematograph May Render to Education and Social Progress*; cit. at pp. 142–3; cf. Maltby and Vasey, 'International Language Problem', 72–3; on the constitution of the committee and its context, Richards, *Age of the Dream Palace*, 49.

[85] *The Film in National Life*, 11, 15, 42, 43.

But the results of this and similar efforts by other groups of patriotic moralists appear to have been scarce indeed in the early 1930s. In one of the many volumes of national self-discovery that kept appearing in those years, a representative member of the governing classes, Major Rawdon Hoare, reflected on a recent encounter at a London garage with a petrol pump attendant. The young man, he claimed, had insisted on speaking to him with an American accent:

> The powerful influence of the cinema had changed this youth from the East End into something that was neither one thing nor the other, into something that had lost the many good qualities of the people belonging to that part of London, and yet had failed dismally to give him the American stamp he so desired. He is only one among millions whose entire lives are being influenced by the American Cinema. What good can all this do to England? Will it create patriotism? Will it create a desire to keep our great Empire together? I doubt it. But quite definitely it *is* creating a race of youths belonging to all classes whose experience of life is based largely on the harrowing and frequently sordid plots of American films.[86]

The choice of protectionism in 1927 had clearly transformed the economic chances of constructing a successful national cinema in Britain. Five years later the American share of the market had fallen from 95 to roughly 70 per cent, and the numbers of British films being produced had gone beyond the figure predicted by the 1927 quota legislation, even discounting the infamous debris produced locally only to legalize additional imports, the so-called 'quota quickies.'[87] Vertically integrated combines had emerged to unite production and exhibition. These groups soon divided neatly in their production strategies: the two leaders—Gaumont-British and British International Pictures—believing in internationalizing their output to try to compete with Hollywood on its own terms, while another—Associated Talking Pictures—insisted on material that was unmistakably British, and designed strictly for the nation's popular audiences. In 1932 the successful Hungarian producer Alexander Korda arrived from Hollywood, set up his own studio, and quickly made his first hit: *The Private Life of Henry VIII*. By cleverly exploiting his old connections in California, the film enjoyed a uniquely effective launch on the American market, was a vast success, and went on to bring beguiling fame and riches to a British production company.[88]

[86] Cit. in Richards, *Age of the Dream Palace*, 57; emphasis in original.

[87] On the costs and benefits of the 1927 legislation, Tom Ryall, *Britain and the American Cinema* (London, 2000), 44–51.

[88] Higson, 'Cultural Policy', 98–109; *The Film in National Life*, 79; on Korda, ibid. 106–7, Trumpbour, *Selling Hollywood*, ch. 5; Peter Miskell, 'Americanization and its Limits: United Artists in the British Market in the 1930s and 1940s', in Wiener and Hampton (eds), *Anglo-American Media Interactions*, 224–5.

In this way cinema conquered a quite new level of legitimization in commercial as well as cultivated minds, and went on to become part of a new 1930s 'common culture', says LeMahieu. Expressions of a different kind of national identity began to emerge, profit oriented, technologically modern, and apparently classless. If this culture was also structurally interlocked with other products of America's mass-communication industries, including their journalism and their light music as well as the films they sent over, it could never be a simple emulation. It was mediated not only by much from the past but also by additional dimensions of the new commonality, for instance its suburban and southern English features.[89]

These truths emerged however long after the developments they characterized. At the time, and especially in the earlier part of the sound era, the new cinema technology had a dramatic dividing effect in the population. The middle and working classes went to separate picture houses in the same town; they liked different stars, different action, and different humour. Above all the discovery that British actors spoke with voices that could only come from the southern English upper middle class, and specifically 'with the accents and mannerisms of the London stage', drove young working people whether from the East End of London itself, or Cardiff or Glasgow, straight into the open arms of Hollywood.[90] In a decade when social documentation and 'mass observation' came into their own, survey after survey would confirm the force of these distinctions. Cinema managers in working-class areas were 'practically unanimous in regarding the majority of British films as unsuitable for their audiences', reported a 1937 symposium:

> British films, one Scottish exhibitor writes, should rather be called English films in a particularly parochial sense: they are more foreign to his audience than the products of Hollywood, over 6000 miles away.[91]

---

[89] LeMahieu, *Culture for Democracy*, 230–1.

[90] Richards, *Age of the Dream Palace*, 24–33; Robert Murphy cit. in Maltby and Vasey, 'Temporary American Citizens', 50; Lary May points out that this process happened in the US too, and drove Hollywood production radically down-market after sound, the most effective way to keep a mass market at a time of severe depression; L. May, *The Big Tomorrow: Hollywood and the Politics of the American Way* (Chicago, 2000), 61–2, 64, 68–77.

[91] Cit. in Richards, *Age of the Dream Palace*, 24; for full survey evidence from the later 1930s and wartime, Jeffrey Richards and Dorothy Sheridan (eds), *Mass Observation at the Movies* (London, 1987); many witnesses comment here on the superiority of American films; comment ibid. 41. On the Scottish experience, the specialist Alastair Michie notes that sound killed off hopes of a specifically Scots production effort, but did launch a new awareness of cinema and hence a new film culture; A. Michie, 'Scotland: Strategies of Centalisation', in Charles Barr (ed.), *All Our Yesterdays: 90 Years of British Cinema* (London, 1986), 256.

The industry would do its best through the decade to produce national films for the popular masses, and even discovered two northern working-class 'stars' in Gracie Fields and George Formby.[92] But cinema enthusiasts were 'young, working class, urban and more often female than male' (Richards), and they overwhelmingly preferred the American product. An emerging young northern author of the time, J. B. Priestley, a man who would develop over decades a complex attraction–repulsion relationship with American mass culture, explained how some of the popular fascination with Hollywood's output arose. It derived from the fact that 'American life has a quicker tempo than English life', that 'truck drivers and clerks, cops and garage hands and their women folk are much more vivid and vital figures than their English equivalents', while 'American speech is snappier, harsher, more vivid'.[93]

The sound movies started to replace 'one kind of English with another which was achieving a vitality, versatility and poetry of its own', comments film historian Peter Stead.[94] This was just the sort of trend the established cultural authorities disliked most, a self-propelled mechanism outwith their control that could cross cultural boundaries as though they were invisible, and undermine traditional sources of moral authority in the three groups most likely to determine the future social identity of the nation: the working-class, young people, and the 'backward races' of the Empire. So the arrival of sound greatly intensified the search for a national cinema that would help renew those traditional mechanisms built in time to guarantee the imperial governing class its own reproduction. This explained why so much emphasis was placed on the minds of young people, and the importance of film in the classroom, as it would be in so many nations throughout the century.[95]

But like them the British were destined to be disappointed in the 1930s, as in all the subsequent decades. In the case of radio (and later television), the governments of the times made sure they had a firm control from the start on the medium's development, for the sake of the moral improvement and education of all the nation's citizens, high or low, among other purposes. This was a key task of the BBC, and one it was

[92] This effort is explored in depth in Higson, 'Cultural Policy', ch. 4.

[93] Cit. in Peter Stead, 'Hollywood's Message to the World: The British Response in the 1930s', *Historical Journal of Film, Radio and Television*, 1/1 (1981), 28; but in his fiction Priestley's characters often expressed dislike of the arrival of Americanisms in everyday English. e.g. Timmy, the old-fashioned comedian in *Let the People Sing*, 36–7.

[94] Stead, 'Hollywood's Message', 31.

[95] Cf. Richards, *Age of the Dream Palace*, ch. 4, 'Our Movie-made children'; Italian Fascist version cit. in R. Maltby, 'The Cinema and the League of Nations', in Higson and Maltby (eds), *'Film Europe' and 'Film America'*, 97; Dutch concerns in Kroes, *If You've Seen One*, 90–1.

proud to succeed in. But in the case of the cinema, the horse had already bolted by the time members of the Establishment had come to contemplate 'national planning' for the moral welfare of young people and all the rest. Hollywood had created its own mass following, and it was up to the institutions of Britain's slowly modernizing democracy to adapt to that fact, rather than the other way around.

British producers demanded and obtained protection for their industry, which did succeed in expanding into the sound-transformed world of newsreels and educational cinema. A new and high-minded movement of documentary film-makers attempted to create a distinctive national idea of social realism in the cinema, based on 'the English love of the open, the English feeling for the more empirical forms of poetry, and the English respect for authenticity', as the group's leading light John Grierson asserted.[96] Although much mocked later for its moralism and self-importance, the group acted at a time when most of government cared little for the industry's challenges, and when censorship was so tight that the President of the British Board of Film Censors could boast with satisfaction that 'there is not a single film showing in London today which deals with the burning issues of the day'. The movement would go on to distinguish itself in World War II, influence thereafter the socially-aware British cinema of the 1950s and 1960s, and contribute, indirectly, to the naturalistic flavour of so much British television output in its years of maturity. In so doing, writes John Caughie, it defined a cinematic tradition of 'independence': independence 'from anything that smacked of the Hollywood "dream factory" ... [and] independence from the need to compete with Hollywood in the market-place.'[97]

But in the early 1930s what distinguished the British situation most clearly was the outcome of the contest over that dividing line that others tried to defend at all costs: the one 'between a national cinema which

---

[96] John Grierson, *Notes for English Producers* (n.d. [April–May 1927]), reproduced as appendix to I. C. Jarvie and Nicholas Pronay (eds), 'John Grierson: A Critical Retrospective', special issue of *Historical Journal of Film, Radio and Television*, 9/3 (1989); cit. at p. 322: Grierson had studied in America on a Rockefeller Foundation grant, had studied Whitman and the public commentator Walter Lippmann, and was intensely aware of the mass appeal of American cinema (Trumpbour, *Selling Hollywood*, 125–6); but he thought its qualities could be combined with the inspiration of the new Russian cinema to produce a fresh cinema tradition in Britain. His main proposal at this stage was for a new genre of 'expeditionary' films, based on the life of the Empire.

[97] On the documentary movement and its inheritance, Higson, 'Cultural Policy', ch. 5; J. Caughie, 'Broadcasting and Cinema: 1: Converging Histories', in Barr (ed.), *All Our Yesterdays*, 198–200; Trumpbour, *Selling Hollywood*, 123, *passim*; Miles and Smith, *Cinema, Literature and Society*, Part II, ch. 6; BBFC President quoted in James Donald, Anne Friedberg, and Laura Marcus (eds), *'Close Up' 1927–1933: Cinema and Modernism* (London, 1998), 273.

enjoyed international recognition and absorption by Hollywood'. In the aftermath of sound and the reinforcement of exclusive nationalism that it provoked, the American film industry began to depend on its English-speaking markets, and British demand above all, in ways that were never foreseen in the silent era. This consequent new double dependence produced remarkable results. During the 1920s, as already mentioned, the US industry earned 35 per cent of its entire foreign earnings in Britain; in the following decade this share rose to 50 per cent; in wartime to 60–70 per cent. In 1933 the UK imported more film than any other nation anywhere, more than twice the amount imported into France, the next largest Western European consumer in that year. Many studios had relied on the domestic market to cover the costs of individual pictures, and looked to the rest of the world to supply the profit margins. Now the British market alone was expected to fulfil this role, a demand that was reinforced as the decade proceeded, film finances worsened, and hostile governments began to deliberately shut out the Americans from their national screens.[98]

The studios began to invest in the new British production combines and turn into full-scale cinema chains their already well-established position in distribution. They pushed forward the sound revolution and encouraged the construction of the 'dream-palaces', those vast, luxuriant temples to mass picture-going that became a feature of the age, luminous beacons of pleasure standing out so much more sharply as the distance from London increased and the shadows of depression deepened.[99] The great companies began to recruit British acting and screenwriting talent, and encouraged the development of a full-scale British film community in Los Angeles. As the industry's MPPDA-managed censorship system was radically tightened up under the pressure of conservative guardians of public morality, it coordinated the clearing of stories with the British Board of Film Censors. Paradoxically however, this institution delegated the script-reading job to 'a rather tetchy retired army officer and a sheltered upper class spinster', whose basic instincts, reports Richards, were chauvinistic and anti-American.[100]

---

[98] On the general situation of the studios and their foreign markets after sound, Vasey, *World According to Hollywood*, ch. 3; on Hollywood and the British market in the 1930s, Miskell, 'Americanization and its Limits', 218–22; Trumpbour, *Selling Hollywood*, ch. 7.

[99] Miskell, 'Americanization and its Limits', 222–5; Miles and Smith, *Cinema, Literature and Society*, 164; these authors point out that cinemas in the depressed areas, although more numerous, were usually much smaller than the 'dream palace' model. But so low were their prices that 'the unemployed could afford to go regularly'.

[100] Ryall, *Britain and the American Cinema*, ch. 3; on relations between the managers of the new Hollywood 'Production Code' and British censors, Glancy, *When Hollywood Loved Britain*, 42; on BBFC personnel Richards, *Age of the Dream Palace*, 109–11.

Above all Hollywood started selling their own history back to the British. Establishing early in the decade a 'taste for the most famous, traditional and antiquated aspects' of the old mother country, the studios succeeded in creating a British, American, and world audience for themes that the London producers had never succeeded in romanticizing convincingly. Mark Glancy has listed the memorable results of this effort:

> Ronald Colman made his talking debut as the British detective in *Bulldog Drummond* (1929) and soon after played the 'amateur cracksman' of *Raffles* (1930). There was a great interest in British horror stories, which resulted in screen classics such as Paramount's *Dr Jekyll and Mr Hyde* (1932), and Universal's *Dracula* (1931), *Frankenstein* (1931) and *The Old Dark House* (1932), as well as romances with supernatural elements, including MGM's *Smiling Through* (1932) and Fox's *Berkeley Square* (1933). 'British' melodramas such as Universal's *Waterloo Bridge* (1931) and Samuel Goldwyn's *Cynara* (1931) used class as a source of romantic conflict. And MGM inaugurated one of its most successful series of films with the British Empire adventure story, *Tarzan the Ape Man* (1932).[101]

In the course of the decade over 150 such titles would emerge, reports Glancy. At a time when British censorship forbade the screen presentation of *any* question of foreign policy, contemporary or otherwise, here was a wave of sympathy for the classic imperial codes of gentlemanly honour and heroism, white supremacy, and national sacrifice. The old romantic view of the Empire was relaunched at a time when its diminishing prestige in the real world was apparent on all sides, and so by flattery its inheritance became inserted into the supposedly modernizing 'common culture' of the epoch.[102]

Of course not everyone was won over. An MP contributing to a debate on a new quota law commented:

> I rather assumed that the chief function of the cinema in this country was to accomplish what I am sure will never be accomplished, or even attempted, in any other way—the annexation of this country by the USA.[103]

---

[101] Glancy, *When Hollywood Loved Britain*, 72; for French envy of Hollywood's new-found love of the British Empire, Trumpbour, *Selling Hollywood*, 229–30.

[102] Glancy, *When Hollywood Loved Britain*, 72; cf. Miles and Smith, *Cinema, Literature and Society*, 177. MGM was the studio with the strongest commitment to Britain; for an example of its films that include gratuitous British plot developments and characters, *China Seas* (Tay Garnett, 1935); the Warner Brothers spectacular *The Adventures of Robin Hood* (William Keighley, 1938), with Errol Flynn and a host of Hollywood Brits, was the most expensive production ever mounted by the studio up to that time, featuring an early use of Technicolor among its attractions.

[103] Cit. in Stead, 'Hollywood's Message', 19; the British film industry remained convinced that Hollywood's basic aim was 'to obliterate every vestige' of it, and that in 1937 the Americans were succeeding like 'the Italian conquest of Abyssinia', quote in Trumpbour, *Selling Hollywood*, 2; further discussion in Chapter 5, n. 76.

Searching for the cinema in ourselves

Responses to the challenge of Hollywood in Europe in the 1920s and early 1930s quickly fell into a highly structured pattern whose durability throughout the twentieth century would supply a striking consistency to relations between the cultures on either side of the Atlantic. In these years and all the way to the 1990s, says Andrew Higson, the British industry sought to come to terms with Los Angeles using four main approaches:

> ... by competing with Hollywood on its own terms and in its own markets; by colluding with Hollywood in the distribution and exhibition of American films in the British market; by trying to protect British producers from the immense power and penetration of the American film industry; and by various forms of product differentiation.[104]

But the evidence of the preceding pages shows that *every* national cinema tried these methods, in varying proportions at different times.[105] It was indeed their duplication and overlap that gave rise to the 'Film Europe' movement in its heyday. The arrival of sound soon paid to this project, and the parallel dissolution of the ambitious political dream of European integration launched by Aristide Briand showed how fragile were the many political premises on which it rested. Instead sound relaunched the illusion that certain national cinemas—particularly the German one—might be able to offer serious competition to what was on offer from across the Atlantic. Yet by the middle of the 1930s this illusion too was dead, at least in the democracies (and the Soviet Union), crushed by the realities of the Depression. Hollywood's capacity for technical and artistic innovation, its financial resources, and quite simply the superior understanding its movie-makers demonstrated of the attraction of music, action, and colour. On average, fifty musicals a year came out of the studio system in its heyday. Claudel, the French Ambassador to the US, told the New York Chamber of Commerce of the new familiarity with American 'methods and manners' spreading everywhere in France through the sound movie, 'carrying new visions of ability and a new vital rhythm'.[106]

In response to this challenge, the decade saw the heyday of European cultural protectionism, the political means by which the State reinforced the commercial and artistic attempts by local movie producers to come to

---

[104] Higson, 'Cultural Policy', 272; on repetition and ineffectuality of most of these tactics, Puttnam, *Undeclared War*, 147, 161, 211.

[105] Cf. Trumpbour, *Selling Hollywood*, 6.

[106] Cit. in Harley, *World-Wide Influences*, 2; figures on musicals and production context in Marsha Siefert, 'Image/Music/Voice: Song Dubbing in Hollywood Musicals', *Journal of Communication* (Spring 1995), 48.

some sort of terms with Hollywood's hegemony. Today's historians explain this reaction in terms of the role politicians and intellectuals (in particular) have traditionally assigned themselves as the mediators and explainers of novelty, the definers of acceptable modernity in each local context. As Romier, the editor of *Le Figaro*, pointed out in 1933: 'the representatives of the spirit are the principle people responsible, in all epochs, for our social future.'[107] Faced with the overwhelming presence of Hollywood around them, established writers and thinkers insisted that by choosing to promote a certain idea of national film identity, they were simply doing their duty of protecting local mores and customs; seeking not to exclude but to arbitrate between the new realities and whatever was thought most precious and characteristic in the inheritance their societies supposedly contributed to Western civilization.[108]

But outside the totalitarian states, the market always had the last word. Cinema-going had become 'the essential social habit of the age', in the words of a famed British historian,[109] and Hollywood had entered into the heart of whatever was new in popular reality between the wars; becoming 'naturalized' everywhere and democratizing technical progress, entertainment, even glamour. Unable to resolve the fundamental contradiction between the cultivated, the commercial, and the emotional impulses of their publics, European cultural establishments failed—and would always fail—to establish any of their cinemas as a complete cultural *industry*. With capitalism buckling and folding in on itself in most nations of the Old World under the weight of the Depression, the Fascist and Nazi movements exulted now that such a challenge should have arisen to test their youthful, virile grip on the future.

---

[107] Lucien Romier, 'La disgrace du capitalisme', *Revue des Deux Mondes* (1 June 1933).

[108] On the moral front, the Catholic Church carried on a parallel crusade from 1929. Its greatest success came when in 1934, at the prompting of the American Catholic Legion of Decency, the MPPDA set up the Production Code Administration, organized under the stern eye of a Jesuit-educated Irish-American, to run a far tighter censorship system; details in Thomas Doherty, *Pre-Code Hollywood: Sex, Immorality and Insurrection in American Cinema, 1930–1934* (New York, 1999), ch. 12; Pope Pius XI's landmark encyclical of 1936 *Vigilanti Cura*, endorsing the wider American Catholic campaign against the alleged sins of the cinema, especially that of Hollywood, with its worldwide influence, is reproduced in the official collection of Vatican statements in this area, *Le Cinéma dans l'Enseignement de l'Eglise* (Vatican City, 1955).

[109] A. J. P. Taylor cit. in Richards, *Age of the Dream Palace*, 11.

4

The 1930s: Capitalism on Trial

PERSISTING THEMES AFTER THE CRASH

By the time Herbert Hoover had come to start the third volume of his memoirs—after a crushing defeat by Franklin Roosevelt in the 1932 Presidential elections—he had retired to Stanford, California, a very bitter man. Hoover took no personal responsibility whatsoever for the onset of the Depression, declaring that his own remedies had begun to work, and were already setting other countries back on the road to prosperity. The former President insisted that Europe was to blame for the slump, meaning in his view a generalized European shiftlessness that in the course of the 1920s had learned how to exploit the weakness and greed of the American banking system. He recalled an address he had made to Congressional leaders in October 1931, which offered an updated and eloquent version of the anti-European refrain so deeply rooted in American official views of the world since the time of Woodrow Wilson's failure:

> The nations of Europe have not found peace. Hates and fears dominate their relations. War injuries have permitted no abatement. The multitude of small democracies created by the Treaty of Versailles have developed excessive nationalism. They have created a maze of trade barriers between each other. Underneath all is the social turmoil of communism and fascism gnawing at the vitals of young democracies.

Hoover acknowledged that the war debt burden was impossible to bear, but condemned the habit of former allies and enemies alike of paying for it using masses of long- and short-term loans, all raised in the American private banking sector, particularly on Wall Street. The only way these obligations could be managed was by repeated bouts of inflation and devaluation. Little wonder that 'nineteen countries in the world, in two years, have gone through revolutions or violent social disturbances...'. In these conditions, who could say what might become of the many victims of the Versailles treaty? 'Whether or not Germany and Central Europe will avoid Russian infiltrated communism or some other "ism" is still in the balance…' At home meanwhile, as unemployment affected nearly a quarter of the workforce and misery and distress spread everywhere, there was general bewilderment at 'the revelation that our government for the first time in peacetime history might have to intervene to support private enterprise'.[1]

Contemporary European views on the origins of the slump of course read very differently. Most interesting in the present context are those that connected explanations of the financial turmoil to the likely future relations between the two civilizations on either side of the Atlantic. But this outlook is not always traceable, not even in the pronouncements of sophisticated experts such as Keynes, or the editors of *The Economist*.[2] Moritz Bonn's *Prosperity* of 1931, already mentioned, did offer one such reflection. The Berlin economist wrote that since the war, America's lesson in democracy had taught the industrial world that 'capitalism can only be maintained as the economic groundwork of life if capitalism guarantees a reasonable income to all concerned'. But should the system fail to meet this most fundamental of its promises, he warned, then it would be changed, perhaps peacefully if democracy had other roots as well as the economic one, otherwise by revolutionary destruction.[3]

---

[1] Herbert Hoover, *The Memoirs of Herbert Hoover*, iii: *The Great Depression, 1929–1941* (New York, 1952), 89–90; details of Hoover's anger at '"the Wall Street crowd" for drawing America into Europe's troubles', and France's in particular, in Boyce, *Great Interwar Crisis*, 305, 386–8; reflections along these lines while in office, including those delivered to H. G. Wells, cit. ibid. 337. Bernard Shaw was among the many who poured scorn on Hoover, telling an American radio audience that 'your President who became famous by feeding the starving millions of war-devastated Europe, cannot feed his own people in time of peace'; transcript published (by the Friends of the Soviet Union) as 'A Little Talk on America' (London, October 1931).

[2] Keynes largely disdained or ignored America during the 1920s, suggests his biographer, Robert Skidelsky, in *John Maynard Keynes*, ii: *The Economist as Saviour, 1920–1937* (London, 1992), 20, 489; there is no hint of a qualitative judgement on almost any aspect of America's functioning in Keynes's published writings of these years, not even in the heart of the 1929–32 crisis in which he was heavily involved. He was surprised to discover the lawlessness of the American banking system, and thought that Britain should reassert its 'rightful' leadership of the world financial system once the crisis had been overcome; cf. John Maynard Keynes, *Collected Writings*, xviii: *Activities 1922–32: The End of Reparations* (London, 1978) and xx: *Activities 1929–1931: Rethinking Employment and Unemployment Policies* (London, 1981). The reporting of *The Economist* during the crisis concentrated strictly on the Wall St. upheaval, and assumed that once the great speculative bubble had been eliminated, a period of 'rest and recuperation' would eventually bring the stock market back in line with the fundamental strength of the US economy; only at the end of May 1930 did the journal acknowledge that a world depression was under way; cf. edition of 31 May 1930; for a very pessimistic British Embassy view that the breakdown was due to 'the failure to preserve the hegemony and ideals of…the Anglo-Saxon race in America, the original ruling class…', Boyce, *Great Interwar Crisis*, 379–80.

[3] Bonn, *Prosperity*, 152–3.

Bonn's later chapters discussed the financial and industrial roots of the crisis, 'its stupendous psychological effect... throughout the world', and its critical effect on the behaviour of those in authority in the US, whose arrogance, he believed, was now forced to give way to a realization of the long-term consequences of their choices:

> A country which wants to play the rôle of the world's banker must be influenced by conceptions of world economy, and... cannot view the financing of the outside world merely as an appendage to the financing of consumers in its own market... the business of Empire is something quite different from the empire of business.[4]

But there was one area of US enterprise that had already learned this lesson and could count on sympathetic ears in official circles on both sides of the Atlantic, wherever the notion of 'interdependence' was taken seriously.[5] The International Chamber of Commerce (ICC) had been founded in 1919 as an organization for the promotion and organization of world peace through ever freer trade, 'a businessmen's league of nations'.[6] At its grand Washington conference held in May 1931, opened by Hoover, there could be no hiding the gravity of the immediate economic situation; the tensions filling the headlines over Austrian banks, gold reserves and currencies, war debts and tariff barriers (the US Congress had raised them to new heights in 1930 amidst intense controversy).[7] But the participants

---

[4] Bonn, *Prosperity*, 182–3; historical confirmation of this judgement in Boyce, *Great Interwar Crisis*, 85, 135, 221, 295, 429.

[5] The concept of 'interdependence' had been popularized by the British political economist Norman Angell, in his best-selling survey of 1910, *The Great Illusion*. History long held Angell in ridicule for his prediction that the ever-tightening network of business connections and economic interests across the industrial world made war between the great powers impossible. Now it sees him—rightly—as an early prophet of globalization; cf. Thomas L. Friedman, *The Lexus and the Olive Tree* (New York, 1999), 197. Angell continued to refine his analysis between the wars. He won the Nobel Peace Prize in 1933.

[6] On the pre-war origins and initial development of the ICC, George L. Ridgeway, *Merchants of Peace* (Boston, 1959), chs 2, 3 (an official history). Its first meeting, at Atlantic City, was a large-scale affair intended as an economic 'corollary to the Peace Conference', ibid. 32.

[7] In June 1930 Congress had passed the notorious Hawley-Smoot Tariff, which raised the duties on some 900 tariffs, even 'extravagantly', according to *The Economist*. The journal reported the intense opposition to the Bill in much of US business and denounced the 'folly' of its passing as a 'festival of vested interests'; edition of 21 June 1930. Twenty four foreign nations made formal protests against the Bill (though not Britain); popular demonstrations, boycotts of US goods, and even physical attacks on American cars were seen in several European nations; for background and details, Joan Hoff Wilson, *American Business and Foreign Policy, 1920–1933* (Lexington, 1971), 88–9, 94–8; Boyce, *Great Interwar Crisis*, 235–6. The war debts question was under intense transatlantic discussion at the time of the conference; in the following month, after long deliberations far from Wall Street, Hoover would declare a moratorium on the payment of war debts and reparations, ibid. 305, but beyond this 'neither Hoover nor Congress was prepared to assist Europe', ibid. 336.

sought to look far beyond the upheaval, towards a world of harmonious Euro-American development that would be post-imperial and free-trading, organized consciously in a new framework of effective rules and mutual understandings. In the short run, the carefully worded analyses of these 'business internationalists' made little impact, but as the 1930s wore on and the attractions of economic nationalism wore off, some of their priorities began to conquer the higher ground.[8]

The Europe–United States Committee of the ICC arrived in Washington bringing a comprehensive series of surveys on the 'economic structure of the two areas' and 'their commercial and financial relations' over the previous thirty years. A particularly brilliant treatment of the 'psychological elements' of Euro-American relations was offered by the leading French commentator on the United States, Professor André Siegfried. Here, the writer demonstrated at length how over the years since the start of the century, the sudden rise of a 'powerful and unexpected rivalry' from America was beginning to transform the Old World's self-awareness, 'Europe's knowledge of Europe'. And there was much in the material presented to the congress that expressed this new kind of supernational consciousness, a highly unusual phenomenon at a time when national governments surviving from day to day competed in protectionism of every sort.[9]

Much of the contemporary talk of 'Europe', especially Siegfried's, was of course deeply pessimistic in tone, reflecting the rise in the 1920s of the 'civilization under threat' mentality, as well as the effects on confidence of the Crash.[10] But on this occasion the Europeans present made determined efforts to counter the general impression that the Old World was finished off economically and spiritually. The Chairman of the Europe–United States Committee was Senator Alberto Pirelli, chief executive of the great Italian rubber company founded by his father, and a member of the Executive Council of the League of Nations. In a diplomatic but eloquent introduction, Pirelli made clear that while the American economy had indeed made 'astounding progress' over the previous twenty years, the Old Continent was making a remarkable recovery for an invalid, and

---

[8] Authorized account in Ridgeway, *Merchants of Peace*, 111–15, who cites the presence of 1,200 business leaders from 37 countries; historical discussion in Rosenberg, *Spreading the American Dream*, 169–70; Hoff Wilson, *American Business*, 98–9.

[9] International Chamber of Commerce, Europe–United States Committee, Monographs Presented for Discussion at the Washington Congress (n.p., 1931); Siegfried, 'Psychological Elements', 18–19; cf. Siegfried, 'L'Europe devant la civilisation américaine', *Revue des Deux Mondes* (15 April 1930); *The Economist* covered the conference with as much enthusiasm as was possible in the circumstances, since the magazine acknowledged that 'in the economic sphere the nations are at war', edition of 16 May 1931.

[10] In 1935 Siegfried would publish *La crise de l'Europe*; cf. Strauss, *Menace in the West*, 82.

looked forward to an epoch of 'renewed youth.'[11] True, every American was born 'thrice as rich' as every European, partly because the size of the American market meant that it included twice as many consumers as the largest European market (Britain's). But the American choice for standardized mass production that derived from the scale and uniformity of its market was not the only choice open to the European economies, with all their traditional distinctions. Might not the slump itself have shown the world the limits of the mass production system? Was there not a fatal mismatch between the power of the American assembly line and the capacity of markets everywhere to absorb its tremendous output?[12]

Above all, said Pirelli, there was the reality of interdependence. This was not just a physical fact of the ever-expanding exchange of goods, services, and people (at least until October 1929), or even of the $15–20 billion the US possessed in credits or investments abroad. Beyond these realities was 'the growth and improvement of means of communication and the spread of more refined tastes even among the less developed social classes, due partly to improved publicity and advertising methods...', novelties that promised to create a single grand transatlantic market one day. If only the continents on either side of the Atlantic could return to the spontaneous process of integration between them that had made the pre-war world such a prosperous one, then this day might soon dawn. In the meanwhile, concluded Pirelli, 'the extent of the present depression is such that it cannot be secured by the action of any single nation or any single continent'.[13]

The cultural paradox of the slump

As the ICC meeting demonstrated, even after the Wall Street collapse of October 1929 and the spread of the Depression to Europe and back again, the force of America's modernizing inspiration and presence was still at work in ways that could profoundly disturb contemporary European opinion. Many of the best-remembered interwar commentaries on the American world of mass production and its implications for Europe's future in fact appeared well after the contraction became worldwide in the first half of 1930: 'the Twenties mood continued into the early Thirties', said a British writer of the time.[14] In England in 1930 the rising literary critic F. R. Leavis produced his damning pamphlet on *Mass Civilisation and Minority*

---

[11] Alberto Pirelli, 'Address by the Chairman', 8–9.
[12] Ibid. 21.
[13] Ibid.; cits at pp. 13, 14, 23.
[14] The writer Ethel Mannin's *Youth in the Twenties: A Chapter of Autobiography* (London, 1971) contained a chapter entitled 'Overflow to the Thirties'; cit. in Savage, *Teenage*, 251, 492.

Culture, with its resonant pages denouncing the alleged 'levelling-down' effects of America's news and entertainment models. Georges Duhamel's diatribe—though originally based on a trip taken in 1928—appeared in 1930, and set off a controversial public debate reviewed in the business newspaper *Le Figaro* in November of the following year.[15] Aron and Dandieu's *Le cancer américain*, yet another attack on the perceived American obsession with turning productivity into a way of life, was a publication of 1931.[16] In 1932 came Aldous Huxley's dystopian novel *Brave New World*, depicting a system of mass regimentation based on unlimited consumption, systematic genetic selection, and the worship of a god named Ford ('For Ford's sake!', say protagonists of the year 632 A.F.—After Ford—in their rare moments of exasperation).

In Germany a philologist had offered in August of 1930 a discussion on 'Americanism: the History of a Term'. The analysis discussed the many common meanings of this reference in the talk of the times, declaring that: 'In the practical professions, in scholarship, in ordinary life, and in the newspapers, one daily hears the terms Americanize, Americanization, and Americanism.' Seen from this perspective, reflects James Ceaser, ' "America", had become a vehicle by which ideas generated in philosophic and intellectual circles in Germany were transferred to the realm of common opinion.'[17]

But other Berlin commentators seemed inclined to face up to the possibility that they had lived in a world of illusion in the roaring 1920s. As a repentant writer in one of the city's illustrated news magazines put it: 'we were watching in a spell-bound state, we saw a picture blinded by optimism.' And the radical playwright Brecht used the past tense when applying his irony to America's alleged influence on 'the interests, thoughts and imagination of mankind':

> What men they were! Their boxers the strongest!
> Their inventors the most adept! Their trains the swiftest!
> So we imitated this renowned race of men

---

[15] F. R. Leavis, *Mass Civilisation and Minority Culture* (Cambridge, 1930), see in particular pp. 6–11; in 1933 Duhamel would publish *L'umanité et l'automate*; debate in *Le Figaro* entitled 'For or Against American Civilisation', from 19 November 1931 to 11 February 1932, comment in Panchisi, *Future Tense*, 121–2.

[16] Robert Aron and Arnaud Dandieu, *Le cancer américain* (Paris, 1931); two other volumes of 1931 were Pierre Laurent, *L'impérialisme économique américain* and Charles Pomaret, *L'Amérique à la conquête de l'Europe*; cit. in Strauss, *Menace in the West*, 97; many of these writers collaborated with the new Catholic journal *Esprit*, founded in 1930 by the intellectual Emmanuel Mounier, a man who developed systematically his own form of American critique; cf. Seth D. Armus, 'The Eternal Enemy: Emmanuel Mounier's *Esprit* and French Anti-Americanism', *French Historical Studies* (Spring 2001), 271–304; cf. Roger, *American Enemy*, 276.

[17] Ceaser, *Reconstructing America*, 162.

Who seemed destined
To rule the world by helping it to progress.[18]

Clearly many of the post-1930 productions were the fruit of projects set
in motion long before the Crash, but the fact that so few were modified
to take account of the new circumstances suggests their authors believed
they wrote in the presence of forces far stronger than a mere stock
market upheaval. Seen from this perspective, *Brave New World* appears
as a curious synthesis. It was based on Huxley's experience of the British
version of the Crash, and the bankruptcy of parliamentary democracy
he perceived in those years. These sentiments, and a growing fear of
America's industrial example, led him to conclude that only a system of
rigidly programmed hedonism would stabilize the relationship between
Fordist mass production and its appropriate consumption in the long
term.[19] What all these writers and critics were proposing implicitly was
that, for better or for worse, certain forms of American power and influence would outlast the economic disarray; the later their arrival the
more likely to endure. Had not America just invented an irresistible
new way to project its vision of the world in the talking motion
picture?

Antonio Gramsci's notes on 'Americanism and Fordism', already mentioned, were concluded in prison during 1934. In their final sections they
face openly the question that had implicitly divided most European observers in the course of the 1920s: whether the distinctive civilization
emerging in America did indeed represent a new phase in Western social
evolution, or was simply an etiolated form of trends visible since the days
of the Industrial Revolution in the Old World, an outgrowth become
vastly enlarged in the limitless spaces of the new continent.[20] According
to the answer, quite different strategies of selection, amalgamation, or resistance to its challenge would be required.

It was in this context that Gramsci at a certain point picked up a phrase
from the playwright Pirandello of April 1929, and began to reflect on it.
The great dramatist had stated:

[18] Gassert, 'Without Concessions', 232; Brecht cit. in Costigliola, *Awkward Dominion*,
184.
[19] David Bradshaw's introduction to the Huxley centenary edition of *Brave New World*
(London, 1994), gives a telling account of the social and cultural context the novel sprang
from, and specifically of the development of Huxley's anti-Americanism in the 1920s; for
the world view of Mustapha Mond, the system's London controller, ibid. 208, 216; cf.
Miles and Smith, *Cinema, Literature and Society*, Part II, ch. 2, esp. pp. 112–21.
[20] As late as 1939 a French commentator saw the US as a magnifying mirror of Europe:
L. Ferrero, *Amérique, miroir grossissant de l'Europe* (Paris, 1939); for an American confirmation of this outlook, Mowrer, *This American World*, 126–7.

Americanism is swamping us. I think that a new beacon of civilisation has been lit over there. The money that runs through the world is American (?!) [Gramsci's interpolation], and behind the money (?!) runs the way of life and the culture.... In Berlin you do not feel the gap between the old and the new Europe, because the structure of the city itself offers no resistance.... In Paris, where there is an historical and artistic structure, where the evidence of an indigent civilisation is present, Americanism is as strident and jarring as the make-up on the face of an aging femme du monde.[21]

But this was the wrong approach, suggested the founder of Italian Communism. There was no American cultural revolution or invasion. In their civilization the basic social divisions and class relationships remained the same as in Europe, and the whole could be identified therefore as nothing more than an 'organic extension and an intensification' of the European way of life.

The problem is rather this; whether America, through the implacable weight of its economic production (and therefore indirectly), will compel or is already compelling Europe to overturn its excessively antiquated economic and social basis.... In other words, whether we are undergoing a transformation of the material bases of European civilisation, which in the long run (though not that long, since in the contemporary period everything happens much faster than in the past ages) will bring about the overthrow of the existing forms of civilisation and the forced birth of the new.[22]

The great wail against 'Americanism', Gramsci went on, arose from those 'old strata' who could see that their time was up, that they would be swept away by the 'new order' that America portended. They were already in the grip 'of a wave of social panic, dissolution and despair'. In this situation the only hope for progress lay in those forced to sweat, suffer, and build with their own hands the new system of production.

It is they who 'must' find for themselves an 'original' and not Americanised, system of living, to turn into 'freedom' what today is 'necessity'.[23]

Italy itself showed very few signs of being 'swamped' by Americanism in the early 1930s. Making an exception for Hollywood's products (but not for much longer), the regime had set in motion its own form of cultural

---

[21] Gramsci, *Selections from the Prison Notebooks of Antonio Gramsci*, ed. tr. Quintin Hoare and Geoffrey Nowell-Smith (New York, 1971), 316.

[22] Ibid. 317; one small sign of the possibilities, thought Gramsci, was the spread of the network of Rotary Clubs to Italy, representing a more modern, emollient, and service-oriented form of capitalism; comment in *Prison Notebooks*, ii, ed. tr. Joseph A. Buttigieg (New York, 1996), 269–71, 273; on the spread of Rotary Clubs to Europe, de Grazia, *Irresistible Empire*, 36–49.

[23] Gramsci, *Selections from the Prison Notebooks*, inverted commas in original.

protectionism with Mussolini's campaign of 1927 for a return to rural values, as Gramsci himself recalled.[24] It was a very special event to see an advertisement for Midas motor oil (an American brand) appear in an Appenine mountain village in the summer of 1931. It was brought by the first car the village had ever seen.[25] In Ignazio Silone's world-famous novel *Fontamara*, of 1933, set in a similar, extraordinarily primitive village in the Abruzzo region, America remains the dream land of would-be emigrants. It only comes nearer home, as a metaphor of self-made riches, when an unknown outsider turns into an over-bearing local magnate thanks to political connections and the magical ingredient of bank credit. 'America is everywhere. Everywhere. You just need to know what to look for,' cries the man.[26]

The rising British playwright, novelist, and social critic, J. B. Priestley, might well have agreed. But his understanding of the assertion would have been very different. You did not need to know what to look for, he might have said, it came to look for you, at least in the most prosperous, up-to-date regions of his beloved country. Born in a Yorkshire schoolmaster's family, Priestley was a man who, in LeMahieu's view, would come to embody in the course of the 1930s the renewed British 'common culture': a synthesis of recently invented and traditional identities that would provide a successful response to the challenge of the three modernities, and help keep the fabric of national life together in the supreme test of World War II. In 1934 he provided a new sort of evidence of the lasting changes in national life being introduced by the force of America's example.

In the autumn of the previous year, Priestley had set out on long journey of exploration in his native land. In his conclusion to the commentary that resulted, a best-seller in its day, Priestley described the intermingling worlds he had discovered on his travels. The first was that of Olde Englande, part myth part real, rural and pastoral, a survivor from the pre-industrial world. The second bore the stamp of the

[24] Gramsci, *Selections from the Prison Notebooks*, inverted commas in original. 287; the main point of the 1927 campaign however was to try to reverse the declining birth rate, thought to be a direct outcome of urbanization and its lifestyle; Bruno P. F. Wanrooij, 'Italian Society under Fascism' in Adrian Lyttelton (ed.), *Liberal and Fascist Italy, 1900–1945* (Oxford, 2002), 187; discussion of the very limited penetration of American models and myths in 1920s Italy in D'Attorre (ed.), *Nemici per la pelle*, 20–3.

[25] Cit. in Victoria de Grazia, 'The Arts of Purchase: How American Publicity Subverted the European Poster, 1920–1940', in Barbara Kruger and Phil Marlani (eds), *Remaking History* (Seattle, 1989), 221.

[26] I. Silone, *Fontamara* (1st edn, Zurich, 1933; 1949 edn repr., Milan, 1988), 42; the publication of *Fontamara* was 'the most exciting Italian–American cultural event of the thirties', says John Diggins; discussion in *Mussolini and Fascism*, 250–1; an equally famous portrait of rural life under Fascism is Carlo Levi *Christ Stopped at Eboli* of 1945; for its discussion of the myth of America in the peasant mental universe, and its alteration as a result of the 1929 Crash, New York 1976 edition, pp. 122–32.

nineteenth-century industrial era and was now filthy and flyblown, the unforgivable product of Victorian capitalism's cynicism and greed. Then there was the new England, the one that had grown up since the War, the product of the age rather than of Britain herself:

> America, I supposed, was its real birthplace. This is the England of arterial and by-pass roads, of filling-stations and factories that look like exhibition buildings, of giant cinemas and dance-halls and cafés, bungalows with tiny garages, cocktail bars, Woolworths, motor-coaches, wireless, hiking, factory-girls made-up to look like actresses, greyhound racing and dirt-tracks, swimming pools, and everything given away for cigarette coupons...

This was a democratic creation undoubtedly, said Priestley, accessible and egalitarian, as its films, wireless, and 'sixpenny-stores' confirmed every day of the week. Unfortunately, he went on, it was a cheap kind of reality, 'a bit too cheap'. It was monotonous, artificial, and deliberately fabricated by profit-driven purveyors of dreams and symbols:

> You feel that too many people in this new England are doing not what they like but what they have been told they would like. (Here is the American influence at work)... this new England is lacking in character, in zest, gusto, flavour, bite, drive, originality and... this is a serious weakness.

Living in a self-contained universe of monotonous hedonism, the new generations inhabiting this England would be 'the perfect subjects for an iron autocracy'.[27] These were the same thoughts that had prompted Huxley's fantasy, and which troubled a wide variety of thinkers across the Channel, in the France of the Third Republic's final years.

French parallels

In Paris the onset of the slump was witnessed at some distance, as official financial arrangements effectively protected the national economy for over two years from its full effects. But the cultural debates of the previous

---

[27] J. B. Priestley, *English Journey* (1934 edn repr., London, 1984), 375–9; for full contextualization, John Baxendale, '"I Had Seen a Lot of Englands": J. B. Priestley, Englishness and the People', *History Workshop Journal* (Spring 2001); on the continuing fascination of American models for British youth in the 1930s, Savage, *Teenage*, 300. The lively fresco of interwar social history—'of the forgettable sort'—written by the poet Robert Graves and the historian Alan Hodge under the title *The Long Weekend: A Social History of Great Britain, 1918–1939* (1940 edn repr., London 1985), offers many more glimpses of the phenomena that had also made Priestley unhappy: cafeteria and milk bars, pp. 295–6; the transformation of the British Press under the influence of American models, pp. 342–3; holiday camps, p. 381, music and dance, pp. 385–6, jitterbugging, pp. 390–1 ('It demanded a capacity for idle nervous excess that the American climate might bestow, but not the English.'), etc.; the authors point out that by no means all these local adoptions succeeded in their various markets.

decade on the meaning of contemporary US experience spilled over directly into politics when one of France's most experienced and prominent commentators on America's experiments, André Tardieu, arrived in the Prime Minister's office in November 1929. The latest in a long line of short-lived interwar Prime Ministers, Tardieu promised a 'prosperity policy' based on a grand project for 'national retooling'. The hope was for a true fresh start, based on the triumph of 'Ford over Marx', in the words of contemporary political campaigning.[28]

But the Crash immediately galvanized the right-wing opposition and the sceptics, and the progressive industrial elite that had supported Tardieu soon found itself isolated and forced on the defensive. The president of the employers' association, Duchemin, denounced the Americans' obsession with 'the mystique of high wages': it was this fantasy that had brought them to ruin. And a leading industrialist, Marthon, gloated that 'the hymn to restraint has succeeded the hymn to production'. In the final analysis, neither left nor right in France believed in modernity based on productivity and rising wages, comments Richard Kuisel, and the local band of technocrats who had done so were now dispersed and forced to look elsewhere for their inspiration.[29]

Yet the 1920s and 1930s brought to France many of the same consumer-oriented social and economic novelties that had so struck Priestley in England. Advertising, magazines, management, motoring, shopping, and leisure activities were all transformed in the course of the decade, at least in the big cities and wherever the majority went on working, and the *expectation* of more change to come in the same uplifting direction began be considered, if not wholly legitimate, at least normal.[30] The task of the arbiters of taste then was to give this impulse a distinctly French 'spin'. Only in this way would it remain orderly, controlled, and compatible with traditional identities and customs, most especially those that F. R. Leavis in England called 'the mature inherited codes of habit and valuation'.[31]

The swelling world of public relations and advertising displayed a variety of interesting responses to this challenge. An architect advertising in the biweekly *Revue des Deux mondes* promised—with illustrations—to build for his readers 'un *Home*'. This was not a living machine or a

---

[28] On Tardieu's career, interest in the United States and book *Devant l'obstacle* (Paris, 1927), Strauss, *Menace in the West*, 71–2; R. Kuisel, *Capitalism and the State in Modern France* (Cambridge, 1981), 90–2.

[29] Kuisel, *Ernest Mercier*, 69–70, 88, 91, 123.

[30] Cf. Panchisi, *Future Tense*, Introduction, 162.

[31] Leavis, *Mass Civilisation*, 6; conflicts over these questions in the case of the remodelling of Paris after World War I in Panchisi, *Future Tense*, ch. 2.

mass-produced housing unit, said the copy, but an expression of the client's personal interpretation of the union between a plot of earth, a habitation, and his own individuality. Being able to turn this vision into a residence of charm and distinction was what made Architect Clement of Le Vésinet 'un spécialiste du *Home*'.[32]

In 1927 the first of a new generation of French low-price chain stores—the *prix uniques*—had opened in Paris, based directly on the latest techniques in retailing in the United States, as well as the experience of Woolworth's in Europe. By the mid-1930s, in spite of some closures due to the Depression, the American chain owned 450 branches in Britain and 70 in Germany. At that time about 160 low-cost stores had been opened in France, reports Ellen Furlough, all sharing the same features of rationalization as applied to location, internal organization, marketing, and pricing. With their careful reproduction of the ambience and selling techniques that had long distinguished American pioneers in the field, the *prix uniques* had created a new kind of consumer, and hence a new social phenomenon. But in the land of the small shopkeeper and artisan, they quickly stirred up opposition and resistance. In 1936, after a three year political battle, a law was passed strongly restricting the further growth of the chains.[33] One parliamentary sponsor of a bill defending traditional retailing paid exalted tribute to 'the vitality of our small commerce and of the middle class, the core of the nation and the backbone of order, method, and savings upon which all our institutions rest'. At a time of intense social unrest and economic anxiety in France, the protectionist refrain found a ready audience.[34]

But official Paris had already found an alternative space for channelling and adjusting traditional home life to the opportunities of the new era. This was the *Salon des Arts Ménagers*, a French exhibition of the home of

---

[32] *Revue des Deux Mondes*, 1 March 1930; among the ironies of this architectural promotion was the fact that American architects, particularly in New York, considered Paris to be the acme of all good taste and 'worked over each French fillip to adapt it for consumption in the US. Parisians were pickier about their Americana'; Ariella Budick, 'Transatlantic transfer of style', review of the exhibition 'Paris/New York: Design, Fashion, Culture, 1925–1940', Museum of the City of New York, 2008–9, *Financial Times*, 29 December 2008. The evolution in these years of a leading French firm in advertising, the Michelin tyre company, is analysed in Stephen L. Harp, *Marketing Michelin: Advertising and Cultural Identity in Twentieth Century France* (Baltimore, 2002).

[33] Ellen Furlough, 'Selling the American Way in Interwar France: Prixs Uniques and the Salons des Arts Menagers', *Journal of Social History*, 26 (1993), 491–519. Hitler's governing programme of 1933 also included a ban on department stores: John Gunther, *Inside Europe* (London, 1936), 40; historical context analysed in de Grazia, *Irresistible Empire*, 154–64.

[34] Furlough, 'Selling the American Way', 503; at the same time modernizing pressures such as the arrival of cash registers were splitting the front of small shopkeepers; de Grazia, *Irresistible Empire*, 163–4.

the future that showed off the latest improvements in domestic science, household management, and consumer durables, all within a framework that the State and the governments of the day could support.[35] Starting in 1923 as the idea of a Taylor-inspired technocrat, Jules-Louis Breton, the event gathered pace throughout the interwar years, attracting over a thousand exhibitors by 1939 and vast crowds, all the while maintaining its official patronage. The emphasis was very much on 'the beautiful and fruitful affirmation of our national industry', as the 1927 official presentation had put it. And although the great American household brands began to appear from the late 1920s onwards, there was, explains Ellen Furlough, 'a nationalist tone to discussions surrounding the Salon, with a constant theme being the preservation of French taste, refinement and elegance'. The overall purpose, as in so many other spheres, was to identify 'a particularly French version of domestic modernity', one that would stand out with its own distinguishing features in contrast with the American standard ideal. A spokeswoman for one edition of the Salon explained:

> If the United States creates households that are laboratories of porcelain and nickel, it is in France that one finds beautiful old furniture, discreetly brilliant ceramics, the intimacy of long silk curtains, books and bibelots, loving and faithful objects...we have made a world-wide reputation for taste and finesse and it should be preserved.[36]

Today's historians, especially of consumer culture and the place of women in it, see much at stake in these anticipations of the post-war World War II scene with its systematic emphasis on private definitions of standards of living, its invitation to affluence, and *embourgeoisement* for all. In particular they see the most conscious and sustained efforts up to this point to reconcile a revolution in material living along lines suggested by American experience, with inherited national customs and hierarchies in all their forms. The struggle for the 'cultural preservation of social differences' (Furlough), particularly those of class and gender, had accompanied the emergence of mass society from the start. It was forced down the national

---

[35] The post-World War I discovery across Europe of the home as a focus for social policy and rationalization movements is discussed in Paul Betts and David Crowley, 'Introduction', *Journal of Contemporary History* (April 2005), Special Issue: 'Domestic Dreamworlds: Notions of Home in Post-1945 Europe', 216–18, 222–3.

[36] Furlough, 'Selling the American Way', 512–15; the British equivalent, the Ideal Home Exhibition, had started in 1908 at the instigation of the *Daily Mail* (which continued to sponsor the show until 2012). It was the true inspiration of the Paris event, claims Deborah Ryan in her officially authorized history of the spectacle, and was at least as effective in promoting modernization in the private sphere of the home, in legitimizing expectations of a new era of material comfort and prosperity to come, and in burnishing the traditions of domesticity and Empire; Deborah S. Ryan, *The Daily Mail Ideal Home Exhibition: The Ideal Home Through the Twentieth Century* (London, 1997).

agenda in the decade of the 1930s by the pressure of all the other battles, whether fought or not fought. But it was not altogether abandoned, since it found a new role in the line-up of protectionisms and nationalisms—economic, political, psychological—which were anxiously mobilized in France to face the crises of the decade.

After the catastrophe of World War II it became clear that a successful search for a French way to be modern was an indispensable condition for healthy survival in the community of nations. But in the 1930s, as democracy collapsed in Germany, and people began to seek shelter from the prospect of another outbreak of civil war in Europe, survival on any terms seemed the only option. Seen from this perspective, and given the 'irreducible particularism' of its behaviour during the financial crisis, as a Parisian commentator put it, the United States as a source of aid and comfort, of anything other than myth and mystification, appeared to be a world further away than ever. Even the heroic Lindbergh had come out as a militant isolationist. As we shall see, all this did not prevent French commentators from producing a constant flow of books on American life and times throughout the decade.[37]

AMERICANISM AND THE TOTALITARIAN MENTALITIES

Italian Fascism and the 'star-spangled Babylon'

Just as the system Benito Mussolini built in Italy was contradictory and incomplete, so its encounter with modernity in American form was divided, magmatic, and shifting. Post-war Italy was of course a much less developed and complex society than the versions on display in the major European powers; the Fascist revolution itself was invented in part to find an Italian way to fill the gap (and to prevent others doing so).[38] But the manner in which a series of overlapping myths of America came and went during the twenty-year Fascist epoch, the role these imaginary Americas played in the Fascist effort to create its own idea of progress, and finally the strength of Italy's many connections in the material world with the

---

[37] Phrase from *Revue des Deux Mondes*, 15 January 1930; sixty-four works appeared between 1933 and 1939, reports B. Galloux-Fournier, 'Un regard sur l'Amérique', p. 322, n. 69, mostly classic travelogues or reports on the New Deal.

[38] These are the dominant themes in today's historiography on Fascism; cf. 'Introduction' and numerous articles in Lyttelton (ed.), *Liberal and Fascist Italy*; Ruth Ben-Ghiat, *Fascist Modernities: Italy, 1922–1945* (Berkeley, 2001); Emilio Gentile, *Fascismo: Storia e interpretazione* (Bari, 2002), ch. 11, 'La modernità totalitaria'.

US: all these elements make the story of the American question in inter-war Italy's evolution a complex and controversial one.

Until 'the great Italian lawgiver' (Churchill) fell under Hitler's sway once and for all, from about 1937 onwards, and so began to compete on his terms with the Führer's notions of the world, the Duce and his nation expressed their own distinctive vision of a possible role for the United States in their future. Elements of it would turn out to be part of the enduring inheritance of Fascism in Italian culture.[39]

In 1929 the officially sponsored *Enciclopedia italiana* included a full-scale entry on 'Americanism'. Here the phenomenon was defined as:

> the admiration, whether naïve or reasoned, but mostly excessive, for American (United States') ideas or things; an admiration which at times even becomes a fashion, in contrast to European cultural traditions.[40]

In its function as 'one of the main mythical metaphors of modernity', says Emilio Gentile, 'Americanism…was perceived ambivalently, as a phenomenon both terrifying and fascinating'.[41] Whenever it was left to writers, critics, and journalists to debate the significance of America in contemporary life, rather than the Duce or other regime personalities, the trend of judgements remained overwhelmingly negative. This is the line of anti-Americanist commentary that has attracted most scholarly attention, not least because of its obvious spillover effects in time.[42] As elsewhere in Europe, America's restless machine and material civilization was heavily condemned: it was alleged to provoke a new rupture between culture and society. Here every aspect of human life was systematically alienated 'by removing it from the spontaneous rhythm of nature and from the soothing dominion of the spirit'. In America 'the tragedy of modernity' had reached its fullest expression, 'a repressive and preventative punishment (from God) for all the other great discoveries of the Renaissance: i.e. gunpowder, humanism and Protestantism': this was the unforgiving view of a Catholic writer from the Church's most conservative wing. The moralizing tone of much commentary was particularly in evidence, since it allowed a sharp contrast to be drawn between the degeneracy thought to be rampant in 'the star-spangled Babylon', and the

---

[39] Cf. Stephen Gundle, 'Il Duce's Cultural Cachet', *History Today* (October 2010). The article was written to accompany a London exhibition on anti-Fascist art and the cult of Mussolini.

[40] Cit. in Emilio Gentile, 'Impending Modernity: Fascism and the Ambivalent Image of the United States', *Journal of Contemporary History*, 28 (1993), 8–9.

[41] Ibid. 7.

[42] Cf. Michela Nacci, *L'antiamericanismo in Italia negli anni trenta* (Milan, 1989); M. Beynet, *L'image de l'Amérique dans la culture italienne de l'entre-deux guerres*, 3 vols (Aix-en-Provence, 1990); Ben-Ghiat, *Fascist Modernities*, 39–44.

stern task of living in the new Roman era, the heroic civilization of the spirit announced by the Duce from his balcony high above the crowd.[43]

After his first long sojourn in the US, the future novelist and film director Mario Soldati wrote:

> America is not just a part of the world. America is a state of mind, a passion. From one moment to another, any European can catch the American disease, revolt against Europe, and become American.[44]

This was the risk the dictators feared most of all, and although a figure like Soldati—an agnostic towards the regime—would become a living demonstration that the change was by no means irreversible, serious efforts were set in motion by some of the currents of Fascism to contain the onset of America's inspiration in the land that had invented 'totalitarianism'. Otherwise the containing effect might be reversed and the force of America's inspiration start to dilute the value of the Fascist revolution itself.[45]

The *Strapaese* movement, for instance, a 1920s product, sought to build a synthesis of what were believed to be the best of traditional values, the ones still prevailing in the heart of local communities, and those of the original Fascist revolution in order to create a new form of ethnic identity. Fighting the threat of 'fads, foreign ideas and modernist civilization', the leader of *Strapaese*, the artist Mino Maccari, called explicitly for 'a modernity of our own, an Italian modernity'. American civilization in Maccari's view was the product of a 'bastard, international, external, mechanical' form of contemporary progress; it was 'a concoction brewed by Jewish bankers, pederasts, war profiteers and brothel-keepers'.[46]

Yet Mussolini's muse, confidante, and lover from his earliest years to the early 1930s was Margherita Sarfatti, a Jewish intellectual and high *borghese* fascinated far more by America than anything rural Italy could offer. It was she who transmitted to the Duce the powerful tug that America exercised over so many in the roaring twenties, and who made strenuous efforts to ensure in return that the governing classes in the US would get to know the meaning of Fascism's great project, and come to develop a highly positive image of it. Manipulating journalists, diplomats, and the

---

[43] Gentile, 'Impending Modernity', 10–13.

[44] Cit. in Wanrooij, 'Italian Society', 193.

[45] Commentators who later wished to defend the behaviour of the Italian people under Fascism, minimizing the extent of its mass support, claimed that this was precisely what had happened: R. De Felice cit. in D'Attorre (ed.), *Nemici per la pelle*, 24; a particularly vivid personal account of the identity clashes of the time was supplied in the 1959 collection *As Others See Us*, by the then celebrated commentator Luigi Barzini Jr; 'from Italy', in Franz M. Joseph (ed.), *As Others See Us: The United States through Foreign Eyes* (Princeton, 1959), 72–7.

[46] Ben-Ghiat, *Fascist Modernities*, 26–7, Gentile, 'Impending Modernity', 11.

many powerful Americans who visited Italy in the 1920s, Mussolini and his English-speaking companion turned the dictator into a US media celebrity with few European rivals. By the end of the decade, the United Press and the Hearst chain of newspapers were able to count on a stream of material coming allegedly from Mussolini's pen, but usually produced by or with Sarfatti. The Duce persuaded the most powerful banks of their day, in New York, to provide loans, trade openings, and tolerance to Italy's war debts. He also imagined that a strong US connection would give him extra weight in European politics, or at least in American policies to Europe.[47] In return, his American admirers—which included William Randolph Hearst himself, the journalist O'Hare McCormick, Louis B. Mayer and Will Hays of Hollywood, Lamont the senior partner in the J. P. Morgan bank, Giannini the head of the Bank of America, Butler the Chancellor of Columbia University, and others—expected that Mussolini would save Italy from communism in exemplary fashion, and, after the Crash of 1929–31, might even have invented a third way between communism and capitalist democracy.[48]

Given all the colourful variety of Italian–American traffic in the 1920s—credits, business, some investment, cinema, tourists, personalities[49]—it would have been surprising had Mussolini turned churlish when the American economy began to devour itself after 1929. But almost a year went by before he offered his own organized reflections on the new situation. In a series of three speeches, the Duce then made clear that although Italy was hit hard by the crisis, and the State would intervene with economic help of every sort for deserving workers and investors (while its bureaucrats would have their salaries cut), there was no question of criticizing America or its capitalist system.

Certainly the collapse of all the dreams of the 1920s had been a great shock as 'we too on this side of the water shared in the euphoria'. And the whole mass-production system was a fallacy—'they can see it themselves now'—clearly demonstrating that Fascism's arrangements were superior. But any sort of general explanation or condemnation was not to be expected. In a radio message of greeting to the American people on New

---

[47] Migone, *Gli Stati Uniti e il fascismo*, 103–5, 117–75, 217, 265–7, 281–6.

[48] Philip V. Cannistraro and Brian R. Sullivan, *Il Duce's Other Woman: The Untold Story of Margherita Sarfatti, Benito Mussolini's Jewish Mistress, and How She Helped Him Come to Power* (New York, 1993), ch. 23; Emilio Gentile portrays Sarfatti as an intellectual who rejected the established anti-Americanism of her peers, and dreamed of a new Euro-American civilization galvanized by Fascism, 'Impending Modernity', 21; Migone, *Gli Stati Uniti e il fascismo*, 305–6.

[49] These are the themes of Diggins, *Mussolini and Fascism*, Part II; for example, on the powerful support of the Morgan banking house, ibid. 147–56; cf. Migone, *Gli Stati Uniti e il fascismo*, ch. 2.

Year's Day 1931, Mussolini emphasized the warmth of his sympathy not only for America's Italian immigrant masses, naturally, but for its scientists and philosophers, its celebrated writers and statesmen. Swearing on his belief in peace and a renewed prosperity, Mussolini sent his warmest greetings to 'the President of your great republic'.[50]

But the crisis period of 1929–32 found most of the Fascist movement adopting a quite different outlook on the American turmoil. Its most typical commentators saw their direst predictions confirmed, rejoiced in America's fall from grace, and announced the appearance of a Fifth Horseman of the Apocalypse, a 'giant figure [who] has no visible contours, whose dark shadow is the only thing we perceive of him in the troubled eyes of the unemployed'.[51] From this perspective the crisis looked like a magnificent purge for the ills of hedonism and self-indulgence that had run riot in the 1920s. Now the Republic had a chance to find its way back to its ancient humanistic and Latin roots in Europe, to leave behind its 'secessionist ideology' and recognize the superior wisdom of the Old World. The Fascist regime, said this argument, should be prepared to meet the United States halfway as it made the painful but unavoidable effort of self-criticism.[52]

As Mussolini's system intensified its hold on Italian society and strengthened its corporatist State against the effects of the capitalist depression, official anti-Americanism tended to become more militant, as did the 'spontaneous' version of the intellectuals. But there was another force at work pushing in the same direction. Consumerist modernity was beginning to catch up with Italy. 'American products—from chewing gum to typewriters and from movies to gramophones—invaded the Italian market', reports a social historian. 'Young men dressed '*alla Fox*', and young women wanted to be slim and have their hair bobbed, trying to look like Hollywood stars.'[53] Market awareness, techniques of merchandizing and advertising all evolved along lines stimulated by American experience when not directly by US companies. Illustrated magazines for modern housewives, movie fans, and company managers emulated their peers in other parts of Europe, as an 'international demonstration effect' was consciously managed by new advertising agencies to ensure respect for local sensibilities even while they were refreshed. In 1927 a magazine

---

[50] Speeches of 1 October 1930, 28 October 1930, and 18 December 1930, radio message of 1 January 1931 in *Scritti e Discorsi di Benito Mussolini: Edizione definitiva VII* (Milan, 1934), 213–18, 223–33, 251–74, 277–9.

[51] Gentile, 'Impending Modernity', 13, 16–17; cf. Nacci, *L'antiamericanismo in Italia negli anni trenta*, ch. 8.

[52] Gentile, 'Impending Modernity', 17–18; Nacci, *L'antiamericanismo in Italia negli anni trenta*, 120–4.

[53] Cit. in Wanrooij, 'Italian Society', 193.

entitled *L'Ufficio moderno*, had been founded to promote an 'Italian form of rationalisation', just as the technocrats were supposed to have done in France. In 1932 it proclaimed that advertising would...

> ...contribute to elevating the lives of the masses...impose new customs and habits. [Advertising campaigns could] become a formidable force that pushes people towards a higher faith, teaching it virtues of prevention, savings, hygiene and a happy life.[54]

But how could 'the higher faith' be reconciled with the 'happy life' as understood by advertisers? In 1931 the Duce's brother Arnaldo complained of 'those who would like to turn the universe into a workshop', and 'those who are mad about machines'. At the same time, he said, the regime had no sympathy 'with the sick decadents who love the streams that carry away the images, dreams and life of restless time'.[55] The following year the Duce himself gave orders to the planners of the tenth anniversary 'Exhibition of the Fascist Revolution' to make sure it was 'a thing of today, therefore very modern and daring...the expression of the kind of art and aesthetics which reflect our yearning, dynamic, escapist and fevered times'. And in an article on 'Technocracy', published in the *New York American* early in 1933, he explained his own version of the belief that technological development expressed an inevitable form of human progress.[56]

Partly as a reflection of Mussolini's admiration for the New Deal—which he saw as inspired by his own methods and principles—the height of the Duce's American fame arrived in 1934–5. In July 1934 the business magazine *Fortune* dedicated a special issue to the Corporate State and its achievements, suggesting that its idea of activist government could well teach US business how to find a way between the anarchy of unfettered capitalism and the menace of Soviet-style collectivism.[57] Margherita Sarfatti made a triumphal diplomatic and lecture tour of the US: 'official Washington received Margherita as if she were Mussolini's consort', say

---

[54] Full contextualization, including story of *L'Uffico moderno*, in Adam Arvidsson, *The Making of a Consumer Society: Marketing and Modernity in Contemporary Italy*, PhD thesis, European University Institute (Florence, 1999), ch. 1, sections I, II; cf. de Grazia, 'The Arts of Purchase', 249–51.

[55] Cit. in Gentile, 'Impending Modernity', 21.

[56] Ibid. 20–1; on Margherita Sarfatti and the 1932 exhibition, Emily Braun, 'The Visual Arts: Modernism and Fascism', in Lyttelton (ed.), *Liberal and Fascist Italy*, 202–5.

[57] Discussion of the *Fortune* special issue in Diggins, *Mussolini and Fascism*, 163–5; for a sympathetic comparison of the NRA and the Corporative State, William G. Welk, 'Fascist Economic Policy and the National Recovery Administration', *Foreign Affairs* (October 1933); for Mussolini's admiration of the New Deal, Maurizio Vaudagna, 'Mussolini and FDR', in Cornelis A. van Minnen and John F. Sears (eds), *FDR and His Contemporaries: Foreign Perceptions of an American President* (New York, 1992), 162–6.

the episode's chroniclers.[58] The year of Mussolini's Ethiopian invasion (1935) saw the leading *New York Times* correspondent in Europe, Anne O'Hare McCormick, reach the utmost point of her long infatuation with the Duce, declaring that whatever the results of his 'dangerously explosive energy', this man with his true dictator's temperament would live forever as the most extraordinary figure of his time.[59]

All this was ruined when the regime mobilized for war and empire to fulfil Mussolini's great dream of reconstructing the Italian people's sense of themselves and their place in the world. A very rapid estrangement then set in between the regime and its transatlantic admirers. The State Department called for a 'moral embargo' and Roosevelt issued his first denunciation of Fascism's 'twin spirits of autocracy and aggression'. The new atmosphere of angry disapproval, with its rioting and political mobilization, even reached the world of popular song. John Diggins reports that the original version of Cole Porter's hit of the moment, 'You're the Tops', was quickly modified to drop the line 'You're the Tops / You're Mussolini'.[60]

Even its former sympathizers began to see that Fascism's pretence of building a distinctive synthesis between militant romanticism, State socialism, and Americanism for the benefit of a vulnerable, needy populace was being undermined by the Depression, and the unwinding of its leader's own delirious ideology. To offset the threat of impoverishment, a new effort of superhuman will was required, proclaimed the Duce. A war to conquer Italy's rightful 'place in the sun' at the expense of the old imperial 'have' nations would galvanize the population and transform it into a swelling race of conquerors and colonizers. None of the totalitarian systems engaged so extensively with post-First World War America as the Italian Fascists did. Mussolini desired US support and sympathy in any form they cared to take, not least to keep the money flowing and US

---

[58] Cannistraro and Sullivan, *Il Duce's Other Woman*, 430: Sarfatti produced an enthusiastic reflection on her experience: *L'America, ricerca della felicita* (Milan, 1937), commentary in Cannistraro and Sullivan, *Il Duce's Other Woman*, 501; but few, if any, of the American elite she so assiduously cultivated were convinced by Sarfatti's zeal. In the White House itself Eleanor Roosevelt made clear to Margherita 'her distaste for Mussolini'; Cannistraro and Sullivan, *Il Duce's Other Woman*, 447.

[59] Cit. with comment in Federica Pinelli and Marco Mariano, *Europa e Stati Uniti secondo il 'New York Times': La corrispondenza estera di Anne O'Hare McCormick, 1920–1954* (Turin, 2000), 132.

[60] Diggins, *Mussolini and Fascism*, 287–91; the US government's displeasure was short-lived, as hope remained in the State Department and the White House until very late in the day that Mussolini could be used to contain Hitler and advance an American-inspired appeasement policy; cf. David F. Schmitz, ' "Speaking the Same Language": The U.S. Response to the Italo-Ethiopian War and the Origins of American Appeasement', in David F. Schmitz and Richard D. Challener (eds), *Appeasement in Europe: A Reassessment of U.S. Policies* (Westport, Conn., 1990); cf. on the divisions in the US governing class that prevented a united front of disapproval, Migone, *Gli Stati Uniti e il fascismo*, 310, *passim*.

neutrality benevolent. But he had not become the living, revolutionary embodiment of a new Latin race in order to adopt America's solutions to the challenge of the three modernities.

Stalin's certainties (and Trotsky's)

At the end of a 1924 lecture series to honour the recently deceased founder of the Soviet Union, Vladimir Ilyich Lenin, the General Secretary of the Soviet Communist Party, Joseph Stalin, invited his students at the Sverdlov Communist University to dedicate their lives in the Party to realizing his vision of its ideal member. This was a being moved by two unstoppable forces: revolutionary fervour and the American practical spirit. A profound understanding of the teachings of Marx and Lenin was indispensable for the true inspiration of a militant, said Stalin, but it risked turning into fanaticism unless joined with that indomitable American energy and realism that stuck to every job until it was done. Yet on this, as on every other comparable occasion, Stalin's admiring endorsement of the American work ethic contained no reflection on the world this spirit had built, much less on its implications for the future of Europe.[61]

What the Soviet leadership did see, as already noted, was an American supremacy in technological development that they felt they could borrow to modernize semi-feudal Russia by means of accelerated industrialization. As the director of the Soviet film agency, Amkino wrote in 1928, trying to broaden the range of film imports from Hollywood:

> America... represents to the Russians a land of incredible efficiency, and in his desire to imitate its ideas the Russian is eager for every bit of news of life in this country.[62]

Stalin and his collaborators appeared to see no political risks in this impulse. The Party told its members that the point was to make the most of Western finance, skills, and technology, and then 'when the lemon was sucked dry', to discard it. Had not Lenin himself sworn that the capitalists would sell the very rope the proletariat would use to hang them?[63] But the capitalists, who were ready to help Russian progress, saw things in exactly the opposite sense, perhaps with a conscious irony. Owen Young, influential head of General Electric, said that investing in Russian industry was to hand the Communists the 'very gun with which they will shoot themselves'. Henry Ford, a hero of Soviet production at the time, agreed:

[61] Giuseppe Stalin, *Questioni del Leninismo* (Moscow, 1946), 89–90.
[62] Parks, *Culture, Conflict*, 19.
[63] Anthony C. Sutton, *Western Technology and Soviet Economic Development*, i: *1917–1930* (Stanford, 1968), 305–8.

both were convinced that communism was a malady of extreme underde-velopment. With access to the promise and then the start of prosperity, extremism would shrivel and liberal democracy emerge triumphant. Ford's decision to promote the huge Gorki car plant in 1929 was for him a gesture of peace.[64]

But the regime had no intention—except perhaps in the eyes of a be-nevolent, doomed theorist such as Nikolai Bukharin—of borrowing Western technology to introduce the proletariat to the joys of mass con-sumption in peacetime. The biggest surge of imports, deals, factory-building, and infrastructure projects, organized by US corporations, came during the frantic period of the first Five Year Plan, 1928–33. Ford, Gen-eral Electric, and the Radio Corporation of America (RCA) were among those signing large-scale contracts at the start of this effort, with GE alone looking forward to $25 million in sales over six years, using credit sup-plied largely by the company itself. Quantities of American engineers and others were said to be at work across Russia in 1930—perhaps two thousand—with many more due to follow. Americans were preferred be-cause they were more open with their money and their credits than the Europeans, were not bound by 'conservative production horizons', and unlike say, Germans, had no political interests whatsoever.[65]

The head of a Stanford research project into this experience concluded at the end of the 1930s, after interviewing a significant number of the engineers, that the central aim of the Soviet Plan was 'to free the country from [its] dependence on foreigners ... ', in other words to transfer enough 'labor power from agricultural and exploitative pursuits to industrial pro-duction (in order), within a few years, to transform Russia into a virtually self-sufficing economic unit'.[66] But as Stalin made very clear, the point of the whole effort was to build as rapidly as possible the defences of true socialism in the one country where the great dream was being realized. In 1931 he warned:

We are fifty or a hundred years behind the most advanced countries.... We must make good this distance in ten years ... or we shall go under.[67]

---

[64] Costigliola, *Awkward Dominion*, 161–4; Sutton, *Western Technology and Soviet Eco-nomic Development*, ii: *1930–1945* (Stanford 1971), 344; Edgar Mowrer was struck by the conviction of the Communists that they could take over American industrial organization and outlook, 'without any taint of the cruel, greedy yet puerile capitalism that inspired them!'; *This American World*, 172.

[65] Sutton, *Western Technology*, ii. 277, 295, 348.

[66] H. H. Fisher (Chairman), 'American Engineers in Russia. Report of the Russia Re-search Committee, Stanford University', Hoover Institution Archives, Russian Subject Collection, Box 20, File 20–52.

[67] Costigliola, *Awkward Dominion*, 158, 162–3; cf. references in Sutton, *Western Tech-nology*, i. 344.

The vast gap between the promise of American technology and Soviet Russia's capacity for absorbing it not only broke the mind and spirit of many of the engineers, but meant that the revolutionary fatherland nearly did go under ten years later. The obsession with quantity over quality, the conviction that revolutionary will would make up for any local technical deficiency, the insistence on copying rather than adapting Western technology, the obsessive political control and the sheer frenzy and violence of the effort: all this guaranteed endless waste, alienation, and frustration. The effort to disguise this reality then took on a ruthless political dynamic of its own.[68]

So because of these contingent circumstances, but also for profound reasons of outlook and dogma, there was never to be an officially developed Soviet analysis of American civilization or 'Americanism' between the wars. Nikolai Bukharin was prepared to recognize that the US was the stronghold of the capitalist system, that its progress was technology based and still 'on the upgrade' in the late 1920s. He also recognized that American workers might be paid up to four times the European average, although this did expose them to the risks of co-optation. In the context of fierce debates in the Soviet leadership about the place of the peasantry in their great projects for forced industrialization, Bukharin also insisted that the US was the place where one could see how a modern, market-based agricultural sector was actually reinforcing general economic development, and that there were lessons for the Soviets in the experience. Without any concessions to the fashionable, ridiculous view that Fordism and advanced technology were opening the way to a new and benign form of production, where class exploitation was eliminated, said Bukharin, the 'exceptional nature of [their] whole situation' and the 'special role' of the United States in world capitalism had to be recognized.[69]

But the General Secretary of the Soviet Party thought otherwise, and in a famous and deadly struggle Stalin made sure his view prevailed. Even after the crisis of 1929 and Germany's plunge towards Nazism, Stalin persisted in his belief that America was simply another version of capitalist imperialism, with whom the USSR could do business when and if necessary. Roosevelt's diplomatic recognition of the Soviet Union in

---

[68] Sutton, *Western Technology*, i. 318–26; the most moving account of the extreme pressures, frustrations, and dangers which even the most sympathetic American engineer encountered was supplied by the exceptional Californian civil engineer Zara Witkin: Michael Gelb (ed.), *An American Engineer in Stalin's Russia: The Memoirs of Zara Witkin* (Berkeley, 1991).

[69] Theodore Draper, *American Communism and Soviet Russia* (New York, 1960), 260, 271–2, 280, 303; N. I. Bukharin, *Selected Writings on the State and the Transition to Socialism*, ed. Richard B. Day (Armonk, New York, 1982), 309–10 (article of September 1928), 347–8 (article of June 1929).

November 1933 proved the point. Didn't the Soviets also enjoy perfectly normal relations at the same time with Mussolini's Italy, he asked the 17th Party Congress in 1934? 'Fascism is not the issue here.' This same attitude, when applied to Nazism itself, of course had lethal consequences, as it lay behind the German Communist Party's underestimation of Hitler's movement, and its notorious line of hostility to the German trade unions and other left parties, which soon led to the destruction of them all.[70]

But the idea of one monolithic capitalism, indivisible into its separate and distinct Fascist, social democrat, and liberal democrat components, was not simply a product of obtuseness or Soviet satisfaction with the spectacle of the world crisis. The diplomat and historian George Kennan, the first well-known Western specialist on the Soviet Union, wrote that for the genuine Leninist the laws governing the operation of human society were truly identical across the world, *except* in the Soviet Union. Only the violent destruction of the existing order everywhere, by those devoted unswervingly to the example and instructions of the Russian comrades, would allow the benefits of the Soviet revolution to spread.[71] Among the militants who, to their chagrin, discovered at first hand the implications of this world outlook were the few thousand members of the Workers (Communist) Party of America.

In February 1929 the 6th Convention of the American organization received a letter from the coordinating body that transmitted Soviet policy to the network of parties throughout the world, the Communist International, the one non-military instrument the Soviets could deploy to project their power abroad. The American party was tiny and marginal in the Comintern's scale of things, but its internal affairs were causing concern. It had taken to factional disputes over the meaning of America's contemporary experience in relation to the prescriptions of the Comintern itself. Everyone appeared guilty of overestimating the significance of American economic expansion, with its alleged basis in technological development: 'The slightest concession to the noisy advertisers of the growth of technique, the slightest vacillation, is an intolerable opportunist mistake', the Executive Committee warned.[72]

When the Comintern cracked the whip its attitude was curiously reminiscent of the Roman Curia's denunciations thirty years earlier of deviationist tendencies in the Catholic Church of the United States. Once

---

[70] George Kennan, *Russia and the West under Lenin and Stalin* (New York, 1960), 190–1, 286–92; Stephen F. Cohen, *Bukharin and the Bolshevik Revolution* (New York, 1973), 359–60.

[71] Kennan, *Russia and the West*, 189.

[72] Letter of February 1929 reproduced in Jane Degras (ed.), *The Communist International, 1919–1943: Documents*, iii: *1929–1943* (London, 1965), 9–16.

again the accusation was of 'Americanization': of over-identification by the local adepts with the dominant values and historical experiences of the land they lived in. In this case they were starting with a favourable and particularist interpretation of the American Revolution, and ending with an invidious view of their nation's recent development along lines that openly subscribed to Bukharin's notions.[73] Unable to understand what was at stake politically (the first stage in the road to Bukharin's liquidation) or analytically (Stalin's insistence that capitalist crisis, war, and revolution were just around the corner), the American leadership was called to account in Moscow in April–May 1929.

There Stalin himself lectured them on their duties, insisting that the work of all parties must be based exclusively on an understanding of:

> ...the general features of capitalism, which are the same for all countries, and not its specific features in any given country. It is on this that the internationalism of the Communist Party is founded...(especially in the Comintern), the holy of holies of the working class.[74]

A specially appointed Comintern jury found the American party leadership guilty of expounding a theory of American 'exceptionalism', a view of the world that separated out the US from the general revolutionary trends so obviously on display elsewhere and, worst of all, risked the unity of the Comintern itself. Their party would have to be reorganized from top to bottom and its leading figures substituted. Stalin in person and in public warned the Americans of the risks of defiance. After sampling these risks, the key officials were divided and scattered from Moscow. The Executive Secretary was expelled from the party and forced to flee incognito in fear for his life. This figure was Jay Lovestone, twenty years later to become America's most formidable trade-union Cold Warrior.[75]

As is well known (to borrow a Stalin phrase), the Soviet Union began to abandon its own form of militant political isolationism from 1934 onwards, and began to seek any form of accommodation in the West that might delay or diminish the impact of the looming world conflict. In this situation all the effort and sacrifice brought on by the Five Year Plan was ever more fervently justified by the regime's leaders. Stalin told the Central Committee of his party that without its heavy industry, the Soviet nation would be defenceless and open to the same fate as China, victim of a Japanese invasion that had brought aggressive imperialism to the very

---

[73] Draper, *American Communism*, 272–5.

[74] This dramatic scene, which in one account included a death threat from Stalin, is recounted ibid. 409–12.

[75] Ibid. 419–29; details in Ted Morgan, *A Covert Life: Jay Lovestone, Communist, Anti-Communist and Spymaster* (New York, 1999), ch. 6.

borders of Russia.[76] The Comintern's leading economist, Evgenii Varga, wrote in 1935 that capitalism was 'now passing through the period of its unevenly proceeding revolutionary collapse', with extreme protectionism, autarchy, and war preparations visible on every side. Rationalization had shown itself to be a mythical good-times philosophy; now mass unemployment and intensified exploitation were the order of the day. Most astonishing was the resort to state control, even fascistization, of economies in a desperate bid to regain stability. The New Deal was the 'most grandiose effort' so far in this sense, but it had introduced competitive currency devaluation, artificial controls on production and consumption, and a scandalous phenomenon unseen in human history: subsidies for the deliberate destruction of agricultural produce. In general, concluded Varga, the only hope for the world was that a second round of revolutions would forestall a second round of wars. Fortunately the 'objective prerequisites' for such an explosion were all in place, declared the Comintern.[77]

+ + + + + +

Stalin's most celebrated antagonist Leon Trotsky, expelled from the Soviet Union in 1929, spent a part of the early 1930s on the run in France. In spite of his many profound differences with his persecutors, he shared with all of them except Stalin intense concern over the dangers of economic nationalism. In early 1934 he provided the readers of the authoritative New York journal *Foreign Affairs* with a vibrant warning of what was at stake:

> Homeward ho! Back to the national hearth! Not only must we correct the mistake of Admiral Perry, who blasted the breach in Japan's 'autarchy,' but a correction must also be made of the much bigger mistake of Christopher Columbus, which resulted in so immoderately extending the arena of human culture.

The political rejection of the economic reality of interdependence was producing 'intolerably acute' tensions between nations, Trotsky declared. The fallout of the Great War had left Europe and America newly dependent on one another, but in ways that had only aggravated the economic stresses caused by their different systems of development. 'Attempts to save economic life by inoculating it with virus from the corpse of nationalism result in blood poisoning which bears the name of fascism.' As a faithful reader of Marx the economist, Trotsky believed that the logic of

---

[76] Stalin, *Questioni del Leninismo*, 79–87 (speech of 7 January 1933).

[77] Eugen Varga, *The Great Crisis and its Political Consequences* (London, 1935), ch. 5 and pp. 169–73; elements in the Comintern thought the US might well be developing towards its own form of fascism; Degras (ed.), *Communist International*, iii. 286; 'objective prerequisites' ibid. 296.

capitalist evolution, or more specifically the law of the productivity of labour that had always driven man to find ways 'to attain the greatest possible quantity of goods with the least expenditure of labor', meant that only a pan-European and world scale of activity was appropriate for the mass-production systems of the contemporary era. The true challenge for Europe in his eyes could be expressed as follows:

> How may the economic unity of Europe be guaranteed, while preserving complete cultural freedom to the peoples living there? How may unified Europe be included within a coördinated world economy?

Rather than face this question, the enfeebled rulers of Europe were trying with lesser or greater desperation to force economic development back into the national framework, using an ever more aggressive form of State capitalism.

Where then did this entirely reactionary development in the Old World leave the United States? There could be no doubt in Trotsky's view that the US had taken the law of the productivity of labour to a new level with its system of 'conveyor, standard or mass production'. But the rest of the world was prepared to defend itself with every means at its disposal, even armed force, rather than face up to the logic of America's experience. This was a choice that would only bring war, ruination, and 'the music of hell'. Eventually 'the basic law of human history must inevitably take revenge on derivative and secondary phenomena', and clear the way for the next world leader:

> Sooner or later American capitalism must open up ways for itself throughout the length and breadth of our entire planet. By what methods? By *all* methods. A high coefficient of productivity denotes also a high coefficient of destructive force. Am I preaching war? Not in the least...

In the meantime decadent fascist nationalism was preparing chaos and devastation everywhere. Competitive capitalism in crisis was 'like a chicken that hatched not a duckling but a crocodile. No wonder she cannot manage her offspring!'[78]

Enter the Führer

In a typical page of the first volume of *Mein Kampf*, which appeared in 1925, Adolf Hitler had used a slightly different metaphor when prophesying his own arrival on the world stage:

> It nearly always takes some stimulus to bring the genius on the scene. The hammer-stroke of Fate which throws one man to the ground suddenly

---

[78] L. Trotsky, 'Nationalism and Economic Life', *Foreign Affairs* (April 1934).

strikes steel in another, and when the shell of everyday life is broken, the previously hidden kernel lies open before the eyes of the astonished world. The world then resists and does not want to believe that the type which is apparently identical with it is suddenly a very different being…[79]

It was of course the great Crash and its consequences in Weimar Germany that provided the vital push Hitler had been waiting for. Historians are united in pointing to the disastrous economic pressures that built up in the country between 1930 and 1932 as the crucial force propelling Hitler to power in January 1933, these and the urge to self-destruction of the state and party system that had half-heartedly tried to build democracy in Germany's unsteady 1920s.[80] But the Nazi leadership did not, it seems, awake to the full significance of the Wall Street Crash until it became clear that it would cause a full-scale banking and industrial crisis in the country. A growing but still marginal political force up to then, Hitler and his party were transformed by the drama, which brought them to the threshold of government from the moment of their first big electoral triumph in September 1930.[81]

In the development of Hitler's world view and his rise to prominence, the American question played what appears at first glance a quite marginal role. It is hardly ever mentioned in the 630-odd pages of *Mein Kampf*, and certainly not in terms of the questions of development it might pose for the future of Germany.[82] On specific issues of policy there were of course violent denunciations. The Versailles Treaty, and the Dawes and Young plans, were all taken as evidence of the fury of the Jews in the latest chapter of their centuries-old drive to a world-engulfing supremacy, a crusade that could count the Bolshevik revolution as another of its successes. The world war itself and especially America's entry into it had of course been developments in the great Jewish plot. Pushed on by this malevolent energy, 'Americans would have girded up their loins anyway, with or without submarines'.[83]

Little wonder that Germany's revival had been manacled from the start. The bankers and the Wall Street speculators behind the reparations plans were of course all assumed to be Jewish, 'the controlling masters of the producers in a nation of one hundred and twenty millions'.

---

[79] A. Hitler, *Mein Kampf* (1943 edn repr., London, 1992), 266.

[80] Wilfried van der Will, 'Culture and the Organization of National Socialist Ideology 1933–1945', in Burns (ed.), *German Cultural Studies*, 105.

[81] Ian Kershaw, *Hitler, 1889–1936: Hubris* (London, 1998), 311, 318, 333.

[82] Ibid. 330, 426; Detlef Junker, 'Hitler's Perception of Franklin D. Roosevelt and the United States of America', in van Minnen and Sears (eds), *FDR and His Contemporaries*, 147–8.

[83] Cit. in Detlef Junker, 'The Continuity of Ambivalence: German Views of America, 1933–1945', in Barclay and Glaser-Schmidt (eds), *Transatlantic Images*, 250.

Fortunately there remained one outstanding American hero, that superior individual who alone had stood unbowed in the face of their onslaught: 'only a single great man, Ford, to their fury still maintains full independence.'[84]

The fundamental quest of course was for an effective, radical, and Germanic response to the challenge of the three modernities, in whatever guise they might appear. As today's specialists have shown, the anti-Weimar right believed that they had solved this conundrum with the formula known now as 'reactionary modernism', a vision that 'claimed that Germany could be technically advanced while remaining true to its soul'. This dream involved appropriating the message of Henry Ford in such a way as to portray his system as one that combined technological progress with a devotion to a hierarchical but enlightened social order. Using this method, devotion to discipline, harmony, and the common good would overcome all the old social clashes of the class war, and provide the values for a collective identity far beyond the blind pursuit of riches and hedonism. At this point the 'romantic, anti-liberal and anti-Western traditions of German nationalism' (Philipp Gassert) might finally be reconciled with the material benefits of scientific development, and a truly fulfilled Germanic *volk* would find a destiny worthy of its name.[85]

Hitler however added his own personal twist to this prospect. In his unpublished *Secret Book* of 1928,[86] the party leader dealt openly with the force of the American inspiration and provided his own reading of the new meaning of interdependence and rising expectations:

> The present-day European dreams of a living standard which he derives as much from the potentialities of Europe as from the actual conditions prevailing in America. International relations have become so easy and close through modern technology and the communication it makes possible, that the European, often without being conscious of it, applies American conditions as a standard for his own life.[87]

The more intense mutual relations between peoples became, so 'the more will living conditions reciprocally leave their mark on each other and seek

---

[84] Hitler, *Mein Kampf*, 583. Comprehensive survey and analysis of the Nazi admiration for Ford and his 'system' in Stefan Johannes Link, 'Rethinking the Ford-NAzi Connection', in Bulletin of the German Historical Instsitute, Fall 2011; readable at http://harvard.academia.edu/StefanLink/Papers/133476/Rethinking_the_Ford-Nazi_Connection.

[85] Grasset, 'Without Concessions', 221, 223–31, which applies the formulations of Jeffrey Herf (*Reactionary Modernism*) to the specific question of Nazi attitudes to the challenge of American modernism.

[86] This dictated work was eventually published in 1961; on its significance Kershaw, *Hitler*, 291–2, D. C. Watt, 'Introduction' to *Mein Kampf*, p. xxviii.

[87] *Hitler's Secret Book* (New York, 1961), 19.

to approximate one another'. This dynamic however would highlight the difference between those who could and those who could not better themselves. Production and productivity were all very well, and lower prices might certainly put 'the individual folk-comrade in a position to own more vital commodities'.[88] But underlying every choice open to the Germans there lay the fundamental problem of sustenance and living space, the one that had driven millions of them to emigrate in the years before the war, to become 'anglicized...and so lost to our people spiritually and ideologically as well'.[89] Only peoples abundantly supplied with land—soil-surface per head of population—could hope to prosper in the world of the future, Hitler insisted, since that would be a universe from which the German industrial economy would be excluded inevitably and forcefully by the British: was that not why they had fought the war?

> The German people's prospects are hopeless. Neither the present living space nor that achieved by a restoration of the borders of 1914 will allow us to lead a life analogous to that of the American people. If we want this, either our people's territory must be considerably enlarged, or the German economy will again have to embark on paths already known to us since the prewar period. Power is necessary in both cases. Specifically, first of all in the sense of a restoration of our people's strength, and then in a military mounting of this strength.[90]

But the Führer's enthusiasms of 1928 never became public, and by the time he came to power himself distinctly different thoughts had taken over. Leaving aside for the moment National Socialist readings of the New Deal, and their effect on Nazi Germany's attitudes to the US from 1933 onwards, a short reflection is required here on another current of thought on the America-as-future question that found in the Third Reich its most comfortable home. This was visible in the anti-bourgeois and anti-materialist line in Nazi thinking, and was articulated by two of the Reich's most distinguished intellectual sympathizers, the philosophers Oswald Spengler and Martin Heidegger. 'There is an inner relationship between Bolshevism and Americanism', Spengler wrote in his 1934

[88] Ibid. 95.

[89] Ibid. 52, 92; for expressions of this concern in Germany at the time of the great emigration, W. T. Stead, 'Americanisation of the World', 67; it was at the root of the new German colonial policy of the time, Stead thought.

[90] *Hitler's Secret Book*, 96; cf. Junker, 'Continuity of Ambivalence', 251–3; the historian who discovered and translated the 'Secret Book', Gerhard Weinberg, points out that the text did foresee a final and definitive war with the US, and that this vision was carried through later in rearmament choices, and in support for Japan; Weinberg, 'Franklin Delano Roosevelt and Adolf Hitler: A Contemporary Comparison Revisited', in Elisabeth Glaser and Hermann Wellenreuther (eds), *Bridging the Atlantic: The Question of American Exceptionalism in Perspective* (Washington DC and Cambridge, 2002), 214–15.

volume *The Year of Decision*, '...life is organized exclusively from the economic side.' The 'Faustian will-to-power' was at work in both of them, 'but translated from organic growth into soulless mechanization'. It dominated every consideration in both societies, and sacrificed every spiritual or cultural resource man had ever possessed for the sake of boundless physical well-being.[91]

This impulse to equate the US and the Soviet Union as the supreme social embodiments of the principle of standardization—the one private in outward form, the other collectivist—had first appeared in French commentaries in the 1920s, and remained a constant in that country at least until the Second World War. 'Between these two gigantic transmitters of constraint, France is still an oasis where a man can breathe a certain air of liberty', intoned a conservative banker at a certain point. 'But make no secret of it: we are threatened.'[92] Italian commentators too denounced the oppressive collectivism dedicated to purely material ends that they perceived in both societies.[93] Spengler took this line of feeling and developed it into a much broader reflection on the relationship between technology and social organization, seeking to demonstrate that in the absence of a clear sense of spiritual duty imposed by farsighted and dauntless leaders, the West was doomed. Spengler saw Russia and America as inevitable outcomes of the logic of the three post-war modernities, with their common Enlightenment roots.[94]

Both Spengler and his admirer Martin Heidegger would have liked to have become inspirational *éminences grises* standing at the shoulder of Hitler, suggests James Ceaser.[95] Neither succeeded, but it was Heidegger who went furthest in expressing hopes that the new regime would save the Western world as a whole by reconnecting 'Being' and national consciousness, and so revitalize Germany's vocation as 'the most metaphysical of nations'.[96] And it was Heidegger who was most successful in creating a

---

[91] Ceaser, *Reconstructing America*, 179; for a full contextualization in the development of anti-materialist thought, Zeev Sternhell, 'Aux sources de l'idéologie fasciste: La révolte socialiste contre le matérialisme', in Yehoshua Arieli and Nathan Rotenstreich (eds), *Totalitarian Democracy and After* (1984 edn repr., London, 2000).

[92] Gagnon, 'French Views', 446–7; Armus, 'Eternal Enemy', 281, passim; Strauss, *Menace in the West*, 89–90, citation ibid. p. 92, n. 29; a particularly violent expression of this sentiment was produced by the novelist Céline in his 1937 pamphlet *Mea Culpa*; for two gentle British versions Bertrand Russell and Dora Russell, *The Prospects of Industrial Civilisation*, p. 8, J. B. Priestley, *Midnight on the Desert: A Chapter of Autobiography* (London, 1937), 122–3.

[93] Nacci, *L'antiamericanismo in Italia negli anni trenta*, ch. 9.

[94] Ceaser, *Reconstructing America*, 175–80; Kroes, *If You've Seen One*, 21.

[95] Ceaser, *Reconstructing America*, 120.

[96] Cit. ibid. 203; on the literary and philosophical context of Heidegger's career at this time, van der Will, 'Culture', 123–7.

type of connection between baleful modernity and the American–Soviet condominium that would endure far beyond the era of the Third Reich. In a series of lectures given in 1935, Heidegger said, among much else:

> From a metaphysical point of view, Russia and America are the same, with the same dreary technological frenzy and the same unrestricted organization of the average man...

They were the predictable outcomes of Western Europe's industrialization experience, with its levelling down, its insistence on 'extension and number', on prosaic routine and outward conformity.[97] The corruption of language, the exaltation of material consumption, and the technical approach to human behaviour and values, as well as the reconfiguration of history for ideological purposes: all these impulses united the two *ersatz* civilizations in Heidegger's world view. Little surprise then that they were to found on the same side in World War II, throughout which the philosopher maintained a degree of support for the Nazi regime until its failure became obvious.[98]

The irony of it all was that not even Nazi Germany could fully resist the irradiant force of American mass culture and the big businesses that stood behind much of it. About 50 books a year on the US appeared during the Nazi era, according to one account. Certain—not all—American advertising techniques were studied intensively and taken over.[99] When Heidegger began to distance himself from the Nazis in the later 1930s, it was partly because he saw them becoming as enthralled as their enemies by modern media and technological development. The American companies Woolworth and General Electric, IBM and General Motors, Ford and Procter & Gamble all either started or expanded their operations under the new regime. The empire of Coca-Cola flourished and even began to imitate the style of Nazism itself. Jazz and Hollywood kept their appeal in spite of government efforts to channel or suppress them.[100] In

---

[97] Ceaser, *Reconstructing America*, 188–9.

[98] Ibid. 209; Heidegger spent no time worrying about 'Americanism' as such, which he considered no more than a catchword that Europeans applied to 'the as-yet-uncomprehended species of the gigantic', and the Americans to their pragmatism. As such it remained 'outside the metaphysical realm', M. Heidegger, *The Question Concerning Technology and Other Essays* (New York, 1977), 135, 153.

[99] Figure reported by Sigmund Skard in his pioneering exploration of 1961 on the spread on 'American Studies' in Europe since the birth of the Republic; the majority—but not all—were written to serve the propaganda purposes of the regime: Skard, *The American Myth and the European Mind: American Studies in Europe, 1776–1960* (Philadelphia, 1961), 78–9; on advertising appropriation, Ross, 'Vision of Prosperity', 67–71; historical debate on the American model in the Nazi era summarized in Schäfer, 'Study of Americanisation', 133–4.

[100] On the ambivalent attitude of the regime towards American popular culture, Junker, 'Continuity of Ambivalence', 255–8; for the remarkable career of Coca-Cola in Germany

1934 the Führer declared that the German must have his cheap automobile just like the American. In 1938 the regime started to build a Ford-inspired plant to produce it. Bewitching images of future prosperity helped to stabilize and legitimize even a regime like the Third Reich. In such a situation what other choice than disaffection lay open to the authentic reactionary modernist, true to the dictates of his soul?[101]

* * * *

The evolution of this functional component of the Third Reich's world outlook reminds us just how far the politics of the American question in Europe could by this time be removed from the specific behaviour of the US as a power, an economy, or a culture. In the 1930s—the last decade of the twentieth century when official America did little of significance to or for Europe (at least not directly)—the romantic, anti-modernist attitude took on an even more forceful life of its own, creating 'powerful symbolic resonances' that might be heard to this day; a rhetoric designed at least in part to work as a form of shock therapy, one that might galvanize the old soul of Europe and reawaken the spirit of the true individual.[102]

But more optimistic and democratic spirits looked at America's achievements in adversity and saw signs of the future that, they thought, the world would find hard to resist. On the basis of a trip along Western highways in 1936, J. B. Priestley paid tribute to the emergence of a trashy but vital new road civilization—'*Gas, Eats, Hot and Cold Drinks:* something like this would be spelt out, in paint by day, in neon lights after dark, all the way from Shanghai to Capetown'. But the same Priestley also saw 'a native genius for large-scale organisation, for concerted effort, for tremendous team work' spreading in Depression-era America. The great new freeway system, the Empire State Building, and above all the stupendous Boulder Dam were the products of a new generation of protagonists,

---

from 1929 onwards, Mark Prendergast, *For God, Country and Coca-Cola* (London, 1994), ch. 13, Jeff Schutts, ' "Die Erfrischende Pause": Marketing Coca-Cola in Hitler's Germany', in Swett et al. (eds), *Selling Modernity*; on the destiny of jazz under Nazism, Michael H. Kater, *Different Drummers: Jazz in the Culture of Nazi Germany* (Oxford, 1992); Savage, *Teenage*, 326–8.

[101] *Hitler's Secret Book*, 98; Hitler's speech opening 1934 Berlin Motor Show cit. in Mazower, *Dark Continent*, 307; *Volkswagen Chronicle*, Historical Notes, Vol. 7 (Wolfsburg, 2003), 4; on the centrality of the motor car to Hitler's view of the future German civilization, Möser, 'Creation of Desire', 218–21; R. J. Overy, *War and Economy in the Third Reich* (Oxford, 1994), ch. 2; in reality not a single Volkswagen reached private hands in the Nazi era, notes Paul Betts, but expectations were set in motion all the same: Betts, 'The New Fascination with Fascism: The Case of Nazi Modernism', *Journal of Contemporary History* (October 2002), 554.

[102] Ceaser, *Reconstructing America*, 189–90, 202; this impulse—and Heidegger's influence—also fed the intensely critical writings on America of the *Esprit* group in Paris; Armus, 'Eternal Enemy', 278.

'the men with the blue prints and the blue jeans'. These were 'new men', building 'a new world, a new way of life'. Of course the Soviets looked to this America for their inspiration. Here they imagined how the 'soul of America under socialism' would develop. But the new men were expressing themselves 'with an ease, force, and natural cohesion beyond Lenin's dreams'. Would the New Deal then be capable of realizing the enormous collective potential these people bore witness to, the possibility of bringing to the world's political and economic problems all the skills they embodied in their triumphs of architecture and of engineering?[103]

[103] Priestley, *Midnight on the Desert*, 54–5, 86–9, 110–12, 124–6.

5

Roosevelt's America:
The Flickering Beacon

DESPERATE REMEDY OR GUIDING LIGHT?

As nations everywhere sought some way out of the ever-deepening shadows of economic misery, defensive nationalism, and even war itself—fears greatly aggravated by the behaviour of Nazism since its triumph in Berlin in early 1933—Franklin D. Roosevelt's defiant new experiment in government inspired intense attention across the world. In Europe meanwhile, there continued to run through much of public opinion 'a phenomenal will to believe in utopia', recalls the historian Mazower. It was an urge that notoriously drove some cultivated minds into the orbit of Fascism, more into sympathy with Soviet Communism, others—such as Bernard Shaw's—into a realm of confusion somewhere between the two.[1] Was this the impulse that provoked such enthusiasm for the New Deal in those who understood that 'capitalism was on trial' (*The Economist* and many others), and who sought a way out of the contemporary muddle that did not involve overturning the entire democratic system?

The last great British utopian, H. G. Wells, was an early admirer of Roosevelt and his effort, its spirit, drive, and direction. Soon the New Deal experiment came to represent for him not just the only hope for the enlightened globalizing revolution of his many dreams, but the last chance for the salvation of *any* sort of open economic life and progress in the industrial world. In 1932 he had written:

> There is, I believe a great and growing stir in the minds of men to fight the sombre destiny that hangs over humanity. The gathering distresses of our race, deepening economic misery, the unrelieved threat of war and the lassitudes of governments are rousing a spirit which is in its essence revolutionary.[2]

---

[1] Mazower, *Dark Continent*, 127; cf. Shaw, 'Little Talk'.
[2] Cit. in Smith, *H. G. Wells*, 303.

If only the organized intelligence of the New Deal could be international-ized and subsumed to the creation of a world community better than the League of Nations, then the worst might be avoided. Unlike lesser peo-ples, who had collapsed into military dictatorships under the weight of the Depression, the Americans were sticking to their Constitution and even its familiar if much ridiculed electoral system. A 'publicist with a world wide audience', as his son recalled, Wells felt it was his duty to bring before opinion everywhere the full significance of the extraordinary performance Roosevelt was directing.[3]

The leading prophet of his time, received in the White House by all but one of the Presidents since Teddy Roosevelt, Wells was delighted by the spirit he found at the centre of every activity in Washington on a visit in early 1934. In his *Experiment in Autobiography* of the same year, the writer recalled his 1906 criticisms of the lack of an idea of the state in America: 'Now they are getting a sense of the state put over them rather rapidly, and they are taking it very ungraciously.' He saw the President as an 'un-limited' person, 'entirely modern' in the openness of his mind and the dynamic of his action. Surrounded by his elite group of enlightened expert advisers—the so-called 'Brains Trust'—the President himself was the central nervous system of the entire enterprise: receiving, expressing, transmitting, combining, and realizing 'exactly what a modern govern-ment ought to be'.[4]

Today Wells's political inheritance seems negligible. A man of universal reputation in the early 1930s, his purely intuitive notions of war and its causes—an over-accumulation of 'social energy' with no organized out-let—appear hopelessly inadequate. But his remedies are not so easily dis-missed, and fed into the politics of the future in Europe in a fashion that left a lasting mark.[5] On the way back from one of his American trips, Wells had written a resounding piece for *Foreign Affairs*. In it he had

---

[3] Wells's old Fabian companion and adversary, George Bernard Shaw, told the Ameri-cans in a famous performance in New York in 1933 to get rid of their 'confounded' Con-stitution, an invitation to anarchy against 'the tyranny of law and order', as he saw it. They should replace it with their own version of socialism, based on the nation's 'irrepressible social instinct, this wonderful surging thing inside itself'; discussion in Spoerri, *Old World and the New*, 165–9.

[4] Wells, *Experiment in Autobiography*, 789–97; cf. John Dizikes, *Britain, Roosevelt and the New Deal: British Opinion, 1932–1938* (New York, 1979), 173–4; Wells had been pondering on the duties of an enlightened elite to modernize government ever since his novel of 1905, *A Modern Utopia*. His updated reflection on the theme is found in *The Open Conspiracy* of 1928. Like many early enthusiasts Wells was soon to be disappointed in the progress of the great experiment, and by 1935—in *The New America: The New World*—he too was denouncing it as a form of neurotic atonement for the overindulgence of the previ-ous era; cf. Conrad, *Imagining America*, 156.

[5] Wells's 1933 volume *The Shape of Things to Come* and its film version *Things to Come* (1936) both received great attention; Smith, *H. G. Wells*, 324–5.

stated his opinion that the general 'state of stress' the world had endured since the Great War was due to the difficulty of passing from an economy of want to one of plenty. It was America's destiny to be the first nation to work out how this transition could be managed:

> The choice before us is war or a new world—a rational liberal collectivist world with an ever rising standard of life and an ever bolder collective enterprise, in science, in art, in every department of living.[6]

Elsewhere in the English-speaking world, a more typical example of the New Deal's influence on the capitalism-on-trial debate can be seen in the writings of Sir Arthur Maitland Steel, a former Minister of Labour and Member of Parliament from the left wing of the British Conservative party. 'If the capitalist system is jettisoned, it will not be because of the merits of others, but because the mass of mankind has lost hope that old order can be improved', judged this Tory, who, unlike his government, was an admirer of the new American response to the crisis.[7]

> The great experiment in the United States...[involves reforms] in industry, in agriculture, in currency, in finance and in public works—experiments which are only possible in a country which is still young, able to repair the effect upon itself of possible mistakes, and careless of the result of such experiments upon neighbouring nations...[8]

Capitalism was facing its supreme test, as its enemies proclaimed and its defenders acknowledged. There was no hope for it if the hardships of the recent years were to be repeated, judged people like Maitland Steel and, in the Labour Party, a leading intellectual like Harold Laski. But now another 'new America' was emerging, said this outlook, confirming the extraordinary energy, youthfulness, and pragmatism of this nation, qualities long known but that were now producing structural and even theoretical innovations to which everyone should pay attention. For the first time, America's semi-mythical civilization—plunged into a misery worse than all but a handful of situations in Europe—appeared to be offering a model of applied politics to correspond to its 1920s teachings in applied economics.[9]

---

[6] 'Civilization on Trial', *Foreign Affairs* (July 1935), 595–9; cf. Smith, *H. G. Wells*, 307–8; in the meantime, said Wells elsewhere, if only the US, Britain, Russia, and France could form a common front for peace, then the worst might be avoided: *Experiment in Autobiography*, 796.

[7] Arthur Steel-Maitland, *The New America* (London, 1934), 206–8.

[8] Ibid. 206.

[9] Laski became a Marxist *and* a keen admirer of Roosevelt during the 1930s. These features, his skills of talking, teaching, and writing, and his energy, gave Laski considerable prestige in the US, a land he considered a model on many levels; Gary Dean Best, *Harold Laski and American Liberalism* (New Brunswick, NJ, 2005), 1–2, 25, 52–9, 85–93; Isaac Kramnick and Barry Sheerman, *Harold Laski: A Life on the Left* (London, 1993), 393–407.

Looking for lessons: The rise of the 'middle way' in Britain

On the last day of 1933 John Maynard Keynes wrote an open letter to the American President:

> Dear Mr President,
> You have made yourself the trustee for those in every country who seek to mend the evils of our condition by reasoned experiment within the framework of the existing social system.
> If you fail, rational change will be gravely prejudiced throughout the world, leaving orthodoxy and revolution to fight it out.
> But if you succeed, new and bolder methods will be tried everywhere, and we may date the first chapter of a new economic era from your accession to office.[10]

In the emergency Keynes added his voice to that of a new group of economists, administrators, and politicians from all three major parties in Britain seeking as urgently as possible a conscious, organized alternative to the apathy and indecision that to them characterized official policy in the crisis, as well as to the extremisms of left and right surging on all sides in Europe. To these people Roosevelt and his actions were shining beacons.[11] Yet the fate of the New Deal in Britain, the nation where cultivated minds probably dedicated more attention to American developments than any other, shows how paradoxical and ambiguous its results would turn out to be.

Like Wilson fifteen years earlier, Roosevelt and his project were embraced most enthusiastically by the progressive moderates in the political spectrum, a small band of people who believed that in the crisis, capitalism and democracy could only be rejoined by an effort of radical reform in favour of social justice and *planned* economic development. The whole would be organized and driven on by the kind of inspired political leadership and governmental energies that had realized prodigies of mobilization in wartime, and which now seemed to be monopolized by the totalitarians. Not by chance, the most enthusiastic of all Roosevelt's would-be emulators in Britain was the former wartime Prime Minister, David Lloyd George, the still famous ex-leader of the Liberal Party. In January 1935, in a wave of publicity, Lloyd George launched his own new programme of planned national reconstruction: *A New Deal for Britain*. It was a political and popular failure.

---

[10] Skidelsky, *John Maynard Keynes*, ii. 492; Roosevelt received Keynes in the White House in May 1934, but there seems to have been little mutual understanding, Skidelsky, *John Maynard Keynes*, ii. 506; Pelling, *America and the British Left*, 134.

[11] Pelling, *America and the British Left*, 133–4; David Reynolds emphasizes though just how small and isolated a group this was; Dimbleby and Reynolds, *An Ocean Apart*, 112.

Quite simply British political culture in the 1930s was not ready for
the sort of determined governmental activism in a framework of parliamentary democracy that Lloyd George's enthusiasm proposed. Although
the trades unions and the most moderate Labourites were keenly interested in importing workable examples from America, true believers in
Socialism would have nothing to do with the old Liberal leader or his
vision. The leading gentleman socialist, Stafford Cripps, derided the plan
as an old-fashioned public works scheme, paying workers 'to make something nobody really wanted very badly...'.

> ...Labour had enough of the control of industrialists....They wanted the
> workers in control, and when Mr. Lloyd George drew the New Deal herring
> across the political track...the workers would realise it was the old red her-
> ring in a new disguise.[12]

Although the National government gave Lloyd George a hearing, the
Prime Minister MacDonald was indifferent, and his Chancellor, Neville
Chamberlain, totally opposed as always to such visions. For the Treasury Minister there could be no question of unbalancing the national
budget on the mere hope that private confidence would thereby take
off, and so overcome the doubts that would inevitably be roused in
banking and official circles everywhere. The conservative *Daily Telegraph*
asked sarcastically: 'Is the wisdom of Washington succeeding better then
the crass ignorance of London?' Was America's performance on unemployment, trade, currency, social insurance any better than Britain's?
'Are they still not relying on colossal loans and piling up colossal
debts?'[13]

As the New Deal zigzagged its way across the western horizon, doubts
began to spread everywhere as to its effectiveness and availability as a
model for any sort of reproduction. On the Left, but not only there, were
the many who thought it might well lurch into an American Fascism if
conditions turned worse. On the business side of the argument were the
sceptics, such as *The Economist*, who could not believe that 'relentless,
searching, expectant pragmatism' alone would supply a lasting solution.
In an October 1936 special survey the magazine commented:

> Relief there has been, but little more than enough to keep the population
> fed, clothed and warmed. Recovery there has been, but only to a point still
> well below the pre-depression level. Reform there has also been, but it is

---

[12] Cit. in Dizikes, *Britain, Roosevelt and the New Deal*, 218–19; cf. Barbara C. Malament, 'British Labour and Roosevelt's New Deal: The Response of the Left and the Unions',
Journal of British Studies (Spring 1978); Pelling, *America and the British Left*, ch. 8;
Dimbleby and Reynolds, *An Ocean Apart*, 112.
[13] Edition of 14 December 1934 cit. ibid. 219.

slight compared with the reformers' blue-prints. The great problems of the country are still un-touched.[14]

Here indeed was the heart of the matter. Was all the mass of New Deal programmes, projects and, propaganda simply a cluster of improvised remedies thrown at the emergency as their authors saw fit? Or was there to be found an underlying consistency in method or objective that would sooner or later bring enduring progress to America's society and its economy, and so bolster all the struggling democracies? At the time, Keynes in his open letter had warned that recovery and reform would not be easy to manage in tandem, and that such innovative agencies as the National Recovery Administration—in comprehensive charge of industrial policy—tended to disguise as recovery what amounted to a programme of reform so radical it risked undermining recovery itself.[15] A fellow Liberal, William Beveridge—later to be the author of the British Welfare State's most celebrated founding document—insisted that the two impulses could not be reconciled. There was no middle way for the emergency; only an orthodox programme of austerity, deflation, and the fearless reduction of public expenditure along the lines embraced by Britain's government of national unity could restore equilibrium.[16]

Today, historians consider it 'trite' to say that Beveridge was right about the fundamental confusion in the New Deal. In a monument of imaginative scholarship of 1998, the American specialist Daniel Rodgers concluded that the significance of all the effort could now be seen in its true, reduced perspective.[17] As was quite clear at the time, economic recovery eluded Roosevelt and his team: that came only with the onset of war. But even the reform element too was much less original and daring than it had once appeared: 'What [the New Dealers] did best was to throw into the breach, with verve and imagination, schemes set in motion years or decades before' elsewhere. So the historical meaning of the experience was not to be found inside it, but outside, in the steady build up of progressive social policy in Europe, which now, in the great emergency, finally found its window of opportunity in America.[18]

'The New Deal was a great, explosive release of the pent-up agenda of the progressive past', writes Rodgers, a vision developed from German

---

[14] Burnet, *America 1843–1993*, 127, 120.

[15] Ibid. 493; in 1935 the NRA was declared unconstitutional by the Supreme Court and forced to close.

[16] Dizikes, *Britain, Roosevelt and the New Deal*, 180–1; cf. Pelling, *America and the British Left*, 138–9.

[17] Daniel T. Rodgers, *Atlantic Crossings: Social Politics in a Progressive Age* (Cambridge, Mass., 1998), ch. 10; on Beveridge, ibid. 415.

[18] Ibid. 415–16.

social insurance, British housing policy, Danish farm support, Australian industrial tribunals, English garden suburbs, and much else besides.[19] With the conventional authority expressed by traditional institutions—business, press, Republican and Democratic conservatism of all kinds—quite discredited, a new elite of policy experts weaned on European reformism seized its chance. A rare event occurred in the flow of modernizing notions across the Atlantic: although not organized as such, the traffic was openly two-way and relatively balanced. Thinking of British social policy in 1938, Roosevelt himself told the journalist Anne O'Hare McCormick: 'In five years I think we have caught up twenty years.... If liberal government continues another ten years we ought to be contemporary somewhere in the late Nineteen Forties.'[20]

These realities did not escape sceptics in nations like Britain. Following on from the caustic remarks already mentioned, the *Daily Telegraph* commented that most of the new American social legislation had been 'established here for two generations'. So the New Deal had nothing to teach: 'the U.S. has imitated, not led; it is in our wake, not our van.' Specific measures produced in London to fight the slump, such as help for the farm, coal, textile, and shipping industries, although often similar to American interventions, owed nothing to that example.[21]

And yet the national political culture was permanently affected by Roosevelt's great effort. Moderate reformists of a new generation continued to be inspired by it and took heart. The Middle Way did not go away. One of the most significant of future Conservative Prime Ministers, Harold Macmillan, produced a book of that title in 1938, and placed himself at the head of a movement of opinion in favour of planned economic reconstruction led by a renewed government machine. The group believed in developing the expertise of an emerging managerial class, and, in emphasizing the need for far greater sophistication and knowledge in economic affairs, soon left Wells behind, while anticipating the impact of

---

[19] On the New Dealers' attention to Swedish experiments in social democracy, Dag Blanck, 'Television, Education, and the Vietnam War: Sweden and the United States During the Postwar Era', in Alexander Stephan (ed.), *The Americanization of Europe: Culture, Diplomacy and Anti-Americanism after 1945* (New York, 2006), 107.

[20] Rodgers, *Atlantic Crossings*, 428; Roosevelt cit. at p. 428; cf. also examples cited in Dimbleby and Reynolds, *An Ocean Apart*, 112; the Secretary of Labour in Roosevelt's Cabinet, Frances Perkins, recalled that there had been 'great shock' when the President had first pointed out how far behind Europe the US was in the field of social security, Perkins, 'Social Security Here and Abroad', *Foreign Affairs* (April 1935), 373.

[21] Dizikes, *Britain, Roosevelt and the New Deal*, 219; on the contrasts and parallels between the New Deal and British government economic policies, John A. Garraty, *The Great Depression* (New York, 1986), 216–17.

Keynes. Keynes's controversial new *General Theory of Employment, Interest and Money* appeared in 1936.[22]

Roosevelt's inspiration in Continental Europe: the Popular Front as 'France's New Deal'

Given the stagnation and corruption of French public life in these years, only an articulate minority, as in Britain, could recognize the force of the new American experiment, and try to imagine how its intuitions might be applied to their own society at some point in a revived future.[23] The debate in public opinion from the 1920s on the wider choices of modernization thereby took a new turn, trying to reconcile the earlier judgements with diagnoses of American experience in the Depression which could be useful to defend or to change France's familiar ways of life. The outpouring of journalism, travel commentary, and social analysis on all things American continued, but deciding what they might mean for the future development of *la Patrie* now assumed a new, politically radicalized urgency.[24]

The historical surveys of today show, not surprisingly, that contemporary French analyses of the New Deal while numerous, were highly selective and designed to support a variety of ideologies and positions under debate at that time on the domestic scene.[25] The new National Recovery Administration received concentrated attention because it seemed to presage the State takeover of all productive life as experimented under totalitarianism. *Le Figaro* called it the 'Bolshevization of America'.[26] The Tennessee Valley Authority—a massive rural development scheme centring on electrification—had no parallels in Europe and so was largely ignored. The monetary reforms involving deliberate inflation, wide-ranging subsidies, and controlled devaluation were universally condemned (just as they were in the US). The questions left open for argument then concerned such problems as whether the New Deal with all its economic priorities reflected a shift in the balance between Wall Street and

---

[22] For the story of the 'Next Five Years Group', Garraty, *Great Depression*, 223–32; Pelling, *America and the British Left*, 135–6.

[23] For a comprehensive overview of national life in this period, Weber, *Hollow Years*; on the emergence of a new technocratic minority in these years, Nord, *France's New Deal*, 25–49.

[24] Galloux-Fournier, 'Un regard sur l'Amérique', 320; Michela Nacci, *La barbarie del comfort: Il modello di vita americano nella cultura francese del '900* (Milan, 1996), ch. 4; Kuisel, *Ernest Mercier*, 12–14; Donald C. Allen, *French Views of America in the 1930s* (New York, 1979), 264–5.

[25] The following paragraphs are based on Nacci, *La barbarie del comfort*; Strauss, *Menace in the West*, ch. 15, and Allen, *French Views*.

[26] Cit. in Emil Lengyel, *The New Deal in Europe* (New York, 1934), 299.

Washington, or was something quite new; whether this was young America again asserting its vigour or a new maturity at work. Had the nation's machine civilization learned the limits of its development, for example, by rediscovering the importance of the land, agriculture, and farmers, realities that old Europe had never forgotten.

In this sort of context, the episode of the Socialist-led Popular Front of 1936–7 can be read as a short-lived and ambiguous attempt to build a distinctive French synthesis of the two impulses of recovery and reform, using selected elements from the New Deal's inspiration. 'America was as much a symbol for an attitude as the exemplar of a policy', writes the specialist Julian Jackson. 'The argument [in Popular Front circles on America]…was not only about how to overcome the problems of the Depression, it was also about the present and future of French society and civilization.'[27] The Front's leader Léon Blum, the most famous of French Socialist leaders before World War II, never missed an opportunity to express his love and admiration for Roosevelt, judging that: 'Roosevelt's boldness has enabled him to change his methods when he recognized that the desired ends had not been achieved. Thus nothing is definitive.' In this way, notes Jackson, the US President's limitless pragmatism 'became Blum's model'.[28]

Accounts of these times have generally tended to separate out the continuous 1930s debate on America's evolution from the specific drama of the Popular Front. In contrast, Jackson's studies on Depression-era France show how bringing the two together helps explain why the politics of modernization in that country have so often revolved around cultural conflicts on the meaning of American innovations great and small. The 1920s perception in which America was seen as prosperous, materialistic, and invidiously modern, gave way to a Depression-era nation that struck progressive French observers for its ability to produce a revolutionary political experiment in a time of crisis, one that seemingly subverted the rules of its own system, while yet declaring undying faith in liberal capitalism.[29] Seeing themselves as both the doctors and the inheritors of a French capitalism in its death throes, the leaders of the Popular Front disputed whether or not the New Deal 'model' might be considered

[27] Julian Jackson, *The Politics of Depression in France, 1932–1936* (Cambridge, 1985), 223.

[28] Blum's speech extolling Roosevelt's victory in the 1936 elections is reproduced in Blum, *L'histoire jugera* (Paris, 1945); his enthusiasm on this occasion hit the American Ambassador particularly forcefully: episode recalled in J. Jackson, *The Popular Front in France: Defending Democracy, 1934–1938* (Cambridge, 1988), 159; the citation opens a chapter on 'the Blum New Deal'; Blum cit. ibid. 169.

[29] Jackson, *Politics of Depression*, 222–3; for the comments of the leading novelist and America-watcher André Maurois, Allen, *French Views*, 254–5.

acceptable as a sort of intermediary regime on the way to full Socialism. Some felt it anticipated a new kind of planned capitalism, organized by the State around the control of credit and key industries.[30] In its brief, frenzied life (May 1936–June 1937) the Popular Front faced crises over the value of the Franc and its industrial policy, over the war danger and rearmament, over social reform and parliamentary politics.[31] It raised huge hopes and brought bewildering disappointment. Its crucial economic and financial policies failed to pull the country out of the Depression, and yet raised near-hysterical opposition on the Right. Its milestone reforms in favour of collective bargaining and the 40-hour week (partly New Deal inspired), as well as paid holidays for workers (adapted from Nazi Germany), all ended by being dismantled or scaled back. Not Marxian and all but unaware of Keynes, its reformism would derive much of its faith and energy from the effort to evolve a pragmatic response to the crisis, referring ever more explicitly—in spite of its revolutionary aspirations—to the real or imagined achievements of the New Deal.[32]

A distinctive Popular Front speciality was the notion of an implied social contract between the working class and the 'progressive' sections of the middle class for the sake of reform, a vision with a long future ahead of it, and not only in France. Although used to justify theoretically the Communist–Socialist alliance at the heart of the Popular Front, America was thought to offer proof of its practical potential, serving to obscure the abandonment of any truly revolutionary perspective in favour of immediate advantages (hence the pro-New Deal leanings of the national trade unions, as in Britain). This effort of projecting some of the emerging categories of French left-wing political culture on to American reality was the obverse of the more common practice of trying to fit developments in the US into familiar French conceptions of the world.[33] The New Deal, and the Popular Front opportunity, provided stimulating new challenges to these practices.

Less materialistic but more nationalistic, certainly more self-conscious and disciplined, the American nation had unexpectedly supplied an en-

---

[30] Garraty, *Great Depression*, 232; Jackson, *Popular Front*, 59–60; Allen, *French Views*, 264; for the evolution of thought on economic planning in 1930s France, R. Kuisel, *Capitalism and the State*, ch. 4.

[31] 'The French New Deal never had a chance since the government was tied on the crucial question of currency', (i.e. the Franc's link to gold), judged the Viennese economist Polanyi in a classic work of 1944, *The Great Transformation* (1944 edn repr., New York, 1957), 229.

[32] As the New Deal waxed and waned so did the faith of Popular Front leaders in its relevance; commentators on the Right oscillated between denouncing the Popular Front's revolutionary tendencies *and* its dedication to the American model, which it said was quite inappropriate in France; Allen, *French Views*, 274–6.

[33] Cf. ibid. 119–20.

tirely different understanding of the relationship between prosperity and democracy, under a capitalism that elsewhere had either broken down or been thoroughly discredited.[34] The good times had shown how private affluence could legitimize and renew democracy as no other force; now in the crisis it was democracy's job to repay the favour.[35] But what could the relevance of such a 'deal' be for a French productive and political system that was so exhausted and conservative, apparently unable to rise to the challenge of saving itself? If successful, where would it leave the hopes for a proper, working-class led revolution that to most on the Left seemed the only prospect worth struggling for? As elsewhere in Europe, history would provide answers to these questions only after World War II, when a second, more heroic reconstruction period finally opened, and a new French elite began to build its own 'middle way'.[36]

The New Deal's greatest attraction: The President

It was of course not the New Deal project but Roosevelt himself, because of his endeavour, creativity, and courage in so many departments, his highly visible and massive assumption of moral responsibility, who succeeded in conquering the enthusiasm of the majority in Europe. For the first time since Wilson a democratic leader had emerged who, against all the odds of his case, had found a thoroughly modern way to fuse his own person with the message he intended to convey. As his admirer Anne McCormick wrote: 'the New Dealer has become so completely both interpreter and interpretation that when Europe now looks towards the United States it focuses its entire attention on the White House.'[37]

The British were quickest to notice the difference, since Roosevelt's Inaugural speech of 1933 was the first of its kind to be transmitted live by

---

[34] Two other economic experiments in Europe that could claim some parentage to the New Deal were those in Belgium and Sweden; on the former, Charles Roger, 'A "New Deal" for Belgium', *Foreign Affairs* (July 1935); on Sweden, Lengyel, *New Deal in Europe*, ch. 15 (this book, by a Hungarian expatriate economist, mainly concentrates on the totalitarian states and the common features they shared in their efforts to go beyond capitalism and parliamentarianism).

[35] But this effort was doomed from the beginning, said Karl Polanyi, by the prevailing orthodoxies concerning self-regulating markets and currency stabilization; *Great Transformation*, 232–4.

[36] This is the main theme of Nord, *France's New Deal*, which emphasizes the continuities of technocratic personalities through the 1930s crises, the Vichy experience and the Resistance, finally emerging triumphant at the moment of Liberation; ibid. ch. 3; see Chapter 6, p. 246 *passim*.

[37] 'Roosevelt as Seen from Abroad', 20 May 1934, in Marion Turner Sheehan (ed.), *The World at Home: Selections from the Writings of Anne O'Hare McCormick* (New York, 1956), 206; for Roosevelt's transforming effect on political communications in his time, Giuliana Muscio, *Hollywood's New Deal* (Philadelphia, 1997), 20–35.

radio into their homes. The well-known diplomat and social commentator Duff Cooper said:

> Even today the ordinary Englishman would hesitate to name the King or President of half a dozen foreign countries, but there is not one home in a million where the name of President Roosevelt is not a household word. The radio has brought him to countless firesides and he is certainly the first President of the United States whose voice has been familiar to Englishmen. In that voice they have heard expression given to sentiments which they recognized as their own, and they have rejoiced at the vision and courage which inspired the speaker.[38]

Elsewhere Roosevelt's ceaseless educational efforts via the radio, his mastery of the press conference, his presence in the new talking newsreels, all produced similar effects. In a famous conversation, Stalin told H. G. Wells of his appreciation for the President's visible 'initiative, courage and determination'. Although a full-blooded capitalist who would never change the class basis of his system (Wells's assertions to the contrary notwithstanding), he was one of its strongest figures.[39]

Mussolini saw an admirable reflection of his own 'intensive culture of dictatorship' in Roosevelt's style, a manner cultivated with 'technique and single-mindedness'. But the American President even trumped the leader of Fascism on his own territory. In an often-quoted passage of Carlo Levi's fictionalized memoir of internal exile *Christ Stopped at Eboli*, the antifascist writer and painter recalled how rare in reality were images of the Duce in the peasant houses he shared in the mountains of the south. Instead 'only Roosevelt and the Madonna of Viggiano never failed to be present'. The Madonna appeared 'fierce, pitiless, mysterious', while the President in contrast looked out from a colour print with his 'sparkling eyes, behind gleaming glasses and hearty grin…'. He appeared as '…a sort of all-powerful Zeus, the benevolent and smiling master of a higher sphere'.[40]

In Paris the novelist André Maurois was one of those who saw most quickly how Roosevelt's style amplified the substance of what he was doing:

---

[38] Cit. in Sheehan (ed.), *World at Home*, 305–6; for Churchill's and Laski's celebrations, ibid. 308.

[39] New Statesman and Nation, *Stalin–Wells Talk: The Verbatim Record and a Discussion* (London, 1934), 6.

[40] Mussolini cit. in Gentile, 'Impending Modernity', 18–19; cf. Vaudagna, 'Mussolini and FDR', 162–3; Levi, *Christ Stopped at Eboli*, 122; (for Hitler and Nazism's early appreciation of Roosevelt's outlook, Junker, 'Hitler's Perception', 150; Garraty, *Great Depression*, 205–7; Nicholas Halasz, *Roosevelt Through Foreign Eyes* (Princeton, 1961), 51, 69, 77–8, 82–3.)

People thought less about the reality of the acts than about the energy of the decision, and the novelty of the experience.... This was an incredible adventure.... One was living in a mad world, but one was living.[41]

The political journalist Saint Jean sounded a note of envy when he suggested that Rooseveltism expressed just the sort of strength that was lacking in contemporary France: '[it] is not a doctrine...all things considered, it only represents a pure manifestation of energy.' The professor of American civilization at the Collège de France, Bernard Faÿ, asserted that Roosevelt's intuitive feel for action came not from his economic understanding or any sort of administrative ability, but from his rapport with the American people. This was his 'true element...it is of them he thinks, it is on them he relies for support, it is to them he looks'. They were the source of his energy, wrote a leading French correspondent in the US, 'a force which is no doubt his own...but which is identified to something passing him by: the spirit of a people who want to feel they are on the march towards a better world.'[42]

There were echoes of the emotional and symbolic impact of Wilson, Ford, and Lindbergh in the *New York Times*'s description of the celebrations in Europe that accompanied Roosevelt's overwhelming victory in 1936: 'Each country in its exaggerated nationalism pictured the triumphant President as one of its heroes...' Dictatorships and democracies alike had joined the chorus of praise, each for its own reasons, but it was his towering place in the popular imagination that was so striking to the New York paper:

Somehow the President's personality has crossed the ocean, leaped all Europe's barriers of language and tradition and made the common man here believe in him. He is liked by millions who are utterly ignorant of the things he has done or the policies he stands for.[43]

Ten years after Roosevelt's death in 1945, the distinguished historian and philosopher Isaiah Berlin was able to recall how:

He was one of the few statesmen in the twentieth or any other century who seemed to have no fear at all of the future.... As the skies of Europe grew darker...he seemed to the poor and the unhappy in Europe a kind of benevolent demigod who alone could and would save them in the end. His moral authority, the degree of confidence which he inspired outside his own country—far more beyond America's frontiers than within them at all times—has no parallel.[44]

---

[41] Lengyel, *New Deal in Europe*, 286.

[42] Cit. in Allen, *French Views*, 251, 256.

[43] McCormick in Sheehan (ed.), *World at Home*, 215–16; *New York Times*, 7 November 1936 cit. in Halasz, *Roosevelt Through Foreign Eyes*, 74–5.

[44] Isaiah Berlin, 'Roosevelt Through European Eyes', *The Atlantic* (August 1955), cits. at pp. 68, 69.

TOWARDS THE NEXT WAR, AND BEYOND IT

Public enemy no. 1

The Economist too celebrated Roosevelt's 1936 victory, and gave him credit for capturing something of that spirit that elsewhere had been corrupted into Fascism. But the British weekly hoped that the President's imagination would now care to look outside his native land for its next challenge: 'it is even conceivable that he may venture to act upon the belief that a great nation such as the United States should have a foreign policy.' Anne McCormick invited Roosevelt to present the US 'as an example of a truth that must be spectacularly demonstrated', showing how to *make democracy succeed*. She expected that just as reform and recovery had been the dominant themes of the first term, now the defence of peace and democracy would be uppermost.[45]

Organized as it is around a small series of old, tight-knit questions—appeasement, isolationism, preparedness—the intense controversy that continues to surround Roosevelt's foreign policies of the late 1930s needs to be largely set aside if we are to understand the fate of the America-as-future question in the decisive few years leading up to the formal US entry into World War II, in December 1941. Seen from this perspective, the Presidential efforts to prepare the American nation for the risk of war appear as less significant than the question of how Roosevelt and his advisers began to think about constructing an alternative world to the one being dragged down to its final destruction in Europe. It is easy to show that the US had identified its key aspirations for the post-war universe well before entering the conflict, and that the general direction they took was recognized by a consensus extending significantly beyond the grounds of the White House. Roosevelt's Four Freedoms speech came in January 1941. A hardly less celebrated pronouncement—the declaration of 'The American Century' by the founder of *Time* and *Life* magazines, the Republican Henry Luce—was offered to public opinion only a few weeks later.[46] Then there was Lend-Lease (March 1941) and the Atlantic Charter (August). So how did the vague, remote, and ineffectual posturings of the Roosevelt administration in the face of the European crisis turn in so short a time—three to four years—into such a formidable new American will-to-power?

[45] *The Economist*, 7 November 1936; McCormick in Sheehan (ed.), *World at Home*, 290, 297.

[46] In 1939 Walter Lippmann had challenged the nation to abandon its timidity and indecision—perfectly reflected in Roosevelt's day-to-day foreign policy making, in his view—and embrace its future at the vanguard of Western civilization: *The American Destiny*, a *Life* reprint (June 1939).

By the late 1930s an intense public debate was developing in America on the nation's rights and duties in a civilization heading towards war. Rather like its equivalent earlier in the century, this started in narrow, elite circles. But it ended by being a great deal more democratic than the 1900s version. It remained meritocratic as long as it was channelled through such institutions as the authoritative Council on Foreign Relations, founded in 1918, and whenever it turned to the sort of economic expertise the New Deal favoured. But the discussion turned democratic after the Nazi outbreak in September 1939, when it expanded into a vast public discussion that lasted for the rest of the war. Eventually it would include journalists and philosophers, publicists, academics, businessmen, the heads of churches, bankers, farm and union leaders, as well as men and women from all over the voluntary sector. The journalist Clarence Streit's *Union Now*, for instance, offered an early one-man analysis of the causes of totalitarian aggressiveness, and included a plea for world government based on extending an American-style constitution to the leading democracies of the West. A best-seller when it appeared in 1939, it eventually fed into the currents that developed the American version of Atlanticism.[47]

What made Franklin Roosevelt's task in concentrating the force of American experience on the world's crises so much harder than that of his cousin Theodore (or even Wilson), was of course the 'isolationist' political culture that so dominated organized public opinion in the 1930s. This nationalistic creed of self-sufficiency, and the corresponding refusal of large parts of the electorate to accept limitations on national sovereignty, seemed to have become—ever since Wilson's humiliation—the default setting of the American popular temper.[48] Between 1935 and 1937 Roosevelt signed into law the infamous Neutrality Acts, which limited very strictly the effective economic and political aid an American President could give either side in an international dispute. The legislation not only gave the world advance notice of American policy whenever a war broke out, but convinced European statesmen that Washington could not be counted on to support any solution to a given crisis. In 1940 Roosevelt won re-election on promises that included a pledge not to send his country's young men into a foreign conflict, and only by extreme dissembling

[47] C. Streit, *Union Now* (New York, 1939); data on Streit from *Current Biography* (New York, 1951), 552–4; on the origins and impact of *Union Now*, Heald, *Transatlantic Vistas*, 220–2.

[48] The classic study of William L. Langer and S. Everett Gleason, *The Challenge to Isolation, 1937–1940* (New York, 1952), opens with a discussion of 'the popular temper'; perspective seventy years on offered in Warren Kimball, 'The Sheriffs: FDR's Postwar World', in David B. Woolner et al. (eds), *FDR's World: War, Peace and Legacies* (London, 2008), 93–5.

and deviousness did the occupant of the White House manage to balance this stance with his efforts to help embattled France and Britain.[49]

But as historians started pointing out not long after the war was won, 1930s isolationism was supremely an anti-European phenomenon. 'On all sides', wrote Langer and Gleason in 1952, 'it was felt again that the European system was basically rotten, that war was endemic on that continent, and that somehow the Europeans had only themselves to blame for their plight.' A letter-writer from the Midwest to *The Economist* at the time of the Munich conference in September 1938 warned: 'Don't try sell us a front-line position in a European war.'[50] Meanwhile America's involvements with other parts of the world, particularly the Caribbean, Latin America, and the Asia region, were becoming much more significant. As the prominent political commentator Walter Lippmann pointed out in 1935, 'America is isolationist as to continental Europe, but it has never been and is not now isolationist in the region of the Caribbean or the Pacific Ocean.'[51]

While relations with Japan involved the most pressing problems of security and trade, the new and constructive attitude to Latin America— culminating in the expansion of Hoover's 'Good Neighbour' policy of benevolent cooperation from 1933 onwards—was meant to have long-term, strategic value. Articulated by convinced anti-Europeanists high up in the State Department, it persuaded Roosevelt that the defence of Western civilization must start with the consolidation of an all-American hemisphere, a vision legitimized historically by Thomas Jefferson's view of the Americas as a universe separate and superior to the corrupt Old World, and then James Monroe's Doctrine of 1823. In the short term, writes the American specialist Harper, this attitude 'meant preventing Europe's internecine quarrels from engulfing the New World', while using ever-stronger language to alert domestic public opinion as to how serious was the risk that this threat could turn into reality.[52]

In the best-known of the speeches Roosevelt employed on this mission, delivered in Chicago in October 1937, the President declared the neces-

[49] Dimbleby and Reynolds, *An Ocean Apart*, 116–24; cf. D. Reynolds, *From Munich to Pearl Harbour: Roosevelt's America and the Origins of the Second World War* (Chicago, 2001).

[50] Langer and Gleason, *Challenge to Isolation*, 13–14; *The Economist*, 17 September 1938.

[51] W. Lippmann, 'Britain and America', *Foreign Affairs* (April 1935), 368; for an alternative historical view, Akira Iriye, *The Cambridge History of American Foreign Relations*, iii: *The Globalizing of America, 1913–1945* (Cambridge, 1993), 139–44; the exclusively anti-European thrust of American 'isolationism' is emphatically reaffirmed in Boyce, *Great Interwar Crisis*, 11, 36, 78, *passim*.

[52] John L. Harper, *American Visions*, 54–60, 64–9.

sity of placing in 'quarantine' those nations afflicted by the contagion of war. But there was an underlying rationale in the world view revealed on this occasion that while recognizing how dangerous were the emergencies of Europe, looked beyond them:

> There is a solidarity and interdependence about the modern world, both technically and morally, which makes it impossible for any nation completely to isolate itself from economic and political upheavals in the rest of the world, especially when such upheavals appear to be spreading and not declining.[53]

Such was the force of isolationist protest that the White House immediately abandoned the call for action that the speech implied, and so came to rely ever more heavily on diplomacy by public gesture and private stealth to make its preferences known abroad. Yet the concept of interdependence announced by Roosevelt on this occasion was not one of his typically casual remarks. He came to see it as the key to a reformed world order, which starting from the example of a peaceful, unified western hemisphere, might eventually bring hope and solace to distraught humanity everywhere.

Interdependence: Where economics and politics met

The Roosevelt administration knew that whatever the rights and wrongs of the European debt saga, it had played a major role in precipitating the great Crash and then aggravating the Depression, when the backwash from Europe's crisis hit American trade, industry, and employment. The man in Washington who worried most about all this was Secretary of State Cordell Hull, an outwardly genteel southern veteran of Congressional politics who had long cherished his own version of Wilsonism, and how America's place in the world should function. In his memoirs, Hull recalled that America's share of world trade had declined from 13.8 per cent to 9.9 per cent between 1929 and 1933; business with Latin America in 1933 was a fourth what it had been in 1929, while exports of high-visibility products like cars were down from $541.4 million to $90.6 million.[54] To Hull, a contemporary foreign policy demanded recognition that the economic and political dimensions of interdependence must be managed together:

> To me it seemed virtually impossible to develop friendly relations with other nations in the political sphere so long as we provoked their animosity in the

---

[53] Cit. in Langer and Gleason, *Challenge to Isolation*, 18.
[54] C. Hull, *The Memoirs of Cordell Hull*, i (New York, 1948), 354, 308.

economic sphere. How could we promote peace with them while waging war on them commercially?[55]

The Smoot–Hawley tariff act had provoked 'formal and emphatic diplomatic protests' from thirty-four nations, the Secretary recalled, and many of them had gone on to open retaliation. The worst case was Great Britain, which in 1932 had finally abandoned its apparently immortal commitment to free trade, and erected tariff walls around its entire empire, including the Dominions. Based on long-held convictions stemming from his understanding of English and local free-trade sages, it became Hull's life mission to fight these trends and promote trade liberalization with every means at his disposal.[56] The effects of the 1930s rivalries in economic nationalism in Europe and Asia only confirmed his beliefs, and as he remained in office longer than any contemporary Secretary of State (until 1944), he was able to develop an American tradition and culture in trade policy that left a lasting mark. Of all the New Deal strategic innovations that carried through to the post-war world, this was one of the most distinctive, enabling the world and the US itself to forget just how intensely protectionist America had been until Hull's era.[57]

Both Roosevelt and Hull explained the rise of the dictatorships in overwhelmingly economic and deterministic terms. They took seriously the arguments the Nazis and Fascists liked to make about the grievances the 'have-not' nations felt towards the 'haves', and casting their perceptions of Japanese imperialism back on to Europe, they took for granted that a fair share of world trade and access to raw materials was what they all wanted underneath. They were well aware that the US and the UK together controlled three-quarters of the globe's minerals, and, with France, 33 per cent of world trade.[58] There was no notion for a European settlement that did not include a reference to raw materials and trade, and even when

---

[55] Ibid. 355.

[56] Anthony Howe, 'Free Trade and the International Order: The Anglo-American Tradition, 1846–1946', in Leventhal and Quinault (eds), *Anglo-American Attitudes*, 155–8; Randall B. Woods, 'FDR and the New Economic Order', in Woolner et al. (eds), *FDR's World*, 176–7; for a spirited denunciation of Hull's 'obsession', Donald Cameron Watt, *How War Came: The Immediate Origins of the Second World War, 1938–1939* (New York, 1989), 126–7.

[57] Hull, *Memoirs*, vol. i, chs 26, 27; the Library of Congress conserves the pamphlets of the Commercial Policy Series, which from 1934 to 1945 spelled out the steps that Hull and his colleagues thought should lead to the creation of a renewed international economic order; in practice of course the US remained highly protectionist, only beginning to dismantle its own tariff walls very gradually from the opening of the GATT (General Agreement on Tariffs and Trade, 1947) era onwards; see Chapter 8.

[58] Rosenberg, *Spreading the American Dream*, 176; Boyce, *Great Interwar Crisis*, 10 (figs from second half of 1920s); cf. Jonathan Marshall, *To Have and To Have Not: Southeast Asian Raw Materials and the Origins of the Pacific War* (Berkeley, 1995), chs 1, 7.

visiting Mussolini and Hitler after war had broken out, in early 1940, the President's emissary Sumner Welles invariably returned to this question.[59] After all if Soviet Russia was not one of the 'war-mongering... bandit... jingoist' nations (Hull) in the 1930s, was this not because the Russians had all the raw materials they could need in their own vast territory?[60]

But that still left to be explained how tiny extremist groups such as the Fascists and the Nazis (and the Bolsheviks for that matter) could become mass movements and take over great nations. Here again it was Hull who spelled out the rationale that would sink deepest into the American official mind. By the time ideological and psychological dimensions had been added to it, it would go on to become one of the key orthodoxies of the Cold War, and beyond. Hull told the British Ambassador in early 1936:

> The most incomprehensible circumstance in the whole modern world is the dominating ability of individuals or one man to arouse the mental processes of the entire population of a country, as in Germany and Italy, to the point where overnight they insist upon being sent into the frontline trenches without delay. When people are employed and they and their families are reasonably comfortable and hence contented, they have no disposition to follow agitators and to enthrone dictators.[61]

Hull had already berated the Italian Ambassador for the invasion of Ethiopia, asking him why Mussolini had not invested $100 million in the country instead of conquering it and spending far more. Now he told the British diplomat that if only Italy had been able to keep up her pre-crisis exports, there would probably have been no military campaign. As for the future, if only a $20 billion increase in international trade could be engineered, and investment to provide work for 12 to 14 million people, then this might make the whole difference between war and peace in Europe.[62] In his memoirs, published in the year the Marshall Plan started, Hull enlarged on the lessons he saw in his long experience:

[59] Rosenberg, *Spreading the American Dream*, 176–7; S. Welles, *Time for Decision* (New York, 1944), 85–6 (conversation with Mussolini), 105–6 (conversation with Hitler).

[60] Stalin too saw the raw materials question as crucial in explaining the aggressiveness of Germany, Italy, and Japan; speech to the 18th Congress of the Communist Party of the Soviet Union, 10 March 1939, in G. Stalin, *Questioni del Leninismo*, 307; but his apologists insisted that the Soviet Union was a pacific nation because it had eliminated the contradictions of capitalism: 'it is utterly senseless to think of a policy of war being adopted by a proletarian state', Bukharin told the readers of *Foreign Affairs* in July 1936 (shortly before being purged); N. Bukharin, 'Imperialism and Communism', *Foreign Affairs* (July 1936), 563–77.

[61] Hull, *Memoirs*, i. 521; comparable reflections in Walter Lippmann, *The Method of Freedom* (New York, 1934).

[62] Hull, *Memoirs*, i. 439, 521.

A people driven to desperation by unemployment, want, and misery, is a constant threat of disorder and chaos, both internal and external. It falls an easy prey to dictators and desperadoes.

In so far as we make it easier for ourselves and everyone else to live, we diminish the pressure on any country to seek economic betterment through war.

The basic approach to the problem of peace is the ordering of the world's economic life so that the masses of the people can work and live in reasonable comfort.

In the long term this meant developing in systematic fashion the promise of mass consumption that pioneering thinkers had signalled in the teens and twenties, as we have seen, to be the unique American contribution to humanity's material progress. New Deal thinkers in business, government, and economic research now began to take on this challenge with specific organizations built for the purpose.[63] In the meanwhile, Hull's diagnosis pushed him to start the comprehensive removal of all barriers to fair and equal international trade. When the Secretary of State obtained from Congress his pioneering Trade Agreements Act in 1934, he felt he was at the very least setting off 'a general movement in the direction of international economic sanity'.[64]

Some anticipations of the future

Through gritted teeth, the British eventually signed a Trade Agreement with the US in 1938, but for reasons that were all political and nothing to do with economics or commerce. Likewise as the Pound sterling slowly became aligned with the Dollar at a value close to its old rate vis-à-vis gold, British exchange-rate policy was guided by a desire not to alienate US authorities 'in order to avoid possible retaliation and in the light of Britain's deteriorating security situation', as later experts explained.[65]

---

[63] Olivier Zunz, *Why the American Century?* (Chicago, 1998), 88–90; David Ekbladh, *The Great American Mission: Modernization and the Creation of an American World Order* (Princeton, 2010), pp. 63–76 and ch. 2 in general.

[64] Hull, *Memoirs*, i. 364, 377; the Hull system did not of course envisage free trade in the literal sense but impartial, non-discriminatory trade on the most-favoured-nation principle; his explanation ibid. 359–61; cf. Lloyd C. Gardner, *Economic Aspects of New Deal Diplomacy* (Madison, 1964), 40–5; Patricia Clavin, 'Shaping the Lessons of History: Britain and the Rhetoric of American Trade Policy, 1930–1960', in Andrew Marrison (ed.), *Free Trade and its Reception, 1815–1960* (London, 1998), 291–5.

[65] Watt, *How War Came*, 128; Harold Van B. Cleveland, 'The International Monetary System in the Interwar Period', in Benjamin M. Rowland (ed.), *Balance of Power or Hegemony: The Interwar Monetary System* (New York, 1976), 55; Clavin, 'Shaping the Lessons of History', 295; Charlie Whitham, 'Seeing the Wood and the Trees: The British Foreign Office and the Anglo-American Trade Agreement of 1938', *Twentieth Century British History*, 16/1 (2005), 29–51.

Overcoming old resentments, France gradually became incorporated into a system of active financial cooperation with the US and in May 1938 the Franc was formally tied to the Pound, itself linked to the Dollar in 1939. The Tripartite Monetary Agreement of 1936 had accelerated these processes and promised mutual support backed by the strength of the American currency. Having refused at Roosevelt's command to take part in international currency stabilization in 1933, and abandoned gold, the US Treasury now acquired the power to lend money to foreign governments to help them stabilize their currencies. With the size of the US system and the growing international use of its currency, 'for all practical purposes, the hierarchy of authority which would govern the postwar system had already been established', said economists.[66]

By the end of the 1930s, however, as the war emergencies in Europe and the Pacific loomed ever larger, Roosevelt had lost whatever faith he once may have had in strictly economic solutions to these crises. Their beneficial effects took far too long to make themselves felt, and seemed to hold no attractions at all to the warmongers. But Hull's Trade Act and the Treasury's Tripartite Agreement held one great merit in the President's eyes: they gave him instruments of economic policy he could use outwith the control of Congress.[67] It was partly because of the real or potential stranglehold of isolationism working through Congress that the New Deal became so adept at inventing new ways to bring its power to bear on reality, and throughout the later 1930s this impulse began to make its effects felt on the projection of American power abroad. As the Lend-Lease Act of 1941 and the Bretton Woods system of 1944, the Truman Doctrine and the Marshall Plan, announced in 1947, all went on to demonstrate, this capacity would also remain as one of the long-term legacies of the Roosevelt era.

While the final ends of all the efforts were often promoted in language that today sounds highly utopian—there was much talk of world disarmament, and it became the fourth of Roosevelt's Four Freedoms, then the final point of the Atlantic Charter—there were few limits to Roosevelt's pragmatism in method. Nationalist in 1933, he shifted tack in 1934 and joined the International Court of Justice in The Hague, as well as the International Labour Office (both League of Nations by-products). In the same year the Export–Import Bank was created, an export credit guarantee agency designed to encourage trade with difficult nations such as

---

[66] Cleveland, 'International Monetary System', 56; Rowland, 'Preparing the American Ascendancy: The Transfer of Economic Power from Britain to the United States, 1933–1944', in Rowland (ed.), *Balance of Power*, 207–12 (cit. at p. 212); Rosenberg, *Spreading the American Dream*, 184; Clavin, 'Shaping the Lessons of History', 293–5.

[67] Cf. Rosenberg, *Spreading the American Dream*, 178.

Soviet Russia, just recognized formally after the Soviets had boasted that they were untouched by the Great Depression, and might be interested in placing up to a billion dollars' worth of business. But at the Bank's head Roosevelt placed an outspoken isolationist, and came to use its loan policy for contingent foreign policy purposes.[68] After Hull's trade law success, an Assistant Secretary of State declared: 'We are to a greater extent than ever before meshing our economy into the world economy', and as Lloyd C. Gardner has pointed out, more legislation designed to open up and maintain trade outlets was passed in those years than in any previous period of national history. But the Neutrality Acts seemed to contradict all the eloquence about the progressive possibilities that might link economics and politics, and they provoked a new wave of diffidence abroad against the background of American ambiguity over the Spanish Civil War.[69]

All the time Roosevelt was under pressure from specific economic interests to make sure that their needs were recognized: 'farmers, exporters, workers all wanted foreign trade and Congress knew it', reports Gardner.[70] The great US oil companies flourished during the 1930s and their global reach became a government-recognized fact. There was New Deal support for rapid expansion of the communications empires being built by the private corporations RCA and ITT, and the importance of civilian air travel in America's international future was recognized with the subsidized expansion of Pan-American Airways throughout Latin America. The Air Commerce Act of 1938 provided a long-lasting framework for the development of America's airline industry, based on well-regulated competition. The Europeans, in contrast, all settled on state-run monopolies, the 'flag carriers', in these years.[71]

Latin America was also the beneficiary of the first-ever State Department-sponsored cultural exchange programme in peacetime, a public–private initiative that among other activities promoted the distribution of American film and radio materials. This small project was significant for being the first to bring the US government into the business and dilemmas of peacetime information and cultural policy, especially the difficulty of

---

[68] Anne McCormick in Sheehan (ed.), *World at Home*, 266–77 (report of 20 January 1935); Rosenberg, *Spreading the American Dream*, 181–4; Gardner, *Economic Aspects*, 35–6.

[69] Gardner, *Economic Aspects*, 93; Rowland (ed.), *Balance of Power*, 205; Clavin, 'Shaping the Lessons of History', 291–5; on Spanish episode: Welles, *Time for Decision*, 57–61; Dominic Tierney, 'Franklin Delano Roosevelt and Covert Aid to the Loyalists in the Spanish Civil War 1936–39', *Journal of Contemporary History* (July 2004).

[70] Gardner, *Economic Aspects*, 97.

[71] On oil, Rosenberg, *Spreading the American Dream*, 164–5; on telecommunications ibid. 183; on Pan-Am, William A. Krusen, *Flying the Andes: The Story of Pan American Grace Airways and Commercial Aviation in Latin America* (Tampa, Fla., 1997).

devising a credible balance between 'information' and 'culture'. But the programme rapidly expanded when Nelson Rockefeller, an heir to the great oil and finance empire of Standard Oil, absorbed it into a much bigger media effort from 1939 on: aimed ostensibly at defending the Americas from Nazi propaganda infiltration, but in practice pushing the original exchange impulse towards ideology and propaganda.[72] Rockefeller's effort also served to add another thread to the many connections linking the New Deal to the movie industry. No business or opinion sector was so directly affected by the rush to war in Europe than Hollywood, and thanks to its famous lobbying arm, the MPPDA, none was more active or effective in making sure its concerns were heeded by the White House.[73]

Gradually forced by deliberate State policy out of key markets in Spain, Germany, Italy, and Japan's sphere of influence in Asia, the war came to Hollywood long before it hit Pearl Harbour.[74] A fresh influx to Los Angeles of brilliant exiles from Nazi-controlled Europe started, and went on to include such luminaries as Billy Wilder, Bertolt Brecht, Fritz Lang, Kurt Weill, Otto Preminger, and many others, over 800 in total.[75] With Hitler's invasions of France and Scandinavia went two more territories, and eastern Europe soon became impenetrable. At the same time, as Britain's plight before the Nazi menace became ever more desperate, and dependence on American aid—material and moral—that much more evident, so Hollywood's effort on behalf of its most crucial overseas market was, as already seen, greatly intensified. In 1938 a Parliamentary Committee tried to rejig the quota system and so raise higher the barriers against alleged American movie influences on 'the development of national character and characteristics'. But the MPPDA and the US Ambassador intervened, and a fairly lax balance was struck that put the converging economic and political interests of both sides well above any consideration of content.[76]

---

[72] Rosenberg, *Spreading the American Dream*, 205–6; Pells, *Not Like Us*, 31–4; Cull, *Cold War*, 11–13; for context Iriye, *Cambridge History of American Foreign Relations*, iii. 155–6.

[73] Muscio, *Hollywood's New Deal*, ch. 2; on Latin America and Hollywood, Vasey, *World According to Hollywood*, 224; for effects of war on film sales 1939–40, Harley, *World-Wide Influences*, 265–7.

[74] The Nazi government banned all American films from Germany and German-occupied territories in August 1940; Harley, *World-Wide Influences*, 18.

[75] Saverio Giovacchino points out that, unlike many other anti-Nazi refugees, the film people were keen to get to America, hoping to match their talents to Hollywood's capacity to reach a mass audience. The result was the development of an influential if temporary form of 'democratic modernism' in America: S. Giovacchino, *Hollywood Modernism: Film and Politics in the Age of the New Deal* (Philadelphia, 2001), 2–5, 27–35; 800 figure cit. ibid. 27; cf. A. Appel Jr, *Nabokov's Dark Cinema* (New York, 1974), 196–9.

[76] P. Stead, 'Hollywood's Message', 21–2, which concludes that in the end 'no government wanted to legislate in matters of style and taste'; for politics of 1938 British quota law, Trumpbour, *Selling Hollywood*, 160–7; for contemporary American comment, Harley, *World-Wide Influences*, 248–9.

One result was that the MGM studio began to make high cost films in Britain reflecting supposed British values (the best known to history is probably *Goodbye Mr Chips*, 1939). Some studios made room in their cinemas for British dramas, mostly historical (*Quality Street*, 1937; *That Hamilton Woman!*, 1940), others made films for the American market glorifying Britain's war effort (famously *Mrs Miniver*, 1942). Occasionally they went to the politically permissible limits in bringing the conflict home to Americans and challenging US neutrality (*The Invader*, released 1942).[77] Transatlantic stars such as Leslie Howard and Douglas Fairbanks Jr put their celebrity at the disposal of governments to fight anti-Europeanism in the US and anti-Americanism in British official circles.[78]

All this reinforced the already close links between the producers' organization and the State Department, to the point where the MPPDA was using the Department's coded cable service and running crisis negotiations with foreign governments in tandem with its officials. As a currency of power the value of the movies appreciated under the shadow of war, because actions to restrict them in some countries had become a highly visible element in a very consistent pattern of political and economic hostility. In the British case they became essential in trying to convince the Americans to join the cause. No industry geared up for American participation in the war before it took place more actively than Hollywood, and in leading the fight against isolationism, it made sure that when payback time came, the industry–government effort to reconquer all those joint markets would be a true joint campaign. The challenge, concludes film industry historian Ian Jarvie, was to orchestrate 'the full majesty of the newly powerful United States in behalf of its loyal and selfless motion picture industry'.[79]

---

[77] K. R. M. Short, 'Cinematic Support for the Anglo-American Détente', in P. M. Taylor (ed.), *Britain and the Cinema in the Second World War* (London, 1988), 122–7; MGM was particularly active in the war effort, putting *Mrs Miniver* (William Wyler, 1942) into production in August 1941; a month later Congress set up a Committee on Propaganda in the Movies; ibid. 126–9; isolationist counter-attack against Hollywood in Trumpbour, *Selling Hollywood*, 75–82; cf. Nicholas John Cull, *Selling War: The British Propaganda Campaign Against American Neutrality in World War II* (New York, 1995), 18–19, 50, 139–40; for a list of 'patriotic' films made in 1938–39, Harley, *World-Wide Influences*, 14.

[78] Fred M. Leventhal, 'Leslie Howard and Douglas Fairbanks, Jr: Promoting the Anglo-American Alliance in Wartime, 1939–43', in Wiener and Hampton (eds), *Anglo-American Media Interactions*, 110–23.

[79] For William Hays statement of March 1939 on Hollywood's efforts to promote peace, democracy, trade, and entertainment, Harley, *World-Wide Influences*, 251–2; Jarvie, *Hollywood's Overseas Campaign*, pp. 351–2 and ch. 12 in general (cit. at p. 375); cf. David Welky, *The Moguls and the Dictators: Hollywood and the Coming of World War II* (Baltimore, 2008).

THE LAST BEST HOPE

Under the pressure of ever less controllable events, the prevailing tone of French and British political attitudes to the United States passed in the final year of peace from scorn and indifference to anxious attentiveness and then open pleading. In 1938 Roosevelt had declared that no one in Europe cared 'a continental damn about what the United States thinks and does', and in fact Chamberlain about the same time was stating that 'the Americans are so rotten...it does not matter...who we send' as Ambassador to Washington.[80] By March 1939 the US President was despairing of British fearfulness and suggesting that they needed 'a good stiff grog'. He couldn't bear their latest 'we who are about to die salute thee' attitude, which seemed to suggest that 'the scepter or the sword or something like that had dropped from their palsied fingers...[and] that the U.S.A. must snatch it up'.[81] The French political elite seems to have placed almost no faith at all in America as it crumbled in despair. The lonely and destitute leader of what he hoped would be a French resistance movement, Charles de Gaulle, concluded in London: 'when all is said and done, Great Britain is an island, France the cape of a continent, America another world.' But from London the French did manage to send another (lesser) man of the future, Jean Monnet, to Washington on an aircraft purchasing mission that would eventually change his and France's economic destiny, far ahead when the war was over.[82]

From early autumn 1939 Roosevelt chose as his preferred alternative contact in Britain a secondary figure in Chamberlain's latest Cabinet, reflecting his inclination to do business by way of informal personal connections. The individual chosen was Winston Leonard Spencer Churchill, ex-Cabinet Minister, lecturer, broadcaster, and historical writer of note, newly restored to the Admiralty. As the President must have foreseen, when that controversial figure took over in May 1940 a quite different spirit blew into the Anglo-American relationship. By then, writes the Canadian historian McKercher, Churchill the politician 'had undergone an intellectual odyssey concerning the United States that lay at the basis of his subsequent embrace of "the special relationship" '.[83] Having been an

---

[80] Cit. in Wayne S. Cole, 'American Appeasement', in Schmitz and Challener (eds), *Appeasement in Europe*, 6.

[81] Harper, *American Visions*, 62; cf. Richard A. Harrison, 'The United States and Great Britain: Presidential Diplomacy and Alternatives to Appeasement in the 1930s', in Schmitz and Challener (eds), *Appeasement in Europe*, 131–2; Halasz, *Roosevelt Through Foreign Eyes*, 148–9.

[82] Watt, *How War Came*, 132; Charles de Gaulle, *The Complete War Memoirs of Charles de Gaulle* (New York, 1998), 104; J. Monnet, *Memoirs* (London, 1978), ch. 6, Part I.

[83] Brian McKercher, 'Churchill, the European Balance of Power and the USA', in R. A. C. Parker (ed.), *Winston Churchill: Studies in Statesmanship* (London, 1995), 43.

admirer of his mother's native America as a land of opportunity, novelty, and vulgar energy before World War I,[84] Churchill in office in the 1920s began to have doubts about the nature of US as a new world power. He saw the economic challenge that it would present to his beloved British Empire, and deplored the selfish irresponsibility it demonstrated in politics. Accepting no liability for the European peace, the Americans had taken four-fifths of the reparations Germany paid to her victims, he claimed, and had enfeebled Britain's recovery by obliging her, albeit indirectly, to return to the Gold Standard. There was bitter rivalry throughout the 1920s over the size of navies and the rights of neutrals in wartime, and Churchill had been at the heart of all the battles, on the side of untrammelled British sovereignty.[85]

Then, of course, the picture began to change, and as Churchill in the political wilderness began to reflect seriously on the geopolitical prospects in Europe and beyond, the inevitability of America became more and more evident. Not America as a system, economy, or any sort of model, of course, but as a strategic force that could maintain the balance of power in the Pacific in friendly hands, and help defend democracy in Europe should his prophecies be confirmed and the worst come to the worst. What was special about Churchill's outlook at the end of the 1930s was not the logic of the strategic analysis, but the kind of political conclusion he drew. A vast effort of persuasion and education would have to be set in motion to convince the far-off American public of the historic responsibility it must shoulder in defending the inheritance of democratic government that the British race had bequeathed to it. The 'English-speaking peoples' must now gird their loins and learn to face their common destiny as a civilization. To this end Churchill began his famous history of all the sentiments, experience, and values that in his eyes united the Empire, the Dominions, and the citizens of the American republic.[86]

The sheer quantity of organized propaganda that in subsequent years went into persuading the Anglo-American 'cousins' to learn to understand each other, and live—and fight—together, reveals how deep was the sea of suspicion and ignorance that kept them apart in 1939.[87] David Reynolds's remarkable history of the three million strong American 'occupation' force that passed through Britain

---

[84] Jennings, *Them and Us*, 22.

[85] Ibid. 49–56; W. S. Churchill, *The Gathering Storm* (Boston, 1948), chs 1–3.

[86] McKercher, 'Churchill', 61–4; Halasz reports a broadcast Churchill made to the US in August 1939 on the Nazi danger, *Roosevelt Through Foreign Eyes*, 150–1.

[87] Reynolds, *Rich Relations: The American Occupation of Britain, 1942–1945* (London, 1995), ch. 11; Cull, *Selling War*, ch. 6; John E. Moser, *Twisting the Lion's Tail: Anglophobia in the United States, 1921–1948* (London, 1999), ch. 6.

between 1942 and 1945 starts by pointing out that up until that time 'America had been far more peripheral to Britain's self-image than Britain was to the cultural identity of the United States'. And he supplies figures that show that the *New York Times* 'devoted nearly 20 per cent of its foreign news coverage to Britain in the period 1933–1941, double that allocated by its London namesake to America in 1936–39 and nearly four times as much as in 1939–41'.[88] When the new US Ambassador to Britain, Joseph Kennedy (father of the future President) had arrived in 1938, he had been dismayed to find that Hollywood's image of the US seemed to hold a monopoly on the popular view. He called—without result—for more serious attention from the British Press 'so that people would believe that something happened there besides gangster shootings, rapes and kidnappings'.[89] There were plenty of Hollywood films representing all the ages of Britain to Americans, but none from Pinewood (opened 1936) portraying an America the British could understand.[90]

The recently invented Gallup Poll confirmed that Britons and Americans preferred each other as 'favourite country' far above any other, and indeed the King and Queen Elizabeth were warmly welcomed in the US on a carefully staged royal visit in the summer of 1939.[91] But as long as majorities against entering a European war reached as high as 96 per cent, there would never be opinion poll support in the US for amending the neutrality laws in favour of anyone, and a strong majority (69 per cent) declared itself opposed to lending money. There was very stiff resistance to the slightest whiff of British pro-war propaganda being aimed at the US, and only 51 per cent said that Roosevelt should return the Royal visit, even though (or perhaps because?) the President enjoyed vastly

---

[88] Reynolds, *Rich Relations*, 35, 32, 36, 38, 82, etc., earlier survey, with figures and similar conclusions in Heindel, *American Impact on Great Britain*, pp. 16–18 and ch. 2 in general.

[89] Dimbleby and Reynolds, *An Ocean Apart*, 113; cf. Heindel, *American Impact on Great Britain*, 15–18 for a detailed survey of Anglo-American press relations 1898–1938. Heindel concluded that coverage of the US in British dailies had not changed since 1918, and that of the 8–16% of total foreign news space dedicated to the US in 1938, 30–40% dwelt on 'sensation and crime'. The birth in 1938 of *Picture Post*, a British version of the famous photo-news magazine invented by Henry Luce, *Life*, must have done something to correct the balance, as it contained a variety of American materials; cf. Savage, *Teenage*, 312.

[90] A *Los Angeles Times* commentator of May 1939 suggested that film after American film with English 'locales, themes and heroes' had transformed traditional US Anglophobia into 'understanding and appreciation of a great people'; cit. in Harley, *World-Wide Influences*, 5.

[91] Their way had been opened by the fervently pro-American Prince of Wales (Edward VIII) in the 1920s and early 1930s; his downfall at the hands of an American divorcee in 1936 did not seem to affect public opinion in the US towards the British monarchy; Jennings, *Them and Us*, chs 12–14.

higher ratings there than he did at home.[92] On the opposite side of the ocean, said other contemporary sources, the British majority regarded their counterparts in America 'with jealous, condescending and irritated, yet profoundly admiring suspicion'.[93]

The cultivated minority had long predicted the disaster of war, with greater or lesser relish, but none of them succeeded in imagining just how profoundly their habits of mind and judgement would be upset by the emerging dependence on America, and the meanings that nation would subsequently bring to the world conflict. One small group continued to sound the alarm over modernization. Just before 'rain stopped play', the poet Robert Graves and the historian Alan Hodges—turned social commentators—were claiming that 'by this time it was taken for granted not only in business [the specific example cited was advertising] but in all departments of everyday life that the United States should set the course and pace, and Great Britain follow'.[94] The all-purpose writer, Priestley, clearly agreed and deplored the trend, to judge from comments in the popular tale he started reading on the radio the day war broke out, *Let the People Sing*. But George Orwell's famous reflections of this time on Englishness and patriotism present a quite different picture. While they denounced many of the same forms of urban modernity that Priestley objected to, they make no reference whatsoever to the American influences behind such developments, even when they are anticipating that the war would only be won with the help of Roosevelt's nation.[95]

---

[92] George H. Gallup, *The Gallup Poll: Public Opinion, 1935–1971*, Vol. 1: *1935–1948* (New York, 1972), polls of 21 July 1939 (on favourite country), 8 December 1939 (96% figure), 3 September 1939 (on neutrality laws), 15 May 1939 (on lending money), 10 July 1939 (on possible Roosevelt visit to GB); on the Royal visit, Peter Bell, 'The Foreign Office and the 1939 Royal Visit to America: Courting the USA in an Era of Isolationism', *Journal of Contemporary History* (October 2002); the article makes clear that the visit was partly a product of the severe shortage of British policy options at that time, and the hope that this form of propaganda *would* be effective; cf. Cull, *Selling War*, pp. 28–9 and ch. 1 in general.

[93] Graves and Hodges, *Long Weekend*, 436.

[94] Ibid. 434.

[95] Priestley, *Let the People Sing*, 13, 19, 36, 38, 82, 137–8, etc.; Orwell, 'My Country Right or Left' and 'The Lion and the Unicorn', both 1940, in G. Orwell, *Essays* (1984 edn repr., London, 2000); only in Orwell's novel *Coming Up for Air* (1939), do we see a brief, Priestley-like denunciation of the Americanized snack bar (1984 edition, pp. 25–7), while his essay deploring the novel *No Orchids for Miss Blandish* (1939) by an English writer who had produced a flawless copy of the American gangster story, led him to worry about the great numbers of English people 'who are partly Americanized in language and, one ought to add, in moral outlook'; in *Essays*, 263.

America as land of exile

There was however another spirit at work in Europe's intelligentsia from Hitler's time onwards that became a unifying cultural factor across the Old World working in America's long-term favour. The English feminist and pacifist writer Vera Brittain wrote these words in 1938 after returning from a visit to New York:

> Thirteen years ago America appeared to me in the guise of an antagonist. Nine years later she became my friend; today she represents the beloved refuge to which I would gladly entrust the lives that I hold most dear. From the forward direction of her aspiring, invincible spirit, freed from the impulse of death that leads ancient cultures to compass their own destruction, arises one sure and certain hope that for those whom she shelters, the dawn of tomorrow will break.[96]

But it was in Hitler's Europe, naturally, that this sentiment echoed most profoundly. Between 1931 and 1941 over 73,000 members of the professional, intellectual, and artistic classes from Germany, or German-occupied territories, chose exile in the United States to lives made impossible in their places of origin or undesirable elsewhere. The irony of America, snubbed for so long as a universe of 'Babbitry' and mechanization, now transformed into the haven of European culture, was not lost on some of the protagonists. But as one émigré wrote in a special survey: 'The noise and vigor of America's pulsing life shake the newly arrived European out of his meditation on the decline of a continent.... He begins to discover America, and this is such an exciting adventure that he wants to present his "America as I see It".'[97]

This was as true for creative artists and performers as it was for the intellectuals, especially if they were Jewish, Marxist, or belonged to any of the categories the Nazis considered 'decadent'. As Phyllis Rose, the biographer of the great jazz dancer Josephine Baker, remarks: 'People who thought of jazz as vital and America as the land of freedom were likely to find themselves before long living in America.' And while all encountered some sort of difficulty in adjustment and assimilation, they could still find the freedom they sought in all sorts of unexpected places. Rose quotes the memory of a German Jewish music publisher who arrived in New York to start life afresh at the end of the 1930s. To this man even a shirt that

---

[96] Cit. in Graves and Hodges, *Long Weekend*, 436–7.

[97] Donald Peterson Kent, *The Refugee Intellectual: The Americanization of the Immigrants 1933–1941* (New York, 1953), 6, 141, Lewis A. Coser, *Refugee Scholars in America: Their Impact and Their Experiences* (New Haven, Conn., 1984), Introduction; Giovacchino, *Hollywood Modernism*, 33.

buttoned up the front instead of being put on over the head possessed remarkable symbolic value:

> You put on a shirt with your eyes open, your head erect, in the proud posture of a free man in a free country.[98]

Anti-fascists who were not able to travel, but could survive unharmed at home, invented an imaginary America on which to project their longings for freedom. This was the case in Italy and France, where a new chapter of creative literature and thinking opened in the 1930s, based on the meanings the leading lights of the future saw not only in the Hollywood cinema but in the great American writers of their era, whose works they rapidly translated. The impulse was clearly anti-regime in political terms, but in publishing in Italian, writers such as Dreiser, Lewis, Dos Passos, Steinbeck, Faulkner, Scott Fitzgerald, Hemingway, and others, novelists and poets such as Pavese and Vittorini, Moravia and Montale, believed they were introducing an idea of liberty and individual dignity whose message rose above the suffocating circumstances of the time. In a remarkably similar process in nominally democratic France, Sartre, Malraux, Camus, and other thinkers acted under the same inspiration. There was a vitality, openness, spontaneity, and a fighting spirit in these American visions that might yet renew the humanism of the Old World with its death wish, and provide a post-totalitarian generation with a new myth to live by. Again freedom was the key concept, 'freedom, freedom for the individual in the face of the unreasonable chains of society', as Cesare Pavese wrote.[99]

When the Cold War broke out, precisely this impulse and these sorts of people would be key targets for America's newly organized strategy of persuasion and enrolment. The preferred instrument would be that unique semi-private, semi-public expression of the nation's ability to project power in a hundred different ways, the great cultural foundation. But the Cold War effort was only conceivable because of the heroic work the foundations had put in between the Wars, building bridges, creating networks, and then, in the late 1930s, bringing to American sanctuary the cream of central Europe's intellectual life. By this time the Rockefeller Foundation alone had twenty years of experience in supporting European

---

[98] Phyllis Rose, *Jazz Cleopatra: Josephine Baker in Her Time* (London, 1991), 126–7; compare Henry James's always elegant heroine Daisy Miller: 'Whenever she put on a Paris dress she felt as if she were in Europe'; 'Daisy Miller' (1878), in Napier Wilt and John Lucas (eds), *Americans and Europe: Selected Tales of Henry James* (Boston, 1965), 116.

[99] This paragraph is based on Lino Pertile, 'Fascism and Literature', in David Forgacs (ed.), *Rethinking Italian Fascism: Capitalism, Populism and Culture* (London, 1986), 181–2; and Louis Menand, 'The Promise of Freedom, the Friend of Authority', in Michael Kazin and Joseph A. McCartin (eds), *Americanism: New Perspectives on the History of an Ideal* (Chapel Hill, NC, 2006), 208–10.

social science and transatlantic exchanges with multi-million dollar investments. Others, such as the Guggenheim Foundation, The Carnegie
Endowment for International Peace, the American Council of Learned
Societies, and the Commonwealth Fund, encouraged the natural sciences
and the growth around the world of disciplines such as psychology, international relations, and economics, greatly contributing to the creation of
the international communities in those areas that their participants soon
took for granted.[100] After 1933 the Foundations and their university connections led the organized effort to save the best and the brightest with
the creation of a special Emergency Committee in Aid of Displaced
German (later Foreign) Scholars. By this and other means over 7,500
writers, creative artists, scientists, and others arrived, with the number
destined to increase (especially from France) after war broke out.[101]

ANNOUNCING THE AMERICAN CENTURY

As Olivier Zunz points out, the long-term effect of this development and
its related internationalization of American intellectual life was to provide
a key cultural pillar for the soon-to-be-proclaimed 'American Century',
'for it is the reorganization of knowledge, not merely the power of capital
accumulation that gave Americans the means to generate prosperity at
home and expand their presence into the world'.[102] For sixty years American businessmen, researchers, university leaders, foundation trustees, and
government officials had been quietly creating 'a vast institutional matrix
of inquiry', a system whose purpose was to turn knowledge of the universe in all its forms into concrete economic, social, and scientific projects
that could, potentially, challenge existing arrangements in any part of the
world. The American system of innovation was clearly ready to emerge by
now as superior to its European competitors, because status barriers were
far lower, interaction was guaranteed, and everyone's moral right to produce original ideas was recognized. 'Consequently, Americans unleashed
an unprecedented level of creative energy among partners who were producers, brokers and users of knowledge.'[103]

[100] On the origins of the Foundations and their efforts in these areas, Ekbladh, *Great
American Mission*, 23–4.
[101] Pells, *Not Like Us*, 22–9; Volker R. Berghahn, 'Philanthropy and Diplomacy in the
"American Century"', in Michael J. Hogan (ed.), *The Ambiguous Legacy: U.S. Foreign relations in the 'American Century'* (Cambridge, 1999), 384–6; cf. Jarrell Jackman and Carla
Borden (eds), *The Muses Flee Hitler: Cultural Transfer and Adaptation* (Washington DC,
1983).
[102] Zunz, *Why the American Century?*, pp. xi–xii.   [103] Ibid. 4–7.

In 1939 this alliance put on its greatest production up to that time: two world's fairs running concurrently, one in San Francisco, one in New York. Just as Europe plunged into the near-death experience of Hitler's war, here was the mass communications, civic and business leadership of the United States daring to organize a pair of immense shows of national pride. While 'Pageant of the Pacific' opened on the west coast, the even grander New York event was dedicated to no less a theme than 'Building the World of Tomorrow'.

In San Francisco the myths of Hollywood and the frontier were fused in the Hall of Western States to set in motion a new legend of post-industrial pleasure: *California*. The souvenir guide proclaimed:

> This is adventure and adventure is a product of leisure, just as leisure in America is a product of industry's efficiency. So adventure sets the pace for the Fair—leisure, travel, recreation, the yearned-for opportunity to gather into one beautiful setting the color of the Western world not at work, but living, playing, roaming over its finest country. This makes industry important only as a contributor to romance. This makes the Fair, instead of a factory manual, a saga of the West.[104]

Buffalo Bill's legend was explicitly updated in San Francisco for a new generation of myth-seekers, people who would enjoy at the same time the spectacle of Pan American's China Clipper flying boat as it took off on its three day voyage to Hong Kong. The Pacific rim was shrunk to the Lagoon of Nations, where pavilions from all over Asia jostled with Good Neighbour allies from south of the Rio Grande and a few others.

The official chronicler of the New York show said its purpose was to exhibit 'the best tools, ideas, industrial techniques and social services available to the average man and woman of today'. Between March 1939 and May 1940 almost 45 million visitors got the message, which was available in as many different forms as the stands of the dozens of corporations and foreign nations (fifty-eight) who took part.[105] Bigger and more technologically spectacular than San Francisco, the New York event offered a theme song written by the Gershwin brothers entitled 'Dawn of a New Day'. It also celebrated the official launch in America, by RCA, of the new medium of television, featuring the image of President Roosevelt as he opened the Fair.[106] The most popular attraction in New York, ahead

---

[104] Cit. in Lisa Rubens, 'Re-Presenting the Nation: The Golden Gate International Exhibition', in Robert W. Rydell and Nancy Gwinn (eds), *Fair Representations: World's Fairs and the Modern World* (Amsterdam, 1994), 134.

[105] *Dictionary of American History*, iv (New York, 1942), 120.

[106] Details of RCA's efforts and context in Ron Becker, '"Hear-and-See" Radio in the World of Tomorrow: RCA and the Presentation of Television at the World's Fair, 1939–1940', *Historical Journal of Film, Radio and Television* (October 2001), 361–78; the Paris fair of 1937 had seen

Fig. 4. View of an unidentified man as he works atop a 32ft tall replica of the Empire State Building in what was billed as the world's largest diorama, the Consolidated Edison City of Lights exhibition at the New York World's Fair, Queens, New York, 1939. The exhibit featured working building lights, elevators, and subways, and was a full city block long.

(Getty Images/Time Life/Margaret Bourke-White)

of Democracity (a vision of the City of Tomorrow set up in the vast dome of the Perisphere), was the Futurama Exhibit by General Motors. This was an enormous scale model of a perfect world, with its 'animated panorama' of cities and country, farms and industries, country clubs and freeways, American life in its most utopian form. Visitors flew over it on

a highly successful pilot project featuring German TV technology and an uplifting mass ideology to go with it, Andreas Fickers, 'Presenting the "Window on the World" to the World: Competing Narratives of the Presentation of Television at the World's Fairs in Paris (1937) and New York (1939)', *Historical Journal of Film, Radio and Television* (August 2008), 298–301; 'whereas "nation" and "education" can be identified as keywords of the television discourse in Paris, "commercialization" and "entertainment" most adequately represent the popular television rhetoric during [the] World's Fair in New York', says Fickers, ibid. 304–5.

'magic moving chairs', and when they left were given a badge emblazoned with the words 'I Have Seen the Future'.[107]

The European nations present all used the occasion to emphasize their ideas of national prestige, their distinctive contributions to Western culture, and above all their links with America and its idea of democracy, since the official pretext for the occasion was the 150th anniversary of George Washington's installation as the first President of the United States. With the exception of Nazi Germany and Franco's Spain, every European nation was present, including a defiant version of Czechoslovakia. The Soviet Union constructed a massive marble and granite pavilion, housing what turned out to be the most popular of all the national exhibits, according to exit polls.[108] Like the Soviets, the imperial nations all chose some form of 'authoritarian monumentality'—as a local architectural review put it—to express the sense of their presence in the world. Within this framework, the French attempted a subtle balance of modernity and history. The historian David Nye describes how industry was subordinated to fine art, the 'scenic beauties of France [and] ... the civilising force of French culture'. Mussolini's Italy offered a 200-foot waterfall and vistas of the neo-classical universe the Duce was building, complete with a selection of his famed dogmas written on the walls, as was customary throughout *la Patria*. The British adapted modern architecture to frame traditional emphases on the Parliament, the Commonwealth, and their way of life. But the Fair represented above all a key moment in the intense British communication campaign aimed at winning over local public opinion to the cause of their national survival. They imported not only an original copy of Magna Carta and exhibited proof of Washington's English roots, but made sure the visit of King George VI and Queen Elizabeth would be the most publicized event of the entire show. It was 'the high point of the British bid to win American sympathy on the eve of the war', judges the historian Nicholas Cull.[109]

Although all the big national pavilions saw millions of visitors, none could match the attractions of the great corporate exhibits. The most successful West European offerings—the British, the French, the Dutch— each displayed the national endeavour to find a particular balance between

---

[107] Jon B. Zachman, 'The Legacy and Meaning of World's Fair Souvenirs', in Rydell and Gwinn (eds), *Fair Representations*; television and Roosevelt cit. in Muscio, *Hollywood's New Deal*, 35; Becker, ' "Hear-and-See" Radio', 364–5: Savage, *Teenage*, 329–30.

[108] David E. Nye, 'European Self-Representations at the New York World's Fair of 1939', in Kroes et al. (eds), *Cultural Transmissions*; poll of 17 May 1939 in Gallup, *Gallup Poll: Public Opinion*, i.

[109] Nye, 'European Self-Representations', 55–7; Cull, *Selling War*, 26–8.

modernity and the inheritance of the past.[110] The Soviet effort may have enjoyed its success because, in contrast, it 'stressed technology almost to the exclusion of all else' and provided an original 'narrative of rapid economic growth', says Nye, citing the success of the replica Moscow subway station.[111] But the corporations present, such as GM, General Electric, AT&T, and Westinghouse, concentrated totally on the future, and did so using their new technology—such as television—to entertain rather than to educate and uplift. The majority of the European shows by contrast looked static, didactic, and rooted in the past. The Germans and the French had already shown off television at the Paris World Fair of 1937, but their notion of it was as a public service like radio, adapted to reconcile education, arts, and technical modernity.[112] Their ideal was the museum, the art gallery, the luxury restaurant. The Americans—exhibitors and public alike—showed they preferred the simulated airplane flight, domestic air conditioning, and long-distance phone calls, the all-electric city just around the corner.[113]

The extended edition of the New York Fair finally closed in spring 1940, by which time its theme had changed to 'Peace and Freedom' and its emphasis had become more nationalistic. A few months later, Henry Luce, the New York publisher who had revolutionized the print media with a fresh generation of mass-market weeklies, proudly proclaimed that 'America is already the intellectual, scientific, and artistic capital of the world'. Against the background of a Western Europe that had entirely succumbed to Nazi-Fascism, with only the British still defying the onslaught, Luce used the editorial column of his *Life* magazine to launch a call for the fullest mobilization of national pride, an effort to turn the revered American Dream into a world-shaking project to build 'The American Century', not something to be imposed but an experience of fulfilment to be shared.

When the American people finally faced up the challenges of their time, said the editorial, they would see that these were to make their nation 'the dynamic leader of world trade', a land 'which will send

---

[110] The Irish effort in the same direction is described in Clair Wills, *That Neutral Island: A Cultural History of Ireland During the Second World War* (London, 2007), 15–21; the modernist pavilion the Irish government offered masked severe strains between the misery of much of the Irish countryside at the time, and the hesitant, conflicted modernization of the towns, says Wills.

[111] Nye, 'European Self-Representations', 60.

[112] Andreas Fickers and Jonathan Bignell, 'Conclusion', in Bignell and Fickers (eds), *European Television History*, 232–4.

[113] Nye, 'European Self-Representations', 63–4; cf. Warren Susman, *Culture as History: The Transformation of American Society in the Twentieth Century* (Washington DC, 2003), ch. 11; David Gelernter, *1939: The Lost World of the Fair* (New York, 1995).

throughout the world its technical and artistic skills', one that would feed hungry people everywhere with its boundless produce, and above all...

> ...the powerhouse from which the ideals [of Western civilization] spread throughout the world and do their mysterious work of lifting the life of mankind from the level of the beasts to what the Psalmist called a little lower than the angels.

Everyone knew that there was already a global form of the States, said Luce:

> American jazz, Hollywood movies, American slang, American machines and patented products, are in fact the only things that every community in the world, from Zanzibar to Hamburg, recognizes in common.

But this was trivial stuff compared to the results the world would see when the people of the United States developed an imagination broad enough to match their inheritance of 'purposes and enterprise and high resolve'. Only then could America realize the full meaning of its freedom:

> It is in this spirit that all of us are called, each to his own measure of capacity, and each in the widest horizon of his vision, to create the first great American Century.[114]

Men like Luce already knew by this time that America could look forward to irresistible supremacy at the war's end, an extraordinary occasion to attempt again the creation of a world order that would approve and enhance the exceptional status in western history of the United States. For the land of opportunity, World War II would be the greatest of them all.

---

[114] Luce editorial of 17 February 1941 reproduced in Hogan (ed.), *The Ambiguous Legacy*, 11–29; discussion ibid., Introduction and chs 1–8; cf. Judis, *Grand Illusion*, 64–6; Stephen J. Whitfield, 'The American Century of Henry R. Luce', in Kazin and McCartin (eds), *Americanism*.

PART II

1941–1960

6

A Very Philosophical War: The Global New Deal and Its Critics

OUR DESTINY, YOUR FUTURE

The peace leader

Just seven weeks after the United States was forced to enter World War II as a combatant, in December 1941, one of Roosevelt's most ardent journalistic admirers, Anne O'Hare McCormick, interviewed the President on the occasion of his sixtieth birthday. She found a man who claimed that he detested being a war leader. But this President was transfixed by his personal sense of history, said McCormick, strong of nerve, cool of temper. Here was the visionary who had proclaimed the advent of the United Nations on the first day of the New Year, because, more than anything else, Roosevelt wanted to be 'the peace leader':

> ... how he would enjoy reconstructing the world! His eye lights up when he turns for a moment from the dreary planning for war to speak of a world without passports, of a Europe with federalized public services, of the ever-normal granary on a world scale, of international control of rubber and other essential raw materials, of a world police force...[1]

By the time Roosevelt came to leave for the Yalta conference three years later, in February 1945, he had gone far to show that the images he had once used when speaking to an admiring writer were much more than flights of fantasy. His latest urgent message to Congress sought approval for another of his comprehensive plans of American action for the peace. At the top of the list was a request for rapid approval of the international agreements the US government had signed in August 1944 for world financial reform. Roosevelt used the occasion to demand also:

---

[1] Report of conversation, printed 25 January 1942, in Sheehan (ed.), *World at Home*, pp. 321–9, cit. at pp. 327–8.

... The establishment of the Food and Agriculture Organization of the United Nations, broadening and strengthening of the Trade Agreements Act of 1934, international agreement for the reduction of trade barriers, the control of cartels and the orderly marketing of world surpluses of certain commodities, a revision of the Export–Import Bank, and an international oil agreement, as well as proposals in the field of civil aviation, shipping and radio and wire communications.

The end of the war, said the President, provided the United States with 'a tremendous opportunity'. Now the American people would have to decide whether to grasp it or not. 'I have said before and I repeat again: This generation has a rendezvous with destiny.'[2]

The New Deal's gaze now turned to the peoples outside America, dreaming that it might touch humanity everywhere. Roosevelt expected that through persuasion and enlightenment, he and his team could convince Americans to support them in a great crusade to save the world by rebuilding it, and took it for granted that the world would wish to go along. It seems that there was never an instant in the whole course of the conflict, whether the US was still out of the war or fully engaged, when the government and its key thinkers were not considering in some parts of their minds how the peace should look once the war had ended, and the leading role the United States would play in building it. Compared to its earlier or later equivalents, in the 1920s and 1990s, this time the American challenge to Europe, and the world beyond it, would be deliberate and conscious, determined to reform America's allies as much as to remodel her enemies.[3] The uncertain, unsettled United States of the 1930s—half in the international system, half out of it—had turned into a revolutionary, even evangelical nation.

The era of the great pronouncements

By January 1941 the stage was already set for this startling conversion. The Four Freedoms address of that month, then the Lend-Lease Act of March and the Atlantic Charter of August, were no simple sloganeering blasts from a far away country still officially neutral. The first of them announced that henceforth America would now take sides and play a full role in the ideological battle. Incorporated in the President's Annual Message to Congress of January 1941, following his second re-election, the

---

[2] *The Public Papers and Addresses of Franklin D. Roosevelt*, xiii: *1944–45 Volume, Victory and the Threshold of Peace* (New York, 1950), 548–54, message of 12 February 1945.

[3] Cf. D. C. Watt, 'U.S. Globalism: The End of the Concert of Europe', in Warren F. Kimball (ed.), *America Unbound: World War II and the Making of a Superpower* (New York, 1992), 45.

pledges featured freedom of speech and of religion, freedom *from* want and from fear of war. And these were to be upheld 'everywhere in the world'.[4]

The Lend-Lease system was rushed into being in March 1941. It was devised to enable the allies to receive war material of all sorts under a variety of credit or 'leasing' arrangements, without committing the government to the war as such. Here now was action of substance, and it was radically new in technique, purpose, and language. That unlooked-for American propensity first glimpsed at the end of the Great War now reappeared: a startling, forceful ability to invent new ways to project power.[5]

There was indeed much more to the Lend-Lease scheme than a simple emergency lifeline. Those who signed up to the full programme, as outlined in a 'Master Agreement', would not only pay for or return at the end of the war the mass of material received while they had been fighting. They would also formally recognize the standards and the objectives that the benefactors were determined to set for what came afterwards. Article VII of the accord spoke of 'the expansion... of production, employment and the exchange and consumption of all peoples... the elimination of all forms of discriminatory treatment in international commerce... the reduction of tariffs and other trade barriers'.[6]

Here was Cordell Hull's long-standing preoccupation with free trade turned by the State Department and the President into another key theme of all the thinking, debating, and plan-making that would go into the American peace. At the same time, in the US Treasury, the first schemes for a world reconstruction bank and a stabilization fund for currencies were emerging.[7] In a book-length public education exercise written in 1943, the Lend-Lease administrator Stettinius evoked the Open Door, the first twentieth-century narrative of American expansion in the world, and imagined 'the return' that would come back to America as a result of all its wartime planning and aid:

---

[4] *The Public Papers and Addresses of Franklin D. Roosevelt*, ix: *1940 Volume, War—and Aid to Democracies* (New York, 1941), 672; context and dissection of Roosevelt's global language and imagery in Alan K. Henrikson, 'FDR and the "World-Wide Arena" ' in Woolner et al. (eds), *FDR's World*, 35–49.

[5] The constrictions of domestic politics had much to do with the form of the first Lend-Lease design; cf. Warren F. Kimball, *The Most Unsordid Act: Lend-Lease, 1939–1945* (Baltimore, 1969); on Congressional opposition to the proposal, Woods, 'FDR and the New Economic Order', 179–80.

[6] Council on Foreign Relations, *The Problem of Lend-Lease: Its, Nature, Implications and Settlement* (New York, April 1944).

[7] Robert Skidelsky, *John Maynard Keynes*, iii: *Fighting for Freedom, 1937–1946* (London, 2000), 239; G. John Ikenberry, 'A World Economy Restored: Expert Consensus and the Anglo-American Postwar Settlement', *International Organization* (Winter 1992), 289–321.

Fig. 5. Edward R. Stettinius Jnr, the American industrialist and statesman, charts the course of American Lend-Lease supplies from America to other nations.

(Getty Images/Hulton Archive)

We have, generation after generation, gone forth to meet the challenge of new frontiers. A Lend-Lease settlement that opens up new peace-time opportunities for a more prosperous America in a more prosperous world will be worth more than all the gold and all the materials we have expended in this war.[8]

The definitive version of the Lend-Lease Master Agreements incorporated the third great 1941 pronouncement of principle and plan: the Atlantic Charter. In the Charter, production, employment, trade, and consumption were defined as 'the material foundations of the liberty and welfare of all peoples'. A pledge to expand them after the war was therefore a fundamental duty of the fighting democracies, whose common philosophical and political aspirations were spelled out here, at least provisionally.[9]

---

[8] Edward Stettinius, *Lend-Lease Weapon for Victory* (New York, 1944), 330–1.

[9] For the development, context, and subsequent history of the Charter, see essays in Douglas Brinkley and David R. Facey-Crowther (eds), *The Atlantic Charter* (London, 1994); for Charter's joint, Anglo-American conception of 'welfare', and the propaganda competition with the Axis powers in this area, Maurizio Vaudagna, 'Social Protection and the Promise of a Secure Future in Wartime Europe and America', in Marco Mariano (ed.), *Defining the Atlantic Community: Culture, Intellectuals and Policies in the Mid-Twentieth Century* (London, 2010), 96–8.

But all along, economic objectives remained central to the vision. Right after the three Charter pledges on self-determination, democracy, and peace came the fourth, promising to every nation equal access to 'the trade and to the raw materials of the world which are needed for their economic prosperity'. In the fifth principle the signatories expressed their wish...

> ...to bring about the fullest collaboration between all nations in the economic field with the object of securing, for all, improved labor standards, economic advancement and social security.[10]

The convictions that came together in the Atlantic Charter, say American historians, added up to a set of reference points that Roosevelt never abandoned, 'whatever short-term, compromises and long-range adjustments he found necessary'.[11]

But would the American people as whole be ready to confront their responsibilities, as well as their opportunities, under the transition to the peace of the Atlantic Charter? Was the democratic public opinion of the nation conscious of the intense worries its own federal government felt that Europhobic unilateralism might rise again in the nation's heartland, and paralyse all of the great Rooseveltian ambitions? How could the people be brought to realize that the old choice of 'separation or entanglement' was not available any more in the world of interdependence?

'The whole American people thinking out loud'

This was Edward Stettinius's characterization of the noisy national discussion set off by the proposals setting up his Lend-Lease administration. It was a debate, he recalled, that 'went on all over the country—on the radio, on street corners, around the stoves in country stores, at Grange and Rotary club and labour union meetings, in college rooms, and in the churches'. Congress was 'flooded with postcards, letters and resolutions'. 'The people made themselves heard, everybody counted.'[12]

By early 1942 the theme of the post-war world and America's place in it had been taken up by a vast panoply of public and private organizations across the nation. The *Bulletin of the Commission to Study the Organization of Peace*, a compendium and guide to all the activity, listed at this time no

---

[10] Charter visible at <http://usinfo.state.gov/usa/infousa/facts/democrac/53.htm>, still available from the Wayback Machine Web archive: <http://wayback.archive.org>.

[11] Lloyd C. Gardner and Warren F. Kimball, 'The United States: Democratic Diplomacy' in David Reynolds et al. (eds), *Allies at War: The Soviet, American and British Experience* (New York, 1994), 399; the Charter was formally cited in the UN Declaration of 1 January 1942, and in the Declaration on Liberated Territories of the Yalta conference, February 1945.

[12] Stettinius, *Lend-Lease Weapon*, 72, 74–5.

less than ninety-one private organizations dedicated to it, supplemented by thirty-two universities and other 'learned societies', seventeen religious groups, and twenty-eight government agencies. Another forty-one foreign or international groups also supplied information and analyses. In stark contrast with the behaviour of nearly every other country, belligerent or neutral, comments the specialist Carlo Santoro, 'this almost obsessive interest in the future... indicated a kind of unconscious or premonitory sensation that the business of decision regarding the future world order lay indeed with the United States itself'.[13]

Vice President Henry Wallace placed himself at the head of the most visionary wing of the many-flavoured movement. By the beginning of 1942 every leading speaker in it had been obliged to promise at least a new world organization to police the peace, a transformed global trade system, and a democracy based on rising purchasing power.[14] But Wallace's eloquence added a religious and populist dimension, which made his commitment to cars, houses, air travel, and access to the middle class for all sound like a ticket to the Promised Land. At the same time, the Vice President made it as clear as possible that the world had become, economically, a single 'neighbourhood', and that its potential bounties could only be guaranteed if peoples everywhere could be offered at least the hope of equal access to them. In this vision, America herself would take an unselfish place in an integrated world system dedicated to rising standards of production, consumption, and living.[15]

By the time that serious choices had to be made on the post-war world, as opposed to debating the possibilities, Roosevelt's administration could even count on influential support among its former adversaries. In the Four Freedoms, 'Mr Roosevelt again states the same major purposes in America's participation in this war—a second crusade to establish American ideals', declared ex-President Herbert Hoover. 'What we must

[13] Carlo Maria Santoro, *Diffidence and Ambition: The Intellectual Sources of U.S. Foreign Policy* (Boulder, Colo., 1992) 34; a sample of the results in James MacGregor Burns, *Roosevelt: The Soldier of Freedom* (New York, 1970), 358; the classic study of all the movements remains Robert A. Divine, *Second Chance: The Triumph of Internationalism in World War II* (New York, 1967).

[14] The Republican President of the US Chamber of Commerce, Eric A. Johnston, produced his own version, *America Unlimited* in 1944. In it the author exhorted the nation's film industry—owners of 'the most powerful medium for influencing people which man has ever built' to start setting 'new styles of living...the doctrine of production must be made completely popular'. In 1945 Johnston took over from Will Hays as president of the MPPDA; details in Trumpbour, *Selling Hollywood*, 89–90.

[15] Henry Wallace, *The Century of the Common Man* (London, 1944); Wallace's vision of a post-war US aviation policy, expressed in *June 1943*, when the Allies had yet to set foot in Europe, is mentioned in Henrikson, 'FDR and the "World-Wide Arena"', 50–1; context of Wallace's campaign in Divine, *Second Chance*, ch. 3, esp. pp. 64–6; for Wallace's personal history and a critique of his wartime vision, Judis, *Grand Illusion*, ch. 2, esp. pp. 59–66.

win now, during the war, are the principles…', added Roosevelt's old opponent of 1940, Wendell Willkie, early in 1943.[16] In a brilliant propaganda move, Roosevelt had loaned Willkie a converted army bomber and crew in 1942, and sent him on a fact-finding tour across the Middle East, Russia, and Asia. The result was a book entitled *One World*, which made this film-industry lawyer from the small-town Midwest one of the first contemporary prophets of globalization.

Willkie's essay was a paean to the principles of interdependence and 'a peace planned on a world basis'. Western civilization and its 'presumed supremacy' would be judged by the outcome of this peace, said Willkie. It was being watched intensely by the peoples of the world now on the march, societies looking for a future for themselves, materially, intellectually, spiritually. The age of imperialism was of course over, whether it be European or Japanese: 'The big house on the hill surrounded by mud huts has lost its awesome charm.' As a result America was becoming a beacon for those nations that had put self-government and economic freedom at the top of their agendas, countries of the future like Turkey, India, and China.[17]

More critical of his own nation than any of the official visionaries—Willkie's travels made him realize how badly America's democratic prestige was compromised by its record in race relations—the ex-Presidential candidate shared with the New Dealers their absolute faith in the link between economic development and democratic freedom.[18] Nutrition, housing, health, education, technical progress, offered together as a package, would transform the present conflict into what Marshall Stalin had called 'a war of liberation', said Willkie, and create the essential premise for the cooperative management of interdependence. So Americans should realize that from now on that their well-being too depended on the prospect of rising living standards across the globe. The peoples of the East were only passing on a message when they had spoken to Willkie: 'They would like the United States and the other United Nations to be partners with them in this grand adventure.'[19]

One World was an instant and extraordinary sales success, selling 2 million copies in its first year, 3 million by 1945. The historian Divine records that it 'enjoyed the most phenomenal sale of any book published in the

[16] *Prefaces to Peace: A Symposium* (New York, 1943), 292, 121; this bestselling volume contained essays by Henry Wallace and Sumner Welles, as well as those by the two Republicans.

[17] W. Willkie, *One World* (New York, 1943), 166–7, 171.

[18] Ibid. 27.

[19] Ibid. 168; impact of anti-imperialist theme explained in Lloyd C. Gardner, 'FDR and the "Colonial Question"', in Woolner et al. (eds), *FDR's World*, 123–6.

United States'.[20] Yet Roosevelt and his team worried incessantly about the persisting weight of isolationist sentiment and its cohorts in Congress, and the question was central to the 1944 election campaign. A correspondent for *The Economist*, reporting from Ohio in April 1945 on 'the American mood', explained why. People in general, said the anonymous reporter, were ready to face up to 'responsibility for helping to preserve world order in general', and believed strongly in collective security and the new world organization. 'But they recoil from specific responsibilities on the Continent of Europe', and tended to leave practical applications of the principle of collective security to be worked out somehow later.[21] This was the attitude that explained why the designs had to be so overarching and universalist, even utopian, and Roosevelt and Hull were deeply aware of it.[22]

Planning, as choice and necessity

Even before the pivotal year of 1941, Roosevelt had lost no opportunity to remind his audiences that improvised, temporary remedies would not be adequate if the peace of the future was to be sustained by economic transformation. Innovations in science and technology had transformed the war, he said, and should be used to promote the new world order.[23] The President's report to Congress on the Yalta Conference of late February 1945 showed how great was his belief in practical planning led—but not monopolized—by government. Whatever true libertarians might think, said Roosevelt, in domestic affairs it had brought 'many benefits to the human race'. Desert areas had been recovered, river valleys developed, social welfare programmes set in motion. Now was the time to apply its lessons for the benefit of relations among nations.[24]

---

[20]   It was also included in *Prefaces to Peace*; sales and marketing details in Divine, *Second Chance*, 105; full context, including criticisms, explained in Howard Jones, 'One World: An American Perspective', in James H. Madison (ed.), *Wendell Willkie: Hoosier Internationalist* (Bloomington, 1992); limits of Willkie's judgements emphasized in André Kaspi, 'One World: A View from France', ibid. The government gave extensive courses on the book to returning German prisoners of war; Zunz, *Why the American Century?*, 185.

[21]   *The Economist*, 7 April 1945.

[22]   Critics at the time and since have portrayed the President and his Secretary of State as slaves to this belief, though Hull for one tried to brake the 'evangelical' impulses of visionaries such as Henry Wallace; Burns, *Roosevelt*, 359–61; Woods, 'FDR and the New Economic Order', 177, 179–81.

[23]   Examples include his radio address before the 8th Pan American Scientific Congress, May 10, 1940, in *The Public Papers and Addresses of Franklin D. Roosevelt*, 1940 volume, cit., pp. 184–7; and 'The President Requests Plans for Future Scientific Research and Development', 20 Nov. 1944, in *The Public Papers and Addresses of Franklin D. Roosevelt*, 1944–45 Volume, cit., pp. 425–7; cf. Ekbladh, op.cit., pp. 68–9, 73.

[24]   Willard Range, *Franklin D. Roosevelt's World Order* (Athens, Ga., 1959), 155.

As early as February 1940 a State Department committee had begun informal and exploratory conversations on post-war planning with the other nations then still neutral (forty-seven in total). They considered two questions to be fundamental: 'the basis of a sound international economic system', and disarmament. These talks, recalled Hull, specifically excluded 'present problems arising from the war'.[25] More significant was the major study campaign launched by the Council on Foreign Relations of New York, which from the first week of the war fed directly into the official thinking. With its large-scale War and Peace Studies Project, based on functional study groups, 'a distillate of ideas and international political culture [from] within the East Coast Establishment' became available to widen the government's perspective. The vast institutional matrix of inquiry of the 1930s now moved into top gear, and the War and Peace Studies teams were among its most significant expressions.[26]

Much of the effort of the New York study groups was dedicated to exploring just how the perceived American experience of the connection between democratic liberty and economic progress might be translated into empirical, universally applicable recipes. Washington of course thought its own inventions in this department as good as any. Among the favourite models was always the Tennessee Valley Authority, the great New Deal system of dams, hydroelectric plants, and irrigation projects that had transformed the prospects of a once-backward rural region. Former Under Secretary of State, Sumner Welles, pinpointed the Danube and the Balkans as the most suitable terrain in Europe for a similar scheme. In his October 1944 contribution to the national debate on the future, entitled *Time for Decision*, Welles wrote:

> The poverty of the masses underlies every problem of the Balkan peoples. Only through a higher standard of living can they develop the social foundation upon which to construct stable national governments…the potentialities inherent in some vast power project which might be established in the Danube valley are unlimited. The electrical power derived from such an installation, cutting across all the national lines of Eastern Europe, could within twenty years create an entirely new industrial civilization in the area.[27]

---

[25] Hull, *Memoirs*, ii. 1628; in 1943 Hull still thought of a question such as the future of Poland as 'a piddling issue' he did not care to contemplate, Warren F. Kimball, *The Juggler: Franklin Roosevelt as Wartime Statesman* (Princeton, 1991), 95. Patrick Hearden, *Architects of Globalism: Building a New World Order During World War II* (Fayetteville, Ark., 2002), 19–20; the official guide to post-war planning in the State Department is Harley A. Notter, *Postwar Foreign Policy Preparation, 1939–1945* (Washington DC, 1949).

[26] Santoro, *Diffidence and Ambition*, ch. 4; cit. at p. 183.

[27] Welles, *Time for Decision*, 152–3, cit. in Ellwood, *Rebuilding Europe: Western Europe, America and Postwar Reconstruction* (London, 1992), 22–3; in 1944 the International Labour Organization published a booklet on *The Tennessee Valley Authority: Lessons*

-Dead-
-Wake-

By this time the planners in and out of government had developed a comprehensive prognosis for the past, present, and future situation of every country to be liberated in Europe. No matter what the nation or its problems, they reiterated their core belief in a direct, almost mechanical connection between prosperity, stability, and peace, and simply applied it to each particular situation. In the case of a country like post-Fascist Italy, the State Department's thinkers looked forward to '[an] economic reconstruction designed to create an expanding economy which will offer the Italian people genuine opportunities for their economic betterment'. Looking at Greece, the experts imagined the 'chain reaction' that might be set off by huge, planned capital inputs into such a poverty-stricken land. For France, 'a thoroughgoing re-orientation of its economic and social life' was demanded, accompanied by a revolution in its values that would 'place less emphasis on security and more emphasis on risk and enterprise', with the state providing 'direction, coherence and encouragement', in a general scheme of industrial and agricultural development'[28]

Always there was trade, meaning ever freer, ever growing, ever more American trade. From the time of Lend-Lease onwards, State Department and Council on Foreign Relations committees would be working on specific schemes for international commerce that, they imagined, would keep the most-favoured-nation principle but go beyond the old Trade Agreements programme. They even began to think seriously about dismantling the daunting tariff system the US Congress had crowned in its panic reaction to the great Crash, and designed an International Trade Organization under the UN to police the new commercial world they dreamed of.[29]

But there were other, far more immediate concerns that drove the administration's experts in the same direction. Especially during his victorious election campaign of 1944, the President had promised the country what he called an 'economic bill of rights', and held out the vision of a new universe of consumption and comfort:

> I look forward to millions of new homes, fit for decent living; to new, low-priced automobiles; new highways; new airplanes and airports; to television;

for International Application; commentary in *The Economist*, 9 December 1944; the centrality of the TVA to liberal American visions of the post-war order is emphasized in Ekbladh, *Great American Mission*, pp. 37–8, and chs 2, 3. Abroad too the TVA acquired a mythical reputation as a vast model of successful development, anticipating the even greater success of the Marshall Plan in this area, and confirming the skills of the Americans in consciously combining the medium and the message in such contexts; ibid. 40–1, 46–8, 73, 85–6.

[28] Ellwood, *Rebuilding Europe*, 21, 24; Cf. Hearden, *Architects of Globalism*, ch. 3.

[29] Hearden, *Architects of Globalism*, ch. 2, on ITO, see State Department, Commercial Policy series, cit. ch. 5, n. 57; Woods, FDR and the New Economic Order', 187.

and other miraculous new inventions and discoveries, made during this war, which will be adapted to the peacetime uses of a peace-loving people.[30]

But all of this depended on making sure the great mass of Americans enjoyed the levels of job security they had become used to as a result of the war. In his State of the Union Address of January 1945, Roosevelt pointed out that full employment had been achieved and maintained throughout the war years because the government had bought half the nation's productive output. Now 60 million new jobs would be needed if no one was to be left behind in the transition to peace. Private enterprise would be relied on to provide them, of course, but could only be expected to do so fully if America's export performance was transformed.[31]

So the economic agencies were told to brace themselves for a fight to convince the heavy majority of protectionists across the land that exports could only flourish if foreigners acquired the rights to sell in America, and so gain the currency needed to pay for what they took in. With the United States massively in credit again in relation to its allies, this necessity was more and more obvious, and there could be no question of repeating the agonies of the 1920s.[32]

But the administration's trade liberals had very few cards to play in their battle against the economic isolationists.[33] This explains the determination they brought to the long, bitter confrontation with Europe's imperial heritage. If the Open Door was to be finally inaugurated in America itself, then doors would have to be seen opening in every corner of Europe's old colonial empires. Against this background, Roosevelt's Washington developed a method of its own for transforming aspirations into objectives, and objectives into policy: this was the grand international conference.

The conference phase

In 1943 a long-felt Presidential urge to 'do something about world agriculture' came to a head. From it came the Hot Springs Agriculture Conference of May–June 1943, from which the old League of Nations Food and Agriculture Organization would emerge transformed. Hot Springs was the

---

[30] F. D. Roosevelt, *Public Papers and Addresses*, xiii. 383–8, Campaign Address from the White House, 2 November 1944.

[31] F. D. Roosevelt, *Public Papers and Addresses*, xiii. 503–5, address of 6 January 1945; Henry Wallace had been saying the same from 1942: *Century of the Common Man*, 40–1.

[32] Cf. Alvin Hansen, *America's Role in the World Economy* (New York, 1945), chs 15, 18, 19, 22.

[33] On the opposition that Roosevelt's 'economic bill of rights' encountered, Vaudagna, 'Social protection', 107.

first demonstration of Roosevelt's functionalist, sector-by-sector approach, seeking through specific international gatherings an institutional solution to the problems each area presented in relation to his overall vision of the post-war universe.[34] By concentrating on sectors such as money, communications, science, education, America's involvement in the outside world could be extended in ways that appeared strictly limited and pragmatic, and so did not provoke the militant isolationists in Congress. To Secretary of State Hull, conferences offered useful tests and experience in international collaboration on the road to the supreme task: creating the United Nations organization.

Although the suggestions of foreigners for conferences were not welcome, as the Australians discovered when they proposed one on employment policy, the government was not entirely averse to sending conference delegates abroad. In the name of the 'intellectual rehabilitation of Europe', the Americans joined the Conference of Allied Education Ministers in London in 1944, one of the impulses that fed into the later creation of UNESCO.[35] Roosevelt got most of the conferences he demanded, but even his power in this area was not unlimited. In 1944 he wanted an immediate conference to plan the management and conservation of the world's resources, especially oil and water. This time though the State Department claimed it was too busy to take on the job, and the idea went no further.[36]

The list of conferences organized by the Administration in the war years is impressive. It reads as follows:

- On food and agriculture, Hot Springs, Virginia, May–June 1943, 38 nations represented.

- On post-war relief and rehabilitation, Atlantic City, New Jersey, November–December 1943, 44 nations represented.

- On the problems of labour and employment, Philadelphia, April 1944, 41 nations represented.

[34] Cf. Divine, *Second Chance*, 116–17; Vice President Wallace's thoughts on aviation policy, and the need for an international authority to make it function, cit., n. 14, fed into the Chicago Aviation Conference of 1944: Henrikson, 'FDR and the "World-Wide Arena" ', 50–1.

[35] Australian proposal and its fate presented in *Foreign Relations of the United States, 1945*, ii (Washington DC, 1967), 1328–60; American participation in the London conference of Allied Education Ministers presented in *Foreign Relations of the United States, 1944*, i (Washington DC, 1966), 964–80; Hull, *Memoirs*, ii. 1654–5.

[36] Range, *Franklin D. Roosevelt's World Order*, 148–9; Roosevelt was not pleased, and tried to insist the Department take notice of the many countries, such as Iran, which could be transformed by development into good customers, 'and although it might take a hundred years to do it, as history goes that was a short time'.

- On international monetary reform, Bretton Woods, New Hampshire, July–August 1944, 44 nations represented.

- On the organization of international security after the war, Dumbarton Oaks, Washington DC, August–October 1944, four great powers represented: Soviet Union, USA, Britain, and China.

- On the organization of civil aviation after the war, Chicago, Illinois, 51 nations represented.

- On problems of war and peace in the Americas, Mexico City, March–April 1945, 21 nations represented.

- For the creation of the new security organization, the United Nations, San Francisco, California, May–June 1945, 50 nations represented.

From many of these events came either a renewal of an institution left over from the League of Nations (in the case of the Food and Agriculture Administration, and the International Labour Organization), or a brand new institution: UNRRA for relief and rehabilitation, the International Monetary Fund for currency stabilization, the International Bank for Reconstruction and Development (later the World Bank), and the greatest achievement, the United Nations Organization. Whatever the fate of these institutions once they encountered the harsh world of reality after the war, all of them (except the transitional UNRRA[37]) survived the shift. Battered and modified by the experience, they would eventually become fundamental pillars of the international order in the twentieth century and afterwards. A State Department proposal of mid-1944 for a grand conference on international economic cooperation produced, after many delays, the Havana Conference of 1947, which gave birth to the General Agreement on Tariffs and Trade and its long negotiating tradition.[38]

Were these successes all the fruits of the collaborative atmosphere of Roosevelt's conferences? It seems unlikely. Although the number of nations present looks impressive, on closer inspection they turn out to be made up of three large but mostly ineffectual blocs: the 20 or so Good Neighbours of Latin and Central America, the exile governments of Europe, and Britain and her Commonwealth. At the best-known of the conferences—that at Bretton Woods, famous as the place of origin of

[37] UNRRA was not meant to be permanent, but its demise, in December 1946, was hastened by Cold War tensions and the urge to restore American primacy in the areas it dealt with; cf. Ellwood, *Rebuilding Europe*, 34–6; on its origins, Hearden, *Architects of Globalism*, 67–8.

[38] Semi-official explanation of International Trade Authority offered in Hansen, *America's Role*, ch. 9; economic conference discussed in Hearden, *Architects of Globalism*, 50–1.

the post-war monetary system—the only struggle that counted was between the British, led memorably by Lord Keynes, and the Americans, represented by a tough and determined Treasury team bent on crowning the dollar as the gold-plated king currency in a world transformed by free trade.[39] The new French liberation government sent a highly significant future Prime Minister and political thinker, Pierre Mendès-France, but his impact on proceedings seems to have been marginal, and many of the delegations were made up of lesser figures.[40] 'It takes a very sophisticated country to be truly rational when it comes to monetary matters', an expert onlooker concluded drily.[41]

As is well-known, after long and exhausting battles with Keynes at Bretton Woods, deriving from the position of the Americans as booming creditors and the British as ever more beleaguered debtors, the Americans got their way in the end.[42] And so it appears to have been on most of these occasions. Few of the designs they brought to these events seem to have been seriously modified as a result of the talking. Many dire warnings were offered up by their foreign interlocutors about the extreme unreality of all the blueprints in relation to the situation likely to emerge on the ground after the war.[43] Usually these predictions turned out to be true, but from a historical perspective this does not diminish their long-term impact, or lessen their interest. The New Dealers of wartime had the power and the will to make sure their ideas were the only game in town. As they alone among the leaders of the United Nations thought comprehensively and consistently of their national future in terms of a new world order, rather than in the narrow, conventional language of geopolitical

---

[39] I am grateful to staff at the Bretton Woods Hotel for supplying me with material on the event. Cf. Hearden, *Architects of Globalism*, 58–64; Skidelsky, *John Maynard Keynes*, iii. 339–57; Ikenberry, 'World Economy Restored', 315–17; Woods, 'FDR and the New Economic Order', 182–3.

[40] Some indication of Mendès-France's view of the event can be gained in the letters included in his *Oeuvres complètes: II Une politique de l'économie, 1943–1954* (Paris, 1985), 44–9, and in his report on the Monetary Conference of Savannah of March 1946, ibid. 192–5; in these papers Mendès-France hints at the methods the Americans used to build a very heavy hegemony—including reliance on the '*total*' (*sic*) support of the Latin American delegations, on the discomfiture of the British, and the marginalized status of the Europeans, clients of no one. Official—sceptical—French reflection on Bretton Woods fifty years later summarized in *Vingtième Siècle*, n. 46 (April–June 1995), 182–4. The Guatemalan delegation at Bretton Woods consisted of a doctoral student from Harvard.

[41] Hansen, *America's Role*, 143.

[42] But the resentments their victory provoked were enduring; cf. David Marquand, 'Keynes was wrong', *Prospect* (March 2001); for a contrasting American view emphasizing synthesis and harmony, Ikenberry, 'World Economy Restored', 317.

[43] French views reflected in a later commentary in *Le Monde*, 7 June 1945, Mendès-France article of 15 September 1946, on proposed International Trade Organization, in Mendès-France, *Oeuvres complètes*, 197–8.

interest, this was not hard to do. When the British, the French, and the Soviets finally felt secure enough to begin serious consideration of the post-war scene, after the start of 1943, they discovered that much of the work had been pre-empted, large parts of the territory already staked out. As we shall see, they were far from happy to find themselves in such a situation.

The President's doctrine of liberation

One of Roosevelt's habits to relieve the frustration he often felt at hostile commentary on his actions, was to dictate to his speechwriters speeches he knew he would never give. On his return from the Casablanca conference of January 1943, the crucial turning point in the shift of all the Allies to sustained thinking on the peace, Roosevelt dictated a few lines on his ideas of America's role in the world economy of the future:

> Some snob asks glibly 'Why should we give a quart of milk a day to every Hottentot?' [a play on a light-hearted suggestion from Vice President Wallace] First of all that type of man would have you believe that that is the great American aim in life. Secondly he deliberately omits the fact that if the population of Dakar and the population of Morocco and the population of Algiers and even the Hottentots could be helped to get a better standard of living, each one of them would have greater capacity to participate more greatly in the trade of the world and by that create employment needs among nations and, incidentally, assure greater markets for producing for the manufacturing nations of the world, including the people of the United States of America.[44]

As such, the words never went out. But the basic ideas behind them were often repeated in one form or another: interdependence, the transformation of sovereignty, the moral responsibility of the leading powers and its link to their self-interest, political egalitarianism, the need to think in the long term ('at least fifty years'[45]), the supremacy of just that factor whose exclusion had ruined Versailles: economics, as planning, as business, as *development*. This word's epochal career was launched by one of the Council on Foreign Relations' economic consultants, Eugene Staley:

> What is economic development? It is a combination of methods by which the capacity of a people to produce (and hence to consume) may be increased. It means introduction to better techniques; installing more and better capital equipment; raising the general level of education and the particular skill of labor and management; and expanding internal and ex-

[44] Samuel I. Rosenman, *Working with Roosevelt* (London, 1952), 346.
[45] Cit. in Range, *Franklin D. Roosevelt's World Order*, 143.

ternal commerce in a manner to take better opportunities for specialization.

Importantly, adds David Ekbladh, the historian who rescued Staley and his context from oblivion, 'Staley and others began to treat the term "modernisation" as synonymous with this process'.[46] In a comment of the time, the New Deal's leading economist, Alvin Hansen, wrote in an educational tract for the masses of 1945:

> It is apparent that the leading countries are far more aware of the basic economic problems in international relations, and see far more realistically now than before what these basic economic problems are.[47]

Roosevelt of course was no economist, but he knew who were the men and women who had been transforming the range and power of management, business, and economic science since the onset of the Great Depression. He was particularly successful at reaching for those individuals, whether in the private or the public sectors, most adept at turning their knowledge into effective direction of the agencies set up to run the national war effort, and at facing the daunting challenge of the transition to the better peace, always present in all of their thoughts, and in all their many private power struggles.[48]

Logically, it seemed obvious to these Americans that once the Japanese were dealt with, the French, the Dutch, and even the British would not simply be returning to their old possessions in South East Asia to carry on as before. 'The age of imperialism is ended', proclaimed Under Secretary of State Sumner Welles in 1942, and Willkie had boomed the same message in *One World*.[49] The vast philosophical and political stakes the government and its allies saw in the battle against Europe's imperial heritage were best explained by Walter Lippmann in 1944:

> It [anti-imperialism] is organic to the American character, and is transmitted on American soil to all whose minds are moulded by the American tradi-

---

[46] Ekbladh, *Great American Mission*, 63–76; cit. at p. 74; for intellectual context ibid. 79–86.

[47] Cf. Warren F. Kimball, 'U.S. Economic Strategy in World War II: Wartime Goals, Peacetime Plans', in Kimball (ed.), *America Unbound*, 147–9; Hansen, *America's Role*, 18–20.

[48] Santoro, *Diffidence and Ambition*, 118, *passim*; Ikenberry, 'World Economy Restored', 300–1; for a highly ironic view of this process seen from the inside, John Kenneth Galbraith, *A Life in Our Times: A Memoir* (London, 1981), chs 8–12.

[49] Cf. Christopher Thorne, *The Issue of War: States, Societies and the Far Eastern Conflict of 1941–1945* (London, 1985), 226–7; the same message brought back after a world tour by five Senators in autumn 1943 had also attracted much publicity, Moser, *Twisting the Lion's Tail*, 158.

tion. It is a deep and pervasive habit of thought because it comes directly from the original conflict in which the colonists became Americans...[50]

From early 1943 onwards, more and more ruthless efforts were being made to ensure this message was understood by all the United Nations, who were now expected to sign a formal Declaration of National Independence. This State Department document was pushed by its sponsors on every big international occasion in 1943, and added to a vast range of pressures, including what Roosevelt called 'pitiless publicity'. Together with the British, the French and the Dutch were the prime targets of this line of action, and as we shall see, they deeply resented it.[51]

The Declaration naturally demanded of the colonial powers that they offer to their dependent peoples, 'continuous efforts towards their political, economic, social and educational advancement'.[52] To reinforce their pressures the Americans pointed to three great and specific experiments they were carrying out across the world, exemplifying the seriousness of their purposes, the success of the results, and the great popularity of their works wherever they went.

The Philippines, captured from the Spanish in 1898 and managed under a form of protectorate until the Japanese invasion, were held up as a specific demonstration of the goodness of America's intentions for the post-colonial peoples under its charge. From the time of the Philippine Independence Act of 1944, said the administration, the US had been working by stages of self-government towards the horizon of complete independence, promised for the time right after the conflict had ended. In this way the islands would join the new 'global civilization', said Roosevelt in 1942, one 'which recognizes no limitations of religion, or of creed, or of race'.[53]

---

[50] *U.S. War Aims* (London, 1944), pp. 18–22, cit. at p. 19; Churchill thought that this was precisely what made it so irrelevant to contemporary conditions in a land such as India, *The Second World War*, iv: *The Hinge of Fate* (London, 1951), 194; historical evolution of American thought in this area in Rhodri Jeffreys-Jones (ed.), *Eagle Against Empire: American Opposition to European Imperialism, 1914–1982* (Aix-en-Provence, 1983), 9–21: cf. Niall Ferguson, *Colossus: The Price of America's Empire* (New York, 2004), ch. 2, 'The Imperialism of Anti-Imperialism'.

[51] Welles cit. in Frank Ninkovich, *The United States and Imperialism* (Oxford, 2001), 234; Declaration discussed in Kimball, *Juggler*, pp. 138–41, quote at p. 151; cf. Hearden, *Architects of Globalism*, pp. 101–4 and ch. 4 in general; Albert E. Kersten, 'The Dutch and the American Anti-Colonialist Tide, 1942–1945', in Jeffreys-Jones (ed.), *Eagle Against Empire*.

[52] A version of the Declaration of March 1943 is reprinted in *Foreign Relations of the United States: The Conferences at Washington and Quebec, 1943* (Washington DC, 1979), 717–20, cit. at p. 719; the document was one of a number of initiatives that launched the UN trusteeship system on its career.

[53] Burns, *Roosevelt*, 178–9, Ninkovich, *United States and Imperialism*, ch. 2, Michael Adas, 'Modernization Theory and the American Revival of the Scientific and Technological

But the New Dealers were convinced that it was their Good Neighbour policy towards the other nations in the western hemisphere that presented the most outstanding, exemplary remedy for all those ailments that had brought the international system, dominated by the Europeans, to its final agony. It is difficult to over-emphasize the intensity of the faith Roosevelt and his followers placed in their policy of creating a distinctly American commonwealth in the western hemisphere, and presenting the results as a complete model of international well-being. Woodrow Wilson had declared that hemispheric unity was 'the only available offset to the follies of Europe'. Herbert Hoover had acted, revising and expanding every form of economic connection, hoping to 'increase the standard of living of all our peoples' and promising a new quality of relationship.[54]

Taken over from Herbert Hoover and then enlarged, the Good Neighbour vision convinced its supporters that the other twenty Central American and Latin republics (except Argentina) shared US values and views of the world. Had they not all declared war alongside America after Pearl Harbour and all signed on to the free trade vision? Were they not an oasis of peaceful coexistence in a world in turmoil?[55] Like Hoover, Roosevelt believed the experience 'should be made universal throughout the world',[56] and a strong current in the State Department, 'Europhobic' and 'hemispheric', in the view of the American historian Harper, sought to promote the inter-American system as the example of 'a regional federation of free and independent peoples'. Even people outside the administration and normally critical of its foreign policies, such as Walter Lippmann, shared the faith that the Good Neighbour policy was, 'a radical innovation in human affairs... the only true substitute for empire'.[57]

The administrations of the United States had of course been taking a direct interest in the affairs of Latin America since the proclamation of the Monroe Doctrine in 1823. But there was another sphere of the world where the government found itself largely as a result of the war, and then

---

Standards of Social Achievement and Human Worth', in David C. Engerman et al. (eds), *Staging Growth: Modernization, Development and the Global Cold War* (Amherst, 2003), 30–2.

[54] William O. Walker III, 'Crucible for Peace: Herbert Hoover, Modernization and Economic Growth in Latin America', *Diplomatic History* (January 2006), 84–90, 108–9; on limits of Hoover's action, Ekbladh, *Great American Mission*, 25.

[55] Latin American setting and perspectives on these beliefs ibid. 90–4; Harper, *American Visions*, 56–7.

[56] F. D. Roosevelt, *Public Papers and Addresses*, xiii. 343, address to Foreign Policy Association of 21 October 1944.

[57] Harper, *American Visions*, 56; cf. Santoro, *Diffidence and Ambition*, ch. 8; Kimball, *Juggler*, ch. 6; Sumner Welles, *The World of the Four Freedoms* (New York, 1943), 74–5; W. Lippmann, *U.S. War Aims*, 51.

quickly identified it as a most suitable trial terrain for some of its ideas on the future progress of the peoples of the world. This region was the lands east of the Mediterranean, between the Russian border and the Indian Ocean, the area traversed by America's key Lend-Lease supply route to Soviet Russia.[58]

Testing the doctrine of liberation in the Middle East

When Wendell Willkie visited Egypt, Iran, and Turkey, and flew over the lands in between, he discovered that American 'soft power' had already arrived: 'we have sent our ideas and our ideals, and our motion pictures and our radio programmes, our engineers and our business men, and our pilots and our soldiers. We cannot now escape the result.'[59] By the end of the war, untrammelled by isolationists of any variety, the New Dealers would be involved with all the paraphernalia of the succeeding decade's great efforts to encourage economic 'development', wherever in the world it was thought to be inadequate by the standards Washington now laid down.[60] The US Ambassador to Egypt said: 'the American system is based on the intent to help backward countries to help themselves in order that they may lay the foundation for real self-dependence.' With our way of employing expert advisers, said a Treasury commentator, the locals were empowered, and everyone shared the benefits.[61]

In January 1944 the State Department opened a new Office of Near Eastern and African Affairs, while the White House had by that time sent its own director of US operations to the region with Ambassador rank. Prompted by the big oil companies, the government had meanwhile decided that 'the oil of Saudi Arabia constitutes one of the world's greatest prizes', as Hull put it. But the lure of petroleum does not explain all the urges that fed the new American interest in what the Secretary of State called the 'Near East'.[62]

Roosevelt's participation in the Teheran conference of late 1943 had vastly stimulated his personal interest in these territories. In a memorandum to the State Department written soon after his return, he depicted Iran as a largely tribal society, of great inequality, 'definitely a

---

[58] Cf. Map 30: Lend Lease, in Martin H. Folly, *The Palgrave Concise Historical Atlas of the Second World War* (London, 2004).

[59] Willkie, *One World*, 26.

[60] Adas, 'Modernization Theory'.

[61] Cit. in Barry Rubin, *The Great Powers in the Middle East, 1941–1947* (London, 1980), 44, 50; Hull, *Memoirs*, ii. 1738; Range, *Franklin D. Roosevelt's World Order*, 156.

[62] For the growth of Hull's and the State Department's interest in the 'Near East', Hull, *Memoirs*, vol. ii, ch. 109, 'The Near East Looms Big'.

very, very backward nation'. Where better then to test the freshly recast, overseas editions of the New Deal's recipes? Here in Iran was a society where the US could show how *dis*-interested its presence was, and how superior its benefits to the locals, not only compared to the selfish, imperialistic British (and the French, in control of neighbouring Syria), but also to the wily, unreliable Soviets, with their totally closed economic system.

> I was rather thrilled by the idea of using Iran as an example of what we could do by an unselfish American policy. We could not take on a more difficult nation than Iran. I should like, however, to have a try at it.[63]

To guarantee peace and stability in the Middle East, concluded the President, reform would have to be promoted everywhere, meaning that governments like Iran's must be prompted to 'improve their economic systems in terms of the production and distribution of wealth', guaranteeing at the same time 'equality of opportunity for all nations'. The dominant position of, for instance, France in the Levant, could no longer be tolerated: 'for such privileges have little place in the type of world for which this war is being fought.'[64]

Even the Palestinian question, rising fast up the ladder of concerns by the end of the conflict, was seen as one obviously amenable to this sort of treatment. At the height of the post-war battles surrounding the birth of Israel, Sumner Welles recalled how Roosevelt had looked forward to the birth of a Jewish–Arab commonwealth in Palestine, whose economic force of attraction might lead to a 'federal union', including Syria, the Lebanon, and Transjordan. In this area 'customs and currency barriers could be gradually eliminated, and...far-reaching projects for irrigation, power development, and the construction of communications might be carried out by common agreement'. It was not the fault of Roosevelt, 'a firm believer in the appeal of reason and of self-interest', if this vision had not been realized, said Welles.[65]

---

[63] Cit. in Rubin, *Great Powers in the Middle East*, 90; a ' "boyish note of enjoyment" was characteristic of Roosevelt's tone when dealing with the lands of the Middle East', said one State Department observer: Herbert Feis, *Seen from E.A: Three International Episodes* (New York, 1947), 122.

[64] Cit. in Rubin, *Great Powers in the Middle East*, 3–4; Roosevelt recited these views for the benefit of Churchill and Stalin at Yalta, following a note from his adviser Harry Hopkins: 'Mr President: When are you going to spring your T.V.A. for Europe?'; episode recalled in Edward A. Stettinius, *Roosevelt and the Russians: The Yalta Conference* (London, 1950), 164–6; for Roosevelt's association with the birth of the TVA, Ekbladh, *Great American Mission*, 49, 52.

[65] S. Welles, *We Need Not Fail* (Boston, 1948), 29–30.

The second great challenge

The Middle Eastern experience foreshadowed many of the themes that would dominate the America-as-future question when it arrived in uniform on Europe's shores after 1943, and also demonstrated how they were not in any way limited to the European arena. All of the New Deal's 'mechanistic idealism' was on display in the Middle East,[66] its strange mixture of utopianism and ruthlessness, of earnest concern for the future of 'the masses' and indifference to local conditions and context, the inclusiveness and at the same time the hubris of a winning, post-imperial power. Development was the mantra—development through trade, exchange, industrialization, technology, scientific knowledge, planning— all premised on an end to empires; the rapid transformation, somehow, of the Atlantic Charter pledges of self-determination into reality, and an unquestioning faith that what had been best for America would be ideal for the rest.[67]

In this context, whatever the compromises and adjustments made along the way, the birth of the United Nations represented the greatest triumph of the New Deal in its new globalist expression. Uniting in one vaulting design the three great themes of this political culture—an improved idea of collective security, ever-freer commerce, rising living standards everywhere—the United Nations vision redefined Wilsonism and turned it into the central rhetorical tradition of American foreign policy in the twentieth century. Only in this way, said the UN's sponsors, could hopes for peace be justified of an intensity equal to the miseries and sacrifices of the war. Everywhere the UN charter was studded with the economic and social promises of the three great declarations of 1941, now turned into the laws of a prototype world government.[68]

---

[66] 'Mechanistic idealism' was a phrase from Dean Acheson, Assistant Secretary of State during the war, whose memoirs are highly critical of the State Department's planning effort: *Present at the Creation: My Years in the State Department* (New York, 1969), 64, 88.

[67] David Ekbladh suggests that the highest expression of this faith was *Democracy on the March*, (New York, 1944), by the charismatic head of the TVA, David Lilienthal; Ekbladh, *Great American Mission*, 81–2.

[68] Cf. Hansen, *America's Role*, ch. 14. Sixty years after the end of the war, historians deplored the fatal legacy of the 'messianic impulse' that Wilsonism had apparently set in motion: Walter LaFeber, 'FDR's Worldviews, 1941–1945', in Woolner et al. (eds), *FDR's World*, 225. This sort of approach was refuted by the intellectual historian Frank Ninkovich in 'Wilsonism, Pre-Wilsonian American Liberalism, and the Atlantic Community', in Mariano (ed.), *Defining the Atlantic Community*, 28–33, and by Warren Kimball in 'Sheriffs', 98–101, which denied any significant connection between Wilson's legacy and the policies of Roosevelt. But all these accounts concentrate on relationships between the Great Powers and reflect a narrow, Cold War-influenced conception of security that ignores the social, economic, and legal dimensions embodied in the Charter, and which Roosevelt's institution-building enhanced; cf. Iriye, *Cambridge History of American Foreign Relations*, iii. 140–1.

But what can America's allies have thought as they witnessed the proclamation of 'the world forged anew'? In spite of the all the wartime conferences with all their participating nations, only the British and the Soviets, some of the time, had been allowed to impinge on the construction of the great new system unfolding before their eyes. If the world was in reality not amenable to government by the UN organization, but one quite unforeseen until very late—of two militarized superpowers, with an enfeebled British Empire in between—just how useful and relevant would the New Deal's vision turn out to be? Why had the Americans put off planning for the world as it really was after the worst war in history, rather than as they imagined it ought to be in the peacetime of their dreams? Above all, if the key allies in Europe had developed their own ideas of what should happen to them when the war was over, why was so little account being taken of these thoughts and aspirations in designing the civilization of the Four Freedoms?

RESPONDING TO THE WORLD'S REFORMER

What America is this?

Even before America had entered the war, those Europeans who were still free to think knew that the United States would dominate whatever came after it. It was obvious that the American economy was getting richer faster than at any time since the 1920s, on the strength of war production for its own defence and for its friends. But the three great pronouncements of 1941 made very clear that this time round money alone would not define what happened next. The problem was that to many on the European side of the Atlantic, the great statements had a totalizing, all-or-nothing air about them that, given all the circumstances, left the allies little choice but to register their feelings of bewildered awe or profound scepticism. Or to wonder, as the former Popular Front Prime Minster Léon Blum did in his prison cell after the Atlantic Charter came out, where this America had been when needed in 1921 or since 1933. An unknown British observer was recorded in 1941 as saying: 'They share a presumption of interfering in the affairs of others without the intention of coping with the consequences.'[69]

Echoing Churchill, a leading British socialist thinker, Brailsford, called the generosity of Lend-Lease 'one of the most remarkable acts of states-

---

[69] Léon Blum, *For All Mankind* (London, 1946), 25; Mass Observation report cited in the *New Statesman*, 3 March 2003.

manship of its kind in the history of civilisation'.[70] But the Director of the French Institute in London, Denis Saurant, claimed that working men in his country, all on the Left, were telling each other '[it] was our own money that the Americans have lent back to us', earned by selling goods in the world while preventing others selling to them.[71] The Soviet Ambassador to London, Maisky, deplored the exclusion of the USSR from the Atlantic Charter's creation and said it seemed to him 'as if England and the USA imagine themselves as almighty God called upon to judge the rest of the sinful world, including my country. You cannot strengthen an alliance on such a basis.'[72]

The nations whom Roosevelt invited to his imposing conferences were often left disoriented by the apparent paradox presented by the dreams of world economic reform that the visionaries of Washington loved to spin, coupled with the brutal lack of sentimentality of the bargains their bureaucrats drove on specific issues such as currencies, oil, and aviation. Whether the Allies liked the American positions on these questions or not, it was at least possible to get a policy on them out of Washington, whereas one on, say Poland or Greece, was completely out of the question until very late in the war. No one among the European observers seemed to take any notice at all of the great public debate going on among Americans about their nation's rightful place in the world, or the efforts of research and analysis under way across the official American establishment.[73] Foreign Secretary Eden told his functionaries: 'They know very little of Europe and it would be unfortunate for the future of the world if United States uninstructed views were to decide the future of the European continent.'[74] Gradually however, it became clear to the others that of all the three great New Deal aspirations for the post-war world—the security organization, freer trade, and raising living standards everywhere—economic liberalism was the one that Roosevelt and his men would stick to with the most coherence and tenacity.[75]

---

[70] H. N. Brailsford, in *The British Commonwealth and the United States in the Post-War*, papers from a conference organized by the National Peace Council (London, November 1941), 46.

[71] Ibid. 53.

[72] Cit. in Lloyd C. Gardner, 'The Atlantic Charter: Idea and Reality, 1942–1945', in Brinkley and Facey-Crowther (eds), *Atlantic Charter*, 52.

[73] On Dutch insensibility, Kersten, 'Dutch', 100–1.

[74] Cit. in Anthony Eden, *Memoirs*, ii (London, 1965), 341; by 'knowledge', of course, the British meant the accumulated and specific historical experience of people, places, and problems.

[75] Cf. Kimball, 'The Atlantic Charter: "With All Deliberate Speed"', in Brinkley and Facey-Crowther (eds), *Atlantic Charter*, 85–8; Woods, 'FDR and the New Economic Order', 183, cites the great Congressional diffidence towards the administration's concept

The emergence of these revolutionary designs struck the surviving free Europeans—nations, neutrals, exile groups—very differently. Obviously the basic circumstances of the war dictated reactions in the first instance. But for those able to look beyond the emergency, above all the British and the French but also the Dutch, it became clear that the urgency and force with which the Americans were making their plans demanded that certain markers be laid down as quickly as possible.[76] A classic example was the writing in London of Geoffrey Crowther, editor of *The Economist*, but also, from September 1943 to December 1945, of *Transatlantic*, a semi-official monthly magazine put out to try to explain America to the British governing classes. Crowther's signed comments in *Transatlantic* always sought to help the two sides understand each other's positions, and to mediate underlying conflicts of culture and psychology, as well as over politics and economics. But on one point he was quite clear: 'it is the survival of Britain but only the prosperity of America that is on the agenda.'[77]

But the survival of *which* Britain?, would always come the response from America. Did the British really expect their American allies to guarantee the survival of the entire British Empire, with all its appurtenances, dominions, colonies, protectorates, and sterling connections?[78] From 1941 onwards, for fifteen years, this was vital, contested terrain between the British and the Americans, which no amount of tactical retreats by both sides—of Cold War, of Special Relationships, of Churchillian nostalgia for wartime race harmony—could conceal or deny.[79] Prime Minister Neville Chamberlain had predicted as much. In January 1940, the architect of the failed foreign policy of the late 1930s wrote: 'Heaven knows I don't want the Americans to fight for us. We should have to pay too dearly for that if they had a right to be in on the peace terms.'[80] Churchill

---

of multilateralism; view of an expert British protagonist in Lord Robbins, *Autobiography of an Economist* (London, 1971), 197–204.

[76] Queen Wilhelmina of the Netherlands made a very carefully prepared speech defending the Dutch colonial experience in December 1942; full discussion in Kersten, 'Dutch', 94–102.

[77] *Transatlantic*, no. 7 (March 1944).

[78] For obvious reasons, the military saw the most immediate, open antagonisms on this question, cf. Brian Holden Reid, 'Tensions in the Supreme Command: Anti-Americanism in the British Army, 1939–45', in Reid and John White (eds), *American Studies: Essays in Honour of Marcus Cunliffe* (London, 1991); in general, Moser, *Twisting the Lion's Tail*, ch. 7.

[79] D. C. Watt, *Succeeding John Bull: America in Britain's Place, 1900–1975* (Cambridge, 1984), chs 5, 11; John Charmley, *Churchill's Grand Alliance: The Anglo-American Special Relationship, 1940–57* (New York, 1995), 252–3; Ferguson, *Colossus*, 66–8; Burk, *Old World, New World*, 560–602.

[80] Cit. in David Reynolds, *From World War to Cold War: Churchill, Roosevelt and the International History of the 1940s* (Oxford, 2006), 183.

of course saw that there was no alternative, and that he was mortgaging the future of the British Empire. But he insisted in February 1942 that 'the key-note of our relations must surely be equality'. He rejected any suggestion of 'tutelage' and tried to stop 'all this fussing about what is to happen after the war'. Throughout, and like many in the British governing class for years afterwards, he believed Britain's 'superior statecraft and experience' would see her through.[81]

Hands off the British Empire!

The Americans had no illusions: the empire of His Majesty King George the Fifth, which had expanded to its greatest extent ever between the world wars, was the chief obstacle to the fulfilment of their goals. Hull said as much to Roosevelt in September 1944.[82] By that time, deep undercurrents of feeling had begun to set American and British views of the post-war world against rather than alongside each other. At the end of a discussion of the outstanding issues in 'economic peace-making', Geoffrey Crowther wrote:

> In England we must not blame the Americans if, in the pride of their strength, they treat other countries' weaknesses with a certain arrogance. We were just the same a hundred years ago.
>   In America, there should be an effort to understand that their wartime enrichment is the result of their fortune, not their virtue. Other countries will emerge from the war so battered and beggared that they cannot be expected to look at the world through a creditor's spectacles.[83]

There was nothing as becoming as optimism, said de Gaulle, 'to those who can afford it'.[84]

In the economic sphere, there were the vast Anglo-American confrontations over currencies, trade policy, and the uses of Lend-Lease, made famous to history by the role of Keynes in their unfolding.[85] But the

---

[81] Cits in Charmley, *Churchill's Grand Alliance*, 49, 155; the effect such attitudes had in feeding anti-European isolationism in the US seems to have escaped all the British observers.

[82] Alan P. Dobson, *The Politics of the Anglo-American Special Relationship, 1940–1987* (Brighton, 1988), 85; Watt, *Succeeding John Bull*, 222–6; Lloyd C. Gardner, 'FDR and the "Colonial Question"', 123–33; Geoffrey Warner, 'Franklin D. Roosevelt and the postwar world', in David Dutton (ed.), *Statecraft and Diplomacy in the Twentieth Century* (Liverpool, 1995), 162; cf. T. R. Fox, *The Super-Powers: The United States, Britain and the Soviet Union—Their Responsibility for Peace* (New York, 1944), ch. 3.

[83] *Transatlantic*, no. 13 (September 1944).

[84] De Gaulle, *Complete War Memoirs*, 572.

[85] Skidelsky, *John Maynard Keynes*, vol. iii, chs 4, 10; Robbins, *Autobiography*, 197–9; Richard N. Gardner, *Sterling–Dollar Diplomacy* (3rd edn, New York, 1996).

disputes over what looked like lesser issues—raw materials (especially oil and rubber), civil aviation, and telecommunications—were often just as hard. 'There was an element of dogmatism in the American case which we all found it very hard to swallow,' recalled a British negotiator.[86] One of the few occasional defenders of the British in Washington, Dean Acheson, Assistant Secretary of State, told the hard-hitters in the US Treasury Department that he could not understand 'the political necessity of so conducting the Lend-Lease program as to bankrupt Britain, or keep the British at the edge of bankruptcy indefinitely'. This was his friend Keynes's argument,[87] and there were many in London who, from August 1941 onwards, saw such action as a form of economic warfare, used to bully the United Kingdom into signing up to the American post-war system without conditions. These methods were not unknown in the so-called Good Neighbour policy, said this point of view, but they were new between democratic allies, and they were noticeably not applied at this stage to the Soviets. In November 1944 *The Economist* wrote: 'The Americans, for all their talk of freedom, want to limit other countries' freedom to do what Americans do not like.'[88]

Not only cynics felt how convenient it was for the Americans that their conversion to free trade should coincide with their rise to economic dominance, and those of Churchill's colleagues who pointed to this ambivalence, such as Eden, the Foreign Secretary, Cripps, the Secretary for India, and Bevin, the Minister of Labour, were not cynics.[89] But they all ex-

---

[86] Robbins, *Autobiography*, 201. The American position on civil aviation was explained for British readers in Joseph Krastner, 'What to do with the World's Air', *Transatlantic*, 3 (March 1944); Crowther, the Editor, told his British readers not be too scared by Krastner's image of out-and-out US predominance in the air, American journalists simply wrote about competition 'much more fiercely' than their British colleagues; detailed overview of the dispute in Alan P. Dobson, 'FDR and the Struggle for a Postwar Civil Aviation Regime: Legacy or Loss?', in Woolner et al. (eds), *FDR's World*.

[87] ... put directly to Stettinius in an otherwise very friendly letter of 18 April 1944, in *The Collected Writings of John Maynard Keynes*, xxiv: *Activities 1944–46: The Transition to Peace* (London, 1979), 27–30. No reply is recorded; Acheson cit. in Dobson, 'FDR and the Struggle', 45; Skidelsky, *John Maynard Keynes*, iii. 103, 337–8; cf. Woods, 'FDR and the New Economic Order', 183.

[88] cf. Alan P. Dobson, *United States Economic Statecraft for Survival, 1933–1991: Of Sanctions, Embargoes and Economic Warfare* (London, 2002), 61–5, Charmley, *Churchill's Grand Alliance*, ch. 8; *The Economist*, 11 November 1944 (the context was the contentious Chicago aviation conference of those weeks; overview in Dobson, 'FDR and the Struggle', 202–3).

[89] Cf. Reynolds, *From World War to Cold War*, 63: the most cynical of the Cabinet, in these areas at least, was the unelected Canadian Press magnate Beaverbrook, guilty of a strong form of anti-Americanism in some eyes: Robbins, *Autobiography*, 204; Beaverbrook's grievances against the US are described in A. J. P. Taylor, *Beaverbrook* (London, 1972), 439–40; his determination to maintain Britain's position as a world power in the face of American economic action ibid. 555–7.

pressed serious doubts about the direction and implications of American world views, well beyond the endlessly discussed confrontations over the conduct of the war. 'Soviet policy is amoral, while American policy is ex-aggeratedly moral, at least where non-American interests are concerned', said Eden.[90] The Lend-Lease Master Agreement was tantamount to 'black-mail', said Labour Ministers. Cripps and Bevin told the Prime Minster that they would prefer imperial 'autarchy' to a heavily tied American loan.[91] The dreams of a Henry Wallace provoked particularly sharp com-ments. The British Ambassador in Washington spoke of his 'apocalyptic version of America as "the chosen of the Lord" in whom the culture of Palestine, Rome, and Britain are to be brought to final fruition'. It was the 'most unbridled expression to date [June 1942] of the view of the new deal as the New Islam, divinely inspired to save the world'.[92] An 'unceas-ing wave of isolationism and anti-Americanism [was] passing over us' by May 1944, said Keynes, and this was well before the great, contentious conferences of the year.[93]

Some became seriously concerned for the prospects of domestic re-newal in this new situation. The intensity of the American debate on the world after the war was matched in the United Kingdom by the serious-ness of efforts to imagine and plan for a rebuilt Britain. Now fears arose, says the historian Dobson, that 'the economic liberalism advocated by Washington would compromise the chances of achieving full employ-ment after the war, and interfere with [the] hopes for massive reform outlined in the famous report by Sir William Beveridge (of late 1942) on health and welfare'. Who knows, asked Keynes, what terms the American would require if Britain should borrow from her for 'a great programme of social amelioration'.[94]

Divided between the impulse to patronize the US, to try to manipulate American power for British ends and to construct a distinctive, national–imperial path to the future, the British Establishment felt that it had

---

[90] Cit. in Charmley, *Churchill's Grand Alliance*, 32; Charmley comments: 'It was against this last rock that Eden's policy recommendations were to be shipwrecked.'

[91] Ibid. 49, 187.

[92] Ibid. 51; other sources cit. in Woods, 'FDR and the New Economic Order', 181.

[93] Ibid. 92; Keynes though remained convinced till the end of his life that the Ameri-cans needed a strong Britain and could be persuaded to do whatever necessary to help his nation. He apparently maintained a lofty detachment from all the evidence and experience that seemed to point in the opposite direction. The comparison is instructive between Keynes's reassuring letter to the Chancellor of 12 December 1944 (*Collected Writings*, xxiv. 192–23) and *The Economist* of 31 December 1944, which saw the normally pro-American journal publish its strongest attack ever on US unilateralism and selfishness over a wide range of issues; cf. Robert Skidelsky, *Keynes* (Oxford, 1996), 100–4.

[94] Dobson, *United States Economic Statecraft*, 67; Charmley, *Churchill's Grand Alliance*, 120; Skidelsky, *Keynes*, 237.

nothing to learn from its transatlantic partner and much to teach. Roosevelt's conferences might look like the method of 'the monkey house', said a leading London figure at Hot Springs, but they were just the kind of occasion the British could dominate with their unity, their personalities, and their preparation.[95] A Foreign Office paper of early 1944 proposed that although 'the American may feel that he is more efficient in business administration, in inventiveness, in techniques, and in mass production', he 'will, almost without realising it, accept Britain in thought, in politics, and in standards generally as an exemplar of quality'. By combining forces, however, 'rivalry' could be avoided and 'community' promoted.[96] On colonies, said Eden, the Americans should stop encouraging native peoples to dream of independence under some updated version of the League of Nations' 'mandate' system, and 'accept colonial responsibilities on the same terms as ourselves'. In any case, concluded Eden in this note to the Prime Minister, the two of them were agreed: 'Hands off the British Empire.'[97]

The Labour Party took it for granted that some of the resources to build the new, more progressive Britain would come from the Empire, and naturally assumed that it defined the nation's status as Great Power.[98] But in the Middle East, India, and South East Asia, the British governing class, like its French and Dutch peers, was forced bit-by-bit to cope with determined and explicit American efforts to undermine its position, with serious short-term repercussions on, for instance, the collaboration of secret intelligence services.[99] London's man in Saudi Arabia criticized the

---

[95] Lionel Robbins in Susan Howson and Donald Moggridge (eds), *The Wartime Diaries of Lionel Robbins and James Meade, 1943–45* (London, 1990), 56–8; preparation included a showing of the new Ministry of Information film *World of Plenty*, on the possibilities of rationalized food production and supply. With an appearance by Roosevelt and a ringing endorsement by H. G. Wells, the film was reportedly a great success; details in Richard Farmer, 'Exploiting a Universal Nostalgia for Steak and Onions: The Ministry of Information and the Promotion of *World of Plenty* (1943)', *Historical Journal of Film, Radio and Television* (June 2010); cf. above, n. 23.

[96] Cit. in Charmley, *Churchill's Grand Alliance*, 89; British observers often remarked disparagingly of American social and political conservatism, compared to progressive, left-moving Britain, e.g. Eden's Private Secretary, cit. in Thorne, *Issue of War*, 241, Harold Nicolson, *Diaries and Letters*, ii (London, 1967), 330.

[97] Cit. in Gardner, 'Atlantic Charter', 70; cf. Eden, *Memoirs*, ii. 513; here Eden implies that the Americans simply wanted to substitute European empires with their own.

[98] Cf. Alan Bullock, *Ernest Bevin: Foreign Secretary, 1945–1951* (New York, 1983), 117; figures such as Keynes of course shared the same outlook, and insisted that that the first step was economic independence from the United States; cf. Letter to Lord Beaverbrook, 27 April 1945, in *Collected Writings*, xxiv. 328–30, and other correspondence in this volume.

[99] Thorne, *Issue of War*, 226–7; David Stafford, *Roosevelt and Churchill: Men of Secrets* (London, 2000), 164–5, 189, 210, 252–5, 271–6, 286–8, 292–3, 302.

Americans for over-playing their hand and 'arous[ing] suspicions as to their good intentions':

> They see a backward country and immediately want to run it on modern lines not realizing that [King] Ibn Saud's strength and prestige in the Moslem world, which is of considerable value to us, lies in his insularity and will be undermined and largely neutralized if there is any large infiltration of Americans or for that matter members of any other Christian power.[100]

Both the British and the French considered the Atlantic Charter a huge provocation in the Arab world in particular, and tried to have it banned. Churchill openly demanded that its application be restricted to Europe; Roosevelt of course replying that its purposes were worldwide. There was no House of Commons debate on it, no radio programme or publicity by the Ministry of Information.[101] But the Americans had the Charter translated into Arabic and circulated it widely in the Middle East, to the particular chagrin of the French, who reportedly did succeed in banning it in North Africa.[102] In central Africa however, in response to the Charter's fame, they organized a special conference at Brazzaville in January 1944, aiming to assert the continuing destiny of France as an imperial power, but promising reforms.[103] For their part, the British made sure that Willkie's *One World*, with its resounding calls for an end to all colonial systems, would not appear in a country such as Egypt, just as they had stopped publication of Wilson's Fourteen Points in Iraq in 1918.[104]

Anthony Eden, as British Foreign Secretary, thought it 'unfortunate' that the Americans could not see how much Britain had done for Arab freedom and development. Others vainly hoped that the US might help shore up the British position, or at least make joint management work effectively, in the name of a 'British Monroe Doctrine' for the Middle

---

[100] Cit. in Rubin, *Great Powers in the Middle East*, 52.

[101] W. Arnold-Forster, *Charters of Peace: A Commentary on the Atlantic Charter and the Declarations of Moscow, Cairo and Teheran* (London, 1944), 133.

[102] But the Algerians came to know of it anyway, and set in motion a mass movement in its name. At the end of the war in Europe, huge popular demonstrations called for national independence. The gathering at Sétif set off a vast regional revolt, which the Resistance government in Paris decided unanimously to repress by force. The thousands of victims became martyrs to the cause of Algerian independence, and the movement was fatefully, permanently radicalized; summary in Martin Evans, 'Algeria and the Liberation: Hope and Betrayal', in H. R. Kedward and Nancy Wood (eds), *The Liberation of France: Image and Event* (Oxford, 1995), 260–5. President Jacques Chirac issued a formal apology for the Sétif massacre in 2005. Polemical film interpretation in *Hors-la-loi* (Rachid Bouchareb, 2010), an Algerian–Belgian–French co-production including support from French official cultural institutions.

[103] Tony Chafer, 'African Perspectives: The Liberation of France and its Impact in French West Africa', in Kedward and Wood (eds), *Liberation of France*, 242–3.

[104] Rubin, *Great Powers in the Middle East*, pp. 24, 135 and p.141, n. 15.

East.[105] Keynes pointed out that Britain's financial agony in 1945 was not due to the cost of the war against Germany but 'wholly' due to the expense of maintaining an imperial presence around the world, and above all in the Middle East.[106] To everyone else involved in the region however, it was obvious that the days of British hegemony were numbered, and that such was the stake of the Americans in the future of big oil alone that the British would be left to fight, 'a stubborn rear-guard action to preserve as much as possible of the political and economic influence on which "the British way of life" depended', as a semi-official historian in London wrote gloomily not long afterwards.[107]

As in the Middle East, the arrival in India of American soldiers, journalists, diplomats, intelligence agents, and plans for independence were actively encouraged by Roosevelt, whose fantasies included a constitutional convention chaired by an American. At the Teheran conference he told Stalin that India needed reform from the bottom up 'somewhat on the Soviet line'. Stalin replied that from bottom up 'would mean a revolution'.[108] The *Bombay Chronicle* expressed a vast wave of excitement when it declared the Atlantic Charter to be the 'Magna Carta of the world'.[109]

All this provoked the most violent of Churchill's reactions against the President he loved so much, and a concerted campaign by the Prime Minister and the Viceroy, Lord Linlithgow, to try to contain the impact of American activism.[110] Such was the force of this British line, and the emotions behind it, that after a Christmas 1941 meeting with Churchill, the President decided to avoid the topic altogether in open discussion, and to oblige the State Department to give up any explicit encouragement to Indian nationalists, no matter how deserving. But Roosevelt did not hesitate to send influential emissaries to the subcontinent, who invariably confirmed his judgements about the appalling conditions there, and pressurized the British on the inevitability of independence.[111] Meanwhile the American press was in 'an uproar,' recalls one account. Distinguished

---

[105] Rubin, *Great Powers in the Middle East*, 26, 57, 90; Watt, *Succeeding John Bull*, 107; George Kirk, *The Middle East in the War*, Survey of International Affairs (Oxford, 1952), 191.

[106] Cabinet Paper of 15 May 1945, in Keynes, *Collected Writings*, xxiv. 264–5.

[107] Kirk, *Middle East in the War*, 368; Charmley, *Churchill's Grand Alliance*, 196–201.

[108] Stafford, *Roosevelt and Churchill*, 219; Gardner, 'Atlantic Charter', 63.

[109] Cit. in Stafford, *Roosevelt and Churchill*, 207; for wide-ranging Japanese responses, Iriye, *Cambridge History of American Foreign Relations*, iii. 34–7.

[110] Churchill's view is briefly expressed in his memoir, *Second World War*, iv. 185–96; cf. D. C. Watt, *Succeeding John Bull*, pp. 234–7 and ch. 11 in general.

[111] Roosevelt's capacity for tactical duplicity on imperial issues is well documented in the Dutch case: Kersten, 'Dutch', 93–4; cf. Gardner, 'FDR and the "Colonial Question"', 128–9.

British visitors were bombarded with imprecations.[112] Leading magazine and newspapers published petitions on India from prominent figures in public life, while Wendell Willkie recounted to a vast radio audience how the Indians he had met on his round-the-world trip couldn't tell 'whether we really do stand for freedom, or what we mean by freedom'. He accused Roosevelt of being 'wishy-washy' on the issue of India.[113]

In response the Prime Minister told one of Roosevelt's India-bound emissaries that Willkie reminded him 'of a Newfoundland dog in a small parlour, which had wiped its paws on a young lady's blouse and swept off the teacups with its tail'.[114] When the Americans tried to reassure the British by insisting on the potential for economic development in such a country, Sir Ronald Campbell, from the Washington embassy, told London that this what he had always feared: 'we will get here a combination of Wallace up-lift and National Association of Manufacturers export drive.' The Undersecretary replied that social conditions anyway must be improved: 'The important thing…is to get [them] off the Independence tack.'[115] The BBC mounted a serious campaign of programmes to rebut American anti-Empire feeling, and dilute American propaganda influence in general, even on its own airwaves.[116] So successful were the British in these efforts that by the end of the war, American media and political attention had shifted its reforming zeal elsewhere, to South East Asia, with results that provoked decades of controversy.[117]

Looking back across the years, British commentators have always acknowledged that 'strains and stresses, impatience, prejudices, misunderstandings and occasional accusations of betrayal' were inevitable in a

---

[112] 'Can't you persuade your aristocrats to relax their hold on Malaya?', the international affairs specialist Barbara Ward was asked after an official lecture, Ward, 'Journey to America', *Horizon* (April 1943), 264.

[113] This paragraph is based on Stafford, *Roosevelt and Churchill*, ch. 15; cf. Gardner, 'Atlantic Charter', 58–65; Allan M. Winkler, 'American Opposition to Imperialism During World War II', in Jeffreys-Jones (ed.), *Eagle Against Empire*, 84–5.

[114] Cit. in Gardner, 'Atlantic Charter', 63.

[115] Ibid. 65; cf. Watt, *Succeeding John Bull*, 233–7.

[116] Thomas Hajkowski, '*Red on the Map*: Empire and Americanization at the BBC, 1942–50', in Wiener and Hampton (eds), *Anglo-American Media Interactions*, 176–83.

[117] This is the topic of Christopher Thorne's monumental volume, *Allies of a Kind: The United States, Britain and the War Against Japan, 1941–1945* (London, 1978), of its sequel, *Issue of War*, and, in part, of the equally imposing work of William Roger Louis, *Imperialism at Bay: The United States and the Decolonization of the British Empire, 1941–1945* (Oxford, 1977); D. C. Watt accuses the Americans of 'populism' and 'arrogance' in this area; *Succeeding John Bull*, 224, *passim*; the Dutch simply insisted on the impeccable nature of their imperial policies in Indonesia and after trying to ignore American impulses to change, attempted their own propaganda campaign in the US; Kersten, 'Dutch', 96, 100, 109; Gerda Jansen Hendriks, 'High Stakes in the East: Dutch Government Films on the Dutch East Indies/Indonesia 1940–1945', paper presented at the Iamhist Conference (Amsterdam, July 2007).

process which saw the US takeover as 'the sole genuinely global power'. The great British encyclopedist Toynbee thought at the end of World War II that compared to the alternatives, '[if] we do get an American empire instead we shall be lucky'.[118] The historians point out, though, that over time the need for cooperation and compromise tended to bring the two sides together, usually on the basis of America's superior strength, and from the great conferences came results that together the Anglo-Americans were normally able to impose on the rest.[119]

But to take a strictly geopolitical or geo-economic view of the American challenge that emerged from World War II means seriously underestimating not only the impact of America's incarnation as liberating armed forces—to be presented in the next chapter—but also the outstanding relevance of America's model of production and consumption for societies whose wartime sufferings and humiliations taught them they had much to learn about the business of staying competitive (surviving), militarily, economically, and politically, in the new world order.[120] Post-liberation France is the key example of this experience.

France: Modernization or decadence?

The new men who emerged from the wartime French experience of occupation, resistance, and exile had other priorities on their minds than salvaging the nation's 'overseas territories'. In the famous first broadcast from London in which de Gaulle launched his mission of Resistance, in June 1940, the General had promised 'when we get back we will re-make France'. The promise was as serious as the very will to resist. It was confirmed four years later in the triumphant hero's first major speech in liberated Paris, and in the detailed reform programme he announced right after the end of the war in Europe.[121] In this latter address de Gaulle pointed out that the instant the armies stopped fighting, a State's key currency of power was no longer military success. Instead...

---

[118] Watt, 'U.S. Globalism', 53; Toynbee cit. in Ferguson, *Colossus*, 68.

[119] Robbins, *Autobiography*, 199–200; Mendès-France, *Oeuvres complètes*, 194; Reynolds, *From World War to Cold War*, 62; Ikenberry speaks of a harmonious Anglo-American community of experts, refuses talk of imposition, and suggests that the Americans hoped that their visions 'would have a normative appeal to elites in other nations', thereby guaranteeing their legitimacy; 'World Economy Restored', 293–8, 320.

[120] *The Economist* discussed the very great American productivity progress during the war, and its implications for Britain's future development, in a series of articles starting 19 August 1944 under the title 'A Policy for Wealth'; the dimness of British official perceptions of these issues is denounced in Corelli Barnett, *The Audit of War: The Illusion and Reality of Britain as a Great Nation* (London, 1986), pp. 226–8, and ch. 9.

[121] *Le Monde*, 20 December 1944, 26 May 1945; Ellwood, *Rebuilding Europe*, 17.

...it is the capacity to live, to work, to produce which become the most pressing condition of the independence and influence of a nation.

The French, he emphasized, must show the world that they had understood this, and not expect to live on charity.[122]

Everywhere there was Resistance, recalled Michel Debré, a key protagonist of the post-war years, in London, Algiers, Paris, Lyons, Toulouse, there one found projects to revitalize the nation by relaunching French politics. Every tradition from Bonapartism on was present, said Debré, and new ones were invented for the occasion. Each of them expected a new kind of action by the State, all of them found—for a while—a means of continuing the celebrated unity of the Resistance experience. But this would be action with a purpose, since every protagonist understood that stagnant, largely rural France had been overwhelmed by technology and economic dynamism in 1940, and not just by the diabolic fury of the Nazis.[123] Léon Blum wrote from his prison cell that the nation's bourgeoisie—myopic, reactionary, selfish—had collapsed and been totally discredited by the defeat. The collaborationist Vichy regime was its last shield against contemporary reality:

> Is it not clear that in every field of productive activity—industry, agriculture, trade, banking—it had never left the rut of its traditions, and in a France inevitably left behind by more powerful countries in the quantity of its production, had been unable to preserve the prestige of our quality?...It had not understood that both its own interests and those of the nation required perpetual modification of the relationship between workers and employers.[124]

Blum declared that modernization meant promoting a democratic revolution: to open the nation to the world, to bring it to a par with the most advanced industrial economies, instilling the habit of continuous renewal and restructuring, distributing the fruits of industrial progress to the masses. This automatically suggested that the State should do the organizing and planning, said Blum, but under the direction of the working classes, who now had a tremendous opportunity to take the lead in constructing a France that would be social democratic, internationalist, and an example for Europe and the world.[125]

---

[122] *Le Monde*, 26 May 1945.
[123] Michel Debré, *La République et son pouvoir* (Paris, 1950), 180–8: cf. Gérard Bossuat, 'The Modernisation of France: A New Economic and Social Order after the Second World War?', in Dominik Geppert (ed.), *The Postwar Challenge: Cultural, Social and Political Change in Western Europe, 1945–58* (Oxford, 2003), 153–4; Nord, *France's New Deal*, ch. 2.
[124] Blum, *L'histoire jugera*, 59–63, cit. at p. 59.
[125] Ibid. 133–9; cf. Francois Bloch-Lainé and Jean Bouvier, *La France restaurée, 1944–1954: Dialogue sur les choix d'une modernisation* (Paris, 1986), 47–51.

The drive to social and economic modernization, combined with a strong recognition of the logic of interdependence, was common in antifascist forces everywhere. But nowhere was it transformed into specific plans as in the French Resistance, exceptionally fortunate in the sort of intellectual talent it could count on. Around de Gaulle in London a commission of experts had already produced by 1942 its own response to the challenges of the Atlantic Charter and Lend-Lease. Influenced by the British wartime experience, the Beveridge social welfare plan, and the writings of Keynes, the Alphand report of 1943 embraced economic stabilization and full employment, as well as nationalization and free trade. It predicted that there would be an economic planning ministry and a world economic organization.[126]

Like their British equivalents, the flow of reform plans that followed Alphand's all took for granted that expanding world trade was one of the keys to full employment, and that consensus on this point would ease the way to the ample American assistance needed to start reconstruction. But there were those who warned of the price likely to be paid for this support. In an outspoken paper delivered to de Gaulle at the end of 1943, the economist and former Popular Front supporter Georges Boris predicted that America's rejection of isolation was complete, 'but they are not cured of imperialism, far from it'. This was expressed in the urge to scatter the presumed benefits of their civilization to peoples everywhere, in a fashion that always employed the language of altruism. The Atlantic Charter said it all.

Boris suggested that the integral liberalism the US was proposing required that America itself must open its borders to the products and money of foreigners, and to the foreigners themselves, as immigrants. But would the people of the US really stand for this? Then again, with America as the indispensable, overwhelming creditor, how could monetary stability be guaranteed, and hence confidence? Waves of credit to Europe would be needed to keep the system functioning while reconstruction was going on. But after that phase, the contradiction between an open world and a closed America would condemn to failure any attempt at general neoliberalism. So the Europeans with their advanced welfare states would have to slow down and allow the Americans to catch up, wasting the advantage of all their reformism, or go through another 1929.

Beyond this the fundamental cultural and psychological differences remained, concluded Boris. The Americans still firmly believed in indi-

---

[126] Nord, *France's New Deal*, 94–111; Bossuat, 'Modernisation of France', 154; full historical and comparative contextualization in Tony Judt, *Postwar: A History of Europe since 1945* (London, 2005), 67–70.

vidual enterprise, the Europeans not at all. The former resented any sort of intervention by the State; the latter expected it to deal with the basic capitalist injustice in the distribution of wealth, which the peoples' sacrifices of wartime had made far more acute. No more big cakes and little cakes: 'the masses' wanted one cake for all, equally cut up. So the Europeans' dependence on the Americans for their basic reconstruction needs would come at a price. There would be political conditioning and manipulation. Together though, united under French leadership, the Europeans would be able to resist this form of hegemony, Boris insisted.[127]

It was not until the businessman and international civil servant Jean Monnet returned to France, after the liberation, that the prospect of a different, more realistic kind of mediation opened up. The providential Monnet had spent his war in Britain and America, organizing friends and winning admiration for his particular combination of vision and practicality. Like the most successful Englishman in Washington, General Dill of the British Supply Mission, Monnet 'had an acute, almost feline understanding of the subtleties of the alliance',[128] a quality that gave him a unique place at the heart of Atlantic relations over the succeeding 15 years. With his special openness to Anglo-American inspiration and ideas, the signatory of France's Lend-Lease master agreement in March 1945 would turn out to be the man to turn all the talk into method, policy, and decisions for France.[129]

In August 1945 Monnet told his leader de Gaulle, when the two were in Washington on an official trip:

> You speak of greatness...but today the French are small. There will only be greatness when the French are of a stature to warrant it. That is how they are. For this purpose they must modernize themselves—because at the moment they are not modern. They need more production and greater productivity. Materially the country needs to be transformed.

De Gaulle had by now realized the great economic weakness of his nation, says Monnet in his memoirs, and knew he had no choice but to ask the Americans for their help. He had just lived through the first atomic explosions, and confessed to Monnet that 'America's dazzling prosperity...had astonished him since his arrival: his knowledge of this enormous country

---

[127] 'La politique américaine: Les données fondamentales du problème', in Georges Boris, *Servir la République: Textes et temoignages* (Paris, 1963), 328–35; commentary and contextualization in Bloch-Lainé and Bouvier, *La France restaurée*, 91–3.

[128] The phrase is applied to Dill by Brian Holden Reid, in Reid, 'Tensions', 286.

[129] Recollection and critiques of Monnet by his peers in Bloch-Lainé and Bouvier, *La France restaurée*, 51, 87, 90–1, 119, *passim*; cf. Nord, *France's New Deal*, 109–11.

had previously been limited and imperfect'.[130] De Gaulle's biographer, Lacouture, presents evidence that these impressions were not new. In his successful July 1944 trip to the US, the leader of the Free French had been 'immensely and instantly impressed by the sight of an America bursting with promise and industrial creativity'.[131] In a memorable phrase, Lacouture makes the following suggestion:

> In considering de Gaulle one should never forget the American euphoria which so brought out everything that was modernist and even futurist in this mediaeval crusader.[132]

Although few at the time or since spotted these aspects of the man, de Gaulle knew how to read at least some of the signs of the times. In a June 1942 speech he saluted the Four Freedoms as 'magnificent', and paid tribute to the American ability to supply an 'international ideal' for the masses who were the protagonists of World War II. Even Henry Wallace received an endorsement. Echoing Wallace's newly invented phraseology, de Gaulle talked of 'the war of the common man'.[133]

But in practice a great tension developed between liberated France's geopolitical situation and the urge of some of its key figures to deal with the 'pitiless reality of everyday life', using, as appropriate, US resources and solutions. Even the British, no lovers of de Gaulle, could see that politically the General and his Free French movement were treated very badly by Roosevelt and Hull.[134] A bitter personality clash between the two men of destiny had broken out from their first encounter. Some have seen the austere soldier as one of the very few men or women not to be overawed by Roosevelt's personal charm and charisma. But a senior State Department observer attributed the antagonism to the incompatibility between de Gaulle's 'acute and unconquerable nationalism' and 'the plans for remodelling the world worked out by Roosevelt'.[135]

Struggles between Washington and de Gaulle broke out over war strategy, the treatment of French North Africa when it was invaded in November 1942, and authority in liberated France after D-Day. The

---

[130] Monnet's biographer emphasizes that de Gaulle and Monnet were not allies, or close in any way, but in this area they could agree, François Duchêne, *Jean Monnet: The First Statesman of Interdependence* (New York, 1994), 146; Bloch-Lainé and Bouvier, *La France restaurée*, 133.

[131] Jean Monnet, *Memoirs* (London, 1978), 228.

[132] Jean Lacouture, *De Gaulle: The Rebel, 1890–1944* (London, 1990), 543.

[133] Charles de Gaulle, *Discours et messages: Pendant la Guerre, Juin 1940–Janvier 1946* (Paris, 1946), 203, speech of 18 June 1942.

[134] Robbins, *Autobiography*, 237.

[135] On the tensions between de Gaulle and Roosevelt, and the subsequent conflicts, Lacouture, *De Gaulle*, ch. 27; (cit. at p. 333), Harper, *American Visions*, 141–4.

Americans persisted in their deeply ambiguous ties with Vichy France until forced by events to relinquish them, and made a messy deal with its representatives in North Africa. Their propaganda then seemed to encourage Arab nationalism in that region, and to undermine the authority of the French empire. At the Casablanca conference of January 1943, Roosevelt had openly urged his host, the Sultan of Morocco, to imagine independence. Some historical analyses suggest that French garrisons were left to be massacred by the Japanese in Indochina rather than encouraged to participate in the area's liberation. De Gaulle attempted to put down markers, insisting in a landmark speech in Brazzaville, in January 1944, that France would reform and relaunch its empire, 'under our sovereignty'. But he was convinced that the American government 'accepted France's permanent eclipse as a fact'.[136]

In general, official France seemed to pay little attention to all this. The new newspaper *Le Monde*, a model of respectability, used the occasion of a private conference of the Institute of Pacific Relations at Hot Springs, Virginia, to allow the government to reject via its scant pages any notion of 'accountability' to others for the working of the French empire.[137] Meanwhile, not surprisingly, de Gaulle took out a reinsurance policy, signing a pact of friendship with Stalin in December 1944. Approved unanimously by the national Consultative assembly, the pact meant that, as the wartime alliance of the Big Three broke down, France had less to worry about from Communism and the Soviet Union than many other western nations.[138]

In his own mind de Gaulle seems to have resolved the tension between American geopolitical action and its world-reforming impulses with the dismissive phrases in his war memoirs where he talks of the 'messianic mission' the United States had chosen, of its 'vast designs':

The United States, amazed at the scale of its own resources, feeling that its dynamism no longer had sufficient scope for action within its own frontiers,

---

[136] J. B. Duroselle, *France and the United States*, ch. 6 (de Gaulle cit. at p. 150); Irwin Wall, *The United States and the Making of Postwar France, 1945–1954* (Cambridge, 1991), 20–9; D. C. Watt, *Succeeding John Bull*, 237–9; Gardner, 'FDR and the "Colonial Question" ', 130–1; Brazzaville speech in de Gaulle, *Discours et messages*, 401–4; Jean Touchard notes that this highly important speech was *not* a charter for decolonization: Touchard, *Le gaullisme* (Paris, 1978), 67–8.

[137] *Le Monde*, 13 January, 19 January, 20 January, 26 January, 1 February, 3 February 1945; the report in this last edition pointed out that all political parties were united in defence of the Empire, and that de Gaulle had told the French they knew how to look after what was their own; Nord, *France's New Deal*, 375, suggests that the armed forces remained particularly attached to the Empire as compensation for their humiliation in the war, with dreadful consequences for the subsequent decolonization process.

[138] The pact was hailed in the first number of *Le Monde*, 19 December 1944.

wishing to aid all those in the world then living in poverty and subjection, yielded in turn to the temptation of intervention, a cause in which the spirit of domination then became enlisted.

Describing his long July 1944 meeting with Roosevelt, the General famously wrote: 'As was only human, his will to power cloaked itself in idealism.'[139] How else to reconcile the American urge to democratic decolonization with the equally strong impulse to install military bases everywhere in the world, including on French territory? But there was apparently never an elaboration of these thoughts that went beyond geopolitical categories, or looked at the society that, at Roosevelt's bidding, was now proposing to set up 'an American Peace...a permanent system of intervention...instituted by international law'.[140]

Glimpses of some of de Gaulle's feelings may be seen in his November 1944 suggestion to Churchill that the British and the French unite against the superpowers, in the name of Europe's world inheritance, 'and a certain conception of man despite the progressive mechanization of society'.[141] Apart from some scant musings of the 1930s on the domination of the dollar in American life, the leader who allowed his aides to portray him as the Jean D'Arc of his day when Wendell Willkie called never developed a line of argument, a 'discourse', about the United States, much less one that could leave him open to accusations of anti-Americanism.[142]

On the other hand, a figure like Monnet never offered one on Americanism, for all his enthusiasms, or even an explanation of what criteria he favoured for selecting what was to be adopted, what adapted, and what rejected from the Anglo-American way of doing things. The historic intelligence that Monnet and his expert colleagues bequeathed to their country, with de Gaulle's benediction, was to show how the lessons of America's scientific and organizational successes might be moulded to French experience, and to convince the Americans it was in their interest to help France in this project.[143] At the same time the planners had to adapt the traditional State very rapidly, so as to supply as fast as possible a response to the large mass of French citizens who genuinely assumed that bour-

---

[139] De Gaulle, *Complete War Memoirs*, 573.

[140] Ibid. 573, 574; Duroselle, a leading post-war French historian, comments that these phrases had 'immense historical significance', as became clear when de Gaulle governed from 1958 to 1969, *France and the United States*, 157.

[141] De Gaulle, *Complete War Memoirs*, 727.

[142] On pre-war reflections, Christopher S. Thompson, 'Prologue to Conflict: de Gaulle and the United States, First Impressions Through 1940', in Robert O. Paxton and Nicholas Wahl (eds), *De Gaulle and the United States: A Centennial Reappraisal* (Oxford and Providence, 1994), 14–16; Paxton ibid. 7, Roger, *American Enemy*, p. 492, n. 117; Lacouture, *De Gaulle*, 334–5; Willkie, *One World*, 20–1.

[143] Cf. Bossuat, 'Modernisation of France', 155; Nord, *France's New Deal*, 111–15.

geois capitalism was dead in their country, and so looked forward enthusiastically to the birth of some new form of socialism in the land with the greatest revolutionary tradition in Europe.[144] But Monnet and de Gaulle refused to see the questions they faced in ideological terms. So bad was the day-to-day situation of surviving and living that a complete social breakdown was what they feared. Without 'a profound social change' it seemed inevitable to de Gaulle that 'the embittered and suffering mass of the workers would founder on disturbances which ran the risk of depriving France of what remained of her substance'.[145]

In December 1945, at the moment when Monnet submitted his first comprehensive planning proposal, the French government applied for a new loan from the Export–Import Bank of $550 million. It also promised to ratify the Bretton Woods accord, devalue the franc, sign a bilateral aviation convention, and forego any increase in quotas or tariffs.[146] Monnet had prepared for the test by importing an expert from the Massachusetts Institute of Technology to teach techniques of national accounting, one of the pre-requisites of the State-run, macroeconomic management systems that the peace was to learn from the war.[147] But the Americans of the time expected more, starting with the rapid adoption by France of the 'commercial policy' that Washington wanted. The US Embassy in Paris made clear to its masters that this would happen only with large dollar credits, but if they did arrive then France would help the other Europeans understand that this would be the key condition of any aid.[148] By this time however, the deepening East–West conflict was beginning to add complicated layers of mutual dependence to the old positions. The Americans needed a strong France to fight Communism and help them reinvent Germany; the French republic, to be strong, needed American aid and support. The trick was to find the political and moral resources to keep these two impulses in a balance favourable to France, so that help could be accepted in a sense conditionally, on French terms.[149]

---

[144] Blum, *L'histoire jugera*, 8–9, 66, 139; Gérard Bossuat points out however that although all were in favour of State-led innovation and reform, there was no agreement on the specific plans required: 'choices were dictated by circumstances'; 'Modernisation of France', 156–7; cf. Nord, *France's New Deal*, 367–73.

[145] De Gaulle, *Complete War Memoirs*, 688.

[146] Wall, *United States and the Making of Postwar France*, 42; Judt, *Postwar*, 70–1.

[147] Monnet, *Memoirs*, 227; cf. Bossuat, 'Modernisation of France', 158–9.

[148] Doc. cit. in Ellwood, *Rebuilding Europe*, 64; full American context of these negotiations presented in Wall, *United States and the Making of Postwar France*, 38–56.

[149] For American scepticism on this approach, John S. Hill, 'American Efforts to Aid French Reconstruction between Lend-Lease and the Marshall Plan', *Journal of Modern History* (September 1992), 515–6; for the self-confidence of the French planners in their own analyses and prescriptions for their country's problems, Nord, *France's New Deal*, 377–8.

The wartime inheritance of feelings, perceptions, and convictions lived on long after the end of hostilities, on both sides. Truman's Washington felt that 'France' suffered from an 'inferiority complex', dreaming of 'grandeur' far beyond its means, and in its frustration expressing contempt for the US as a civilization, and scorn for its values. Communism there was a cancerous outgrowth of poverty, and nothing more. The masses would befriend America when they clearly saw what the global New Deal could do for them.[150] For their part the French economic planners never bothered to take issue with this outlook, but emphasized their agreement with those elements of American policy that seemed most useful to them—like economic liberalism—pleading always and above all that the Open Door be opened in America itself. In a big campaign in Washington and New York, Léon Blum insisted that 'prosperity has become indivisible like peace and justice'. He saluted the Roosevelt tradition for facing up to the logic of interdependence, and creating a new kind of international community. But Blum's campaign was not a success, and the money eventually allotted far less than the negotiators had hoped for.[151]

All this strengthened the Gaullist diffidence and defiance, which crept into the wider intellectual debate at the end of the war, crossing the ideological divides and putting down the deepest roots of all. In a remarkable novel of 1954, which confirmed her fame as a writer, Simone de Beauvoir evoked a group of left-wing friends from literary and political circles, whose self-appointed job it was to express the hopes and fears of the generation that had been young at the liberation. Whatever their individual positions, the group as a whole was endowed by its creator with remarkable powers of foresight on the coming confrontations:

> I shook my head and Scriassine resumed heatedly: 'Don't you see? What weight will the message of French writers have when the earth is ruled by either Russia or the United States? No-one will understand them anymore; very few will even speak their language.' …
>   'I know Dubreuilh believes in peace and the possibility of maintaining a free and independent Europe,' Scriassine said. 'But even brilliant minds can

---

[150] State Department document of September 1946 cit. in Wall, *United States and the Making of Postwar France*, 58–9.

[151] Blum, *L'Oeuvre de Leon Blum* (Paris, 1958), 197–200; the context was the long, disorderly negotiation leading to the 'Blum-Byrnes' loan accords of May 1946, Wall, *United States and the Making of Postwar France*, 38–56, Bloch-Lainé and Bouvier, *La France restaurée*, 90–1, 129; Bossuat, 'Modernisation of France', 158; Nord, *France's New Deal*, 153; for the vast controversy surrounding the fate of the French film industry after these accords, which included a weighty quota agreement, Trumpbour, *Selling Hollywood*, 266–70.

sometimes be mistaken,' he added with an indulgent smile. 'We'll be annexed by Russia or colonised by America, of that you can be sure.' ...

'Nevertheless, certain conditions would be less unfavourable than others,' he said confidently. 'If Russia wins, there's no problem: it's the end of civilisation and the end of all of us. But if America should win, the disaster wouldn't be quite so bad. If we were able to give her certain values while maintaining some of our own ideas, there'd be some hope that future generations would one day re-establish the ties with our own culture and traditions. But to succeed in that would require the total mobilisation of all our potential.'[152]

The longer the war had gone on—and almost no one predicted that the agony would endure beyond autumn 1944—the more it changed the short- and long-term meanings of the America-as-future question in Europe and the wider world. But even as they clutched for a space between the two emerging giants of the era, thinking Europeans knew that the challenges presented by the causes of the war had not gone away, had not been crowded out by its consequences. As their wartime reflections demonstrated, the new American will-to-power shook up many an intellectual's dream of the world to be built when the fighting finally stopped.

PROGRESS REDISCOVERED? EUROPEAN THINKERS AND AMERICA'S PROPOSITIONS IN WORLD WAR II

Contemplating the new superpower

Almost until the very end of the conflict, the fog of war hung heavily over the Atlantic. How else to explain the large gap of understanding across the ocean between 'thinking people'—George Orwell's phrase—about the meaning of what was to come afterwards? In January 1943 Orwell himself, in a characteristically gloomy mood, wrote:

Now ... the tide begins to turn and immediately the dreary world which the American millionaires and their British hangers-on intend to impose upon us begins to take shape. The British people, in the mass, don't want such a world, and might say so fairly vigorously when the Nazis are out of the way.[153]

---

[152] S. de Beauvoir, *The Mandarins*, translation of Paris edition of 1954 (London, 1957), 43–4.

[153] Letter from England to *Partisan Review*, 3 January 1943, in *The Collected Essays, Journalism and Letters of George Orwell*, ii: *My Country Right or Left, 1940–1943* (Harmondsworth, 1970), 282.

What this 'dreary world' looked like Orwell did not care to spell out, but he clearly thought that any form of substantial continuity with the pre-war era would be a defeat for the popular, democratic revolution he believed in.

But the point here is not so much the content as the occasion of Orwell's musing. The author of *Animal Farm* (1944) was writing to a small, American left-wing magazine of political culture, *Partisan Review*, using one of the few channels that allowed European opinion—or what was left of it—to filter through regularly to a prime American audience.[154] By this phase in the war, traffic in the other direction was far more voluminous, certainly as far as Britain and the liberated countries were concerned. For the British there were Washington correspondents, radio journalists, visitors, and a limited but steady supply of books. All the key tracts on America's view of the post-war world were quickly published in London, and from there they could spread through exile communities and underground channels to the rest of Europe. This was a great change compared to the early days of the war when very few American books were published in Britain, and the US itself only hit the headlines 'during Presidential elections or after some phenomenal behaviour on the part of the weather', as the writer and lecturer Vera Brittain complained.[155]

For their part, senior American journalists had always been present in London, and from the time when American troops began to arrive in southern Italy in July 1943, the important American newspapers and magazines such as the *New York Times* and the *Saturday Evening Post* quickly sent key reporters describing conditions in 'liberated' Europe. Meanwhile distinguished magazines, including the *Atlantic Monthly* and *Harpers*, habitually reserved space for prominent exiles living in America, men such as Thomas Mann, Joseph Schumpeter, Hans Kühn, Franz Neumann, and Jacques Maritain. Many of these, even minor figures, succeeded in publishing their books in America, though whatever their long-term fame, few seem to have made much impact at the time. Although Schumpeter did quite well with his *Capitalism, Socialism and Democracy*, of 1942, the most prominent exception to this rule was another Austrian economist Friedrich Hayek, a refugee in Britain rather than the US. His powerful denunciation of collectivism in all its forms, *The Road*

---

[154] Context and reception explained in Irving Howe, 'Orwell in America', in Rob Kroes (ed.), *Nineteen Eighty-Four and the Apocalyptic Imagination in America* (Amsterdam, 1985), 21–4.

[155] Vera Brittain in National Peace Council, *The British Commonwealth and the United States in the Post-War*, 10–11.

to Serfdom, gave Professor Hayek several weeks of celebrity status on Wall Street in the first half of 1945.[156]

Yet moments of genuine, intellectual dialogue between the two sides of the ocean appear to have been very rare. *The Listener*, the BBC's weekly magazine that published transcripts of its most important talks and much else besides, recorded one such in January 1944. This was an impromptu discussion between Ed Murrow, the famed CBS correspondent in London, and a small group of British luminaries, now mostly forgotten, on the meaning of Churchill's phrase, 'We mean to hold our own', referring obviously to the row over the future of the Empire. Broadcast in the BBC North American Service, the debate predicted that the US would need the British Empire, and not just for bases, while Murrow told the British: 'you feel about the French empire what we feel about yours.'[157]

But *The Listener* recorded no similar encounters in these years, and on the question of the Empire indeed went out of its way to strengthen pro-Empire programming, in part as an antidote to the swelling American influence on this and so many other questions dear to British hearts. At the same time the Corporation was making strenuous efforts to bring its output to American listeners via US radio stations of all sorts.[158] So the impression that remains is of two quite separate worlds of elaboration and discussion. Not surprisingly, few of the cultivated minds of Europe who passed through World War II were in a position to reflect on America in the way they'd been used to in the 1920s or 1930s. So great was the upheaval, so tragic the confirmation of all the predictions of catastrophe, so baleful the failure of all the hopes placed in the previous round of post-war visions, that the best the thinkers could hope for was a voice in the debates going on everywhere about renewal in their own country or—in the case of the many distinguished exiles—wherever they had come to rest.[159]

---

[156] J. A. Schumpeter, *Capitalism, Socialism and Democracy* (1st edn, New York, 1942); reception described in Thomas K. McCraw, 'Introduction', to 2008 edition, p. xxv; F. A. Hayek, *The Road to Serfdom* (London, 1944); a *Reader's Digest* compression of the book supplied its author with a mass audience and a lasting reputation; on Hayek's reception, ironical views of Isaiah Berlin in H. G. Nicholas (ed.), *Washington Despatches, 1941–1945* (London, 1981), entries of 31 March, 6 May, 11 June 1945.

[157] *The Listener*, 13 January 1944.

[158] Hajkowski, 'Red on the Map', 176–85; cf. Maurice Gorham, *Sound and Fury: Twenty-One Years in the BBC* (London, 1948), 109–35. Gorham was the Director of the BBC's North American Service after 1942; his memoir contains much commentary on arrangements, initiatives, and people, but none at all on content, or on the BBC's deep diffidence of American radio and its potential influence in Britain.

[159] According to their Italian peers, the group of French exiles in America was particularly isolated and self-referential, even arrogant, with a few distinguished exceptions such as the writer André Maurois, the philosopher Jacques Maritain, and the anthropologist, Claude Lévi-Strauss; details in Bénédicte Deschamps, 'Salvemini e gli intellettuali fuorusciti

Thomas Mann was one of those who made the most of his new situation in California. A Rotarian since 1929, admirer of the New Deal, Mann became a naturalized American citizen in 1944. He made clear to fellow Rotarians in the United States his conviction that 'the preservation and stewardship of the West's cultural inheritance has passed to America'.[160] Like so many, Mann too commented on the 'contraction' of the world caused by communications technology and the aeroplane, but felt that this opened the way to new ideas of world community and mutual responsibility. He told a Library of Congress audience in October 1943 that a Magna Carta of universal human rights was needed, with the American Bill of Rights as a possible model.[161]

Mann saw America as a land of 'courageous progressivity... [which] gives us premonitions of the coming world in its egalitarianism and in its feeling that work disgraces no-body. The common possessions of opportunities for enjoyment and education are largely achieved.' If everyone smoked the same cigarettes, ate the same ice cream, saw the same movies, heard the same music on the radio, and wore similar clothing, this was no cause for regret but a sign that freedom and equality were developing and modifying each other in the American context. Class differences would disappear over time as the right to work and the duty to work became accessible to all. If this sounded 'communistic', so be it. Fear of communism as such was superstitious and childish, just like the German bourgeoisie's fear of social democracy in the 1880s. The new world would be social democratic, with America showing the way to common rights of ownership and the enjoyment of earthly goods.[162]

But the case of fellow German émigré Theodore Adorno, a leading figure in the creation of the Frankfurt School of Social Research, highlights some of the paradoxes of the exile's view of the democracy-as-prosperity question. Adorno spent eleven years in the US, and never forgot his debt of 'existential' gratitude to the country. His highly influential *Dialectic of Enlightenment*, written in 1944–5 with fellow Frankfurter Max Horkheimer, was based to a large extent on material and observations gathered in America on what they saw as the application of mass-production techniques to the standardization and co-optation of consciousness via enter-

francesi negli Stati Uniti (1940–1944): Un'incontro mancato', in Patrizia Audenino (ed.), *Il prezzo della libertà: Gaetano Salvemini in esilio* (Soveria Mannelli, 2009), 80–2.

[160] On Mann and Rotary, de Grazia, *Irresistible Empire*, 19–24.

[161] T. Mann, *The War and the Future*, Library of Congress (Washington DC, 13 October 1943), 22.

[162] Ibid. 19–21; on Mann's background and American experience, Coser, *Refugee Scholars*, 239–42. The author points out that although happy to adopt the role of passing public commentator, Mann never dealt with American themes in his fiction; ibid. 242.

tainment.[163] Yet Adorno's interest in the American nation's progress or problems, its wartime evolution and developing impact on the world, seems to have been minimal. Only those phenomena that might have 'prognostic value' for the future of Europe were taken seriously, particularly any evidence that might confirm the unhappy refugee's conviction that fascist authoritarianism was 'a universal tendency' that could spring up at any time anywhere. What terrified Adorno most of all, says the German political philosopher Offe, was the threat of a merger between 'European totalitarianism' and 'the American entertainments industry'. In July 1945 he felt certain that the obvious coming clash between the United States and Soviet Russia would 'push American capitalism in a fascist direction'.[164]

Because the post-war settlement, the breakdown of the wartime alliance, and the onset of the 'Cold War' weighed so heavily on the decades that followed in Europe, few care to recall today the sort of arguments about the future that circulated in the wartime years *before* the Communist question became unavoidable, and before the concept of 'totalitarianism' had taken over so many intellectual debates about right and wrong in the world. American observers— and exiles such as Jacques Maritain—all took it for granted that the United States and its designs would play the key role in the great reconstruction of peace[165], but this was far from clear to their peers who had remained in beleaguered Europe. Those free (or paid) to think about the future in that part of the world were, not surprisingly, much less sanguine and optimist than was the norm across the Atlantic. But they could still imagine a democratic order built by Europeans themselves, with the Americans providing no more than the material help needed to make reconstruction work and keep Germany down.

---

[163] 'The Culture Industry: Enlightenment as Mass Deception', in Adorno and Horkheimer, *Dialectic of Enlightenment* (Amsterdam, 1947); the essay offers no reflection on the relationship between American politics, economics, or society and the development of the 'culture industries', but assumes they are a typical, theoretically definable, phenomenon of Western capitalism in that phase of its development, whether under democratic or fascist control. Adorno's existence in America explained in Lorenz Jäger, *Adorno: A Political Biography* (Oxford, 2004), ch. 9; production of the *Dialectic of Enlightenment* and discussion of the concept of 'culture industry' ibid. ch. 10; cf. Coser, *Refugee Scholars*, 90–4.

[164] Claus Offe, *Reflections on America: Tocqueville, Weber and Adorno in the United States* (Cambridge, 2005), ch. 4, esp. pp. 73–80; Offe makes clear that Adorno radically revised his opinions of America and his experiences there in his later years, leaving his readers with 'two [*sic*] pictures of America that simply do not go together and are each as unconvincing as the other', ibid. 87–92; Adorno's own 1969 account of his intellectual evolution in the US in Donald Fleming and Bernard Bailyn (eds), *The Intellectual Migration: Europe and America, 1930–1960* (Cambridge, Mass., 1969), ch. 7.

[165] An intensely moral and uplifting view of this prospect was offered by Maritain in his broadcast 'America's Role in the New Europe', reproduced in *The Commonweal* (February 26 1943).

At a May 1945 meeting in Paris of the progressive Catholic group around the journal *Esprit*, Michel Colmert summed up a wide range of local thought on the choices facing the Old World:

> Most European countries are, in varying degrees, in a transitional phase between capitalism and socialism. The old system can only be revived by massive aid from outside, and the new one is in a state of helpless infancy owing to the physical and moral destitution of the working masses. Any attempt to build a [socialist] system in a single country is doomed to failure...

The French Resistance, said Colmert, had provided a blueprint for a progressive national reconstruction effort. Now, this example should be proposed to the other liberated nations, so as to create...

> ...a European New Deal for the prevention of starvation and unemployment, the restoration of transport and the distribution of credit.... France today is in a wretched state, but that is no reason why she should not try to promote a democratic order from which famine and fascism are excluded once and for all.

In terms of international politics, this meant that the choice lay between 'total submission to Anglo-American capitalism—which not even America demands of us, let alone Britain—and an independent policy with some degree of federalism'.[166]

'The peoples of Europe mean to be independent and not to be the satellites of anyone', the prominent British historian A. J. P. Taylor told listeners to the BBC's Home Service in November 1945. They wanted Socialism and the Rights of Man, 'economic collectivism and intellectual individualism'. They wanted what the Communists had to offer 'but they do not want it in the Communist way'. They wanted liberty for themselves but no liberty for Fascists and their supporters, types like the big landowners and international bankers. This means that the Right was dead, capitalism silent and discredited. Nationalization and state control of foreign trade would be universal. Not surprisingly then:

> Nobody in Europe believes in the American way of life—that is in private enterprise: or rather, those who believe in it are a defeated party and a party which seems to have no more future than the Jacobites in England after 1688.[167]

---

[166] Walter Lipgens (ed.), *Documents on the History of European Integration*, iii (Berlin, 1988), 29–31.

[167] 'The European revolution', *The Listener*, 22 November 1945; Jacques Maritain had made similar points in his 1943 broadcast; 'America's Role in the New Europe'.

Always under ferocious attack in the US as enemies of 'private enterprise', the New Dealers thought they had found their own solution to the problem of reconciling collectivism and democracy, of finding a new balance between State and market. But that was not how things appeared to European thinkers. Even after the Bretton Woods accords had been signed, *The Economist* still considered America an unlikely model in this area, since the agreements had still to be turned into reality via Congress, and the US was the nation 'least persuaded of the necessity of taking positive action to control the economic environment of human activities'.[168] Echoing Thomas Mann, the most distinguished British philosopher of his day, Bertrand Russell, wrote that the biggest question of all at the end of the war remained 'the combination of democracy with central control over the economic life of the community'. At a time when his peers from central Europe, in exile in various parts of Britain, the US, or New Zealand, were writing monumental tomes which insisted that the two could not in any way be combined without producing totalitarianism, Russell declared his belief in the moral capacity of Britain to offer a new route out of this dilemma.[169]

Although Joseph Schumpeter was also convinced that Britain, thanks to the political genius of its governing class, would find a workable synthesis of collectivism and parliamentary democracy, the best-selling philosophical book of the era, Hayek's *Road to Serfdom*, insisted that, on the contrary, the British were sacrificing the nation's character to their new ideas of socialism.[170] Likewise Karl Popper's *The Open Society and Its Enemies*, written in 1943 but published in 1945, warned heavily that large-scale 'planning' of any sort must inevitably compromise freedom, as did the speeches of another of the distinguished émigré economists from Vienna, Ludwig von Mises.[171] The problem was 'mass man' and the ruthlessness of his craving for absolute unanimity, security, and comfort. The philosopher Herman Rauschning, the former newspaper editor Leopold Schwarzschild, and the theologian Hans Kühn in Harvard, all declared that self-appointed tribunes of the people such as Hitler and Stalin had not conquered 'the masses' but simply portrayed and represented them. These two diabolical figures could only have come out of the Germany or the Russia of those years, conceded Kühn, but the rise of the masses and

[168] *The Economist*, 29 July 1944.
[169] Thomas Mann, 'How To Win the Peace', *Atlantic Monthly* (February 1942); Russell, 'Where Do We Go Now?', *The Listener* (11 January 1945).
[170] Schumpeter, *Capitalism, Socialism*, 229–31; Hayek, *Road to Serfdom*, 78, 83, 90.
[171] Cf. *Selected Writings of Ludwig von Mises*, iii: *The Political Economy of International Reform and Reconstruction*, ed. Richard M. Ebeling (Indianapolis, 2000); on the Austrian school of economics and its welcome in America, Coser, *Refugee Scholars*, 137–45.

their demands, combined with their capacity to break the constraints of tradition and destroy 'all higher values' (Rauschning) were challenges that no Western democracy could ignore.[172]

Schumpeter, Popper, and Rauschning were, in their way, optimists, and a great act of faith must have been required for Rauschning to place his money—in 1941—on the future construction of a 'Pax Atlantica' led by Great Britain.[173] Hayek and Schwarzschild in contrast were pessimists, pouring scorn on the then current fashion for constructing visions of a 'welfare state', or for spreading democracy via a device such as the United Nations, which obviously required the Big Three to agree among themselves perpetually if peace was to be kept. Von Mises believed that the Bretton Woods institutions would inevitably bring 'world inflation on an unprecedented scale'. Far better a return to a rigid gold standard all round, with America leading by example. Von Mises contemplated with the calmest equanimity his own prediction that Europe after the war would 'have to go through a long period of extreme poverty', while the blameless entrepreneurs returned to rebuild their businesses, the banks their savings deposits, and the masses their will to work more and consume less.[174]

But all of these writers were eventually forced to come to some sort of terms with the *political* reality that the mass man's demands for greater economic comfort and security could not and would not be ignored by the surviving Western democracies. From 1941 onwards, among all the other projects, one great priority for the post-war world had been defined on both sides of the Atlantic, and that was the need to raise living standards 'everywhere'. Love it or hate it (as men like Hayek, von Mises, and Schwarzschild did openly), once this vast aspiration had been taken up by the government and public opinion of the United States, and identified as a supreme purpose of America's participation in the conflict, then there

---

[172] Hayek, *Road to Serfdom*, 90; Popper explained the wartime purpose of his book in *Unended Quest: An Intellectual Autobiography* (London, 1976), 115; Herman Rauschning, *The Redemption of Democracy: The Coming Atlantic Empire* (New York, 1941), esp. pp. 51, 84–5, 97, 167–8; Leopold Schwarzschild, *Primer of the Coming World* (London, 1944), esp. chs 20, 26; Hans Kühn, 'The Mass Man: Hitler', *Atlantic Monthly* (April 1944); much of this writing reflected the great influence of *The Revolt of the Masses*, by the Spanish philosopher and social commentator Ortega y Gasset; see Chapter 4.

[173] Rauschning, *Redemption of Democracy*, 104, 137, 236.

[174] Schwarzschild, *Primer*, 131; von Mises, *Selected Writings*, iii. 27, 29, *passim*, 103, *passim*; background, American experience and lasting influence of von Mises in Coser, *Refugee Scholars*, 140–2. Schumpeter remained convinced of the possibility of true, American-style capitalism—with the wartime shackles of collectivist politics and bureaucracy removed—to achieve impressive growth rates. He is the only one of these writers to use the language of 'growth' and Gross National Product (*Capitalism, Socialism*, 114–15, 131–3, 383–4). But his analyses, dense and learned as they are, reflect very little of the specific political or economic evolution of the war.

could be no avoiding its challenges to the sickly European capitalism of the time.

An economist from the Royal Institute of International Affairs summed up the sense of this development when he told the readers of *Harper's* magazine:

> In whatever terms the proposition is put, everybody seems to agree that the greatest hope for the postwar world is a higher living standard for all.[175]

A British supporter of the United Nations project, Walter Arnold-Forster, emphasized how great was the distance between the commitments to expansion that everyone had signed up to in the Lend-Lease Act and at the Hot Springs Food Conference, and all the exhortations to frugality, sacrifice, and 'drastic economy' that had so racked Western societies in the interwar years. As the Four Freedoms had first pointed out to the world, 'the economic and social foundations of democracy are not less important than the political ones'.[176] The Labour Party's most vociferous intellectual, Harold Laski, agreed passionately and thought the Four Freedoms and Lend-Lease revolutionary ideas, and indeed the only ones produced by the United Nations. But to work, their promise had to be fulfilled, and seen by the masses everywhere to be so:

> Our chief concern [in building the post-war order] must be to remember that democracy and freedom flourish when economic systems expand and not otherwise... this means, quite simply, raising the standard of life all over the world, and particularly in those areas—China, India, South East Europe, South America—where it is today pitifully low...

Nor could this be done by an Anglo-American bloc alone:

> the productive potentialities of modern industry and agriculture imply an inter-connected world market.[177]

The Economist of wartime never shared the ebullience of the American outlook on the peace, and irked by too many blows to British national pride, commented caustically on the 'Americans with their usual impetuosity to make a million overnight', and their urge to put 'two motorcars in every European barn and a chicken in every Zulu's pot'.[178] But the

---

[175] Allan G. B. Fisher, 'The Clash Between Progress and Security', *Harper's* (July 1944).

[176] W. Arnold-Forster, *Charters of Peace*, ch. 2; cits at pp. 51, 91.

[177] Laski wartime correspondence in Best, *Harold Laski*, 120–3; quotes from Laski, *Reflections on the Revolution of Our Time* (London, 1943), 207, 208, 210. This was the thinking that produced the Ministry of Agriculture film 'World of Plenty', on the reforms imaginable after the war in a world of organized food production; discussion in Farmer, 'Exploiting a Universal Nostalgia'; on its success at the Hot Springs conference, above, n. 95.

[178] *The Economist*, 3 February 1945.

magazine clearly understood the logic of the swelling prosperity–democracy vision as it rose up across the Atlantic. It reprinted the clauses in the founding documents of the World Bank and the International Monetary Fund that bound those institutions to the growth of trade, investment, employment, and living standards among their members, and reported on developments such as the 1944 mission of British cotton textile experts to the United States, which went to study (again) why the average American cotton worker produced from one-and-a-quarter to ten times as much as his British peer.[179]

Not in the Empire, much less in redistribution, would be found the key to expansion in *The Economist*'s view: the only hope was a revolution in national productivity. In an August 1944 discussion of 'A Policy for Wealth', the editors complained how little attention was being paid to the sources of the prosperity everyone seemed to take for granted after the war. With the Imperial legacy liquidated, and exports likely to be very difficult, there was only one way forward—to get to American levels of capital investment, technological development, and 'horsepower per head'. A 'raging, blaring campaign of propaganda' was needed on this front, since only through wealth creation this way could the nation meet that 'demand for reforms which arose insistently in the British people, as the war gave urgency to the hopes and aspirations of many decades'.[180]

In the course of the conflict, the most prominent thinker on the European side of the Atlantic to develop the line of argument linking democracy and prosperity was probably the historian and *Times* editorialist E. H. Carr. In an autobiographical sketch of 1980, Carr partly disowned his reflections of 1942 on *The Conditions of Peace*; he called them 'highly utopian'. Utopianism had been a common refuge for European intellectuals at such a time, he suggested, but 'after all, it was on the basis of such visions that a lot of real constructive work was done'.[181] In his wartime text, Carr started with the discrediting of democracy itself,

---

[179] *The Economist*, 29 July 1944, 28 October 1944.
[180] Ibid. 19 August, 26 August 1944, 14 October 1944, 4 November 1944; at best, however, the magazine did not expect Britain to reach America's 1944 levels of productivity before 1972.
[181] Carr, *Conditions of Peace* (London, 1942); 'An Autobiography' (1980), in Michael Cox (ed.), *E. H. Carr: A Critical Appraisal* (Basingstoke, 2004), p. xix. On utopias, Karl Polanyi's *The Great Transformation*, of 1944, still influential to this day, denounced the utopianism of Anglo-American liberalism, with its quasi-religious faith—as Polanyi saw it—in self-regulating markets in capital, labour, and property, and the belief in 'sound money' as its supreme symbol. This faith had done a great deal to undermine interwar democracy in Polanyi's view: pp. 26–30, 231–4. The book was written while Polanyi was in exile in America, helped by a grant from the Rockefeller Foundation; on his background and American experience, Coser, *Refugee Scholars*, 169–73.

a theme that, he said, had become 'stale, unprofitable and "inert"'... it is difficult to recall a single significant European exposition of democracy as a driving force in the modern world'. Liberal democracy had lost all credibility because, defying the general extension of the franchise, producers' groups and the State's bureaucracy between them had mortified whatever progress the masses thought they might have made through acquiring the vote. Now the totalitarian states had apparently demonstrated that they could provide better standards of economic equality and security than those of the democracies. The test for true democrats was no less than redefining 'liberty' itself, but now 'in economic terms'.[182]

Carr cared very little for America, but he was willing to acknowledge that under Roosevelt an attempt had been made to recast democracy in the direction of a much wider kind of social and economic opportunity.[183] In Europe this effort had 'hardly yet begun'. Yet everywhere the people as consumers were calling upon the State to harness its capacities to their interests. A massive shift of power in their favour had started to take place, which the producers—whether they be industrialists, trade unionists, or farmers—had tried to resist at every turn, said Carr, even at the cost of a slump. 'The demand for prosperity has spread and deepened', and beggar-my-neighbour nationalism had shown its utter inability to cope with this change. Interdependence was not just an underlying reality of technological development, but a psychological trend, visible even in such a marginal and poverty-stricken country as Ireland. As evidence, Carr quoted Sean O'Faolain's *Irish Journey* of 1940, a J. B. Priestley-like exploration of the divided island by one of its leading writers. At the end of this travelogue a young correspondent to the *Irish Press* is quoted as complaining how the world had shrunk, and how the contemporary blessings of modernity were being deliberately withheld from the new generations of Eire by those of their elders terrified of jazz, dancing, and cosmopolitanism in all its forms.[184]

---

[182] Carr, *Conditions*, ch. 2, cf. Laski, *Reflections*, 33–5, 130–2, 206; like Carr, Karl Polanyi believed that the nineteenth-century principle of laissez-faire was by this time totally discredited, and that the 'primacy of society' over market mechanisms had to be secured in a new 'balance of freedoms'. But he seems to have been unaware of the demands for prosperity that were rising from below to challenge all traditional forms of democracy and liberty; *Great Transformation*, 250–6.

[183] On Carr's disinterest or disdain for America, Jonathan Haslam, *The Vices of Integrity: E. H. Carr, 1892–1982* (London, 1999), 74; Carr on Roosevelt in *Conditions*, 31–2.

[184] Carr, *Conditions*, chs 3, 4; O'Faolain quoted (wrongly) at pp. 59–60; cf. O'Faolain, *An Irish Journey* (London, 1940), 304–6; life, professional development, and cultural context of O'Faolain in Wills, *That Neutral Island*, 5–14, 279–81, 290–8.

Carr doubtless read the whole of the young man's letter to the *Irish Press*, as reproduced by O'Faolain. Among its passages were these sentences, striking from such a rarely considered, pinched part of Europe:

> Within the past twenty years the standards of life have jumped—jumped is too weak a word—they have soared dizzily. With the change this small country grew a shade smaller; it could no longer provide more than a fraction of its children with the standard they had been taught to expect.
>
> Some years ago a responsible newspaper (*The Irish Press*, I think) made the suggestion that 'frugal sufficiency' should be our highest ambition. I was a senior schoolboy then; this statement aroused derisive laughter among my schoolmates. Who wanted frugal sufficiency, anyhow? We all wanted 'sports-eights' and we meant to get them...
>
> Our attitude to wealth (adequate living means) in general has undergone a radical change. We expect it...

Moralistic, xenophobic cultural protectionism was useless, said the unnamed writer, as was 'the lingering war mentality which fails to distinguish between British and modern'. All that contemporary youths like him wanted—'as fiercely as the youth of Britain or America wanted'— was 'the things that modern life had taught us to expect'.[185]

In reality, before such young people found their dreams fulfilled in Ireland itself, and not in emigration, decades would have to pass. The Prime Minister was the Republic's founding father, Eamon De Valera, the American-born former leader of fighting Irish republicanism. In 1943 he imagined the future development of his native land in terms quite different from those of O'Faolain's young man:

> The Ireland which we have dreamed of would be the home of a people who valued material wealth only as the basis of right living, of a people who were satisfied with frugal comfort and devoted their leisure to things of the spirit—a land whose countryside would be bright with cosy homesteads, whose fields and villages would be joyous with the sounds of industry, with the romping of sturdy children, the contests of athletic youth and the laughter of comely maidens, whose firesides would be the forums for the wisdom of old age. It would, in a word, be the home of a people living the life that God desires that man should live.

De Valera recognized that material development of his country was a necessity, since too many Irish people were living without the minimum standards 'of comfort and leisure' needed to make the best of their God-given talents. But many more enjoyed this level already, and so should be ready 'to cultivate the things of the mind, and in particular those which

---

[185] O'Faolain, *Irish Journey*, 305–6; the 'sports-eight' refers to the racy, eight-cylinder, 'sports' cars fashionable in upper circles in America in those years.

mark us out as a distinct nation'.[186] But as Irish historians have pointed out, this vision was never likely to catch on. Workers, farmers, and people in general wanted more. 'The pressure to become the same as the rest of the West was already mounting', writes Tom Inglis.[187]

So to a practical mind such as E. H. Carr's, writing in 1942, and looking for sources of hope for the embattled democracies in the West, the challenge of rising expectations looked unpostponable. Like most contemporary left-of-centre thinkers, his solution lay in planned, collective consumption. Carr's was one of many in Europe and America that demanded a post-war project that would couple the popular moral and social energies of the war to the potentialities of state action revealed by the war experience itself, leaving far behind considerations of price and profit and '[substituting] welfare for wealth as our governing purpose'.[188]

Carr almost never mentioned American experience in his peroration, but there were obvious parallels with the visions of Willkie, Roosevelt, Wallace, and the other New Dealers. All of them demanded an organized revival and liberation of world trade; all wanted to set down basic standards of health, education, and job security for their peoples; all saw the need to give capitalist democracy a new moral purpose and legitimacy by redefining its dominant ideas of progress. All could see that, as Carr put it:

> There has probably never been a time when so many people in so many parts of the world were not only looking for guidance, but were themselves so eager to make their own contribution to the building of a new order.[189]

But there was a crucial transatlantic difference. The analysis of a man like Carr, as well as his sentiments and experience, led him to demand from the future a 'call for common sacrifice for a recognised common good...self-sacrifice on the scale requisite to enable civilisation to survive', a generally shared moral purpose comparable in its general charisma and collective exaltation to the mobilization for war.[190] American leaders by way of contrast felt that the notion of 'sacrifice' had to be limited to the

---

[186] M. Moynihan (ed.), *Speeches and Statements by Eamon de Valera, 1917–1973* (Dublin, 1980), 466–7; on de Valera and context of this speech Tom Inglis, *Global Ireland* (New York, 2008), 146–8; cf. Gabriel Doherty and Dermot Keogh (eds), *De Valera's Ireland* (Cork, 2003).

[187] Inglis, *Global Ireland*, 148.

[188] Carr, *Conditions*, 95–101, cit. at p. 97.

[189] Ibid. 112.

[190] Ibid. 111, 116; Harold Laski developed Carr's line of thought further, but Laski lost credibility after 1943 when his proto-Marxism led him to exalt the Soviet system as the only complete answer to the challenge of democratizing economic development; cf. Laski, *Reflections*, chs 1, 4, 6; cf. Kramnick and Sheerman, *Harold Laski*, 421–69.

phase of actual military combat, and could be justified even then only by the promise of higher individual, *private* standards as soon as possible once the victory was won.

Even a man as dedicated to guaranteeing minimum levels of welfare as Henry Wallace was writing in 1943 that 'we need the driving force of self-interest to get most of the work of the world done'. Social security would offer background support in bad times, said Wallace, but 'the spirit of free competition will and must continue to be one of our main driving forces', rewarding individual effort and achievement with the chance to enter 'what has been called the "middle class"'. Here the 'representative American of the future' would enjoy 'a home of his own' with all the modern scientific conveniences (which Wallace listed down to its rugs), 'a car neither old nor ramshackle', 'his decent share of recreation...vacations, high-school and college for his children, horse-racing, football, baseball, golf, or tennis, as his taste is inclined'. These, explained the Vice President, 'together with ample food, make up the American way of life'. By turning the nation's 'great productivity for war [into] an equally great productivity for peace', this way of living could be spread from the minority 'to the great mass of our people'.[191]

But there was at least one wartime thinker who could see through the various approaches the leaders of the democracies were inventing to persuade their masses to fight the war to its end, and make it worth their while to do so. In a remarkable reflection of 1943 entitled *The Making of Tomorrow*, the French journalist and historian Raoul de Roussy de Sales, long based in Washington, argued that the 'way of life' model that radiated from the US provoked not admiration but confusion at home and abroad, over its meanings and its purposes. Domestically Americans were 'rather apt to forget that the adoption by other people of American methods and tastes does not mean the adoption of American thoughts and ideals'. In the world the talk, more often than not scornful, was all of 'Americanization'. But that term referred only to the irresistible pull of the nation's images of material success, of the mass-production system, of Hollywood, Coca-Cola, motor cars, fridges, radios, 'and other good gadgetry'. Against this background, the spirit of the nation's political experiment and its lessons for 'the general trend of civilization' were very hard to discern from outside.[192]

De Sales, like Thomas Mann, was one of the few upper-class European admirers of the American experiment in its form of that time. He clearly moved in a frame of reference inspired by the 'American Century' vision

---

[191] 'Horatio Alger Is Not Dead' (January 1943), ch. 10, in Wallace, *Century of the Common Man*, 47–8.

[192] Raoul de Roussy de Sales, *The Making of Tomorrow* (London, 1943), 290–1.

of Luce, as well as by the commitment to a better world written into the Four Freedoms and the Atlantic Charter. He also saw some of the limits of these pronouncements. The Charter for instance upheld the right of 'self-determination', but understood this promise to mean sovereignty, not necessarily representation. It also set up an awkward tension between the political and the economic, between the world of nation states and universal trade liberalism.[193] More broadly, de Sales feared that like contemporary socialism, Western capitalism as a whole had never faced up to its own 'inner contradictions' and as a result 'Fascism and Nazism are now threatening to destroy both and to impose on the whole world the simplified solution of pure force'.[194] Capitalism was not automatically democratic, nor was democracy automatically capitalistic. Until the Western versions of these doctrines understood that they must genuinely fulfil their promises of equality, opportunity, and freedom, suspicion would always surround their practice and performance. Instead of being mutually reinforcing, they might well end up at odds with each other. The France of the 1930s had revealed just what the stakes were. Similar circumstances could produce similar results anywhere, said de Sales, with messianic nationalism—'one of the worst evils of these times' used as the supreme weapon to destroy civilization. The 'feeling of permanent urgency and relentless effort' that Roosevelt had mobilized to push forward his New Deal was now needed to inspire true democrats the world over.[195]

The message and its destination

De Sales did not live to see the various stages of the wartime New Deal's evolution after 1943, and its relentless development of specific, if highly abstract, designs that would supposedly project a revamped version of the Roosevelt experiment on a global scale. But de Sales did understand the American dedication to the concept of a '*standard of living*', which 'assumed that the improvement of physical conditions for all would have an uplifting effect on the soul and on the intelligence'. In complete contrast with so many European critics, such as the wartime Adorno and Horkheimer, he insisted that 'more and better food, more motor cars and more radios [meant] more culture, better morals'.[196] But even de Sales' brilliant and unique analysis could not envisage how this conception would come to animate so much of the organized projection of American

---

[193] Ibid. 282, 325–6.   [194] Ibid. 108.   [195] Ibid. ch. 2 and pp. 326–7.
[196] Ibid. 45–6; on the invention and development of the concept of the 'standard of living' in the US between the wars, de Grazia, *Irresistible Empire*, ch. 2.

power—political, cultural, economic—after World War II, or how it would be linked by the New Dealers and their successors to the promotion of democracy against all its adversaries, of whatever lineage.

In 1939 Vera Micheles Dean, journalist, political scientist, and international relations expert, had written that what Nazism and Communism shared was a...

> ... revolt of the dispossessed classes against industrial capitalism and such remnants of feudalism as the aristocracy, the officer class and a politically minded church. Both... sought to provide the masses with material opportunities and a taste of power hitherto reserved for a social elite.... Both, paradoxical as it may seem, represented an effort to realize the promises held out by the political democracy of the 19th century, which the possessing classes had too often failed to translate into terms of economic democracy in an age of mass production.[197]

This was the key American perception and understanding of the roots of the world wars, of the great depression, of totalitarianism, which fed the determination of that nation's government to place the peace of the world on a different, non-European footing. De Sales quoted Herbert Hoover, who, in September 1941, had said 'we have grown steadily apart from the ideas of Europe. Every one of our ancestors came here to get away from this dread turmoil...'[198] But the contemporary logic of interdependence, which was psychological, technological, and economic as well as strategic, meant not only that the United States was forced to promote the well-being of the world's peoples if its own standard of living was to be maintained at the levels Americans had become used to in wartime. The same urge drove America on to save all the nations from Europe's ancient propensity to start continental civil wars and then drag the rest into them. Whether the national interest was defined broadly or narrowly, Roosevelt's grand design had to be made to function, preferably sooner if not later.[199]

But how many of the 'thinking people' in Europe understood the purpose behind all the declarations? A caricature of their debate might suggest that while the Marxist tradition—European Communist and some socialist parties, the Frankfurt School—saw the masses as victims of new, subtle, and particularly effective forms of capitalist domination, to conservatives it was liberal capitalism that was the victim of the masses. This was what the very influential current of thought inspired so radically by

---

[197] V. M. Dean, *Europe in Retreat* (New York, 1939), pp. xv–xvi.
[198] De Sales, *Making of Tomorrow*, 320.
[199] Historic, civilizational perspective lying behind this outlook offered in Ninkovich, 'Wilsonism', 34–43.

Ortega y Gasset's *Revolt of the Masses* stated in a variety of languages (mostly German). Both left and right did however share one conviction: that the great European traditions of liberal individualism founded in Athens and Rome, in mortal danger for fifty years, now risked being crushed forever by total war and its protagonists. In 1944 T. S. Eliot took up the old refrain. The real enemy was industrialism, stifling and homogenizing all human life, totalitarianism its definitive political expression. Adorno and Horkheimer declared 'the culture industry as a whole has moulded men as a type unfailingly reproduced in every product.... Pseudo-individuality is rife.... The defiant reserve or elegant appearance of the individual on show is mass produced like Yale locks, whose only difference can be measured in fractions of millimetres. The peculiarity of the self is a monopoly commodity determined by society...'[200]

In contrast with all this, American ebullience positively embraced the revolution of rising expectations that it saw in progress across the world, and saw in that upsurge of demands not a source of fear and hatred but one of unparalleled opportunity. Commenting on an article describing the impact of America's armies in the world, famed less for their fighting skills than for their opulence, the sociologist David Potter wrote later:

> ...the United States has certainly played a far greater part than any other country in displaying to the world the variety and magic of the new abundance, and it has done more than any other to disseminate the belief that this abundance may actually be placed within the grasp of ordinary men and women. The films that have come out of Hollywood, for instance, have presented conspicuous consumption not as a mere practice but, one might say, as a system and an act of faith.[201]

Potter wrote his essay to lament the failure of this proposition, recounting all the disappointments and setbacks it had encountered by the mid-1950s, how the Americans had found themselves preaching the democratic faith 'in places where the economic prerequisites for democracy' had never been established.

Yet the Americans of World War II had quickly been proved right when they had understood that the war provided a unique opportunity for radical change, and gave scope to impulses and energies in America and outside it that could remake the world. They did not have to wait long to see the confirmation of their belief that the end of the European empires was at hand. They had also been the fastest to understand the full implications of 'interdependence', and had been correct when they understood that a

---

[200] Eliot, 'The Man of Letters and the Future of Europe', *Horizon* (December 1944); Adorno and Horkheimer, *Dialectic of Enlightenment*, 127, 154.
[201] Potter, *People of Plenty*, 136.

revolution of popular expectations had taken place in the twentieth century that the liberal democracies ignored at their peril, and which the American experiment was—in its unmistakable way—intensely ready to meet. The connection they made in this way between prosperity and democracy, and the propositions they derived from this belief, would return to challenge successive generations of believers in liberal freedoms. At the same time their faith in the capacity of the public and private institutions of the United States to invent new ways to project national power would be repeatedly upheld.

But there were just as many facts of international life that the New Dealers of wartime Washington could not and would not face up to. Most obvious was the irreducible persistence in the world of the 'power politics' they all deplored, specifically the geopolitical realities created by the outcome of the war as such.[202] Nor could they conceive either the scale and depth of the misery the conflict had brought, nor understand how the more total it had become—with America's armies, weapons, and propaganda playing their special part—the more Europe's 'dread turmoil' had been aggravated, and the further away it had become from the universe of the Four Freedoms, Bretton Woods, and all the rest.[203]

But most importantly, wartime opinion in the United States could not grasp the fact that amidst all the death and wreckage, the Europeans (not to mention those Middle Eastern peoples the New Dealers fancied as guinea pigs), had worked out their own programmes for meeting those hopes and aspirations of decades that the war had brought so compellingly to the surface. Everywhere in Europe the Left was the great beneficiary of this surge in popular feeling. Left-wing parties, trade unions, and social movements were swelling everywhere. 'Private enterprise', said so many, had had its day, and was not a credible option. And the workings of private enterprise America as a many-faced power system, so enthralling seen from inside, were understood through quite different, far more pragmatic eyes by all the others without exception. World War II was the pivotal moment in the history of the American modernizing challenge to Europe, because the challenge was open, organized, and conscious in a way it had never been before and would never be again. As ever, some

---

[202] As this contradiction became obvious, opposition to European colonial empires was the first standard to be sacrificed; cf. Winkler, 'American Opposition', 86–7; Gardner, 'FDR and the "Colonial Question"', 134, *passim*; the basic failure was 'the absence of an integrated worldview', writes Walter LaFeber, i.e. a coherent set of operative conceptions that would link the broad visions to realities and capabilities within and without America, LaFeber in Woolner et al. (eds), *FDR's World*.

[203] There is no trace of any of these problems, for instance, in Alvin Hansen's 1945 discussion of *America's Role in the World Economy*, though Hansen was at the time the leading economist in Harvard and a 'Special Economic Adviser' to the Federal Reserve.

welcomed it, some dreaded it, all were forced to come to terms with it. But precisely because the balance of every form of power between the two sides was so skewed at the end of the war, the battle over those terms was all the more intense.

* * * *

There were, however, Americans far away from their mother country who had come to recognize this reality, had been brought face to face with it very quickly, indeed the moment they stepped on foreign shores. These were the men and women of their nation's great armed forces as they prepared to enter Hitler's Europe in 1943. They were hailed as liberators, just as the propaganda had promised. But it would not take long for many more complex and contradictory feelings to surface among the people they had come all that way to save.

7

'The Most Revolutionary Force': When American Armies Arrive...

LIBERATION, OCCUPATION... MODERNIZATION?

The man who would launch the phrase 'the revolution of rising expectations' on its distinguished career was Harlan A. Cleveland, at the time a Deputy Administrator of the Marshall Plan. The occasion was a university speech, delivered right after the outbreak of the Korean War in June 1950. Everything that had happened in Asia in the previous months—most prominently the Chinese revolution of May 1949—seemed to confirm this young New Dealer's faith in the prescriptions of his wartime predecessors. The Communists were not the true 'revolutionists', claimed Cleveland, they were just trying to 'stamp their trademark on the revolutionary ferment which is so apparent throughout Asia'. And where did this ferment come from? It came from the consciousness of the Asian peasant—just like the French worker—that everywhere in the globe people could have access, for the first time in history, to enough food, clothing, shelter to begin to satisfy all their basic human needs. Everywhere the dispossessed could see that 'an expanding economy and a rising standard of living' were within their reach, and they were acting accordingly.

But, asked Cleveland, who started this unprecedented process of physical and mental change anyway? And he supplied his own answer:

> Was it not we ourselves, we and our colleagues of the Western world, who showed what could be done by the application of modern science and modern ideas about organization to the problem of earning a living? Wasn't the American GI, with his wrist watch and his flash-light, his jeep and his airplane, one of the most revolutionary forces that has ever been let loose in the world?... The revolution that is now endemic in Asia is

not Communism—it might better be called the *"revolution of rising expectations"*.[1]

A writer in *Harper's Magazine* had already laid claim to the notion that the America's armed forces were exceptional because they were the agents of revolutionary social change. This time though the rhetorical question was placed on the lips of the expectant masses. What was it, asked Isabel Lundberg, that...

> ...the native population everywhere wanted of the G.I., the Air Force pilot, the gob and the Seabee? They wanted what the vast majority of the world's population, European and non-European, wants: the wrist-watch, fountain pen, cigarettes, flashlight, chocolate bars, chewing gum, cameras, pocket knives, pills to kill pain, vaccines to save lives, hospital beds with clean sheets, hand soap, gadgets and gewgaws of every description, the jeep, the truck and *white bread*....To be able to afford white bread is a dream that awaits fulfilment for billions of the world's population. To afford it signifies that one enjoys all the comforts of life.[2]

Reporting from desolate Vienna in August 1945, Anne O'Hare McCormick of the *New York Times* was also convinced that 'occupying armies, wherever they are, are examples of systems they represent'. As for the 'well-fed, well-equipped, opulent doughboy', his effect had been to leave behind, 'a rosy and disturbing vision of a plenty more widespread than any other country has achieved...[he] sowed in his wake the fertile seeds of envy and rebellion'.[3] Of course not everyone got the message, at least not right away. An American army officer who had spent time in Italy was quoted as saying after the war, in deliberately provocative fashion, that the Italians were far too obsessed with politics and far too little concerned with 'the rival claims of cornflakes or cigarettes'. They needed to be taught that domestic prosperity, calm, and freedom itself depended not on politics, but on the commodities the film stars used, and all the other wondrous products that delivered smooth legs, healthy intestines, slim bodies, and vigorous blood.[4]

---

[1] *Reflections on the 'Revolution of Rising Expectations'*, Address before the Colgate University Conference on American Foreign Policy, 9 July 1950, in National Archives, Washington DC, Record Group 469, Assistant Administrator for Program. Deputy Assistant Administrator, Subject Files of Harlan Cleveland; (emphasis added).

[2] Isabel Cary Lundberg, 'World Revolution, American Plan', *Harper's* (December 1948), cit. in Potter, *People of Plenty*, 135–6; emphasis in original (Potter cites this text in 1954 in order to criticize the hubris that lay behind it). 'Gob' was a generic, popular reference to a US Navy sailor. The Seabees were members of the Navy's Construction Battalions.

[3] *New York Times*, 1 August 1945.

[4] Marshall McLuhan, *Understanding Media: The Extensions of Man* (New York, 1964), 203; McLuhan, a celebrity media anthropologist in his day, commented: 'The army officer was probably right. Any community that wants to expedite and maximise the exchange of goods and services has simply got to homogenize its social life', ibid. 204.

But the power of example brought responsibility, suggested the Chicago historian W. H. McNeill, an officer in the first American military mission to Greece of 1945. It was not just a moral duty but in the strategic interests of Greece's new sponsors to make sure that the bounties of their armies and their dollars were put to good use. The democracy-as-prosperity question was moving on, becoming more complex and at the same time more immediate. But in Greece too meeting expectations was the underlying challenge:

> If economic conditions could be so improved that every Greek was able to live as well as he had been brought up to expect, it seems probable that the excessive concern and fanaticism which the people now manifest for political parties and programs would diminish. Circumstances might then become propitious for the gradual emergence of a community of ideas that would embrace almost the whole population, and permit genuine democratic government to be established. Economic prosperity could not guarantee stable and popular government, but it would certainly make its achievement more probable.[5]

Greece of course had neither been liberated nor occupied by the Americans, but its national experience in these years—when placed in comparison with those countries that knew some form of both those processes—demonstrated to Europeans that the arrival of the military might of the United States brought with it a variety of interventions, an unpredictable range of presences, which didn't cease in the normal way when the armies went home.[6] Instead it evolved over time. Liberation, Allied occupation, Truman Doctrine, Marshall Plan, NATO: all the West European nations knew some combination of these experiences, usually in that sequence. It was certainly possible to be liberated without being occupied, insisted the French. It could even happen that one's country was occupied without being liberated, the British would respond in their ironical way.[7] But Italy, Austria, and Germany all went through a variety of the processes of liberation/occupation after the collapse of first Fascism then Nazism, and as all became caught up in the Cold War they saw too in their politics some of the side effects of the Truman Doctrine of ideological confrontation. Then came the vital and irresistible Marshall Plan offer, which they all either joined willingly or were co-opted into from the beginning. With the construction of NATO from 1951 onwards, responding to strong European pressures, the American armed forces returned and began

[5] William Hardy McNeill, *The Greek Dilemma* (London, 1947), 223–4.

[6] Cf. James Edward Miller, *The United States and the Making of Modern Greece: History and Power, 1950–1974* (Chapel Hill, NC, 2009), 19–20, ch. 1.

[7] Hence the subtitle of David Reynolds's study of the impact of the millions of US forces personnel who passed through Britain in the course of the war: *Rich Relations: The American Occupation of Britain 1942–1945*.

constructing bases for a long stay. What began to look like a chain of encounters emerged stretching back to 1942, changing its form and declared purpose according to circumstances, but always bringing certain
fundamental challenges.

The revolutionary force

No matter how friendly the intentions of foreign armies upon their arrival in
a given territory, no matter how short their stay, their presence always involves some form of dilution, suspension, or transfer of sovereignty from
local peoples to those armies. The question then arises of how willingly that
transfer takes place, how to manage the conflicts that inevitably arise, in
direct proportion of number and intensity to the length of time those armies
remain.[8] The mythical British popular complaint against the Americans that
they were 'over-sexed, over-paid and over here' brilliantly encapsulates those
tensions, especially in its third phrase. Wherever the American armies went,
there were indeed everyday misunderstandings between the soldiery and the
local populations, especially and always over the vast gap between the opulence of their lifestyle and the near-starvation of the peoples they were liberating.[9] But nowhere was the sovereignty issue more exposed than in the
endless complaints about the impulse of the Americans to take over every
building, road, port, energy supply, restaurant, cinema, theatre, and other
physical resource that they might conceivably need: the plague of 'requisitioning'. Local men thought 'their' women were being requisitioned.

Every expeditionary army in history has provoked some form of resentment in these areas wherever it landed, in the case of 'liberators' as soon
as the initial euphoria wears off. But the wry British phrase also implies
there was a different and new quality about the Americans in uniform.
Experience soon suggested that a series of highly visible factors contributed to the impact of these forces when they arrived from across the Atlantic, and to the reception that subsequently greeted them:

1. The inheritance in any liberated territory of all the prevailing myths
   of America there, and of all the previous, direct experiences of its
   people of the reality of the US in all its forms.[10]

---

[8] Cf. Eric Carlton, *Occupation: The Policies and Practices of Military Conquerors*
(London, 1992), 1, 5.

[9] The problem was seen immediately in North Africa, which became a major learning
experience; Edwin P. Hoyt, *The GI's War: American Soldiers in Europe during World War II*
(New York, 2000), 267.

[10] German case in Detlef Junker, 'The Continuity of Ambivalence: German Views of
America, 1933–1945', in Barclay and Glaser-Schmidt (eds), *Transatlantic Images*; cf. Hilary
Footitt, *War and Liberation in France: Living with the Liberators* (London, 2004), 28;
Wagnleitner, *Coca- Colonization*, 27, 44.

2. The explicit ideology that the liberators brought. One legend said that the military banknotes the Americans brought to Italy bore the Four Freedoms printed on their reverse side. Obviously Wilsonian and Rooseveltian, the fighting 'United Nations' promised in their propaganda salvation from all the misery, backwardness, class struggle, and wars of all the centuries.[11]

3. The dynamism, technology, material comforts and subliminal messages of the American way of making war. The opulence flowed everywhere, blinding, distorting, often corrupting everything it came into contact with. Scholars would demonstrate later that this was not the casual thoughtlessness of a newly rich nation, but the key technique chosen by the General Staff under George Marshall to hold together armed forces that were *not* fighting to defend home and hearth; a huge, raw mass of young individuals in uniform from a land with scarce military traditions, and a strong commitment to citizen democracy.[12]

4. The uniquely American might of popular music and Hollywood films. Everywhere the armed forces went, the movie industry followed right behind. With 4000 of its people in military service, and permission to act as 'the only commercial set-up' functioning in the war zones, Hollywood was determined to recapture markets, parade the products of the years of absence, turn the war itself into legend, myth, and entertainment, and exalt the American way of life. For its part the State Department expected that the industry would send abroad films that would 'reflect credit on the good name of this country and its institutions'.[13]

5. An almost complete lack of preparation—historical, cultural, mental—for all the responsibilities awaiting a force of liberation in modern times. There were paper plans and schemes; there were sixty-day courses in a specially created school. But no one knew how to apply

---

[11] The president of the US National Conference of Christians and Jews said that the task of America's young soldiers was 'to become missionary-minded in sharing the American Idea [*sic*] with the rest of the world...', cit. in Savage, *Teenage*, 371; on US propaganda apparatus in World War II, Cull, *Cold War*, 13–21.

[12] Reynolds, *Rich Relations*, ch. 6; rawness vividly evoked in Hoyt, *GI's War*, p. xvii, ch. 2–4, based on individual accounts; Savage, *Teenage*, 368–9; some of the extraordinary privileges of the US citizen in uniform are listed in Franklin M. Davis, *Come as a Conqueror: The United States Army's Occupation of Germany, 1945–1949* (New York, 1967), 35–6.

[13] Wagnleitner, *Coca-Colonization*, 237–9; Paul Swann, 'The Little State Department: Washington and Hollywood's Rhetoric of the Postwar Audience', in Ellwood and Kroes (eds), *Hollywood in Europe*; details of State Department and MPPDA plans for recreating post-war US film markets abroad in Trumpbour, *Selling Hollywood*, p. 89 and ch. 3.

the lessons taught there, how to balance control and local initiative, civil and military priorities, relations with Allies and relations with the liberated peoples.[14] Southern Italy 'turned into a laboratory where we tested out our theories', recalled a semi-official report of 1948.[15]

6. Together with all the apparent confidence and swagger, a self-critical attitude that would quickly emerge in newspaper reports, then filter into official reports and hearings, and into memoirs, novels, films. The paradoxes of 'imposed democracy'—of peoples 'forced to be free'—escaped no one, at the time or later. John Hersey's *A Bell for Adano* was written by a rising reporter from *Time* magazine to highlight the difficulties of bringing democracy to pre-modern societies like the villages of Sicily, burdened by time and Fascism. Although written as a novel, the text predicted that America was coming into the world with its armies, and would be judged by them and their men. Over sixty years later, Hershey's prediction would be acknowledged in an apparently quite different context.[16]

But trying to democratize Sicily was just one of the reasons why the American experience of liberation and occupation in Italy—the site of the first Allied invasion of continental Europe, from July 1943 onwards—produced so many unmissable precedents.

LIBERATION, OCCUPATION, AND BEYOND: THE ITALIAN EXPERIENCE

The Anglo-American armies spent more time liberating Italy during World War II than any other enemy-occupied territory. The campaign dragged on far longer than expected, and although a scaled-down sideshow by the end (May 1945), the experience made a vast impression on every level of society, and left a lasting legacy of images, symbols, memories, legends, and controversies. A writer from the south of the country recalled how, 'modern civilization cheerfully and noisily penetrated cities and towns…the fabulous and far away America, country dear to the dreams and labors of the fathers, had come among us.'[17] Although a joint

---

[14] Cf. Davis, *Come as a Conqueror*, 20–6, 50–2.

[15] Merle Fainsod, 'The Development of American Military Government Policy during World War II', in C. J. Friedrich et al. (eds), *American Experiences in Military Government in World War II* (New York, 1948); cit. at p. 31.

[16] Robert D. Kaplan, 'Supremacy by Stealth', in *Atlantic Monthly*, July/August 2003, 69.

[17] Giuseppe Galasso cit. in Stephen Gundle, *Between Hollywood and Moscow: The Italian Communists and the Challenge of Mass Culture, 1943–1991* (Durham, NC, 2000), 32.

Anglo-American war effort, with the British very firmly in charge most of the time, militarily and politically, it was the Americans who were seen to hold the keys to the future, and who went on to provide most of the aid, the money, and the propaganda, including a grand backlog of Hollywood films. 'The central encounter was between Italy and America', wrote a later onlooker.[18]

To manage their presence in the country the armies brought with them an elaborate military officialdom. First there was 'Allied Military Government' right behind the battle-lines, whose official orders were simply to do whatever it took to 'prevent disease and unrest'. But these soldiers soon found themselves faced with bigger challenges. As a Washington-based political scientist recalled in 1948:

> The adjustments of modern society were so delicate and the impact of modern war so comprehensive that an elaborate web of non-military activities had to be organized merely to protect the military advantages gained.... Nothing delayed for long the interest of the indigenous population in food, clothing, work and some sort of social organization. This meant in effect that the Allied Military Command was the final authority to whom these claims were presented.[19]

After AMG came the apparatus of so-called 'civil affairs', which took a longer view, and was supposed to restart local government, the law and order system, the shattered economy. But in Italy the armies were also expected to organize the destruction of Fascism and supervise the transition to a post-Fascist State. So an Allied Control Commission was put in a place, a stultifying piece of Anglo-American military bureaucracy that in British eyes was meant additionally to prepare the Italians for a punitive peace treaty, and thereby teach them a lesson. The unwritten objectives were even more demanding. According to journalists, the Allied officials were expected to reflect the intentions of the United Nations towards the liberated continent, and to demonstrate the capacity of the democracies to reorganize war-torn Europe. Italy was just the first case. Taken together, these challenges caused much unease in the top commands of the British and American armed forces. Commenting on the Nazi use of terror to keep peoples in occupied countries in order, Harold Macmillan, the British Resident Minister on the spot in Italy, said: 'civilised armies, defending high principles,

---

[18] John A. Davis, 'Introduction', in Davis (ed.), *Italy and America, 1943–44: Italian, American and Italian American Experiences of the Liberation of the Mezzogiorno* (Naples, 1997), 17.

[19] William Reitzel, *The Mediterranean: Its Role in American Foreign Policy* (New York, 1948), 14.

cannot find this easy way out. They start as conquerors but soon find themselves trustees.'[20]

But in part because the Allies could not decide whether the Italians were to be treated as potential friends or defeated enemies, the net result of all their activities was profoundly ambiguous, and continued to generate argument in all the succeeding decades.[21] The American army was different from all the others present not just because of the lavishness of its facilities and its relatively lax discipline, but also as a result of its detached attitude to the Italian people and their politics. It was the army of a nation with—until this time—an extremely small stake in the country it was fighting over. The result was that the long, drawn-out process of liberation gradually turned in many areas into a special kind of occupation.[22] In the second of Roberto Rossellini's neo-realist film classics, *Paisà* of 1946, the stages of this evolution are vividly depicted, with the effects of the black market, poverty, and mass prostitution in Rome and the south particularly in evidence. An African-American soldier is brought to realize that there are people in Naples much worse off materially than he is, people who consider him a conquering hero. In the middle section of the film, set in Rome, time, money, and idleness seem to turn every American soldier into a prostitute's potential client. Unemployment and starvation corrupt the finest local girl.[23]

In Sicily, the Italo-American 'town majors' of AMG attempted single-handedly to teach democracy to the bemused locals, or so Hersey's *A Bell for Adano* would have us believe.[24] But liberated Naples presented a very different order of challenge, and the records of that experience from all sides—official material, memoirs, diaries, films, plays, novels—portray something like a clash of civilizations erupting along with Vesuvius in the old Bourbon city. For the American soldiery, the bombed out, starving metropolis allegedly represented everything they hated about the Old World. 'In August, 1944, the port of Naples was a flytrap of bustle and efficiency and robbery in the midst of ruin and panic', wrote the novelist John Horne Burns in his post-war masterpiece *The Gallery*. Looking at

---

[20] Detailed discussion in Ellwood, *Italy 1943–1945: The Politics of Liberation* (Leicester, 1985), ch. 3, Macmillan cit. at p. 50.

[21] Early semi-official assessment in George C. S. Benson and Maurice Neufeld, 'American Military Government in Italy', in Friedrich et al. (eds), *American Experiences*; some sixtieth anniversary debates captured in Eric Gobetti (ed.), *1943–1945: La Lunga liberazione* (Milan, 2007).

[22] Ellwood, *Italy 1943–1945*, ch. 7.

[23] Full contextualization in Christopher Wagstaff, 'Italian Cinema of the Resistance and Liberation', in Davis (ed.), *Italy and America*, esp. pp. 538–9.

[24] Hersey, *A Bell for Adano*; discussion in Ellwood, *Italy 1943–1945*, 139–40.

the rubbish floating in the seawater, one of his soldier characters says simply, 'Europe drains into the Bay of Naples.'[25]

The soldiers 'figured it this way', wrote Burns:

> These Ginsoes have made war on us; so it doesn't matter what we do to them, boost their prices, shatter their economy, and shack up with their women...

Burns the narrator comments:

> In the broadest sense we promised the Italians security and democracy if they came over to our side. All we actually did was to knock the hell out of *their* system and give them nothing to put in its place. ... I remember that my heart finally broke in Naples. ... I found out that America was a country just like any other, except that she had more material wealth and more advanced plumbing. ... And I found out that outside the propaganda writers...Americans were very poor spiritually. Their ideals were something to make dollars on. They had bankrupt souls. Perhaps this is true of most of the people of the twentieth century. Therefore my heart broke.[26]

In their desperate struggle for survival, many Neapolitans seemed to take pride in flaunting their anti-modernism. A British diarist claimed, with ample evidence, that the war had pushed them 'back into the Middle Ages'.[27] Yet the playwright Eduardo De Filippo took a different view. His play *Napoli milionaria*, written and set in the midst of the liberation/occupation experience, became a triumphant symbol of the Neapolitan spirit in adversity, and made him a national hero. Later he recalled:

> The new century, this twentieth century did not reach Naples until the arrival of the Allies; here in Naples, it seems to me, the Second World War made a hundred years pass overnight.[28]

The greatest Italian novel of the war, Curzio Malaparte's *La Pelle*, also set largely in Naples, emphasized instead national abjection. In Malaparte's deeply pessimistic world view, self-abasement turns into a form of exhibitionism. As such it represents a generalized defiance of the Anglo-Americans' logic of liberation, especially their bizarre blend of moralism and materialism. Malaparte rejected the conventional definitions of victory and defeat, liberation and occupation. Once an unorthodox Fascist, now a liaison officer

---

[25] John Horne Burns, *The Gallery* (New York, 1947), 223; Gore Vidal considered this the best novel of World War II: preface to *Williwaw* (London, 1970), 9.

[26] Burns, *Gallery*, 280–2, emphasis in original.

[27] Norman Lewis, *Naples '44* (London, 1978), 108, 132, 145, 151.

[28] Cit. in Moe Nelson, 'Naples '44/"Tammurriata Nera", *Ladri di Bicicletta*', in Davis (ed.), *Italy and America*, 442; on the play, Gabriella Gribaudi, 'Napoli 1943–45: La costruzione di un'epopea', in Davis (ed.), *Italy and America*, 303–5; the piece was written from direct experience and first staged in May 1945.

Fig. 6. Liberators at ease in Italy.
(Getty Images/Time Life/Margaret Bourke-White)

between the Allies and the remains of the Italian armies, the writer declared that the Neapolitans, with all their centuries of foreign invasions, were never likely to feel *defeated* just because a new invader had arrived. As for these Allied armies, it was useless for them to claim to liberate people and at the same time want to make them feel defeated. Either they were free or they were defeated. In truth, claimed Malaparte, the Neapolitans felt neither.[29]

As in all the liberated territories of Europe, it was women who bore the brunt of the paradoxes and contradictions the Allies brought with them.

---

[29] C. Malaparte, *La pelle* (1st edn, Milan, 1949; Milan, 1991), 4; similar sentiments are expressed by the old man the young American flyers find in a Roman *bordello* in Joseph Heller's *Catch-22* (1962 edn repr., London, 1982), 258–60; full discussion of Malaparte, Burns, Lewis, and others in John Gatt-Rutter, 'Naples 1944: Liberation and Literature', in Davis (ed.), *Italy and America*.

At the beginning, all kinds of collaboration was on display between the newly arrived soldiery and local women, writes Maria Porzio: 'from the positive sort—dates, engagements, marriages—to the illegal kind, centred on the ever-swelling market in Allied goods.'[30] The Americans' opulence and generosity conquered many a heart, and made up in some way for the recent bombardments and the plague of requisitioning. But from the start of 1944, serious noises of indignation began to come from various local authorities, provoked by 'the frequency of crimes, especially of robbery and rape, caused by Allied military personnel'.[31] As starvation spread, so did conflicts over prostitution: local police had arrested 14,000 women by December 1944, and their reports spoke of up to 40,000 people involved in the sex market. The police, the Church, leading local figures all protested, upset in particular by the contribution of coloured soldiers (not just African-Americans) to the commerce.[32] Some local men saw their male sovereignty and pride under threat. Bands of Italian soldiers appeared who set about cutting off the hair of women said to have sold themselves to the riches and promises of the Allied soldiery.[33]

During the winter of 1943–4 'Naples was probably the worst-governed city in the Western world', said an American officer veteran of the experience, 'and it was not much better a year later'.[34] But once the armies started moving northwards again, after the end of May 1944, things generally improved, and although economic breakdown and near-starvation were everywhere, the liberation of Rome in June and Florence in August presented only occasional outbreaks of the deep miseries of the south. Local peoples began to take initiative on their own account, and in Tuscany there was 'a nearly complete administrative organization established by determined and purposeful anti-Fascist forces', reported the Office of Strategic Services, the new American political intelligence organization.[35]

In this way the Anglo-Americans first encountered on the ground the Communist question they had started to worry about in high politics, in Italy as elsewhere, from early in 1943. For Italian anti-Fascism was deeply conditioned by the presence in its midst of Stalin's most significant fol-

---

[30] Maria Porzio, *Arrivano gli Alleati! Amori e violenze nell'Italia liberata* (Bari, 2011), 66.

[31] Ibid. 74, citation from a police report.

[32] Ibid. 100, *passim*.

[33] Cit. ibid. 139.

[34] Cit. in Ellwood, *Italy 1943–1945*, 49; Naples remained under Allied Military Government from 1 October 1943 to 1 January 1946.

[35] Roger Absalom (ed.), *Perugia Liberata: Documenti anglo-americani sull'occupazione alleata di Perugia (1944–1945)* (Florence, 2001), 3–20; OSS cit. in Ellwood, *Italy 1943–1945*, 152.

lower in the West, Palmiro Togliatti, newly returned from Moscow to head the national Communist Party. From March 1943 on, its members and presence began to swell in every direction, its fighters came to dominate the armed Resistance movement behind German lines, and its allies included the formidable Yugoslav Communist movement under its renowned leader Tito. By the time the Allies were ready to liberate the north, in spring 1945, they had almost convinced themselves that a Red revolution would take place if they didn't get there fast enough.[36] In apparently similar conditions just such an outbreak had already taken place, in Athens in December 1944. It had been repressed by the British in blood, much to the discomfiture of their high-principled American allies.[37]

But a conviction soon spread that economic misery alone explained the vast growth of the Communist Party in Italy, as in Greece, Yugoslavia, and elsewhere at the end of the war. It was a 'communism of the belly', said the founder of political Catholicism, Don Sturzo. It was this same situation after World War I that had produced Fascism, said the Allied Control Commission. Ship food now to stop Communism, said Treasury Secretary Henry Morgenthau and Herbert Hoover in Washington.[38] Where then did this leave the much-vaunted plans for world economic expansion, ever freer trade and development, the ones brought to the Allied Control Commission by an eminent businessman and politician, Henry F. Grady? His permanent departure after a few weeks symbolized very effectively the vast distance between Washington's great designs and the uncontrollable material difficulties that a broken-down nation like Italy presented. By mid-1944 the State Department planners found themselves obliged to make space for 'certain measures to meet emergency conditions which are not in harmony with [our] long-term objectives'.[39]

It was indeed hard to see any revolution of rising expectations at work in the desolate peninsula of those years, where the battle for survival meant so much to so many. Instead a different kind of aspiration began to emerge. The total discrediting of Fascism and the inability of Italy's own forces to destroy Nazi-Fascism unaided meant that a nation that had once vaunted its national pride and great power ambitions was now in a state of humiliating dependence on the victorious armies of Britain and the United States. But from the era of the great pronouncements, the Italians came to believe that only the Americans possessed a future for the world worth the name. And only they—unlike the British, the Russians, the French, and all the others who had outstanding accounts to settle with

---

[36] Ellwood, *Italy 1943–1945*, chs 8–10.   [37] Ibid. 121–4, 135–6.
[38] Ibid. 90–2, 97–8, 224.   [39] Ibid. 128–30.

Fascism's successors—seemed willing to imagine that the Italians might one day be part of it.

There was however a fateful political ambivalence in this outlook. The Left and the northern Resistance movements wanted to reconstruct Italian democracy on their terms, and so demanded more autonomy from Allied control as time went on. Just so, the Right and Fascism's inheritors began a none-too-subtle campaign to persuade the Americans that it was in their interest to stay. As the peninsula quickly evolved into a major battleground in the emerging East–West confrontation, these pressures became more and more intense. Mussolini's successor, Marshal Badoglio, Count Sforza, the Foreign Minister, and his Ambassador in Washington, Cardinals in the Vatican, all provide examples of the language being used to entice the Americans to invest their political, moral, and financial capital in post-Fascist Italy.[40]

But the wartime Americans took little or no notice of this sort of solicitation, which was never expressed in their conceptual language. Washington's interest in Italy remained marginal until the very end of the war, and although some of its functionaries on the spot thought of reforming the State bureaucracy, or its education system, or the labour market, Allied military government was not designed for reconstruction, let alone renewal.[41] The British remained convinced that the only real hope for influence lay in aid, raw materials, food, and money, meaning that they had no choice but to encourage the Americans to 'take the lead', and to get 'well-embedded' in the country. 'They must be made to realize what a terribly important responsibility it is and that we cannot get away from it', said Harold Alexander, the Supreme Allied Commander.[42]

But there were Americans able to pick up the message and try to pass it on back home. These were the senior journalists sent to the battlefront from the American newspapers. They were a forceful group but, on this issue, not one with great influence. The *Christian Science Monitor*, the *Chicago Daily News*, the *New York Times*, the *Saturday Evening Post*, and others, were well represented and eloquent. They constantly bemoaned

[40] Roosevelt's Special representative to the Vatican, Myron C. Taylor, had been sending him similar messages for many months, cf. doc. 155, Taylor to Roosevelt, 17 July 1944, in Ennio Di Nolfo, *Vaticano e Stati Uniti, 1939–1952: Dalle carte di Myron C. Taylor* (Milan, 1978), 327–31; similar pressures on the US in Greece described in Miller, *United States and the Making of Modern Greece*, 20.

[41] On reformism in general, Ellwood, *Italy 1943–1945*, 146–8; on educational reform, Steven F. White, 'Liberal Antipodes: Omodeo, Smith and the Struggle over Schooling, Naples and Salerno, 1944', in Davis (ed.), *Italy and America*; on labour market reforms, Federico Romero, *Gli Stati Uniti e il sindacalismo europeo, 1944–1951* (Rome, 1989), ch. 2.

[42] Comments from the Supreme Allied Commander and the British Resident Minister cit. in Ellwood, *Italy 1943–1945*, 200.

the lack of American purpose, presence, and power in the land, and insisted that Italy was a test case for the future of Europe.[43] A feature writer for the *New York Herald Tribune*, John Chabot Smith, even supplied an outline plan for America's future role in Italy. His premise, in a long article of July 1945, was simple: 'Everyone said win the war first. Now no-one knows what to do.' According to Smith, the objective circumstances were clear to all concerned: everything in Italy depended on US aid, especially economic and military. But the army had big plans to demobilize and/or send large contingents of its forces to the Pacific theatre of war. Those who had originally pressed for a strong United States presence in Italy had been conservatives fearing mob rule and civil war. But now many Americans were coming round to the same opinion. They were concerned, said Smith, of the risk of civil war in the country, provoked by the revolutionary forces of the Left. The conservatives meanwhile had stopped simply asking for Allied charity, and were preparing to face the conditions of poverty and disorder that fed Leftism:

> ...there is growing disposition among some Italian and American officials and businessmen to look deeper into the problems of economic reconstruction and into the possibilities of developing a permanently higher standard of living.[44]

The 'hands-off' era was over, concluded the New York journalist: indeed many Italians and Americans 'would like to see the U.S. take a more direct hand in Italian politics'. But more than two unhappy years were to pass before the United States was able to combine this sort of awareness with effective means of direct intervention on the ground. Nevertheless, in the economic sphere as in others, the line of succession from the military governors of the Allied Control Commission to the technocrats of the European Recovery Program was a direct one.[45]

FRANCE: LIBERATION OR *LIBÉRATION*?

In the course of the war, no one on any of the sides understood the dilemmas, risks, and opportunities of the liberation/occupation experience better than the leader of the French anti-Nazi resistance, Charles de Gaulle. In his war memoirs, de Gaulle reminds his readers that other ter-

---

[43] Examples ibid. 116, 119, 121.
[44] *New York Herald Tribune*, 8 July 1945.
[45] cf. James Edward Miller, *The United States and Italy, 1940–1950: The Politics and Diplomacy of Stabilization* (Chapel Hill, NC, 1986), 176–84; John Lamberton Harper, *America and the Reconstruction of Italy, 1943–1948* (Cambridge, 1986), chs 1, 3.

ritories had been liberated and occupied well before the Allies succeeded in reaching Italy and France. The French North African territories had gone through the experience from the end of 1942. Then there was the special case of Iran, notes de Gaulle, not liberated but occupied by the Russians in the north and the British in the south from 1941. The General recalls how he took it upon himself to lecture the Shah of Iran on the behaviour of a leader in such a situation, how he must present himself to his nation's occupiers to ensure a minimum of dignity and sovereignty, and to win their respect.[46]

If anyone had the qualifications to give lessons on this subject, it was indeed de Gaulle. The unbending General was the only leader of a liberated nation who succeeded in avoiding the construction of any form of military government on his territory. Based in Algiers until June 1944, and with the Italian experience before his eyes, de Gaulle developed an overriding determination to avoid transferring even the slightest expression of French national sovereignty into the hands of an Allied occupation regime, the only possible exception being the battle zone itself.[47] In the General's vision, the national Committee of Liberation, grouping all the principal forces of the Resistance, would turn into the provisional Government of the Republic immediately when the fighting was over. So no duplicate power, not even for a day, even though the Republic did not in practice exist. In principle however it did. *L'État c'est moi!*: never was the phrase more literally appropriate, as de Gaulle made clear when he insisted that with his arrival in Paris right after the expulsion of the Germans in August 1944, he had caused 'the figure and the authority of the State to appear at once'.[48] At the end of September, the Allied Command announced the transfer of its powers to the French public administration. De Gaulle comments, 'naturally the Allies transferred nothing because they held no such powers: they could not hand over what they did not possess.'[49]

But de Gaulle had triumphed not simply through the force of his personal will, formidable as it was. He had also won through because the Allies were unable to decide how to organize their relations—as governments and armies—with the real or 'virtual' authorities they found in

---

[46] De Gaulle, *Complete War Memoirs*, 733–4; full conceptual discussion of the French idea of 'liberation' in Michael Kelly, *The Cultural and Intellectual Rebuilding of France after the Second World War* (London, 2004), 35–44.

[47] Memorandum of September 1943 cit. in de Gaulle, *Complete War Memoirs*, 543; Kelly, *Cultural and Intellectual Rebuilding*, 42.

[48] De Gaulle, *Complete War Memoirs*, 646; Kelly, *Cultural and Intellectual Rebuilding*, 62, 65–6.

[49] De Gaulle, *Complete War Memoirs*, 662.

place in the territories they liberated. There were no fully developed plans for France, certainly none formally agreed between all the Allies—including the Soviets—and between the governments and the military commands. The British had bet on de Gaulle from the beginning. The Americans said they believed in continuity—meaning Vichy—and practiced wait-and-see. In the meantime they delegated all the local political questions to the military commands on the spot, a responsibility that their Generals, led by the Supreme Allied Commander Eisenhower, repeatedly tried to refuse. In the event the Allied commands ordered that 'any semblance of military government in France was to be scrupulously avoided', and that the activities normally associated with military government—restarting food, work, law, order—would on French soil be termed 'civil affairs'.[50]

All these developments combined to ensure that the liberation experience in France did not in general create the violent swings of feeling towards the Allied armies and their soldiery, the enduring traumas, which left such deep marks in the collective memory and the identity politics of countries like Italy or Greece, not to mention Germany. No great novels, plays, or films celebrate or even debate what the arrival of the Anglo-Americans meant, no matter how tumultuous it appeared at the time, especially in the north and the east of the country.[51] The legacy of their presence appears fitfully in such works as Simone de Beauvoir's portrayal of the left-wing intellectuals at the time, *The Mandarins*, with its heavy, ironic references to 'the great liberating nation, the nation in which fountains spout streams of fruit juices and ice cream'.[52]

But there was another, specifically French factor, which created its own inheritance of attitudes and sentiments towards the liberators. Beyond their obvious, fundamental differences in values and geopolitics, at the official level a curious continuum of diffidence emerged between Vichy and de Gaulle's Free French movement, a reserve that they shared concerning America's ever more forceful impulse to present itself as a model of contemporary civilization. The historian Robert Paxton points out that both sides sought the aid and support of the United States, while seeking at the same time to limit America's wider influence which they considered

---

[50] Hilary Footitt and John Simmonds, *France 1943–45: The Politics of Liberation* (Leicester, 1987), 9–10; Merritt Y. Hughes, 'Civil Affairs in France', in Friedrich et al. (eds), *American Experiences*; cit. at p. 148.

[51] The Franco-Moroccan film, *Indigènes* (Rachid Bouchareb, 2006), celebrates the participation—up to 65% of the total—of soldiers from Algeria, Morocco, Tunisia, Senegal, and other colonies in the invasion/liberation of southern France in August 1944.

[52] De Beauvoir, *Mandarins*, 90.

likely to be invidious and suffocating.[53] The Vichy regime, says Paxton, was the first French government to put in place an explicit policy for limiting American cultural infiltration. Taking over two of the 1930s currents of anti-Americanism, the anti-modernism of the far Right and the 'corporatist and personalist' critique of bourgeois conformism, Vichy set out to use them in its project of rebuilding French identity in a more hierarchical, patriotic, and religious key. Anticipating the campaigns of many a French government over the succeeding decades, Vichy insisted that the minds of young people were the key battleground: the continuity of the great European cultures must be defended on this terrain against the seductive, facile pleasures of the American way of life.[54]

As for the Gaullists, a distinguished American witness of the liberation, H. Stuart Hughes, recalled a feature of the process that impressed him particularly:

> Those who knew the French on the morrow of victory can recall the patronizing tone they frequently took towards their American or British liberators—a tone brought to a perfection of unruffled assurance in the greatest literary classic of the Second World War, the memoirs of General de Gaulle.[55]

Sharing them, de Gaulle had done nothing to allay the fears of his Resistance allies about the implications of the various political approaches and methods the Americans and the British were bringing with them as they approached France. The constitutional planning body that was preparing designs for a new republic warned that 'imposing English and American law on the West might bring very serious consequences. Western civilization is not mono-lingual or mono-religious.'[56] The nearer the liberation came, the more attitudes to the nations bringing it hardened, a common impulse that had a strong and clear unifying effect on the Resistance front. Its newspaper said:

> We want France in War, the France of the Resistance to keep its independence. When the Allies arrive on our territory, France will receive them with

---

[53] Robert O. Paxton, 'Collaborateurs et Resistants', in Denis Lacorne, Jaques Rupnik, and Marie-France Toinet (eds), *L'Amérique dans les Têtes: Un Siècle de Fascinations et d'Aversions* (Paris, 1986), 72–3.

[54] Ibid. 77; on the phenomenon of the *Zazous*—dandified young rebels who adored American jazz, dancing, and cinema—and Vichy's repression of them, Savage, *Teenage*, 386–90; in *War and Liberation*, Hilary Footitt points out however that the Vichy press's enemy no. 1 always remained the British, pp. 13–14; context of Vichy policy in Kelly, *Cultural and Intellectual Rebuilding*, 17–18, 25–7, 29–32.

[55] Hughes, *The Obstructed Path: French Social Thought in the Years of Desperation, 1930–1960* (New York, 1968), 8.

[56] Cit. in Footitt, *War and Liberation*, 18.

joy, but she'll welcome them as friends, that's to say she'll stay in charge of her own house.[57]

And everywhere the Allies *were* received with joy, with 'hope and fervour, when even those who were not heroic began to live vicariously with the heroes in an atmosphere of passionate anticipation', recalled a young Jewish Austrian—Stanley Hoffmann—who escaped to America, and a brilliant future, after four years of Vichy existence. Nothing could surpass 'the bliss of being alive at the end of an unspeakable ordeal, the bliss of being happy with and proud of the people with whom one has survived', Hoffmann went on. All the meannesses of the war were forgiven, 'because of the price paid, and because of the slowly opening eyes, the *revanche* that was also a redemption'.[58]

The great array of sentiments produced by the encounter between the hopes, expectations, and fears of the peoples of France and their friendly invaders has by now been very effectively surveyed by time and historians. The host–guest conception that they highlight was the way the local populations everywhere expressed their sense of welcome, their impression of the temporary, fleeting meaning of the relationship, of a double rite of passage: back to some sort of peacetime normality, forwards to reconstruction and renewal, always trying to keep full control of their own destinies. In Normandy movement and destruction were the key themes, reflecting the trauma of an experience in which so much of the damage was caused by the liberators themselves. At least the Normandy phase, which saw the region as a starting point on a journey of two million soldiers eastwards, was relatively short-lived.[59] The Allied masses and their tanks crashed through; the French stood and looked, appalled at the wreckage of war, and exasperated at being simply spectators. Out of sympathy and in a form of expiation, all the Allied armies gave gifts—biscuits, cigarettes, sweets, cans. But none of the generosity made as much of an impression as white bread. One old man broke down and embraced the American soldiers who gave it away: 'Then he ran home [said a witness], to distribute this miraculous food, like the blessed wafer, to all the inhabitants of the house and the neighbours.'[60]

After violent battles over the key northern port of Cherbourg, the Americans handed over to its Mayor a version of the French flag made out

---

[57] Ibid. 20.

[58] Stanley Hoffmann, *Decline or Renewal? France since the 1930s* (New York, 1974), 60.

[59] GI experiences of the Normandy war in Hoyt, *GI's War*, chs 30–32.

[60] Footitt, *War and Liberation*, ch. 2; cit. at p. 57. The Normandy experience is the setting for the classic French film of liberation, *La bataille du rail* (Réné Clément, 1946), in which the Allies make no appearance.

of parachutes used in D-Day, as a mark of respect for French sovereignty and identity. But everyone realized—including the American command itself—that what happened next was a very heavy form of occupation, in practical ways often more burdensome than the German version. Many Cherbourgeois, to name but one instance, had difficulty adapting to the presence of large numbers of African-American troops in their midst.[61] Public relations efforts and starting to hand over as much responsibility as possible to local authorities—always the key criterion for the start of an end to occupation—were the obvious means to keep control of the situation. But within the months the locals clearly began to feel swamped. Friction was rising over the usual questions: money, women, requisitioning, regulations. Even when the military handed back the cinema, the first anywhere, the films shown were British and American. The more the authorities on both sides attempted to manage the contrasts, the more they became apparent. Finally, four months after their arrival, the Mayor offered a grand reception for the liberators, and used the occasion to remind them what lay behind the differences of outlook that had become so apparent:

> The Frenchman lives with his past, a past of which he is justly proud and which he endeavours to preserve from the hand of modernism. He refuses any idea of over-organization...he is capable of the best and the worst, disappointing his friends one day, and then showing the day after that he has unquenched vitality.

In reply the commanding General acknowledged how many difficulties there had been, and the cultural differences that had sometimes provoked them. He asked his hosts to understand that the Americans were a new nation, and just getting to know how a foreign land like France functioned. But he made a stirring promise: 'Our army is young, and when it goes back home after the Liberation of Europe, it will take back with it the spirit of France.'[62]

But the spirit of France the French most liked to point to afterwards was the one on display in the south. Here the French 'army of the interior', the Resistance movement, and its local authorities were able to show a degree of initiative that turned the Allies into grateful observers and friends, as much as armoured conquerors of the enemy. There would be no military government of any sort in Provence, and as so many towns had liberated themselves, and started their own reorganizations, sovereignty was never as heavily compromised as in the north. But, just as in northern Italy, the more the local populations had shown the way and

---

[61] Footitt, *War and Liberation*, 73–7.   [62] Ibid. ch. 3; cits at pp. 92, 93.

taken matters into their own hands, the more the situation highlighted the leading role that the forces of the political Left expected to play in the future government of their region. Once more London and Washington worried if this meant revolution, civil war, or a Soviet thrust into France, and found the urge to moderation and Republican unity of the French Communist party deeply suspect.[63] Again as in Italy, the military on the ground were pragmatic. They focused on the campaign and their supply lines, delegating civilian jobs to whatever civilian authorities seemed best able to handle them.[64]

The liberating armies in Provence were as everywhere multinational, but once more it was the Americans who caught the eye of local peoples. Comments by French soldiers and workers in the docks referred to the superb equipment the US military brought, and their technical inventiveness. 'This technical expertise was largely represented [by the relaunched local newspapers] as positive, symbolizing a post-war modernity that was exciting and worthy of emulation', comments the historian Footitt. The Allied public relations team helped to restart a key Marseilles newspaper, *Mid-Soir*. One of its first photographs 'showed a large American military policeman on an impressive motorbike, under the heading: "Goodbye German police and bon voyage! You've been magnificently replaced by these men-machines, so much more sympathetic"'.[65] But it was the rediscovered Hollywood cinema that made the biggest splash: 'Hollywood has reconquered Marseille', exclaimed *Midi-Soir*. At a time to look forward, said the newspaper, 'American films were so much a symbol of a happy life that we were certain that their return would coincide for us with a return to sunny days and happiness'.[66]

Not right away though. The time period that transformed a liberation into something much less desirable, more contentious and unruly, was measured in roughly two months in the Marseilles area. Allied authorities commented later: 'At the conclusion of eleven weeks...criticisms and rumours were becoming endemic. Misconceptions of American ideas and policies were starting to cascade.' Tensions over food, work, and differing conceptions of law and order intensified. Local commentators spoke of 'humiliation' and 'disillusion'.[67]

In the Rheims area, in eastern France, the same evolution took even less time, as the stakes were much higher. The war continued close by, and the weight of soldiers and machinery was all the greater. A vast forward military complex was established, and local voices of government felt

---

[63] Cf. Footitt and Simmonds, *France 1943–1945*, 104–5, 108–10, 150, 186–92.
[64] Footitt, *War and Liberation*, 100–6.   [65] Ibid. 107.
[66] Ibid.   [67] Ibid. 112, 119.

themselves pushed aside. Requisitioning started immediately on a very large scale, in complete disorder but involving communications, industry, housing, shops, leisure facilities, even the water supply.[68] The Americans employed thousands but they did not provide food to match, and the familiar contrast between the profligacy of the liberators and the penury of the locals soon appeared. A flourishing black market in goods and sex was the inevitable consequence. Politics swung to the Left even more markedly than elsewhere, and the Communist Party enjoyed overwhelming success in the first municipal elections of April 1945.[69]

The language of occupation began to be used even by the French authorities in official reports, and there was much invidious comparison with the behaviour of the Germans.[70] When the Rheims area was turned into a vast transit camp for demobilizing American soldiers after the end of the war, all the devices used up to that time to bridge the gaps of understanding and custom between the hosts and the guests—political, public relations, informal—rapidly began to break down, and two separate antagonistic blocs began to emerge. Two long years were to pass before the last of the GIs left the area, by which time the American authorities had started to resent very intensely their treatment as 'foreigners'.[71]

As in liberation experiences everywhere, France demonstrated that the key priorities of a liberating army wishing to stabilize the situation once the battle has finished or passed on must always be *food, work, law, order*. Around these objectives the French, the Resistance in all its forms, and the Allied soldiery made—at least in the early weeks from June 1944 onwards—common cause. But the American armies promised more than just stabilization. At the beginning they had told themselves that theirs was the 'best dressed, best fed, best equipped Liberating Army now on earth'. So they must act correspondingly in France, where local peoples trusted them more than the soldiers of any other nation, and looked up to the US 'as the friend of the oppressed and the liberator of the enslaved'. Even at the end, when cohesion and discipline were breaking down, American commanders tried to exhort their men to remember that they were 'Ambassadors of Good Will', and examples of the ' "American Way of Life" to others less fortunate than ourselves'.[72]

---

[68] Footitt, *War and Liberation*, 156–7.

[69] On the sex market, Mary Louise Roberts, 'The Price of Discretion: Prostitution, Venereal Disease and the American Military in France, 1944–1946', *American Historical Review* (October 2010), 1002–30. This analysis demonstrates how the ruthlessness of the American armies in their use of prostitutes revealed all the attitudes of a force of occupation.

[70] Footitt, *War and Liberation*, 156–67.

[71] Ibid. 168–74.   [72] Cit. ibid. 30, 163.

But when this inspiration was taken seriously the results were disappointment. In Provence, where relations had started out so well, on a basis of mutual respect and support, local voices expressed disillusionment and dismay, not rancour, as the promise of American support failed to turn into reality. In November 1944 the leader of the Resistance front for Provence, Daniel Georges, wrote an article expressing some of the key frustrations of the liberated peoples of the area. The problem was no longer the necessities of survival, but one of attitudes. The Americans were accused of taking no interest in the society hosting them, of ignoring local aspirations—especially the desire to enrol and take part in the war—of simply using local resources on their way to somewhere else. 'The burden of Georges's complaint was that the Americans were simply not interested in helping France to develop a bright and independent future of her own', comments Footitt. 'The USA represented much that was highly desirable for an aggressively resurgent national identity like that of France. Gradually, however relationships cooled with misunderstandings and misconceptions on both sides.' Unrealistic expectations met limits of time, patience, attention, and interest which were surprising in such an outgoing, forward-looking new superpower, anxiously proclaiming its urge to remodel the world.[73]

'THIS HUGE MODERNISTIC MUSTERING': THE FRIENDLY OCCUPATION OF BRITAIN

Everyone agreed: when the mass of the American armies went off to take part in the great cross-Channel assault of June 1944, the towns and countryside of England suddenly felt empty. A presence of 1.5 million soldiers was reduced by half in the days and weeks after D-Day, leaving the 300,000 flying crew and ground staff of the 8th Airforce as the only major US military presence in the land.[74] Marshalling for the invasion of France had 'made clear the scale of the American presence', writes David Reynolds; it 'put the American occupation in a different perspective'. Vast areas along the coast and most of the south western towns had been totally taken over by the D-Day armies. The scale and sophistication of 'this huge modernistic mustering' (Reynolds) left lasting impressions. The military historian John Keegan, then a schoolboy, eloquently recalled how the country area to which his family had been evacuated was swamped by the GIs and their machinery:

[73] Ibid. 119–21.   [74] Reynolds, *Rich Relations*, 394.

How different they looked from our own jumble-sale-quality champions, beautifully clothed in smooth khakis as fine in cut and quality as a British officer's ... and armed with glistening, modern, automatic weapons. ... More striking still were the number, size and elegance of the vehicles in which they paraded about the country-side in stately convoy. The British Army's transport was a sad collection of underpowered makeshifts, whose dun paint flaked from their tin-pot bodywork. The Americans travelled in magnificent, gleaming, olive-green, pressed steel, four-wheel-drive juggernauts, decked with what car salesmen would call optional extras of a sort never seen on their domestic equivalents: deep-treaded spare tyres, winches, towing cables, fire extinguishers. There were towering GMC six-by-sixes, compact and powerful Dodge four-by-fours, and pilot fishing the rest or buzzing nimbly about the lanes on independent errands like the beach-buggies of an era still thirty years ahead, tiny and entrancing Jeeps, caparisoned with whiplash aerials and sketchy canvas hoods which drummed with the rhythm of a cowboy's saddlebags rising and falling to the canter of his horse across the prairie.[75]

Once more the medium was the message, and it was conveyed with a drive and spontaneity as striking as it was forceful.

Between the start of their arrival and the demobilization after VE Day in May 1945, nearly three million Americans in uniform passed through Britain. At the peak, in May 1944, they 'occupied 100,000 buildings, either newly built or requisitioned, ranging from small Nissen huts, cottages and bell tents to sprawling hangars, workshops and assembly plants in more than 1,100 cities, towns and villages'.[76] In Norfolk and Suffolk alone 426,000 airmen were concentrated. There was said to be an air force base every eight miles in East Anglia. For every two local residents of Wiltshire there was one American in early 1944. In a civil engineering project unprecedented in scale and intensity in the British Isles, some 500 airfields were brought into operation; 116 new hospitals were built to deal with 90,000 sick or wounded soldiers at any one time.[77]

This colossal operation required a vast joint planning staff, and a mobilization of resources of every kind: human, economic, territorial, mental. It was given a special unified code name: BOLERO, and its task, said the supreme American commander on the spot, Eisenhower, was 'appalling'. Because it required a quite different sort of collaboration than ever seen

---

[75] Cit. in Juliet Gardiner, *'Over Here': The GIs in Wartime Britain* (London, 1992), 185; cf. Reynolds, *Rich Relations*, 368–9.

[76] Gardiner, *'Over Here'*, 41.

[77] Reynolds, *Rich Relations*, pp. 109, 112, 115, 116, and ch. 7 in general (detailed maps of presence, pp. 110–11), fluctuations discussed pp. 102–5. John Schlesinger's 1979 film *Yanks* vividly depicts the arrival of a large US infantry division, and its encampment, near a small town on the Yorkshire–Lancashire border. Discussion below, pp. 303–4.

before between two national command structures, there were—inevitably—continuous disputes: 'over objectives, strategies, tactics, command networks and responsibilities' (Gardiner). 'The rhythm was erratic, the orchestra ever-changing, and no-one seemed sure of the tune.' (Reynolds.) Conflicts blew up over basic military priorities, over supply needs—more troops or more cargo?—and between the demands of the various categories of personnel: combat, air, and service (this latter mass nearly half the total at some stages). The early stages of the influx were particularly chaotic. Yet under the pressures of time, circumstance, and force—calculations that changed constantly—the job somehow got done. As D-Day approached the 'pulsating crescendo of men and supplies' began to take shape in a fashion corresponding roughly to what the high commands had imagined.[78]

But there were certain peculiarities about the new American presence that made clear to those who cared to notice that the whole vast enterprise entailed a significant surrender of British national sovereignty, that a variety of occupation was indeed under way. It was partial and temporary, and it was—formally at least—accepted. But its outlines were unmistakable, and its historical implications not long in making themselves visible. Partly it was the result of an asymmetry of power that became more and more apparent as the war went on, and was openly acknowledged after D-Day. 'We shall have to play second fiddle—safe but no longer powerful', one citizen told a survey conducted by Mass Observation, the voluntary organization that collected so many British voices on the nation's war experience.[79] But beyond this fact of life, there were certain specific features of the 'friendly invasion' that could only have been expressed by the institutions and politics of the United States, and these would turn out to be remarkably enduring.

'I'll never take an order from a Britisher': so declared the first of the commanders of the US bomber force on his arrival on English soil, in February 1942. And very quickly the Chief of the General Staff in Washington, George C. Marshall, laid down the official line: cooperation with Allies was one thing—and might indeed be exceptionally close in the British case—but integration with them was very different. This could not be contemplated: 'the forces of the United States are to be maintained as a separate and distinct component of the combined forces', said Marshall's directive.[80] Because Britain was where the Americans were coming to, their commanders worried at first that they would be silently

[78] Gardiner, *'Over Here'*, 41, Reynolds, *Rich Relations*, 89–90, 92–3.
[79] Cit. in *New Statesman*, 3 March 2003; cf. Angus Calder, *The People's War: Britain 1939–1945* (London, 1969), 266.
[80] Reynolds, *Rich Relations*, 94.

subsumed into the British war effort. By the end, it was the British who had to struggle to make sure they were not 'submerged' by the huge build-up of American strategic power in every direction.[81] Much of the strenuous Anglo-American diplomacy, military and political, of the kind that made Eisenhower famous, was in fact necessary to bridge the gap between the different ideas of cooperation and autonomy prevailing on the two sides, in a war where military success was as always the key currency of political power.

One of the questions arising from these tensions that was least discussed in public was policy for the accommodation and management of the massed American armies arriving in the British Isles. In reality it was one of the most revealing. More than any other British adaptation, it was the evolution of the legal position of the soldiery that bestowed on the friendly invasion the contours of a formal occupation. Reynolds explains:

> ...in peace or war, British troops in Britain remained liable to ordinary courts for any breaches of the civil or criminal law, such as theft from or assault on civilians. This was true in peacetime in America but *not* in war, under Article 74 of the U.S. Articles of War.

To the consternation of British authorities, the Americans now insisted that this rule applied whether US troops were stationed at home or abroad:

> The American demand for exclusive extraterritorial jurisdiction over its soldiers therefore clashed with the British insistence on the exclusive "rule of law".

So, in contrast with the numerous other Allied forces present in the UK, the arrival of the Americans set off an irreconcilable clash in legal principle. 'It was also argued that American public opinion would resent foreign courts exercising jurisdiction over U.S. citizens.'[82] In the end His Majesty's Government simply swallowed its pride and backed down. A special law was passed in great haste in the summer of 1942, which conceded the American official position, and created an unprecedented, extraterritorial jurisdiction on British soil. The 'adamantine rigidity' of the US case had won through, comments Reynolds. 'But the main reason was quite simply that the United States was a far more important and powerful Ally than, say, Canada or Poland.'[83]

---

[81] Example of divergences and compromises over bombing strategy discussed ibid. 300–1.

[82] Ibid. 145–6 (emphasis in original).   [83] Ibid. 146–7.

Among those most struck at the time by the implications was George Orwell, who linked the act explicitly to street scenes that made him feel that 'Britain is now Occupied Territory'. But it was 'fixed policy', said Orwell, 'not to criticise our allies, nor to answer their criticisms of us.... Not one person in ten knows of the existence of this agreement; the newspapers barely reported it and refrained from commenting on it.'[84] While 'the worst kind of trouble' that Orwell predicted never arrived— for reasons discussed below—history has revealed the importance and the invidiousness of the precedent. American armed forces abroad from this time on would expect to enjoy a different kind of sovereignty to those of other nations.

A far more visible example of the same truth touched every form of contact between the soldiery and their British hosts: money. The point here was not simply that the Americans were 'overpaid' by any local standard of the time, but that all the laws and army provisions of Washington were directed to the end of making sure that the GI and his officers, as members of a citizen army, had as much of their spending power in their pockets as they chose to put there. Once again, for good or ill, here was an American exception. Every other army kept back a part of its soldiers' pay so as to boost saving, spare the foreign currency reserves, and limit the impact of troop spending on stretched or devastated local economies. But in the United States 'army pay was almost entirely a function of domestic politics' (Reynolds). This reality was accompanied by Chief of Staff George Marshall's conviction that in an army not fighting to defend its homeland, morale was almost entirely a function of material comforts of the domestic kind. The net result was not only that many GIs lived better in uniform than the natives, but better than the most of them had done as civilians back home in Depression-era America. The pay of privates and corporals in US uniform was 'five times that of a British soldier', Orwell pointed out.[85]

The US authorities knew that the pay issue was going to cause friction in rationed, war-battered Britain. In *Instructions for American Servicemen in Britain 1942*, issued to all troops destined for that country, the General Staff warned:

DON'T BE A SHOW OFF. The British dislike bragging and showing off. American wages and soldiers' pay are the highest in the world. When pay day comes it would be sound practice to learn to spend your money in ac-

---

[84] Orwell, 'As I Please' (a column in the left-wing weekly *Tribune*), 3 December 1943, in *The Collected Essays, Journalism and Letters of George Orwell*, iii: *As I Please, 1943–1945* (Harmondsworth, 1970), 72–3.

[85] Ibid. 73; details and comparisons of British and US troop pay in Gardiner, 'Over Here', 56, 62–3.

cordance to British standards.... They won't think any better of you for throwing your money around: they are more likely to feel that you haven't learned the common sense virtues of thrift. The British 'Tommy' is apt to be especially touchy about the difference between his wages and yours... don't rub him the wrong way.[86]

Prickly minds like George Orwell's were of course rubbed the wrong way: 'I rarely see American and British soldiers together. You can't have really close and friendly relations with somebody whose income is five times your own.'[87]

One of the more obvious reasons the GIs had so much disposable income was that all of their basic material needs were to be found on the great bases they constructed, and so much else—'cigarettes, chocolate, tinned fruit, tinned ham, razor blades etc.'—at their extraordinary Post Exchange stores. Though the soldiers soon became famous for their big-heartedness, here was another form of extraterritoriality that could provoke envy. Arnold Toynbee, the great historian, was quoted as calling the PX: 'a lodestone to the American exile and an offense to the native of the country, setting up a caste barrier and losing much goodwill.'[88] A *Times* correspondent visiting a base taken over from the RAF was thrilled at being taken on 'an impossibly fast journey to America'. But every trace of the Royal Air Force had disappeared:

> The aircraft are American, and so are the petrol trailers, lorries, mobile workshops, bomb trolleys, 'jeeps' (powerful little passenger cars), salvage vehicles, and all the thousand and one pieces of equipment without which an air force could not function... the Americans are not relying on this country for even the smallest items; they have actually brought with them their own dustbins—garbage cans, they call them.[89]

And so the list went on. The American Red Cross opened its own lavish and largely exclusive leisure facilities for the GIs. The US authorities demanded—and got—a separate radio network for their men and women, since the GIs were loud in denouncing the stuffiness, to their ears, of the BBC's output. The Corporation, which had never hitherto faced a rival, was greatly discomfited, and denounced the US impulse to isolation and

---

[86] *Instructions for American Servicemen in Britain, 1942* (1942 edn repr., Oxford, 2004); cf. Jonathan Croall, *Don't You Know There's a War On? The People's Voice, 1939–45* (London, 1989), 78; in Schlesinger's *Yanks*, the protagonist, an army cook played by Richard Gere, embarrasses his local-town girlfriend by successfully bribing a landlady into providing more drink.

[87] 'As I Please', 17 December 1943, in Orwell, *Collected Essays*, iii. 78.

[88] Cit. in Robert O. Mead, *Atlantic Legacy: Essays in American–European Cultural History* (New York, 1969), 186.

[89] Reynolds, *Rich Relations*, 295–6; discussion ibid. 296–7.

'separatism': 'all they require from this country is a piece of land to camp on until the "second front" opens…'[90]

The separatism also brought great official embarrassment when it came to managing the presence of the 130,000 African-American GIs who passed through the land. Most of the US armed services of the day were officially and rigidly segregationist. In anguish the British government felt obliged to support this policy in practice, out of the highest consideration for Anglo-American relations and Congressional politics. In public though they could not condone it, knowing that the British people generally were seriously disconcerted by the racial attitudes of the US army, air force, and navy, and so many of their members.[91]

All this meant that the American occupation of Britain was consciously managed by the authorities at every level, on both sides of the ocean, with the utmost delicacy and seriousness. It was a topic 'avoided in the press and utterly taboo on the air', complained George Orwell in 1943; there was 'a careful censorship of the radio to cut out anything the Americans might object to'.[92] None of the other territories liberated and occupied by the US armed forces saw such an effort at organized public relations, nor did any of the two nations' other allies. While Churchill, Roosevelt, and the top soldiers handled the diplomacy of the situation, the planners and general staff succeeded together in setting up Operation Bolero for all the logistics. But that still left the problem of getting the peoples of the two worlds to live and work alongside each other on the ground, of managing hopes, fears, prejudices, expectations, and disappointments, so as to win the war *and* open the way for a new order afterwards. A British writer told an American audience:

> …when American soldiers landed in Great Britain we made the mistake of thinking that because they spoke English they were just like ourselves. The attitude of the American soldiers was naturally the same. They expected a home from home and what they found was, to all intents and purposes, a foreign country.[93]

---

[90] On ARC facilities, Gardiner, *'Over Here'*, ch. 9, 'Islands of Little America', eloquent denunciation of consequences of separatism by Assistant Controller of BBC cit. in Gorham, *Sound and Fury*, 134; Reynolds, *Rich Relations*, 154–61.

[91] Gardiner, *'Over Here'*, ch. 14 and p. 150 in particular, Reynolds, *Rich Relations*, ch. 14; Savage, *Teenage*, 420–1. The African-American writer Ralph Ellison spent a significant part of the war as an ordinary seaman stationed in south Wales; the effects of the experiences he knew there on his ethnic, national, and intellectual identity are discussed in detail in Daniel G. Williams, ' "If we only had some of what they have": Ralph Ellison in Wales', *Comparative American Studies*, 4/1 (2006).

[92] Orwell, *Collected Essays*, iii. 55, 77; cf. Reynolds, *Rich Relations*, 184.

[93] Cit. in Gardiner, *'Over Here'*, 38; cf. Orwell, *Collected Essays*, ii, 'Letter to Partisan Review', 3 January 1943, 320–1: 'the cultural differences are very deep, perhaps irreconcilable…'

It wasn't just their foreignness that had to be handled, in a land already coping with Canadian, Polish, Czech, Norwegian, French, and Commonwealth soldiery.[94] It was also because they were seen on both sides, in so many ways, as a wave of the future that so much attention was paid to how the impact and reception of the Americans functioned in wartime Britain. 'Are you our destiny?' was a question that resurfaced once more, and soon began to disturb souls at every level of society, and not just among the almost 38,000 women who would become GI brides. The long pre-history of this hope—or fear—in Great Britain had come into sharp focus as soon as the friendly occupation started happening.[95] No one thought the Americans aimed to alter the island race in any deliberate fashion (though many would have liked to change the climate, the food, and the leisure facilities, preferably instantly). After all the British were working out very consciously the social contract they wanted to see put in place by a new government after the war and, as already seen, it had nothing to do with American visions. But the GIs and all their forms of opulence made at least some of the British realize that there were other things they had been missing besides secure jobs, and decent schools, hospitals, and pensions: 'emancipation was the promise that Britain and America held out to its youth as a reward for their war efforts', writes Jon Savage.[96]

If ever there was need for confirmation of the 'soft power' theory of America's impact on the world, it must be surely found among the young women of Britain between 1942 and 1945. 'The G.I. found it easy to establish rapport with people his own age, especially girls, because Hollywood films and American music had preceded him as ambassadors', wrote the GI historian Lee Kennett.[97] Nowhere in Europe was popular feeling so well documented as it was during that experience, and what all the surveys, opinion polls, interviews of the time, and later confirm is that, as an ex-serviceman put it: 'never in history has there been such a conquest of women by men as was won by the American army in Britain in World War II.' One of the many women witnesses on record recalled:

---

[94] Comparisons of the time reported and discussed in Croall, *Don't You Know There's a War On?*, 78.

[95] Partly summarized in Reynolds, *Rich Relations*, ch. 3, cf. Savage, *Teenage*, 416; a contemporary popular expression of the common destiny question reproduced in Simon Garfield, *Our Hidden Lives: The Everyday Diaries of a Forgotten Britain, 1945–1948* (London, 2004), 109: Harold Nicolson deploring the disappearance of everyday amenities for his class such as taxis: 'we shall have to walk and live a Woolworth life hereafter', he complained in 1941 (4 June 1941).

[96] Savage, *Teenage*, p. 421 and ch. 27 in general.

[97] Ibid. 461.

I suppose we were as jubilant as everyone else in the country when the Americans came into the war. In Bournemouth we had seen troops of almost every colour and nationality, but when these GIs hit town, commandeering our homes and our countryside, we were captivated at once. With their smooth, beautifully tailored uniforms, one could hardly tell a private from a colonel. They swaggered, they boasted and they threw their money about, bringing a shot in the arm to business, such as it was, and an enormous lift to the female population.[98]

The lax discipline, lack of soldiery spirit, and conspicuous consumption of the invaders upset plenty of male minds, cultivated and otherwise. By mid-1944 even the GIs themselves could tell the British were getting 'edgy'.[99] But like so many products of American popular culture, America's servicemen seemed to young women to possess built-in features not easily found elsewhere. 'It as if the cinema had come to life', recalled a woman who went onto have a screen career of her own. 'They were so handsome and well groomed and *clean.*' Another pointed out that 'they used deodorants and after-shave—things unknown to 99 per cent of British men'. Others talked of the exuberance, drive, and confidence, while a woman Red Cross worker recalled how the GIs 'brought with them colour, romance, warmth—and a tremendous hospitality to our dark, shadowed island'.[100]

Although every film made featuring uniformed Americans in Britain dealt with the jealousies and conflicts all this provoked,[101] the most graphic of them came long after the end of the war. In John Schlesinger's 1979 production of *Yanks*, set, as already mentioned, in small-town northern

---

[98] Cit. in Gardiner, *'Over Here'*, 110; a typical encounter is reconstructed 'verbatim' in Hoyt, *GI's War*, 73–4. Not all the girls were amused. Decades later, a female shop-steward still remembered the jealousies and resentment provoked by GI opulence and carefree spending, in Croall, *Don't You Know There's a War On?*, 78; graphic novelistic rendering, set in Liverpool, in Annie Groves, *The Grafton Girls* (London, 2007).

[99] GI reaction to British testiness reported in Hoyt, *GI's War*, 290. The celebrated wartime writer and broadcaster J. B. Priestley gave a glimpse of working-class male resentment in the character of Tommy Loftus, a non-combatant, in his instant end-of-war novel *Three Men in New Suits* (1945 edn repr., London, 1984).

[100] Cit. in Gardiner, *'Over Here'*, 52–3, 111–12 (emphasis in original); cumulative effect of Hollywood films and GI presence emphasized in Savage, *Teenage*, 418; GI experiences of the encounter recounted—with poems—in Hoyt, *GI's War*, 73–4, 283–90. The other North Americans in Europe—the Canadians—could also provoke the same reactions on occasion, as the Dutch liberation experience testified; summary in David Stafford, *Endgame 1945: Victory, Retribution, Liberation* (London, 2007), 350–2.

[101] Wartime cinema-society relationship explained in Calder, *People's War*, 367–73. The Ministry of Information promoted the production of a number of films in the cause of Anglo-American understanding, particularly *A Yank in the RAF* (Lou Edelmen, 1941), *The Way to the Stars* (Anthony Asquith, 1945), *A Matter of Life and Death* (Michael Powell and Emeric Pressburger, 1946). In 1982 London Weekend Television produced a 12-hour miniseries dedicated to the same themes, *We'll Meet Again*, set in a small Suffolk town.

England, Hollywood glamour in the form of Richard Gere plays an ordinary small-town American boy interpreting the Hollywood glamour of
1943. Matt's looks, wealth, manners, and generosity confirm all the stereotypes. He soon sweeps the shopkeeper's comely daughter off her feet,
and her small, shy, poorly kitted local lad into oblivion. Through many
painful vicissitudes, love triumphs and the two are reunited by cheers and
waves across a huge crowd—including numbers of fatherless children—as
Matt's packed troop train pulls out of Keighley station. Meanwhile his
superior officer has seduced the naval captain's wife in the big house
(Vanessa Redgrave), by flying her to Northern Ireland in a bomber, and
plying her with Coca-Cola and slot-machines.[102]

At the time cinema was used extensively by the authorities as they tried
to manage the inevitable surges of feelings on both sides as the war wore
on and illusions wore off.[103] Not everyone enjoyed the consequences.
J. B. Priestley's demobilization novel *Three Men in New Suits* of 1945,
presents one of its ex-soldier heroes as a great admirer of the American
Army, but disgusted by the American takeover of his local cinema, complete with preachy documentaries, fatuous comedies, and ludicrously im-
probable war dramas, all dedicated to putting over 'tasty...slabs of the
American way of life'.[104]

But seen from a longer, broader perspective, the friendly occupation
brought changes in the ways the British regarded themselves and the world
that turned out to be enduring. 'It was so drab when they had gone', lamented one English woman. 'The whole world had been opened up to me
and then it was closed down again....We realised how confining England
was.' A schoolboy claimed that: 'The Yanks introduced a whole new concept of life to the British Isles.' A *New York Times* correspondent told of
beliefs in England that the Labour Party's great victory of July 1945 was in
part a product of the GI presence. The contrasts of wealth and misery had
been too strong, feeding—especially among young people—the 'fertile
seeds of envy and rebellion...[the British] voted for automobiles, better
clothes, mass production factories, more spending power, more conveniences. They voted socialist, in other words, in order to enjoy some of the
fruits of American capitalism.' The claim would have seemed laughable at

---

[102] Origins, construction and unhappy commercial and artistic fate of film recounted in
William J. Mann, *Edge of Midnight: The Life of John Schlesinger* (London, 2004), chs 14–15
and pp. 426–7.
[103] A glimpse of the documentary material made for this purpose may be seen in episode
4 of the BBC's 1984 series on Anglo-American relations in the twentieth century, *An Ocean
Apart*; discussion of propaganda problems in Orwell, *Collected Essays*, ii, cit. 'Letter to
Partisan Review', 3 January 1943, 321–2.
[104] Priestley, *Three Men in New Suits*, 91–2.

the time, yet within a very few years—after the British had well and truly founded their Welfare State—there was every sign that the revolution of rising expectations was breaking through in their country. The American armies had camped such a long time on British soil that by the end, one conclusion seemed obvious: it wasn't the American troops who were over-paid; it was the British who were underpaid.[105]

* * *

Truly the youth of America, the GI incarnated not just its wealth and new-found power. 'In an unhappy and uncertain world he seemed happy and confident of the future', said Ms McCormick of the *New York Times*. ' "America must be a happy country," was the comment the GI commonly provoked.'[106] But while huge numbers of GIs headed from Britain for home on the first available transport in June 1945, his peers on the Con-tinent were coming to grips with the much sterner tasks of taking over nations and peoples that were defeated, bombed-out, starving enemies. After the final end of the war in Europe, and following on from their very ambiguous experiences in Italy and France, the liberators now arrived in the land where, as Ms McCormick said, 'Hitler tasted his greatest tri-umph': Austria.

AUSTRIA: 'RECREATING A NATION'?

It was on 3rd May 1945, at eight o'clock in the evening, that the first American troops, coming from Germany, entered Innsbruck. The red-white-red flag of Austria flew from every house and an enormous throng greeted the car of Major Sheldon D. Elliot, the first American officer to come into contact with civilian Austria. Half Innsbruck crowded the streets as Elliot was jubilantly escorted to the sea of the government of the province—the Tyrol *Landhaus*. A huge American flag was unfurled when he entered.[107]

With these lines, Karl Gruber, Austria's first post-war foreign minister, opens his memoir of his years in office up to 1953. In Innsbruck Gruber had been leader of the small, local anti-Nazi resistance network, and stepped forward to greet Major Elliott as the head of a self-appointed new government of the province. Within the next few days and weeks he would quickly get used to these liberators and their ways, their 'astonish-

---

[105] McCormick, *New York Times*, 1 August 1945; Gardiner, '*Over Here*', 211–13; testi-mony of a contemporary working-class youth on the impact of US film on popular expec-tations cit. in Savage, *Teenage*, 411.

[106] McCormick, *New York Times*, 1 August 1945.

[107] Karl Gruber, *Between Life and Liberty: Austria in the Postwar World* (London, 1955), 15.

ing' quantities of materials and machinery, their heavy-handed attempts at communication—both official and personal—, their hopelessly confused bureaucracy, and their deep lack of political and psychological preparation for entering Austria, let alone such a special region as the Tyrol.[108]

By the time, ten years later, when the Austrians finally regained their sovereignty with the State Treaty, they were thoroughly fed up with all their occupiers, and Minister Gruber did not hesitate to say so in public.[109] In his memoir, he denounced the entire overreaching apparatus, and claimed that a thousand men would have been sufficient 'to maintain order'. But with his nation on the fault-line between the West and the new Soviet version of liberation/occupation, there was never any chance that such a solution would emerge. By December 1945 there were 47,000 US army personnel in two divisions, 40,000 French forces in one division, 65,000 British in two divisions, and 200,000 Soviets in seventeen divisions. The official American report that included these figures calculated there was roughly 'one member of the occupation forces for every 20 Austrians'. The first head of government in Vienna, Karl Renner, talked of 'four elephants in a row boat'.[110]

As in the case of Italy, the Allies had great difficulty in striking a balance between liberation and occupation in Austria. Apart from the their enduring reluctance to make commitments and offer hostages to fortune, the basic problem was the same: was this nation to be considered one of Hitler's willing accomplices, or—via the Anschluß of 1938—among the first victims of his brutal designs? It was the British who, as in Italy, took the lead in deciding what should happen, since much American deliberation had ended with the country 'left hanging between East and West', as a contemporary said, with the President as usual seeking to take as little specific responsibility as possible.[111] By the end of 1943 the British and the Americans had decided that they favoured an independent, reconstituted Austria in an organized Danube framework of some sort. The Moscow Foreign Ministers Conference of November 1943—present only

---

[108] Gruber, *Between Life and Liberty*, 24; most of the units had been expecting Stuttgart, and found themselves in western Austria through the fortunes of war.

[109] Gruber cit. in Günther Bishof, 'Austria—a Colony in the U.S. Postwar "Empire"?', in John G. Blair and Reinhold Wagnleitner (eds), *Empire: American Studies* (Tübingen, 1997), 123–4.

[110] Gruber, *Between Life and Liberty*, 46; personnel figures and Renner quoted in William B. Bader, *Austria Between East and West, 1945–1955* (Stanford, 1966), 55; the figures quoted give no indication of distribution.

[111] Cf. remarks by the first American High Commissioner to Austria, the former head of the 15th Army Group in Italy, Gen. Mark Clark in his memoir *Calculated Risk* (New York, 1950), 460.

the British, the Americans, and the Soviets—issued a proclamation that would weigh very heavily indeed, far more than its promulgators had intended, on the Austrians' own idea of their post-war future. Based on the notion that Austro-German solidarity must be broken up by treating Austria *better* than post-Nazi Germany, the Moscow Declaration officially recognized the nation as Hitler's first victim, promised to re-establish a free and independent Austrian nation, and encouraged 'the Austrian people themselves, to find that political and economic security which is the only basis for a lasting peace'. As with the Italians, the Austrians were reminded however that they could not escape responsibility for their role in Hitler's war, 'and that in the final settlement account will be taken of [their] own contribution to [their] liberation'.[112]

Although the Declaration produced none of the signs of revolt it was designed for, it did establish and announce the principle that the Austrians were to be treated differently from the Germans, and as the liberation finally came the Anglo-American armies were being told by the Combined Chiefs of Staff in Washington that they could permit themselves to be 'more friendly' to the natives than in Germany: 'There will be no need to discourage some degree of fraternization.' A British official history explains that '[t]he Germans were to be made to taste defeat. The Austrians were to be liberated from German domination and their country restored to freedom and independence.'[113]

In the spirit of these vague but comforting notions, General Mark W. Clark, the American High Commissioner, newly arrived from a field command in Italy, was happy to attend the improvised Salzburg Festival of music in August 1945, where he reportedly 'unfurled the insignia for his troops, the olive branch and the colors of Austria'. In his memoirs Clark recalled how much effort he had put into convincing the Austrians 'that we had come in peace—with good will...to feed them, to help them open their schools. To do everything in the world to make life more...livable for them....I had an educational program right down to every commander— personally to see to it that their men understood that they were to be courteous—polite—none of this arrogance...we were there to help.'[114]

---

[112] Ibid. 20–5; Moscow Declaration and preliminary documents reproduced with discussion in Robert H. Keyserlingk, *Austria in World War II: An Anglo-American Dilemma* (Kingston and Montreal, 1988), ch. 5 and Appendix 3.

[113] Cit. in F. S. V. Donnison, *Civil Affairs and Military Government in North-West Europe, 1944–1946* (London, 1961), 284; critical view of these promises in Keyserlingk, *Austria in World War II*, 158–66.

[114] Cit. in Hans A. Schmitt (ed.), *U.S. Occupation in Europe after World War II* (Lawrence, Kan., 1978), 147; the first festival is described in Donald R. Whitnah and Florentine E. Whitnah, *Salzburg Under Siege: U.S. Occupation, 1945–1955* (Westport, Conn., 1991), 15–16 (the author was a military government officer in Salzburg, his wife a local girl).

In November 1945 a writer in a Salzburg newspaper vividly portrayed local reactions to the realities of the American presence:

> We have so much to tell you. So much between us is still new and unexplained…do not be hurt if we grumble, some thought you would let us wallow in white bread and canned goods, forgetting that you also have to feed millions of others who are starving.…You require so much paperwork, so many questions, so bureaucratic—Do you mistrust us yet? Believe us, we admire you! We are such a little country, we do not expect you to understand out neutrality.…We smile about some of the things you do. We cannot always keep step with your rhythm or accept the fact that you put your feet on a desk, are almost happy that you are so outward!…We, too, ask of you that you do not judge us quickly. We also possess something of your will to live and vitality which made you a great country.[115]

What happened next depended on three crucial, interlocking factors: (*a*) the hard work of establishing military government as such;[116] (*b*) the relative success of Austrian political forces in re-establishing credible national and local authorities; (*c*) the ever-greater difficulty in reconciling Western and Soviet interests in Austria. As the wartime alliance broke down irreparably, central Europe turned into an arena of struggle for geopolitical and ideological domination, with Vienna—occupied by the Soviets in April—one of its pivots. More than any other reality, the onset of the East–West conflict brought the Americans to understand just how much their influence and example might make a difference in 'the difficult and delicate task of re-creating a foreign country', as a semi-official report described it soon afterwards.[117] With the appalling experience before their eyes of the Soviet 'liberation' of eastern Austria, where plunder, pillage, and mass rape had been the order of the day, the Western powers knew that they must do better, and do it fast.

In reality progress was hard to come by. A *New York Times* correspondent writing from Vienna in September 1945 talked of a state of 'suspended animation' throughout the economies of central Europe. 'Vienna is heartbreaking', wrote the well-known author John Dos Passos, now a war correspondent, a few weeks later, 'The shivering misery of the people in the streets, the burnt-out filigree of Saint Stephens' Cathedral, the shattered baroque façades, the boarded-up shops, the grassgrown ruins, seem more touching here than in the cities of Germany proper. Perhaps it is

---

[115] Cit. in Whitnah and Whitnah, *Salzburg Under Siege*, 18.
[116] Early account in George C. S. Benson, 'American Military Government in Austria, May 1945–February 1946', in Friedrich et al. (eds), *American Experiences*; this emphasizes the complexity of the task and the lack of any definite plan for facing it.
[117] Ibid. 172.

because the destruction was not so complete. Much of the frame of the city remains.'[118]

A year later the economic life of the country collapsed as winter set in. An official American poll of March 1947 found that 43 per cent of the Viennese felt the Allies were hindering the reconstruction of their country, while only 23 per cent approved of Allied economic action. In mid-1948 things were not much better, at least at the psychological level. The nation was a 'study in inertia', said a British commentator, with the locals living 'under a cloud of self-pity, unrelieved by hope or incentive to do anything themselves to better their lot'. 'The Americans take pride in the fact that they are feeding Austria', said the *New York Times*. 'The Soviets rely on the fact that they are in a position to starve her.' Many agreed with *The Economist* when it predicted that the Soviets might well succeed in splitting the country.[119]

It was in this context that the Americans decided to participate directly in the rebuilding of an Austrian sense of self and national identity, setting out to work among a population that they knew to be starving, deeply aggrieved, and in many ways nostalgic not just for the Third Reich but even more so for the days of the Hapsburg Empire. As the Austrian historian Ingrid Bauer has put it: 'It was only with great emotional difficulty that many Austrians could grasp that their defeat in World War II could have been, simultaneously, an act of liberation.'[120] With the British and the French lacking the resources to make much of an impact, and often inclined to think first of Austria as a defeated enemy, it was the United States that decided it must construct a vast operation of mental and moral reconstruction.[121]

Run by the military, this strategy would not simply eradicate Nazism, but put before Austrian public opinion the option of a different kind of future. The lessons of America's national experience would be presented as an inspiration, since its social system clearly 'superseded all [others] not only materially but morally as well'. The benefits of pluralistic, liberal

---

[118] *New York Times*, 5 October 1947; John Dos Passos, *Tour of Duty* (Boston, 1946), 279–80.

[119] Opinion poll and *The Economist* quoted in Reinhold Wagnleitner (ed.), *Understanding Austria: The Political Reports and Analyses of Martin F. Herz* (Salzburg, 1984), 129, 375–6; other cits in Ellwood, *Rebuilding Europe*, 31, 132–3.

[120] Bauer, '"Austria's Prestige Dragged into the Dirt"? The "GI-Brides" and Postwar Austrian Society (1945–1955)', in Günther Bischof, Anton Pelinka, and Erika Thurner (eds), *Contemporary Austrian Studies*, vi: *Women in Austria* (New Brunswick, NJ, 1998), 41.

[121] The memoir and documentary compilation of Martin F. Herz, the Political Officer to the US Legation in Vienna, 1945–48, gives an idea of how this official American consciousness developed; e.g. doc. of 8 October 1945, in Wagnleitner (ed.), *Understanding Austria*, 54–5.

democracy and free market economics would be taught, contemporary American culture of every kind would be brought in, and a model of modernity would be offered as far removed from the temptations of atavism as it was possible to be. 'Democratic decontamination', 'cultural rejuvenation', 'an alteration of consciousness', 'reorientation', all these terms could be applied to the effort of information–education–propaganda that emerged as the Americans gradually defined their civilizing mission in this Cold War frontier country.[122]

In his monumental study of this great cultural project, a landmark contribution to the history of the politics of Americanization in Europe, the Salzburg historian Reinhold Wagnleitner makes clear above all that no matter how urgent and desperate the demands for food, work, and security in post-war Austria, the battle for minds and hearts was never forgotten. And in the long term, he believes, its impact can be considered as great as all the other forms of American presence put together: 'It hardly seems presumptuous to assert that the dreams of the "American dream" (nightmares were not included, there were already enough of those) played an absolutely decisive role in the political developments of the Second Republic...'

> Regardless of how much the Austrian population actually knew about the United States, regardless of how twisted the images might have been (and still are), the United States stood for wealth, a comfortable standard of living for the masses, freedom, modernity, the culture of consumption and a peaceful life.[123]

In the summer of 1945 the key currency of American power was not the army or its men, but the stuff they brought, in quantities that none of the other liberators could even dream of:

> Even though the real behaviour of the GIs in many ways was hardly distinguishable from the soldiers of other occupation armies, they had one tremendous advantage—their seemingly endless access to goods. They brought dollars and even harder currencies—food, cigarettes, nylons, penicillin—all the necessities of survival for the plagued, hungry, confused people.[124]

But by the time the economic situation had begun to be stabilized in mid-1947, it was the information, education, and propaganda campaigns that had become the most prominent part of the American presence. Their official purpose was 'to utilize every possible material and psychological

---

[122] Wagnleitner, *Coca-Colonization*, 66–7.

[123] Ibid. chs 2, 9; cit. at pp. 277–8.

[124] Ibid. 68–9; the food question recurs vividly in the memoir of the military government officer Whitnah; *Salzburg Under Siege*, 78, 96, 98–9, 110, etc.; on the general opulence of the occupiers, ibid. 110–11.

means to create respect, if not admiration, for the American attitude, and thereby to vitiate the propaganda of competing political philosophies'. In the early years they 'controlled the presentation of films, theater, opera, concerts, newspapers, magazines, books, pamphlets, advertisements, radio, news agencies, the school system, even puppet theaters, circus exhibitions, carnival festivities, balls, religious processions, and local country fairs'.[125] Via a 'total control of Austrian cultural life', the American effort aimed to reach 'the entire population', particularly the professional classes, the politically conscious working class, youth, and active members of the Catholic church. Often the emphases shifted between information and education, between propaganda and psychological warfare, according to the perceived exigencies of the Cold War, and to the realization that lambasting the Soviets was not enough: 'It is hardly necessary for us to prove further to the Austrians that they should dislike the Russians', said an American official at one point.[126]

By the time the Marshall Plan started to work in mid-1948—the true lifebelt for the Austrian economy as a whole—the Americans had launched the biggest and most profitable newspaper in the country, the *Wiener Kurier,* introduced US magazines and press agencies, and trained a new generation of journalists.[127] They had created the most popular national radio station—*Rot-Weiss-Rot* (named after the colours of the national flag)—and turned it into an instrument for broadcasting deep behind the Iron Curtain. They had created a network of twelve Information Centers (later called 'America Houses', as in Germany) for 'projecting democratic ideals and the American way of life', using books, films, music, news media, talks, and warm, comfortable rooms. To the school system the Americans brought de-nazification, social sciences, curriculum reform, and English. Even the latest in teacher-training, school furniture, and audio-visual equipment was on offer. In the theatre, whether they liked it or not, Austrian audiences were introduced to American drama.

The most sacred terrain of all—classical music—was turned into a battleground for '*cultural hegemony*' (Wagnleitner). Here the American challenge faced opposition not only from a significant Soviet effort, but also from the ingrained conservatism and insularity of the locals. Only under heavy pressure 'and with great distaste' did the Salzburg Festival admit an American composition and performers in 1946. Jazz too arrived to Austrian ears, impetuously crossing the Atlantic, and—'*this cannot be stressed*

[125] Wagnleitner, *Coca-Colonisation*, 72; sample of the experience of schools in Salzburg in Whitnah and Whitnah, *Salzburg Under Siege*, 79–80.
[126] Wagnleitner, *Coca-Colonisation*, 72–4.
[127] Ibid. ch. 3; for official American views of the *Kurier*, Herz in Wagnleitner (ed.), *Understanding Austria*, 158, 186–7, 629–30.

enough—turned into one of 'the most exportable commodities—second, perhaps, only to dollars'.[128]

Or to the Hollywood motion picture? By the end of the conflict, Hollywood had drawn up detailed and specific plans for every one of the markets it had been forced to abandon in the 1930s. Its plan for Austria was completed in January 1945, and included a list of production, distribution, and financial conditions the US government was expected to impose on the country.[129] Within months the joint Hollywood–US Army film operation had taken control of distribution of the movies of all of the occupying powers throughout the country, and had even set up an office in the Soviet zone. By the end of 1946, American features, shorts, and newsreels were common in the Soviet-controlled territories, while no Soviet products at all were allowed in the US zone. Meanwhile, every one of Hollywood's commercial demands had been satisfied by the Austrian government, including full control of any reborn Austrian film industry that might appear. In March 1947, the special body Hollywood had created at the end of the war to coordinate its return to its blocked markets around the world—the Motion Picture Export Association—took over full control of the film sector from the Army. To judge from the quantity of US films of all sorts dominating Austrian screens during the occupation, and the fully documented figures of people seeing them, the great information–education–entertainment effort found its greatest success via the medium of the moving picture.[130]

Austrian historians who ponder the theme of the 'Americanization' or 'Westernization' of their nation after the Second World War—making inevitable comparisons with West Germany—all emphasize the role of the occupation experience, and its centrality in that effort of national redefinition that went on as soon as physical survival was guaranteed in the beleaguered country. In the long term, they say, the methods the Americans used to socialize and legitimize their hegemony made certain key sectors of the populace—especially youth and women—' "mature" enough for the central message of the American way of life: *the culture of consumption*'.[131]

---

[128] Wagnleitner, *Coca-Colonisation*, chs 3–7, quotes at pp. 193, 197, 202 (emphases in original); 1946 Salzburg Festival described in Whitnah and Whitnah, *Salzburg Under Siege*, 91, 112.

[129] Wagnleitner, *Coca-Colonisation*, 236–9, 256; contextualization in Swann, 'Little State Department', Trumpbour, *Selling Hollywood*, 91–5; on worries of US diplomats of impact of Hollywood's products on sensibilities around the world devastated by war and misery, ibid. 95–8.

[130] Wagnleitner, *Coca-Colonization*, 256–67.

[131] Ibid. 271 (emphasis in original); cf. Günther Bischof and Anton Pelinka (eds), Contemporary Austrian Studies, xii: *The Americanization/Westernization of Austria* (New Brunswick, NJ, 2004); Günther Bischof, 'Two Sides of the Coin: The Americanization of Austria and Austrian Anti-Americanism', in Stephan (ed.), *Americanization of Europe*.

The GIs, says Wagnleitner, played their own role in this transformation: 'while [they] did not always act like victors, they certainly looked the part.' They could supply extraordinary forms of provocation and inspiration:

> In 1946, the starving and freezing people of Salzburg were quite impressed when they learned that the U.S. occupation army managed to feed its fifteen thousand troops sixty thousand portions of ice cream as dessert on a daily basis.

An army fighting on its stomach in this fashion invited all sorts of disparagement and scorn from traditionalists of every hue. But the 'daily demonstration of abundance and wealth' left its mark, endearing the GIs 'to large groups of the young who had had more than enough of senseless order and military marching music'. In the 1950s they would turn into the 'children of schmaltz and Coca-Cola'.[132]

But in the years right after the war few of these silent transformations were on display.[133] The only group that seemed to have a glimpse of the revolution of rising expectations was those young women from rural western Austria who began to spend time in wealthy Switzerland to make money. They would be the ones most likely to strike up friendships with the GIs in their neighbourhood on their return. The phenomenon of these *Amibräute*, as they were derisively known, 'was simply the manifestation of a shifted horizon of expectations on the part of young females in general', judges Ingrid Bauer. Through the GIs, these women had 'instant access to . . . money, leisure time and pleasure'. They anticipated the 'hedonistic intensification of life' that the rest of society would come to know only years later.[134]

But they paid a heavy price for the privilege. In the conservative media, in bishops' sermons, in police reports, and elsewhere, they were accused of a form of betrayal of 'Austrian honour', and their lifestyle evoked much disparaging comment at a time of 'dreary forced frugality'. 'Honourable' women were directed by one newspaper letter writer to show their contempt directly to the 'chocolate girls', and to 'boycott all those who besmirch your honor and that of your family and drag Austria's good name into the dirt'.[135] At the same time the reconstruction of national identity

---

[132] Wagnleitner, 'The Empire of the Fun, or Talkin' Soviet Union Blues: The Sound of Freedom and U.S. Cultural Hegemony in Europe', in Hogan (ed.), *Ambiguous Legacy*, 474; Wagnleitner, *Coca-Colonization*, ch. 9.

[133] There is no mention of them in the day-by-day memoir of the military government officer Whitnah, even in the generally positive summing up; *Salzburg Under Siege*, ch. 12.

[134] Ingrid Bauer, 'Americanizing/Westernizing Austrian Women: Three Scenarios from the 1950s to the 1970s', in Bischof and Pelinka (eds), *Contemporary Austrian Studies*, xii. 172.

[135] Cit. in Bauer, 'Austria's Prestige', 44.

that took place after the war—'re-Austrification'—was an overwhelmingly conservative movement. If technological and economic renovation there had to be, then the family—and the women in it in particular— were expected to be a stronghold of rediscovered traditional values.[136]

As elsewhere in Europe, a general post-war return to the home was also a form of revolt against an excess of modernity, whether of the warlike or peacetime varieties, an attempt by the traditional sources of authority to restore moral and social hierarchies in the family and in the nation. In Austria this meant coming to terms with the meaning of seven years of membership of the Third Reich, at least as much as understanding the world of the Four Freedoms, the GIs, and Hollywood. Returning veterans were the most bitter at the liberators' threat to their manliness, already compromised by defeat. 'They took five years to achieve victory over German soldiers but he [the foreign soldier] only needs five minutes for the conquest of some Austrian women!', wrote one pamphleteer.[137]

In a vast cultural effort to reconstruct national identity in terms of victimhood, the Moscow Declaration acquired an extraordinary symbolic status. A play and even a film script were based on it. The most conservative forms of the new patriotism looked back to the glory days of the Habsburgs, and lauded those cultural figures who had stood by their country throughout the dark days of Nazism: in other words returning refugees and exiles were not welcome.[138] In Richard Billinger's play *The House*, of 1949, the 'house' symbolizes Austrian tradition and links with the past (writes Michael Mitchell). 'The owner's younger brother Max, who returns in the uniform of a US officer and talking about Europe and Europeanism, is described by his brother as "an adventurer, a reckless figure who missed the dark years", concluding that "he who doesn't defend the house loses it"; the ghost of their mother appears, telling Max to leave the house immediately.'[139]

---

[136] Cit. in Bauer, 'Austria's Prestige', 42–4, 50.

[137] Ibid. 47–8; this quote came from the French zone, but would have been even more appropriate in the US-controlled areas: Bauer, ' "The GI Bride": On the (De)Construction of an Austrian Postwar Stereotype', in Claire Duchen and Irene Bandhauer-Schöffmann (eds), *When the War Was Over: Women, War and Peace in Europe, 1940–1956* (London, 2000), 223, 226–9.

[138] Helga Embacher, 'Unwelcome in Austria: Returnees and Concentration Camp Survivors', in Duchen and Bandhauer-Schöffmann (eds), *When the War Was Over*, 194–206.

[139] Michael Mitchell, 'Restoration or Renewal? Csokor, the Austrian PEN Club and the re-Establishment of Literary Life in Austria, 1945–55', in Anthony Bushell (ed.), *Austria 1945–1955: Studies in Political and Cultural Re-Emergence* (Cardiff, 1996), cit. at p. 81, n. 21. I am grateful to John Clifford for the translation of these lines. The Austrian play may be compared to Heinrich Böll's 1954 novel *Unguarded House*, in which a dilapidated family home serves as 'a central metaphor for Germany's haunted past', as Paul Betts and David Crowley explain in 'Introduction', 213–14.

Under the impact of Allied attempts at de-Nazification, protests against tutelage soon began to be heard from officials and politicians. The Mayor of Vienna led the way in telling the Allies they had no right to give the Austrians lessons in diplomacy and education. The nation was capable of 'de-Germanizing' itself, rediscovering its own cultural heritage and just how radically different it was from that of the Prussians. The Mozart of Salzburg was contrasted with the Wagner of Bayreuth. An American journalist visiting Vienna felt that the majority of Austrians, 'having mentally mislaid the Hitler years...filled the void with Austrian patriotism....Austria was in fashion now, as symbolised by the ubiquitous peasant hats few would have worn in Vienna before the war....Everything German was out, even the way the Viennese now spoke that language.'[140] The historians Bischof and Pelinka sum up: 'War memorials commemorated the war as a dutiful and heroic struggle for the *Heimat*...emblems and official historical commemorations centered on Austria as victim...the war memoirs of soldiers and generals insisted on pure and simple *Pflichterfüllung*, only having done their duty.'[141]

The Cold War provided an excellent alibi for every sort of reconciliation and compromise. General Clark said: 'The Soviets here...use de-Nazification as a means for justifying large numbers of troops in Austria. I...will not allow the Soviets to make immediate political capital out of this subject.' Since the construction of a distinct and renewed national identity was an explicit part of the policies of the Western powers, especially of the United States, the Austrians' wish to reconstruct their past, present, and future according to their own tastes and priorities had to be respected, no matter how much from the recent past was rehabilitated in the process.[142] For their part the culturally superior Austrians— 'who did not feel defeated intellectually by the outcome of the war' (Wagnleitner)—could always rely on anti-Communism. In this way they could justify to themselves their need to lean, hopefully temporarily, on an alien power whose force entirely depended on its technology and wealth. Indeed cultural conservatism could be justified by insisting

---

[140] Cit. in Hella Pick, *Guilty Victim: Austria from the Holocaust to Haider* (London, 2000), 45; Austrian government demand for a scaled-down occupation run by the UN reported in the *New York Times*, 24 April 1946.

[141] Robert Knight, 'Narratives in Postwar Austrian Historiography', in Bushell (ed.), *Austria 1945–1955*, 18–28; Bischof and Pelinka (eds), Contemporary Austrian Studies, v: *Austrian Historical Memory and National Identity* (New Brunswick, NJ, 1997), 1–4.

[142] John Bunzl, 'American Attitudes towards Austria and Austria-German relations since 1945', in David F. Good and Ruth Wodak (eds), *From World War to Waldheim: Culture and Politics in Austria and the United States* (New York, 1999), 21–3; glimpses of Salburg experience in Whitnah and Whitnah, *Salzburg Under Siege*, 21, 77, 124.

that propaganda and information coming from outside might be more acceptable and effective, if only it was adjusted to meet traditional Austrian tastes.[143]

Americans began to respect the taboos and self-deceptions, and the founding myths like the Moscow Declaration, needed to begin the long social and moral healing process of the post-war years. As time went on they lessened the pressure to modernize on institutions like schools and universities, and the party system. Some Austrian forms of conservatism had become useful.[144] For their part Austrians were largely grateful for the Marshall Plan, for the 60 per cent of their food that in 1950 still came as an American gift, and for the 20 per cent of the machinery in use in the US zone supplied on the same basis. The 'warm, comfortable' hatred they felt for the Russians helped make sure this relationship would endure.[145] But for how long would the supervision and the division persist? Who would have thought that the competing claims of the four powers who had 'liberated' Austria in the spring of 1945 would still be justifying their occupation of the country ten years later?

GERMANY: OCCUPATION BLUES

Struggling to adapt

It was not obvious to anyone in 1945 or 1946 that the United States would emerge to lead a Western drive for a new German nation. None of the occupiers looked good or behaved well in the ruins of Hitler's Reich, but after the propaganda and the build-up, it was a great surprise to all concerned to see the leading conquerors of the western half of Germany fall so quickly into confusion and disorder in their zone, a shame to themselves and to many others. Observers such as the CBS correspondent Howard Smith talked in 1949 of 'a long, grating, complex tragedy of errors, relieved only very occasionally by any act of constructive intelligence'.[146]

The most eloquent of the agonized later critiques of the US military's activities in Germany begins its section on planning with these words:

[143] Wagnleitner, *Coca-Colonization*, 112, 128.

[144] Anton Pelinka, 'Taboos and Self-deception: The Second Republic's Reconstruction of History', in Bischof and Pelinka (eds), *Contemporary Austrian Studies*, v. 94–100.

[145] Howard K. Smith, *The State of Europe* (London, 1950), 132–3 (Howard was chief CBS correspondent in Europe at the time).

[146] Smith, *State of Europe*, 101.

The troops now [in 1945] realigning themselves within Germany...shifted and adjusted according to a concept that had as complicated an evolution and development as anything since the blueprint for Armageddon referred to in Revelation 16.... There were a number of reasons for this.[147]

In this version of an often-told tale, written by the ex-military government officer Franklin Davis, the military were only partly to blame. Their experience in the past, including a spell in the Rhineland itself from 1919 to 1923, and such places as the Philippines, was certainly of little help. 'What was new was the tremendous scope and sweep of occupation operations, the higher degree of specialization, and the complexity of the politico-military relationships. These complexities for the most part were not recognized sufficiently in advance...the problems of occupation...were only dim shadows beyond the victory beacons.'[148]

In the war years there had been long and inconclusive confrontations between the Pentagon and the State Department over occupation policies of all sorts, and Germany in particular. Experience in North Africa had dramatized the problems but done little to clarify them, and the long drawn-out Italian campaign seems to have been thought completely irrelevant.[149] President Roosevelt had not been helpful. His pronouncement in early 1943 about 'unconditional surrender' had been made without any regard for the weight of total responsibility this would place on the forces of occupation. At the Quebec conference of September 1944 he notoriously allowed himself to be swayed by his friend, the Treasury Secretary Morgenthau, into endorsing a drastic, radical plan for the deindustrialization of Germany and its conversion 'into a country primarily agricultural and pastoral in its character'.[150] The vast revulsion at home and abroad against this vision forced Roosevelt to distance himself from the plan, but Morgenthau persisted, knowing he could count on solid support in high military circles, and leverage in key committees. Faced with these divisions, Roosevelt fell back on a favourite tactic: procrastination. With US forces already inside German territory, in late October 1944 the President told his Secretary of State officially that he

---

[147] Davis, *Come as a Conqueror*, 19.

[148] Ibid. 20.

[149] Ibid. chs, 2, 4, 5; Hearden, *Architects of Globalism*, ch. 9. Italy is barely mentioned in Friedrich et al. (eds), *American Experiences* (cf. p. 197), and rarely anywhere else. Robert Murphy, State Department political adviser to the Supreme Commander in the Mediterranean, and then to the Military Governors Eisenhower and Clay in Berlin, seems to have contributed little to the planning process; cf. Murphy, *Diplomat Among Warriors* (London, 1964), ch. 16.

[150] Details and key memorandum in Dale Clark, 'Conflicts over Planning at Staff Headquarters', in Friedrich et al. (eds), *American Experiences*, 221–31.

wanted no serious plans to be made: 'I dislike making detailed plans for a country which we do not yet occupy...'[151]

When Nazi Germany finally surrendered in May 1945, two big American army groups stood on the territory. But from that point on the US armed forces rapidly broke up. By the end of the year no less than two and a half million troops had left Germany and Europe, so that 'it was the forces that replaced them...[that would] create the history of the occupation'.[152] A presence of 300,000 troops was planned for this job, but even this could not satisfy the mass of conscripts who used every sort of pressure to return home. By 1948 the occupying army was down to about 100,000. In January 1946 a separate Constabulary force of 30,000 had been created to try to stiffen morale and discipline among the remaining soldiery, as much as in the local population.[153] The official Military Government apparatus meanwhile dwindled from 12,000 in December 1945—'much less than either the British peak which I understand exceeded 26,000', said the military governor General Lucius D. Clay, 'or even the French peak for a much smaller zone of occupation'[154]—to 7,600 people in 1946, 5,000 in 1947, and 2,500 in spring 1949. 'Corresponding British strength was then about 12,000 and French strength about 8000', recorded Clay. Of the American force only 94 were officers or ordinary conscript soldiers. The others were all either American or German civilians, following the Army's long-standing policy of 'handing over' as much responsibility as possible first to other US government departments, then to local German authorities refashioned for the purpose.[155]

'The Army in Germany was left manned by young replacements fresh from the States, officered by a few career professionals and late arrivals', wrote Franklin Davis. 'Collectively, this force was asked to accomplish tasks it neither understood, nor in truth cared very much about.' Although it looked the same as the wartime army, and possessed the same gear and even more privileges, underneath, 'there was little gristle and no real spirit'. The vast, hysterical demobilization had 'drained away as well the soul of a victorious army—its professionalism'.[156] Yet this army was 'all-powerful as befitting conquerors and the Germans were defenseless easy targets...guilty of all kinds of things'. In this situation the individual soldier was given to understand that he was 'the source of virtually all

[151] Memorandum cit. in Davis, *Come as a Conqueror*, 34.
[152] Ibid. 48.
[153] Davis, ibid., 118; Lucius D. Clay, *Decision in Germany* (New York, 1950), 62, 64, 231.
[154] Clay, *Decision in Germany*, 65.
[155] Ibid. 66.
[156] Davis, *Come as a Conqueror*, 136.

power', where his spirit of vengeance or generosity depended on his training, his leaders, and the restraints of the rules. Especially in the first year, none of these were strong enough to keep order, writes Davis:

> Thus the occupation soldier found himself in a cultural netherland where only his own conscience and his own code would keep him standing tall in the midst of disillusion, immorality and tragedy...this was not sufficient armor to withstand the cultural shock of occupation duty.[157]

Yet this leftover army and its version of military government had immense responsibilities. The American zone covered a vast swathe of southern and western Germany, including such major cities as Frankfurt, Munich, and Stuttgart, as well as sectors in Berlin and Bremerhaven in the north. The total population was about 19 million people, plus an ever-swelling population of refugees and 'displaced persons': about 2 million in mid-1945. Berlin was 75 per cent destroyed—it looked 'like a city of the dead' said Clay—Frankfurt 60 per cent. Munich 75 per cent. Smaller towns registered up to 90 per cent destruction. Transport, housing, utilities, and public services were wrecked; the food situation was particularly desperate. The struggle for survival dominated every calculation.[158]

Three years went by—'the desperate years'—before the American military regime was able to stabilize the situation in its zone. There were four phases of improvised evolution: (*a*) the earliest, from July 1945, run under the auspices of Pentagon directive JCS 1067, with 'strict military controls and far-reaching measures of punishment and purgation'; (*b*) the new more positive prospect authorized by the Secretary of State Byrnes in September 1946, who declared that American forces would stay 'as long as an occupation force is required in Germany'; (*c*) the radical shift to reconstruction and cooperation opened up by the Marshall Plan announcement of June 1947, and the production of a fresh directive, JCS 1779, a month later; (*d*) the decisive moment of the currency reform of June 1948, and the commitment to defend the Western position in Berlin by means of an airlift in the same days.[159]

But these shifts came about only because most of the previous programmes and declarations broke down or proved impossible to operate. The principles of the occupation had been agreed by all the Allies (except the French, not present) at the Potsdam conference of July 1945, and they

[157] Ibid. 112–14.

[158] Clay cit. in Michael Ermarth (ed.), *America and the Shaping of German Society 1945–1955* (Providence and Oxford, 1993), Introduction, p. 4; Davis, *Come as a Conqueror*, 108–9, 181–4; on Berlin, Stafford, *Endgame*, 476–81.

[159] Based on a scheme in Ermarth (ed.), *America and the Shaping of German Society*, 7.

revolved round disarmament, demilitarization, de-Nazification, and de-centralization. They took for granted that the destruction of Germany's potential to make war implied 'the elimination of the nation's economic and industrial power blocs, including much of the physical plant they had created'.[160]

There was much overlap between this vision and the one spelled out by JCS 1067, noted the Harvard political scientist C. J. Friedrich in a semi-official commentary of 1948, especially the notion that as the directive put it: 'Germany will not be occupied for the purpose of liberation but as a defeated enemy nation.... The principal Allied objective is to prevent Germany from ever again becoming a threat to the peace of the world.'[161] But the Potsdam declaration went further in that it gave a glimpse of the possibility of economic and political rehabilitation. The occupation was now expected to guarantee a basic living standard. In politics, parties were to be permitted and a democratic local government. The educational system would be democratized. The entire population was to be 're-educated'. The Potsdam document promised freedom of speech, press, and religion, and guaranteed the rule of law under a reformed judicial system. It excluded however, the creation of any central government. Full sovereignty was placed in the hands of a unitary Allied Control Council, composed of the military governors of the four occupying powers. Eventually Germany would get a Peace Treaty that would bring this situation to a proper end.[162]

But the great Potsdam principles 'soon fell afoul of inner contradictions and manifest impracticalities', says the specialist Michael Ermarth; from the apparently simplest ('non-fraternization' between US soldiers and the local populations) to the most ambitious (the purge of all Nazis), position after position had to be abandoned, watered down, revised, or simply handed over to the Germans to deal with. 'We cannot re-educate twenty million people if we are never to speak to them', protested the British General Montgomery.[163] The handling of the food, fuel, and refugee situations moved from crisis to crisis: the US zone was relying on millions of dollars' worth of food and relief packages from private and voluntary agencies in the US and elsewhere in the early years, as well as official imports and its own resources. Yet it could rarely

---

[160] Friedrich et al. (eds), *American Experiences*, 384–5; comment in Merle Fainsod, 'The Development of American Military Government Policy during World War II', in Friedrich et al. (eds), *American Experiences*, 44–5.

[161] Cit. in Appendix A, in Friedrich et al. (eds), *American Experiences*.

[162] Fainsod, 'Development of American Military Government Policy'; Potsdam Declaration in Friedrich (eds), *American Experiences*, 42–5.

[163] Cit. in Stafford, *Endgame*, 483.

bring consumption up to a decent minimum.[164] The democracy-as-prosperity question appeared to many to be falling back on its old brutal underpinning of pure determinism. Clay wrote to his superiors:

> We have insisted on democratic process in the U.S. zone and have maintained a strict neutrality between political parties. As a result the Communist Party has made little inroad. However there is no choice between becoming a communist on 1,500 calories [a day, in the Soviet zone] and a believer in democracy on 1000 calories. It is my sincere belief that our proposed ration allowance in Germany will not only defeat our objectives in middle Europe but will pave the way to a Communist Europe.[165]

The more complex questions produced frank bewilderment. In March 1946 the German-born State Department consultant, Hans Speir, wrote:

> It is difficult to maintain that we are working toward the 're-education' of the Germans—whatever that may mean—or are making progress in a definite direction. In the Western zones, the food problem almost seems to be growing worse by the day; the Germans do not know what our policy is regarding the Ruhr, or what policy we pursue on the issue of a central government…[166]

As for de-Nazification, 'military government officers in the field felt time and again that the job was impossible', said the Friedrich report of 1948. They fought against it, said another early account. Basic practical realities came first; if producing results meant bringing back the old, unscreened native operators, then so be it. But then some other part of the machine would object strongly, and confusion would set in. Unpredictability, great arbitrariness, and local alienation were the result.[167] 'The Americans could never make up their minds whether they wanted Nazis plus efficiency or Democrats plus possibly a period of inefficiency in administration', wrote

---

[164] The classic survey is John Gimbel, *The American Occupation of Germany: Politics and the Military, 1945–1949* (Stanford, 1968); for the 1947–8 crisis of occupation policy, ch. 11, 'Dissension in Germany'.

[165] Cit. in Ellwood, *Rebuilding Europe*, 54; one of the first British directives to the Allied Control Commission said: 'Decent average democracy can only grow out of a reasonable standard of living'; cit. in D. C. Watt, *Britain Looks to Germany: British Opinion and Policy Towards Germany since 1945* (London, 1965), 69.

[166] Cit. in Ellwood, *Rebuilding Europe*, 53; the ups and downs of the re-education effort in the US zone are described in James F. Tent, *Mission on the Rhine: Reeducation and Denazification in American-Occupied Germany* (Chicago, 1982), and in Jessica C. E. Gienow-Hecht, *Transmission Impossible: American Journalism as Cultural Diplomacy in Postwar Germany, 1945–1955* (Baton Rouge, 1999), 5–9, 14–15.

[167] Fundamental dilemmas summarized in John Gimbel, *A German Community under American Occupation: Marburg, 1945–52* (Stanford, 1961), 7–8; cf. Konrad H. Jarausch, *After Hitler: Recivilizing Germans, 1945–1995* (Oxford, 2006), 48–55.

the correspondent Howard Smith in 1949. 'Be-Kind-To-Germans weeks alternated with Don't-Forget-What-the-Bastards-Did-At-Malmédy weeks.' A young military government officer pleaded with the correspondent Dos Passos: 'for God's sake, tell me what we are trying to do.'[168]

Cultivated minds from America were most upset. It was the lifestyle of the military government men themselves that most dismayed the distinguished literary critic F. O. Matthiesen on a visit to the American 'compound' in Heidelberg in mid-1947: 'how can such a group come into any real relationship with the impoverished country and people surrounding them, living as they do entirely apart, in an imported American world, complete with milk and orange juice, ice cream and Coca-Cola?' It looked as though they were becoming 'the civil servants of the new American empire', and yet were totally unfitted for their unprecedented role.[169]

The situation and behaviour of the ordinary American soldiery produced intense official dismay in the early years. Far from being the happy warriors bestowing their myths and their models on the benighted Germans, as some of the Press seemed to imagine, the occupation soldiers appeared often to betray the basic civilizing mission they had been explicitly entrusted with. George Kennan, diplomat, policy planner, and intellectual familiar with Germany, was one of their most eloquent critics. His memoirs vividly explain why he had developed 'an almost neurotic distaste' for his nation's occupation regime in Germany after two visits there:

> Each time I had come away with a sense of sheer horror at the spectacle of this horde of my compatriots and their dependents camping in luxury amid the ruins of a shattered national community, ignorant of the past, oblivious to the abundant evidences of present tragedy all around them, inhabiting the very same sequestered villas that the Gestapo and the SS had just abandoned, and enjoying the same privileges, flaunting their silly supermarket luxuries in the face of a veritable ocean of deprivation, hunger, and wretchedness, setting an example of empty materialism and cultural poverty before a people desperately in need of spiritual and intellectual guidance...
>
> That many Germans merited punishment was clear; but their delinquency was not the proof of our virtue.... In the presence of [the German] tragedy

[168] Friedrich et al. (eds), *American Experiences*, pp. 243–4 and ch. 12; Smith, *State of Europe*, 105 (the Nazi atrocity at Malmédy in December 1944, resulting in the deaths of over 100 US soldiers, is described in Stafford, *Endgame*, 125); Dos Passos, *Anglo-Saxon Century*, 251; Gienow-Hecht, *Transmission Impossible*, 15.

[169] F. O. Matthiessen, *From the Heart of Europe* (New York, 1948), 7. Matthiessen was on his way to give the opening speech at the first session of the now-celebrated Salzburg Seminar, just founded on the private initiative of a group of Harvard students and their friends; details ibid. 9–11.

even the victors had, to my mind, a certain duty of self-effacement and humility.[170]

The ex-participant Franklin Davis explained the background. The paternalistic Pentagon looked after its soldiers particularly well in Germany, 'in a manner befitting a conquering army'. The soldier had access to the best of requisitioned houses and staff. In the vast post exchanges his 'every want was anticipated and provided for...and there was more liquor than a man could drink':

> ...Doughnut shacks, snack bars, service clubs, transient billets, stage shows, travel tours, cheap recreation—all these catered to the soldier for prices that had to be paid to be believed.

Living in a 'low-overhead economic dreamworld'—including a virtually unlimited black market that could transform $1 million of monthly pay into $3 million in remittances in *July 1945*—'the rallying cry of the Occupation Army was "You never had it so good"'.[171]

But higher authority knew this was not the way to enhance the credibility of America or America's objectives in Germany, and was eventually forced to find other means for convincing the Germans of their government's seriousness of purpose. In the meantime, concluded the official economist E. F. Penrose afterwards:

> If it is desired to demonstrate a better way of life and conduct to a people, the aim will not be achieved by planting in their midst an army made up largely of raw youth, separated by thousands of miles from the restraint of family and neighbourhood, subject to new temptations against which nothing in the experience of the majority of them is proof,... little ground is left for hoping that the prestige of the occupying powers will be as great at the end as it was at the beginning of the occupation.[172]

Varieties of German response

From the beginning there were plenty of voices at home and on the ground ready to tell the Americans that they had set out on the wrong track. Among them was an element none of the Allies had seriously included in their imaginings and plans, that of the anti-Nazi or non-Nazi

---

[170] George F. Kennan, *Memoirs 1925–1950* (Boston, 1967), 428–9. Kennan's March 1949 visit and his further reflections, based on a detailed diary, follow on pp. 429–42.

[171] Davis, *Come as a Conqueror*, 114–15, 138–9, 150–1, ch. 10; cf. also ch. 6, 'An Occupation Day'; on the black market, Harold Zink, *The United States in Germany, 1945–1955* (Princeton, 1957), 136–40.

[172] E. F. Penrose, *Economic Planning for the Peace* (Princeton, 1953), 308–9.

Germans. The most striking of these in the early months was the émigré intellectual Heinrich Hauser, 'novelist, adventure-writer and journalist-commentator'. His 1945 production *The German Talks Back* enjoyed an immediate *succès de scandale* on its launch in the United States, and it is not difficult to see why. Here was the voice of 1920s 'reactionary modernism' transplanted into the new world.[173]

A well-born engineer and writer who had worked in warehouses and farms across America during the war, Hauser was particularly pessimistic about the functions of the occupation and its 'human representatives'. The first two phases of attempted 'Americanization' in Germany—in the Weimar era and via the émigré elite—had failed, he believed. So would the third one using the tools of military government. Its display of opulence and materialism in the ravaged land would create uncontrollable expectations, and a vast backlash that could only favour Communism.

In Hauser's vision 'Bolshevization and Americanization' were once again twin evils to be fought in the name of an alternative modernity. This would be unmistakably German, Prussian even. What Hauser searched for was 'a sort of ethico-cultural elixir', says his rediscoverer, Michael Ermarth, a spirit that would reinvent Germany along militant socialist lines, self-reliant, hard-working, and proud of 'how many things it can do without'.[174] Like Malaparte in Italy, Hauser insisted that the prospect of the hedonistic, matriarchal civilization from across the Atlantic attempting to castigate and demilitarize the wretched Volk, all the while preaching freedom, democracy, and 're-education', looked ridiculous. Even those best disposed to work constructively with the occupiers—the intelligentsia—would soon be repelled and thereby driven straight into the arms of Stalin.[175]

In the same fashion as Heidegger, Spengler, and others, Hauser despised the American infatuation with technology: 'the war had revealed the uncontrollable "demonism of technology," which was akin to the "satanism" of Nazism itself.' The only alternative for Germany was a well-organized, mass return to the land with science and technology reapplied to increase food production, and conserve nature: 'never again will we be in a position to set three thousand pounds of steel and a hundred horsepower in motion just to send our wives on a shopping spree . . .' The two worlds, the old and the new, were destined to part company. As for Germany,

---

[173] Michael Ermarth, '*The German Talks Back:* Heinrich Hauser and German Attitudes toward Americanization after World War II', in Ermarth (ed.), *America and the Shaping of German Society.*

[174] Ibid. 112, 114, 124; on the myth of the 'other Prussia' and its values, ibid. p. 124, n. 39.

[175] Ibid. 115–27.

'[t]his is the kind of atonement for which we [Germans] can work: [to] dive through the turmoil of mechanical civilisation and save the soul that was drowned by it.'[176]

Although never taken particularly seriously, Hauser's work caused some controversy in the US and was banned in Germany until the author returned as a magazine editor in 1947.[177] On the ground, meanwhile, 'Germans greeted the "long-term visit" of the Allied occupiers with a paradoxical mixture of fear and hope', writes the German historian Konrad Jarausch. Even as they stooped under the weight of defeat, poverty, and awakening guilt, there was a widespread impulse—especially among the most conservative elements—to sneer at the victors, and at the Americans in particular. A journalist who wrote an 'American Primer' in 1945 warned that they were 'not be measured according to our standards', and immediately proceeded to do so. Thus the 'nation of immigrants' appeared to be made up of conformist 'personality types'; it was a land of standardizers, moralizers, hypocrites, interested in novelty for its own sake.[178] The Protestant Bishop of Baden-Wurtemberg, in the US zone, contrasted the 'political peoples who know how to conquer and rule—in all these things they have a natural talent, which lends them superiority', with the 'ingenious, creative people in a spiritual sense, chosen by God, to transmit to mankind spiritual goods in art and religion and noble cultivation'. Bishop Wurm believed that the catastrophe would soon bring out these gifts in his flock.[179]

Only in 1947 did a recognizable public opinion begin to emerge, since until then newspapers and radio were under strict control, political parties had just begun to grow, and the first local elections had only recently been held. Up to that time only the voices of individuals or small groups stood out to express the sentiments of the conquered at their fate. And where these were considered too critical of military government, particu-

---

[176] Ibid. 125–6; following this logic Hauser went so far as to approve the Morgenthau plan, insisting that the Germans would defiantly create a new society of their own out of it; ibid. 125–5.

[177] Ibid. 128–30; Ermarth notes that while Hauser was 'arrantly misguided' on the prospects for American policy, and the aspirations of the post-war Germans, many elements of his thought fitted into a line of conservative German critiques of the American models of modernity that continued well into the era of the Federal Republic.

[178] Jarausch, *After Hitler*, 103.

[179] Cit. in Michael Ermarth, ' "Unconditional Americanization?" German Identity, Cultural Criticism, and the West-Option, 1945–1955', unpublished paper, p. 2. Ermarth points out that Wurm was 'soon bitterly disillusioned with the trends of West German development, which he and others did not hesitate to disparage as abject Americanism', ibid. 3; for the efforts of the Omgus newspaper *Neue Zeitung* to turn high culture into a means to persuade the German middle classes to abandon their fear of modernity, Gienow-Hecht, *Transmission Impossible*, 65, *passim*.

larly of the 'forced-to-be-free' paradox, they were liable to find themselves banned.[180] Yet it was a peculiarity of the occupation all the way through that in spite of its own unhappiness and self-criticism, military government continually sought out evaluations by the Germans in polls and reports of all sorts. Faced most usually—especially in the disaster years—with silence or alienation, the Americans made particular efforts at the local level to solicit comments from people they thought to be representative in some special way.

In the small university town of Marburg, 60 miles north of Frankfurt, scene of the classic occupation study by the American historian John Gimbel, the military administration did this repeatedly, often selecting the types thought to be the most 'respectable' and moderate among the non-Nazi survivors, including the clergy. In fact—commented Gimbel—these were the very people most likely to be upset by the presence of the conquerors, and angry at their prescriptions. Thus in June 1945 a former school administrator's report denounced requisitioning, the ban on fraternization, the material waste and the hypocrisy of the regime the military had set up, and its almost racist treatment of the Germans as a nation of war criminals. A few months later these impressions were confirmed by a newspaper editor the Americans themselves had appointed, a man who emphasized too the iniquities of de-Nazification. In November came a major report from an embryonic, cross-party political committee. Together with now-familiar list of complaints came an additional emphasis on the disorderly conduct of American troops, their violence, and impulse to loot. Particularly irksome were details such as the strict rationing of electricity for locals, 'while houses requisitioned by the occupation forces could be seen to have lights burning from top to common both in the night and during the day'. All in all, commented Gimbel, the Marburgers contemplated their relations with the occupiers in terms of 'utter helplessness', simply taking as given the benefits they brought.[181]

Just how seriously the military regime took its own opinion polls is hard to say.[182] They were certainly carried out with all the rigour the technique could muster at the time, were frequent, comprehensive, and detailed. 'Some Germans crawling from their refuges... encountered something unique in the history of warfare: batteries of foreign soldiers

---

[180] Such was the fate of the periodical *Der Ruf* (The Cry), founded in April 1946 by a group of ex POWs from American camps; Keith Bullivant and C. Jane Rice, 'Reconstruction and Integration: The Culture of West German Stabilization, 1945 to 1968', in Burns (ed.), *German Cultural Studies*, 211; Gienow-Hecht, *Transmission Impossible*, 142; Ralph Willett, *The Americanization of Germany, 1945–1949* (London, 1989), 2–3.

[181] Gimbel, *German Community*, 75–84.

[182] General Clay wrote: 'We had much faith in these polls, although it was shattered somewhat by the election at home in November 1948', Clay, *Decision in Germany*, 283.

asking them—in German—to respond to questionnaires', writes Richard Merritt, the historian of this effort. In other words, the Psychological Warfare Division had arrived, and with it squads of social psychologists and sociologists, ready to apply the newest techniques of the social sciences to discover 'the moods and concerns of the defeated Germans'. After years of enduring the totalitarian approach to public opinion, the culture shock among the interviewees was palpable.[183]

In spite of much other evidence to the contrary, the polls gave a consistently benign impression of German attitudes to the 'Ami's', but then few people, it appeared, actually knew any of their conquerors. In September 1946, 66 per cent of those interviewed claimed that they neither knew nor had talked to any US soldier. In November 1947 only 25 per cent said they knew one. In late 1947, 58 per cent denied that Americans cornered German food for themselves, while 64 per cent denied that Americans wasted food. Only 21 per cent said that American negligence destroyed German property. In 1951, when 'asked what was the most significant error made by the occupation forces had been, only 1 in 7 respondents in a national sample cited the troops' luxurious style of life and behavior'.[184]

In September 1946, 75 per cent of those interviewed described the Americans as friendly. In October 1946 almost two thirds attributed positive traits to the occupiers, while over a third emphasized negative ones. 47 per cent found they were 'kind, helpful, good-natured, courteous and neat'. On the other hand, 14 per cent said they were undisciplined, drank too much, and chased after the local women. But 55 per cent gave no response on the negative side. Requisitioning was prominent among the complaints, but even then only featured in 19 per cent of responses. Even in autumn 1949, 60 per cent of those polled attributed good or very good behaviour to Allied troops, while only 4 per cent said it was bad or very bad. Unlike almost any other occupation in modern history, the approval rating apparently went up as time went on.[185]

But the Germans 'flatly denied the moral superiority of the Allies', comments Merritt, and scorned their fighting skills. In spite of this, 'the public attitude towards the U.S. occupation troops themselves, occasional misdeeds notwithstanding, was acceptance. The quality, character and

---

[183] Richard L. Merritt, *Democracy Imposed: U.S. Occupation Policy and the German Public, 1945–1949* (New Haven, Conn., 1995), 70–1.

[184] Ibid. 253–4; reparations policy was condemned as the biggest error, followed by the 'soft' policy to the Soviet Union and the 'defamation of the Germans', cit. in Gerard Braunthal, 'The Anglo-Saxon Model of Democracy in the West German Political Consciousness after World War II', *Archiv für Sozialgeschichte*, 18 (1978), 249.

[185] Merritt, *Democracy Imposed*, 254–5.

behaviour of the American occupiers did not yield bitter and disruptive resentment—though the basis for such a reaction existed, had recalcitrant nationalists chosen to exploit it.... The [Allied zone] Germans acquiesced because few alternatives were available', and knew on which side they wished to place themselves in the looming confrontation with the Soviets.[186] In the meantime, intense but pacific German resistance to the early non-fraternization policy, to de-Nazification, and to industrial dismantling, registered in many other places beside the military's opinion surveys, and eventually produced the policy changes the occupied peoples demanded.[187]

In the long run there were three principal reasons why the 'collision' between the occupiers and the locals avoided the worst sort of confrontations and slowly evolved into something approaching peaceful coexistence. The restraints as well as the comforts that the army system placed on the troops began to turn into forms of outreach from 1947 onwards, with organized as well as spontaneous social, youth, and cultural programmes. Then again Soviet behaviour in their zone, and the unfolding 'Cold War'—identified as such by Walter Lippmann in September 1947—made the Western occupiers look better every day, although no one doubted that only the Americans had the resources to make a difference. But there was a third factor at work that no one had taken into account at the beginning of the occupation. This was—say Franklin Davis and many other authors—'the influence of the German women'.[188]

'The hour of the women'

'The first human contact with the Allies was via us women.'[189] So wrote one of the many witnesses whose memories have survived, and been incorporated in a vast German effort to reconstruct a form of national identity partly on the basis of what happened in those years. Through women Germans discovered that Allies were not so censorious or fearsome as the official public relations machine in the early years made them out to be. Witnesses talked of 'soldiers who appeared extraordinarily rested and well-cared for', while an actress who later married one of them said: 'they

---

[186] Merritt, *Democracy Imposed*, 259, 269; the polls also documented, however, intense diffidence towards the black troops in the occupying forces; ibid. 257–8.

[187] Ibid. 261, 266.

[188] Davis, *Come as a Conqueror*, 115; Zink, *United States in Germany*, 137–8; Stafford, *Endgame*, 480–1.

[189] Elizabeth Heineman, 'The Hour of the Woman: Memories of Germany's "Crisis Years" and West German National Identity', *American Historical Review* (April 1996), 390.

had beautiful teeth, they were so healthy, clean and well-fed.' Another feminine voice talked of them sitting in outdoor cafes reading 'funny books' and drinking Coke from a straw. She wished she could 'erase all the sad memories of the past and act as young and spirited as they did'. Petra Goedde comments that contacts with GIs 'enabled young women to tap some of that material abundance and carefree leisure time'.[190]

For their part the local women helped American men to overcome or at least cope with some of their inhibitions, the stereotypes they had brought with them, and their sense of existential alienation. It was the women who quietly convinced the Americans that their stern non-fraternization policies could never work, and as such opened the way to the end of the notion of undifferentiated, collective guilt. They made sure that when non-fraternization was finally dropped in October 1945, a great boom of relations would take place: 'Army investigators estimated that 50 to 90 per cent of American troops "fraternized" with German women in 1946; among married servicemen, one in eight had "found a home"—that is, entered a relatively stable relationship—in Germany.' By the end of 1947, 2,262 women had married occupation soldiers.[191]

The love market generated controversy then and forever after. Until the currency reform of June 1948, which largely killed it off, female company and sex were among the major items available in the all-encompassing barter economy. Once more, the Americans supplied the demand, the locals the supply. Some women offered domestic services, others the warmth and comfort of a home environment, still others brought Germany luxury items and souvenirs to the market. The Americans could provide almost any material good, but what mattered above all in the desperate years was food. 'Some women resorted to prostitution to save themselves and their families from starvation', reports Petra Goedde, '[f]or others it became an additional source of income...whatever the original motivation, food had become a central aspect of American-German interactions.'[192]

Many observers, Allies and German, thought commercial sex had achieved the same status, provoking a great deal of unease among authorities on both sides of the relationship, as well as among the male and older population in general. The Yanks sweetheart was 'no heroine', comments Elizabeth Heineman. 'She became the symbol of Germany's moral decline—and, as such, implied that the decline occurred with the collapse

---

[190] Petra Goedde, *GIs and Germans: Culture, Gender and Foreign Relations, 1945–1949* (New Haven, Conn., 2003), 106–7.
[191] Heineman, 'Hour of the Woman', p. 381 and n. 68; Goedde, *GIs and Germans*, 42–60, 71–9; Stafford, *Endgame*, 493–5.
[192] Goedde, *GIs and Germans*, 91; for semi-official American views, Davis, *Come as a Conqueror*, 115–17; Zink, *United States in Germany*, 137–8.

of, rather than during, Nazi rule.'[193] Just as in Austria, Veronika Danke-schon (Veronika Thank-You-Very-Much, whose initials were 'VD') was seen as a great slur on national honour, and yet another threat to the posi-tive heritage in the German national identity. She got pleasure out of what to others was bitter material necessity, and confirmed that the loss of national self-determination extended to the sexual order. Here was the true meaning of defeat. In Hans Habe's novel *Off Limits*, a best-seller of 1955, the prostitute becomes a metaphor for the entire society in which she lives. The character is killed off in the novel after the currency reform, but the Yanks are depicted in general here as missionaries 'with the Bible in one hand and the knout in the other... "unless you are willing I shall have to use force" '. The message, says Elizabeth Heineman, was that the West Germans had to attain their own form of national sovereignty and oblige the foreigner to return home.[194]

The end of the beginning

Opinion polls conducted in 1951 revealed that by this time, West Germans were sick and tired of all the occupiers. Although the Russians generated by far the strongest antagonism, even the Americans were de-plored by almost half of the sample. In a separate investigation, 70 per cent of Germans in the western zones thought that the 1945–8 years were the worst to live through in the entire century. Eventually the Americans too came to recognize that, as one of them put it, the sentence they and their allies had imposed on the conquered was 'four years of hard labour on quarter rations in a prison camp called Germany'.[195]

But in July 1947 the Joint Chiefs had issued a new directive for the direction of the American occupation, and following right on from the Marshall Plan announcement, the prospect of an opening up of policy, together with a new and positive flexibility, began to change horizons in many directions. The Americans would now openly take the lead in the western zones. The hand that punished would give way to the guiding hand. Re-education would become 'reorientation', and move from the periphery to the centre of occupation policy. In November 1947 Secre-

---

[193] Heineman, 'Hour of the Woman', 380–1; cf. Jarausch, *After Hitler*, 32.

[194] Heineman, 'Hour of the Woman', 383–6; The ambiguous feelings and behaviour produced on both sides by these realities are effectively dramatized in the Billy Wilder film, *A Foreign Affair* of 1949 (see below, n. 212), and by Rainer Fassbinder's *The Marriage of Maria Braun* of 1978 (see below, n. 225).

[195] Polls quoted in Heineman, 'Hour of the Woman', p. 387, n. 82, and in Michael Geyer, 'America in Germany: Power and the Pursuit of Americanization', in Frank Tromm-ler and Elliot Shore (eds), *The German–American Encounter: Conflict and Cooperation between Two Cultures* (New York, 2001), 123; Tent, *Mission on the Rhine*, 280.

tary of State Marshall finally stated openly that German economic revival was essential to the recovery of Europe as a whole. For this purpose de-Nazification was expected to come to a swift end. A proper linkage between economic, cultural, and social recovery was apparently now to be on offer.[196]

It was, obviously, the pressure of the confrontation with the Soviets that had brought about this great turnaround, and not all the Germans were impressed. Soon afterwards one writer recalled—in a prestigious American social science journal—the 'wavering, confused, half-hearted policy of co-operation, help and reconstruction' of this period. The conquerors had turned into an 'uneasy and implausible mixture of conquistador and social worker'. While they continued to rule Germany by force of arms, and maintained an absolute monopoly of the executive, legislative, and judicial functions by way of their military government, 'they set out to educate her to democracy by force of argument'. In 1945 they had insisted on the strictest compliance with the rules that obliged cooperation with the Soviets. Only two years on the Soviets had become public enemy no. 1, and the Americans had done little to admit or explain their reversal. So changes in attitudes towards the Germans appeared to be governed not by experience or reflection, but by Soviet policy: 'the Americans seemed never to have an independent political purpose of their own, and no insight into what they should do in Germany.'[197]

It was clear that the Americans had never provided themselves with a clear idea of the Germany they wished to rebuild after 1945; perhaps none of the Allies did, not even the Soviets. In Frank Capra's Pentagon-commissioned film of early 1945, *Your Job in Germany*, the tone is entirely negative. The Germans are portrayed in the commentary as a people diseased with the urge to conquer and dominate. Blood and iron were the rule of recent Germany history. Over pictures of attractive old cities, pretty girls, and cute children, the storyline warns that the Nazi 'thinking, training and trickery remain; . . . practically everything you believe in they've been trained to hate'. Soldiers were instructed to be 'aloof, watchful and suspicious' avoiding even the slightest form of contact. Whatever it took to break the vicious cycle of war and phony peace (images of explosions and beer-garden dancing) would be done: 'This is your job in Germany.'[198]

---

[196] Zink, *United States in Germany*, 96–7; Gimbel, *American Occupation*, 172; Tent, *Mission on the Rhine*, 282–3, 318; the July 1947 directive, n. 1779, is reproduced in Friedrich et al. (eds), *American Experiences*, 402–15.

[197] Norbert Muhlen, 'America and American Occupation in German Eyes', *Annals of the American Academy of Political and Social Science* (September 1954), 52–61, cits at pp. 55–7.

[198] I am grateful to the Imperial War Museum London, for a viewing of this film.

It was certainly possible to find accord all around on the negative aspects as enshrined in the Potsdam Declaration, and by 1947 this outlook had spread to cover experiments in socialism in the US zone (as it had in the British and French zones as well). But none of the great visions of wartime gave the slightest clue as to how to behave in a nation that had surrendered unconditionally once the basic conditions of food, work, law, and order had been stabilized if not satisfied. In July 1945 Archibald MacLeish, Assistant Secretary of State, and resident cultivated mind, had warned the Secretary that 'common agreement as to the American purpose in the occupation of Germany does not exist'.[199]

At the time, and for years afterwards, it seemed to many that democratization was a fetish that, in spite of its proclamations about enhancing the sense and practice of German responsibility, in reality boiled down to reproducing the American system as far as possible in the conquered land. Some Germans felt that their new freedoms did not include the freedom to do things the Americans did not like.[200] Bavaria was the scene of a notorious confrontation between its resurrected, and deeply conservative, educational establishment, and the would-be importers of the US model of secondary education. This was a battle that the Americans largely lost.[201] Until the Marshall Plan's effects began to be felt, the proclaimed two-way link between democracy and material well-being was treated with particular scepticism. A *New York Times* reporter found German youth entirely cynical towards all forms of political promise. They had been fooled once, she believed, and now took the attitude that 'if this democracy we hear so much about is the real thing, if it brings work, food, comfortable living, and above all, security, well, then we'll support it. But, meanwhile, we'll wait and see.'[202]

But, whatever the reasons for the great shift, the search for a new basis of legitimacy that characterized American occupation policy after 1947 produced effects that to many German observers have come to be seen in terms that are much more positive. Although seeking to preserve their

---

[199] Smith, *State of Europe*, 126, Carolyn Eisenberg, 'The Limits of Democracy: U.S. Policy and Rights of German Labor, 1945–1949', in Ermarth (ed.), *America and the Shaping of German Society*; detailed analysis of ambiguous consequences as seen in the story of the official Omgus newspaper *Neue Zeitung* in Gienow-Hecht, *Transmission Impossible*, ch. 7 and Conclusions.

[200] Muhlen, 'America and American Occupation in German Eyes', 56–9; the impression was confirmed by critical authors such as Gimbel, *German Community*, 4.

[201] Full details in Tent, *Mission on the Rhine*, ch. 4; they also lost the battle to teach baseball—thought to be a paradigm of democracy—to children who preferred soccer, Goedde, *GIs and Germans*, 145.

[202] *New York Times* report of 25 November 1945 cit. in Goedde, *GIs and Germans*, 134–5; intellectual versions in Ermarth, 'Unconditional Americanization?', 3–4; for pessimism of *Neue Zeitung* over youth, Gienow-Hecht, *Transmission Impossible*, 73–7.

authority, they say, the Americans stopped emphasizing the difference between losers and winners. Giving up on transformation, they settled for a kind of reformation, which given the real conditions, 'ended being a series of transactions', and a deepening trust in traditional German structures: in politics, business, and culture.[203] Perhaps for this reason Heinrich Hauser, upon his return to Germany in 1948, was able to congratulate the Germans for the grace with which his fellow citizens bore the burdens of their occupation, and above all 'their absence of hate'.[204]

Whenever the occupiers attempted to apply to force to achieve their results they sooner or later failed, say today's German historians. Where they sought to build consensus, a sort of seeding process began to start whose benefits few now doubt. As in Austria, 'America Houses' were a prime example, together with new exchange programmes that by 1952 would bring more than 3,000 public officials, trade unionists, media professionals, judges, doctors, churchmen, women's leaders, and 'young potential leaders' to the United States. The democratization of the Press and the reform of radio broadcasting should also be included in this context.[205]

The transactional evolution of relations was nowhere more visible than in the cinema. Movie theatres were quickly reopened in large numbers, and the audiences arrived. But when it became apparent that military government and the State Department would *not* allow Hollywood to create a monopoly and eliminate a renascent rival,[206] then spite arose in Los Angeles and the studios organized a sort of boycott, providing only mediocre, B-movie fare, which local audiences soon made clear they would not tolerate. At this point the authorities brought in the émigré film director Eric Pommer. A man last seen in Chapter 3 telling the Weimar-era studios what they should learn from the success of America's celluloid fantasies, Pommer—by now an American citizen— believed at this point that in seeking 'to imbue the German mind with new and better ideals...Germans of sincere intent can do more than foreigners'.[207]

---

[203] Peter K. Breit, 'Culture as Authority: American and German Transactions', in Reiner Pommerin (ed.), *The American Impact on Postwar Germany* (Providence and Oxford, 1995), 125–6, 128.

[204] Ermarth, 'German Talks Back', 110.

[205] Hans Woller, 'Germany in Transition from Stalingrad (1943) to Currency Reform (1948)', in Ermarth (ed.), *America and the Shaping of German Society*, 33–4; Braunthal, 'Anglo-Saxon Model', 254–5 (the French and British governments also promoted exchange programmes, the French version being particularly extensive and enduring).

[206] Details in Trumpbour, *Selling Hollywood*, 101–3.

[207] Heide Fehrenbach, *Cinema in Democratizing Germany: Reconstructing National Identity after Hitler* (Chapel Hill, NC, 1995), 62–5, cit. at p. 64.

But the hapless Pommer was squeezed from without and within. The Hollywood producers' lobby sought to undermine him, and manoeuvred at every level to make sure their output would be dominant in the long run. In the meantime, film had become an area, like the school and university system, where those anxious to recover and rebuild a distinctive German national identity felt able to make their voices heard. Conservative voices in churches, schools, the public administration, and elsewhere, were anxious that Godless Hollywood, with its commercialism and amorality should not reinvade the fatherland, or what was left of it, and organized a barrage of complaint revolving around the issue of censorship.[208] When it became clear that audiences overwhelmingly preferred films from the native tradition, with familiar images, language, and stars, and rejected the 'carefree escapism and incomprehensible humour' of the American imports, then the military regime knew it must fashion a compromise.[209]

In the stultified and deeply compromised world of classical music, the incubation phenomenon could also be seen. Here the impulse to sneer at American notions, and to resent any intervention in this world's efforts to reconstruct itself, was particularly strong. But an in-depth study by David Monod into the 'chiaroscuro' of German music reveals that the 1947 shift 'from rule to role modelling to winning friends' produced its effects in the long run. The military government men, seriously understaffed and under-resourced in the early years, 'were deeply divided and lacked clear policy guidance'. So they chose the easiest, cheapest course, and allowed the local experts to decide. In their turn these people rehabilitated former Nazis without the slightest scruple, and quickly reasserted the innate German superiority in this and in so many other areas of cultural life. Yet it was the American cultural officers, with integrity and dedication, who made work whatever worked, and the most serious local figures appreciated this. The official effort succeeded in pushing through important structural reforms and 'encouraged new thinking about the freedom of the arts and how to ensure them'. The innovations 'took root and provided the structural foundations for a more democratic and liberal administration of cultural life'.[210]

---

[208] Samples of popular reaction in Trumpbour, *Selling Hollywood*, 99–101.

[209] Ibid. 64–8; Fehrenbach, 'Cinema, Spectatorship, and the Problem of Postwar German Identity', in Pommerin (ed.), *American Impact*, 166–9; Fehrenbach, 'Persistent Myths of Americanization: German Reconstruction and the Renationalization of Postwar Cinema, 1945–1965', in Fehrenbach and Uta G. Poiger (eds), *Transactions, Transgressions, Transformations: American Culture in Western Europe and Japan* (New York, 2000), 87–91; for the newspaper *Neue Zeitung* as one of the compromises, Gienow-Hecht, *Transmission Impossible*, ch. 4.

[210] David F. Monod, *Settling Scores: German Music, Denazification, and the Americans, 1945–1953* (Chapel Hill, NC, 2005), 5–10, 262–3.

Volker Berghahn sums up: 'The American occupation of Germany did see the application of direct force to achieve its aims, but not in any major and brutal way. Rather it was based on the idea that any recasting of the country's political, economic and socio-cultural structures and traditions would only succeed through negotiation, blending and voluntary acceptance by the large majority of people.'[211] But this was not so obvious at first. Both sides of the relationship experienced an intense learning process.[212] The Germans came to understand that whatever their motives, the Americans of the currency reform, the Berlin airlift, and the Marshall Plan were seriously committed to the renaissance of a version of their nation. It may have been divided down the middle, but it was not lobotomized. Western Germany moved to the heart of America's—and the West's—geopolitical and ideal preoccupations in these years.

At the same time the Americans of the early Cold War—so adept at inventing new ways to project their powers—were learning that they too had to adapt, if these inventions were to achieve the effects of legitimization and participation they so ardently hoped for. Berghahn quotes Edward Mason, Harvard economist and key member of the influential Committee of Economic Development, to make this crucial point:

Of all the institutions and policies known to history . . . those imposed by the victors on a vanquished enemy are likely to be the most impermanent. The

---

[211] Berghahn, 'Conceptualizing the American Impact on Germany: West German Society and the Problem of Americanization', paper presented at the German Historical Institute conference at Washington DC (March 1999), p. 5, <http://www.ghi-dc.org/conpotweb/westernpapers/berghahn.pdf>, still accessible from the Wayback Machine Web archive: <http://wayback.archive.org>.

[212] At a certain point the American military authorities decided it was time that their re-education efforts be turned away from the Germans and directed to their own people back home. The medium they chose was an entertainment film, directed by one of Hollywood's most distinguished refugees from the German-speaking world, Billy Wilder. The title was *A Foreign Affair* (1949). A visiting Congressional delegation, featuring an outspoken Congresswoman from Iowa come to fumigate the 'moral malaria' she believes is ravaging honest American troops, soon discover that reality is more complex than their home-made pre-conceptions. Certainly some American soldiers are compromised: with the black market, the free-flowing alcohol, and 'gorgeous boobytraps', such as the sensuous and world-weary nightclub singer Erika (played by Marlene Dietrich). But the main message comes from the compromised officer Jimmy Pringle and his stern but humane superior, Colonel Plummer. It states that occupation is a 'tough, thankless, lonely job', involving soldiers who are expected to be ruthless in combat then wise instantly afterwards, the human embodiment of abstract ideals. As for the Germans, theirs was a country with 'open graves and closed hearts' (says Plummer), and a strong suicidal impulse. What the occupation had tried to do was recreate free men in a civilized state, to give them some dignity and above all rekindle 'the will to live'. By the end Congresswoman Frost (*sic*) has thawed to the point of throwing herself into the arms of Captain Pringle. Erika however, is left silent and empty-handed, with her secret Nazi lover dead at her feet. History of the film's production in Willett, *Americanization of Germany*, ch. 3.

only lasting structural changes that can be made in the German economic and political system will have to be made, in the absence of continuous occupation, by the Germans themselves.[213]

This does not mean that the reform process was left to chance, goodwill, or the market. It was always 'deliberately planned, consciously advanced and actively manipulated' (Berghahn), and would become more so as the Cold War intensified, and the loyalty of the Germans became an ever-higher stake.[214] But by March 1948 General Clay was musing: 'Somehow we have to find out what is the true essence of democracy rather than what is the true essence of what Americans would like... [we] have got to distinguish between reforms that we would like to have because we say we do them at home [and] the Continental practice.'[215] A month later the Marshall Plan had passed into law as the 'European Recovery Program', and it included the western zones of Germany. In 1945 Heinrich Hauser had poured scorn on the inability of the Americans either to preach their gospel of liberty or 'bring the bread that the masses crave much more than liberty'.[216] In its own fashion the Marshall Plan would do both, as well as help to build the American–German synthesis embodied in the Basic Law of 1949, foundation stone of the Federal Republic, and much of what followed.[217]

CONCLUSION: LEARNING THE HARD WAY

Of all the nations that sent their military to Europe from 1942 onwards, none more than the Americans might have recognized themselves in the dictum that Josef Stalin formulated in early 1945, when speaking to a visiting delegation of Yugoslav Communists:

> This war is not as in the past; whoever occupies a territory imposes on it his own social system. Everyone imposes his system as far as his army has power to do so. It cannot be otherwise.[218]

But why could it not be otherwise? Stalin's mental picture was not the one shared by the peoples who greeted the liberating armies from across the

---

[213] Berghahn, 'Conceptualizing the American Impact on Germany', 5.

[214] In contrast, Gienow-Hecht emphasizes the contradictions that crept into official information and education policy as the Cold War intensified; *Transmission Impossible*, 147, 180–2.

[215] Cit. in Diethelm Prowe, 'Democratization as Conservative Restabilization: The Impact of American Policy', in Jeffry M. Diefendorf et al. (eds), *American Policy and the Reconstruction of West Germany, 1945–1955* (Washington DC and Cambridge, 1993), 329.

[216] Cit. in Ermarth, 'German Talks Back', 113.

[217] Berghahn, 'Conceptualizing the American Impact on Germany', 6, 7.

[218] Milovan Djilas, *Conversations with Stalin* (London, 1963), 90.

ocean, neither in 1943 nor in all the subsequent years when so much collective mental effort was spent in reconstructing the meaning of World War II and its aftermath. Years afterwards Milovan Djilas, the dissident, disillusioned Yugoslav resistance leader who had originally reported Stalin's pronouncement, wrote: 'It is the fatal, unforgiveable error of conquerors to ordain the destinies of men and nations according to wartime views and circumstances.'[219] Having no time to learn anything from their on-going experiences elsewhere, the Americans tried to do the same in Germany under the scheme of retribution and suspicion spelled out in JCS 1067 and 'Your Job in Germany'. The result was the judgement a veteran British relief worker offered afterwards after many months in Bavaria:

> All large armies of occupation are disastrous. They strangle the conquered and demoralise and make helpless the conqueror.[220]

But the peoples of the American zone in south-west Germany, women in the lead, eventually gave their occupiers the opportunity to change, and ensured that things evolved in directions never foreseen in 1945–6. The official turnaround involved much hesitancy, and of course might never have happened without the Cold War's new pressures. In 1949 Clay's civilian successor, John J. McCloy, commented:

> Naturally American ideas have had some effects, but sometimes I suspect we have mostly convinced our friends and left our enemies untouched. People who have a natural bent for our way of doing things were eager to learn. The others admitted a few American traits, our efficiency, our machines, our financial part, perhaps, and seldom bothered to go to the source of our power, which is liberty. Some Germans follow our leadership only because we have defeated them. Has our experiment been successful? I wish I could say yes. I don't know. It will take years to know.[221]

In Europe, Germany and Austria were the only nations that the Americans decided consciously to remake. Not by chance these were nations whose territory they shared with the new Cold War rival, the Soviet Union. By improvisation, exhortation, and inducements, the transatlantic conquerors absorbed their British and French partners, and after 1947 set out to construct a different Western path to the future. In Germany enhanced democratization was to be the key to this project, including an embryonic central government, federalism, political parties, the respect of basic human rights, and a vastly expanded educational and cultural programme. The Washington authorities insisted that they did not 'wish to impose [their] own historically developed forms of democracy and social

---

[219] Cit. in Ellwood, *Rebuilding Europe*, 56.
[220] Cit. in Stafford, *Endgame*, 507–8.   [221] Cit. in Mead, *Atlantic Legacy*, 185.

organization', and expected that others would follow suit.[222] In Austria a complete model of American modernity was offered as inspiration, but Austria identities had not been totally devastated by Nazism or war, and soon found ways of reasserting themselves.

Elsewhere, American armies left Italy in 1947 and started to arrive—in the form of military advisers—in Greece. They left few visible traces of their presence in either country, but plenty of memories, completely eclipsing the British, the hegemonic power in that part of the Mediterranean world up until then. In one later account, the arrival of the Americans in Italy was alleged to have set in motion the subterranean psychological processes—was it a revolution of expectations?—that produced the great internal migrations of the boom era of the 1950s.[223] For sure their presence left memories whose sweetness could be related directly to its brevity or otherwise. In the northern city of Bologna, the Allies remained for roughly six weeks. A 1995 celebration of the city's liberation, published by the Press of the former Communist Party, dwelt on the music and dancing the Americans had brought, the baseball and Camel cigarettes, the colour-filled images of a renewed way of life, and an undreamt-of prosperity. But a memoir from Naples, where the Allies stayed over 18 months, published in the same year by another Communist writer, offered a pained and bitter portrait of the experience, seen as prelude to a long-term occupation under the flag of NATO. Similar sentiments seem to underlie Patrick Quignard's *L'occupation américaine* of 1994, a querulous novel set in the France of the late 1950s, which presents a view of the American military presence as continuous from the liberation onwards, the latest in a long series of invaders of the Orléans region stretching back to the Celts, the Germans, and the Romans.[224]

These were memories mainly from the Left. The Right in France wanted the Americans out. Their Italian peers wanted the Americans to stay, in 1947, in 1948, and in 1949. In Austria conservatives were far more sceptical; in Germany their attitudes gradually evolved as the Americans

---

[222] Cits from JCS 1779 in Friedrich et al. (eds), *American Experiences*, 403–4, 413–14.

[223] Eugenio Scalfari, *L'autunno delle Repubblica* (Milan, 1969), 95–6; in a short story that remained unpublished until 2007, Curzio Malaparte claimed that the total defeat of 1943 had sparked an exodus of people from Sicily, led by women, who saw an opportunity to escape from misery and to search for a land that gave them plenty, justice, order, and dignity. Malaparte however did not link this mass movement to the arrival of the Allies, but to an age-old pattern in which the defeat of the existing order always brought an 'opportunity for liberty' to the poorest people; Malaparte, *Il compagno di viaggio* (Milan, 2007), 74–5.

[224] 'C'era una volta l'America', supplement to *L'Unità*, Emilia-Romagna edition, 21 April 1995; Ermanno Rea, *Mistero napoletano: Vita e passione di una comunista negli anni della guerra fredda* (Turin, 1995), 28, 60–3; P. Quignard, *L'occupation américaine* (Paris, 1994); this latter novel was set—not by chance—in a time when popular anxiety over the American military presence in France was at its height, writes Hilary Footitt, in 'American

demonstrated the depth of their commitment to a new, capitalist Germany, and as the Soviet ex-ally behaved ever more badly in its zone and eastern Europe in general. But the true revolution of material expectations that an American army could inspire only happened in western Germany after the GI's return on a massive, long-term scale after 1951, under the auspices of NATO. A 'Gold Rush' atmosphere broke out, reports Maria Höhn, requiring a great crusade by the defenders of reborn German moral integrity for its containment. And once again women were the key protagonists.[225]

Like all the other armed forces of the West, the US army was not happy to be entrusted with the job of carrying out a social revolution. It had dodged the issue in Italy, had no such intention in France, and made sure others—including the locals—did the work in Austria. In Germany only the seriousness of the security situation, inside the western zones as well as in Berlin, delayed the departure that General Clay longed for, and his replacement by a civilian. By the time this finally happened, conservative Germans knew they had won their battles over de-Nazification, dismantling, and re-education, and could look forward to unstinting American support, even if in only half a nation. But this still left unanswered the question of Germany's place in the new diminished Europe. Officially, everyone recognized that without a German economic revival, there could be no recovery for the rest of the Old World, and vice versa. But to make this happen, and to reconcile this project with the long-standing ambitions of the Roosevelt heritage, required a different sort of projection of American power. Traditional forms of military, political, and economic intervention were not enough. What was needed was another display of that remarkable American talent for inventing new ways to project national power, so visible from January 1941 onwards. The Cold War supplied the occasion and the urgency. But the design was a classic New Deal product—the last of an impressive line. It was called the European Recovery Program, but was better known by the name the Press instantly bestowed on it: 'the Marshall Plan'.

Forces in France: Communist Representations of US Deployment', in Simona Tobia (ed.), *Cold War History*, Special Issue, 'Europe Americanized?' (February 2011).

[225] Maria Höhn, *GIs and Fräuleins: The German–American Encounter in 1950s West Germany* (Chapel Hill, NC, 2002), 19, 31–6, 39–51, 226–9; yet the German film expert Thomas Elsaesser insists that the millions of GIs who passed through the Federal Republic in all the post-war years 'seem to have left virtually no trace in the German cinema'. The one major, partial, exception is Rainer Werner Fassbinder's *Marriage of Maria Braun* (1978), a highly allegorical film in which the heroine survives by bestowing her 'love' on an African-American GI, only to kill him when the husband she married under the Anglo-American bombs finally returns from the war; cf. T. P. Elsaesser, 'German Postwar Cinema and Hollywood', in Ellwood and Kroes (eds), *Hollywood in Europe*, 285.

8

Reflating Europe with the Marshall Plan

'THE FORCEFUL DREAD...'

The Western Europe that the Marshall Plan stepped into was a sad place indeed. On the basis of a visit early in 1947, the editor of the journal *Foreign Affairs*, Hamilton Fish Armstrong, painted a grim fresco of all the misery. Beyond the 'complete absorption in the problem of how to live', there was the breakdown of all the traditional systems of legitimacy. Old Europe's political passions had gone, declaimed Armstrong. Now a vote could be captured by a bucket of coal, a packet of cigarettes, an ounce of bread. The American–Soviet split meant nothing in such circumstances: 'the present currency for winning esteem in mainly material [so that] the advantage lies with us if we choose to exercise it...we can use our calories and our machines to reveal the weakness of the Communist apparatus of production and distribution.' In the meantime statesmanship was at a discount as politicians struggled, each in his own myopic way, to fill the 'empty national breadbasket...empty national coalbin...empty national treasury'.[1]

This article appeared in the same number of *Foreign Affairs* that made the diplomat George Kennan famous. In his classic analysis of 'The Sources of Soviet Conduct', Kennan warned: 'the palsied decrepitude of the capitalist world is the keystone of Communist philosophy.' Kennan and his team of State Department policy planners shared the belief that Europe's difficulties stemmed not just from all the evident causes, but from something deeper: 'a profound exhaustion of physical plant and spiritual vigor', coming on top of a historical 'maladjustment' of economic nature, 'which makes European society vulnerable to exploitation by any and all totalitarian movements and which Russian communism is now exploiting'.[2]

---

[1] Armstrong, 'Europe Revisited', *Foreign Affairs* (July 1947), cit. in Ellwood, *Rebuilding Europe*, 75–6.

[2] Original documents cit. in Ellwood, *Rebuilding Europe*, 92.

Was the refined intellectual Kennan over-impressed by the outpourings of the post-war cultivated minds he may have read? Geoffrey Crowther, the editor of *The Economist*, tried hard to fight the consensus of the declinists on a trip to the US in early 1948, but his was a minority voice.[3] The majority sounded more like the diplomat and writer Harold Nicolson, one of the most cultivated commentators of his day on the British side. At the end of 1948 Nicolson talked of the 'forceful dread under which we all live today', a fear that 'renders security—actual *physical* security—the main centre of our desires'.[4] In the July–August 1947 issue of the American liberal journal *Partisan Review*, while discussing the topic of European unity, George Orwell proclaimed that 'capitalism itself has manifestly no future'. Orwell expressed his hope that even the United States might soon be taking a turn in the direction of socialism. As on many other occasions in this period, the author of *Animal Farm* was quite clear that the outlook was 'very dark', that the chances of atomic war in the future were high, and that the Socialist United States of Europe—'the only worthwhile political objective today'—was in practical reality quite out of the question:

> [But] the greatest difficulty of all is the apathy and conservatism of people everywhere, their unawareness of danger, their inability to imagine anything new—in general as [the philosopher] Bertrand Russell put it recently, the unwillingness of the human race to acquiesce in its own survival.[5]

Soon afterwards T. S. Eliot wrote: 'We can assert with some confidence that our period is one of decline...and that the evidence of this decline is visible in every department of human activity.' Commenting, Orwell said: 'in any case...we cannot reverse the present trend by conscious action.' Conscious action could of course make it worse in some respects, and the appearance of his dystopian novel *1984* in June 1949, together with Orwell's assertion that the totalitarian scenario described therein could happen anywhere, including England, can hardly have helped to lighten the atmosphere.[6]

While today's economic historians insist that the great post-war production and investment boom in Western Europe was already under way in the late 1940s, on the surface, at the level of lived experience, all was darkness and anxiety. Orwell's friend Arthur Koestler reported in *The Observer* in

---

[3] Geoffrey Crowther, *The Economic Reconstruction of Europe* (Claremont, 1948), 28–9.

[4] H. Nicolson, *The Future of the English-Speaking Peoples*, text of speech of November 1948 (Glasgow, 1949) (emphasis in original), 8.

[5] G. Orwell, 'Toward European Unity', *Partisan Review* (July–August 1947), reproduced in *The Collected Essays, Journalism and Letters of George Orwell*, iv: *In Front of Your Nose, 1945–1950* (1968 edn repr., Harmondsworth, 1980); cits at pp. 425, 426.

[6] Orwell, 'Review', *Observer* (28 November 1948), reproduced ibid.; cits at p. 517.

February 1948 how an authoritative French opinion poll of the previous summer had asked the question: 'Do you believe that at the present moment things are going well or badly with France?' The answers, summarized Koestler, were: Going well: 0 per cent. Rather well: 4 per cent. Badly, or rather badly: 93 per cent. No opinion: 4 per cent. The author commented:

> The near-unanimity of the answers shows that the series of convulsions which constitute post-war French history are not a surface disturbance, but rather the result of what is called here a *lame du fond*, a ground swell which affects all the basic values of life.[7]

Reading the French press and intellectual output, writes the historian Pascal Ory, one can see that:

> the decisive... break in French self-confidence (a confidence shown up in all its ingenuousness in 1938) came less in 1940 or in 1945 (when it still had its myths to fall back on) than between 1946 and 1948...

The incontestable hegemony of the superpowers, the eruption of the Cold War within the country as well as all around it, the burden of the empire, the disillusionments after the bright promises of the liberation period, especially the stark dependence on the Americans, all contributed to the new sense of anguish and disorientation. The Vichy and pre-war complaints that 'the nation lacked foresight, discipline and order' returned to common currency, and even the scarce film output began to reflect the dominant tones of pessimism and disillusion.[8]

While civil war raged in Greece, Italy saw an unprecedented Cold War propaganda battle in the general elections of April 1948. Both sides used clandestine outside support in order to mobilize fear, with the Americans and the Vatican presenting the confrontation as one between religion and liberty on one side, against atheism and slavery on the other. The victory of the conservative bloc only partially reassured the Americans, who felt that without long-term reform and social modernization, the Communists could come to power by democratic means at any time and the country 'would be an object of our charity for many years to come'.[9]

---

[7] Articles reprinted in Arthur Koestler, 'Land of Bread and Wine', *The Trail of the Dinosaur* (London, 1955), 40–2, cit. at p. 40.

[8] P. Ory in J. Becker and F. Knipping (eds), *Power in Europe? Great Britain, France, Italy and Germany in a Postwar World, 1945–1950* (Berlin and New York, 1986), 397–407, cit. at pp. 399–400. Atmosphere and events powerfully evoked in Anthony Beevor and Artemis Cooper, *Paris after the Liberation, 1944–1949* (2nd edn of 2004 repr., London, 2007), ch. 26. The total contrast with the analyses of the political economists is striking; cf. Irwin Wall, 'The Marshall Plan and French Politics', in Martin Schain (ed.), *The Marshall Plan: Fifty Years After* (New York, 2001), 167–83.

[9] H. K. Smith, *State of Europe*, 207–11; cf. Ellwood, 'The 1948 Elections in Italy: A Cold War Propaganda Battle', *Historical Journal of Film, Radio and Television*, 13/1 (1993).

Meanwhile in West Germany the editor of the weekly *Der Spiegel* seemed to express a widely held sentiment when he complained of an all-pervading powerlessness, 'a political no-man's land in the heads of the puzzled people of Europe'.[10]

Across Europe writers and opinion-makers poured out their dirge of desperation, very often seeing in America not the great beacon of hope but the source of pestilences that only the choice of a 'Third Way', if not Communism itself, could guard against.[11] In Britain a Mass Observation survey of 1947 discovered that a third of middle-class Britons regarded Americans unfavourably, and only a quarter said they were real admirers. The organization commented that 'despite their central heating, business efficiency and industrial superiority', Americans were considered to be 'still the younger cousins'. There was resentment in the inferiority and dependence that the British now sensed. Harold Nicolson lamented that 'we must remain more dependent upon the United States than is gratifying to our pride'. Fortunately the English-speaking world was united 'by a community of needs, traditions and feelings... if we also are not to surrender to a materialist fallacy that sentiment and those ideals must be ever-present'. Geoffrey Crowther of *The Economist* felt obliged to point out to his American audiences that 'to accept the role of followership is a difficult psychological adjustment to make... there are often signs of almost insurmountable psychological reluctance to accept the new status'.[12]

In a large-scale survey of opinion among leading Europeans from all walks of life, carried out for the Common Council of American Unity (a prominent New York civil rights group), it was discovered that while all looked to America for economic, military, 'and even a degree of moral' leadership, 'serious doubts' were present about the qualifications of the US to exercise this responsibility. American policy was seen as unreliable, American society as too materialistic, dominated by Big Business and 'not capable of coping with the deeper issues involved' in contemporary struggles. The survey found even elementary concepts such as 'democracy' and 'freedom' to be misunderstood in Europe, and a significant degree of opposition present to capitalism itself, as well as to communism.[13]

---

[10] Cit. in Ellwood, *Rebuilding Europe*, 124.

[11] Full context in Tony Judt, *Postwar*, 203–21; cf. Jessica C. E. Gienow-Hecht, ' "How Good Are We?" Culture and the Cold War', in Giles Scott-Smith and Hans Krabbendam (eds), *The Cultural Cold War in Western Europe, 1945–1960* (London, 2003), 270–1.

[12] Mass Observation cit. in Robert Taylor, ' "Immature, immoral, vulgar, materialistic...":
How Britons viewed Yanks in the 1940s', *New Statesman* (3 March 2003); Nicolson, *Future*, 24, 29; Crowther, *Economic Reconstruction*, 76–7.

[13] Common Council of American Unity, *European Beliefs regarding the United States 1949* (New York, 1949), 6–8. I am grateful to Madeline Vadkerty, formerly of USIA, for

In such a context the Truman Doctrine of March 1947, which provided a rationale for immediate military and economic aid to Greece and Turkey, had worrying aspects. It effectively announced that the United Nations could play no useful role in the new situation, and—as Hamilton Fish Armstrong put it—seemed to declare that 'everyone must now choose sides in an ideological battle'. In reality, said Armstrong—America's task was to move on from relief to reconstruction: 'first we must give; then we must invest; whenever possible we must buy; and eventually we may hope to begin getting our money back.' What was needed was a plan, drawn up cooperatively by the Europeans, but with the best American brains involved 'to give it reality'. Capital goods and raw material imports, mutual aid principles, currency stabilization measures, would all be treated in the plan, which perhaps could be supervised by the new UN Economic Commission for Europe. Above all America would like to demonstrate her 'native confidence' in what she stood for: not just a political and economic system that had produced 'the highest standard of living the world has ever known', but one capable of extension and improvement to meet modern needs and desires, capable of projecting its example in the knowledge that, in contrast with the Soviets, 'Europe wants what we can give'.[14]

Even as Armstrong prepared his article, just such a plan was forthcoming from the government of the United States. The English literary critic Cyril Connolly commented:

> As Europe becomes more helpless the Americans are compelled to become far-seeing and responsible, as Rome was forced by the long decline of Greece to produce an Augustus, a Virgil. *Our impotence liberates their potentialities.*[15]

THE VISIONARIES

> ...we had a goal; we had fire in our bellies; we worked like hell; we had tough, disciplined thinking, and we could program, strive for and see results.[16]

drawing my attention to this document. In tandem with the State Department information agency, the Council responded with a vast 'Letters from America' campaign, supplied by immigrant communities across the US for mother countries, as well as sending materials for newspaper editorials and radio programmes abroad; details in Cull, *Cold War*, 57–8.

[14] Armstrong, cit. in Ellwood, *Rebuilding Europe*, 75–7.

[15] Connolly cit., with emphasis, in Vann Woodward, *Old World's New World*, 78; indeed many plans for European salvation were on offer in the US; cf. Ellwood, *Rebuilding Europe*, 57, 79.

[16] James C. Warren Jr, 'Those Who Made the Stabilization Program a Success', in Constantine C. Menges (ed.), *The Marshall Plan From Those Who Made it Succeed* (Lanham, Md., 1999), 190.

So rejoiced one of the veterans of the Marshall Plan's headquarters in Greece, fifty years after the great experience. With the Plan, the American modernizing challenge to Europe took human form, arrived with people, projects, propaganda, set up office in not just a few crucial countries, but from the top to the bottom of the Old World. Its highly motivated experts, all on temporary loan from somewhere else, deployed their own very special kind of fix-it appeal. They brought dollars and political clout, but also a distinctive language for communicating their methods, their techniques, images, convictions. For a short, intense period a new American team presence arrived in Europe, incarnated in those few hundred technocrats and their masters all dedicated to finding ways to translate the successes of the American economic experience into recipes for the salvation of others. Theirs was the peculiar mix of inventiveness and dogma, of energy and complacency, of adaptability and righteousness, which left such an indelible mark on the European experience of the Plan. They were the ones, they said, who knew how to rescue the Old World from its backwardness and spiritual paralysis, how to restore hope, rebuild the capitalists' elemental confidence in the future, above all to turn American myth into American model. 'You Too Can Be Like Us': that was the subtext of the Marshall Plan, its 'promissory note', and the chosen few of the great project came among the Europeans to show just how the miracle could be performed.

Secretary of State George Marshall had said of course that 'the initiative must come from the Europeans', in his speech launching the great proposition in June 1947. He repeated: 'the program should be a joint one.' From its inception then a special type of mutuality was, officially, to be the guiding principle of the exercise. The classic work by Hadley Arkes on the Plan's evolution in its Washington context long ago confirmed this disposition. Arkes highlighted Marshall's insistence that 'only a coherent program with thorough coordination could work. It was the commitment to a new degree of cooperation that made the Marshall Plan different.'[17]

But what if the partner nations and governments had visions of the European Recovery Program—the project's formal title—that differed in some significant way from those of the American planners when choices came to be made? From the beginning everyone involved in it was aware of the tension between mutuality and hierarchy in the working of the Program, a source of strain that could only be managed, said Arkes, deli-

---

[17] Hadley Arkes, *Bureaucracy, the Marshall Plan and the National Interest* (Princeton, 1972), ch. 7; cf. the explanation of the mutuality principle offered by Paul Hoffman, the head of the Marshall Plan, in a reflection offered soon after leaving the job: *Peace Can Be Won* (Garden City, NY, 1951), 41–2.

cately, through 'the elasticity of self-denial'. Each side of course demonstrated its own limits to this elasticity, and it was in the give-and-take struggles over these limits or boundaries that many of the long-term political, economic, and cultural differences between the players became most visible.

While every European government was and remained deeply grateful for the support and the consideration offered by the Marshall Plan, especially in the frantic early months, its experience over time was a far more contentious affair than the golden myths it left behind would have us believe. Familiarity bred exasperation. But most of the battles sooner or later came down to two issues, which were easy to state, often very difficult to face.

On the American side the key question was this: how could the bankrupt, half-desperate Europeans be made to learn the democratic, progressive lessons of American history in time to save themselves from their own past and the embrace of Communism?

But from the European angle there were two other, quite different queries: how could the aid beneficiaries keep their overweening American sponsors happy while defending their customary methods of organizing governance and consensus building, of the State and the market, of production and consumption? At the same time, how could they preserve the ideas of a happier future they had painfully worked out for themselves during and after the Second World War?

In countries like France, Italy, and Greece, the language of anti-communism could to some extent bridge the mental gap between all the parties to the Marshall Plan experiment, as it would in the world of the North Atlantic Treaty of April 1949. But what of participating nations where no communist threat existed? Across northern Europe, from Ireland, through Britain to Scandinavia were societies that also yearned for ERP dollars, and at the same time sought to make their own deal with what the Americans were offering and demanding in exchange. If dependence there was to be for a while, it must in any case be *conditional*.

Facts of life at the start of the European Recovery Program

The 'Marshall Plan' came into being informally, with 'a few remarks' on the state of Europe by Secretary of State George C. Marshall at a Harvard academic ceremony in June 1947. These suggested that an emergency was under way, and that urgent economic action was required to save the very basis of human existence in the Old World. A short, almost cryptic paragraph invited the Europeans to agree among themselves on 'the requirements of the situation', thence on the part each nation would take 'in order to give proper effect to whatever action might be undertaken by this government'. The Europeans should take the initiative, the Secretary made clear, while the US would initially provide 'friendly aid in the drafting of a European program…and support of such a program as far as it may be practical for us to do so'. Above all those wishing to take part must understand that 'a cure rather than a palliative' was being sought. Afterwards Marshall characterized his speech as 'something between a hint and a suggestion', and professed embarrassment that it should have been dubbed a 'Plan' by the President and the press, with his name 'tagged to it'.[18]

Within less than two weeks, the French and British foreign ministers had set in motion a Conference on European Economic Cooperation (CEEC), which, in stages between the end of June and the end of September, with the help of fourteen other governments from the top to the bottom of Western Europe, plus representatives from the Western occupied zones in Germany, prepared a report to the US Government on the total economic aid thought to be needed by all of them. A grand total of $22 billion was cited. The immediate priority was to stop the haemorrhage of dollars from Europe caused by the need to find in America basic supplies of food, fuel, and raw materials, which in normal times would either have been produced locally or imported from colonies and other parts of the world. While the West Europeans faced bankruptcy, the Americans were building a huge, unusable, balance of payments of surplus. This was the so-called 'dollar gap'. As in the game of Monopoly, world trade was shuddering to a halt because one of the players had accumulated all the money. To restart it, the Bank would have to redistribute the cash.[19]

After a long winter of discussion, some stopgap help, and greatly increased tension in East–West relations, the European Recovery Program was born officially with an act of Congress signed by Truman in April 1948. To administer the project a new federal agency, the Economic Cooperation Administration (ECA), was brought into being at the same

[18] Original text of speech online at: <http://www.trumanlibrary.org/whistlestop/study_collections/marshall/large/documents/index.php?documentdate=1947-06-05&documentid=8-7&pagenumber=1>; context in Ellwood, *Rebuilding Europe*, 82–6.

[19] Ellwood, *Rebuilding Europe*, 86–7; Timothy Healey, 'William Clayton, Negotiating the Marshall Plan, and European Economic Integration', *Diplomatic History* (April 2011), 240–5; this was the occasion when the Soviets arrived to take part, walking out after three days and obliging Poles, Czechs, and Finns to cancel their expressed interest in the Plan. Besides Great Britain, France, and the German zones, the nations present were Austria, Belgium, Denmark, Greece, Iceland, Ireland, Italy, Luxemburg, the Netherlands, Norway, Portugal, Sweden, Switzerland, Turkey.

time, headed by a Republican businessman, Paul G. Hoffmann. Expenditure began to flow immediately. In the same month the CEEC became the Organization for European Economic Cooperation, with its headquarters in Paris. The Belgian Prime Minister and Foreign Minister, Paul Henri Spaak, was appointed chairman of its governing council. By July it would begin working on specific systems for the allocation of American aid.[20]

From the beginning a Special Representative of ECA had been installed in Paris, with the formal purpose of organizing liaison between the OEEC and the ECA, but with the added intention—made clear by Congress—of spurring a more general process of economic cooperation between the European participants. The role of Special Representative was assigned to the distinguished businessman, diplomat, and former Governor of New York, Averell Harriman, Chairman of a Presidential Committee that had done much to prepare the ground for the act of Congress. In a highly unusual move, both ECA head Hoffmann, a car salesman become head of an automobile corporation, and Harriman, an American grandee, were given Cabinet rank in the US government.[21]

The Programme's Congressional enactment identified the supreme objective as creating in Western Europe 'a healthy economy independent of extraordinary outside assistance' by 1952. To this end, commented the economic historian Imanuel Wexler, 'the act stipulated a recovery plan based on four specific endeavours: (1) a strong production effort, (2) expansion of foreign trade, (3) the creation and maintenance of internal financial stability, and (4) the development of [European] economic cooperation.' More broadly, wrote the British economist Barbara Ward shortly afterwards, the act aimed 'to balance Europe's budget at a level of consumption—in other words a standard of living—high enough to give political stability'. How would this be achieved? By seeking, said Ms Ward, 'an industrial and agricultural expansion equal to the tremendous increase in the American economy between 1940 and 1944'. This implied, among other tasks, doubling exports to the United States and the western hemisphere in general, while increasing them to the rest of the world by a third. Above all such advances could only be based on permanent structural change in the European economies, singly and together, *as*

---

[20] Detailed political background to the birth of the ERP in Arkes, *Bureaucracy*, chs 3 4 5; for the OEEC, Daniel Barbezat, 'The Marshall Plan and the Origin of the OEEC', in OECD, *Explorations in OEEC History*, ed. Richard T. Griffiths (Paris, 1997); ERP/OEEC chronology ibid. Annex 2; full, tortuous political history of OEEC birth in Alan S. Milward, *The Reconstruction of Western Europe, 1945–1951* (London, 1984) ch. 5.

[21] Origins and significance of this position—an anomaly in American governmental institutions—in Arkes, *Bureaucracy*, 138–45.

a whole. This, it would soon emerge, was what the phrase 'a cure rather than a palliative' meant, nothing less.[22]

While the OEEC confronted the task of turning the Congressional indicators into specific plans and requests, coordinated across Europe, American embassies in each of the participant nations were obtaining signatures on bilateral pacts that spelled out the obligations of governments towards their new sponsors. If mutuality should fail, hierarchy was always available in the background. Recognition was required of the authority of the ECA, the Office of the Special Representative (OSR) in Paris, and the ERP 'Mission' that would be set up in each national capital. A formal committee would link the local government to the Mission, in order to supervise the running of the programme on the ground.

The committee's key task was to make plans for spending productively the sums in the new 'Counterpart Fund', a characterizing feature of the whole operation, and the one that aroused most controversy at the time. This was a specially created account at each national bank that would contain the proceeds from the local sale of ERP-supplied goods. Much of the 'aid', it turned out, would not be as free, or as liquid, as the Europeans had imagined. It would instead most often be merchandise, sold to the highest bidder, public or private, or to whomsoever requested it. Their payments would then go back not to the US, but into the new Fund. From the Counterpart Fund would come the money to help pay for national reconstruction and modernization efforts.

At the same time the ECA would keep 5 per cent of the Fund for its own purposes. This figure would pay for the operating costs of the ECA Mission in each country. More remarkably it would underwrite the information and public relations effort that would explain to every nation's citizens where the Plan came from, how it functioned and what they could expect to get out of it. The Marshall Planners were not just technocrats: they would emerge as exceptionally determined educators in the economics of advanced, American-style market capitalism. But the Europeans would be paying for their own education.

The ERP was clearly a mighty weapon in the Cold War. Ambassador Harriman went so far in 1949 as to characterize the whole effort as a 'fire-fighting operation'. Marshall's successor as Secretary of State, Dean Acheson, the individual who, in his own words, 'probably made as many

---

[22] Cit. in Ellwood, *Rebuilding Europe*, 88–91; cf. Theodore Geiger, a veteran, in Menges (ed.), *Marshall Plan*, 27–8; the role of Will Clayton, a cotton magnate become undersecretary of state for economic affairs in 1946, in fathering the Marshall Plan, and especially its insistence on future of economic integration for Europe, is highlighted in Healey, 'William Clayton'.

speeches and answered as many questions about the Marshall Plan as any man alive', remembered that 'what citizens and the representatives in Congress always wanted to learn in the last analysis was how Marshall Aid operated to block the extension of Soviet power and the acceptance of Communist economic and political organization and alignment'.[23] Against the Plan indeed stood the forces of the Cominform, an international propaganda organization set up in October 1947 by the Kremlin with the explicit purpose of combating the Marshall Plan, internationally and—using local Communist parties—within each participating nation. At a time when Communist forces were leading armed insurgency in Greece, looked capable of taking power politically in Italy, seemed to threaten chaos in France, and knew what they wanted in Germany— unlike the West at this stage—the Cold War gave an urgency to the Program that concentrated minds everywhere.[24]

Yet the great project was born in an atmosphere of deep political suspicion in Washington: in Congress, in the traditional Federal agencies, and across the party and lobby systems. Many considered the inheritance of the New Deal and its latter-day exponents with great scepticism, and also reacted against any sign of deeper American involvement with the woes of Europe. Even those who were willing to look abroad for America's future were split between the 'business progressives' who supported expanded trade, living standards, and democratic reform as the keys to peace, and their conservative critics, who emphasized national security, military readiness, and trade protection.[25]

As a result Congress kept unusually firm control over the design and launch of this new means of projecting American power, and hedged it

---

[23] Ellwood, *Rebuilding Europe*, 92, 161. The Soviets had abruptly left the original CEEC conference when they discovered just how serious was the requirement to build an integrated recovery plan for the whole of Europe—hence with Germany inside it—which Washington would then inspect and approve.

[24] The Cominform's purposes however went much beyond organizing opposition to the ERP, and led to a significant tightening up of control by the Soviets of local Communist parties, harking back to the days of the Comintern (1919–1943), Vojtech Mastny, *The Cold War and Soviet Insecurity: The Stalin Years* (Oxford, 1996), 27–34. The ERP contained its own secret 'political action arm', the Office of Policy Coordination, run jointly with the CIA, but funded from Counterpart monies, for the purpose of psychological warfare and emergency political action in the case of revolution or invasion; details in Sallie Pisani, *The CIA and the Marshall Plan* (Lawrence, Kan., 1991), 67–79; for the Cold War context that gave birth to Marshall Plan propaganda, Günter Bischof, 'Introduction', in Günter Bischof and Dieter Stiefel (eds), *Images of the Marshall Plan in Europe: Films, Photographs, Exhibits, Posters* (Innsbruck, 2009), 9–13.

[25] Jacqueline McGlade, 'From Business Reform Programme to Production Drive: The Transformation of US Technical Assistance to Western Europe', in Matthias Kipping and Ove Bjarnar (eds), *The Americanisation of European Business: The Marshall Plan and the Transfer of US Management Models* (London, 1998), 20–4.

round with restrictions of every kind. It was on their insistence that the new agency should be separate from the State Department, that it should be headed by a private sector personality, that it should be temporary (four years only), and that it should be obliged to come back to Capitol Hill every year to justify its efforts and plead for its budget. On Congress's insistence loans would be used as well as grants in the scheme of aid, money that would pay for goods (and advice) produced in America, not handed over in some form of cash. They also made clear that the amounts of support would start diminishing as soon as possible after the first year. Wherever possible private sector channels and resources were to be used to supply the goods. Investment, however, was another matter. The US private banks and the capital markets in general were of course out of the picture: the first post-war period and the Great Crash had taught them too many painful lessons in Europe. Hence the importance of the Counterpart Funds, whose use for investment participating governments and Missions would—in theory—plan together.[26]

As a result of all the diffidence, the machinery of the Program was full of safeguards, and so became extremely intricate and time-consuming. Loan and grant decisions made by ECA were obliged to pass through the National Advisory Council, a Treasury subsidiary, for final approval, while the loan element was run administratively by yet another agency, the Export–Import Bank.[27] The OEEC was required to evaluate the national import and reconstruction budgets, as was the ECA. Meanwhile, to get material access to the Marshall Plan resources eventually allocated after these checks at the general level, State agencies and importers were obliged to go through repeated layers of financial, technical, and procedural vetting.[28]

Yet the ERP staff on the ground were under immense pressure to get instant results, newsworthy jumps in production, immediately visible improvements in housing, transport, energy, industry, agriculture, downturns in communist votes by the next election, enthusiastic endorsement of every American proposal in time for the next Congressional fact-finding tour or budget hearing. They were under direct orders to close the 'dollar gap' as soon as possible, preferably by encouraging European manufacturers

---

[26] On the fears of the capital markets, Barry Eichengreen, 'The Market and the Marshall Plan', in Schain (ed.), *Marshall Plan*, 137–8.

[27] Arkes, *Bureaucracy*, 162.

[28] For the specific experience of a large Italian company attempting to navigate this maze, Ellwood, 'The Limits of Americanisation and the Emergence of an Alternative Model: The Marshall Plan in Emilia-Romagna', in Kipping and Bjarnar (eds), *Americanisation of European Business*, 158–9; the company was on the verge of bankruptcy by the time machinery ordered in July 1948 arrived—in November 1950.

to export a lot more to the US. They were expected to keep the American taxpayer convinced, to take a frontline position in the psychological war against Communism, and to build consensus at every level of European society for their efforts. Above all they were charged with promoting reconstruction and structural change in a fashion that would, in the space of four years, deliver some form of reorganized, integrated, European economy:

> The word "structural"...was the word of the hour', recalled Harold van Buren Cleveland, a senior American administrator. 'Everything was a structural problem: the dollar problem was a structural problem, European industry was in such a structural state that it couldn't possibly compete with the United States; there was a structural inability of Europe to have a sufficient level or growth of productivity to compete with the almighty U.S. economy. And so on.[29]

In his monumental work of scholarship dedicated to the Anglo-American confrontation set off by the demand for change-by-integration, the great string attached to all the support, Michael Hogan explains the Americans' reasoning. In the short term the effects would be political and strategic, setting off a revolutionary shift in Franco-German relations that, among other benefits, should eventually enable Western Europe to stand up for itself against the East. But there were other, no less ambitious designs for the long term:

> The economic assumptions grew fundamentally out of the American experience at home, where a large internal economy integrated by free-market forces and central institutions of coordination and control seemed to have laid the groundwork for a new era of economic growth and social stability. An economic United States of Europe would bring similar benefits.... Besides creating a framework for controlling the Germans and containing the Soviets, it would limit Communist inroads, dissolve class tensions through a shared abundance, and set the continental countries on the path to a multilateral system of world trade.[30]

Of course nothing could have been further from the minds of the European diplomats and experts who were given the heavy job of meeting Marshall's original challenge. The crucial meeting to turn the American invitation into a concrete recovery design made-in-Europe opened in July

---

[29] Harold van B. Cleveland, 'If There Had Been No Marshall Plan...', in Stanley Hoffmann and Charles Maier (eds), *The Marshall Plan: A Retrospective* (Boulder, Colo., 1984), 63.

[30] M. J. Hogan, *The Marshall Plan: America, Britain and the Reconstruction of Western Europe, 1947–1952* (Cambridge, 1987), 27; cf. official statements from ERP legislation reproduced in Arkes, *Bureaucracy*, 366–8; cf. Healey, 'William Clayton', 233–4, 242–3.

1947. 'I recall spending long days in the rooms of the Grand Palais', wrote Robert Marjolin, the French Secretary General, 'and in sweltering heat, trying to reconcile programmes of which almost all had been drawn up on differing premisses or even by pure guesswork. Most of the governments represented did not have a national plan and some not even an overall picture of the national economy.'[31]

No one knew how Congress would react to their efforts, nor even how much money was really available. There were endless other difficulties. Many of the participants lacked the staff, the statistics, or the mentality to do the kind of planning required, and in any case none had ever even thought of doing it on a collective basis. A senior British participant, Eric Roll, recalled 'the time when we sent out our original questionnaires on import programs, on the basis of which we were going to produce a list of requirements'. Leaving a meeting at 2 a.m. with a colleague, he came across the office of the Greek delegate, who was still working, laboriously filling in the questionnaires:

> We said 'But this is not for you, this is to be sent to Athens for the people there to fill in.' He said, 'You don't really think that anybody in Athens will know anything about this and will be able to fill it in. I can just invent the figures myself.'[32]

The outcome of all the to-ings and fro-ings at the start was summarized at a fiftieth anniversary conference by one of the most senior veterans, the former Deputy Administrator Harlan Cleveland:

> It was not, of course, a 'plan'. It was a continuous international happening, with frequent course corrections. From watching the Marshall Plan begin, and from helping with some of those course corrections, I first derived a definition of 'planning' that I later used in teaching public administration. Real planning is improvisation on a general sense of direction. The Marshall Plan was a brilliant series of improvisations on a deceptively simple theme: Europe needed help and only America could supply it.[33]

---

[31] Robert Marjolin, *Architect of European Unity: Memoirs, 1911–1986* (London, 1989), 184–5.

[32] Eric Roll, 'The Marshall Plan as Anglo-American Response', in Hoffmann and Maier (eds), *Marshall Plan*, 43; for a detailed account, from a witness, of the discomfort of the Austrian bureaucracy in these circumstances, Hans Seidel, 'Austria's Economic Policy and the Marshall Plan', in Günter Bischof, Anton Pelinka, and Dieter Stiefel (eds), *Contemporary Austrian Studies*, viii: *The Marshall Plan in Austria* (New Brunswick, NJ, 2000), 274–5.

[33] H. Cleveland, 'The Marshall Plan: Reflections in Retrospect', in Hans H. J. Labohm (ed.) *The Fiftieth Anniversary of the Marshall Plan in Retrospect and Prospect*, Report of the Seminar organized by the Clingendael Institute (The Hague, May 1997), 4.

THE 'CLASSIC' ERA OF THE MARSHALL PLAN:
SPRING 1948–SUMMER 1950

In the light of what happened to the European Recovery Program after the outbreak of the Korean War in June 1950—its rapid subordination to military demands—the early years of the experience soon came to be seen by all concerned as the golden epoch of pure economic action and rewards. A veteran of the Greek experience, Jim Warren, evoked a time of 'results-oriented planning of a tough and imaginative, taut and inspired character. And there was another difference: there was a certain "moral authority".'[34] A colleague, C. William Kontos from the Civil Government Division of the Greek Mission, spoke later of his experience of reshaping the country's public administration, 'a novel task for Americans'.

Kontos claimed to have personally reorganized the Greek postal system and its patent office, and recalled travelling all over the country, handing out building supplies and checking the work in progress: 'we funded schools, bridges, culverts, roads, water-mains, clinics, slaughter-houses', as well as resurrecting power systems, rebuilding housing, supplying food and raw materials. Later came efforts to re-establish democratic trade unions, stabilize the currency, reform tax collection, and start industrialization, all this right after years of war, civil war, and devastation in which other Americans had played quite different roles, following the military script of the Truman Doctrine. At its height the ERP provided almost 50 per cent of Greek GNP, and paid for 64 per cent of its civilian imports.[35]

By the end of 1949 just under $6 billion had been spent by the ECA managers on goods and services for the participating countries, 86 per cent of which had been in the form of grants—not loans—to pay for these imports. In order of proportion the major beneficiaries had been Britain, France, West Germany, and then Italy. Food, feeds, and fertilizer had been the most requested items, followed by raw materials and semi-finished goods, fuel, machinery, and vehicles. The sale of these and all the other imports had brought a total of $4.3 billion to the national 'Counterpart Funds'.

'Few could doubt that the money had been well spent', declared the Council on Foreign Relations of New York in a comment on the first year.

---

[34] James C. Warren, in Menges (ed.), *Marshall Plan*, 190.

[35] C. William Kontos, ibid. 169–70; Greece had been a prime beneficiary of the Truman Doctrine, receiving military aid that enabled government forces to end the civil war in their favour in October 1949; figs. from H. Jones, 'A New Kind of War': America's Global Strategy and the Truman Doctrine in Greece (New York, 1989), ch. 13, n. 20; cf. Stelios Zachariou, 'Struggle for Survival: American Aid and Greek Reconstruction', in Schain (ed.), *Marshall Plan*, 160.

They pointed to the rise of nearly a quarter in the total output of goods and services that the ERP countries had enjoyed between 1947 and 1949, and asserted that the 'over-all index of production, based on 1938, rose to 115 in 1949, as compared with 77 in 1946 and 87 in 1947'. Agriculture too had recovered, and progress on the inflation front was considered 'uneven but definitely encouraging'. The foreign trade of the member states was back to its pre-war levels, but its most remarkable feature was the increase of 50 per cent over the previous two years on trade between them. In contrast, against all hopes, exports to the United States had stagnated. The notorious 'dollar gap' loomed as large as ever.[36]

But it was the psychological effects of the Plan that attracted the most comment and celebration. As early as October 1948 the *New York Herald Tribune* had published the results of a survey that declared the ERP four times over 'a success'—in recovery, cooperation, investment, and as American foreign policy.[37] It had been 'of inestimable value' said a Dutch official commentary later, because its impact on business confidence had unlocked expectations of profits to come, and hence investment. The prospect of large flows of goods and investment funds from America had played their part in releasing stocks in Germany at the time of the crucial and historic currency reform in June 1948.[38]

For the first anniversary of the Plan the eminent French philosopher, Raymond Aron, paid eloquent tribute in the daily newspaper *Le Figaro* and over the radio to the results of the American gesture, and once again it was the effects on confidence that gained most of the appreciation. Aron spoke of the return of 'a sense of hope and confidence', or 'restored courage and reawakened energy', transforming, 'almost at once, the psychological atmosphere of the "cold war"'. A new sense of solidarity had emerged, said Aron, providing an occasion without precedent to bring about what has been the centuries-old dream of philosophers, and what is today an imperious necessity of history—the unity of Europe. It was up to the Europeans themselves, Aron concluded, 'not to lose this unique opportunity'.[39]

Uniting or dividing Europe? The politics of the Marshall Plan in the first phase

Such attitudes, expressed in even more decisive terms by an equally eminent and much more powerful Frenchman, Jean Monnet, revealed the

---

[36] Ellwood, *Rebuilding Europe*, 155–6.
[37] Cit. in Menges (ed.), *Marshall Plan*, 113.
[38] Ellwood, *Rebuilding Europe*, 156.
[39] Cit. ibid. 164.

potential for division implicit in the ERP's great ambition for a united Western Europe. Although Hoffman and Harriman complained in late 1948 that the Marshall Plan was 'less successful, less understood, and less appreciated in France than in any other Western European nation',[40] no one on his side of the Atlantic understood better than the providential Monnet what the New Deal coalition behind the Marshall Plan wanted from the project, and how it expected the ERP to function. His long wartime experience in the Allied planning machinery in Washington, then his return there as part of a governmental delegation seeking a big loan in 1946, all taught him what to say and how to say it.[41] Under Monnet's guidance and that of his colleague Jean Fourastié, France became the first European nation to embrace openly the twin Marshall Plan principles of productivity and integration as the keys to a new kind of economic expansion.[42]

Later celebrated as supreme among all the patron saints of Europe's economic integration, Monnet in reality had only become an enthusiast for this cause—says the economic historian Alan Milward—when in 1948 he realized how vital was its place in the new American scheme of things. All the while of course, say Milward and others, the undisguised priority of Monnet was not so much the reform of Europe but the revitalization of the French State and its national economy.[43] For this purpose the beguiling and inventive businessman-turned-technocrat had set up his own official planning machinery, and using American experts and American-bred techniques of economic policy management, made it work throughout some of the most uncertain days of the Fourth Republic. The Counterpart Fund would be its lifeblood.[44]

---

[40] Cit. in Brian A. McKenzie, *Remaking France: Americanization, Public Diplomacy, and the Marshall Plan* (New York, 2005), 38.

[41] J. Monnet, *Memoirs* (London, 1978), chs 7, 10; François Duchêne, *Jean Monnet: The First Statesman of Interdependence* (New York, 1994), 87–97, 131–7, 158–9.

[42] On Monnet Plan and American inspiration, Stewart Patrick, 'Embedded Liberalism in France? American Hegemony, the Monnet Plan and Postwar Multilateralism', in Schain (ed.), *Marshall Plan*, 227; on Monnet's experience of negotiating the French loan of 1946, and the understanding it gave him of prevalent lines of thought in Washington and New York, ibid. 230–3; Jean Fourastié was a tireless educator on the productivity theme, using articles and books such as *La productivité* (Paris, 1952 and 1968), La *Grand espoir du XX siècle* (Paris, 1949 and 1958), *Machinisme et bienêtre* (Paris, 1951 and 1962); Monnet's tribute to him in *Memoirs*, 276–7.

[43] Alan S. Milward, *The European Rescue of the Nation State* (2nd edn, London, 2000), 335; cf. John Gillingham, *European Integration, 1950–2003: Superstate or New Market Economy?* (Cambridge, 2003), ch. 2. Monnet claimed he had first reached his conclusions in favour of a federal Europe in August 1943; cf. letter to Committee of National Liberation cited in Monnet, *Memoirs*, 222.

[44] Monnet, *Memoirs*, ch. 11; Duchêne, *Jean Monnet*, 173, 178–9; Healey, 'William Clayton', 253.

How very different were views of the Marshall Plan's prospects on the other side of the Channel. The Foreign Office under the Labour stalwart Ernest Bevin had reacted instantly to the Marshall 'hint' and raced the French to be first to convene a conference of likely beneficiaries. Having understood quickly that cooperation rather than competition was to be the order of the day, the British nevertheless tried to carve out for themselves a special deal with the State Department, even before the Congressional Act was passed, in part because of the urgency of their financial situation, but also because they could not contemplate being treated 'as merely another European country'. For the sake of jointly leading the CEEC, they temporarily swallowed American objections to this outlook and ensured that one of their men, Sir Oliver Franks, would preside over its succeeding efforts.[45] But this was just the beginning.

At the heart of Michael Hogan's great study are the details of how and why the British government fought so tenaciously over the ERP years against the American vision of a structurally reformed Europe, with the United Kingdom at its heart. As generally recognized, Bevin and his Labour colleagues were determined to preserve the status of Britain as a Great Power at the head of a revitalized Commonwealth and Sterling area, pivot—or bridge—of an Atlantic system linking America to Western Europe indirectly. But the lengths gone to in order not to modify imperial preferences, not to be treated on a par with France, Germany, Italy, etc., not to concede authority of any real sort to the OEEC, not to support its later projects for modest regional customs unions, not to alter arrangements in the Sterling area even minimally, not to support Monnet's 1950 plan for a European Coal and Steel Community—measures prompted or encouraged by the Americans with tireless determination and patience—taken together these episodes make up a story with implications for all the following years.[46] The British had no time for the logic of interdependence, least of all institutionalized in a non-elected body located in Paris. It seemed there was no time in London for reflections on the breakdown of the international system between the wars, on changes

---

[45] William C. Cromwell, 'The Marshall Plan, Britain and the Cold War', *Review of International Studies* (October 1982), 238, 242–3.

[46] *The Economist* noted how strange it was that Britain should be as anxious to get the US involved in Europe, as they themselves were to get out of it; Burnet, *America 1843–1993*, 150; the magazine found the Foreign Office's attitude to Europe irrational to the point of being incomprehensible, edition of 12 April 1952; cf. Healey, 'William Clayton', 252, internal Whitehall discussions of integration visions in light of Marshall Plan ibid. 244–50; rejection of American pressure to abolish imperial preferences ibid. p. 255, n. 131.

in the nature of sovereignty, or even on the sources of the Communist challenge.[47]

Yet Britain obviously needed US aid, and Bevin continued as energetically as feasible—in his own fashion—Churchill's old wartime policy of getting the Americans well-embedded in Europe. And the other European powers were no less determined to do likewise, each in its own way. The trick was to avoid surrendering the recognized national priorities and objectives to America's grand design and ideology (especially the free trade version), while recognizing of course that American aid was as generous as it was indispensable, that lessons from the past had to be learned in order to rebuild the international system, and that the new East–West confrontation was very dangerous.[48]

The distinguished Italian diplomat and historian Sergio Romano suggested later that as military sovereignty was abandoned in 1949 with the North Atlantic Treaty, so economic sovereignty had to be defended by West European governments before their national constituencies with whatever means were available. 'Of course we needed an alibi in order to do this... and the alibi was Europe.' Starting to make use of the cause of European unity in this way enabled the OEEC's members to conceal from Washington how little was effectively being conceded to its designs, while hiding from national electorates the depth of their dependence on America.[49] 'The European states wanted only to restore their own economies and to reacquire and strengthen their national sovereignty', said Romano. 'There is no doubt that most European countries would have preferred not to go into any link, political or military, with the United States.' (Nor of course would most Americans have freely chosen the burdens of the ERP and the North Atlantic Treaty.[50])

[47] For a Treasury discussion of the merits and demerits of a West European economic union, docs 24–27, in Sir Richard Clarke, *Anglo-American Economic Collaboration in War and Peace, 1942–1949* (Oxford, 1982), 190–210; cf. Healey, 'William Clayton', 238–9.

[48] For an Austrian reflection on this tension, Seidel, 'Austria's Economic Policy', 276; for Jean Monnet's—after the outbreak of the Korean War—Duchêne, *Jean Monnet*, 228.

[49] The tactic also allowed the Europeans to manipulate the implicit contradiction between the general American commitment to multilateralism, the Bretton Woods institutions and GATT on the one hand, and on the other their specific insistence on a free trade area in Western Europe with discriminating external tariffs; cf. Healey, 'William Clayton', 249–51.

[50] Romano remarks in Ellwood (ed.), *The Marshall Plan Forty Years After: Lessons for the International System Today* (Bologna, 1989), 104–5; cf. Robert Latham, 'Cooperation and Community in Europe: What the Marshall Plan Proposed, NATO Disposed', in Schain (ed.), *Marshall Plan*.

A CASE STUDY: STRUGGLING TO MAKE THE MARSHALL PLAN WORK IN ITALY

Perhaps it was inevitable that a comment such as Romano's should have come from an Italian who was both a diplomat and a historian. Facing the full reality of Italy's weakness in the new international order was not easy for the Italian governments of the time, anxious as they were to understand what levels of power and autonomy might be enjoyed in future by a people whose recent history consisted of defeat, occupation, liberation, and retribution. The discovery that the Cold War would develop inside the nation, as well as all around it, provoked in its early post-war ruling groups the deepest sense of exposure and helplessness.

Even as the Marshall Plan was being prepared, Italy had been the scene of the first great ideological confrontation of the Cold War. For the occasion of the first general election under the new Republican constitution in spring 1948, both of the main Left–Right party blocs obtained heavy backing from their superpower sponsors, and set in motion an unprecedented mobilization of propaganda weapons of every type. Marshall himself declared that should the Left win, the country would be excluded from the benefits of the ERP.[51] Vividly remembered, celebrated, and excoriated to this day, 18 April inaugurated the long era of Christian Democrat rule in Italy, and the country was said to have 'chosen sides' once and for all. Many American observers however were very unhappy with what they witnessed in the election campaign. Journalists such as Howard Smith of CBS denounced their government's alliance with 'social elements...whose aims have nothing to do with democracy'. This comment on the local bourgeoisie was echoed by an Embassy counsellor, Henry Tasca: these people were mostly 'disorganized or disoriented and incapable of realizing their social responsibilities'. They thought only of their own immediate selfish interests, and were capable of any compromise rather than recognizing the need for long-term reform and social modernization.[52]

To avoid continuing dependence on America, and provide a new legitimacy for democracy based on the hope of a better life under its rules, were among the key ambitions of the Marshall Plan in Italy when it finally got under way in the country in June 1948. All too aware that, uniquely in the West, the local Communists were a mass party strong enough to stand a serious chance of coming to power by democratic means, the Plan was accompanied in Italy by a vast propaganda operation, the strongest in any

[51] Miller, *United States and Italy*, 243–9.
[52] Ellwood, '1948 Elections in Italy'.

of the sixteen participating countries. This set out to ensure that every Italian citizen, at every level of society, understood the nature of what it was the Americans were offering, and why.[53]

But there was a delicate problem of hierarchy and sovereignty at the heart of the Marshall Plan presence in such a troubled land. As Howard Jones comments about the Greek case, it was generally assumed that America 'had the leverage to dictate policy [in the country]...because of the aid program'; but whether the Greeks or the Italians carried out the conditions of the programme or not, the aid would still continue, such was the nature and symbolic importance of the American commitment. Hence it was America's 'clients' who determined the use to which the aid was put in the last instance, the result of a learning and negotiating process that was invariably painful for both sides. The 'elasticity of self-denial' was as often as not stretched to breaking point.[54]

The Plan in Italy was carried out in an atmosphere of latent civil war. The tumultuous elections of April 1948 had been followed by an attempt on the Communist leader Palmiro Togliatti's life in July, and an insurrectionary reaction by his followers that brought democracy to the brink. With two million surplus workers left over from Fascism's wasteful industrialization, and as many more left to choose between destitution or emigration, intense social battles went on in the cities, the countryside, the north, and the south, putting immediate pressure on governments as well as on the leadership of the Communist–Socialist opposition. As a fully paid-up member of the Cominform, the Communist Party's official line was militantly anti-ERP. A 1949 pamphlet entitled *The Marshall Plan and the Communists*, written for a wide party readership, compared the world hierarchy implied in America's designs with the benefits of egalitarian

---

[53] Cf. Ellwood, 'Italian Modernisation and the Propaganda of the Marshall Plan', in Luciano Cheles and Luciano Sponza (eds), *The Art of Persuasion: Political Communication in Italy from 1945 to the 1990s* (Manchester, 2001); on radio propaganda, Simona Tobia, 'Advertising America: VOA and Italy', in Tobia (ed.), *Cold War History*, Special Issue, 'Europe Americanized?' (February 2011); Sallie Pisani however insists that in the high-level US government strategic view of the world, Italy was not a particularly significant place, except as a location for military bases, and that there was little hope of changing minds or mentalities there, *CIA and the Marshall Plan*, ch. 6.

[54] H. Jones, 'New Kind of War', 73, Miller, *United States and the Making of Modern Greece*, 24–9. In the Italian case, more perhaps than in any other, this process has been explored in detail by today's scholars, going beyond the old fixations with its Cold War origins or its economic outcomes, to focus on the evolving political confrontation with American power that the Marshall Plan produced; cf. Chiarella Esposito, *America's Feeble Weapon: Funding the Marshall Plan in France and Italy, 1948–1950* (Westport, Conn., 1994); Carlo Spagnolo, *La stabilizzazione incompiuta: Il piano Marshall in Italia (1947–1952)* (Rome, 2001); Mauro Campus, *L'Italia, gli Stati Uniti e il piano Marshall, 1947–1951* (Rome, 2008); Francesca Fauri, *Il piano Marshall e l'Italia* (Bologna, 2010).

participation in the 'Assistance Committee' run under the auspices of the Soviet Union and its allies. With the North Atlantic Treaty confirming the warlike nature of true US intentions, said the Party, the whole scheme could now be seen in its malevolent entirety, promising 'misery and hunger for the workers'.[55]

But as a senior Marshall Plan administrator in Italy, Vince Barnett, later recalled, 'what the Communists preached was one thing, what they practiced was something else.' This strange party, whose members remained like the rest of the population overwhelmingly Catholic, gathered the votes of the masses because it was the one that credibly stood for change, said Barnett, the only force offering serious opposition to the complacency and corruption of the dominant forces.[56] So there was serious practical interest in the Marshall Plan at various levels of the party beyond its official core. The Party's economists tried to predict the positive as well as the negative results of the Plan, and took part in a rather sophisticated debate on its meaning which included government experts.[57] More striking was the welcome the Plan received when it arrived in the Party's showcase city, Bologna, heart of the Communist-dominated Emilia-Romagna region in the north-east. An ERP documentary film of early 1950 on the propaganda campaign nationwide remarked that Bologna had given the greatest welcome yet seen to the ERP exhibits and movies, and there were images of the respected mayor of Bologna, Giuseppe Dozza, walking round the town centre with the Rome Mission Chief, David Zellerbach. At the formal reception in the Town Hall, Dozza surprised his guests by suggesting that only if the Left's 'social innovations' were accepted did the Marshall Plan have a real chance of success.[58]

Faced with this weight of challenge from the Communists, the transient coalitions in charge in Rome looked to the Marshall Plan for aid that would bring visible benefits as fast as possible, the kind the Soviet Union could never supply. They demanded food, coal, raw materials for factories, and they wanted cash. They also sought as free a hand in making use of these resources as they could possibly squeeze out of the ERP/OEEC machinery.

---

[55] Italian Communist Party (PCI), *Il Piano Marshall e i comunisti*, pamphlet in series 'Problemi economici' (Rome, 1949).

[56] Video interview with Vince Barnett, August 1993, carried out by Linda and Eric Christenson, Washington DC.

[57] Ellwood, 'Limits of Americanisation', 150–1, 155.

[58] Ibid. 160–1, documentary film 'Talking to the Italians', ECA (n.d. [early 1950]), conserved in National Archives, Washington DC; the ERP's limited contributions to Emilia-Romagna's progress were recorded in another documentary: 'Emilia' (n.d. [1950]); discussion in Ellwood, 'Limits of Americanisation', 161–2.

In this way the stage was set for a protracted struggle between the ECA and the Italian State that coloured the entire Marshall Plan experience in the country. There was indeed little compatibility between the logic of the intricate political manoeuvres the Christian Democrat leader De Gasperi carried on to keep his party and his coalitions together, and the demands for radical change to boost economic progress emanating constantly from the Mission and ECA. In particular the Christian Democrats and the country contained a right wing that was nationalist and yet anti-State, terrified of the class war yet anti-welfare, anti-social concessions, essentially anti-democratic. This was a Right that had only partially digested the meaning of Italy's defeat in the war, and thought that suppressing inflation should take precedence over the nation's encounter with popular democracy. Even those who could contemplate these developments, such as the distinguished economist at the head of the Bank of Italy, Luigi Einaudi, were rigorous liberals of the nineteenth-century type, who believed in accumulated savings as the only possible source for sound investment and sound money. The Einaudi school thought the entire ERP an unnecessary interference with natural markets and national sovereignty. They deplored the Counterpart Funds in particular as a shabby form of disguised taxation, harmfully increasing the power of the State in the economy.[59]

The clash of policies that ensued has been described in detail elsewhere. At its most intense it led to overt, official criticisms by ECA and the Rome Mission of the incapacity—even unwillingness—of De Gasperi's governments to take on their full Marshall Plan responsibilities, and a temporary suspension of aid in 1949, followed by a reduction in 1950.[60] Land reform was the classic case of these conflicts. By succeeding in creating a distinction between agricultural modernization and the reform of land holding, the Italian authorities managed to provoke splits in the local ERP administration that seriously hampered its effectiveness. The Christian Democrats in Rome knew that land reform was indispensable, but dreaded the reactions of the small landowning class in the south, even more than they feared the occupations and uprisings of thousands of peasants. At every turn the Rome authorities felt the need to organize forms of cultural protectionism against the influence of the outsiders, whose basic instinct to

[59] Spagnolo, *La stabilizzazione incompiuta*, ch. 4; Einaudi's view best expressed in 'Un scritto inedito: Sul cosidetto fondo lire', ed. P. Ciocca and E. Tuccimei, in *Annali della Fondazione Luigi Einaudi*, xxv (1991). This essay makes no reference whatsoever to the Cold War social and international context in which the Marshall Plan worked. Einaudi was also Treasury Minster at the time, and went on to become the first President of the Italian Republic.
[60] Miller, *United States and Italy*, 249–53; Pisani, *CIA and the Marshall Plan*, 109–10; Spagnolo, *La stabilizzazione incompiuta*, ch. 5.

introduce market mechanisms into agriculture, as elsewhere, was rejected by everyone. So the only leverage the US possessed came with the money it brought. In a time of systematic deflation, American resources were thought to be the only means available to pay off the injured parties in the process of change.[61]

Southern Italy was too difficult for the Marshall Plan, as it would be for most of the succeeding national and supernational efforts on its behalf. Yet, as elsewhere, a longer-term perspective reveals the gradual emergence of a distorted but enduring development pattern in Italy in these years. The emphasis in Marshall imports shifted from 'maccheroni' (i.e. grain and food) to 'macchinari' (machine tools), and the beneficiaries were not only pro-ERP firms like Fiat and the steel industry, but electricity generators, and the oil and chemical sectors. Renewed pressure from late 1949 on brought concrete initiatives for land reform and southern development, both supported controversially by Counterpart funds and the ERP. When the new Southern Development Fund was launched in 1950, de Gasperi made explicit reference to the New Deal's Tennessee Valley Authority as an inspiration. In the final accounting, Italy would turn out to be the third largest recipient of ERP support, after Great Britain and France.[62] But the forced encounter of cultures and mentalities that the experience witnessed says much about the politics of modernization in Italy and elsewhere in the era of the Marshall Plan.

The key question in the country, according to a *New York Times* correspondent, Michael L. Hoffmann, writing from Rome in June 1949, was not the defeat of communism. It was instead whether the country could develop its own authentic, viable form of capitalism. A real capitalistic mentality, unafraid of risks, enthusiastically in favour of individual initiative, was 'as rare in Italy as a communist on Wall St.', according to Hoffman's sources. The market was divided horizontally, a huge gap separating the luxury level from that of the workers and peasants:

> Italian industrialists have never shown much interest in the job of adapting their products to the mass market, with the result that the scale of their operations remains small and their costs high. The idea of persuading the low income consumer to feel the need for something he's never had, using

---

[61] This paragraph is based on Emanuele Bernardi, *La riforma agraria in Italia e gli Stati Uniti: Guerra fredda, Piano Marshall e interventi per il Mezzogiorno negli anni del centrismo degasperiano* (Bologna, 2006); full discussion in the *International History Review* (June 2007), 428–30.

[62] V. Zamagni, *Dalla periferia al centro: La seconda rinascita economica dell'Italia, 1861–1990* (Bologna, 1990), 415–27; Spagnolo, *La stabilizzazione incompiuta*, 255–8; Italy received a total of $1.575 billion in grants and loans; for context Ellwood, 'Limits of Americanisation', 153–4.

advertising, and then to give it to him at a price he can afford, could be the Marshall Plan's biggest contribution to Italy—if it gets anywhere.

Italian conservatives were far too inclined to use force to hold communism down, Hoffmann insisted, instead of trying the remedy of mass consumption and mass production. Italian industrialists rigged the feeble market there was and encouraged the unemployed to emigrate. If this mentality could be changed, Marshall Plan administrators expected other obstacles such as high interest rates and the obsession with frugality to disappear as a consequence, Michael Hoffmann reported.[63]

Two and a half years after the start of the ERP in Italy, the Mission head Mike Dayton told a businessmen's gathering in Genoa that industrial leaders in the country were even more wayward than the national government in their attitude to the great project, and accused them of paying lip service only 'to the need for raising the standard of living and to the basic principles of low cost and high production... of all the firms in Italy, you can count those who practice these precepts on the fingers of your two hands'. Economic leadership stood for more than conniving, cartelizing, monopolizing, and controlling for the profit of the few. It meant giving to the 'little men and women who are the backbone of the country, something to justify their support of democracy'. Then in a rhetorical flourish deliberately calculated to shock, the exasperated American asked:

> Gentlemen, is there anyone here who believes that half-measures, half-cooperation and timid support of a plan to vitalise democracy, can win anything except the privilege of hanging from the arcade of a filling station, should we lose?

This unseemly reference to Benito Mussolini's fate in April 1945 got Dayton into much trouble.[64]

But it was specifically at the head of the principal industrialists association, in the formidable and influential figure of Angelo Costa, that the ERP men found one of their most unpersuadable adversaries. Exasperated by the ceaseless preaching and pressuring of the Marshall Planners, which increased visibly after the Korean outbreak, Costa accused them of understanding little or nothing of the context in which they were operating. The Genovese shipping magnate explained that to begin with, unlike

---

[63] *New York Times*, 3 June 1949.

[64] Speech of 19 October 1950, to American Chamber of Commerce for Italy, Genoa Branch, in National Archives, Record group 286, OSR 824, Central Secretariat Permanent Country Subject Files, 'Italy 1951' sub-file. Carlo Spagnolo points out that the speech embarrassed De Gasperi and probably played into the hands of the Right, *La stabilizzazione incompiuta*, 282.

those of the American constitution, the institutions of the Italian State did not rest on a firm foundation of historical legitimacy. Instead the laws of Rome were regarded as a form of legalized robbery, and as such were systematically evaded. As for the economic planning demanded by the ERP, with targets for investments, GNP, imports, etc., this could only cause damage and in fact the country had already recovered from the war without any of such devices.

Costa was implicitly opposed to the spread of large-scale industry and urbanization, and now expressed all his scepticism concerning the culture of productivity and high wages. No matter how cheap synthetic fibres became, he insisted, Italian women would always prefer clothes made in the home with natural materials; tinned food might be sold very cheaply, but Italian traditions of cooking would always be preferred. Small firms and traditional artisan skills would be central to Italy's future just as they had been in the past. As for the concept of productivity, it ignored the basic difference between Italy and America: there capital was cheap, labour expensive; at home the situation was the opposite.[65]

Costa was a practicing Catholic and the Church of Rome provided yet another source of difficulty. The Vatican was quite clear that militant communism in all its forms was enemy no. 1, and had demonstrated its fervour in this belief with its all-out effort in the 1948 elections and with an anathema pronounced against Marxist-inspired political parties and their members in 1949. Yet the Vatican refused to embrace America in an unrestricted alliance against the forces of evil. Diplomatic efforts to set in motion a sort of Holy War were checked for various reasons (including Congress's refusal to include Spain in the ERP).[66] But more serious were the doubts about US values and lifestyles that, dating back to the end of the nineteenth century, now took on more urgent form. Like conservative thinkers in the 1930s, Pio XII was inclined to see common defects in Soviet communism and Americanism: an obsession with material output, technical progress, and consumption, a standard of life defined economically. But only in America were individualism and secularization so openly proclaimed and encouraged, only there was licentiousness commercialized and godlessness so flaunted. That was why the mass media held such awful responsibilities, as the Pope had reminded a group of Hollywood producers in 1946.[67]

---

[65] Ellwood, *Rebuilding Europe*, 196.

[66] E. Di Nolfo, *Vaticano e Stati Uniti*, 552–73.

[67] On Vatican and west, P. Scoppola, *La repubblica dei partiti: Profilo storico della democrazia in Italia, 1945–1990* (Bologna, 1991), 155; on Papal audience of Hollywood producers' group, Ellwood (ed.), 'Il Rapporto Harmon (Rapporto di un gruppo di dirigenti dell'industria cinematografica americana, 1945)', *Mezzosecolo*, 3 (Turin, 1982).

The Vatican made its own efforts to come to terms with the revolutions of modern democracy—Pius XII was the first to use openly the word 'progress'—and had no doubts of the short-term benefits of American aid in all its forms. But while the Vatican and Christian Democrat politicians everywhere were encouraging the emergence of a strong state that was socially oriented and unmistakably national, Marshall Plan propaganda insisted on purveying a vision of life that was private, economically based, and thought to meet universal material aspirations. Only after years of frustration did the Marshall Plan eventually make a serious effort to face up to this profound difference of needs and hopes.[68]

FAITH IN THE FUTURE AS FAITH IN CONSUMPTION

What the Americans in Europe in the late 1940s considered the heart of the matter, the great wager they made in bringing confidence and faith in the future back to the Old World, was that given the chance and the choice, ordinary Europeans wanted what ordinary Americans—supposedly—already possessed. Or at the very least they aspired to similar lifestyles, social opportunities, and getting and spending patterns. Frustrating these legitimate desires, said this point of view, betrayed the fundamental promise of the mass-production system acting in an age of mass democracy. Now that democracy had triumphed in the war, and had even been materially extended in countries where women had finally been given the vote, ruling groups who wished to re-establish their basic legitimacy could no longer put off the encounter with the obvious popular desire for a higher standard of living. So the old New Deal conviction that full bellies and steady jobs cut the roots of political extremism had evolved. By 1949 one version took the form of President Truman's Point Four programme, which combined memories of the TVA and the fruits of the Marshall Plan experience into a vision of permanent, official American action across the world in favour of development. The Cold War of the 1950s and 1960s would see its fullest evolution.[69]

Another line of thought, specifically applicable to Europe, was expressed by the young Chicago historian W. H. McNeill when he saw the Marshall Plan arrive in Greece:

[68] Doc. cit. in Ellwood, *Rebuilding Europe*, 165–6.
[69] Ekbladh, *Great American Mission*, 97–102, 111–13.

If economic conditions could be so improved that every Greek was able to live as well as he had been brought up to expect, it seems probable that the excessive concern and fanaticism which the people now manifest for political parties and programs would diminish.

The mental, cognitive dimension of the aid challenge was therefore at least as significant as the material one, and the shift from relief to structural change and modernization would take place in individual minds as well as in the farms, factories, shops, offices, and government departments. McNeill continues:

> Circumstances might then be propitious, for the gradual emergence of a community of ideas that would embrace almost the whole population, and permit genuine democratic government to be established. Economic prosperity could not guarantee stable and popular government, but it would certainly make its achievement more probable.[70]

When, shortly after the start of the Korean war, one of the ECA's deputy administrators, Harlan Cleveland, launched the phrase 'the revolution of rising expectations' on its distinguished international career, he explained what he had in mind in one of the most important speeches ECA ever produced. The 'basic wants of modern man' was the theme of Cleveland's discourse, and he provided a list of them. These were no longer the simple Four Freedoms of Rooseveltian memory, but the four senses of belonging and identity in modern society. They were, explained Cleveland: a sense of security, a sense of achievement, a sense of equity, and a sense of participation. Modern ideas of democracy, coupled with the revolutions in science and technology, had brought an atmosphere of constant change, of dynamic growth to every individual's and every society's sense of its own worth. The result was that an expanding economy and a rising standard of living were now believed to be achievable by both 'the Chinese peasant and the French worker'. But the decisive fact of America's role in these processes was that it had convinced working people everywhere that they had a *legitimate right of access* to these benefits of modern Western development.[71]

---

[70] McNeill, *Greek Dilemma*, 223–4; McNeill kept reflecting on his Greek experience throughout his long and distinguished career; a 2005 commentary in 'Afterword: World History and Globalization', in A. G. Hopkins (ed.), *Global History: Interactions Between the Universal and the Local* (London, 2006), 287–8.

[71] 'Reflections on the "Revolution of Rising Expectations"', cit. A letter to Cleveland of August 1950 from Paul Hoffman, called it 'one of the best addresses I have ever read on the work of the ECA', ibid.

So the Marshall Plan in Europe was never just an abstract affair of economic numbers: loans, grants, production, productivity, integration, etc., even if these were its key operating tools. Nor was it merely another weapon in America's Cold War anti-Communist crusade. With its mass information campaign, the ERP effort aimed to get as close as possible to the people it was benefitting, at all levels of society, and particularly in the relations between the citizen and the state. The challenge was to channel attitudes, mentalities, and expectations in the direction Americans understood as democratic progress: ever wider access to the opportunities of material satisfaction. Based on this conviction, the Marshall Plan evolved into a complete model of investment, production, and consumption. Because it provided the means, productivity would eventually emerge as the key concept for getting results. Ever more efficient and cheaper production would be managed scientifically by forward-looking industrialists, and guided on rational economic lines by the State. This would transform the ancient battle between reactionary capitalists and revolutionary workers into a constructive, dynamic relationship, uniting enlightened producers and contented consumers. *Growth* would resolve all the difficulties, overcome all the challenges, just as in America.[72]

Pointing out that the word 'growth' appeared first in its contemporary guise within Truman's Council of Economic Advisers in 1949, the historian Charles Maier calls this epochal development, 'the politics of productivity'. It was expressed in more prosaic terms at the time by one of the directors of the ERP field headquarters in Paris: 'What the European worker wants first of all', he wrote, was 'a promise of a larger stake in his country's economy—enough income to enjoy better food, a new suit, a picnic or the movies, less cramped living quarters, a chance to retire when he is old'.[73] Beyond anti-communism, beyond the figures

---

[72] In a cautionary reading of Marshall Plan information culture in all its forms, Victoria de Grazia warns that the Marshall Planners were dead set against putting 'the cart of consumption...before the horse of productivity', and suggests that Marshall Plan films in particular offered a distinctly restrained and restraining view of the promises of the American model of production and consumption. But as the Paul Hoffman message (cit. n.74 below) and many others suggest, the promise of rewards to come was very explicit, *as long as* Europeans worked hard to meet the demands of the model; the 'yes you can' message was always a conditional one; de Grazia, 'Visualizing the Marshall Plan: The Pleasures of American Consumer Democracy or the Pains of "the Greatest Structural Adjustment Program in History"?', in Bischof and Stiefel (eds), *Images of the Marshall Plan*; quote at p. 27.

[73] Charles S. Maier, ' "The Politics of Productivity": Foundation of American International Foreign Economic Policy after World War II', in Peter J. Katzenstein (ed.), *Between Power and Plenty: Foreign Economic Policies of Advanced Industrial States* (Madison, 1978); memo from Henry S. Reuss to A. Friendly, 25 February 1949, in National Archives, Record Group 286, OSR Information Division, Office of Director, 'Publicity and Information 1949' sub-file.

on production and trade, beyond even the vision of a new era of European cooperation, this was the promise of the Marshall Plan in its heyday, and it was the task of its great propaganda drive to bring that promise home to Europeans everywhere. In his memoirs, Administrator Hoffman wrote:

> They learned that this is the land of full shelves and bulging shops, made possible by high productivity and good wages, and that its prosperity may be emulated elsewhere by those who will work towards it.[74]

THE CLASH OF CIVILIZATIONS

Historians down to today have documented in some detail the various forms of resistance the Marshall Planners encountered in their daily efforts to bring the participating countries up to these standards. All the elements of the ERP's New Deal for Western Europe met political and economic barriers of every sort in the short term, but there were varieties of cultural opposition on display from the top to the bottom of Europe that revealed too some of the profounder difficulties in reaching minds and hearts.[75]

Danish farmers refused to contemplate any form of Danish industrialization as a threat not only to their own political power but as a danger to their status and the nation's identity.[76] In Britain the productivity message of standardization failed to function partly because managers refused to support a State-run British Standards Institute, while for trade unions the prospect of more mechanization and productivity found very few takers. In Sweden management and unions in the engineering sector for long refused to contemplate the introduction of time-and-motion systems as proposed by American efficiency experts, preferring their own consensus

---

[74] Paul G. Hoffman, *Peace Can Be Won*, 53; on propaganda drive, see below, p. 36, *passim*.

[75] Cf. Hogan, *Marshall Plan*, 444–5, Milward, *Reconstruction*, 92, 114–20; an extreme example perhaps was that of Norway, where by March 1950 the Finance Minister was reported to be 'extremely disturbed, angry and generally disgusted at the whole business'. He pointed out that the American 'fetish' of trade liberalization in Europe, for instance, bore no relation to the continuing protectionism of most American industry and business; Helge Pharo, 'Norway, the United States and the Marshall Plan, 1947–52', in OECD, *Explorations*, 79.

[76] Viebeke Sorensen, *Social Democratic Government in Denmark under the Marshall Plan, 1947–1950*, PhD thesis, European University Institute (Florence, 1987); cf. Leon Dalgas Jensen, 'Denmark', in Labohm (ed.), *Fiftieth Anniversary*, 21–4.

model. In Norway regional and cooperative networks used the national State, as elsewhere, to defend themselves against the American push for large-scale industry.[77] The Austrians refused point blank to reform their railways and their banking system as the Americans desired, and ignored suggestions that they abolish 'the institutions and organization upon which the Austrian system of social partnership was based', in the words of an expert local witness. The Greeks refused currency conversion because the majority believed in gold sovereigns as the only truly reliable form of monetary exchange.[78]

Later the ECA veterans would acknowledge that they had learned amusing lessons in life along the way. A Paris administrator, Everett Bellows, recalled how...

> ...one of my textile manufacturing experts came into my office, completely bewildered. 'What's the problem?', I asked. He told me that he recently spoken to a manufacturer in Lyons. He had asked the French patron, 'Wouldn't you like to make more money?', and the answer came back, 'No. Not particularly.' 'So what do I do now?', was this expert's question. In another incident a British executive was asked, 'Wouldn't you like to see more competition in England?' His answer was, 'On the whole, no.'[79]

Ireland, at the time refusing GATT, the World Bank, and the North Atlantic Treaty, was also the kind of country that, because of the role of the Catholic Church, linked the arrival of the Marshall Plan to all the other varieties of American challenge on display, particularly the Hollywood film.[80] The Prime Minister was still De Valera, last seen in 1943 recommending to his countrymen the joys of frugal comfort and humble peasant spirituality. Although there were protagonists of the Irish political scene, such as the internationally minded foreign minister Sean MacBride,

[77] Kipping and Bjarnar (eds), *Americanisation of European Business*, chs 6 7 8; on Britain, Nick Tiratsoo, 'Limits of Americanisation: The US Productivity Gospel in Britain', in Becky Conekin, Frank Mort, and Chris Waters (eds), *Moments of Modernity: Reconstructing Britain, 1945–1964* (London, 1999), 96–113, David Kynaston, *Austerity Britain, 1945–51* (London, 2008), 467. Kynaston reports how (like the *Daily Mail* in the 1920s), the *Daily Mirror* in the late 1940s took up the American industrial example and attempted to convert readers to its lessons.

[78] On Austria, Seidel, 'Austria's Economic Policy', 276, 278–9; details of the Greek gold panic in James C. Warren, 'Origins of the "Greek Economic Miracle": The Truman Doctrine and Marshall Plan Development and Stabilization Programs', in Eugene T. Rossides (ed.), *The Truman Doctrine of Aid to Greece: A Fifty Year Retrospective* (New York and Washington DC, 1998), 88–98.

[79] Menges (ed.), *Marshall Plan*, 23.

[80] Bernadette Whelan, *Ireland and the Marshall Plan, 1947–57* (Dublin, 2000), ch. 9; Inglis, *Global Ireland*, 144–6.

who understood the development potential of the ERP and sought to increase the scarce weight of Ireland in European councils,[81] an undercurrent of scepticism was detectable on many sides.

The Irish government and its officials 'were not particularly enthusiastic about the Marshall Plan as such', writes the historian Brian Girvin. The Finance Ministry in particular, deeply in thrall to the Treasury in London, echoed much conservative economic thinking in Europe when it stated that Counterpart additions to the money supply would simply weaken the will of private investors and cause inflation.[82] Even the Dublin Mission's elementary efforts to help the Republic earn dollars by boosting tourism ran into disbelievers. If the standards were to be those of the US hotel industry, there was little or no will to reach them in these years among Irish hoteliers or in the government. The national tourist board had been dissolved, and was only restored under pressure from the Mission. There was also a feeling that tourists might bring different tastes and awkward demands, perhaps flout the Church-inspired restrictions on drinking and socializing. 'If we are going to cater for tourists... and if we are prepared to stoop to such a low level it will be a bad day for our country', said a Labour party member in a 1952 debate.[83]

So it was perhaps not surprising that a man like Professor Stanford, holder of the chair of classics at Trinity College, Dublin, should propose to the Council of Europe in 1951 that its members should close their cultural institutions to American tourists for a day 'to demonstrate our distrust of American values'. Here was a man indignant that the Council

[81] *Ireland's Economy: Radio Eireann talks on Ireland's part in the Marshall Plan, (March–April 1949)* (Dublin, n.d. [1949]). This pamphlet contains three talks by MacBride, four by ECA representatives in Ireland. I am grateful to Bernadette Whelan for bringing it to my attention.

[82] Brian Girvin, 'Ireland and the Marshall Plan: A Cargo Cult in the North Atlantic?', inOECD, *Explorations*, 64; Whelan, *Ireland and the Marshall Plan*, 249–50; Ireland received only loans and almost no grants under the ERP, as a result of Congressional doubt about its war record, and the ECA's distaste at Irish attempts to use it to garner American support on the partition question. Irish officials pressed for Counterpart to be used exclusively to pay off the ERP loans. But this approach was disputed by political leaders, and some development work was started; Girvin, 'Ireland and the Marshall Plan', 68.

[83] Whelan, *Ireland and the Marshall Plan*, 340. How very different were attitudes in another Catholic country, Austria, where ERP funds made a 'decisive' contribution to the massive relaunch and modernization of the tourist industry in these years, says Günter Bischof. However the bulk of customers was from West Germany, not the US; details in Bischof, '"Conquering the Foreigner": The Marshall Plan and the Revival of Postwar Austrian Tourism', in Bischof, Pelinka, and Stiefel (eds), *Contemporary Austrian Studies*, viii; the ERP's educational efforts contributed significantly to the revival of the French tourist industry, suggests McKenzie, and it became one of the first to show how American methods could be used to strengthen the nation's identity and presence on the world tourist market, *Remaking France*, ch. 3.

itself showed signs of Americanization, having provided recent American guests with lists of economic statistics instead of 'lists of newly built churches and art galleries and newly written poetry and songs'.[84] But a contemporary of Professor Stanford's, the municipal engineer of the city of Cork, offered a more balanced expression of the cultural scepticism so common at the time:

> Europeans had a cord running through the tradition of their culture...a nostalgia of the past. Because of it they could never ungrudgingly admire the present, whether their own achievements or those of the great continent across the water....In the Marshall Plan, America showed they had the vision which Europe needed and they also had the wealth and power to help Europe....Speaking as an Irishman...his nationality was so rugged and robust that it could not be overthrown, undermined or peacefully penetrated in any way whatsoever.[85]

This comment followed on from a public effort by the ECA Chief in Ireland, Paul Miller, to convince his beneficiaries that the purpose of the Plan was not to 'Americanize Ireland'. But the Irish would indeed be required to understand that life and liberty outside the Soviet orbit meant embracing the free-enterprise system, said Miller, a system that worked only when every economy played its part, providing its citizens with 'the necessities of life and [maintaining] a standard of living somewhat in terms of what people aspire to in this day and age'.[86]

ADAPTING THE MARSHALL PLAN TO EUROPEAN REALITY: THE PROPAGANDA FRONT AFTER 1949

From the very beginning the ECA planners had been aware that to tackle the many obstacles of understanding that their efforts were likely to encounter in countries such as Ireland, they would have to go over the heads of the local governing classes and speak directly to the mass of the populace. Ambitious in its aims from the beginning, the ERP 'Information Program' had evolved by the end of 1949 into the largest propaganda operation directed by one country to a group of others ever seen in peacetime.[87]

---

[84] Whelan, *Ireland and the Marshall Plan*, 341.
[85] Ibid. 393.
[86] Ibid. 392.
[87] The key countries were considered to be France, the Anglo-American Bizone in Germany and Italy. A second band contained Greece, Turkey, Austria, and the French Zone of Germany. A third included the UK (where the campaign acknowledged the sovereignty of the government's efforts), and Sweden. The fourth band comprised the remaining nations.

There is no mystery about the operating principles that the information staff (mainly journalists and broadcasters, *not* advertisers or public relations people), applied in their campaign. They were arrived at fairly quickly and changed little up to the outbreak of the Korean War. A January 1950 report by the information director in Rome explained:

> Carry the message of the Marshall Plan to the people. Carry it to them directly—it won't permeate down. And give it to them so that they can understand it.

The basic thrust then was for a truly mass programme using 'every method possible... to reach Giuseppe in the factory or Giovanni in the fields', or as the Paris office put it, 'slugging it out way down among the masses'. More specifically ERP Information divisions were expected to increase the sense of national identification and participation in the Plan, and to direct special attention to key target groups, particularly trade unionists, agricultural workers, housewives—as managers of the 'economics of the household'—and executives in business, industry, and the State. They were enjoined to avoid direct confrontation with the massive waves of Communist propaganda directed against the Plan, and remember that— as the State Department put it—'the richness of America is distasteful to many.... In many countries men work harder and live more modestly than Americans...' Above all they were requested to be respectful of every form of local sovereignty, and avoid accusations that ERP sought to impose the US free-enterprise system on the rest of the world.[88]

When applied on the ground these methods proved extremely flexible, and no idea seemed too large or daring for the Information program in its heyday. As long as they were directed at workers, managers, or employers, the key words everywhere were always mass production, scientific management, and above all productivity. In each country there were specialized reviews on the subject, joint committees, trips to inspect American factories, conferences, and eventually, in some places, even 'productivity villages' where model factories and workers' communities could be seen in action.[89] For other groups in society—State employees, teachers, fami-

---

[88] Adapted from Ellwood, 'What Winning Stories Teach: The Marshall Plan and Atlanticism as Enduring Narratives', in Mariano (ed.), *Defining the Atlantic Community*; for operational origins of Marshall Plan information efforts, Cull, *Cold War*, 44–5, State Department quote at ibid. 44.

[89] The Anglo-American Productivity Committee was the showpiece of these efforts, and the heart of the educational campaign in Britain; details in Rhiannon Vickers, *Manipulating Hegemony: State Power, Labour and the Marshall Plan in Britain* (Basingstoke, 2000), ch. 7; for the failure of its efforts to alter 'the pathologies of British management', Jim Tomlinson and Nick Tiratsoo, 'Americanisation Beyond the Mass Production Paradigm: The Case of British Industry', in Kipping and Bjarnar (eds), *Americanisation of European Business*.

lies, even schoolchildren—the promises were more jobs, higher living standards, peace in Europe through cooperation and trade. With special treatments of these questions for each different communications medium, the Information Program came to think in terms of tens of documentary films, hundreds of radio programmes, thousands of mobile films shows, millions of copies of its pamphlets, and tens of millions of spectators for its exhibitions and films.[90]

It was in this context that West Berlin was transformed into a showcase for Western—especially American—civilization and ideology. Citizens of the West and the East were presented with an ever-increasing variety of experiences 'trumpeting the Marshall Plan's social contract, which conflated democratic freedom with rising private consumption'.[91] East Berliners were used to crossing over the sector divides to buy clothes and food, or see foreign films. In 1950 they and indeed the whole city were invited to the 'George Marshall-Haus', an exhibition and conference centre, which also included a complete American suburban home, with all the fittings. Police had to be called to control the crowds. In 1951 Berliners were treated to the first large-screen displays of television, both black and white and colour, showing live entertainment. Soon after came the latest version of the 'ideal home' concept, a vast display of household design progress revolving round American interpretations of the concept of modernism in the functioning of everyday life. 'Modern design is intended to implement the lives of free individuals', wrote the exhibition's creator. All these events were huge propaganda successes for the Marshall Planners and their sponsors.[92]

The phase of disillusionment

But away from Berlin, the Americans were never to be satisfied with the progress achieved by their great efforts of persuasion and education. The campaign had been set up in part because, as its director Al Friendly—one of America's leading journalists and broadcasters—put it, not only did the Europeans not know about American aid, 'they don't even know

[90] Ellwood, 'What Winning Stories Teach', 112–14; for the experience of the French mission's exhibitions policy, McKenzie, *Remaking France*, ch. 2; comparative studies in Bischof and Stiefel (eds), *Images of the Marshall Plan*.

[91] Greg Castillo, 'Domesticating the Cold War: Household Consumption as Propaganda in Marshall Plan Germany', in Betts and Crowley (eds), *Journal of Contemporary History* (April 2005), Special Issue: 'Domestic Dreamworlds: Notions of Home in Post-1945 Europe', 263.

[92] Cit. ibid. 263, 271 (emphasis in original). The organizers were aware, writes Greg Castillo, that the sophisticated contemporary taste attributed to the average American of the time was not seriously meant to be taken as typical of reality; ibid. 272.

their own countries are cooperating with each other'. Yet the ERP was intended especially to promote European self-help, stimulating cooperation and coordination without outside interference: that was the whole point of the OEEC, in which the US did not sit. Thus a basic tension emerged in the campaign that sometimes worked creatively, often not, especially as this weakness was exploited ceaselessly by the Comintern's aggressive campaign of opposition. The director of the Industrial Division in Holland said pithily: 'the United States was paying the piper and it was always a great problem how loudly we could call the tune.'[93]

The self-evident rightness of the Plan's goals and methods turned out to be harder to project than expected, and gradually awareness spread of the difficulties of applying abstract principles and concepts to complex and often chaotic local situations. The outcome was disappointment with the short-term results, especially when measured in terms of the rise and fall of support for left parties and unions. '[T]he European workman listens listlessly while we tell him we are saving Europe, unconvinced that it *his* Europe we are saving', complained a senior staff member in Paris in September 1949.[94]

In the early days it had not been difficult for the Information Officers to perceive that the working people of Europe were not particularly interested in the Marshall Plan battle against Communism. Even less did they show any faith in the Plan's hope of continent-wide financial stability by 1952, because this in the popular view meant stability for the traditional ruling groups, not for them. Instead, said an expert in the Paris headquarters, 'what the European workman mainly wants, I believe, is a promise of a larger stake in his country's economy—enough income to enjoy better food, a new suit, a picnic or the movies, less cramped quarters, a chance to retire when he is old.'

But by the end of 1949, experience and extensive opinion polling had brought a significant shift in outlook, to the point where the strategists felt obliged to realize that 'the majority of Europeans today' had one overriding concern of their own: *security*. What did they mean by security? It was easy to state: 'employment, health and old-age benefits. It means further that a man's life, when begun, contains the reasonable assurance and expectation of a rational progress towards a reasonable conclusion.'[95] An-

---

[93] Ellwood, *Rebuilding Europe*, 165; McKenzie points out too that the tunes came from various American propaganda agencies—the United States Information Service, Voice of America, State Department, and others—and often competed with each other or worked at cross purposes, *Remaking France*, 38–9.

[94] Ellwood, *Rebuilding Europe*, 165 (emphasis in original document); for parallel, detailed reflections on French situation, McKenzie, *Remaking France*, 207–8.

[95] The French Mission's trade union associates told it that a full employment and retraining promise must be incorporated in any programme aiming to improve productivity, McKenzie, *Remaking France*, 215.

other commentary noted that the concept of higher standards of living was 'rapidly becoming anathematic to Europeans'. But the basic ERP objectives of higher productivity and European 'economic unification' would not be affected in any way, felt the writer, since only by these means could the Europeans in fact achieve the social security they so anxiously sought. In the meantime the Marshall Plan would from this time on have to recognize the legitimacy of welfare capitalism, insisting simply that it be applied, as doctrine and reality, without restriction in all Europe.[96]

Learning from experience?

In spite of this growing awareness in the public relations departments of need for adaptation, other evidence shows that as time went on, the Marshall Plan as economic operation became less and less pluralistic, and tended to ever more explicit direction of European reconstruction and modernization. Even before the Korean emergency, technical assistance for instance was radically overhauled to produce an 'activist thrust' under which Americans would teach and their European peers learn how to perform more effectively on the new frontiers of business and industry.[97] On the ground, power was already shifting to the country missions in putting ever greater pressure on the trade, investment, and monetary policies of their host governments, not least because the OEEC had found aid allocation an 'intolerable burden' and had almost given up trying. It would never become the embryo of a European government, as its American sponsors had originally imagined.[98]

Yet the Marshall Planners were more convinced than ever that Western Europe had no choice but to unite. In August 1949 Harlan Cleveland had deplored the continuing 'economic nationalism' of the ERP's participating nations, and demanded a vast new sweep of integration. If only a European equivalent of the American Interstate Commerce Commission could be built, all trade and payments barriers would be eliminated. Then a single currency and a harmonized banking system might organize a grand unified market.[99] Paul Hoffman endorsed this outlook in a speech to the OEEC of October 1949, billed as no less significant than Marshall's original Harvard address. A single large market governed by new central

[96] Ellwood, *Rebuilding Europe*, 165–6; cf. James Williamson, 'British Socialism and the Marshall Plan', *History Today* (January 2008).
[97] Jacqueline McGlade, 'From Business Reform Programme to Production Drive: The Transformation of US Technical Assistance to Western Europe', in Kipping and Bjarnar (eds), *Americanisation of European Business*, 26–7.
[98] Milward, *Reconstruction*, 180–211.
[99] Doc. cit. in Ellwood, *Rebuilding Europe*, 154.

institutions, as in America, would 'improve [Europe's] competitive position in the world and thus more clearly satisfy the expectations and needs of its people'. Observers were struck by the bluntness and urgency of Hoffman's peroration, which included demands that the OEEC prepare a new liberalizing scheme covering all the key economic policies by early 1950. But the ECA Administrator was looking over his shoulder, as much as he was preaching to the Europeans. With the Cold War entering its most critical phase, Hoffman's operation was simply not getting results fast enough for its paymasters.[100]

After the Korean outbreak in June 1950 the full weight of the militant Cold Warriors and the business protectionists bore down on the ERP. The project was shortened in time and radically transformed, opening the way to the era of general rearmament and 'Mutual Security'.[101] Congressional amendments to the original ERP Act provided $400 million more for a new drive to persuade European employers and workers to 'accept the American definition of the social and economic desirabilities of productivity', but now so that military output could be increased as well as consumer goods.[102] There was no question of a choice between guns and butter, which the Europeans would refuse. While the CIA and the psychological warriors worked to manipulate the world of organized labour according to Cold War priorities, the Marshall Planners tried to make sure unions and workers at every level were included in the relaunched technical assistance and exchange programmes. This now meant teaching that the benefits of new technologies and methods must be shared equally 'amongst the three basic groups—labour, stockholders and consumers', providing in this way, among other benefits, 'one of the underlying solutions to the Communist problem'.[103]

Among the inspirers of the new Congressional drive was Senator William Benton, distinguished founder of the *Encyclopædia Britannica* in America and of the Benton and Bowles advertising agency, a major figure in the

---

[100] Ibid. 158–9; full context explained in Milward, *Reconstruction*, ch. 9, esp. pp. 296–8; Hogan, *Marshall Plan*, 271–9; quote by Secretary of State Dean Acheson on lack of progress in Latham, 'Cooperation and Community', 71.

[101] Covert action was also stepped up significantly, Pisani, *CIA and the Marshall Plan*, 78.

[102] Bent Boel, *The European Productivity Agency and Transatlantic Relations, 1953–1961* (Copenhagen, 2003), 30–5; French experience of this shift described in McKenzie, *Remaking France*, 217–18, 250–1.

[103] Cf. testimony in Menges (ed.), *Marshall Plan*, in particular that of Herbert E. Weiner, Labour Division, ERP Mission to Britain, Ralph L. Trisko, Chairman of the OEEC Coal Committee, and James C. Warren; Anthony Carew, *Labour under the Marshall Plan: The Politics of Productivity and the Marketing of Management Science* (Manchester, 1987), ch. 10; detailed presentation of the difficulties of preaching this form of enlightened capitalism in McKenzie, *Remaking France*, 251–2.

development of United States official communication efforts since World War II. Now a Senator, Benton took to touring the capitals of Europe himself, in order to explain that while *Europeans believed in capital, Americans believed in capitalism,* and showing that the difference was about untrammelled competition, or as a fellow believer in ECA put it, 'overcoming tariff barriers, restrictive trade practices and the other inhibiting forces to trade and a higher standard of living'. Meanwhile the ERP's original director Paul Hoffman resigned in exhaustion, its administration was annexed by the State Department, and the whole thrust of the effort was shifted towards military production and ideological mobilization.[104]

But the propaganda effort remains interesting because it shows how the proponents of the ERP on the ground tried hard to adapt the new policy goals to their recognition that the European search for 'stability, self-confidence and therefore self-respect' depended on their successful recognition of local priorities, in particular the construction of the welfare state regardless of the pressure of the Cold War. The propagandists were by this time under no illusions as to the difficulties they faced. In a top-level analysis of November 1950, it was admitted that doubts persisted in 'much too great a segment of the European population' around the question of...

> ... whether the US policy was aimed at progressive improvement in general living standards or was designed more to shore up economic and social systems which are not popular and to restore to power conservative and reactionary vested interests.

The top Americans in Europe considered they had been 'led down the garden path' in countries such as France and Italy, where their investments showed so few signs of paying social or political dividends. They believed, said a British observer, 'that really strenuous efforts... from the masses cannot be expected unless "social justice" figured as part and parcel' of all future schemes to raise production for defence.[105] In this view the British version of welfare socialism, long regarded with suspicion in Washington, now acquired new prestige because it seemed to provide a third way, a proof that democratic capitalism was capable of providing a functioning alternative to the radical urge for social justice incarnated in the mass of communist voters of countries like France, Italy, and Greece.[106]

---

[104] Ellwood, *Rebuilding Europe*, 181; McGlade, *Remaking France*, 27–8; for the government career of Benton, Cull, *Cold War*, 24–6, 28–40.

[105] Docs cit. in Ellwood, *Rebuilding Europe*, 180; for survey results in France in various periods of the Plan, Roland Cayrol, 'French Public Opinion and the Marshall Plan: The Communists and Others', in Schain (ed.), *Marshall Plan.*

[106] D. C. Watt, 'American Aid to Britain and the Problem of Socialism, 1945–51', in Watt (ed.), *Personalities and Policies: Studies in the Formation of British Foreign Policy in the Twentieth Century* (London, 1965), esp. pp. 76–80.

From summer 1950, the organization of the information campaign changed in response to the recognized need for more effective contact with local reality. In a country like Italy a system of subcontracts began to delegate to local scriptwriters and directors the fabrication of film propaganda material using schemes furnished by the sponsor but translated into the visual and spoken language of the Italian context. In this way the '*Organizzazione Epoca*' was born, set up not to proclaim but to conceal the American origins of its operations. In 'Epoca' films America as such was nowhere to be seen; instead they displayed the Italian achievements of the Plan: new housing projects, efforts to boost agriculture, irrigation schemes, make-work projects of every kind, always collective efforts that would provide employment, security, and implicitly hope of a better life to come for the mass of the population.[107]

In 1952 the Irish mission sponsored a locally produced docudrama entitled *The Promise of Barty O'Brien,* written by the prominent writer Sean O'Faolain and acted by professionals from the Abbey Theatre, Dublin. This striking film makes no effort to hide the conflicts that arise when the propositions of American-style modernity—represented in this case by the electrification of a poor Irish farm—meet the resistance of traditional ways. The farmer's son becomes a technician, thanks to ERP help, but the old man resists until the final proof of the benefits of electric current are—with the turn of a switch—lit up for all to see. Respect is paid to the centrality of agriculture in Ireland's life and prospects, and the difficulties of the country's struggle to reconcile traditional identities with the call of modernity are faced directly.[108]

In contrast the Mission in France never learned how to build up the local production of means of persuasion, much less a demand for them. Bruce McKenzie relates how in 1952 the Mission sponsored the release of *Jour de Peine*, in principle a film homage to the struggle of French factory workers trying to organize a strike for better wages. But the result, it soon emerged, was far from the hopes of the film's producers. The psychological warriors had created a pro-US trade union in France, Force Ouvrière, and the point of the production was to demonstrate that this union was just as effective on the shop floor as its communist rival, the CGT, which was well ahead in strength and militancy in most factories and working-class areas. But the film alienated both unionists and managers, the first group because it ignored the existence of competing unions, the second because it 'unintentionally emphasized the CGT doctrine of striking for any reason or none at all'. Its pro-consen-

---

[107] Ellwood, 'Italian Modernisation', 39–41.
[108] Whelan, *Ireland and the Marshall Plan*, 379–81.

sus ending angered everyone, and there were calls for it to be changed or not shown at all.[109]

The experience confirmed the radical judgements of a French official, J. Constant, in a report to the French Foreign Ministry written in 1952, after months of collaboration on the ground with the information effort. Whether fighting Communism or boosting their vision of democratic progress, the Americans had failed to 'understand and love' the country in which they were called to operate: 'It is indispensable to know its history, traditions, and principles, but even more important and difficult is to sense the beat of its heart.' The result was that their audience was alienated and their enemies provided with free ammunition. The benevolent audacity of the Plan had backfired, because 'the French refuse to admit that without America France would not exist'. The elites were indifferent; working people reacted 'violently'. By Constant's tally, comments Bruce McKenzie, 'three-quarters of the films produced by the ECA were such an insult to French national pride that they could not be shown in France.' ECA films, concluded Constant, 'provoke antipathy and risk creating a climate of enmity that is dangerous to the security of our alliance.'[110]

Fig. 7. French opposition to the Marshall Plan included this satirical view of petrol imports as encouraging unnecessary traffic and congestion.
(AKG Images)

---

[109] McKenzie, *Remaking France*, 235; cf. *Selling Democracy: Films of the Marshall Plan, 1947–1955* (Berlin International Film Festival, 2004), Filmography, p. 4.
[110] McKenzie, *Remaking France*, 59–60.

THE PARADOX OF THE MARSHALL PLAN

Through the thick and thin of the early post-war era, the French and all the other West European states built political and economic systems that were socially oriented, inclusive, and directed towards dealing with the miseries handed down to their peoples from the past. But the messages of the Marshall Plan offered with unequalled energy and invention a quite different prospect, the model of a good society that was private, consumerist, and oriented towards the future. Explicitly they declared: 'prosperity makes you free', implicitly they suggested that only the American way could meet the demands of the 'revolution of rising expectations'. How then to reconcile such vastly differing impulses, in such a context as the early Cold War, where restoring any sort of faith in the coming years seemed so problematical and urgent?

A typical American response was supplied in an April 1951 article in *Foreign Affairs* by one of the ERP's most influential brains, Richard M. Bissell. At the end of a tightly-knit argument about how to reconcile reconstruction and rearmament, Bissell made clear that only structural changes in Europe's economic structure would suffice to restore vigour to its capitalism and hope to its masses. There was renewed emphasis on trade unions, and their potential role in promoting and enjoying the benefits of productivity. There was recognition, if reluctant, that the European-style welfare system was here to stay. There was of course formal acknowledgement that nothing could be imposed, no matter how great the temptation to do so. But in the end, said Bissell, the US could lead only by the force of its example and its powerful appeal across all sections of European society:

> Coca-Cola and Hollywood movies may be regarded as two products of a shallow and crude civilization. But American machinery, American labor relations, and American management and engineering are everywhere respected....What is needed is a peaceful revolution which can incorporate into the European economic system certain established and attractive features of our own, ranging from high volumes to collective bargaining.... (This) will require a profound shift in social attitudes, attuning them to the mid-twentieth century.[111]

---

[111] Richard M. Bissell Jr, 'The Impact of Rearmament on the Free World Economy', *Foreign Affairs* (April 1951), 385–405, cit. at pp. 404–5; these features were less established than Bissell assumed: on the struggle around them at the Ford Motor Company in the context of the early Cold War years, Mark Rupert, *Producing Hegemony*, 165–73.

But many Europeans doubted whether the two impulses of social welfare and American-style economic growth could ever be reconciled. Scottish industrialists, for example, felt that the nation's disastrous housing situation—with 40 per cent of popular housing over seventy years old—was the greatest barrier to the health and morale of their workers, to the development of new plant in new places, and hence to higher productivity.[112] In any case no small country could match the scale or efficiency of the US domestic markets for goods and capital. Although notions such as 'quality control' and 'market research' sounded interesting to Scottish business ears, there was still a need for traditional conceptions of value and craftsmanship, whether a Scotsman made brushes in a time-honoured workshop in the shadow of Edinburgh Castle, or a Scotswoman produced clocks in a new American factory. Yet as the Scottish Council (Development and Industry) ruefully acknowledged at the end of 1952, 'Whether we like it or not, our civilization and standard of living is [*sic*] tied to expanding markets and an expanding economy.'[113]

The editor of *The Economist*, Geoffrey Crowther, told BBC radio listeners in 1950 that Americans paid 'too high a price for their wealth ... [there was] too much competition ... too much personal instability and unhappiness'. And Mass Observation's interviewers found their public as dubious as ever about the transatlantic 'cousins'. They were accused of 'wealthy condescension', of 'sermonizing', of worshipping Mammon and hugeness. Although there was respect for their success and can-do spirit in some voices, more typical was the vicar who said: 'Their strident vitality makes me want to shrink into myself.' As David Kynaston suggests, the Ealing film comedies of the era showed a way to do this.[114]

Leading French observers were no less sceptical. André Siegfried, once more a prominent commentator on transatlantic relations, told the readers of *Foreign Affairs* in 1952 that the American universe of making and

---

[112] On the centrality of housing to post-war social challenges across Europe, and the impact of American wartime propaganda on the subject, Betts and Crowley, 'Introduction', 219–23.

[113] Paragraph based on The Scottish Council (Development and Industry), Annual Reports 1950–1952, its monthly publication *Scotland*, and the annual *Survey of Economic Conditions in Scotland*, published by the Clydesdale and North of Scotland Bank Ltd, 1948–1952. These reveal that Scottish industry was keenly aware of the need for technological innovation and changes in attitudes to management and markets, but was hampered by capital shortages and the weight of Treasury and other controls from London. Although local schemes encouraged IBM, NCR, and other US firms to put down enduring roots in Scotland in these years, the Marshall Plan's only significant contribution was in part-financing BP's Grangemouth refinery, a major facility to this day.

[114] Evidence and Kynaston comments in Kynaston, *Austerity Britain*, 468–9; the last of the Ealing-style comedies, with its vaguely anti-American flavour, is discussed in Chapter 9, n. 163.

getting was unthinkable in the 'established and rigid European system'. Siegfried highlighted all the contrasts that put Western Europe at a disadvantage compared to the United States: 'It can be said truthfully that in Europe technical progress does not necessarily "pay". There are too many people and too few raw materials; the social system is too complicated.'[115] In Rome, in the national Senate, the Bolognese economist Paolo Fortunati, sitting for the Communist party, declared that he 'wanted to make clear... the irrationality of these economic paradises in which *everybody* is supposed to start getting *better and better off* right away'.[116]

Very soon, much sooner than anyone imagined, Europe's development was to prove these voices wrong, their lack of faith in the future out of tune with the popular mood of the times, and their doubts misplaced. They saw all of the immediate limits of the ERP's operations, but they failed to see how it helped legitimize 'the revolution in which the ordinary citizen [demands] that he share in the benefits of industrialism', as an American critic of European scepticism put it, in other words how it turned the revolution of rising expectations into something like a self-fulfilling prophecy.[117]

The paradox of the Marshall Plan is that the closer observers get to the record of the European Recovery Program, the more limited its empirical achievements appear, yet this does nothing to diminish the long-term significance its protagonists and admirers have always insisted on. In strictly economic terms a consensus has been reached by historians that the role of Marshall Aid was marginal, but that this margin was critical.[118] The dollar gap was not closed, and from 1950 on required vast new

---

[115] Siegfried, 'Can Europe Use American Methods?', *Foreign Affairs* (July 1952), cit. in Ellwood, *Rebuilding Europe*, 209; Jacques Tati's film comedy *Jour de Fête* (1949) offers a satirical expression of the same sentiment. A village postman in deepest rural France is 'converted' by visiting American film documentaries into believing that he must become speedy and efficient. His efforts meet ridicule and humiliation, and he regains the way back to happiness only when he stops trying to act 'à l'Americain'. I have discussed this and related films in 'European Cinema's Satire of Americanization 1949 to 1959', in *Selling Democracy: Friendly Persuasion*, Berlin International Film Festival/German Historical Museum (Berlin, 2006).

[116] Cit. in Ellwood, 'Limits of Americanisation', 165 (emphasis in original). It was to overcome this sort of scepticism, and the realities that produced it, that the European Productivity Agency was born, as a branch of the OEEC, in May 1953. Half funded by the US, its specific task was to continue the ERP/Mutual Security productivity campaign, and ensure support for the defence drive at all levels of economic activity; cf. Boel, *European Productivity Agency*.

[117] Quote from Perry Miller, 'The Reimportation of Ideas', in Bertrand Russell et al., *The Impact of America on European Culture* (Boston, 1951), 85; Miller's article was the response of a distinguished American literary critic to a series of essays by English and an Irish writer on the subject of the title.

[118] French judgement in this sense in Duchêne, *Jean Monnet*, 173.

quantities of military dollars for its management. While production generally stood well above the target levels by 1952, consumption standards, wages, and employment rarely did so. Investment had already taken off at the end of the war, and continued at record levels until the 1960s.[119]

The Plan's push for integration produced its greatest achievement in 1950, with the birth of the European Payments Union, a form of virtual central bank. Attached to the OEEC, this short-lived but essential institution would hasten trade and payments liberalization inside Western Europe. As the boom of exports between the West Europeans themselves turned out to be a key feature of the 'economic miracles' of the 1950s, the EPU can be seen as a useful temporary bridge linking the Marshall Plan to the 1957 Treaty of Rome and the birth of the Common Market.[120] In general though none of the European nations were willing to give anything but the smallest concessions to the maximalist demands for integration, even unification, that accompanied the ERP with ever greater stridency as time went on, especially as they invariably included a relaunched German economy of some sort. Indeed in Alan Milward's hypothesis, the limited degree of long-term integration that did eventually emerge, such as Jean Monnet's plan of 1950 for a Coal and Steel Community, in part stemmed from accumulated resistance to American pressures.[121]

Meanwhile every nation had its own distinctive story of adjustment to tell. Economically the Plan mattered far more in Greece, France, Austria, and Holland than it did in Ireland, Norway, or Belgium. For some nations, such as Italy, it was perhaps truly decisive for one year only; for others, such as Denmark, for securing raw materials and energy supplies. For some, such as the German occupation zones, food mattered most; for others, like Italy and Greece, help with rebuilding railways, roads, power supplies, gave the most lasting benefit. In the France of the Monnet Plan industrial investment came first; in Britain the Counterpart Fund was entirely used to pay wartime debts and refloat sterling.

But both Austria and Sweden, each in its own way, believe that their successful anchorage in the West dates back to the Plan. Perhaps Germany

---

[119] Imanuel Wexler, *The Marshall Plan Revisited: The European Recovery Program in Economic Perspective* (Westport, Conn., 1983), 149–50; the most severe debunking is that of Irwin Wall, 'The Marshall Plan and French Politics', in Schain (ed.), *Marshall Plan*.

[120] Monika Dickhaus, '"It is only the provisional that lasts": The European Payments Union', in OECD, *Explorations*.

[121] Milward, *Reconstruction*, 211; this is not to minimize the historical precedents they created in the successful, institutionalized, management of interdependence; cf. Ellwood, *Rebuilding Europe*, 171; detailed account of halting progress to Schuman Plan in Duchêne, *Jean Monnet*, 187–206; later tributes to American far-sightedness on the need for integration cited in Healey, 'William Clayton', 255–6.

was the nation that benefitted most overall, as the dynamic of integration opened by the ERP allowed the new Federal Republic of 1949 to grow in strength and respectability while calming the suspicions of its neighbours. The hoped-for revolution in Franco-German relations did indeed come about. Whatever its other origins in short-term, Cold War necessities, no political development heightened the contrast with the first post-war era more than this one.[122]

As for attitudes, what often struck Europeans at the time—and some Americans—was the sheer utopianism of the ERP, the massive abstractions, illusions, and ideological constructs that characterized so much of the original design. The notion that the European state system could be remade in four years by a new agency in Washington, run by private sector management types, is still as hard to believe today as it was then. Did Hoffman, Cleveland, Bissell, and their colleagues seriously believe that the Europeans would do by 1952 what in reality they eventually succeeded in doing, in rather weaker form, only in 1992, with the Maastricht Treaty?[123] If 'you too can be like us' was the implicit message of the Plan, the Europeans soon learned from their contacts with the Missions, the propaganda, and visits and exchanges to ask: 'or as you imagine yourselves to be?'[124] The historian of contemporary Greece, W. H. McNeill, newly returned to the country in the 1970s, reflected on the limits of what had been done, and decided that no amount of money or bluster could cancel the original sin of 'naively assum[ing] that Greek society was essentially the same as American society, and needed only a few pointers to duplicate the American New Deal'.[125]

And yet who can deny the eventual, long-term success of the Marshall Plan's key exhortations and invitations, its assumption that to 'catch up'

---

[122] Milward, *Reconstruction*, 92–106; Spagnolo, *La stabilizzazione incompiuta*, 280; Bischof, 'Conquering the Foreigner'; papers in Labohm (ed.), *Fiftieth Anniversary*.

[123] But in 1952 the British had forced Washington to recognize that they would never participate in the American unity vision; in 1992 they signed up for the new European Union, albeit reluctantly; cf. Burk, *Old World, New World*, 586–7. Over the intervening period the US had repeatedly pressed the British to join in the European project wholeheartedly; US perspective explained by former US Ambassador to the UK, Raymond Seitz, in his memoir *Over Here* (London, 1998), 307–9, 333–4.

[124] This question lies at the heart of the Spanish film satire of the myth of the Marshall Plan, *Bienvenido Mister Marshall* (Luis G. Berlanga, 1952. Spain was excluded from the Marshall Plan because of the Francoist dictatorship). Here a poor, isolated village dresses up to celebrate the arrival of a US delegation, believed to be bringing promises of money and progress. But the Americans speed through in their cars, ignoring all the locals, who have no choice but to re-embrace their time-honoured values: the land, their work, the village community; discussion in Ellwood, 'European Cinema's Satire', de Grazia, *Irresistible Empire*, 336–8.

[125] McNeill, *The Metamorphosis of Greece since World War II* (Oxford, 1978), 94–5.

with American production and consumption was the only economic policy Europeans should ever seriously apply? Impelled by their reading of history, the challenges of the times, and of course by their own will-to-power, far-sighted elements in the leadership of the United States temporarily chose a massive and complex formal intervention, a quick fix, to inject sustenance into Europe's sickly capitalism lest it give way and the Communist hordes rush in. The technocrats' attempt to modernize institutions and attitudes on what they believed was America's own pattern represented the highest point, the most explicit one, in that twentieth-century trend that superimposed America's model of modernization on whatever efforts European societies were making to meet the challenges of the three modernities of 1920: mass democracy, mass production, mass communication. Every participating nation in the Marshall Plan showed examples of how this reformism was blunted, how difficult it was to manage interdependence when the American and the West European sides believed in such different ideas of the road to the future. But on one point all the players were united: if only Europe could grow economically with the American way or some local variation of it, everything might be possible. And when the Old World's great boom did indeed finally arrive after 1954, 'catch-up growth' would turn out to be the great force driving it onwards and upwards.[126]

---

[126] N. F. R. Crafts, 'The Golden Age of Economic Growth in Postwar Europe, 1950–1973', *Economic History Review* (August 1995), 445.

9

The 1950s: Going for Growth

MEETING THE DEMAND, FULFILLING THE EXPECTATIONS

In 1960 the OEEC, the Organization for European Economic Cooperation, the agency set up in 1948 to organize the European response to the
Marshall Plan, was refounded under the combined inspiration of Jean
Monnet and his friends in Washington. With the US and Canada now
entering as full members, it became the OECD, the Organization for
Economic Cooperation and Development. Article 1 of its founding convention states the agency's purpose as:

> to achieve the highest sustainable economic growth and employment and a
> rising standard of living in Member countries, while maintaining financial
> stability, and thus to contribute to the development of the world economy.

Ten years earlier almost all of these objectives would have been familiar to
European statesmen and their advisers. Robert Marjolin, first Secretary
General of the OEEC, talked in his memoirs about 'we of the "growth"
generation'.[1] Responding to critics in the French parliament in 1949, Jean
Monnet had supplied 'a new economic analysis':

> We are in a world undergoing a total transformation. You can no longer
> think of the future in the context of the past. We Europeans are still haunted
> by past notions of security and stability. Today the principle idea is that of
> expansion. That is what is happening in the United States. They are always
> ready to evolve and search out progress.

So the Frenchman should take on 'the psychology of an American...the
disposition to change constantly'.[2] But the arrival from America of the

---

[1] Marjolin, *Architect of European Unity*, 185.

[2] Cit. in Kuisel, *Capitalism and the State*, 244; the long effort to educate French people
to the idea of growth and abundance is analysed in Sophie Chaveau, 'Il consumo di massa
in Francia dopo il 1945', in Stefano Cavazza and Emanuela Scarpellini (eds), *La rivoluzione
dei consumi: Società di massa e benessere in Europa, 1945–2000* (Bologna, 2010).

concept and language of economic growth as a supreme goal of policy, well beyond military security or full employment, brought a significant evolution in the *general* idea of progress, not just to France but to Europe and the West.[3] With the unprecedented success of the European economies in the 1950s and 1960s came the canonization of the growth idea and its propagation as a full-scale model of society, rooted in the apparently hard, incontestable numbers of production and consumption. Article 2 of the Rome Treaty of 1957, founding the European Economic Community, states:

> It shall be the aim of the Community, by establishing a Common Market and progressively approximating the economic policies of member States, to promote throughout the Community a harmonious development of economic activities, a continuous and balanced expansion, an accelerated raising of the standard of living and closer relations between its Member States.

'The Common Market even promised a "second America"', say French commentators: 'It was a problem, but also the triumph of Marshall aid policy.'[4] In reality, with a change of generation and the arrival of the economic 'miracles' in Europe had come a new complexity in the Euro-American relationship. Seen in longer-term perspective, the era outwardly dominated by the Cold War is just as likely to be remembered for the encounter, in the post-war reconstruction process, of what were becoming the two dominant models of modernization in the West, two different approaches to the problem of bringing the new possibilities of expanding production and economic management to the salvation of capitalist democracy.

In a hundred different ways since the war—most explicitly in the Marshall Plan—the Americans had made their experience of consumerist prosperity available for emulation. Personalities, products, magazines, advertising, films, television, fashions, 'lifestyles'—all served to project abroad the American Dream's 'promise of an ever-increasing prosperity for an ever-increasing majority', and revolutionize in the process the range and force of American power.[5] But the recent experience of the West Europeans made them much more interested in release from the inheritance of the first industrial revolutions, and from the nightmares of two World Wars and the intervening depression. So they had used the vastly expanded capabilities of the State to build a variety of systems that, whether

[3] These pages are built on reflections first advanced in Ellwood, *Rebuilding Europe*, Ch. 12.
[4] Duchêne, *Jean Monnet*, 322.
[5] This is a central theme of de Grazia, *Irresistible Empire*, which rightly takes the story back to the era of the First World War. Phrase on American Dream by E. N. Luttwak in the *Times Literary Supplement*, 10 June 1994.

Catholic, Protestant, social democrat, or labourite in their origins, were united by their determination to fulfil a number of basic pledges forged from the suffering of the past and the equalizing pressure of wartime: social insurance, redistribution, universal healthcare, pensions, and education, and of course full employment.[6] As the social historian Victoria de Grazia has noted, all this implied two clearly distinct conceptions of the relationship between the state and the market, of the future of class structures and of course, 'different notions of the rights and duties of citizens'.[7]

The Marshall Plan experience had convinced all of those involved in it that the only way to reconcile these two impulses was through heightened production, exchange, and consumption, all undergirded by economic integration and surging productivity, so that—if everyone played their part according to the script—prices could come down and markets expand. The new wealth created by this benign process could then be spent as each society saw fit.[8] This consensus had been celebrated in the European Manifesto, signed by OEEC ministers with much American prompting and many concessions to national susceptibilities, in August 1951. While re-emphasizing European cooperation and trade and payments liberalization in particular, the declaration placed supreme emphasis on the goal of a 25 per cent production increase in five years. The means? Improved labour productivity with guaranteed redistribution of the proceeds: 'By this large increase in production, improvement in living standards and further social progress can in the course of this period be achieved while meeting defense requirements.'[9]

Two years later, in May 1953, came the European Productivity Agency, born as an 'operating arm' of the OEEC. Half funded by the United

---

[6] Cf. Milward, *European Rescue*, 337; Paul Addison explains that the welfare state and the mixed economy were 'the social equivalent of the Maginot Line, a chain of fortresses designed to protect the public in general, and the working classes in particular, from the consequences of another great slump', Paul Addison, *No Turning Back: The Peacetime Revolutions in Postwar Britain* (Oxford, 2010), 50.

[7] On different roads to 'consumer modernity', de Grazia, *Irresistible Empire*, 343–4. As the Marshall Planners had understood, it was in America's Cold War interest to find ways to bridge the gap between these models and emphasize the welfare element in the New Deal heritage; cultural policy was thought to be a useful instrument in this effort cf. Schäfer, 'Study of Americanisation', 134–6.

[8] The ERP/MSA film *Productivity—Key to Plenty*, of 1953, insisted that the purpose of increased wealth was to spread the benefits of material well-being, especially increased leisure, to the individual family and thence to the community.

[9] Ellwood, *Rebuilding Europe*, 182–3; comprehensive survey of US support for European integration in Geir Lundestad, *'Empire' by Integration: The United States and European Integration, 1945–1997* (Oxford, 1998), esp. chs 3–5.

States, its job was to continue the great crusade for ever more productive efficiency, and ensure long-term support for the Cold War defence drive at all levels of economic activity.[10] In Britain the Anglo-American Productivity Council was immediately taken over by the new agency, just as its chief publicist, the economist Graham Hutton, was publishing his panegyric to productivity, entitled *We Too Can Prosper*. It proclaimed more efficient output to be:

> ...the brightest hope for every man, woman and child that the standard of living can be maintained and improved. Its importance and the universal concern in its achievement therefore cannot be exaggerated.[11]

Hutton's equivalent in France, Jean Fourastié, the greatest economic educator of his era, was telling his readers how to reconcile *Machinisme et Bienêtre*. 'On the threshold of the 1950s', says a leading historian of this period, J. P. Rioux, 'no-one better than he expressed the ideology of progress and modernity, or wrote the history of a future which was to be that of comfort and work.'[12]

From the middle of the decade the terms of the subsequent convergence and confrontation of the two Atlantic models, with all their variations, were becoming clear. The OEEC's 6th report, published in March 1955, was entitled 'From Recovery towards Economic Strength'. The introduction explained:

> The task which Western Europe now faces is to build a better economy than that existing before the war. For Member countries have completed—indeed exceeded—the economic recovery which, when the Marshall Plan began, was no more than a hope and, according to the first report of the OEEC (1948), a doubtful hope at that. Their recent achievements have paved the way for further progress.

The OEEC admitted at this point that its members were not likely to fulfil the target of the European Manifesto, and that while they had improved consumption by 12 per cent over the pre-war level, America's increase had been 45 per cent. Military dollars continued to compensate for inadequate exports to the US, whose level had in fact declined. But the

---

[10] Boel, *European Productivity Agency*, Ch. 1. The EPA is not mentioned by Lundestad, who insists instead that in the last analysis, US support for European integration, almost always much stronger than sentiment in Europe itself, reflected political and defence priorities, particularly the containment of Germany and the strengthening of NATO; *'Empire' by Integration*, 9, 16, 22–3, 33–4, 83, 135–8.

[11] Graham Hutton, *We Too Can Prosper* (London, 1953), 5; cf. Anglo-American Council on Productivity, *Final Report of the Council* (London, September 1952); Vickers, *Manipulating Hegemony*, 128–30; Carew, *Labour under the Marshall Plan*, 184–6.

[12] Fourastié, *Machinisime et bienêtre*, cit.; on Fourastié's ambiguities, de Grazia, *Irresistible Empire*, 365.

organization was proud to point out that 80 per cent of trade between its members had been liberalized (if agriculture and invisibles were excluded), and that productivity had increased between 15 and 20 per cent compared to the immediate pre-war phase. Yet not enough had been done in this direction, which should now, asserted the OEEC, be 'one of the central and most constant preoccupations of governments…':

> In the 1930's the great common problem was unemployment, and in the postwar years it was reconstruction; today, however, the problem of raising productivity has pre-eminence.

Only by recognizing this priority could Western Europe turn into reality the two great watchwords for the future: '*expansion* and *liberalization*'.[13]

When the OEEC came to write its seventh report, at the beginning of 1956, it confirmed that 'a new phase of postwar economic development' was under way, with total output 'on a sharply rising trend' for the third consecutive year. But by far the most portentous novelty in the report's text was the use of new words to describe and characterize the processes unfolding. Alongside 'upsurge', 'expansion', 'development', and 'prosperity', there now appeared the phrase 'economic growth'.[14] In the remainder of the decade, as the consumer durable-led 'miracles' surged forth in Western Europe, this word 'growth'—and its associated numbers of gross national product (GNP), gross domestic product (GDP), unit costs per capita/per hour and all the rest[15]—came to sum up the newness of the era and to dominate the objectives of economic policy, if not of all policy, for governing classes throughout the Old World. Finally, it seemed, the West Europeans had learned how to organize for themselves 'built-in, automatic, incremental economic growth extending indefinitely into the future'. A common narrative of material progress, expressed too in more freely convertible currencies, began to unite its beneficiaries on both sides of the Atlantic. The new OECD decided at the end of 1961 to *plan for* a 50 per cent increase in the GNP of the West European region by 1970.[16]

---

[13] 6th Report of the OEEC, Paris, March 1955 (emphasis in original).

[14] 7th Report of the OEEC, Paris, March 1956.

[15] H. W. Arndt, *The Rise and Fall of Economic Growth: A Study in Contemporary Thought* (Melbourne, 1978), pp. 50–1 and Ch. 4 in general.

[16] Howard Temperley, 'The Affluent Society Revisited', in Cristina Giorcelli and Rob Kroes (eds), *Living with America, 1946–1996* (Amsterdam, 1997), 73; the productivity-growth philosophy was also taken up unhesitatingly in the Communist East of Europe, but its ends were supposedly dedicated entirely to the good of the collective; for its evolution in East Germany, Ina Merkel, 'Consumer Culture in the GDR, or How the Struggle for Anti-Modernity Was Lost on the Battleground of Consumer Culture', in Strasser et al. (eds), *Getting and Spending*.

In 1961 the book that was to be the bible of the growth philosophy appeared: *The Stages of Economic Growth*, a historical view of growth as the culmination of a long development process by a distinguished MIT economist W. W. Rostow. Its subtitle was 'a Non-Communist Manifesto': it sought very consciously to offer a liberal alternative to the determinism of the classical Marxist analysis, and at the same time a practical programme to apply to all the rest of the world where the desire to possess what the West possessed was thought to be rising rapidly.[17] The five stages of growth delineated by Rostow passed from traditional society, through the beginnings of industrialization to 'take-off' and maturity, before blooming in 'the age of high mass consumption'.

In this supreme phase all consumption, as well as production, took place on a mass scale. Urbanization accompanied the triumph of the white collar classes and 'society ceased to accept the further extension of modern technology as an over-riding objective'. Instead:

> ...Western societies have chosen to allocate increased resources to social welfare and security. The emergence of the welfare state is one manifestation of a society's moving beyond technical maturity; but it is also at this stage that resources tend increasingly to be directed to the production of consumers' durables and to the diffusion of services on a mass basis, if consumers' sovereignty reigns. The sewing-machine, the bicycle, and then the various electric-powered household gadgets were gradually diffused.[18]

But one innovation above all supplied the mainspring of the new way of life:

> Historically...the decisive element has been the cheap mass automobile with its quite revolutionary effects—social as well as economic—on the life and expectations of society.

America had invented the age of mass consumption with Fordism, said Rostow, had embraced it as a way of life in the 1920s, and pressed it to its

---

[17] Background and context of Rostow's work in Ekbladh, *Great American Mission*, 173–5, 183–9, Mark H. Haefele, 'Walt Rostow's Stages of Economic Growth: Ideas and Action', in Engerman et al. (eds), *Staging Growth*.

[18] Following the classic studies gathered in Richard Wightman and T. J. Jackson Lears (eds), *The Culture of Consumption: Critical Essays in American History, 1880–1980* (New York, 1983), and in Susman, *Culture as History*, these processes attracted ever more attention from historians; for a series of research essays on the theories and practice of consumption in Europe and America in the twentieth century, Strasser et al. (eds), *Getting and Spending*; cf. Matthew Hilton, 'The Fable of the Sheep, or, Private Virtues, Public Vices: The Consumer Revolution of the Twentieth Century', *Past and Present* (August 2002); Martin Daunton and Matthew Hilton (eds), *The Politics of Consumption: Material Culture and Citizenship in Europe and America* (Oxford, 2001); Marie Emmanuel Chessel, 'From America to Europe: Educating Consumers', review essay, *Contemporary European History* (February 2002).

'logical conclusion' in the post-war decade. Now it was the turn of Western Europe and Japan to fully enter this phase, 'accounting for a momentum in their economies quite unexpected in the immediate post-war years'. With its strong narrative, technological determinism, and self-confident accessibility, say Rostow's later critics, *The Stages of Economic Growth* specified the essential characteristics of the American model of modernity, and rationalized its propagation around the globe as a key weapon in the Cold War.[19]

PROGRESS REDEFINED: THE POLITICS OF GROWTH IN EUROPE

In Western Europe—except possibly in West Germany—the new consumer prosperity was not thought of as a blessing of the Cold War. Instead it looked as though the revolution of rising expectations had finally come to pass. At the heart of the extraordinary expansion of the 1950s was a spirit that was truly unprecedented, said the economic historian Michael Postan in his 1967 account of the post-war experience. 'What was really remarkable...was that economic growth was so powerfully propelled by public sentiments and policies.... In all European countries economic growth became a universal creed and a common expectation to which governments were expected to conform.' Full employment had developed 'into a policy and economic philosophy much wider in its implications... all classes of society gradually came to expect continued—indeed perpetual—rises in the material standards of life'. Politicians and economists nurtured this optimism: 'their policies and plans came to be geared to certain irreducible *minima* of growth... in this way fast growth, rather than just growth, became the principle of state of policy.'[20]

---

[19] Walt Whitman Rostow, *The Stages of Economic Growth: A Non-Communist Manifesto* (Cambridge, 1960), pp. 10–11 and Ch. 6 in general (cit. at p. 11); comprehensive critique of Rostow and his work in Gilman, *Mandarins of the Future*, pp. 161–4, 190–202, and Ch. 5 in general; Ekbladh, *Great American Mission*, 186–7; Engerman et al. (eds), *Staging Growth* (various essays); on the 'golden age' of 1950s prosperity in Europe, E. J. Hobsbawm, *Age of Extremes: The Short Twentieth Century, 1914–1991* (London, 1994), 268–81; Crafts, 'Golden Age of Economic Growth'.

[20] Michael M. Postan, *An Economic History of Western Europe, 1945–1964* (London, 1967), 25; Charles Maier, 'The Two Postwar Eras and the Conditions for Stability in Twentieth Century Western Europe', *American Historical Review* (April 1981); for a contemporary discussion by a leading Labour Party thinker of the time, C. A. R. Crosland, *The Future of Socialism*, abridged version for US market of original 1956 edition (Westport, Conn., 1957), Ch. 11, 'The Pattern of Consumption'; comment in Hilton, 'Fable of the Sheep', 241; Crosland is discussed further below, after n. 72.

Writing in the 1970s on the French case, Jean-Paul Rioux confirmed Postan's judgement. Beyond the specific economic factors, whose exact weight remained impossible to measure:

> ... growth occurred because it was actively sought after, because behaviour had changed, because knowledge had increased: thus the French were prepared to accept growth even before they could actually promote it. A new-found confidence in the future, a taste for education, possibly a less-deferential attitude to the status quo, were all changes as important as the rate of capital formation or the intensity of competition. In the final analysis then, an explanation of the economic leads us back to the domains of the social and the mental.[21]

And in none of these spheres was any external influence so powerful or all-pervasive in these years as that of the United States. If European governments had hoped for a prosperity that would last long enough to build and launch the welfare state, the Americans expected enduring, dynamic growth. The economic 'miracles' were so called because they had never been imagined by anyone on the spot, but 'there was a tide in the affairs of mankind' flowing in the 1950s, said *The Economist*, and there could be no doubt which way it had been running. As Postan eloquently explained:

> Transatlantic inspiration to European policies of growth ... came not only from what the U.S.A. gave or preached but also from what the U.S.A. was. ... Both openly and discreetly the wish to catch up with the U.S.A. became the ambition of governments and the public. ... American affluence and American levels of consumption—motor cars, domestic gadgets, and all—were held up as rewards to come. In short, America's very presence provided an impulse to European growth and a measure of its achievements.[22]

The changes in market relationships involved in the 'era of high mass consumption' touched every social class and brought new groups forward to enjoy its benefits: the workers in the advanced technology factories, working women, youth. American myth and American model merged in the Hollywood cinema, in its final phase of mass influence in the years 1945–54.[23] While productivity and integration stood as the keys to the

---

[21] J. P. Rioux, *The Fourth Republic, 1944–1958* (Cambridge, 1987), 335; cf. Chaveau, 'Il consumo di massa in Francia dopo il 1945', 37–8.

[22] *The Economist*, 26 December 1959; Postan, *Economic History of Western Europe*, 49; many later historians have cautioned that modernization was a complex and multifarious process, with the American model just one factor among many in its evolution, e.g. Chessel, 'From America to Europe', 175.

[23] Pierre Sorlin, *Europe Cinemas, European Societies* (London, 1991), Ch. 3.

supply side, a force like Hollywood's worked on the demand side of the economic and social transformations, speeding and channelling the changes in mentality and behaviour. 'The production of desires preceded the purchase of goods.'[24] Thus if 'You Too Can Be Like Us' had been the inspirational message of Marshall Plan documentaries, the continuing waves of feature films showed how, and where the road might lead.[25]

A detailed analysis of European attitudes to America, supplied to the US intelligence services by an anonymous Italian observer just after the elections of June 1953, suggested how these mechanisms worked. 'Ninety-five per cent of all Europeans—friends and enemies of America—judge American society by what they see at the cinema', said the report. It went on to declare that from Hollywood's products many had taken away a dreadful impression of the country, of its crime and corruption, and of the venality and brutality of its ruling groups in particular. But the medium...

> ...was useful above all in reinforcing the European admiration for the American standard of living, for American technique. A Plymouth or a Chevrolet is considered a great luxury even in countries, such as Italy, which have important car industries of their own. The possession of a refrigerator is sufficient on its own to identify a family as belonging to the richest levels of the bourgeoisie. Undoubtedly film has given the US a propaganda triumph, to the extent that it has reminded Europeans of their traditionally optimistic vision of the "American paradise".[26]

In 1950s Liverpool, with its old American connections, Hollywood's musicals were used as a special means to cope with the deprivation and inequality of everyday life. Taking over the role of the wartime GIs as a 'cipher for...women's fantasies and aspirations' about plenty and opportunity, the films offered a wonderland for emotional investment by women (and not only them), who found in such classics as *Calamity Jane* (1953) the way to define an ideal future in the terms of their own, personal 'American Dream'. Life as such films portrayed it 'gave [Americans] the impression that if they struggled there was something at the end of it', said a working-class interviewee forty years later, in sharp contrast with everyday experience in the hard-up, bombed-out city on Merseyside. The 1950s musicals may have functioned as an escapist fantasy for most cinema-goers in these pre-affluence years, yet they still succeeded in

[24] Mazower, *Dark Continent*, 307.
[25] Cf. Ellwood, 'Italian Modernisation'; in France US officials worried that the country was being swamped by an 'an oppressive mass and volume' of American fiction, films, print media, photos, fearing a backlash; McKenzie, *Remaking France*, 221–2.
[26] Original document quoted in Ellwood, 'Italian Modernisation', 44.

legitimizing the belief that participation in a world of difference, modernity, and plenty was possible for everyone if only it could be found.[27]

As progress was redefined in economic, consumerist, terms and the very bases of democratic legitimacy shifted, politics began to adapt.[28] Berlin's population was among the first to experience the change. That 'American invention' Ludwig Erhard had opened the October 1950 trade fair in the new George Marshall-Haus declaring the fledgling federal republic to be 'a free nation of consumers', in which citizens could choose their own forms of personal and social welfare. This vision was turned into the keynote of the Christian Democrat campaign in the general elections of April 1953. On his way to becoming the Federal republic's most famous economics minister, Erhard told a technical fair in Hanover that the aim should be to 'go beyond the people's basic needs and their day-to-day demands'. Accordingly:

> We must see to it that in German households, and particularly in working class households, durable goods, such as refrigerators, washing machines, vacuum cleaners amongst others, will be used.[29]

For Erhard, his party's victory confirmed the rightness of this vision, fruit of the 'social harmony' that came from 'that trinity, which for every modern market economist must be the ideal picture':

> Rising production and productivity accompanied by rising nominal wages, and the increase in prosperity, thanks to stable or lower prices, [bringing] all-round benefits.

Prosperity for All was the title of the book collecting speeches such as this one from the distinctive economy minister, whose vision always assumed that a beneficent state would always oversee the great expansion. Over the subsequent years, say today's German historians, the Federal Republic's economic success and its 'belief in unlimited economic growth' were fundamental forces in shaping that artificial nation's sense of identity, realities

---

[27] This paragraph is based on Joanne Lacey, 'Seeing Through Happiness: Hollywood Musicals and the Construction of the American Dream in Liverpool in the 1950s', *Journal of Popular British Cinema*, 2 (1999), 54–65; context explained in Christine Geraghty, *British Cinema in the Fifties: Gendre, Genre and the 'New Look'* (London, 2000), 29–35.

[28] Cf. Martin Conway, 'The Rise and Fall of Western Europe's Democratic Age, 1945–1973', *Contemporary European History*, 13/1 (2004); the Cold War dimension of this adaptation is discussed in de Grazia, *Irresistible Empire*, 350–8.

[29] Official US propaganda efforts from 1952 exalting this vision reported in de Grazia, *Irresistible Empire*, 352–3, Castillo, 'Domesticating the Cold War', 273–4; among the features of the great Berlin exhibit of September 1952 was a replay of the airlift of 1948–1949, but this time importing stylish furniture rather than food and coal; ibid. 274. Again, the entire exhibition proved a vast popular success, in spite of official US worries over its invidiousness; ibid. 278–9.

'that muted nationalism and any strong initiatives to overcome the division of Germany'.[30]

The great milestone in the British recognition process came with R. A. Butler's speech as Chancellor to the Conservative Party conference in October 1954. It was on this occasion that a famous pledge was made, based on the expected steady increase of Britain's GNP at an average of 4 per cent per year:

> …I see no reason why, in the next quarter of a century, if we run our policy properly and soundly, we should not double our standard of living in this country.

It was a call, rejoiced *The Economist*, 'for a return to the theory and practice of capitalism', an invitation to imitate the United States, where the progressive effects of their vast increases in wealth could be seen in the wholesale 'levelling-up' of the living standard of the poor, which was a comprehensive response to leftism in all its forms.[31]

Looking back on 1954 in its annual survey, the magazine admitted it had never believed possible an increase in British output at the rate of 6 per cent per annum, and was happy to offer congratulations all round for the 'remarkably satisfactory showing in exports'. The fruits of the newly created wealth had largely gone, of course, on a 'splurge on consumer durables', of which the supreme example was the motor car. Furniture, television, and radio, and other items of 'domestic equipment', came next in the order of preferences, buoyed by hire purchase.[32] A particularly striking and unexpected change had taken place in the labour market. In contrast with a predicted 'natural increase' of 55,000, mostly men, the workforce had expanded by 175,000–200,000, of which 120,000 were women entering or re-entering the working population.[33]

The British General Election of 1955 was not conducted in growth terms, though it had been preceded by an expansionary budget and a

---

[30] L. Erhard, *Prosperity through Competition* (London, 1958), 57, 51; Castillo, 'Domesticating the Cold War', 268; de Grazia, *Irresistible Empire*, 359; H. J. Schröder, 'The Economic Reconstruction of West Germany in the Context of International Relations, 1945–1949', in Schröder (ed.), *Confrontation and Cooperation*, cit. in Ellwood, *Rebuilding Europe*, 228; sceptical West German views of these developments recalled in Wirsching, 'From Work to Consumption', 14.

[31] *The Economist*, 16 October 1954; context explained in Addison, *No Turning Back*, 42–4.

[32] On the central importance of improved domestic living standards in 1950s Britain (as elsewhere in Western Europe), Claire Langhamer, 'The Meanings of Home in Postwar Britain', in Betts and Crowley (eds); cf. Addison, *No Turning Back*, 54–5.

[33] *The Economist*, 1 January 1955.

government 'Economic Survey' for the year that transposed the American message in language doubtless appropriate to British conditions at the time: 'Productivity should benefit... from the added incentive to effort which the prospect of rising consumption affords... general confidence in the possibilities of expansion will do much to ensure that expansion is in fact achieved.' A revolution of rising aspirations, with roots in the 1930s if not earlier, was indeed turning into a transformation of expectations.[34]

So the 1959 election under Harold Macmillan's premiership was carried on in quite new tones by British political standards. 'Compared with pre-war, most people are a good deal better off', agreed the leader of the opposition, Gaitskell. The consequences were worrying for a Labour politician: 'There are signs of the breaking up of traditional political loyalties.' The movement of workers' retail cooperatives, for example, had looked to the post-war Labour governments for a programme of economic planning, trade regulation, and food control. Within a decade the coops' members too were forced to recognize that, as British historians put it, 'polarisation between worker and management was dissolving into the subtler hierarchies of a world based upon "status symbols", as measured by consumer goods—badges of the new affluence.'[35] Labour accused the Tories of substituting these symbols for issues, of selling Macmillan like a detergent, and of introducing 'the worst sort of Americanization'. But in reality both the major parties were busy submerging the important choices in a generalized consensus on domesticity, the mixed economy, and the Welfare State, all tied together by the dynamics of growth. Bogdanor and Skidelsky wrote in 1970:

> Economic growth was essential to the consensus. It enabled the Conservatives to offer for the first time a viable alternative to Socialism with their idea of a property-owning democracy. No-one need be defeated in the class war because no war being fought. Capitalism could provide affluence for the working class while at the same time preserving the gains of the well-to-do...
>
> For the Labour Party, on the other hand, growth seemed to promise victory to the working class in the class struggle without the necessity of having

[34] Cit. ibid. 2 April 1955; Langhamer, 'Meanings of Home', 342–3, 355–62; as recently as 1946 fewer than half the visitors to 'ideal home' exhibitions believed that they would ever own the items on display, ibid. 350.

[35] Frank Trentmann, 'Bread, Milk and Democracy: Consumption and Citizenship in Twentieth-Century Britain', in Daunton and Hilton (eds), *Politics of Consumption*, 157; Hilton, 'Fable of the Sheep', 241; in 1957 the Consumers' Association had been founded, based on US and Swedish models. The success of its guide to consumer durables, *Which?*, quickly turned it into a mass movement and permanent institution of British life with its own political ambitions, ibid. 229, *passim*.

to do battle with capitalism. Redistribution could be financed from the proceeds of growth without hurting the better-off.[36]

With increases of at least 4 per cent in GNP per year, any government could hope to strike a balance between private and public consumption without conflict, at least without any of the familiar, economically rooted conflicts of the past. 'You've never had it so good', was a slogan Macmillan reportedly took over from the 1952 Democratic Party campaign in the US, and his decisive victory in 1959 ensured its attachment to a memorable slice of British post-war life.[37]

In France 1954 had seen the launch of Jean Monnet's Second Plan, seeking to use coordinated productivity increases to build a modern economy 'capable of responding to the challenge of free trade and able to offer the consumer a wide choice'. In France too, cars led the way to the growth revolution: they more than doubled in number between 1951 and 1958. In late 1955 the first major productivity bargain was negotiated in French industry, at the Renault plant. It brought guaranteed future wage increases and fringe benefits in exchange for 'a measure of labour peace and acceptance by the unions that the pursuit of efficiency was in the interests of both sides'.[38] The pact was one of the most visible fruits of the non-inflationary expansion at last established. In Rioux's account:

> Economic growth was rising by 5 per cent a year, national income had grown by 25 per cent between 1952 and 1955; trade was expanding, notably in the most dynamic sectors, and in 1955, for the first time since the war, the commercial balance was positive. And higher demand in turn stimulated production; increased currency earnings eased the budgetary imbalance, reducing the humiliation of the search for foreign loans and advances...the steady diffusion of growth's economic and social benefits fostered a climate of peace and optimism...[39]

By this time the centrist politicians who wrangled incessantly for control of the Fourth Republic had also learned 'that for the bulk of the population

---

[36] A celebrated radical critique of this outlook was offered by a group of prominent Left intellectuals, in and out of the Labour Party, led by the historian E. P. Thompson: *Out of Apathy* (London, 1960).

[37] David Butler, *The British General Election of 1955* (London, 1956); Vernon Bogdanor and Robert Skidelsky, *The Age of Affluence, 1951–1964* (London, 1970), 10–11; Lawrence Black, *The Political Culture of the Left in Affluent Britain, 1951–64* (London, 2003), Ch. 6; on the American origins of the election slogan, Harry Hopkins, *The New Look: A Social History of the Forties and Fifties in Britain* (London, 1963), 455.

[38] Rioux, *Fourth Republic*, 318, 327; Carew, *Labour under the Marshall Plan*, 216.

[39] Cf. de Grazia, *Irresistible Empire*, 360–2; the spread of the benefits of growth may have been steady but it was not even. Rural areas were largely excluded at this stage and there was much scepticism about the new trends: de Grazia, *Irresistible Empire*, 361, Kuisel, *Capitalism and the State*, 105.

sharing the fruits of expansion and economic modernisation, with better standards of living, improved amenities, and more social services, counted for more than questions over the Atlantic Alliance, Europe, Germany, and colonial wars'.[40] Although these were indeed the questions that dominated formal politics and elections as the Fourth Republic staggered towards its collapse in 1958, underneath the surface a fundamental historical shift in values had occurred. Economic considerations were replacing politics, the 'mission civilisatrice', the nation's cultural aura, gold and savings, in France's evaluation of her own power. Modernization understood in the terms of growth gained priority, writes Robert Frank: 'presented either as an absolute precondition of the power of France or as an end in itself, a replacement ideal.'[41]

In a country like Italy where Catholic influence was so strong, adapting the culture of solidarity and austerity to the new opportunities seemed at first sight extremely problematic.[42] The ruling Christian Democrats appeared to walk into the era of '*il boom*' looking backwards, more concerned with spreading their influence in the underdeveloped South than organizing the arrival of prosperity in the North. The party secretary (and former economics professor), Fanfani, struggled hard to reconcile the traditional priorities with the new spirit of expansion as he addressed his party's congress in late 1956:

> Politically we work to carry out the second industrial revolution, the personal, solidaristic and hence Christian revolution, even as we favour technical progress. That progress which multiplies goods and reduces human effort will lessen the hardness of the struggle for existence, lessen burdens in the economic sector, lessen the weight and number of temptations wherever misery prevails. That progress will bring a greater abundance of goods, an easier escape from hard times for individuals, for groups, for peoples.

At the same congress a possible means to this end was adopted, an economic framework plan of the French type that promised to bring full employment, eliminate the North–South gap, and balance the foreign payments accounts. How? By 5 per cent growth a year and a series of institutional and structural innovations. But the design was never transformed into working legislation. It was neither liberal enough for the good times nor sufficiently protectionist for the bad ones, and so had little

---

[40] Rioux, *Fourth Republic*, 240–1, 243.

[41] Robert Frank, 'The French Dilemma: Modernization with Dependence or Independence and Decline', in Josef Becker and Frans Knipping (eds), *Power in Europe?*, cf. Kuisel, *Seducing the French*, 104–5.

[42] Stefano Cavazza, 'Dal consumo desiderato al consumo realizzato: L'avvento della società dei consumi nell'Italia postbellica', in Cavazza and Scarpellini (eds), *La rivoluzione dei consumi*, 64–5.

appeal for an industrial culture still—apart from Fiat and a few others—deeply wedded to the old ways. At the same time it cut across the Christian Democrats' own methods for organizing patronage in the public sector, institutionalized in a new Ministry of Public Intervention.[43]

Europe's largest Communist party failed completely to see the potential for expansion in the Italian economy, short of a revolution, and refused to acknowledge that the nation's capitalism had any serious future of its own until the start of the 1960s. Along with a Third International-style reluctance to recognize that the model of development inspired by America might be something new and different (Gramsci's heritage notwithstanding), there went a conviction that any sort of deliberate wealth creation in the Italian setting would only make things worse. It would aggravate the age-old gaps between the classes, create new forms of misery, divide even further the north from the south, town from country.[44] If export-led (which it was by 1958, stimulated by the new Common Market), the expansion risked exposing the national economy to the uncertainties of world economic cycles, especially the vagaries of the money markets, and leave the working class defenceless against the perpetual threats of deflation and unemployment. As the object of systematic persecution and discrimination in the industry that counted most in the great expansion—motor vehicles—it was perhaps not surprising that the party should take a dim view of the boom's impact on national life. But its refusal to admit that the euphoric growth unfolding across the Western world might have any positive benefits, and that the working masses in Italy too were learning to expect genuinely improved living standards as a result of their efforts, all this left the party seriously short of political traction when the boom's effects turned out to be enduring.[45]

So the language of growth politics never took hold in 1950s Italy. There was little or no connection between the declared policies of office holders, their actual behavior, and the performance of the real economy. And

[43] Paul Ginsborg, *A History of Contemporary Italy: Society and Politics, 1943–1988* (London, 1990), 205–6, 222–3 (cit. at p. 205, n. 21); Silvio Lanaro, *Storia dell'Italia repubblicana* (1992 edn repr., Padua, 2001), 33, 197, 235; on the limited horizons and expectations of Italian industrial and banking culture in the early 1950s, Angelo Varni, 'La grande trasformazione', in Antonio Cardini (ed.), *Il miracolo economico italiano (1958–1963)* (Bologna, 2006), 50–3.

[44] Gundle, *Between Hollywood and Moscow*, 21, 76–7, 82–3.

[45] Ibid. 89–91; cf. Lanaro, *Storia dell'Italia repubblicana*, 316, which insists on the rigidity of the Party's Marxist intellectual schemes. In fact as the only serious opposition to the ruling Christian Democrats with their deep conservatism and refusal to face up to the conflicts produced by modernization, the Communist vote increased to over 25% by 1963; cf. Simona Colarizi, 'I partiti politici di fronte al cambiamento di costume', in Cardini (ed.), *Il miracolo economico italiano*, 234–8.

voters were not encouraged to expect any, least of all in terms of numerical pledges on growth, employment, inflation, etc.[46] The keys to economic policy were entrusted to the central bank, whose aims focused on stability and maintaining the exchange value of the Lira. While the problematic south knew its own story of economic progress, no one could imagine that its endemic problems had been solved. In general, trends in consumption lagged some way behind rises in income.[47]

Yet the outcome of Italy's 'miracle' (even more unexpected than the others) has led historians to consider 'Americanization' as 'the major factor in Italy's transformation' in these years, meaning specifically 'that the exposure to new domestic ideas and lifestyles imported from the USA was instrumental in remaking the social and cultural expectations of Italian society', in the eyes of the architectural historian Paolo Scrivano.[48] And this transformation cut across the left–right political polarization produced by the Cold War, add Luigi Bruti Liberati and others.[49] Certainly the country's need for a strong development model became more deeply felt as new aspirations began to emerge and the technological possibilities of fulfilling them became available quite quickly. Urbanization (7–8 million moved to the cities in the 1950s), the spread of welfare, the development projects, and the DC system for spreading its influence by distributing public money, all pushed consumption upwards at an average rate of 5 to 6 per cent per year. Fascism had attempted to dissolve the boundaries between the State and the individual, between the nation and

---

[46] Cavazza, 'Dal consumo desiderato al consumo realizzato', 66–8; yet because Italy's was in fact the fastest growing of all the West European economies in these years, as the sociologist Alessandro Pizzorno noted in 1964, 'all the goals of the Vanoni plan [except Southern development] had already been surpassed in 1961, three years earlier than expected': 'The Individualistic Mobilization of Europe', *Daedalus*, Special Issue, 'A New Europe?' (Winter 1964), 203, 223 (note 9).

[47] On monetary policy and the contradictory progress of the south, Vera Zamagni, *Dalla periferia al centro: La seconda rinascita economica dell'Italia, 1861–1990* (2nd edn, Bologna, 1993), 436, 470–7; on consumption trends, Cavazza, 'Dal consumo desiderato al consumo realizzato', 56.

[48] Paolo Scrivano, 'Signs of Americanization in Italian Domestic Life: Italy's Postwar Conversion to Consumerism', in Betts and Crowley (eds), 317; on the role of the new medium of television with its many American borrowings in this transformation, Barbara Rossi, 'Televisione: Le immagini del "miracolo"', in Cardini (ed.), *Il miracolo economico italiano*, and below, pp. 417–18; 'As for the Italian miracle', wrote Raymond Aron, 'if almost no-one had demonstrated its impossibility, it was primarily because no one had conceived of its possibility'; 'Old Nations, New Europe', *Daedalus*, Special Issue, 'A New Europe?' (Winter 1964), 43.

[49] Luigi Bruti Liberati, 'Witch-Hunts and *Corriere della Sera*: A Conservative Perception of American Political Values in Cold War Italy: The 1950s', in Tobia (ed.), *Cold War History*, Special Issue, 'Europe Americanized?' (February 2011), 70; cf. Gundle, *Between Hollywood and Moscow*, 93–9.

the masses. In a contrast visible in every film, advertisement, and glossy magazine, the American model of modernity put the individual and the family back at the centre of progress, privatizing collective behaviour and domesticating social space in a rebuilt home. 'A common pattern emerged', says the economic historian Vera Zamagni, 'which succeeded in homogenizing the Italians and at the same time preserved their localistic traditions.'[50]

In no country was the impact of the motor car revolution more tremendous, led by a company, Fiat, which had been a privileged beneficiary of ERP aid and made no secret of its admiration for American methods of production, distribution, and selling.[51] Yet the car that put the Italians on wheels, the Fiat 600 of 1955, was a small utility vehicle, in no way resembling the Detroit product. It was a highly visible example of what Scrivano has called 'an unusual capacity for remaking and hybridizing imported transatlantic models'. As the great source of novelties and methods in the new Europe, America's propositions were always taken up, in this stage like all the others, as far as they were useful and adaptable and no further.[52]

A SENSE OF RIGHTFUL CONFIRMATION?

Seen from the outside though, it all looked so good. To Americans watching the rebirth of Western Europe and the blossoming of the economic miracles in the 1950s, everything they had stood for, argued over, and invested in since World War II seemed triumphantly justified. An 'Americanization of economic thinking' was under way, said the foreign editor of *Business Week* in early 1955: 'More and more the Europeans believe in economic growth built in large measure around an expanding consumer market.'[53] Around the same time the *New York Times* reported a recent

---

[50] Lanaro, *Storia dell'Italia repubblicana*, 239–69, Gundle, *Between Hollywood and Moscow*, 80–1; Scrivano, 'Signs of Americanization', 338; Vera Zamagni, 'Evolution of the Economy', in Patrick McCarthy (ed.), *Italy since 1945* (Oxford, 2000), 42–55; Bruti Liberati emphasizes however the sense of unease felt in many conservative, middle-class circles by the American cultural challenge; 'Witch-Hunts', 70–1.

[51] Details of 'mass motorization' and Fiat's role in Stefano Maggi, 'La 600 e il telefono: Una rivoluzione sociale', in Cardini (ed.), *Il miracolo economico italiano*, 96–106.

[52] Scrivano, 'Signs of Americanization', 317; on aspects of the motor car revolution, ibid. 331–2, 338–9; other examples from the European motor-car industry cited in Mazower, *Dark Continent*, 314–15; the limits of adoption were also highly visible in the experience of West German industry in its rebuilding process, cf. Volker Berghahn, *The Americanisation of West German Industry, 1945–1973* (Leamington Spa, 1986), 181, 187, 250–9.

[53] Howard P. Whidden, 'Birth of a Mass Market—Western Europe', *Harvard Business Review* (May–June 1955). This survey is unusual for the richness of its statistical data, and its inclusion of Switzerland and Sweden in its picture of consumption-led economic expansion.

tour by the head of a leading US advertising agency through Western Europe, and quoted his judgement that 'the urge to follow the American way of life is strong in a number of countries. . . . There is also considerable prestige attached to ownership of modern American products, including cars.' As a result, said the ad man, American-style retailing with self-service groceries, chain-stores, and 'instalment-selling' (hire purchase) was expanding to deal with all those now entering the middle class, 'realizing [their] desire for a better life after so many years of a hardship economy . . .'. If American companies could introduce 'product preference and consumer-opinion surveys' to these markets, and so understand the modifications they needed to make to their products, they would find plenty of business.[54]

A year later the *New York Times* correspondent Michael Hoffman reported from Bonn on the 'widening Americanization' of Europe. He cited snack bars, jukeboxes, television aerials, Coca-Cola, and 'young women running about in slacks' as among the most notable pieces of evidence, with the arrival of American-style soft drinks and TV programmes provoking the most controversy. There were indeed plenty of signs of resistance to all this from cultural conservatives, ranging from Italian cafe owners who lived in dread of the day when their clients could afford TV in their own homes, to those Communists who had tried to keep Coca-Cola out of France.[55] But 'the invasion' was steaming ahead:

> Hamburgers with onion, electric mixers in the kitchen, father washing the dishes because the maid gets a day off, soap in hotel bathrooms—where will it all end?[56]

In a remarkable anticipation of much-later discussions of 'globalization', the Reuters news agency reported in mid-1955 the results of a worldwide survey of its correspondents in response to the simple question: 'Is all the free world being Americanized?' Included were comments from Tokyo and Melbourne, from Canada and Brazil, as well as from the Middle East and Europe. The Reuters correspondents described how new processes of change and development were undoubtedly arriving with the spread of American power in all its new variety of forms. But the transitions were varied and uneven, and their effects not always the ones that might be predicted.[57]

---

[54] *New York Times*, 8 May 1955; on arrival of first marketing surveys in the early 1960s, de Grazia, *Irresistible Empire*, 366–7.
[55] On the slow spread of supermarkets in West Germany, Rainer Gries, ' "Serve Yourself!": The History and Theory of Self-Service in West and East Germany', in Swett et al. (eds), *Selling Modernity*, 309–12.
[56] *New York Times*, 24 June 1956.
[57] Ibid. 21 August 1955.

In Iran—the 'desert' that Franklin Roosevelt had once dreamed of transforming—'Americanization' had already reached the point where Muslim leaders were mobilizing to put a stop to it. Hollywood was a particularly disturbing presence in such a setting, as it was in a country like Spain, where American films were thought by some however to be a positive influence, breaking down that country's isolation and encouraging the emergence of a new middle class.[58] Greece was described as resisting the adoption of American clothes, food, mass-communication styles, and mass-production methods, although 'teenagers' were known to be much more receptive to them than the older generations. Still, the great effort to bring the Greek road system, industry, and farming into the twentieth century was continuing under official US auspices, and the national department of foreign commerce was being directly run by an American, in the employ of the Greek government.[59]

But it was in the major countries of Western Europe that the greatest American impact was in evidence, according to the Reuters survey. In each of them, different emphases and preferences could be seen, but the underlying patterns were clear: American methods and customs were being adopted, even 'without acknowledgment of the source. They become part of life in a natural way, especially where the younger people are concerned.' Everyone mentioned popcorn, Coca-Cola, blue jeans, and hamburgers. The new socializing effects of Hollywood and jazz and transatlantic dance music were also commented on widely (and rock 'n' roll was just around the corner[60]). But more long-lasting would be the changes to factories and farms, to advertising and shops and restaurants.

In the face of all these challenges the British were responding with a determination 'to stay more doggedly British than ever'. But they were bound to succumb: 'They stubbornly resist central heating, but it is making inroads. And women of all classes are demanding kitchens planned on American lines. Frozen food is becoming more popular and self-service shops are coming into vogue.'[61] Working-class teenagers in

---

[58] Ibid.; cf. Graham and Labanyi, 'Editors' Introduction', in Graham and Labanyi (eds), *Spanish Cultural Studies*, Section 1, p. 170; Labanyi, 'Censorship', 210; Peter Evans, 'Cifesa: Cinema and Authoritarian Aesthetics', in Graham and Labanyi (eds), *Spanish Cultural Studies*, 220, 222.

[59] *New York Times* (n. 54 above); ibid. 23 October 1955; cf. Miller, *United States and the Making of Modern Greece*, 66–9, which underlines the impulse of leading Greek political figures to adapt American ideas of growth and productivity to local conditions and their personal political priorities.

[60] Cf. Stephen Gundle, 'Adriano Celentano and the Origins of Rock 'n' Roll in Italy', *Journal of Modern Italian Studies* (October 2006).

[61] *New York Times* (n. 54 above); on the impact of the American kitchen in Europe—in part promoted by US information services—Greg Castillo, 'The American "Fat Kitchen" in Europe: Postwar Domestic Modernity and Marshall Plan Strategies of Enchantment', in

particular liked the new leisure products, comic strips, advertising, and commercial television, all of them infused with American styles. Industry was adopting personnel relations and public relations. Nonetheless, Britain was the nation with the strongest low-intensity anti-Americanism, and there was much deploring among 'thoughtful people' of the 'candy-floss' standards said to be taking hold.[62]

In France only a few of the American influences were thought likely to be long-lasting. Again young people were likely to be the chief beneficiaries, since they were the ones most enthusiastic about jukeboxes, snack bars, and 'le be-bob', and the sense of personal liberation that went with them. Meanwhile the 'little shop around the corner' stayed at the centre of distribution because of the lack of refrigerators. On the output front the 'principle of the small independent proprietor remains the basis of most industry and agriculture in spite of all the campaigns for more mass production'.[63]

In Naples twenty years of mingling with American servicemen had brought a new sense of 'hurry and urgency' to that sleepy old city, according to the Reuters man on the spot.[64] In general, though, US influence in Italy touched only the big cities and the few big factories. Teenagers could be seen in such centres as Florence, Genoa, and Rome wearing blue jeans and sports shirts, while their mothers were lured by the advertisements for 'American-style kitchen furniture' and washing machines. But in the villages, 'especially those in poverty-stricken southern Italy', the inhabitants knew there was such a place as the United States 'only because an uncle emigrated there thirty years ago'.[65]

While comments such as these showed the limits of the survey's 'snapshot' character, its judgement that West Germany was the nation caught

---

Ruth Oldenziel and Karin Zachmann (eds), *Cold War Kitchen: Americanization, Technology, and European Users* (Cambridge, Mass., 2009); on the early, post-rationing spread of supermarkets, G. Shaw, L. Curth, and A. Alexander, 'Selling Self-Service and the Supermarket: The Americanisation of Food Retailing in Britain, 1945–60', *Business History* (October 2004), 572–3; the Anglo-American Productivity Council had been 'particularly influential' in this development, say the authors; French experience analysed in Chaveau, 'Il consumo di massa in Francia dopo il 1945', 42–4.

[62] *New York Times* (n. 54 above); the 'candy-floss' reference was an allusion to the writings of the pioneering critic of popular culture Richard Hoggart, later summed up in his *Uses of Literacy* (1957); see below, n. 76.

[63] *New York Times* (n. 54 above); Kuisel, *Seducing the French*, Ch. 5; de Grazia, *Irresistible Empire*, 386.

[64] *New York Times* (n. 54 above); bitter-sweet recollections from a local Communist writer in Rea, *Mistero napoletano*, 102, 154, 326–7, *passim*.

[65] *New York Times* (n. 54 above); cf. Percy Allum, 'Italian Society Transformed', in McCarthy (ed.), *Italy since 1945*, 15–16, 19–20; for the transformation of national ideals of feminine beauty under the impact of these developments, Stephen Gundle, *Bellissima: Feminine Beauty and the Ideal of Italy* (New Haven, Conn., 2007), pp. 170–3 and Ch. 8 in general.

up in the most intense relationship with America mass culture has become generally accepted over the years.[66] Ludwig Erhard now appeared as the champion of the free enterprise way, and German trade unions, with their emphasis on economic gains rather than political power, looked closer to the American equivalent than those in neighbouring countries. Architects followed transatlantic building methods, advertising was 'high-powered', and 'the prominent place given to American authors in the playbills of German theaters show that the country is willing to accept American ideas'. But there was still a long way to go: 'a working man with his own car is almost unknown. Television is still in its infancy. The equality of women exists only on paper.'[67]

'The least one can report', concluded Michael Hoffman of the *New York Times* in 1956, 'is that a permanent-looking layer of American customs has spread itself across the old Continent in the past ten years, to the consternation of the elite, the delight of the masses, and the solid satisfaction of the vendors.'[68] This was an astute remark, but it left open as many questions as it briefly answered. No one doubted the prodigious force of the changes under way—Jean Fourastié talked of the resolution of 'the tragic and millenary problems of man's poverty and impotence'—but what of the underlying dynamics, the push and the pull, in this process of superimposition. Who or what were the mechanisms of transmission of America's influences? Was this a repetition of the 1920s European experience of American modernity, or were there new dimensions of it to cope with? How did the differentials in its impact function; what united, what divided the various elements of society as they evolved their responses to whatever America was offering (or supposed to be offering)? Was it even certain that the United States was the prime originator of what was going on, or simply one expression of a general process of Western democratic development in the direction of social participation through purchasing power?[69]

---

[66] Cf. Volker Berghahn, 'Conceptualizing the American Impact on Germany: West German Society and the Problem of Americanization', paper presented at the German Historical Institute conference at Washington DC (March 1999), <http://www.ghi-dc.org/conpotweb/westernpapers/berghahn.pdf>, still accessible from the Wayback Machine Web archive: <http://wayback.archive.org>; summary of debate in Schäfer, 'Study of Americanisation', 129–32, 136–40.

[67] Detailed picture of local consumption patterns at this time in Michael Wildt, 'Plurality of Taste: Food and Consumption in West Germany during the 1950s', *History Workshop Journal*, 39/1 (1995); Greg Castillo details the efforts of the East German authorities to compete with these displays of Western success; 'Domesticating the Cold War', 283–6.

[68] *New York Times*, 24 June 1956.

[69] Cf. Conway, 'Rise and Fall', 86; de Grazia, *Irresistible Empire*, 342–4, 359–66; Heide Fehrenbach and Uta G. Poiger, 'Introduction: Americanization Reconsidered', in Fehrenbach and Poiger (eds), *Transactions,* xviii–xxiv.

The eminent French social scientist, Raymond Aron, declared that it was easy to make lists of 'phenomena, institutions, amusements' that had crossed the ocean and had 'acquired citizens' rights' in Europe as elsewhere. But this was not 'Americanization' as so many alleged with scorn, it was simply 'the universalizing of phenomena linked to the development of material civilization'.[70] Jean Fourastié's celebration of the 'thirty glorious years', famed in France[71] and the most evocative of all the surveys documenting the vast progress in human welfare in the West brought by the long era of growth, assigns no significance of any sort to the American inspiration, and makes almost no reference to it at all.[72]

Contemporary discussions in Britain, focusing not so much on the causes but on the consequences of affluence, dedicate little or no space to transatlantic models, whether good or bad. Two seminal books of the 1950s prove the point. Anthony Crosland's *The Future of Socialism*, of 1956, a large-scale discussion of the implications for the traditional Left of the new realities, insisted that while Labour's hard core continued to argue over old issues and grievances as if nothing had changed, its traditional supporters were opting in droves for a private world of individualistic consumerism. This was giving them access sooner rather than later to the middle classes, and hence to a radical change in identity and outlook. The book also addressed the fact that the welfare state model of development was going nowhere politically, least of all among young people, who at best took it for granted.[73]

---

[70] R. Aron, 'From France', in Franz M. Joseph (ed.), *As Others See Us*, 60; this line of argument has been well developed by social analysts over the years; the historian of consumerism Frank Trentmann sees an uncoupling of the American model from Europe's version of the consumer society apparent from the 1960s; comment on Wirsching, 'From Work to Consumption', 27–8.

[71] Saluting the appearance of the 2004 edition of the book, Jean-Marc Daniel talked of Fourastié's moral and historical vision, as well as his empirical contribution to the definition of productivity and its results. He also enjoyed pointing out that Fourastié had expected the trend rate of productivity growth over the period (5–6%) to be maintained, with the result that the working week in the years 2000–5 would be 30–5 hours; *Le Monde*, 22 June 2004. Fourastié himself seems to have come to believe by the 1970s that the 'revolution of rising expectations' had gone much too far, in a vulgar, consumerist direction: Régis Boulat, 'Jean Fourastié ou le prophète repenti', *Vingtième Siècle* (July–September 2006), 123.

[72] ...except in a short afterword, where the author dedicates a line to the useful experience of ERP-sponsored information missions to the US for members of Monnet's planning team: *Machinisme et bienêtre*, 276.

[73] *The Economist*, in its end-of-decade celebration of the 'roaring' 1950s, made no mention of the likely causes of the boom, concentrating on the political consequences of an enlarged middle class: edition of 26 December 1959; for a contemporary view that emphasized the individualism but doubted the social mobility, Ralf Dahrendorf, 'Recent Changes in the Class Structure of European Societies', *Daedalus*, Special Issue, 'The New Europe?' (Winter 1964), 256–9; on youth and welfare state Kenneth Allsop, *The Angry Decade* (1958 edn repr., Wendover, 1985), 19, 35, 79, 206; for historical perspective on these processes almost fifty years afterwards, Conway, 'Rise and Fall'.

Crosland rejected what he alleged was the traditional anti-American-ism of the Left, half-ideological, half-Cold War oriented,[74] and never hesitated to point to American examples of best practice (just as he did to Sweden's). But he declared that the trend to managerialism in business, the shift from a society dominated not by work but by leisure and consumption, the success at the same time of full employment and social security policies, all this was general in the West and not the product of one particular experience. The problem for the British was that theirs was 'probably the least competitive nation in the world', with persistent problems of class resentment and diffidence of individual effort. If the Left wished to defend, much less enhance, its traditional values of equality, welfare, and cultural and educational progress for all, it had no alternative but to look differently at the concepts of profit and productivity. Rapid economic growth would be vital for a Labour victory and a Labour agenda once in power.[75]

Even more celebrated in the canon of left thinking on contemporary modernity in this era was—and still is—Richard Hoggart's *Uses of Literacy* of 1957. This pioneering reflection on the state of popular culture at the time—particularly 'publications and entertainments'—by a man who had come from working-class roots and maintained his contact with them, is often thought of as a prime witness to the baleful influence of American stereotypes and icons.[76] In reality, apart from a few Orwell or Priestley-style jibes at young men with 'an American slouch...living in a myth world' feebly absorbed from the obvious transatlantic media, Hoggart makes little explicit reference to the power relations in the production of contemporary mass culture, much less who might be in charge of them. His anxieties are addressed elsewhere, and like many in Britain at this time, Hoggart seemed to echo older, Victorian voices, such as

---

[74] 'It was easier to find a scapegoat than to question the edifying vision of the good, uncorrupted taste of the workers that had so long been an article of faith', wrote the historian and America specialist Denis W. Brogan in 1959, 'From England', in Joseph (ed.), *As Others See Us*, 16.

[75] Crosland, *Future of Socialism*, Ch. 16; for contemporary rebuttal, Thompson (ed.), *Out of Apathy*; historical significance of Crosland discussed in Black, *Political Culture*, 92–3, 106–8, 129–30. This points out how indebted 'revisionists' such as Crosland were to American critics of contemporary capitalism such as J. K. Galbraith, David Riesman, and Vance Packard; on Crosland's view of America, David Reisman, *Crosland's Future: Opportunity and Outcome* (Basingstoke, 1997), 145–52; cf. Stephen Brooke, 'Atlantic Crossing? American Views of Capitalism and British Socialist Thought, 1932–1962', *Twentieth Century British History*, 2/2 (1991), 120–5.

[76] E.g. Richard Weight, *Patriots: National Identity in Britain, 1940–2000* (London, 2003), 305–6; Black, *Political Culture*, 85–6, which offers a discussion of the impact of Hoggart's work at the time.

Matthew Arnold's, in his critique of the latest wave of commercialism and its customs.[77]

But Hoggart's attention did focus on the younger generations, and as such it was starting to look unusual in marginalizing the American influences on what was happening in this key social area. With the emergence of the 'teen' phenomenon, after 1956–7, no later commentator would think of discussing social trends in Britain or elsewhere in Europe without reference to youth and its new American dreams.[78] If there was one area of social life where the American inspiration turned the latest phase of capitalist economic progress into something more than just good times, prosperity, or even affluence, and instead into the new reality and culture of 'growth', it was the change in the passage of generations, the transformation of adolescents up and down Europe into a whole new category of real or potential *consumers*. In this emerging group the revolution of rising expectations made its biggest, easiest conquests. Yet the results of the transformation very rarely corresponded to what the 1950s promoters of growth might have predicted, whether in politics, behaviour, or taste. These new protagonists of the social scene, it turned out, had minds of their own, and quite different uses for the American inspiration than those their parents might have imagined.

TEENAGERS IN THEIR OWN RIGHT

As Tony Richardson's 1959 film classic *Look Back in Anger* opens, the misanthropic and self-hating protagonist is seen playing jazz for dancers in a smoky nightclub. Jimmy Porter's apparent skill belies his scorn for all around him:

> I must say it's pretty dreary living in the American Age—unless you're American of course. Perhaps all our children will be American. That's a thought, isn't it?

Was Jimmy Porter the first 1950s anti-hero to embrace the possibilities of America's cultural creativity and at the same time openly express anti-Americanist sentiments? Compared to what came right after him though (the play on which the film was based had opened in 1956), Jimmy was

---

[77] Dick Hebdige, 'Towards a Cartography of Taste, 1935–1962', Ch. 3 of Hebdige, *Hiding the Light: On Images and Things* (London, 1988), 50–3. This influential essay remained for years a rare exploration of the politics of mass culture in Britain in terms that included 'the spectre of Americanisation'.

[78] Cf. Christopher Booker, *The Neophiliacs* (London, 1970), 79; Addison, *No Turning Back*, 179.

already looking old-fashioned: he was *not* a teenager. Colin MacInnes's novel, *Absolute Beginners*, also from 1959, set in a fashionable corner of London's new youth culture, implicitly explained what was wrong with him. The teen culture, declared the narrator, had burst upon England the year before, in 1958. And, among its many other galvanizing effects, it had swept away Jimmy Porter's entire outlook on the world, including its defeatism about the influence of America.[79]

This subject had inevitably arisen when one of the protagonists in *Absolute Beginners* tried unsuccessfully to start a gay affair with an American. His friend the narrator attempts to comfort him, suggesting that he mustn't become anti-American just because he's rejected: 'It's a sure sign of total defeat to be anti-Yank.' The conversation continues:

'But I thought,' said lovelorn Fabulous... 'you didn't approve of the American influence. I mean, I know you don't care for Elvis [Presley], and you do like Tommy [Steele].'

'Now listen, glamour puss,' I said... 'because I want English kids to be English kids, not West Ken[sington] Yanks and bogus imitation Americans, that doesn't mean I'm *anti* the whole US thing. On the contrary I'm starting up an anti-anti-American movement, because I just despise the hatred and jealousy of Yanks there is around, and think it's a sure sign of defeat and weakness...'

'The thing is,' I said, 'to support the local product. America launched the teenage movement, there's no denying, and Frankie S[inatra], after all, was, in his way, the very first teenager. But we've got to produce our own variety, and not imitate the Americans—or the Ruskis, or anybody for that matter...'[80]

As the novel and a myriad of other sources across Britain and Europe make clear, it was the new wealth of young people—especially working-class young people—that turned them into a distinctive social grouping with a status and an identity of its own, and an ever-changing variety of internal codes and categories, just as their American predecessors in the 1920s and 1940s.[81] Because they were such a self-consciously conspicuous product of

---

[79] C. MacInnes, *Absolute Beginners* (1959 edn repr., London, 1964); on Jimmy Porter's literary, moral, and historical significance, Allsop, *Angry Decade*, 104–13.

[80] MacInnes, *Absolute Beginners*, 58–9; contextualization and comment in Arthur Marwick, *The Sixties: Cultural Revolution in Britain, France, Italy and the United States, c.1958–c.1974* (Oxford, 1998), 55–8.

[81] Conceptual discussion in Marwick, *Sixties*, 41–4; American precedents in Savage, *Teenage*, chs 15, 29; for British case of 1950s, John Benson, *The Rise of Consumer Society in Britain, 1880–1980* (London, 1994), Ch. 7, Bill Osgerby, *Youth in Britain since 1945* (Oxford, 1998), Addison, *No Turning Back*, 178–9 (which cites the pioneering market research survey *The Teenage Consumer* of 1959); for the Netherlands, Mel van Elteren, 'American Life by Proxy: Dutch Youth and Sense of Place', in George McKay (ed.), *Yankee Go*

the new kind of consumerist prosperity, the late 1950s generation of young people of working-class origin quickly turned into its prime symbols. Their most typical representatives spoke, spent, dressed, and moved differently from any previous sample of the age group.[82] They seemed anxious to stake out areas of freedom in the family, the school, and the street, the class system, even the workplace, which had never been subject to negotiation before. Their American inspiration and connotations were obvious—in their leisure patterns and lifestyles—but above all they refused to be labelled, and in building the sort of critical relationship with whatever the US was offering implied in the conversation above, they developed mechanisms of adaptation that turned out to be all their own.

An Italian historian of popular culture, Franco Minganti, has explained:

> The 1950s were crucial for redefining the status of youth in Italy, particularly in the social climate of pervasive cultural eclecticism. Italian adolescents developed a distinct lifestyle and became a distinct social group. They mixed American, British and French imports with a revolutionary outcome…youth as a world apart, a world of its own, almost a class in itself. Youths tended to slip out from under the control of traditional institutions, with their own meeting points and sites of empowerment (jukebox bars), their own time (the night), their own uniforms (jeans and highly stylized fashions).

As the analysis implies, the relationship with whatever America was offering was not a straightforward one:

> In spite of criticisms by cultural conservatives, these adolescent styles did not represent a passive integration into alien—namely American—music and fashion. Rather adolescents used these styles to mark their difference from previous generations of Italians and from Italian tradition.[83]

Popular music and films were the two great areas of creative production and consumption the new generation looked to for its inspiration, enabling adolescents to enjoy an original rite of passage where they could make their own choices before facing the heavy challenges of adulthood. And in this area of transition, America's commercial mass-cultural industries reigned supreme, the advertisers in particular having spotted that the

---

Home (and take me with U) (Sheffield, 1997); for Germany, Kaspar Maase, 'Establishing Cultural Democracy: Youth, "Americanization", and the Irresistible Rise of Popular Culture', in Hanna Schissler (ed.), *The Miracle Years: A Cultural History of West Germany, 1949–1968* (Princeton, 2001).

[82] British experience in Addison, *No Turning Back*, 97.

[83] F. Minganti, 'Jukebox Boys: Postwar Italian Music and the Culture of Covering', in Fehrenbach and Poiger (eds), *Transactions*, 154.

Fig. 8. A crowd dances to 'Rock Around the Clock', starring Bill Haley and His Comets, Manchester, England, September 1956.

(Getty Images/Hulton Archive)

mass of babies springing forth right after the war promised rich pickings in the very near future.[84] Rock 'n' roll—the music and the films—was their first big export to the new markets of the matching European teenager boom, and its uniquely American features were obvious in every note, in each of the original stars, and in every frame of the movies that launched the first craze: *Blackboard Jungle* in 1955, and in 1956 *Rock Around the Clock* and *The Girl Can't Help It*.[85]

As the new youth heroes and heroines of rock added to the freshly discovered talents of Marlon Brando, James Dean, and Montgomery

[84] Osgerby, *Youth in Britain*, 45–7.
[85] On the impact in Britain of *Rock Around the Clock* as music and film, Nigel Fountain and Anjana Ahuja, 'The Tale of Haley the Comet', *The Guardian* (12 April 1994). Paul McCartney testified to the impact of *The Girl Can't Help It* (Frank Tashlin, 1956) on his circle of friends in a BBC World Service radio series of 1999. The film contained sequences featuring many of the emerging African-American rock stars of the time, including Fats Domino, Little Richard, and The Platters. Its title song is listed among the fifteen that, in their view, most influenced the development of the Rolling Stones: *Rolling Stones: Music that Matters to Them* (2002).

Clift, then were quickly followed by Elvis Presley and his imitators, an unexpected wave of freshness and energy swept over the Old World. In 1955 the emerging London critic Kenneth Tynan had complained of Britain's 'cultural fatigue', a place that its young people saw as 'somehow shrunken and inhibited, desperately behind the times', a land where 'the earth is somehow waning in fertility'. In such a context the arrival of the new wave of pop output from across the Atlantic felt profoundly liberating. As one of Tynan's successors, the Anglo-Irish writer Alexander Cockburn, recalled: 'Here was escape from airless provincialism, BBC good taste and the mandates of the class system.'[86]

But the energy and anti-authoritarianism of youth's new attitudes and behaviour soon had the watchdogs of traditional standards on the alert. Reflexes first developed between the wars, or before, suddenly reappeared. The characteristic 1950s panic over 'juvenile delinquency' had started as early as 1953 in Britain, when illustrated weeklies like *Picture Post* had first sounded the alarm about youth crime and linked it to rising working-class wages, changing leisure fashions and of course exposure to American imports such as comic strips, films, and popular music. A chain of associations—'between youth, the future, America and crime'—slowly but irreversibly became 'thoroughly sedimented' in the common sense of cultural conservatism in Britain, suggests Dick Hebdige. A list of coded words appeared in the social commentary of the day, which amounted to 'a shorthand for all manner of imagined decadence'. They included 'streamlined', 'slick', 'shiny', 'chromium-plated', 'candy-floss', even 'modern' itself. Once consolidated 'as signs of the perfidious "American influence"...', they could be invoked to characterize all sorts of anti-social behaviour, and explain a variety of undesirable trends of the times, from the collapse of traditional sources of authority to the rising divorce rate, even the loss of Empire.[87]

As West Germany groped for a mid-twentieth-century ordinariness of its own under capitalism, remarkably similar reflexes quickly appeared. Historians record how the combined effects of the new rock 'n' roll heroes produced among the propertied classes '...the frightening vision of the masses getting out of control and throwing off the harness of civilization. These fears are elicited by the sight of working-class youths breaking cul-

---

[86] K. Tynan, 'British Cultural Fatigue', *Atlantic Monthly* (November 1955); A. Cockburn, 'The Two-Way Street', *The Guardian* (12 May 1995); the BBC had strenuously resisted the arrival of rock 'n' roll, Hebdige, *Hiding the Light*, 55–6; an understanding of the difficulties involved in the transition can be gained from the 1958 map of *The Angry Decade*, offered by the critic Kenneth Allsop. This was a brilliant guide to the mid-decade malaise in Britain and elsewhere, but was heedless of the youth culture explosion about to happen.

[87] Hebdige, *Hiding the Light*, 57–8.

tural rules of how to behave in a concert.'[88] Although similar reactions, especially rioting at rock concerts, accompanied the new youth culture wherever it appeared in Europe,[89] in a nation such as West Germany, where 'normality' and 'normalization' were the code words of the time, they were more virulent. Echoing the right-wing anti-Americanism first heard during the Weimar era, the 1950s middle-class hatred of popular culture—particularly in its youthful American form—was, says Maase, 'an articulation of a strange mixture of repressed nationalism and racism with dominant features of classism', a symptom of the difficulty 'of accepting modern mass democracy'. Already a victim of its own economic success, the Federal Republic had thrown up a wave of working-class, youthful earners whose legitimacy was to be found in their spending power, and whose tastes and lifestyles could not but clash with the dominant norms and authority patterns of the times, not least because they invited imitation on the other side of the Iron Curtain.[90]

But as the historian Uta Poiger has shown, these norms and patterns were not deeply rooted. Brando and Elvis arrived just as the West and East German political and educational systems were attempting, each in its own way, to consolidate a redefinition of ideals of citizenship, masculinity and femininity, and working-class behaviour, which had been going on since the establishment of their respective states. As had already happened in the first post-war era, and would happen again after 1989, American popular culture cut across this effort, even threatened to undermine it. While one West German newspaper responded by denouncing juvenile crime as an 'expression of American civilisation', East German official statements exalted their State's efforts at reconstructing 'the great cultural heritage of the German people', and deploring West Germany as a land invaded by 'American non-culture, nationalist-supremacist race hatred, gangster movies, trash novels, boogie-woogie etc. [all] supposed to prepare the adolescents for murder, killings and war'.[91] So with the added

---

[88] Maase, 'Establishing Cultural Democracy', 430–4, 438.

[89] Dutch case described in similar terms in Marja Roholl, 'Uncle Sam: An Example for All?' in Hans Loeber (ed.), *Dutch–American Relations, 1945–1969* (Asse, 1992), 134–44; Austrian case in Wagnleitner (ed.), *Understanding Austria*, 215–21; Italian case in Bruno Wanrooij, 'Dollars and Decency; Italian Catholics and Hollywood', in Ellwood and Kroes (eds), *Hollywood in Europe*, 261–5.

[90] Maase, 'Establishing Cultural Democracy', 432–4; Hanna Schissler, ' "Normalization" as Project: Some Thoughts on Gender Relations in West Germany during the 1950s', in Schissler (ed.), *Miracle Years*, 359–60; on invitation to imitation in East, Merkel, 'Consumer Culture in the GDR', 284–5; Uwe Breitenborn, ' "Memphis Tennessee" in Borstendorf: Boundaries Set and Transcended in East German Television Entertainment', *Historical Journal of Film, Radio and Television* (August 2004), 398–9.

[91] Uta G. Poiger, 'Rebels with a Cause? American Popular Culture, the 1956 Youth Riots, and New Conceptions of Masculinity in East and West Germany', in Pommerin (ed.), *American Impact*; cits at pp. 99, 103.

aggravation of the youth question as a new area of contention in the East–West struggle, 'traditional cultural élites...teachers, critics, representatives of the churches, [and] politicians' united in a campaign against 'filth and trash' in which America and 'Americanization' took the strain. The main difference was one of degree: no restraint in the East, due respect to where ultimate power lay in the case of the Federal Republic.[92]

The defiant attitude of the new German youth culture, says Maase, posed the fundamental question: 'How was a democratic way of dealing with the cultural desires and practices of the majority supposed to look?'[93] Every society was obliged to face up to this key question sooner or later, in the context of contemporary processes such as the Cold War and decolonization that went well beyond the ambit of the single nation state. And while, unwittingly, they all chose very similar mechanisms for dealing with it, the results that emerged in the 1950s proved to be as distinctive and enduring as the peoples that produced them. America provided in many cases the stimulus and the urgency, in some cases the pretext, but such inventions as television for all were products of the logic of the times. Nations were free to choose how to respond to the challenge, but—as in so many cases in the twentieth century where technological development fed into the dynamics of push and pull in the marketplace—they could not escape making a choice.

Nothing was more successful at showing what a demotic culture for the new generations might look like than the films for popular enjoyment that suddenly appeared in Italy in these years. The output of post-war Cinecittà became one of the most successful mechanisms anywhere for reconciling the latest American challenge with local efforts at cultural democratization—'devoid of a formalised national ethos', in Federico Romero's phrase—and the celebrated '*commedia all'italiana*' showed it off with pride.[94] This became the classic form of Italian popular cinema, the one that discovered Sophia Loren and Marcello Mastroianni, Gina Lollobrigida and Vittorio Gassman, as well as a host of celebrated directors from De Sica to Zavattini and Fellini. Among the actors who emerged at this time was the youthful Alberto Sordi, who rose to stardom with his Christmas 1954 success, *Un americano a Roma*. It remains to this

---

[92] Maase, 'Establishing Cultural Democracy', 444–6; on the impact of western models of popular household consumption in eastern bloc countries, Chessel, 'From America to Europe', 173–4; Anne Kaminsky, ' "True Advertising Means Promoting a Good Things Through a Good Form": Advertising in the German Democratic Republic', in Swett et al. (eds), *Selling Modernity*, 262–9.

[93] Maase, 'Establishing Cultural Democracy', 445 (emphasis added).

[94] Cit. in Ellwood, 'Containing Modernity, Domesticating America in Italy', in Stephan (ed.), *Americanization of Europe*, 253–4.

day the most celebrated example of the use of the cinema as a form of cultural shelter.

The story of a Roman working-class youth infatuated with everything American, Nando Mericoni's sole ambition—misunderstood as he is at home—is a ticket to the land of his dreams, evidently fabricated by Hollywood. After a series of humiliations, Nando threatens to commit suicide from the top of the Colosseum unless he is allowed to emigrate. The denouement, involving a scuffle with the American Ambassador himself, lands Nando in hospital, but to the dismay of all around his infatuation with the US remains as strong as ever. Sordi, Italy's most celebrated and best-loved screen comic until his death in 2003, was an actor who liked to give his career its full historical significance. He enjoyed explaining over the years that his 'comédie humaine' was a way of using irony to reconcile Italians to the changes going on all around them. In the case of *Un americano a Roma*, he told a critic that by including episodes that pilloried behaviour such as Marlon Brando's in *The Wild One* (1954), he would save Italian youth from the temptation of imitating him. In this way the film's essentially defensive nature was revealed, showing how the bombardment of novelties from America could be demystified and dealt with on terms that left the locals much preferring their own traditions.[95]

THE BIRTH PAINS OF TELEVISION

The most significant of the Italian 'commedia' films all reflect an anxiety of control, an apprehension about how, in a situation of continuous and painful upheaval, society could continue to invent means for maintaining some sort of order in the balance between tradition and innovation, between the inheritance of the past and the modernity of technology, mass consumption, and ever-expanding mobility. An eloquent expression of the tensions provoked by attempts at the deliberate management of this situation is visible in official attitudes towards the new medium of television. Transmission in Italy began in 1954 in the hands of RAI, the State radio broadcaster. Controlled nominally by Parliament, materially by one of the more conservative elements of the ruling Christian Democrat party, its original guiding principles seem to Italian historians to have been taken

---

[95] Detailed treatment in Ellwood, '*Un americano a Roma*: A 1950s Satire of Americanization', *Modern Italy* (Autumn 1996); the Italian 'covers' of famous American rock songs of the era very often served an identical function, reports Franco Minganti, 'Jukebox Boys', 150–1.

directly from the instructions handed down to the cinema industry by the Roman Curia in 1941.[96]

In RAI's light entertainment programmes, taking over and adapting familiar American television formats might be permitted to get the service started. So successful was the kind of intuitive experimentation that emerged from this process that according to one local commentator, 'when television aspired to a faraway American dream, it most clearly found its originality'.[97] But in the transmissions that counted most, especially the evening news bulletins, no concession was to be made to the notion of entertainment that pervaded every American offering. Even the on-screen advertising—produced almost exclusively at first by the Italian branches of the big American agencies—was rigorously regulated to make sure its commercial and persuasive effects were strictly contained.[98]

Elsewhere in Europe, says the media historian Jérôme Bourdon, 'at a time when official public policy stressed the national character of public service broadcasting…something different was happening at the professional level. American television provided a source of inspiration, and sometimes a solution, to specific problems of programme elaboration.' As at the birth of radio, in its own domain each system sought to strike a distinctive but plausible balance between the perceived needs of the national community as interpreted by those running the State, and the urge to conquer a lasting mass audience with light entertainment.[99]

But television was much more demanding technically and financially than radio, and so required an input of advertising in most cases to cover at least part of the costs. This fact, together with the sheer speed at which the new invention was introduced, dictated that existing and reliable American experiences were inevitably drawn on. How? Bourdon writes: 'In those early days of public service, professionals in all countries, as the British did when ITV started, boasted of their ability to domesticate the

---

[96] Lanaro, *Storia dell'Italia repubblicana*, 214; details of Church's interest in the new medium in Giulia Guazzaloca, 'Le principali culture politiche italiane di fronte al *boom* della televisione', in Cavazza and Scarpellini (eds), *La rivoluzione dei consumi*, 312–2.

[97] Cit. in Jérôme Bourdon, 'Self-Inflicted Imperialism as Early "Global Culture"? The Early Americanisation of European Televisions', unpublished ms, 18; cf. Enrico Menduni, 'La nascita della televisione in Italia', in Cardini (ed.), *Il miracolo economico italiano*, 126–9.

[98] cf. Gundle, *Between Hollywood and Moscow*, 77–80; Lanaro, *Storia dell'Italia repubblicana*, 215–17, 273–5; on the forms of cultural protectionism put in place by the authorities against excessive American influence, Guazzaloca, 'Le principali culture politiche italiane di fronte al *boom* della televisione', 346–53; on the very particular nature of TV publicity—which taught people how to become consumers but within a very tightly controlled linguistic and visual framework, Rossi, 'Televisione', 157–65.

[99] Knut Hickethier, 'Early TV: Imagining and Realising Television', in Bignell and Fickers (eds), *European Television History*, 75–6.

American formats, to bring to them some national colour (e.g. by slowing down the pace, incorporating them into longer shows).' With little or no connection to the US studios themselves or to what was happening to the American TV system at the time, European producers went to the US, 'simply watched TV, liked an idea, a visual detail, and freely picked it up. We will find many examples of these "American television pilgrimages", but nowhere as much as in the cases of England and Spain.'[100]

Spanish, Italian, and German television (in both West and East) would take over the American quiz and variety show templates—*The 64,000 Dollar Question* was the most copied—and lengthen them, turn them into something more grandiose and theatrical, and so create a quite different sense of occasion. The Swedish variety even had academic hosts and judges, and it was generally thought appropriate to suggest that the knowledge being tested was 'serious', so that the State should not be seen as neglecting its educational responsibilities.[101] This was appropriate for an audience as yet limited in TV sophistication and numbers. In the Mediterranean countries, the most popular shows—the quizzes—were watched in bars or piazzas and drew large numbers for a true community experience.[102] Their presenters quickly became popular heroes and eventually national monuments, figures like Mike Bongiorno (i.e. Mike Goodday), an Italo-American who flourished for decades in the ambience of State television's quiz shows before transferring his loyalties to Silvio Berlusconi, the 1970s pioneer of independent, profit-oriented television in Italy.

Doubters, such as the Swedish journalist Ingvar Orre, fought against 'this notion that we needed to become American because we now have television', but this was not a view that carried much weight among the broadcasting authorities.[103] In France it did. Early television developed 'in an atmosphere hostile to game shows', writes Bourdon delicately. Something

---

[100] Bourdon, 'Self-Inflicted Imperialism', 7, 18; Swedish case in Ulf Jonas Bjork, ' "It's Better to Steal the Idea": Swedish Television Copies Programs from America, 1957–1969', *Historical Journal of Film, Radio and Television* (June 2009), 219–27. The author makes clear that programmes were not often simply copied, but 'reworked' according to a series of criteria that changed in time; cf. Ib Bondebjerg et al., 'American Television: Point of Reference or European Nightmare?', in Bignell and Fickers (eds), *European Television History*, 156–7.

[101] Cf. Bjork, 'It's Better to Steal the Idea', 219–20.

[102] The most popular quiz programme, based on *The 64,000 Dollar Question,* was forced to move from Saturday to Thursday nights after united protests from cinema owners, reported the *New York Times* (n. 54 above); a glimpse of the Greek experience in McNeill, 'Afterword', 288; 'the effect of exposure to American forms of TV entertainment on Greek family patterns and other folkways was profound', says McNeill. As part of a general communications revolution, they contributed in particular to mass migration, urbanization, and the disintegration of traditional patterns of belief and expectation.

[103] Bjork, 'It's Better to Steal the Idea', 220.

of this environment is conveyed by the comment attributed to a prominent Catholic priest, Raymond Bruckberger: 'I always think of Bernanos's words: "Man has greater need for illusions than he has for bread." The danger of television is obvious.'[104] Consequently those entrusted to inform, educate, and entertain by way of the new medium were expected to reinforce national unity and cohesion, with special emphasis on the family as the rock that society should cling to in a time of rapid change.[105] There were almost no pilgrimages to the United States and few concessions to the lower orders of public taste. If quizzes there were to be, they would come later and feature vocabulary and mathematics, or knowledge of the cinema. News was for journalists (not 'newscasters'), who read out what they had written in a group, pretending and being granted little attention from other journalists or the political class.[106] In general the Fourth republic's political class showed scarce interest in television, and did little to promote its development technically or socially. In the United States 64.5 per cent of households possessed a TV by 1960; in France the figure was 13 per cent. The West Germans had bought 4.6 million sets by this time, the French only 1.5 million; even the Italians had more.[107]

In Britain 4.5 million television sets had already been sold by 1955 (compared to 260,500 in France); five years later 81.8 per cent of the population enjoyed direct access to TV, powerful reasons to explain why it was Great Britain that saw the most intense and revealing struggle over the boundaries between the native, the natural, and the made-in-America in the new mass medium.[108] Because of the world prestige of the BBC, a model in Europe and far beyond, Britain had for years been the crucial nation of reference in this sector. So when governing circles in London opened a debate in 1952 about the possible launch of what would be Europe's first privately owned, *commercial* television channel, far more was at stake than the desire of one part of the ruling Conservative Party

---

[104] Bourdon, 'Self-Inflicted Imperialism', 11; Kuisel, *Seducing the French*, 117. Georges Bernanos (1888–1948) had been French Catholicism's best-known novelist and essayist in the 1920s–40s; after the war he produced *La France contre les robots* (Paris, 1947).

[105] Marie-Françoise Levy, 'Television, Family and Society in France, 1949–1968', *Historical Journal of Film, Radio and Television* (June 1998), 200–4; on the centrality of the family, the home, and the traditional roles of women, in efforts to restore historic ideas of social stability in the shadow of war and Cold War, Betts and Crowley, 'Introduction', 231–5.

[106] Bourdon, 'Self-Inflicted Imperialism', 11, 14.

[107] Bourdon, *Haute fidélité: Pouvoir et télévision, 1935–1994* (Paris, 1994), 48–9; but the numbers had started to increase rapidly after 1958, says Bourdon, ibid. 53; on television-set prices as the key to new forms of consumerism, Chaveau, 'Il consumo di massa in Francia dopo il 1945', 39–42.

[108] Figures for 1955 cit. in Chapman, *Cinemas of the World*, 237; for 1960 Addison, *No Turning Back*, 56.

to push back the frontiers of the State, and open up an attractive new business opportunity. Bourdon writes:

> This country elaborated the notion of 'two models' of broadcasting which would, in the fifties and the sixties, pervade all the European debates about television, and later would enter all the communications textbooks: an American, commercial, competitive model, and a European, regulated, public service model.[109]

At the time the key distinction pitted those who believed there should be no commercial dimension to television at all against those who believed it was inevitable, but should be unmistakably British in nature; in practice this meant as unlike the system thought to be prevailing in the United States as possible. Given that the British were on the point of surrendering in the battle to dominate their local film market—a dwindling reality in any case—it was no surprise that a great deal of political capital should be devoted to the television contest.[110] The flag bearer for Labour and the anti-commercializers, the Member of Parliament Christopher Mayhew, affirmed that if TV was 'going to be a dominant force in our national life', then it was necessary to 'make sure it has ideals and integrity, or it will ruin us'. For television journalist Peter Black the debate was about 'nothing less than whether Britain should be free or sober'.[111]

It was inevitable that American practice should have been dragged into this most paradigmatic case of the politics of modernization in Western Europe after World War II. As already mentioned, the very structure and organizing culture of the BBC had from its birth been developed to offer an alternative to the perceived chaos and vulgarity of American broadcasting, and its success during the war and at climatic moments of national pride, such as the Coronation of 1953, had given it a status beyond reproach in the panoply of national institutions.[112] The Corporation's

---

[109] Bourdon, 'Self-Inflicted Imperialism', 4; in reality a good deal of interaction between the two sides developed over the years; cf. Bondebjerg et al., 'American Television', 163–4.

[110] Weight, *Patriots*, 242–3; contextualization in Tom O'Malley, ' "Typically Anti-American"? The Labour Movement, America and Broadcasting in Britain, from Beveridge to Pilkington, 1949–62', in Wiener and Hampton (eds), *Anglo-American Media Interactions*, 234–41; for comparable Swedish debate, Mats Björkin, 'European Television Audiences: Localising the Viewers', in Bignell and Fickers (eds), *European Television History*, 221–2.

[111] Lawrence Black, 'Whose Finger on the Button? Cultural Control versus Free Choice, Labour and the Politics of TV in the 1950s and 1960s', paper delivered at the conference *Governing Television? Politics and TV in Europe, 1945–1975*, University of Bologna (Bologna, May 2004), 4–5; cf. Black, *Political Culture*, Ch. 5; O'Malley, 'Typically Anti-American', 241–4.

[112] Valeria Camporesi, *Mass Culture and National Traditions: The BBC and American Broadcasting, 1922–1954* (Florence, 2000), Ch. 1. The Coronation was the first European television 'event', transmitted *live* into five countries. Shaping 'a new horizon of televisual

founding director general, Lord Reith, told a Parliamentary Committee investigating the new TV proposals that the arrival of American-style for-profit television could be compared to the introduction of bubonic plague in the fourteenth century.[113] The American channels had also covered the Coronation, but notoriously they had interrupted it with advertisements, 'using slogans like "Queen of the Road" to sell cars and featuring the TV chimp "J. Fred Muggs"', says Lawrence Black. Defenders of the status quo predicted that the tastes of advertisers would inevitably dominate any form of commercial TV, meaning that the lowest common denominator in audiences would be targeted, for the sake of the numbers.[114]

But the leader of the public service-only group, Mayhew, revealed that his concerns went well beyond the television sector, crucial though it was obviously going to be. Becoming dependent on the US TV market for imports or even exports endangered 'our whole national culture and way of life... it would be an excellent thing if we British asserted ourselves a bit against the whole cultural impact of America'.[115] To this end Mayhew set up a National Television Council in 1953, counting among its members such cultivated minds as Bertrand Russell, E. M. Forster, and Harold Nicolson, and among its sympathizers the whole of the Labour Party leadership and its most committed followers. *Britain Unites Against Commercial Television* was the title of the Council's manifesto, and although very poor compared to its Conservative-funded rival, the Popular Television Association, the group's concerns and its prestige ensured that when the licences to run commercial television were handed out in 1955, they would be hedged around with a mass of qualifications about quality and choice. These would be managed by an Establishment-run body called the Independent Television Authority. Parliament only narrowly defeated a proposal to include among its many rules and norms a ban on 'aliens' (i.e. Americans) from joining its ruling council.[116]

But the runaway success of commercial television soon forced the cultural conservatives on the defensive. 'By the summer of 1957 ITV had 73 per cent of a growing audience compared to the BBC's 27 per cent',

---

expectations', the cultural significance and impact of the transmission 'cannot be over-estimated', write Bignell and Fickers, in the Introduction to their history of European television; *European Television History*, 8.

[113] Cit. in Trumpbour, *Selling Hollywood*, 1.

[114] Camporesi, 'There are no kangaroos in Kent', 46–7; Black, 'Whose Finger on the Button?', 4–5; O'Malley, 'Typically Anti-American', 243–4.

[115] Cit. in Black, 'Whose Finger on the Button?', 5.

[116] Ibid. 4–6; Camporesi, 'There are no kangaroos in Kent', 47–8; Black, 'Whose Finger on the Button?', 6 (I am indebted to Lawrence Black for details of the 'aliens' rule); Peter Gurney, 'The Battle of the Consumer in Postwar Britain', *Journal of Modern History* (December 2005), 969–72; Weight, *Patriots*, 242–7.

reports Lawrence Black. After a period of genuflection to the official values of the ITA, the bosses in charge of the swelling private companies took the brakes off and started to adapt their output to what they saw as mass tastes, instead of trying to mould them as the high-minded defenders of the BBC tradition demanded. 'Let's face it once and for all', said one executive. 'The public likes girls, wrestling, bright musicals, quiz shows and real-life drama. From now on, what the public wants, it's going to get.'[117] This meant downplaying news, current affairs, factual programming of all sorts in the schedules, and emphasizing above all light entertainment. And here American precedents and examples reigned supreme, at least in the early phases: crime films, westerns, variety shows, situation comedies, and above all quizzes: 'In January 1957, there were no less than ten quizzes broadcast each week on ITV', writes Bourdon, 'most of them copies of American formats, among which *The 64.000 Dollar Question, Spot the Tune, Double your Money, Twenty One, Beat the Clock.* Those were prime time programmes then, as in the United States.'[118] A contemporary observer remarked that in spite all the cautions and safeguards, the prophecies of the doomsayers had been proved right: commercial television did indeed bring 'a strain of garishness and Americanisation that to English viewers...was quite new'. But this, it appeared, was the aura of success.[119]

The BBC of course was forced to adapt, bringing in its own American or American-style shows (e.g. the long-running *What's My Line* and *This is Your Life*[120]), though it never used the language of 'newscasters' or 'quizmasters' as ITV did. The Labour Party pressed for reform of the entire commercial sector, but before it obtained any satisfaction, had to endure ITV's transmission of the weekly Western *Rawhide* at just the time on election night in 1959 when the leadership thought the majority of their voters went to the polling stations. Naturally all of the Tories celebrated their triumphant victory next day, including the large numbers who deplored commercial television just as much as Labour did.[121]

---

[117] Black, 'Whose Finger on the Button?', 6, Weight, *Patriots*, 250–1; Paul Addison offers the programming schedule on the two rival networks for 3rd May 1957 in Addison, *No Turning Back*, 57.

[118] Bourdon, 'Self-Inflicted Imperialism', 7; Weight, *Patriots*, 251.

[119] Booker, *Neophiliacs*, 37, 103; British television advertising however was consciously adapted from the start to accommodate the presumed tastes of the distinctive British 'character': Becky Conekin, Frank Mort, and Chris Waters (eds), *Moments of Modernity*, 65–6.

[120] Weight, *Patriots*, 252–3.

[121] Black, 'Whose Finger on the Button?', 12.

IS THIS TOMORROW? DOUBTERS,
SCEPTICS, REBELS

Renewed arguments about 'Americanization' in the 1950s reflected an awareness that the ability of the Americans to project their way of life, or at the very least to render it so easily accessible, expressed powers more challenging than the variety bought by their dollars or manipulated by their national security state. On that side of the Atlantic, creative energies were at work that were far more dynamic and appealing than those that had built the welfare state after the war in Western Europe. What the US now displayed, to greater effect than ever before, was its capacity to invent, produce, and distribute popular culture on an unrivalled, industrial scale. This was a power potential almost wholly lacking in the Old World at the time, and one that brought back old worries to its governing elites, but now with a new intensity. In 1954 the Swiss philosopher Jeanne Hersch expressed concerns that would return in cycles throughout the rest of the century and beyond:

> The Americans make us uneasy because, without wishing us ill, they put things before us for our taking, things which are so ready to hand and so convenient that we accept them, finding perhaps that they satisfy our fundamental temptations....Masses of American products are forced upon us by artificial means, especially where films are concerned....Even when we can make a choice between products, we are influenced by a sort of force within ourselves, which we fear because it is indeterminate and indefinable...the threat we feel hanging over us is not something evil; it is a vacuum, such as is produced by rapid movement.[122]

In England J. B. Priestley was back on the attack. In 1955 the writer and broadcaster would publish his own grand denunciation of the mass-production-for-mass-consumption society, termed by him 'Admass', and inspired more or less directly by the American experience:

> This is my name for the whole system of an increasing productivity, plus inflation, plus a rising standard of material living, plus high pressure advertising and salesmanship, plus mass communications, plus cultural democracy and the creation of the mass mind, the mass man....Most Americans

---

[122] UNESCO, *The Old World and the New: Their Cultural and Moral Relations, International Forums of San Paolo and Geneva, 1954* (1956), cit. in R. Kuisel, *Seducing the French*, 114. It was partly in response to such sentiments that the Harvard sociologist Daniel Bell produced one of the most famous texts of the era, *The End of Ideology: On the Exhaustion of Political Ideas in the Fifties* (1960; rev. edn, Cambridge, Mass., 2000). A celebration of the political and cultural fruits of growth, the text strongly suggested that the wrong-headed critics of mass society had always been and still were all European: pp. 22–30, 38, 99.

(though not all; they have some fine rebels) have been Admassians for the last thirty years; the English, and probably most West Europeans, only since the war.[123]

Unlike most other commentators, however, Priestley went out of his way to insist he was not anti-American, or guilty of the anti-Americanism that critics in the US accused him of as they read this proclamation. He denounced the wilful compounding by them of everything America was and stood for with their specific preferences in the politics and foreign policy of their government:

> It is as if when friends from New York arrived outside our door in [London], I did not invite them in until I had made sure they were in full agreement with our policy in Cyprus and were enthusiastic admirers of Eden, Butler and Macmillan...
>
> When Mrs. Smith tells Mr. Smith that his trousers are baggy and he needs a haircut, nobody accuses her of being anti-Smith.[124]

Well to the left of Priestley, and a man of the future rather than the past, the British social commentator Stuart Hall declared at the end of the decade that the new prosperity of the era was not 'a solid affair of genuine wealth and well-being', but a narrow and subjective set of 'feelings', revolving around certain desires and aspirations that could be expressed in material, consumerist terms. As such there was no reproduction of the 'American' pattern, said Hall. Over there, working people were seeing some of the true benefits of secure access to more goods, including improved status, comfort, and self-respect. But in a country like Britain, 'a more muted, confusing pattern' still prevailed...

> ...where we defined our interests as human beings in terms of the things we *might*—or others might—conceivably possess, although we did not seem to have very many of them *yet*. [Meanwhile] the second-hand car, the washing machine or the telly did not become 'status symbols' in the American sense—providing the working class with insignias of social position, and smoothing out the way into middle class. But they acquired, in consciousness, a social importance out of all proportion to their *use*, or our needs.[125]

But it was the variety of French critiques of the new realities that gained most notoriety, then and later. This was the era that laid the basis for the

---

[123] J. B. Priestley and J. Hawkes, *Journey Down the Rainbow* (London, 1955), 43–5; British context explained in Hilton, 'Fable of the Sheep', 232.

[124] J. B. Priestley, 'Who is Anti-American?' (1957), in *Essays of Five Decades* (London, 1969); personal and political context discussed in Black, *Political Culture*, 84–9, 143–5.

[125] Stuart Hall, 'The Supply of Demand', in Thompson (ed.), *Out of Apathy*, 74 (emphasis in original); Hall pointed out that this American pattern might well be have been imaginary, ibid.

contemporary reputation of French anti-Americanism, and became the model for all those historians—especially in France itself—who would later demonstrate how far away such attitudes were from any specific behaviour of the United States towards France as power, economy, or culture.[126] Although the arguments were very often a *reprise* of those first heard in the 1920s, this time round they were—in spite of the intense Cold War divisions of the times—generally less violent and nihilistic.[127] Their point of course was just as it had been then: the future direction of French society and national identity, the effectiveness of the means available for defining the nation's sense of itself in the new era, the kind of responses to offer to the radiant presence of the American way, specifically—as Richard Kuisel explains—its 'consumerism, conformity, mass culture and optimism'.[128]

This was after all a time when everyone could see that reconstruction in France had been successfully completed in economic terms, while the political future of the Republic and its empire continued to be surrounded by the deepest shadows. As the sociologist and America specialist Michel Crozier put it, the alternative was between 'stagnation and irrevocable decline on the one hand and transformation of the modes of action on the other'. He was referring to the prospects of French business, but the dilemma was clearly felt widely. 'A will for renewal is nevertheless apparent', he insisted. America in this situation—and it was true for Europe as a whole, said Crozier—could not be the source of models to be copied literally, it should rather be seen as 'a stimulus and not a solution'. The important point was that a choice *had* to be made: 'the old dichotomy between principles and means...persists as a pragmatic problem that cannot be eliminated.'[129]

The cultivated minds debated this problem at length, but in the end always understood their role as to defend the nation's cultural heritage, their 'civilization', against the influences driving *la patrie* to converge on the transatlantic model. The editor of *Esprit*, the review of the socially engaged Catholic intellectuals, noted in 1960:

---

[126] Marie-France Toinet, 'French Pique and *Piques Françaises*', *Annals* of the American Academy of Political Science (May 1988); Pierre Guerlain, 'Pride and Prejudice in the Saga of Anti-Americanism', in Stephen Fender (ed.), *American and European National Identities: Faces in the Mirror* (Keele, 1996), and references at p. 139, n. 12; Roger, *American Enemy*, 439–45.

[127] Survey of the relationship between Cold War positions and anti-Americanism in Michel Winock, 'La guerre froide', in Lacorne, Rupnik, and Toinet (eds), *L'Amérique dans les Têtes*.

[128] Kuisel, *Seducing the French*, 110.

[129] M. Crozier, 'The Cultural Revolution: Notes on the Changes in the Intellectual Climate in France', *Daedalus*, Special Issue, 'A New Europe?' (Winter 1964), 530–42.

Ten years ago we could still look down on the snack bars, the supermarkets, the striptease houses, and the entire acquisitive society. Now all that has more or less taken hold in Europe. This society is not yet ours, but it—or one that resembles it—could be our children's. The United States is a laboratory exhibiting life forms into which we have entered whether we like it or not.[130]

In the presence of such forces, how could the universal meaning of the nation's encounter with destiny be relaunched at a time when the overseas empire was facing its death throes (and partly through deliberate American action)? How might 'the vulnerability of cultural circles to the masses' lack of culture', that Raymond Aron saw in America, be prevented from spreading across the ocean?[131] If the Italians had their popular film comedy and the British their commercial television, where were the cultural resources that France could deploy to domesticate the affluent society?

The most obvious temptation was to reject America in all its forms, and settle in a mood of 'resigned resentment' for an entrenched defence of the traditional national ideology of *la Grande Culture*.[132] This was a conception that was autarchic, exclusive, elitist, and revolved around the reproduction via the school system of the idea of 'classic' books, theatre, and music, with poetry as the highest aspiration. Even the inheritance of traditional popular music was acknowledged as part of this scene, and with its internally driven renewal at this time, thanks to such figures as Gilbert Bécaud, Juliette Greco, Georges Brassens, and above all Jacques Brel, the rock 'n' roll invasion was held off for several years. Only with the affirmation of the Elvis-inspired Johnny Hallyday from 1959 onwards was the corner turned. Elvis himself and the entire rock movement were of course regarded as 'illiterate' by the custodians of the higher orders of culture.[133]

But France did succeed in producing its own particular response to the field of force of the American example, and the wave of young people coming to maturity at the end of the 1950s was at the heart of it. Cinema was their preferred battleground and in searching for an answer to the new challenge of television, as well as to the old one of Hollywood, they brought the familiar European techniques of adoption, adaptation, and improvement to a new level of complexity. Like West Germany, with its

---

[130] Jean-Marie Domenach, 'Le modèle américain', *Esprit* (July–August 1960), cit. in Kuisel, *Seducing the French*, 109; full survey of the debate ibid. Ch. 5; cf. Introduction, pp. 25–30 and section II in Lacorne, Rupnik, and Toinet (eds), *L'Amérique dans les Têtes*; Roger, *American Enemy*, 324–37, 396–405.

[131] R. Aron, 'From France', in Joseph (ed.), *As Others See Us*, 68.

[132] Cf. Roger, *American Enemy*, 330, *passim*; phrase 'resigned resentment' at p. 332.

[133] Paul Yonnet, *Jeux, Modes et Masses: La société française et le moderne, 1945–1985* (Paris, 1985), 192–203; cf. Marwick, *Sixties*, 95–107.

Der Spiegel and *Der Zeit* (founded in 1946 and 1949 respectively), and Italy with its *L'Espresso* (1955) and *Panorama* (1962), France had invented its own version of the American weekly news magazine in 1953 with *L'Express*. It was this publication that in August 1957 sponsored a large-scale survey of 'the succession of generations', and declared in a series of commentaries on the results that 'a new wave' of youth was arriving, bearing 'new moral values' and presenting them with 'refreshing, never before seen frankness'.[134]

By spring 1959 the phrase '*nouvelle vague*' had entered the daily vocabulary of the media and a myth was born. It was rooted specifically in the apparent revolution in the nation's cinema, with new actors and actresses—Brigitte Bardot, Jean-Paul Belmondo, Jeanne Moreau, Alain Delon, and others—new directors (sixty-seven made their first features in the 1959–60 years), and new kinds of film, deliberately provocative in style, subject matter, and intended audience. The dominant creative force in European cinema for two generations had now arrived, and it was exclusively the work of a group of young people with a special talent for fantasy, liberty, and iconoclasm. Their example set off 'new waves' through France's neighbours, which enriched the distinctiveness of national film cultures even if they did not create a pan-European impulse to match that of the 1920s.[135]

What the most memorable of these waves shared—the French and the German varieties—was a peculiar regard for the vast American component in the cultural formation of their leading figures. In a celebrated scene in a late film from the German output, Wim Wenders's *Kings of the Road* (1975), one of the two protagonists, sitting in an abandoned US army post along the border with the East, discovers that he cannot get the lyrics of a rock tune from his mind. He comments, half-jokingly, 'the Yanks have colonised our subconscious'. As a leading European film historian, Thomas Elsaesser, points out, this is not simple anti-Americanism. The remark is offered 'both approvingly and critically', a clue to the 'multi-layered and suitably ambiguous' response of the film's setting, characters, and director to the heritage deposited by America in all its forms in the lives of the post-war generation and the society around them.[136]

---

[134] The commentaries were published by their editor Françoise Giroud as *La Nouvelle Vague: Portraits de la jeunesse* (Paris, 1958).

[135] Figure on directors cit. in Chapman, *Cinemas of the World*, 241; general introduction to 'nouvelles vagues' ibid. Ch. 9; Sorlin, *Europe Cinemas*, 139–49; Marwick, *Sixties*, 174–5; Michel Marie, *The French New Wave: An Artistic School* (Oxford, 2003), Ch. 1.

[136] Thomas Elsaesser, 'German Postwar Cinema and Hollywood', in Ellwood and Kroes (eds), *Hollywood in Europe*, 287.

In the French case, the specific inheritance in question was Hollywood itself. What the intellectuals who became film-makers in the New Wave expected from things American, says Elsaesser, 'were works of fiction that could serve as creative models, representative of their own situation and embodying specifically modern tensions—between intellect and emotion, action and reflection, consciousness and instinct, choice and spontaneity.'[137] Homages to the American film industry's people and their inventions abounded in the new French productions, signs of an admiration that never extended to the nation's society or economy—much less its foreign policy—but which embraced the Hollywood idea of cinematic technique and quality, the 'visual orchestration of the story' (Elsaesser), the development of genres, and the taste for the peculiar undersides as well as the glossy surfaces of American life. Just as Hollywood had deconstructed and reassembled so much classic European culture, now a rejuvenated Western European spirit would repay the compliment. It was an outstanding example of what Michel Crozier was referring to when he remarked in 1964: 'It is only to the extent that they have lost their feeling of inferiority to America that the young Europeans have begun, in turn, to respect it.'[138]

WHEN THE OLD DISCIPLINES
BECOME RELAXED . . .

But the generations still in command were not convinced. The relative sexual frankness of many of the new films, and the rise to international stardom of their piquant incarnation Brigitte Bardot, produced a backlash. The fact that Bardot's career had flourished in the United States— where films like *And God Created Woman* (1956) began to upstage local products still bound by the censorship rules of the 1930s[139]—only confirmed the old notion that there, to the West, lay perdition. Religious groups in France mobilized in outrage over the new manners, and in the atmosphere surrounding the return to power in 1958 of General Charles de Gaulle, a man who could hardly have been more traditionalist in his personal demeanour, censorship was significantly tightened up.[140]

---

[137] Thomas Elsaesser, 'Two Decades in Another Country: *Hollywood and the Cinéphiles*', in C. W. E. Bigsby (ed.), *Superculture: American Popular Culture and Europe* (London, 1975), 211.

[138] Visual evidence in Bigsby (ed.), *Superculture*, after p. 130; Sorlin, *Europe Cinemas*, 140–2; Crozier, 'Cultural Revolution', 534 (note).

[139] Pells, *Not Like Us*, 222.

[140] Marwick, *Sixties*, 175.

Thirty years later conservative critics such as the historians Norman Stone in Britain and Ernst Nolte in Germany seemed to regret that too little had been done in this direction at the time. Deploring the crisis of political legitimacy in the West after the Cold War and attributing it to the 'decline of class differences, [the] role of the mass media in politics, [the] spread of hedonistic culture', Professor Stone explained that the roots of the phenomena were all to be found in the post-war experience of 'Americanization':

> It goes back very obviously to the 1950's, but you can take it back to Hollywood in the 1930's. Democracy, Reader's Digest, rock music and the easy prosperity of 'gadgets' spread. Sensible people saw that this changed the nature of politics...
>
> Prosperity and democracy create their own social problems because the old disciplines become relaxed...[141]

Conservatives of the left and the right were deeply aware of this mechanism at work in the Europe of the 1950s, of the breakdown of old hierarchies of respect and respectability, and they did their best to thwart it.[142] Although West Germany's economic success effectively underpinned the delicate democratization process in that country, conservatives nevertheless tried 'vehemently' to ward off the social and cultural implications of the process, writes Michael Wildt, and expressed a 'deep distrust of the sovereignty of the individual', especially in his or her doings in the marketplace.[143] Eventually the tensions of the protectionist effort became too much, hence the great wave of youthful revolt at the end of the following decade.

The French elite should not have been as surprised as they were by their own experience of the same confrontation. In his 1959 study of *The Rise of the Young*, the distinguished social and economic commentator Alfred Sauvy had warned:

> The young won't let themselves be subdued. If we try to do it, if we keep our old methods, our old houses, the young will explode the whole system according to biological law.[144]

---

[141] *Sunday Times*, 25 July 1993.

[142] The later work of the eminent English novelist Evelyn Waugh is a prime example of this effort, suggests Dick Hebdige, *Hiding the Light*, 49–50.

[143] Michael Wildt, 'Continuities and Discontinuities of Consumer Mentality in West Germany in the 1950s', in Richard Bessel and Dirk Schumann (eds), *Life after Death: Approaches to a Cultural and Social History of Europe During the 1940s and 1950s* (Cambridge, 2003), 215.

[144] Cit. in Levy, 'Television, Family and Society in France', 204; Henri-George Clouzot's *La vérité* (1960), featuring Brigitte Bardot on trial for murder, is one of the best film sources showing these tensions at work; cf. Pascal Ory, *L'avventure culturelle française, 1945–1989* (Paris, 1989), 156–61.

As the German case shows, disputes over recognition and legitimacy in popular taste were crucial to the modernization of European democracy in these years. In the Federal Republic the American inspiration worked on two of the key fronts of this argument, reconciling the traditional middle classes to pluralism and continuous change, while providing the new youth culture with icons, symbols, and myths that would eventually—after much agony but no 'revolution'—help young people acquire proper recognition for their distinctive role in contemporary consumer society.[145]

But all concerned were aware that these processes did bring with them a great crumbling of traditional cultural hierarchies and frontiers. There were plenty of small examples as well as all the big ones. 'We are not thinking of the future in terms of saloon bars and public bars', announced the Chairman of a major British beer producer in 1958, suggesting that even the hallowed division between the 'smart' and the 'working' sections of British pubs was up for negotiation.[146] The phenomena that Priestley called 'Admass' 'carried further that erosion of old frontiers that was so much part of the times', commented Hopkins. A 'new, more fluid, and dare one say it, more neurotic social structure' appeared, said Christopher Booker in *The Neophiliacs* shortly afterwards, 'in which no-one any longer knew with quite such certainty who or where they stood all the familiar landmarks were being eroded, nothing any longer seemed to be quite so real'.[147]

As the ever-spreading consumption of objects and leisure confirmed the legitimacy of rising expectations, the old distinctions which to cultivated minds separated quality from quantity finally dissolved. Leavis's pre-war distress over the threats to standards that he thought classical was now justified, it seemed. An equally distinguished successor, George Steiner, would lament the triumph of those processes that had brought about the collapse of the 'hierarchised, definitional value-gradients' on which 'civilisation itself' was based. In this view of the world, America's single-minded idea of the future of democracy and its bright cultural expansiveness had a lot to answer for. They had appropriated Western man's modern search for individual empowerment and self-realization, pushed it in one particular, hedonistic direction, and turned it into a huge commercial enterprise, heedless or contemptuous of every pre-existing

---

[145] Maase, 'Establishing Cultural Democracy', 445–6; Diethelm Prowe, 'The "Miracle" of the Political-Culture Shift: Democratization Between Americanization and Conservative Reintegration', in Schissler (ed.), *Miracle Years*; Berghahn, 'Recasting Bourgeois Germany', in Schissler (ed.), *Miracle Years*, 337.

[146] Hopkins, *New Look*, 462.

[147] Ibid. 231–2; Booker, *Neophiliacs*, 228–9.

standard of taste and sensibility. If this was precisely why the new generations liked it and bought into it (at very cheap prices compared to the
traditional products of 'high culture'), if this was the answer to the question of what 'a democratic way of dealing with the cultural desires and
practices of the majority' was supposed to look like, then there would be
no more hierarchies and so no more values. 'Americanization' would rule
supreme.[148]

Official America responds: Projecting the nation's message in an age of consumerism

It was partly to combat this sort of mentality, thought deeply injurious to
the ongoing ideological battle with the Soviet Union, that the US government took such an interested, activist attitude towards organized cultural
policies of every sort in the 1950s. The point was to 'prove' to the rest of
the world—as Daniel Bell put it in 1958—'that the United States has a
culture too', and that that culture should be seen as well-intentioned,
even idealistic in its underlying drives and character. At its best, said this
line of argument, it could match the highest standards of European creativity.[149] Exhibitions, art, music, dance, and photo extravaganzas were put
on to attract millions of people to this message, and very often succeeded—at least in terms of tickets sold—in doing so.[150] The study of
America in schools and universities, strongly encouraged by the State Department, the new United States Information Agency (USIA), and their
allies in the great private foundations, encouraged all those who believed,
as a German 'Americanist' did, that the US 'was the overwhelming entity
with which everyone had to be acquainted, if you were intellectually enterprising at all'.[151]

---

[148] Leavis cit. in Chapter 4, n. 29; Hebdige, *Hiding the Light*, 72; Betts and Crowley,
'Introduction', 231; Steiner cit. in Robert Hewison, *Culture and Consensus: England, Art
and Politics since 1940* (London, 1995), 155; French equivalents of this critique discussed
in Kuisel, *Seducing the French*, 126–8. The discussion in this paragraph owes much to
Winfried Fluck, 'The Americanization of Modern Culture', in Agata Preis-Smith and Piotr
Skurowski (eds), *Cultural Policy or the Politics of Culture?* (Warsaw, 1999).

[149] Details and discussion in Pells, *Not Like Us*, chs 3, 4; the role of President Eisenhower
in encouraging official information, educational efforts, and psychological efforts is emphasized in Cull, *Cold War*, Ch. 2; on interest in promoting overseas appreciation of 'American cultural achievement and aspirations', ibid. 114; cf. Bell, *End of Ideology*, 101.

[150] Details in Cull, *Cold War*, 115–18.

[151] Cit. in Pells, *Not Like Us*, 103; on overall phenomenon of growth of American Studies, ibid. Ch. 4; on the large-scale exchange programmes involving universities, Oliver
Schmidt, 'Small Atlantic World: U.S. Philanthropy and Expanding International Exchange
of Scholars after 1945', in Jessica C. E. Gienow-Hecht and Frank Schumacher (eds), *Culture and International History*, 120–6; a typical product of the interest of the foundations
was the volume edited by Joseph (ed.), *As Others See Us*.

Yet the results of all the activity proved ambiguous, and generated controversy from that era of the 1950s down to the present. One reason was the bitter, intensely ideological Cold War context, which, among other deplorable consequences, led to the deliberate blurring of the line between cultural promotion and psychological warfare, with all its shady, clandestine connotations.[152] Even its admirers recognized that the drives to build networks and sympathy often appeared intrusive, artificial, politically as much as culturally motivated, and over-reliant on the fluctuating 'spiritual power of [American] leadership'.[153] Hollywood, it was alleged abroad, had far more influence over time for good or ill than any instrumental cultural policy could produce.[154] There was little two-way flow, and recipients around the world of US invitations often wondered why official policy did not encourage a better acquaintance in America of the peoples they were supposed to be benefitting.[155] While ready to acknowledge the beneficent purposes and effects of many American cultural exports, official or otherwise, allies everywhere insisted they would all be nourishing their own, native arts of living.[156] Meanwhile, the USIA was expected to organize support for its government's foreign policies as well as for the national cultural heritage, unlike the comparable agencies of other nations, and there could be no doubting the Cold War significance of an operation like the semi-private, semi-public Congress for Cultural Freedom.[157]

The historian Jessica Gienow-Hecht has noted that there is a significant distinction to be made between the 'You too can be like us' invitation of the Marshall Plan, 'and the plea for recognition that "We are the

---

[152] Jessica C. E. Gienow-Hecht, ' "How Good Are We?" Culture and the Cold War', in G. Scott-Smith and H. Krabbendam (eds), *The Cultural Cold War in Western Europe, 1945–1960* (London, 2003), 269–74; on the USIA's troubles in the late 1950s, Cull, *Cold War*, 142–5.

[153] Pells, *Not Like Us*, 103; Skard, *American Myth*, 95, 110.

[154] Cf. contributions from Britain, Turkey, India, Philippines, Canada, Chile in Joseph (ed.), *As Others See Us*.

[155] Ibid. contributions from Yugoslavia, Iran, Egypt, India, Philippines, Mexico, Canada, Chile; at the end of his great history of the US Information Agency, Nicholas Cull concludes that over the years, 'the U.S. government conceived of the agency as a way to address the world rather than as a mechanism for understanding it', *Cold War*, 487.

[156] Joseph (ed.), *As Others See Us*, every contribution.

[157] This did not mean that its objectives were not shared in good faith by its members. Only when its extensive, hitherto concealed, CIA funding was finally revealed from the late 1960s on did its credibility receive a fatal blow; discussion in Krabbendam and Scott-Smith, 'Introduction: Boundaries to Freedom', (and other articles), in Scott-Smith and Krabbendam (eds), *Cultural Cold War*; on the destructive, long-term consequences of the strain between foreign policy advocacy and cultural work in general, Cull, *Cold War*, 489–90, 498–9, 503–4.

same as you" (as implied in countless USIA programs in the 1950s)'.[158] In the earlier phase the propaganda came direct. In the latter it often used networks of carefully chosen mediating agents, local intellectual leaders, and opinion-makers who had become convinced of the worth of American values, and of some of the lessons American experience held for the future of Europe.[159] Although this approach evolved into a successful and distinctive American method for picking out and hopefully influencing the future rulers of allied nations,[160] the risks inherent in these network building activities were always in evidence; not all the efforts could be counted on to produce the desired results. The editor of *Esprit*'s reflections on the state of America and its impact in the world, cited above, came as a result of a State Department-sponsored trip. But Jean-Marie Domenach's observations read like the text of a traditional traveller's tale. Although admiring of the nation's capacity for innovation and self-renewal, the author was deeply sceptical of its ideological and moral absolutism, as well as its materialism, and felt the world was drifting away from the United States as a nation, even as 'Americanization' spread.[161]

So, as 'the chromium horde' of cars bore down on the first big waves of American-style supermarkets in Europe, the contentious features of an era known later as post-modernism began to loom large on the horizon. At the same time, under the flashy surface, a new generation of people, thoughts, and feelings was bubbling up. In the following decade it quickly emerged that the Europe now blossoming was as a whole no more in thrall to America's stars of screen, rock concert, or fashion than it was to the world of its own literary critics. The 'psychic dam' of the 1950s was ready to burst, and its waters would sweep away outmoded dogmas, stereotypes, and prejudices of every kind.[162]

---

[158] Gienow-Hecht, 'How Good Are We?', 280.

[159] Cf. Volker Berghahn, *America and the Intellectual Cold Wars in Europe* (Princeton, 2001), esp. pp. 168–77.

[160] Richard Pells lists a few of the future European national leaders who arrived in the US on fellowships and travel grants in these years, *Not Like Us*, 87. In later years, the biggest success story from this generation was considered by the American authorities to be Margaret Thatcher: story of her first, sponsored, arrival in the US and impressions in Cull, *Cold War*, 279–80.

[161] Sections II and III in succeeding numbers of *Esprit*, 1960 (n. 130 above); comment in Kuisel, *Seducing the French*, 116; an earlier unhappy brush between Domenach and official America is recounted ibid. p. 256, n. 1; discussion of risks of official cultural activities in Pells, *Not Like Us*, 87.

[162] Concept of 'psychic dam' in Ian Macdonald, *Revolution in the Head: The Beatles' Records and the Sixties* (London, 1995), 6.

THE END OF IDEOLOGY? FROM 'THE FIFTIES' TO 'THE SIXTIES'

The year 1960 saw the release of *It Started in Naples*, a late Clark Gable feature involving a rich Philadelphia lawyer's search-and-rescue mission in a poor but lively version of the island of Capri, where 'Mr Hamilton' hopes to find his late brother's son, now a local street urchin. While teaching the little boy the joys of the hamburger and how to eat it in his luxury hotel suite, and confirming the by-now familiar American obsessions with personal hygiene and baseball, the hero attempts to convince the boy and his family of how much better his prospects would be if he was removed to Philadelphia. But the visitor's well-meaning efforts to convert the local lad to the American dream, and save him from what looks like poverty, are rebuffed by the boy himself, his flamboyant folk-mother (Sophia Loren), and all the indignant local community. Only when Mr Hamilton abandons his American stuffiness and settles for the locals on their terms, including 'Auntie' Sophia's, does he find the start of the way to happiness. The British commentator Harry Hopkins wrote:

> Europe, in short, was at last giving hints that it might yet succeed in assimilating the Americans as America had assimilated Europeans.

In his colourful 1964 survey of post-war Britain down to that time, Hopkins stated flatly:

> The American Century which in 1946, in the face of Europe's debility, had seemed so unchallengeable—and so galling—fifteen years later, in the face of Europe's re-equipment, consolidation and resurgence, was already over.[163]

Although there were voices in succeeding years who would flatly deny such a conclusion and tried to set off alarms with words like 'take over', 'invasion', and 'occupation',[164] most contemporary observers tended to

---

[163] Hopkins, *New Look*, 456; the old ways reasserted themselves against American modernizing pushiness in the last of the Ealing-style comedies, *The Battle of the Sexes* (Charles Crichton, 1960). Here an energetic female American management consultant (played by Constance Cummings) attempts to convert an old-fashioned Scottish tweed business to contemporary business methods and man-made fibres. She is rebuffed by the inhabitants of the Dickensian counting-house, led by Mr McPherson (Peter Sellers). One old European trope of America—the independent woman—meets a new one of the 1950s: the management consultant; discussion in Ellwood, 'European Cinema's Satire'.

[164] Cf. Francis Williams, *The American Invasion* (London, 1962); James McMillan and Bernard Harris, *The American Take-Over of Britain* (London, 1968). These books were both based on the rapidly expanding American business and investment presence in Europe, a phenomenon that greatly accelerated after the creation of the Common Market in 1957. The most famous production in this genre was Jean-Jacques Servan-Schreiber's *Le défi*

express similar sentiments. At the very least they agreed that a restored balance of vitality, self-confidence, and faith in the future between Western Europe and the US had started to push to the background the fears of 'Americanization' that had plagued the 1950s, and this was a perception later historians would share.[165] Whatever one-way 'Americanization' process had been set in motion—and there were plenty of examples of invidious reproduction, from supermarkets to management consultancy, from high-rise architecture to popular music—it was now practically completed, thought the commentators. In particular the patent rights on contemporary youth and popular culture had run out, argued Harry Hopkins. Jeans, jukeboxes, snack food, and much of the rest had taken on a universal life of their own, and become involved in trends that saw them mixed up everywhere with...

> ...Italian-styled scooters and suits, Spanish holidays, Scandinavian furniture and light fittings, Scotch whisky, Chinese and Indian restaurants, Sartre, Sagan, Henry Moore and Jackson Pollock, Anna Magnani and Tommy Steele, Beckett and Osborne, Tennessee Williams and T. S. Eliot, cheap French wine and French Impressionists, calypsos and espresso bars...

The old distinctions that normally kept such items well in their place on the time-honoured gradient of cultural significance had indeed broken down, it seemed. But that did not mean the transatlantic way was taking over.[166]

Like the dollar itself, America's traditional currencies of power were starting to look over-valued. Even the absolute supremacy of US technical prowess was gone, said Hopkins:

> ...America no longer monopolised that 'secret', that vaunted 'know-how' from which had flowed so much of her unique prestige and magnetism in the Forties. The spell was broken. The sputniks were in orbit and that orbit was global.

The democracy of mass production and mass consumption, and the 're-production in postwar England of basic American conditions', were creat-

---

américain (*The American Challenge*) of 1967. Its extraordinary impact is described in John Ardagh, *The New France* (London, 1977), 711–12; historical perspective in Kuisel, *Seducing the French*, 178–80, 206–10, de Grazia, *Irresistible Empire*, 367–8.

[165] Eric Larrabee, 'Transcripts of a Transatlantic Dialogue', *Daedalus*, Special Issue, 'A New Europe?' (Winter 1964), 463; cf. Mazower, *Dark Continent*, 315–16; Marwick, *Sixties*, 363.

[166] Hopkins, *New Look*, 456, Larrabee, 'Transcripts', 464; on the impact of Swedish concepts of modernity that linked new forms of domesticity to democratization and citizenship, Betts and Crowley, 'Introduction', 228–30.

ing not derivative but parallel phenomena, Hopkins concluded. The reform of secondary education, the mobilization of consumers, the advance of the service sector and suburbia, and many another cultural trend, might be seen to have American precedents, but they were developments with a logic and momentum of their own by this time, which functioned in terms invented by local agents and exigencies.[167]

Everywhere there were signs that a different post-war phase was opening. The newly decolonized nations and the non-aligned movement offered challenges that America's conceptions of freedom were having ever-greater difficulty in meeting.[168] In 1959 the US ran a serious balance of payments deficit with the other industrial nations for the first time. As for the Cold War, it had become clear after 1953 that West Europeans took a different view of it, and refused to shoulder the endlessly increasing burden of expenditure for armaments that the military-industrial complexes in the US and the USSR demanded. Instead they repeatedly sought political or economic alternatives to the military logic of the arms race. The British had for long demanded 'summit' meetings with the Russians. Now—in 1958—returned the formidable figure of Charles de Gaulle, who would over the succeeding years challenge the Atlanticist arrangements from top to bottom. Even the evolution of the European Economic Community and its policies towards the Eastern bloc after 1957 might be seen with hindsight as fitting into the same logic. The arrival in the White House of such a brilliant political figure as the young John F. Kennedy in 1960 would not be enough to block these trends, and there was much reflection in foreign policy circles on the implications for America of the miraculous rebirth of the continent's self-confidence, what the veteran Europe-watcher Edgar Ansel Mowrer called its defiant, distinctive 'relevance to the future'.[169] The historian Ronald Steel's *End of Alliance* of 1964 would turn out to be particularly prescient:

[167] Hopkins, *New Look*, 455; Dahrendorf, 'Recent Changes', 262; Kuisel, *Seducing the French*, 129–30; a large-scale survey of the outcome of the processes described here was offered in 1964 by the American management specialist, Edward A. McReary, *The Americanization of Europe* (Garden City, NY, 1964). In spite of its title, and its starting point in the rapid expansion of US business and investment in Europe, the penetrating discussion makes clear just how important were the distinctions between what had been exported from the US, and what the trends of the times had created on the ground. The volume was in many ways a latter-day equivalent of the journalist Mowrer's study of 1928, *This American World*, see Chapter 2.

[168] For the problems faced in the late 1950s by official US information and cultural policy in Vietnam, Latin America, the Middle East, and even Britain, Cull, *Cold War*, 156–9, 183–4.

[169] E. A. Mowrer, 'The Fifth Europe', *Horizon* (March 1963), 4–9; Jean Monnet's thoughts and actions of the time—he appears to have been a key inspirer of the shift from OEEC to OECD—in Duchêne, *Jean Monnet*, 322–5; cf. Lundestad, *'Empire' by Integration*, 52–6, 86–92, 148–50.

In the sense that it seizes upon the new kind of loyalty being created in Europe, and upon the desire to be both separate and different from America, Gaullism is far stronger than de Gaulle and is likely to outlive its chief exponent just as Bonapartism survived the demise of Napoleon.[170]

For the most part then, West European societies were free to resist the projection of American power in all its forms, to take what they wanted from the American model and to 'seek our own particular accommodation with technological society while holding on to our own lifeline of continuity in these seas of change', as Hopkins said of Britain.[171] The arrival of mass television broadcasting, providing a distinct expression of national consciousness and identity in households every evening, was the most striking and enduring example of this mechanism at work.[172] Entirely free the West Europeans were not: the imperatives of the Cold War and generalized anti-Communism remained dominant themes in the Old World's politics all through the post-war period and caused continuous tension between defence, welfare, and individual priorities in the ways societies spent their new-found wealth. As the Soviets and the Americans vied to promise the most dazzling consumerist future for their populations on such occasions as the American National Exhibition in Moscow of summer 1959, some Europeans recalled (for the last time?) their old judgements about the similarities of those two civilizations, both so relentlessly dedicated to organization and output.[173]

The dilemmas of the nuclear age, and the transition to the new model of modernization, left the West Germans 'oscillating between cosmic fear and satisfaction with their prosperity', said an Italian observer of them.[174]

[170] R. Steel, *End of Alliance* (New York, 1964), 79–81; on de Gaulle's attitudes to America as a nation, his restoration of French self-respect and the consequent dimunition of 1950s reflex anti-Americanism, Michael M. Harrison, 'La solution gaulliste', in Lacorne, Rupnik, and Toinet (eds), *L'Amérique dans les Têtes*.

[171] Hopkins, *New Look*, 457; cf. Larrabee, 'Transcripts', 463.

[172] State-run, monopoly television seemed to organize the 'daily plebiscite' that guaranteed the individual citizen's loyalty to the nation in the famous conception of the French historian Ernest Renan; short version of 1882 speech launching this view at: <http://www.nationalismproject.org/what/renan.htm>; cf. Bignell and Fickers (eds), *European Television History*, 128, 130, 231.

[173] On the Moscow exhibition, scene of the famous 'kitchen debate' between Soviet leader Nikita Kruschev and Vice President Richard Nixon on the prospects for affluence under their respective systems, Betts and Crowley, 'Introduction', 224–5, Castillo, 'Domesticating the Cold War', 261–2, 283–4, Cull, *Cold War*, 162–9; on the debate itself, its background and consequences, Cristina Carbone, 'Staging the Kitchen Debate: How Splitnik Got Normalized in the United States', in Oldenziel and Zachmann (eds), *Cold War Kitchen*; on equivalence of systems, Allsop, *Angry Decade*, 208, Domenach, 'Le modèle américain', III, *Esprit* (October 1960), 1522, Mowrer, 'Fifth Europe', 9 (quoting Denis de Rougemont).

[174] Cit. in Ellwood, *Rebuilding Europe*, 240.

The British were said to be 'in a state of physical well-being hitherto un-equalled and on the brink of a mass nervous breakdown hitherto impos-sible'.[175] It was the reality of tumultuous expansion of course, which served to make these tensions politically manageable, thereby fostering the spread of the growth consensus and sidelining all those who com-plained of the 'spiritual dry rot' of the age.[176]

So, in the sphere of practical politics and economics, if not of ideals, of all those three great, specific themes the United States brought to the post-war world—collective security, free trade, and rising living stand-ards—none was more successful than the latter, in its new incarnation as 'growth'. This was the drive that brought the decrepit local versions of capitalism through their near-death experiences after 1945, and effec-tively guaranteed the transition from stabilization to recovery and on to modernization in Western Europe. The 'revolution of rising expectations' that some peoples in Europe and elsewhere had expressed ever since the first post-war era, if not earlier, had been fulfilled by consumption, what-ever the misgivings of traditional authorities at the outcome, and no matter how many were abandoned by the wayside.[177]

But personal consumption was only one element of the dynamic that turned rapidly rising gross national product from a promise into a chal-lenge. The West Europeans discovered by the end of the 1950s that while they could have growth without welfare (this was a favourite complaint of working-class parties, as well as a common negative stereotype of the US[178]), it was not possible to run the welfare state without growth: demand for its services tended to expand exponentially unless explicitly held down and rationed. Yet there were just as many long, historical fac-tors impinging on growth rates in the various nations as there were recent ones organizing and planning the expansion of the 'mixed economy'. The

---

[175] Allsop, *Angry Decade*, 195.

[176] Ibid. 192; François Bédarida, *A Social History of England, 1851–1990* (2nd edn, London, 1991), 250–2. The change in morals of these years would have deep and enduring effects; practising Christianity started an accelerated, long-term decline in Western Europe at this time, which in the British case was still continuing at the start of the twenty-first century and threatening the extinction of the national churches: Callum G. Brown, *The Death of Christian Britain* (London, 2001), 6–7, 174–5. The effects of the crusade by the American evangelist Billy Graham, hugely visible in 1954 and 1955, turned out to be ephemeral. On the very mixed reception that accompanied Graham's long experience of preaching in Europe, R. Laurence Moore, 'American Religion as Cultural Imperialism', in Moore and Maurizio Vaudagna (eds), *The American Century in Europe* (Ithaca, 2003), 163–5.

[177] Pizzorno, 'Individualistic Mobilization', 218–21; de Grazia, *Irresistible Empire*, 373–4; on the struggle to keep rising expectations under control in East Germany, Merkel, 'Con-sumer Culture in the GDR', 285–6.

[178] Alain Touraine, 'Management and the Working Class in Western Europe', *Daedalus*, Special Issue, 'A New Europe?' (Winter 1964), 327.

result was the appearance of unprecedented strains on old institutions: the family, the company, the community, the education system, parliamentary democracy itself. In Britain Anthony Crosland wrote: '...so far from Utopia coming steadily into view, new and more subtle social problems, hitherto concealed by a national obsession with material standards, now come to the surface and demand attention.' The youthful rebellions of the 1960s, which fed each other across the Atlantic, were just the most conspicuous symptom of these difficulties.[179]

At the start of that decade the US business expert Edward McReary had proclaimed: 'The American Evolution has come to Europe.' He offered a remarkable survey of the role of the New World's inspiration in the era of the economic miracles. Debunking the title of his own book, McReary insisted that 'Americanization' was far too glib and facile a term to use to characterize the changes taking place, a crude tool that naysayers employed in their resentment at the breakdown of old hierarchies and loyalties, and their substitution with accessible abundance. Instead America the rib of the Old World, which since its foundation had acted as Europe's 'alter ego and goad', its 'standing accusation and moral annoyance', had reappeared after 1945 as 'shell-shocked Europe's shield and source of plasma of all sorts—monetary, technical, humorous, escapist'.[180] Along the way the United States had invented the first consumer society, 'it got there first'. Now rather than start from scratch, the European allies were appropriating the best of it and reinventing the rest, tackling in their own way questions of social and individual development that had been there since political democracy first looked the industrial revolution in the face. Perhaps it was the energy produced by this clash or confrontation of models and experiences that laid the basis for the unprecedented, unimaginable success of the West in the fifteen years following the end of Hitler's war.

---

[179] Crosland, *Future of Socialism*, 97; cf. 'Protest in the Growth Society', in Mazower, *Dark Continent*, 316–25; on the discovery of the costs of mass car use, Addison, *No Turning Back*, 171–2.

[180] McReary, *Americanization of Europe*, 260, 265.

PART III

1989–2009

10

After the Cold War: The Age of 'Soft Power'

THE THIRD WAVE

The 1990s saw the Western world's third post-war era of the twentieth century. As in the two previous experiences, nations and societies began to think of the consequences for them of the recent conflict's outcome, how power had shifted and changed in the meantime, who was up and who was down. The unexpected, rushed end of the 45-year confrontation between the Soviet bloc and the West left no doubt as to who had lost the Cold War, but found the Western side divided and hesitant. The late 1980s had not been good years for the American economy, and there could be no talk of a new Marshall Plan: the United States couldn't afford it, not, at least, on the scale of the original.[1] There was much complaint of imperial overstretch, of uncertain leadership, of domestic challenges unfaced, and rivals in Asia preparing to overtake the lone superpower. Japan looked ready to present itself as the world's economic leader and a new model of modernity.[2]

The Europe of the Economic Community, which in 1990 comprised twelve states, was galvanized by the end of the Cold War. A process of integration accelerating since 1986, reinforced by some good years of growth, had produced a resounding design for further integration of markets, laws,

---

[1] Burnet, *America 1843–1993*, 260, in fact between 1992 and 1997 US official policy provided $4.9 billion in aid to Russia (others, of course, provided much more); numbers and critique of this operation in Janine R. Wedel, 'Aid to Russia', *Foreign Policy in Focus* (September 1998), at: <http://www.fpif.org/reports/aid_to_russia/>; official policy of USAid/Russia at: <http://russia.usaid.gov>.

[2] A 1991 lament by the leading political scientist Samuel Huntington is quoted in R. J. Johnston, 'The United States, the "Triumph of Democracy" and the "End of History"', in David Slater and Peter J. Taylor (eds), *The American Century: Consensus and Coercion in the Projection of American Power* (Oxford, 1999), 159; the most famous declinist text of the times was Paul Kennedy, *The Rise and Fall of the Great Powers: Economic Change and Military Conflict, 1500 to 2000* (New York, 1987).

standards, and institutions.[3] With the collapse of the Soviet empire, its newly liberated members immediately looked to Brussels for their salvation and future prosperity, a responsibility for which the EC was not ready or, it soon transpired, willing. A reunited Germany produced an even greater rumbling in the foundations of the Community, and much trepidation, especially among the French and the British, about the future behaviour of the new powerhouse in the centre of Europe. Wouldn't this scaled-up Germany inevitably want to present itself as leader and model astride the Old World?[4]

The well-known Mexican writer and commentator Jorge Castaneda talked of 'these new poles, Germany and Japan', and his belief in the meaning of their rise to prominence:

> These economic powers today have neither the ideological message or the cultural ambition to transform 'the history of their success' into a recipe for others. But if logic and history have any sense, it's only a question of time.[5]

In less than ten years this prophesy looked hopelessly out of place. The competitors floundered, while the United States, against a multitude of other predictions, flourished.

In a longer-term perspective, the third post-war period showed just how much had been gained by the West Europeans in their unique story of recovery since 1945, and yet how unprepared they were for the new freedom of strategic manoeuvre in the world that the end of the Cold War brought them. By the time the 'European Union' was officially born in 1993, its GNP had overtaken America's—$6 trillion compared to $5.2 trillion—and, as American observers noted, 'with only 6.4 per cent of the world's population ... this economic superpower accounted for over one-third of global production and 42 per cent of both world imports and exports'. A vast area of economic interdependence had grown up:

> America ran trade deficits with the European Union every year since 1983, while it remained a key export destination not only for U.S. commodities but

---

[3] Cf. Frans Andriessen, 'Europe at the Crossroads', April 1990, in Center for International Affairs, *Allies or Adversaries? U.S.–European Relations in the Paul-Henri Spaak Lectures, Harvard University, 1985–1992*, 88–103; Andriessen was Vice President of the European Commission at the time.

[4] The Pentagon apparently feared that Germany (and Japan) might now be tempted to a strategy of substantial rearmament, including nuclear weapons; draft strategy document discussed in *International Herald Tribune*, 9 March 1992; on French and British fears of Germany, Tony Judt, *Postwar*, 639, 718–20.

[5] J. Castaneda, 'La revanche des pauvres', *Nouvel observateur* (6–12 February 1992); on the subsequent fate of these two 'models', Ronald Dore, *Stock Market Capitalism: Welfare Capitalism, Japan and Germany versus the Anglo-Saxons* (Oxford, 2000).

for services like cable television. Two-fifths of U.S. overseas investment, and one-quarter of all U.S. exports, went to the European Union (in the early 90s)... roughly 55% of all foreign direct investment in America, mostly in manufacturing, wholesale trade and petroleum, was European... and 40% in Europe came from the United States's investments mainly in manufacturing and finance and insurance. Three million people were employed in America by European-owned companies or subsidiaries...[6]

The US appreciated Europe's ability to speak with one voice on the key issue of trade liberalization, and the successful conclusion in 1993 of the GATT negotiating process begun in 1947 seemed to justify the decades of effort American trade negotiators had dedicated at home and abroad to the grand Rooseveltian vision of free trade 'everywhere in the world' (FDR's refrain in the Four Freedoms speech of 1941).[7] At the GATT's concluding ceremonies, the US representatives used language that could easily have come from a speech by the New Deal Secretary of State Cordell Hull. An ever more open world-trade system, said Vice President Gore, would bring 'mutual prosperity, growth and partnership', thereby creating jobs and fostering social progress. The vision of the US Trade Representative Michael Kantor completed the virtuous circle:

> The key for maintaining growth is to build up the middle class throughout the countries of the world. Enabling people to move from poverty to the middle class is a process which assures them the ability to buy our products as well as those from their own countries. It reinforces democracy and stability in those countries. Finally it reinforces the world trade system and is essential for its future success.[8]

After the end of the Cold War, the great Wilsonian–New Deal economic vision of World War II—raising living standards everywhere—seemed to become the supreme definition of progress throughout the world. Asking himself in 1992 who would go on to 'own' the twenty-first century—Japan,

---

[6] Alfred E. Eckes Jr and Thomas W. Zeiler, *Globalization and the American Century* (Cambridge, 2003), 225–6; a German commentator, Werner Weidenfeld, noted how little of this reality was known to the wider public on either side of the ocean: W. Weidenfeld, *America and Europe: Is the Break Inevitable?* (Gütersloh, 1996), 121.

[7] Michael Smith, 'European Integration and American Power: Reflex, Resistance and Reconfiguration', in Slater and Taylor (eds), *American Century*, 145–6; full history of trade negotiations in B. M. Hoekman and M. M. Kostecki, *The Political Economy of the World Trading System* (1995). But the GATT–WTO transition was almost halted at the last minute by an intense Euro-American dispute over trade in film and television productions; see below, p. 469, *passim*.

[8] Gore speech, Marrakesh, 14 April 1994, reproduced courtesy of United States Information Service, Rome; Kantor speech in *La Voce*, Rome, 15 April 1994; on the ambiguous historical legacy of American efforts to promote democracy by way of trade and growth, R. J. Johnston, 'United States', 158–62.

Europe, or America—the MIT economist Lester Thurow declaimed: 'The 19th century belonged to Great Britain. The 20th century belongs to the United States; we generate the world's highest per capita overall standard of living.'[9] But it was not the physical facts of production and consumption that gave the US its post-Cold War hegemony, or even its military supremacy, but its continuing ideological, political, and cultural ability to transform the history of its successes into recipes for others. The openness of the age's new communication system—the Internet—was a proof of this enduring reality, a true source of cultural power and prestige.[10]

Beyond the obvious propositions of security and prosperity, there was indeed always a third dimension of American power at work conditioning and colouring the transatlantic relationship once more, as clearly after the Cold War as in the two previous post-war eras. The urge of US mass culture to project its presence into Europe—as now across the globe—in an endlessly shifting variety of forms and directions, represented a pervasive force for change that Europeans could never ignore, were always obliged to come to some sort of terms with. By the end of the century, to measure the penetrative power of the industries and cultures bringing Euro Disney and CNN, *Jurassic Park* and *Baywatch*, the Internet, Microsoft Windows, and all the rest, meant discovering just how Europe's characteristic twentieth-century impulse to respond to America as myth and model of modernity had evolved by the 1990s.

A HEIGHTENED CULTURAL AWARENESS

In the general transatlantic euphoria accompanying the end of the Cold War, few people took much notice of the extraordinary assertion made by the American Secretary of State in Berlin, in December 1989, right after the destruction of the city's infamous dividing wall. 'America', said James Baker, 'is and will remain a European power'. Perhaps too much was going on in those tumultuous months for the phrase to attract the atten-

---

[9] *Washington Post/Guardian Weekly*, 26 April 1992.

[10] Manuel Castells, *The Internet Galaxy: Reflections on the Internet, Business, and Society* (Oxford, 2001), 23–9; in *Inventing the Internet* (Cambridge, Mass., 1999), Janet Abate shows that the Net did not simply spread from the US to the rest of the world: 'its global reach resulted from the convergence of many streams of network development', all reflecting local ideas of sovereignty and development, and huge inequality in telecommunications infrastructure. 'The point was not whether these countries would adopt an "American" technology, it was whether and how they would connect their existing national or private networks to the Internet.' By January 1990, 250 non-US networks were linked to the US master-net; by April 1995 the figure was 22,000; *Inventing the Internet*, 209–12.

tion it deserved.[11] The two post-war halves of Germany would soon be reunited—in October 1990. The ancient enemy, the Soviet Union, in its death throes, would officially cease to exist on 31 December 1991. The West Europeans braced themselves to receive a vast wave of new applicants to join their integration process, and in 1992, by way of the Maastricht Treaty, launched the European Union, with great new ambitions in defence, in money, in markets, and—above all—in membership. For its part, the administration of George H. W. Bush invented the proposition of the 'New World Order', and in the Gulf War of 1991 tried to make it function. Whatever the short-term success of the anti-Iraq operation, the phrase never took hold in the public imagination anywhere, and would never enjoy anything like the success of the two new American notions born—or reborn—around the same time: *globalization* and *soft power*, which are discussed further on.

By the middle of the 1990s James Baker's successors had to concede that the United States power most Europeans were obliged to come to terms with was not the F-15s that flew low over Bosnia or Bavaria or the Scottish Highlands. Instead it was the local manifestations of America's unique, unflagging capacity to invent, produce, and market popular culture for the world. US films and television occupied up to 80–90 per cent of European markets, the McDonalds empire planned to open eighty franchises per year in France alone in 1996,[12] Foot Locker shoe stores with their definition in English sprang up in every city centre. The 'colonization of the subconscious'—a famous quote from the 1976 Wim Wenders film *Kings of the Road*—was visible in the continuing imprint of American icons in car, food, and fashion advertisements everywhere in post Cold War Europe, west and east.

A pattern of projection and adaptation across the twentieth century became clear. This third post-war wave resembled in some striking ways the first one of the 1920s: spontaneous, chaotic, market-oriented, with cultural concerns particularly prominent, and the US government encouraging the forces of commerce and finance to make the most of the freedoms they demanded. Again America's economy surged ahead while Europe's failed to gain momentum, as its leading power, Germany, once more paid reparations and indemnities: this time to its own eastern half.

---

[11] Address by Secretary of State Baker Before the Berlin Press Club, Berlin, 12 December 1989, in *American Foreign Policy: Current Documents 1989* (Washington DC, 1990), doc. 126. In the same speech Baker went as far as to suggest that a new bilateral treaty might be contemplated. A joint Transatlantic Declaration came instead in November 1990. The hopes of these months dwindled into the New Transatlantic Agenda agreed at the US–EU Madrid summit, December 1995.

[12] *Europe on the Road*, Channel 4 (GB), 3 August 1996.

After World War I the notion of 'interdependence' had emerged from the writings of the experts to characterize certain features of transatlantic economic relations. Now its vastly expanded, post-Cold War version was recast as 'globalization'. Seen from this perspective, the second wave of US power projection, after 1941, began to look anomalous. Organized by the Federal government and intensely self-conscious, it built institutions, preached multilateralism, and projected America's strategic presence and ideology into every corner of the globe. The 1990s version was led instead by markets, not by Washington.

Aware of history, Baker's Berlin declaration had been pronounced, among other reasons, to assure the world, and Europeans in particular, that official America would not behave as it had done after 1919. Yet certain patterns of the 1920s reasserted themselves quite clearly. With the Cold War connections based on security and Atlanticism fading in significance, America's role as creator and seller of uniquely appealing models and myths became more prominent. No longer held up as a comprehensive model of society, American products, fashions, stars, symbols, icons, and languages (including the computer versions) reconfirmed their ubiquitous and compelling features, available for appropriation, adaptation—and rejection—by everyone.[13]

The 'American challenge', identified in 1967 by the French media entrepreneur Jean-Jacques Servan-Schreiber in a pioneering and far-sighted bestseller with that title, was prevalently technological innovation. (The book was particularly prescient on the future of computers and information technology.) But Servan-Schreiber had also spelled out the meaning of the new wave of American business expansionism in Western Europe. This was the drive of the biggest US corporations to set up bases in the member states of the European Economic Community, taking advantage of the region's new integration process.[14] As elements of this trend reappeared impressively in the wake of the Single European Act of 1986 and the Maastricht Treaty,[15] European governments, opinion leaders, and analysts found themselves once more coming to terms with the combined, cumulative impact of America's power presence in all its dimensions, from its strategic bases (generally shrinking) to its financial and telecoms services (expanding everywhere as privatization accelerated); from ever more efficient manufacturing to *Jurassic Park* (1993), MTV, Windows 95, and above all the extraordinary new open communications system, the Inter-

---

[13] Cf. Iriye, *Cultural Internationalism*, 171–2.
[14] Servan-Schreiber, *Le défi americain (The American Challenge)*, cf. Ch. 9, n.164. For a 1960s American view of the same processes, McReary, *Americanization of Europe*.
[15] *Business Week*, 7 October 1996; Peter Dicken, 'Global Shift—the Role of United States Transnational Corporations', in Slater and Taylor (eds), *American Century*, 48.

net, described in 1999 as 'a star with the US at its center'.[16] Interwar Europeans had dreamed of replicating California's Hollywood on their own soil, and some had succeeded. Now from the same state came Silicon Valley, heart of the booming software industry. Promptly, ambitious West European governments—as well as many others—worried about how to copy it.[17]

Those in America who rejoiced at this situation wrote sentences such as this one:

> ...the realpolitik of the Information Age is that setting technological standards, defining software standards, producing the most popular information products, and leading in the related development of the global trade in services are as essential to the well-being of any would-be leader as once were the resources needed to support empire or industry.

According to this associate of Henry Kissinger, a renewed *Pax Americana* could be built around these successes. David Rothkopf invited the American people not to shy away from the horizons and opportunities this unique informal empire would open up. Not everyone was convinced, even in America. 'McWorld' was Benjamin R. Barber's name for the universal predominance of the nation's mass-cultural corporations. To him it appeared that, 'in a quite literal sense, we *are* the world'. Every conventional notion of democracy, citizenship, and civil society was threatened by their greed and lowest-common-denominator commercialism, argued Barber.[18]

Among the consequences in Europe of the third wave of post-war confrontations was the reappearance with remarkable consistency—and now in many other parts of the world as well—of those traditional elite patterns of concern over 'Americanization', 'homogenization', and 'cultural imperialism' which, as we have seen, established themselves as rhetorical fixtures in Western Europe debates in the era between the two World Wars. This time round though, the stakes seemed higher. As conflicts over

---

[16] Cit. in Castells, *Internet Galaxy*, 209. But the very openness of Internet allowed non-American protagonists to flourish in an ambience that although hierarchical, contained none of the barriers to entry into the US market familiar to traditional media: *The Economist*, 25 May 1996.

[17] Debate over absence of Silicon Valley in France in *Libération*, 12 May 1995; myth of Silicon Valley in Japan in Dore, *Stock Market Capitalism*, 234. Wikipedia, the free Internet encyclopedia founded in 2001, claims to list the technology centres in the US and the world founded with 'the name "silicon" or "valley" to describe their own areas as a result of the success of Silicon Valley in California'; at: <http://en.wikipedia.org/wiki/List_of_technology_centers>.

[18] David Rothkop, 'In Praise of Cultural Imperialism? Effects of Globalization on Culture', *Foreign Policy* (June 1997); similar sentiments in Eckes Jr and Zeiler, *Globalization*, 243; Benjamin R. Barber, *Jihad vs McWorld: How Globalism and Tribalism are Reshaping the World* (New York, 1996), 7, 8, 61 (emphasis in original), 86, 97.

communal, national, and supranational loyalties become ever more prominent in European politics, so the debate over the renewed American challenge encountered the rising wave of anxiety about the future of identities in the Old World, whether individual or collective. In a country like Germany, struggling still to come to terms with the double trauma of the end of the Cold War and reunification, the resulting friction produced for a time extraordinary levels of alienation and acrimony over the alleged effects of America's multiple influences.[19]

Elsewhere a wide variety of responses was on display. Commentators such as Geoff Mulgan, of the prominent London think tank Demos, suggested that the European Commission's decades-long efforts to foster a common sense of European identity had failed, and that on many counts (he specifically cited films, music, and fast food), 'Europe is united not by Europeanness but by the influence of the United States'. The sociologist Colin Crouch suggested that 'both Norwegians and Greeks probably find more that is familiar within the US than in each other's countries'. Talking of cinema, the legendary French film director, Jean-Luc Godard, expressed similar sentiments.[20] Yet the 1990s debate in the major nations of the Old World on America's role as a cultural power in Europe suggested that whatever experiences they have might be going through in common, reactions to it were as different as persisting local interests and sensibilities. Just as the old Washington technique of *divide et impera* so often gave the US the last word among its squabbling allies in the Cold War, so the latest American challenge was provoking (though unwittingly) a hardening of attitudes, a striking of defensive, protectionist postures that seemed likely to increase divisions among the Europeans rather than unite them.

What they shared: Some European perceptions and judgements on the cultural dimensions of American power in the 1990s

The 1996 electoral process in the US was probably the one that set off the most typical of all the 1990s waves of reflection among America's allies on the state of health—political, economic, and social—of their relationship with the superpower they all (except, perhaps, the British) wished they did not have to depend on. Once more the 'America and us' syndrome

[19] M. Ermarth, 'German Reunification as Self-Inflicted Americanization: Critical Views on the Course of Contemporary Development,' in Wagnleitner and May (eds), *'Here, There and Everywhere'*.

[20] G. Mulgan, 'Case of Mistaken Euro-identity', *Times Higher Education Supplement* (20 September 1996); C. Crouch, 'Continental Drift: Are European and American Societies Drifting Apart?', paper presented at the Europaeum Conference (Oxford, September 1994), 3; J-L. Godard press conference in context of film festival, *'Il cinema ritrovato'*, Cineteca comunale di Bologna (Bologna, 9 July 1998).

could be seen on display in TV documentaries, public debates, colour supplements, and books produced by each national media culture for the occasion. The difference this time though was that in one form or other the 'Americanization question' kept appearing on the mass-media agenda everywhere, a pretext for discussing the local reception of the full range of US models, symbols, and popular culture products.

Cambio 16, one of Spain's most prominent weekly magazines, declared in July 1996 that 'American fashions and life-styles have invaded our society', and provided the usual range of examples from food and fashion to films and 'the incomprehensible rap'. But the magazine warned that 'appearances can be deceiving... the bottom line is that Spaniards can't stand them'. Citing a survey carried out locally for the American Embassy, the paper claimed that half of the thousand interviewees had a negative opinion of the US, with one out of five giving very unfavourable opinions, a trend shown to be rising over time. While paradoxically appreciating US strategic leadership in the world rather more in recent years, the percentage of those identifying with perceived US moral and social values varied from as little as 12 per cent (lifestyle) to no more than 18 per cent (family life).[21] Attacking the imperialism of US corporations and the impulse of the US film, television, and pulp-fiction media to reinvent the term 'cultural homogeneity', a writer condemned the Americans for underestimating the intelligence of 'the colonized':

> Even so we must accept our destiny as colonized [people], adore our god Sam, make sure that the great emperor Bill [Clinton] is happy with our submission. We don't want him to get angry and deprive us of all his *merchandising*, like he did to the man with the beard in the little island south of Florida.[22]

The Madrid survey might be usefully compared with a very similar effort commissioned and published by *Le Monde* of Paris less than a week before the US election. Here too negative attitudes prevailed and were also seen to be on a rising trend from at least 1988, the date of an identical enquiry.[23] The proportion of those viewing the US 'sympathetically' had declined from 54 per cent to 35 per cent, antipathy increasing from

---

[21] Fatima Ramirez, 'Come te ODIO, AMOR' (*sic*), *Cambio 16* (15 July 1996).

[22] Emiliano Gonzalez, 'Made in USA', *Cambio 16* (15 July 1996).

[23] The year 1988 probably represented a high-point in a wave of sympathy for the new American 'model' of the decade represented by Ronald Reagan, which had run through important sectors of public opinion since 1981, the year of the Socialist President Mitterand's election. The paradox was only apparent. Details, including poll data, in Jacques Rupnik, 'Anti-Americanism and the Modern: The image of the United States in French public opinion', in John Gaffney (ed.), *France and Modernisation* (Aldershot, 1988), 189–205.

38 per cent to 46 per cent. *Le Monde*'s reporter comments: 'No matter that CNN is present in many public places, that young French people sport Nikes, jeans and baseball hats, that New York is a top destination for French tourists, America as such provokes at best indifference rather than enthusiasm.... America's image deteriorates in parallel with the success of its popular culture in France.' While the US was ever more closely associated with violence, inequality, and racism—rather than dynamism, liberty, and generosity as in the past—French interviewees were overwhelmingly convinced that their own social system, and its welfare state in particular, worked better than anything the US could offer. Even though, noted *Le Monde* with exclamation marks, the US unemployment rate was 5 per cent while France's was stuck at 12 per cent.

While consuming ever more of it, the interviewees—no less than 70 per cent of them—deplored the 'excessive' cultural influence of the US on their TV screens; 59 per cent felt likewise over the cinema. Yet the sample was unmoved by the penetration of the English language in their lives. Perversely repudiating their national government's militancy over the question, 54 per cent of the sample saw nothing to be concerned about, not even in the field of popular music, in which recent legislation had required radio stations to broadcast at least 40 per cent of locally produced material. A rising concern, however, was American-style fast food, 30 per cent judging its presence excessive, a figure up from 10 per cent in 1988, and perhaps reflecting the closing of over seven hundred bistro's and cafes in the country in the previous two years, two hundred in Paris alone. While a net erosion in America's capital of sympathy in France was obvious, concluded *Le Monde*, French people were just as inclined to consume what America was offering as to deplore themselves for doing so: '*hypocrisie ou sentiment de culpabilité?*' [24]

Italy's contribution to this panorama appeared in a new review of geopolitics *liMes* (*sic*). In an edition of September 1996 entirely dedicated to America and its relationship with Italy, the number also appeared to coincide with the Presidential election. Offering a much less serious attempt at public-opinion measurement, *liMes* asked its sample three straightforward questions on their sense of identity and attachment, and on national security: i.e. who they wished to be defended by in case of attack (there was no reference to any effort Italy's own armed forces might make in this situation). In their responses the interviewees revealed a rather mild sen-

---

[24] Alain Frachon, 'L'image des Etats-Unis ne cesse de se dégrader en France', *Le Monde* (31 October 1996); food data from 'Europe on the Road' and *Unità* (Italy), 13 October 1996. Parliament later acted to close the tax gap that favoured fast foods over cafes, ordering a rise in value added tax on all takeaway meals to 20.6%.

timental belonging to their country, but insisted nevertheless that they would overwhelmingly prefer to be citizens of Italy rather than any other state (including a breakaway state of the north of the peninsula). Only 1.7 per cent chose the US as their preferred source of citizenship.

On defence, however, the picture was very different. The US alone was far and away the preferred shield and protector, with 37.5 per cent choosing the American ally (48.5 per cent in the south). In contrast 11 per cent looked to Europe, while only 5.7 per cent placed their faith in NATO. So Italy could not be considered an American colony, commented the survey's editors: 'our relationship with the United States is more cynical than many suspected. To Coca-Cola we prefer the Sixth Fleet.'[25]

In an important intervention in the same journal, the Deputy Prime Minister, the Left Democrat Walter Veltroni, emphasized his absolute belief in the continuing role of NATO and Atlanticism in general. What gave Veltroni's remarks their piquancy was not just their timing (shortly after the American-sponsored Dayton accords had halted the conflicts in ex-Yugoslavia), but the fact that the youthful and media-friendly Deputy Prime Minister had always been at the same time a lifelong member of the Italian Communist Party, until its conversion into the Democratic Party of the Left, and a fervent admirer and consumer of American popular culture.[26] Having acclaimed President Clinton's 1992 victory when editor of the ex-Communist Party's daily, *Unità*, Veltroni now insisted that Europe's renewed social democracy and Clinton's liberalism—'in the noblest sense of the word'—were one and the same thing.[27]

Not for the first time, Veltroni made much of the cultural heritage that bound him to the US. Citing a long list of books and films that inspired his American fascination, Veltroni said that for his generation of the 1960s the mental equation was 'America = movement = discovery = conquest of new frontiers'. Obsessed with the search for novelty, this generation inevitably looked to Kennedy and then to the 'other America' of the opposition to the war in Vietnam. Caught at this point between Europe and America he felt closer to the US. Paradoxically however he claimed to be as worried as the French over US cultural colonialism. The answer, he suggested, was not be found in protectionism on the French model:

> I think that what is needed is a European cultural market big enough and united enough to produce a common taste and language, strong enough to compete with the USA.... National states working together to build a European cultural identity: that is the way to get European unification, since the

---

[25] *liMes*, no. 4 (1996); survey and editorial comments pp. 7–10.
[26] He was also Minister of Culture in the new government.
[27] W. Veltroni, 'Vogliamo gli Stati Uniti d'Europa', *liMes*, 4 (1996), 23–9.

economic-financial route alone will not be sufficient. This alliance between equals—the United States of America and the United States of Europe—will be the best guarantee for the future of the West, for our future.[28]

America discovers how others view the power of its popular culture

To the American commentators who cared to reflect on the new prominence of America's cultural power in the post-Cold War world, Europe was only one element of the panorama. At the end of 1998, the *Washington Post* ran a series of big articles dedicated to 'The Global Power of US Culture'. The occasion was the discovery that international sales of American software and entertainment products had overtaken aerospace and agribusiness to become America's greatest export industry. Since the end of the Cold War its sales had risen 94 per cent, said the reports, and to the old familiar names such as Disney, Readers Digest, Hollywood, and McDonalds, were added the new world brands, Gap, Tower Records and MTV, Blockbuster, Starbucks, Wal-Mart, Bloomberg, the Simpsons, Michael Jordan, and the all-conquering empire of Microsoft.[29] Experts speculated on the reasons for the success of this 'invasion', pointing to the agency of the English language, the old American business propensities for scale, risk and sensitivity to markets, the 'appealing myths of the United States itself: individuality, wealth, progress, tolerance, optimism'. A TV director and scriptwriter was quoted as saying: 'to the world we offer the magical possibility of transformation.'[30]

From the beginning though, the *Post* series made it clear that the great surge of American cultural exports was *not* being welcomed with uncritical acclaim and unalloyed joy, that everywhere 'the love affair [was] fraught with turbulence and passion, ambivalence and confusion'. This was particularly the case in a country to which the series dedicated a whole article, Malaysia, where, it was said, a new hybrid culture was emerging, with great difficulty, and where the government had set in motion a huge effort of protectionism to defend its own notions of sovereignty, modernity, and identity, and in so doing its own cultural authority.[31] Clearly Malaysia was

---

[28] Ibid., 29.

[29] Numbers and analysis of the overall growth of the American trade surplus in private services from the mid-1980s on in P. W. Daniels, 'Overseas Investment by US Service Enterprises', in Slater and Taylor (eds), *American Century*, 68–70. On Michael Jordan as world show business/cultural phenomenon, Walter LaFeber, *Michael Jordan and the New Global Capitalism* (New York, 1999).

[30] *Washington Post*, 25 October 1998.

[31] Ibid. 26 October 1998.

simply the latest in a long line of nations attempting the same sort of defence; Mexico, India, and Iran were also quoted, showing how experiences and choices first made in Europe were now being reproduced across the world.[32] Above all the old European mechanism for containing and domesticating the challenge of American mass culture was going global. 'In country after country', said the concluding article, 'the evidence is not of cloned Americana but of native translation...consuming countries pick and choose what they like from the cafeteria of American cultural products, to adapt it to their tastes and uses, to plagiarize and imitate in their own tongues and styles, and of course to reject it and move on.'[33]

All this was just one of the outcomes of the great new processes that the American foreign policy class and its followers in the elite media now identified with a name well-known to social scientists: globalization.[34] The link between America's mass-culture industries and the worldwide integration of technology, finance, and free market capitalism that lay at the heart of 'globalization', was described in these terms by the most famed champion of the new reality, Thomas L. Friedman of the *New York Times*, in 1999:

> We Americans are the apostles of the Fast World, the prophets of the free market and the high priests of high tech. We want 'enlargement' of both our values and our Pizza Huts. We want the world to follow our lead and become democratic and capitalistic, with a Website in every pot, a Pepsi on every lip, Microsoft Windows in every computer and with everyone, everywhere, pumping their own gas.[35]

'Globalization-is-U.S.', proclaimed Friedman. But he warned that it came at a heavy price for its lead-nation, demanding a sense of responsibility, of proportion, and above all awareness that as 'the biggest beneficiaries and drivers of globalization, we are unwittingly putting enormous pressures on the rest of the world'. Accusations of 'global arrogance' were on the rise, suspicions of yet another form of American imperialism:

> Global arrogance is when your culture and economic clout are so powerful and widely diffused that you don't need to occupy other people to influence

---

[32] In 1995 the Indian government banned satellite dishes; Iriye, *Cultural Internationalism*, 172.

[33] *Washington Post*, 28 October 1998.

[34] The evolution of the concept of 'globalization' is traced in part in A. G. Hopkins, 'The History of Globalization—and the Globalization of History?', in A. G. Hopkins (ed.), *Globalization in World History*. The discussion in Anthony Giddens, *The Consequences of Modernity* (Cambridge, 1990), shows it to be well established among sociologists by that time.

[35] Friedman, 'A Manifesto for the Fast World', *New York Times Magazine*, Section 6 (28 March 1999).

their lives.... The Iranians aren't the only ones talking about America as 'the capital of global arrogance.' The French, Germans, Indonesians, Indians and Russians also call us that now.

In most countries, people can no longer distinguish between American power, American exports, American cultural assaults, American cultural exports and plain old globalization.[36]

As in the 1920s, the societies, groups, and individuals most exposed to these new, unsought forms of modernity were often reacting badly. The main difference this time round though was that Americans and their friends abroad no longer doubted what name to give to this form of hostility: *anti-Americanism* it was termed, by a wide range of commentators inside and outside the US, all talking as if definitions of modernity with hegemonic aspirations from the same source had not provoked similar reactions abroad seventy years before, and many times since.[37] In the 1990s, the fretful foreign policy community of the lone superpower produced a series of specific responses in the face of hostility to 'America' based on fears of globalization. Two of these are particularly worth mentioning in the present context, since they would affect much transatlantic, even global, debate about the new realities, and as such condition them for many years.

Samuel Huntington, a Harvard political scientist who claimed to be a disciple of Reinhold Niebuhr, attempted as his mentor had done in 1930 to warn the US—and the West in general—that it should not mistake the latest successes of its mass-culture products, services, and icons for a new form of effortless hegemony, legitimated by worldwide love for Spielberg's films, Microsoft's software, Starbuck's coffee, CNN's news bulletins, and all the rest. In an anguished reflection on America's post-Cold War 'security environment', Huntington warned that with the world becoming ever smaller, 'civilization consciousness' was increasing, a 'return to the roots phenomenon' that would want to 'shape the world in non-Western ways'. Western modernity was accepted in regions like Asia conditionally,

---

[36] Friedman, 'A Manifesto for the Fast World',; the article anticipated Friedman's book, *The Lexus and the Olive Tree* (New York, 1999).

[37] The transatlantic academic community made strenuous efforts in the 1990s to explain to Americans the origins and meaning of the cultural dynamics at work; cf. Pells, *Not Like Us*, Kroes, *If You've Seen One*, Wagnleitner and May (eds), *'Here, There and Everywhere'*, Iriye, *Cultural Internationalism*. Pells in particular insisted on the European origins of much of what passed for American productions: 'What Americans have done more brilliantly than their competitors overseas is repackage the cultural products we receive from abroad and then re-transmit them to the rest of the planet'; Pells, 'American Culture Goes Global, or Does It?', *The Chronicle of Higher Education* (12 April 2002), p. B8; for an early survey of the factor of American mass culture in global/local tensions, Gregory Claeys, 'Mass Culture and World Culture: On "Americanisation" and the Politics of Cultural Protectionism', *Diogenes*, 34/136 (1986); cf. Iriye, *Cultural Internationalism*, 157–601.

on terms defined in an increasingly aggressive fashion by traditional culture and values. Islamic fundamentalism was only the most radical expression of a widespread cultural trend, with ominous geopolitical implications for the West.[38]

This was the reasoning that led Huntington to develop his much-discussed 'clash-of-civilizations' thesis. In a further extension of it, America's foremost analyst of international relations turned his attention explicitly to the worldwide surge in prominence of the nation's popular culture since the end of the Cold War. His fellow citizens were given a warning: they should not take this 'success' for any sort of universal embrace of the American way of life:

> The argument that the spread of pop culture and consumer goods around the world represents the triumph of Western civilization depreciates the strength of other cultures while trivializing Western culture by identifying it with fatty foods, faded pants and fizzy drinks. The essence of Western culture is the Magna Carta, not the Magna Mac.

Taking a broad, anthropological view of culture, Huntington insisted that the pressures of economic development, which originated in the West, were producing new fractures within and between societies of all sorts. 'Indigenization' was on display everywhere as the fault-lines of globalization appeared around issues such as language and religion. The projection of Western images, products, and values in the context of globalization was provoking responses ranging from 'skepticism to intense opposition: What is universalism to the West is imperialism to the rest.' Repeating Reinhold Niebuhr's numerous warnings on the need to face up to the gap so often visible between declared Western principles, and actual practice, Huntington demanded that America and its allies in Europe shore up their own societies morally first of all, and then look to strengthen their common heritage of institutions and understandings.[39]

---

[38] Samuel P. Huntington, 'The Clash of Civilizations?', *Foreign Affairs* (Summer 1993); cits at pp. 25, 26; the article anticipated *The Clash of Civilizations and the Remaking of World Order* (New York, 1996); for a critique of this prognosis from a Middle Eastern perspective, Geoffrey D. Schad, 'Competing Forms of Globalization in the Middle East: From the Ottoman Empire to the Nation State, 1918–1967', in Hopkins (ed.), *Global History*, 213–16; for the 1960s–1970s origins of the linked concepts of the 'Third World' and 'cultural diversity', Iriye, *Cultural Internationalism*, 160–5.

[39] Samuel P. Huntington, 'The West: Unique, Not Universal', *Foreign Affairs* (November/December 1996); cits at pp. 29, 40; even before World War II Niebuhr had warned that the new power of the US would inevitably attract envy, hostility, and accusations of hypocrisy, since no nation could in reality live up to America's many declarations of high moral principle: 'The Awkward Imperialist', *Atlantic Monthly* (June 1930); 'The Perils of American Power', *Atlantic Monthly* (June 1932); cf. *The Irony of American History* (1952 edn repr. New York, 2008).

'Culture follows power', declared Professor Huntington, using a civilizational definition of 'culture' and a traditional—i.e. military, political, economic—idea of the key currencies of power. But other experts were not so convinced of these definitions, nor of the cause-and-effect sequence that the Harvard man presumed. The Japan specialist Ron Dore, for instance, suggested that 'indigenization' was by no means so predictable or uniform, and that where local cultures failed to develop the self-confidence and coherence to assert themselves in the New World Order, then 'the "soft" cultural power of the hegemon' would most likely fill the void. As Japan's business model had weakened in the 1990s, he suggested, so the younger generations of aspiring corporate types in that country were turning *en masse* to the MBA courses offered by the ever-swelling numbers of US business schools, there to be 'brainwashed' with effects likely to be 'baleful'.[40]

Dore's reference to 'soft power' was one of many clues to the success of another American cultural product of the era, the notion of 'soft power' itself. Devised in 1990 by the political scientist Joseph S. Nye Jr, a colleague of Huntington's at Harvard, the idea came from the conviction that the cultural advantages of the West had substantially contributed to the collapse of the Soviet Union, and so discredited the notions of the declinists of the time that the era of American hegemony was fading. At the same time Professor Nye recognized that the dynamic of interdependence integral to globalization was upsetting established hierarchies and currencies of power everywhere. So traditional expressions of American hegemony were being devalued, not just by the end of the Cold War itself, but as transnational corporations, non-governmental organizations, newly born or reborn states, and other protagonists of the international scene made their weight felt in their own ways. The evolution of information flows, the transformation of financial markets, the differences between the haves and the have-nots in the worlds of education and technology, all these factors were rapidly altering the equations of interdependence, which (like globalization) really meant not 'harmony', but 'unevenly balanced mutual dependence'.[41]

In this situation, a nation's 'broad ideological appeal' was crucial. Its creeds, norms, and culture, incarnated in functioning institutions both public and private, should serve to enhance its legitimacy. This would enable it to structure situations, set agenda, and launch narratives whose effect, hopefully, would be to 'get other countries to *want* what it

---

[40] 'Dore on Huntington', *Prospect* (March 1997), 71; elaboration of this line of reasoning in Dore, *Stock Market Capitalism*, ch. 3 and pp. 219–21; full conceptual discussion in A. G. Hopkins, 'Introduction', in Hopkins (ed.), *Global History*.

[41] Nye Jr, 'Soft Power', *Foreign Policy* (Fall 1990), 154–61; cit. at p. 158.

wants... [to] develop preferences or define their interests in ways consistent with its own'. Bodies like the IMF and GATT showed the mechanism at work in favour of America, said Nye, but so did the transnational corporations, the great majority of whom had their headquarters in the US.[42] After the Cold War, the nation's popular culture now revealed itself to be a true source for the renewal of hegemony and authority based on a forceful, living consensus. 'American popular culture, embodied in products and communications, has widespread appeal', Nye argued. Citing Japanese and Soviet youth fashion, Nicaraguan television, and the symbolic use of the Statue of Liberty in the Chinese student uprisings of 1989, Nye felt there was interest everywhere 'in American democracy and culture'. Updating the messages of Henry Luce and the Marshall Planner Richard Bissell, he went on:

> Of course, there is an element of triviality and fad in popular behaviour, but it is also true that a country that stands astride popular channels of communication has more opportunities to get its message across and to affect the preferences of others.[43]

Nye went on from this kind of reasoning to make a crucial conceptual leap. The man who would be an Assistant Secretary for Defence in the Clinton years suggested that America's seductive or 'co-optive' potential might be mobilized in the future to achieve important foreign policy objectives, with the traditional forms of power remaining in the background. The aim, said Nye, was to arrive at a condition where others spontaneously shared American perceptions, values, and objectives, or, as a British commentator put it, to develop 'the capacity to make other peoples want what Americans want, from Hollywood's products to Coca-Cola to free elections'.[44] Traditional European elite views of the relationship between power and 'influence', all military and economic, began to look narrow and static compared to Nye's formulation.[45] Apart from its handiness as

---

[42] Ibid. 166–8, emphasis in original; further elaboration of these propositions in G. John Ikenberry and Charles Kupchan, 'Socialization and Hegemonic Power', *International Organization* 44/3 (1990), 283–315; Gramscian conceptions of the relationship between power, 'ideology', and hegemony were clearly influential in the development of the 'soft power' formula; cf. Fontana, 'Political Space', 345, 355–7.

[43] Nye Jr, 'Soft Power', 168–9, 155.

[44] Ibid. 167–8; Martin Walker, 'Flawed Vision of the New Imperial Rome', *Guardian Weekly* (27 January 1991).

[45] A good example of the conventional view is to be found in the contribution of the British diplomat and banker Sir Michael Palliser to the Harvard collection *Allies or Adversaries?*, published in 2000, but including essays from earlier years; Palliser, 'Forty Years On: The Nature of United States Power and European Influence', November 1985, esp. pp. 29–32, 35.

conceptual gadget that even politicians could use in public, the appeal of the notion lay in the fact that it gave a name to one of the processes by which the knowledge industries and their customers took over some of the commanding heights of post-industrial economies, a reality that globalization brought before the eyes of the world with ever-increasing speed.[46] Nye meanwhile urged his fellow Americans to stop worrying about their so-called decline, and realize that too much anxiety would only breed nationalism and protectionism. Instead they should wake up to the possibilities offered by a different kind of 'transnational interdependence'. To outsiders, Nye emphasized that compared to them, the United States possessed a 'broader range of power resources—military, economic, scientific, cultural and ideological—', and so was likely to be the big winner in the era of globalization. Wasn't that the reason so many people were willing to risk even their lives to come there?[47]

Seen from the other side of the Atlantic Ocean, however, the picture rarely looked so simple. To France's leading international relations expert, Dominique Moïsi, 'soft power' looked like a typical expression of a time when the United States felt at ease in a world where the ability to convince and seduce through old and new technologies alike complemented so well the burdens of its vast military presence in the world.[48] But if the mutual dependence between the US and the rest was in fact 'unevenly balanced', as Nye himself admitted, or the connections were 'asymmetrical', as a German expert put it diplomatically, who was to deal with all the tensions that constant exposure to this lopsided reality would bring?[49] How would each side's long experience of transatlantic encounters weigh on the third great wave of post-war adaptations? The fault-lines of 'globalization' were quickly becoming clear: women's dress, language, religion, education, mass

---

[46] Cf. Susan Strange, *States and Markets* (2nd edn, London, 1994); this emphasizes the role of knowledge as a form of 'structural power', creating new global hierarchies of capability: ibid. 136.

[47] Nye Jr, 'Soft Power', 155, 170; further elaboration in Joseph S. Nye Jr and William A. Owens, 'America's Information Edge', *Foreign Affairs* (March/April 1996). Here Nye and Owens bring a distinctly harder, security-oriented tone to their argument, suggesting that government must use the nation's lead in information technology 'to increase the effectiveness of its military forces and make the world safe for soft power, America's inherent comparative advantage', ibid. 35.

[48] Dominique Moïsi, '9 novembre 1989–11 septembre 2001: L'âge de la mondialisation', in Anne-Marie Le Gloannec and Alexander Smolar (eds), *Entre Kant et Kosovo: Études offertes à Pierre Hassner* (Paris, 2003), 167.

[49] Kaspar Maase, '"Americanization", "Americanness" and "Americanisms": Time for a Change in Perspective?', paper presented at the German Historical Institute conference at Washington DC (25–7 March 1999), 2 <http://web.archive.org/web/20000917091046/http://www.ghi-de.org/conpotweb/westernpapers/maase.pdf>.

media, transnational business, everyday consumption (especially food). So what sort of spiritual resources would societies now need in order to construct for themselves a stable, manageable position in all the confusion of the global and the local, and at the same time contribute to what Vaclav Havel, the Czech playwright and President, called a 'peaceful, post-modern culture of co-existence'?[50]

'SOFT POWER' CONFRONTATIONS OF THE 1990s

The Europeans, like everyone else, were at first unable to decide whether the sudden rise to fame of the notions of 'globalization' and 'soft power' was the product of reality or myth. Were they perhaps no more than ideological symptoms of American triumphalism, accompanying the end of the Cold War and the apparent success of Anglo-American ideals of borderless markets, smart technology, and super-fast information?[51] Or, more seriously, did they reflect an acceleration of international capitalism's permanent impulse to expansion, producing a transcendent new phenomenon of convergence, a 'flee-floating process without strong national roots', which would *supersede* all the previous century's worries about modernity and modernization?[52] Since the new spin on the concept of globalization emerged from the US at a specific early-1990s moment, might it not express an awareness of America's own growing dependence on the world's economy and geopolitics, a way to accentuate the internationalization of

---

[50] Vaclav Havel, the playwright, opposition leader, and early President of the new Czech republic, was among the foremost thinkers bringing a perspective of moral philosophy to these questions, e.g. speech delivered at Philadelphia, 4 July 1994, at <http://www.worldtrans.org/whole/havelspeech.html>, speech delivered at closing of the Forum 2000 Conference, Prague, 13 October 1999, at <http://www.vaclavhavel.cz>. Havel never distinguished between European and American roles, but of a common Euro-American civilization that had come to 'encompass the whole world', and so brought all to share its benefits and, increasingly, its dangers; speech at New Delhi, 8 February 1994 at Ibid.

[51] Paul Hirst and Graham Thomson, *Globalization in Question: The International Economy and the Possibilities of Governance* (2nd edn, Cambridge, 1999); this locates the origins of the concept in the 1970s–80s, and emphasizes its ideological uses as a pretext for generalized liberalization and deregulation, and the devaluation of all forms of government supervision of economic processes; cf. Castells, *Internet Galaxy*, 276.

[52] A. G. Hopkins, 'The History of Globalization—and the Globalization of History?', in Hopkins (ed.), *Globalization in World History*, 32. The sense of the bewilderment caused by the sudden rise to fame of the globalization 'discourse' in the early 1990s is well expressed in Roger Hart, 'Universals of Yesteryear: Hegel's Modernity in an Age of Globalization', in Hopkins (ed.), *Global History*, 66–7; cf. Niall Ferguson, 'Full Marx', *Financial Times* (17 August 2002).

a vast, self-contained country?[53] The Rome scholar Rita Di Leo has traced the emergence of the word and issue of 'globalization' in the leading foreign policy journals of the US, identifying the years 1993–4 as the key phase, concurrent with the arrival of President Bill Clinton. And indeed Clinton was a man who embraced globalization fervently, declaring: 'We must tear down the wall in our thinking between domestic and foreign policy.'[54]

When historians looked at the phenomenon, they decided that contemporary globalization had of course many precedents, but that it always 'involves the extension, intensification, and quickening velocity of flows of people, products and ideas that shape the world. It integrates regions and continents; it compresses time and space; it prompts imitation and resistance.' In historical comparison, 'the importance of cultural expressions of globalization' appeared to be more apparent this time round, 'whether they appear in the debate over the emergence of a "global civil society" or at a popular level with reference to what has been called "Cocacolonization"'. In any event, the process could never be contemplated as 'simply the result of a dominating center activating lesser peripheries, but is jointly produced by all parties to the process'.[55] But on whose terms? With what sort of political, economic, and cultural resources could all the other parties negotiate with the biggest of them all in the late twentieth-century version of the phenomenon?

Like so many other regions of the planet, *all* the nations of the Old World between the Atlantic and the Urals, and from Iceland to Turkey, found themselves facing up to a relentless series of broadly cultural innovations and initiatives, originating across the ocean, which repeatedly yet unpredictably mixed up traditional forms of power-presence and the force of America's popular culture, thereby heightening the general sensitivity to the American thrust at the heart of so many of globalization's processes of the time:

- In 1990 came demands from all sides, but especially from the US, for a new European Marshall Plan in favour of the nations of the

---

[53] US foreign direct investment doubled in the 1980s, and tripled again in the 1990s, to $1.3 trillion; (well over half of this was placed in Europe), Eckes Jr and Zeiler, *Globalization*, 213–14; the question is adapted from David Reynolds, 'American Globalism', in Hopkins (ed.), *Globalization in World History*, 257.

[54] R. Di Leo, *Il primato Americano: Il punto di vista degli Stati uniti dopo la caduta del muro di Berlino* (Bologna, 2000), ch. 2; on Clinton and globalization, Alfred G. A. Valladão, *The Twenty-First Century will be American* (London, 1996), 114–15; Andrew J. Bacevich, *American Empire: The Realities and Consequences of U.S. Diplomacy* (Cambridge, Mass., 2002), 37–42, cit. at p. 38.

[55] Philip D. Curtin, *The World and the West: The European Challenge and the Overseas Response in the Age of Empire* (Cambridge, 2002), 136; Hopkins, 'Introduction' in Hopkins (ed.), *Global History*, 3, 5; Hopkins, 'The History of Globalization', 15.

former Soviet bloc; meanwhile the first Russian Pizza Hut opened in Moscow in November of that year.

- In spring 1991 the first Gulf War broke out. Traditional news channels around the world found themselves competing with the Cable News Network (CNN), the first 24-hour dedicated news channel, promising live images from the war for Kuwait and all those to follow.[56]

- In October 1992 the Euro Disney amusement park opened in Paris, amidst political and cultural controversy. In November 1992 President Bush signed a law allowing commercial usage of the Internet computerized communications system developed by US defence and scientific organizations, and others. In the same month William Jefferson Clinton was elected President of the United States, promising a new era of 'Third Way' politics between liberalism and 'neo-conservatism'.

- In 1993 came demands from the Hollywood lobbying machine for full liberalization of international film and television markets in the context of the final round of GATT tariff negotiations (the Uruguay Round). The French government led a Europe-wide campaign of opposition. Vice President Al Gore launched the concept of the coming 'information superhighway', which would hopefully democratize access to high-speed communications technology.

- In 1994 Stephen Spielberg's *Schindler's List* arrived in the midst of Germany's early post-Cold War identity debate. The World Trade Organization was born, fulfilling a long-held dream of American trade internationalists.

- By 1995 the Internet had become established as a vast, interactive communications system with extraordinary implications for the future of business and social life everywhere. The Microsoft Corporation of Seattle consolidated its hold on everyday software with the launch of Windows 95. At the prompting of the US, the OECD in Paris proposed a Multilateral Agreement on Investments (MAI). Its official purpose was to agree upon general rules for the conduct of transnational corporate investment.

- In 1996 the Olympic Games were staged in Atlanta, Georgia with major sponsorship from the Coca-Cola Company, based in that city.

---

[56] Rise, role, and impact of CNN in Eckes Jr and Zeiler, *Globalization*, 222–4; commercial impact in Asia and Europe in Valladão, *Twenty-First Century will be American*, 145–7.

The most prominent rock/popstar of the decade, Madonna, starred in *Evita*, a film biography of Eva Perón.

- In 1997 James Cameron's *Titanic* set out on its career as the most successful film ever, taking approximately $600 million in Europe in its first year.[57] In Britain, Tony Blair, elected Prime Minister with much inspiration from Clinton's experience, soon emerged as a European champion of the reinvigorated American economic model.[58]

- In 1998 the World Economic Forum in Davos, Switzerland was 'dominated by the US', said the press, and Hillary Clinton, 'the first lady of the world', was identified as 'the real star of the show'. French commentators recalled a Jean-Paul Sartre question of the early 1950s: 'is America universal because it is imperial, or is it the other way round?'[59] But the MAI was stopped, defeated by 'one of the first global debates and political movements in history'. In Europe, France led the opposition to what was seen as a decisive shift of power from governments to supernational corporations.[60]

- In 1999 the Dow Jones share index of the New York stock exchange broke through the 10,000 mark for the first time ever. The first general meeting of the WTO took place in Seattle, to be disrupted by the new 'no-global' movement, galvanized by the struggle over MAI, and empowered by the Internet.[61]

---

[57] Figures at <http://www.boxofficemojo.com/movies/?page=intl&id=titanic.htm>.

[58] According to the veteran American political scientist Seymour Martin Lipset, Blair's emergence and his embrace of Clinton's 'Third Way' vision were but symptoms of a much wider convergence of European reformist parties on an '"American" path', meaning more respect for the workings of free-market capitalism, far less for the traditional claims of the welfare state; Lipset, 'The Americanization of the European Left', *Journal of Democracy* (April 2001).

[59] Dominique Moïsi, 'America the Triumphant', *Financial Times* (9 February 1998); according to Thomas Friedman of the *New York Times*, America had already been the star at Davos in 1997; Friedman, 'Cut Out for Globalization and Feeling Quite Good', *International Herald Tribune* (10 February 1997).

[60] Dennis M. Ray, 'The Multilateral Agreement on Investment: Implications for Entrepreneurship and New Venture Development', at <http://globalization.icaap.org/content/v7.1/Ray.html>; the general reasons for rejection were spelled out by a Canadian journalist, David Crane; article at <http://www.globalpolicy.org/component/content/article/209/43212.html>; French media opposition recorded at <http://www.highbeam.com/doc/181-53104822.html>; official American abandonment in *Financial Times* (14 February 1998).

[61] Background to Seattle confrontation, and brief history of anti-globalization movement in *The Economist* (11 December 1999). The magazine, which considered the event a disaster from the trade liberalization point of view, described the protesters as 'a model of everything the trade negotiators were not. They were well-organized and they built unusual coalitions. They also had a clear agenda and they were masterly users of the media'; cf. Eckes Jr and Zeiler, *Globalization*, 254–6.

- In 2000 the merger of America Online (founded in 1989), and the Time Warner corporation created the largest media complex in the world, with a value equal to 30 per cent of Spain's GNP.[62] But it soon emerged as a disaster, and the bubble of speculative fervour revolving round Silicon Valley's software industries burst in March–April 2000.

Faced by this daunting wave of novelties, a sort of cultural panic arose during the 1990s in some sectors of European opinion. 'Britain in 1997 has been Americanised', wrote the London *Guardian*'s economics correspondent. 'Almost every provincial town has a greenfield development complete with multiplex cinema, tenpin bowling, a fast-food joint and acres of parking space.'[63] The spread of the McDonald's hamburger chain provoked a wide variety of protests all over the Old World (and elsewhere), from Glasgow to Cracow, from Hampstead to Rome, the Vatican, and Venice, as well as several corners of France. In the small country town of Millau, in the south-west of the country, the destruction of a McDonald's building site by an activist sheep farmer, José Bové, created a new anti-global, national hero.[64]

Although the Old World's intellectuals no longer enjoyed anything like the status they had taken for granted in the 1920s, this did not prevent them from expressing themselves on the American presence in the dilated fashion that had come so naturally to their predecessors between the wars.[65] A French writer, Jean Cau, described Paris's Euro Disney park as:

> …a horror made of cardboard, plastic and appalling colors, a construction of hardened chewing gum and idiotic folklore taken straight out of comic books written for obese Americans…[66]

---

[62] Context and data in *International Herald Tribune*, 17 January 2000, *Le Monde Interactif*, 31 May 2000.

[63] *The Guardian*, 30 April 1997.

[64] Spread of McDonald's in Europe and elsewhere, and backlash, analysed in de Grazia, *Irresistible Empire*, 468–71, 477; Hampstead controversy in *The Times*, 6 August 1992; semi-official Catholic attack on McDonald's in *Avvenire*, 8 November 2000; early phases of Bové story in *Le Monde*, 1 July 2000, *Nouvel observateur*, 6–12 July 2000, and in J. Bové and François Dufour, *Le monde n'est pas une marchandise: Des paysans contre la malbouffe* (Paris, 2000); in April 2000, the manager of a McDonald's outlet in Brittany was killed in a terrorist attack by local separatists; reaction and comment by head of McDonald's in France in *Le Figaro*, 24 April 2000.

[65] On the decline in the status of intellectuals in Europe, Judt, *Postwar*, 785–6.

[66] Cit. in Miles Orvell, 'Understanding Disneyland: American Mass Culture and the European Gaze', in Rob Kroes et al. (eds), *Cultural Transmissions and Receptions: American Mass Culture and Europe* (Amsterdam, 1993), 240; background to Euro Disney enterprise, and controversies, in *Newsweek*, 13 April 1992, *LeMonde/Guardian Weekly*, 26 April 1992.

Fig. 9. 'California Dreaming'. David Simonds's cartoon of 1997 accompanied an article in *The Guardian* denouncing the alleged 'Americanization' of Britain.

(British Cartoon Archive, University of Kent, reproduced by courtesy of David Simonds and *The Guardian*)

For some intellectuals 'McDonaldization' had already became a metaphor for the worst sort of social standardization, and for the continuity of the sins of industrialization in post-industrial life, as in this sample from an ex-socialist, now 'left-nationalist' writer in Germany:

> This melting down and stamping into uniformity—this McDonaldization—all eating and drinking the same (oh, what a state of prosperity and welfare!)—this is not the 'multicultural society' but inhumanity itself, utterly desolate.[67]

In other German examples cited by the specialist Michael Ermarth, a former senior editor of *Stern* magazine, in a book on his nation's Americanized fate, provided a picture of 'a fulminating process leading to utter perdition'. A historian produced one more 'scourge in a long tradition of apoplectic and often apocalyptic German commentary'; a 'left-national political scientist' declared that 'from American diapers to American warheads, no-one in this country can get away from "the American way of life and death"....'. Others called for systematic 'de-Americanization', invoking with heavy irony the de-Nazification process the American themselves carried out after World War II.[68]

---

[67] Cit. in Michael Ermarth, 'German Reunification', 251; general treatise on McDonaldization as a metaphor and model for contemporary practices of industrial efficiency, George Ritzer, *The McDonaldization of Society* (Thousand Oaks, Calif., 1996).

[68] Ermarth, 'German Reunification', 251–3.

In an eloquent caricature of this sort of thinking in the world, the British journalist Polly Toynbee wrote in 1999:

> Sometimes it seems as if a tidal wave of the worst Western culture is creeping across the globe like a giant strawberry milkshake.... Imagine it in satellite pictures, every canyon and crevice pink with it and all of it flowing out the USA. Just as world maps were once pink with the colonies of the British empire, now they are pink with US strawberry shake, for 'cultural globalisation' is often just a synonym for Americanisation. Created in the coke-crazed brains of Hollywood producers, US movies have become universal storyboards of global dreams—sugary and sentimental, violent and pornographic, all beautiful people and happy endings where the good guy always wins and so does the USA.[69]

'Culture panic', said Toynbee, 'is a close cousin of "moral panic" (moral decline), "intellectual panic" (dumbing down), and "patriotic panic" (loss of national identity).' As uncontrolled emotions, gut reactions, they should all be resisted, deconstructed, and rebuilt, in order to understand 'what is good about cultural globalisation, what is dangerous, what is inevitable and what might be tamed and regulated to our advantage'. Blind, undifferentiating anti-Americanism was to be rejected, not least because all of the West was involved in pushing its culture onto the world. Europeans in particular should realize that cross-fertilization was the lifeblood of their own modern ascent, and was obviously sought out consciously by every non-Western society where religious or nationalistic fundamentalism was not in charge.[70]

Salman Rushdie worried about the outbreak of a 'war on American culture', and denounced those who were happy to buy Nike shoes and Gap clothes, and watch MTV, while at the same time deploring the allegedly globalizing power of Americanization. Rushdie reported how a British literary festival had staged a debate on the motion that '[it] is the duty of every European to resist American culture', and how happy he had been to oppose it. Defending the 'purity' of a nation's presumed cultural identity was what totalitarian regimes specialized in, said the Anglo-Indian novelist. Contemporary reality with all its freedoms was very different:

> Is not mélange, adulteration, impurity, pick 'n' mix at the heart of the idea of the modern, and hasn't it been that way for most of this all-shook-up century?

[69] P. Toynbee. 'Who's Afraid of Global Culture?', in Anthony Giddens and Will Hutton (eds), *Global Capitalism* (New York, 2000), 191.
[70] Ibid. 192–7.

To defend ourselves from all the forms of 'tyranny, bigotry, intolerance and fanaticism' of the times meant defending the universal value of freedom, said Rushdie. 'Sneakers, burgers, blue jeans and music videos aren't the enemy... out there are real tyrants to defeat. Let's keep our eyes on the prize.'[71]

But the 'culture panic' of the 1990s acquired for a time its own political momentum. At the 'Third Way' meeting in Florence of 1999, between the centre-left leaders of the US, France, Britain, Italy, and Germany, the American President found himself presented with urgent pleas by European leaders such as Prime Minister Jospin and Chancellor Schroeder for the US to respect all the forms of 'cultural diversity' on display in the Old World.[72] In 2000, the President of France, Jacques Chirac, speaking before the official *Conférence de la Francophonie,* sounded a grave alarm: the Internet, he said, could lead to the 'complete eradication' of some of the world's minority languages. Even French—'the world's ninth most popular language and the fifth most popular on the Internet' in one account—was said by Chirac to be facing an uncertain future.[73]

These initiatives came when memories were still fresh of the great transatlantic confrontation over free trade in television programmes and feature films of 1993. Three years later Dominique Moïsi of Paris wrote that in spite of all the 1990s technological innovations in the world of mass media, it was in the cinema that the world continued to see the supreme version of America's triumph as 'a diluted version of the Roman empire'. The universality of its messages, based on the triumph of the individual, had originated in Europe, said Moïsi, but the ubiquity and familiarity of the movie product were due to the power of a cultural industry over time, and its capacity to represent the miseries and the grandeurs of America's multicultural society.[74] Somewhat as in the 1920s, the world of the cinema industry demonstrated better than most the new stakes emerging in the

---

[71] S. Rushdie, 'Rethinking the War on American Culture', *New York Times* (5 March 1999).

[72] Jospin reportedly mentioned this question directly to American President Clinton; cf. *Le Monde,* 23 November 1999; Schroeder had already made his support of French cultural policy clear in an interview with *Le Monde,* 20 November 1999: 'It is absolutely necessary that we launch a common initiative to oppose this huge American dominion and reinforce the identity of Europe as a pole of cultural creativity.' Italian policy along these lines was expressed by the Minister of Culture Giovanna Melandri in *L'Unità,* 13 November 1999; there was no sign of a British position on these issues.

[73] Chirac quoted in Chris Woodford, *The Internet: A Historical Encyclopedia,* ii: *Issues* (Santa Barbara, 2005), 175; occasionally American commentators would concede that the defenders of cultural diversity might have a point, and that the US would not take easily to a massive presence of Latin American or Middle Eastern culture on their territory, e.g. Charles William Maynes, 'The Perils of (and for) an Imperial America', *Foreign Policy* (Summer 1998), 38.

[74] *Financial Times,* 19 April 1996.

transatlantic cultural power game of the 1990s, the incongruities in the worldwide experience of 'globalization', and how specific questions of popular culture could reveal key issues in the transatlantic politics of modernization in the 1990s.

Cinema and the European experience of globalization

In many of the various crises of identity felt in European countries after the end of the Cold War, film, specifically American film, played its part: Should Scotland be seen in *Braveheart* terms (as dreamed up by Hollywood), or in the features of the local anti-heroes of *Trainspotting*?[75] Could *Jurassic Park* really have been a threat to French cultural sovereignty, as the (conservative) minister of culture declared on its appearance? Did *Schindler's List* really 'take over' the [German] intellectuals' main theme: coming to terms with the past', as a senior Frankfurt editorialist wrote? Was the success of *Titanic* a challenge to the snobbism and envy of Europe's culture ministers in their efforts to educate and elevate the masses, as alleged by the American historian Richard Pells?[76]

'Globalization is creating a cultural hegemony, encroaching on distinct national identities and voices', émigré Yugoslav film-maker Emil Kusturica said in a 1998 interview published in Italy, and the controversial head of the BBC, John Birt, expressed similar thoughts soon afterwards.[77] Statements like these came at a time when the imbalance of creative and economic power between Hollywood and the European film industry was the subject of ever more bitter reflection in West European capitals, a trend that reached a climax in the late 1993 Franco-American dispute over the inclusion of film and television products in the final round of the GATT free trade negotiations.

Transatlantic conflicts in this area in the early 1990s started out from a situation in which US productions accounted for 81 per cent of EC cinema screenings in 1991, over 70 per cent of European box-office takings, and 54 per cent of all dramas and comedies broadcast on television.

---

[75] The Scottish National Party regularly distributed its promotional material outside cinemas showing Mel Gibson's film of 1995, on the anti-English fighter and martyr William Wallace. In contrast a leading Scottish journalist, John Lloyd, denounced the cultural desperation behind the Scots' embrace of 'kitsch nationalism from Los Angeles', in *Scotland on Sunday*, 31 March 1996.

[76] Minister Toubon quoted in *Le Monde*, 14 September 1993; Pells was the author of a series of polemical articles in the *International Herald Tribune*, December 1997–July 1998, focusing on the issue of American film in Europe; I have discussed these cases in 'The American Challenge Renewed: U.S. Cultural Power and Europe's Identity Debates', *The Brown Journal of World Affairs* (Winter/Spring 1997).

[77] Kusturica interview in *Filmaker's Magazine* (Milan, December 1998); J. Birt, 'Holding on to Auntie', *Prospect* (February 1999).

In 1992 US audio-visual exports to the EC were worth $3.6 billion compared to a mere $288 million worth of comparable European exports to America.[78] The year 1993 would be the first in which Hollywood's overseas revenues would be greater than those from its home markets. Meanwhile, under this and other pressures of globalization, a small group of giant media conglomerates was taking control of the industry: Time Warner, Sony-Columbia, News Corporation-Fox, Viacom-Paramount, Disney-Capital Cities/ABC, NBC Universal.[79]

As in the 1920s and the 1950s, the most significant specific sources of the confrontations of 1993 were always to be found in questions of distribution, screen time, and access to markets generally. Two issues of this type dominated: the incapacity of the EC to enforce an agreement with the US 'majors' in 1989 under which their free access to the European market would be conditional upon financial support to the European industry,[80] and the arrival of American satellite television in Europe, using Britain as a launch pad, since Britain was the country that refused to apply the key EC directive of 1989 requiring that at least 50 per cent of TV broadcast time should be reserved for local production.[81]

At this point the Europeans began to remember that by insisting on subtitling, on restricting access to distribution channels, and other means, the US had 'kept down' the foreign share of their cinema audience to a level that was barely visible. The leading German director Wim Wenders protested to an Italian journalist in October 1993:

> The fact that American cinema controls European markets 70–90%, while the Europeans are present in 1% of their market does not show that they make better films than us. It shows the force of American military, political and industrial power, sustained by a ferocious protectionism.

President Mitterand of France was reported to have declared at the same time that no single country 'should be allowed to control the images of the whole world', and in a formal speech in Poland explained the logic of the French position:

> Creations of the spirit are not just commodities; the elements of culture are not pure business. Defending the pluralism of works of art and the freedom of the public to choose is a duty. What is at stake is the cultural identity of all our nations. It is the right of all peoples to their own culture. It is the

---

[78] *Financial Times*, 10 November 1993, *Le Monde* 15 September, 18 September 1993; further figures in Barber, *Jihad vs McWorld*, 91, 93, 95, 330, and Appendix B, 'Twenty-Two Countries' Top Ten Grossing Films, 1991'.
[79] Alejandro Pardo, *The Europe–Hollywood Coopetition: Cooperation and Competition in the Global Film Industry* (Pamplona, 2007), 21–2.
[80] *Le Monde*, 15 September 1993.   [81] Ibid. 18 September 1993.

freedom to create our own images. A society which abandons to others the way of showing itself, that is to say the way of presenting itself to itself, is a society enslaved.[82]

The Franco-American row of 1993—patched over but not resolved to allow the entire GATT process to conclude 'successfully' and give way to the World Trade Organization—saw the mobilization of all the major currencies of American power: economic, political, and mass cultural, not to mention the Commerce and State Departments, the CIA, and the President himself.[83] The confrontation also demonstrated how the value of these currencies could as ever be 'hardened' by the strictly pragmatic attitude to the border dividing the public and the private sector in American official action, since the Hollywood industry was once again able to call upon its deep and abiding ties with Washington, and with President Clinton personally, to make its views felt.[84] The stakes of the contest at the time had been well described by the film critic of the London *Guardian*, after the 1990 Berlin film award ceremony, one of a number of devices adopted by official policy to protect and stimulate the European film and television industry:

> If film-making in Europe collapses, as it already has in what used to be termed Eastern Europe (we have already virtually kissed goodbye to the Hungarian and Polish cinemas that have given us so much remarkable work even under the moral constraints of the Communist system), it can only prove a devastating blow to the concept of film as something more than entertainment.... The question is: how do we save the European cinema, which includes our own, without placing it totally in thrall to American money—and ultimately American values?[85]

By the mid-1990s though, it was clear that film-making in Europe would not collapse. Audiences were returning in the larger markets—partly in response to the 'multiplex' phenomenon—while the industry itself had reorganized, with large new groups such as the French Canal

---

[82] Wenders in *La Stampa*, 27 October 1993; Mitterand cit. in interview with Jean-Pierre Rappeneau, director of *Cyrano de Bergerac*, *The Independent*, 5 November 1993; full background in Jean-Pierre Jeancolas, 'From the Blum–Byrnes Agreement to the GATT affair', in G. Nowell-Smith and S. Ricci (eds), *Hollywood and Europe: Economics, Culture, National Identity, 1945–95* (London, 1998), excerpt from Poland speech ibid. 57–9.

[83] Vivid personal-historical account in Puttnam, *Undeclared War*, 3–8, 340–3; later reflection of French Minister of Culture Jack Lang in Thomas Paris (ed.), *Quelle diversité face à Hollywood*, special edition of *CinémAction* (2002), 205; for the long history of Lang's action on these questions, David L. Looseley, *The Politics of Fun: Cultural Policy and Debate in Contemporary France* (Oxford, 1995), esp. chs 4, 8.

[84] Puttnam, *Undeclared War*, 266–70, 350.

[85] 'Hollywood is the enemy', *The Guardian*, 29 November 1990; cf. Barber, *Jihad vs McWorld*, 90–7.

Plus, Anglo-Dutch Polygram, and the German Bertelsmann emerging as major players, hoping to feed the explosion of demand fed by new technology and the opening up of markets in the former eastern bloc.[86] After the GATT row, the Hollywood bloc began to invest in European film schools, and stepped up co-productions. The EU meanwhile had taken steps to strengthen its own hand in the field of culture by including it in the proposed Maastricht Treaty, and a number of new funding initiatives in the EU and the Council of Europe supported film production and distribution.[87]

The entire question had in any case become vastly more complicated at the structural level by the time because of advances in technology (satellite and digital television, the prospective merging of computer, TV and telephone services), the large-scale privatization of national telecommunications companies, and the reorganization of the sector at the corporate level, with a significant rush of transatlantic alliances and American investment in the emerging European media empires.[88] That this was all simply part of a global trend—confirmed by the eruption of the Internet and the World Wide Web between 1994 and 1995—did nothing to deter the growth of a further set of fears concerning the future of traditional values and identities. Chancellor Kohl of Germany insisted:

> We need stronger co-operation in order to assure the cultural identity of Europe and thereby the durability of the Federal republic as an industrial and cultural nation. It is already foreseeable that as a result of new satellite technology we will be confronted with a veritable avalanche of overseas productions. This development carries with it the danger of cultural levelling, if we do not succeed in asserting ourselves in international cultural creativity with European and German productions.[89]

[86] For an official report on the European cinema audience in 1997, <http://www.medi-asalles.it/yearb98/ybrune98.htm#ing>. This emphasizes that the box office continued to be dominated by American productions, while European films had the greatest difficulty in finding markets outside their country of origin; the analysis is confirmed in Pardo, *Europe–Hollywood Coopetition*, §3.2.

[87] Richard Collins, 'Unity in Diversity? The European Single Market in Broadcasting and the Audiovisual, 1982–1992', *Journal of Common Market Studies* (March 1994); Pardo, *Europe–Hollywood Coopetition*, §6.4; on MPAA efforts, interview with its veteran secretary, Jack Valenti, in *Newsweek*, 26 May 1997; on EU initiatives, *The European*, 10–16 October 1996.

[88] *Time*, 27 February 1995; *International Herald Tribune*, 20 March, 21 March 1996; *Le Monde diplomatique*, May 1997; Puttnam, *Undeclared War*, 352–4; Pardo, *Europe–Hollywood Coopetition*, p. 24, ch. 5.

[89] Cit. in Michael Ermarth, 'Cultural Protectionism in "Media Mediae": "Normal" Germany Confronts Post-Modern Americanization Over the Last Decade (1987–1997)', paper delivered at the Forlì conference, University of Bologna (Bologna, March 1997). In the name of these concerns, the French and Italian culture ministries proposed extensive formal cooperation, starting with the extension of 'Arte', the Franco-German high quality

The Internet explosion caused even more dismay among the governing classes. At a time when French linguistic protectionism had extended to pop songs, the Internet was seen as yet another weapon of penetration of the English language, a death threat to the pioneering domestic network Minitel and 'the latest and most sinister example of American "cultural imperialism"', according to the Gaullist administration of President Chirac' (the London *Times* reported). The culture minister in the Juppé government denounced the fact that 90 per cent of the Internet was in English, and that typing in 'Bonaparte' or 'de Gaulle' brought him only responses from data banks in the United States.[90]

The *Financial Times* commented:

> In a growing number of countries, borderless information and entertainment media are viewed, not as a positive force for integration, but as a divisive threat to national integrity and cultural values.

Active cultural protectionism was on the increase, noted the London newspaper, touching Ireland, Portugal, Belgium, and the European Parliament as well as France, and involving quotas and local content requirements of various sorts in radio and television programming.[91]

But with the arrival of the multi-screen cinema centre—the 'multiplexes'—in Europe, many American-owned, and the new digital 'platforms' offered by the Internet, the old problem of a quite different scale and dynamism of operations between the American and the European industries returned.[92] Even the Italian government—normally quite indifferent to these issues—let out a squeal of horror when it began to look as though a News International-led combination might control the 200+ channels soon to be available from new satellite clusters.[93] David Puttnam, the most successful British movie producer since the Second World War, thought that the answer lay in radically modernized distribution and marketing in Europe, led by the European Union. The *Financial Times* blamed fragmentation, undercapitalization, and poor business professionalism in production, but also the stranglehold of the big US distributors.[94] A leading

---

television channel to include Italian state television; report in *Corriere della Sera*, 13 December 1996. Little seems to have come from the discussions. 'Arte' never became available on terrestrial channels in Italy.

[90] *The Times*, 13 February 1996; similar concerns at the EU level reported in *European Voice*, 6–12 June 1996.

[91] Cf. *European Voice*, 7–13 November 1996; in November 1996 in the European Parliament, the free-marketeers won the most important vote on the issue at that time.

[92] Pardo, *Europe–Hollywood Coopetition*, 28, 111.

[93] Interview with Telecommunications Minister S. Cardinale in *La Stampa*, 27 December 1998.

[94] *Financial Times*, 'How to Spend It' supplement, 33 (February 1999); cf. Pardo, *Europe–Hollywood Coopetition*, 30, 103–5.

London expert, Geoffrey Nowell-Smith, said instead that the European cinema 'needs to re-discover the present, forget rural idylls and plunge into urban nightmares, reconnecting with the mythologies of everyday fear and desire'. Yet he himself, editor of the *Oxford History of World Cinema*, wrote that 'realism was not the commodity audiences required of cinema', and that the old cliché was as true as ever: Hollywood's strength in an entertainment-led market derived from its success as the world's 'biggest fabricator of fantasy'.[95]

Why the film and television industries should, over the decades, have generated the most intensely favourable and hostile attitudes to the American presence in all its forms was best expressed by David Puttnam. In his grand history of the twentieth-century transatlantic confrontation in the movie sector, the film adviser to the 1997 Labour government of Tony Blair wrote:

> Some try to persuade us that films and television are a business just like any other. They are not. Films and television shape attitudes, create conventions of style and behaviour, reinforce or undermine the wider values of society. At a time when the most highly developed nations...are, almost without exception going through a crisis of social disintegration, it is inconceivable that we should pretend that film and television do not have a major impact on our lives. Creative artists, and those who work with them, have a heavy moral responsibility to challenge, inspire, question and affirm as well as to entertain. Movies are more than fun, and more than big business. They are power.[96]

EUROPE'S 'AMERICAN CENTURY': FACING THE THIRD WAVE

By any objective standard America stood triumphant in the world as the twentieth century came to an end, and its citizens were prouder of their country than those of any other nation: 75 per cent claimed to share this feeling (at the other end of the scale were former West Germans at 17 per cent).[97] The late 1980s economic malaise had been magnificently overcome, with eight years of growth. In the year 2000 President Clinton told Congress in his Annual Economic Report:

> We are on the brink of marking the longest expansion in our Nation's history. More than 20 million new jobs have been created since Vice President Gore

---

[95] Nowell-Smith and Ricci (eds), *Hollywood and Europe*, Introduction.
[96] Puttnam, *Undeclared War*, 350.   [97] Judt, *Postwar*, p. 799, n. 12.

and I took office in January 1993. We now have the lowest unemployment rate in 30 years—even as core inflation has reached its lowest level since 1965.

This expansion has been both deep and broad, reaching Americans of all races, ethnicities, and income levels.... In 1999 we had the largest dollar surplus in the Federal budget on record and the largest in proportion to our economy since 1951 ... we are now on track to eliminate the Nation's publicly held debt by 2013. Our fiscal discipline has paid off in lower interest rates, higher private investment and stronger productivity growth.[98]

Accompanying the President's account was the Annual Report of his Council of Economic Advisers. This opened with a dance poster from 1900, advertising a new 'march and two steps' called 'Dawn of the Century'. A historian was quoted recalling America's extraordinary productive and educational strength at that time: 'I don't think we can understand what it was like in 1900 unless you think of optimism, of hope, of buoyancy, for the United States everything seemed to be going right.' The Council of Economic Advisers was proud to have helped the Clinton administration to reproduce these conditions: 'The mood of optimism that prevailed at the dawn of the 20th century prevails today as well.'[99]

'In 1999, the ninth year of the expansion,' the report went on, 'GDP grew by 4.0 per cent and 2.7 million payroll jobs were created.' What were the causes of such a boom? After investment in information and other high technologies, the report of the Economic Advisers listed enhanced participation in the global economy as a key factor: 'between 1991 and 1999 [international] trade...as a share of GDP rose by 4.8 percentage point, compared with increases of 1.5 and 3.5 percentage points during the expansions of the 1960s and the 1980s, respectively.' After Canada, the European Union was the country's most important trade partner, if exports and imports were added together. Transatlantic trade had grown 61 per cent between 1991 and 1998. The 'story of this country's integration into the world economy' had suddenly accelerated and intensified.[100]

Corporate America had certainly played its part. Among the new names of the decade arriving or expanding transnationally were financial giants such as Citibank, Lehman Brothers, and the consulting firm Arthur

---

[98] *Annual Economic Report of the President 2000* (Washington DC, 2000), at <http://w3.access.gpo.gov/usbudget/fy2001/pdf/2000_erp.pdf>, still accessible from the Wayback Machine Web archive: <http://wayback.archive.org>.

[99] Ibid. 21.

[100] Ibid. pp. 30, 34, 205, and ch. 6 in general; transatlantic trade figure in Maya Eichler, 'The Role of Identity in European–U.S. Relations', in Gustav E. Gustenau et al. (eds), *Europe–USA: Diverging Partners*, Austrian Institute of International Affairs (Baden-Baden, 2006), 259.

Andersen. Ratings agencies, such as Moody's and Standard and Poor's, emerged from nowhere to determine the credit worthiness of public and private bodies across the globe.[101] But traditional brands also made their mark. 'By the turn of the century, McDonald's was selling more burgers and products abroad than in the United States', reported Eckes and Zeiler. 'It had 26,462 restaurants in 119 countries (12,624 in the United States, 5,011 in Europe, 5,704 in Asia, and 1,323 in Latin America).' Following attacks on its restaurants in Davos and Prague in 2000, to accompany meetings of the World Economic Forum and the IMF respectively, McDonald's chief executive explained to *Foreign Policy* magazine why protesters singled out his company in these terms:

> If you're going to have that kind of [global] presence, you're going to have that kind of attention. And we're in a world today where people focus a lot of pent-up frustration about a lot of issues on a single concept called globalization—a concept that is much more complicated than some of the people who write and talk about it want to admit.[102]

Meanwhile, continued Eckes and Zeiler, 'by 2002, Wal-Mart, America's largest retailer, had become the world's largest corporation.... With some 1,200 stores outside the United States, Wal-Mart employed more than 1.2 million people—more than any other firm.... In 2001, foreign sales of $32bn. equalled companywide sales a decade earlier.' Britain and Germany were the favoured nations for Wal-Mart's ambitious plans in Europe.[103]

Although America was the world's largest debtor in 2000, with $2 trillion in outstanding obligations, this reflected in part the fact that foreign assets in the US surpassed those held by American firms and individuals abroad.[104] The dollar remained the linchpin of the international financial system. In spite of the deep Asia crisis of 1997–8, the 'Washington consensus' of multilateral stabilization, development, and deregulation continued to enjoy unchallenged ideological supremacy, centring on the ever-freer, ever-faster, ever-bigger flows in 'tradable financial value' at the heart of the new era of globalization.[105] China agreed to accept this vision

[101] On Lehman Brothers and Arthur Andersen, Daniels, 'Overseas Investment', 78–80; on the ratings agencies, Friedman, *Lexus*, 32–3, 91–2.

[102] Eckes Jr and Zeiler, *Globalization*, 214, 244; *Foreign Policy*, May/June 2001.

[103] Eckes Jr and Zeiler, *Globalization*, 244; on Wal-Mart's plans for Germany, the *Financial Times*, 11 February 1999 said that innovation in such a conservative country could only come when 'more foreigners come into the market and bring with them the best practice from their home markets'. On Wal-Mart's European plans after its acquisition of the British chain Asda in 1999, *Business Week*, 24 January 2000.

[104] Eckes Jr and Zeiler, *Globalization*, 209.

[105] Manuel Castells, 'Information Technology and Global Capitalism', in Giddens and Hutton (eds), *Global Capitalism*, 53–7. But the new financial flows were far less regulated

in return for starting talks for admission to the WTO—with the US—in 1999.[106] (Russia, on the other hand, was in no condition to make this leap.) The historian Thomas McCormick wrote:

> By most criteria for hegemony, America superbly fulfilled its systemic responsibilities even as it served its national interests—market for distress goods, lender of last resort and governor of international rules of economic behavior.... Presumably an economic locomotive of such enduring dynamism could pull a whole trainload of global trading partners, including the European Union, into a new era, a new economy—especially, so it was argued, if they were wise enough to junk their rigid, over-regulated labor and capital markets (Europe's social capitalism) in favour of flexible, deregulated ones (American free enterprise capitalism).[107]

Yet America's leading thinkers and commentators were not satisfied, much less happy, with the condition of their country or its place in the world. No Kipling emerged to preach a resonant 'Lest We Forget' message to the citizens of the lone superpower. Instead waves of foreign policy experts competed to draw up baleful lists of risks and dangers. 'The end of the Cold War increased American power, but decreased American hegemony', wrote the liberal historian McCormick.[108] The conservative Professor Huntington expanded on the theme, listing the many features of American primacy in the usual hierarchical order—economic, philosophical, military, technological, cultural—but then concluding that 'American influence falls far short of that'.[109] A leading neo-conservative, Irving Kristol, said that the world had 'never seen an imperium of this kind.... In its favor it lack[ed] the brute coercion that characterized European imperialism. But it also lack[ed] the authentic missionary spirit [of] that older imperialism, which aimed to establish the rule of law while spreading Christianity.' What it did 'offer the world' was 'a growth economy, a consumerist society, popular elections and a dominant secular-hedonistic ethos', a combination that was 'hard to resist—and equally hard to respect

---

than the long-standing channels of trade and investment; on the dangers of this situation, Robert Kuttner, 'The Role of Governments in the Global Economy', in Giddens and Hutton (eds), *Global Capitalism*, 153–4.

[106] *Annual Economic Report of the President 2000*, 221–2; China's accession process was completed in September 2001; on the heavyweight corporate lobbying behind this development, Kuttner, 'Role of Governments', 149.

[107] T. McCormick, 'American Hegemony and European Autonomy, 1989–2003: One Framework for Understanding the War in Iraq', in Lloyd C. Gardner and Marilyn B. Young (eds), *The New American Empire: A 21st Century Teach-In on U.S. Foreign Policy* (New York, 2005), 87.

[108] Ibid. 107.

[109] Huntington quoted in David Campbell, 'Contradictions of a Lone Superpower', in Slater and Taylor (eds), *American Century*, 234.

in its populist vulgarity...an imperium with a minimum of moral substance'.[110]

Many other media and elite observers seemed to feel their country was beleaguered, at the least misunderstood, under siege from forces and groups around the world who were motivated by every sort of grievance and envy, large or small, comprehensible or otherwise. Thought to be typical were attacks such as the following, from a Mexican intellectual writing in an Anglo-Latin essay collection:

> The United States is the most aggressive superpower in applying and disseminating the new structural systems of domination and appropriation. Globalization American style includes the principal policies adopted and promoted by the great powers and obedient governments. American neo-liberalism not only tries to impose and succeeds in imposing American ways of governing, but American neo-liberal and neo-conservative concepts and discourses have become words-acts, discourse structures of the super-power's hegemonized globalization.
>
> The problem is not resolved with an anti-Americanism that is no more than superficial and aggressive xenophobia. What is required is a distinction between the greatness and meanness of America in the history of world domination and appropriation.[111]

The latter phrases showed some of the dangers of bundling all the complaints from without into the catch-all term of 'anti-Americanism'. The age-old gap between the intensity of criticism about the state of the nation permitted within America, and what was considered acceptable on the lips of foreigners, surfaced repeatedly in the 1990s. More than ever the latter were likely to be accused of 'anti-Americanism', a formula that blurred every form of distinction. The great British traveller Anthony Trollope had noted in 1862 how so many of the individuals he had met reacted with 'extreme displeasure when anything is said disrespectful of [their] country....Any touch comes at once upon the network of [their] nerves and puts in operation all [their] organs of feeling...'[112] One hundred and thirty years later, many outside observers thought that little had changed. While nationalism flourished everywhere, said the British political economist Susan Strange in 1994, nowhere was this more obvious

[110] Kristol in *Wall Street Journal*, 18 August 1997 (I am grateful to Mario Del Pero for bringing this article to my attention); cf. Donald Kagan and Frederick W. Kagan, *While America Sleeps: Self-Delusion, Military Weakness and the Threat to Peace Today* (New York, 2000), 340, 424; articles and bibliography in 'U.S. Dominance: Is It Good for the World?', *Foreign Policy* (Summer 1998).

[111] Pablo González Casanova, 'The Americanization of the World', in Slater and Taylor (eds), *American Century*, 328–9, 332.

[112] Anthony Trollope, *North America* (1862 edn repr., London, 1992), 214.

than in the US. The talk was all of international community and globalization, said Strange, but 'in the US the reaction of any injury to Americans, even to American armed forces, is such that... the pursuit of national interest and the defence of national *amour propre* always comes first'.[113] The more the nation prospered and attracted admirers and emulators, the more those who heard only the critics tended to insist crossly on the motto invented for the British Crown by the fourteenth-century Knights of the Garter: *'Honi Soit Qui Mal Y Pense'* (Ashamed be they who think evil thereon).[114]

Yet in the 1990s the US people and government did little in practice to counter what appeared as a widespread disinclination to give due respect to 'America' as model, ideology, or way of life, a tendency even, in some quarters, to blame the US for the ills and inequalities produced by globalization. In a Washington debate of 2000 around the question 'We're #1, Now What?', the head of Foreign Policy Studies at the prestigious Brookings Institution of Washington said: 'The American people aren't isolationist, but they're indifferent...' The former chairman of the House of Representative Foreign Relations Committee, Lee Hamilton, concurred:

> ...there are very strong unilateralist tendencies in this country, very strong tendencies not to get involved in the world.... I remember talking to President-elect Bill Clinton in 1992, and he said: Lee, I went through the entire campaign and nobody asked me a question about foreign policy except a couple of news people.[115]

Journalists and experts sounded alarms over the decline in coverage of foreign issues in mainstream US television and print media after the end of the Cold War. The journalists noted the commercial pressures that had arisen as the nation's great television channels and newspapers had gradually come under the control of transnational corporations. Their competition with the new cable, satellite, and Internet providers had increased choice but had led inevitably to a power shift from the producer to the consumer. The result was the stories that would sell on the streets got the coverage, and those that wouldn't didn't, 'which is

---

[113] Strange, *States and Markets*, 130.

[114] Example of US response to perceived hostility to all people and things American in Paul Hollander, *Anti-Americanism: Critiques at Home and Abroad, 1965–1990* (New York, 1992), ch. 8; dissenting view in William Pfaff, 'Sole Superpower Status Goes to America's Head', *International Herald Tribune* (18–19 January 1997); cf. Chapter 11.

[115] Comments by Richard Haas at a Brookings Institution seminar on 'American Primacy: We're #1, Now What?', 18 October 2000; the seminar provided a comprehensive survey/debate on the policy issues of the 2000 Presidential election as seen from Washington: transcript at <http://www.brookings.edu/events/2000/1018defense.aspx>.

why there are few foreign affairs covers these days', said a 'deeply worried' veteran newsman.[116] Experts such as Joe Nye reported that between 1989 and 2000 TV networks 'cut their foreign news content by two-thirds.... The president of MSNBC blamed "a national fog of materialism and disinterest and avoidance".' Only 7 per cent of those interviewed in 1997 felt that the President should be concentrating his attention on foreign affairs; 86 per cent thought the homeland should come first.[117]

Funding for the traditional activities of 'public diplomacy' declined from approximately $1.1 billion in 1992 to approximate $450 million in 1999. Cultural centres and libraries were closed to save money and please elements in Congress. Between 1993 and 1998 the United States Information Agency lost a third of its funding and staff, and in 1999 was finally folded into the State Department.[118] Only in its dying days did the Clinton administration make a gesture towards redressing the balance with a special 'White House Conference on Culture and Diplomacy', coordinated by the First Lady.[119] The historian Bruce Mazlish wrote: 'The most powerful actor on the global stage seems resolutely determined not to live in the world it is helping to create through globalisation.'[120]

---

[116] Specific figures on decline of foreign coverage in '*New York Times*, 1981–2000', in Stuart N. Soroka, 'Media, Public Opinion and Foreign Policy', *Harvard International Journal of Press/Politics* (Winter 2003), Table 1, p. 31; decline of television news coverage documented in Garrick Utley, 'The Shrinking of Foreign News: From Broadcast to Narrowcast', *Foreign Affairs* (March–April, 1997), 5–6; comment from Don Oberdorfer, 'A Journalist to His Profession: "I Am Deeply Worried"', *Harvard International Journal of Press/Politics* (Winter 1996), 149.

[117] Nye Jr, *The Paradox of American Power: Why the World's Only Superpower Can't Go It Alone* (New York, 2002), p. ix; Pew Research Center for the People and the Press, 'Public Indifferent About NATO Expansion', report of 24 January 1997; other sources cit. in *Foreign Affairs*, Summer 1998, 48; the State Department's chief spokesman, Nicholas Burns, expressed his concerns over public awareness in 'Talking to the World About Foreign Policy', *Harvard International Journal of Press/Politics* (Fall 1996), 14.

[118] Richard T. Arndt, *The First Resort of Kings: American Cultural Diplomacy in the Twentieth Century* (Washington DC, 2005), 540; cf. Kristin M. Lord, *Voices of America: U.S. Public Diplomacy for the 21st Century*, Brookings Institution (Washington DC, 2008); for graph on spending 1957–2007, p. 37; the process had started under President Bush Sr and in spite of the apparent success of official efforts of communication and persuasion at the time of the Gulf War, 1990–1; details in Nicholas J. Cull, 'Speeding the Strange Death of American Public Diplomacy: The George H. W. Bush Administration and the U.S. Information Agency', *Diplomatic History* (January 2010).

[119] White House conference of 28 November 2000 documented at <http://www.state.gov/r/whconf/final_rpt.html>, still accessible from the Wayback Machine Web archive: <http://wayback.archive.org>.

[120] Bruce Mazlish et al. (eds), *The Paradox of a Global USA* (Stanford, 2007), 1.

PARADOXES OF HEGEMONY

So the great 'American Century' enterprise of bringing the world up to scratch by exhortation, example, and exchange, undertaken for decades by official Washington, was much shrunken by end of the 1990s and left often to private initiative. The successors of those, like Henry Luce, who had believed in America's mission to 'transform the world after [its] own image...the dominant rhetorical engine pulling American foreign policy through the 20th century', as a prominent Washington commentator put it, now left this job in Europe to opinion-makers.[121] These included the most distinguished and internationalist politicians, businessmen, and journalists who crowded events like the World Economic Forum held each year in Switzerland. In the 1990s its American protagonists felt it was their duty to communicate to the world the realities of globalized modernity as Bill Clinton's 'Washington Consensus' understood them.

In Europe the message was amplified in various forms by the columnists of transplanted newspapers such as the *Wall Street Journal Europe*, the *International Herald Tribune*, *Business Week*, and echoed by their European fellow believers, particularly *The Economist*. All told their readers repeatedly that they had no choice but to follow the late 1990s American model of success if they wished seriously to tackle the chronic local problems of high unemployment, an aging population and a burdensome welfare state, and thereby accede to all the benefits of globalization. A typical example from 1999 read like this:

> Alongside the annual World Economic Forum here [in Davos], the *Wall Street Journal Europe* invited six senior American and European politicians, business leaders and consultants to discuss the challenges facing Europe's economies. Their verdict: Europe's job markets must be further deregulated if Europeans want to remain competitive in an increasingly global economy. And governments must find ways to encourage capital to finance the growth industries of the 21st century.[122]

Among the group, the President of NASDAQ—'America's vast, over-the-counter broker network'—thought the Europeans should invent better

---

[121] Phrases from review by Jonathan Yardley of Judis, *Grand Illusion*, in *Washington Post/ Guardian Weekly*, 13 December 1992.

[122] *Wall Street Journal Europe*, 2 February 1999; in another session the newspaper convened 'senior executives from the technology industry', from both sides of the Atlantic. Their verdict: the Europeans were 'stymied by fear of failure, over-bearing regulation and limited access to venture capital...[and] many Europeans don't accept technology as a part of everyday life'; ibid. For other versions of this stance, *Wall Street Journal*, 2 February 1999 (on job markets), *International Herald Tribune*, 23 February 1999 (on agriculture and society), *La Stampa*, 1 March 1999 (on information technology), *The Economist*, March 1999 (on the film industry).

ways to fund new businesses. The Chairman of Cambridge (Mass.) Energy Associates, Daniel Yergin, deplored the Europeans for being so 'inward-looking...euro preoccupied', especially when compared to their past. Percy Barnevik, the Swedish head of a long EU study on improving European competitiveness, showed that he had got the message:

> Europe can become more competitive by benchmarking against America and Japan....You have to create an entrepreneurial climate where it is easy to hire and easy to fire. You have to encourage people to take responsibility for themselves.[123]

The European Union promptly set out to answer this call, urged on by Prime Minister Tony Blair and Chancellor Gerhard Schroëder of Germany, who in a joint declaration of 1999 said that the knowledge-based service economy was the inevitable route to the future, and Europe must adapt to it. Seizing the modernizing opportunities of the time would 'offer Europe a chance to catch up with the United States'.[124] The result was the official Lisbon Agenda of March 2000, which talked of building 'a competitive, dynamic, knowledge-based economy', with no social exclusion and full employment, by 2010. Yet commentators like *The Economist* were far from satisfied:

> At the end of a summit devoted mainly to 'employment, economic reform and social cohesion', the [EU's leaders]...produced an 18-page blueprint for 'radical transformation of the European economy' chock-a-block with digital literacy and the like. But admit that Europe is learning from A******? [*sic*] No thanks.
> ...As the American economy has gone on growing, as the American stockmarket has refused obstinately to crash, and as the dollar has humiliated the Euro, so the Europeans have found their long-accumulating envy of the American boom turning into mild panic.

The magazine demanded more tax cuts, more freedom to fire workers, more selection in immigration, and less embarrassment over the source of the EU's new 'onrush of liberalism'.[125]

---

[123] Ibid.; meanwhile corporate and official Japan was busy benchmarking against America, and attempting to apply the same methods: Dore, *Stock Market Capitalism*, ch. 4; *International Herald Tribune*, 25 January 2000.

[124] Tony Blair and Gerhard Schroëder, 'The Third Way/Die Neue Mitte', reproduced in Bodo Hombach, *The Politics of the New Centre* (London, 2000), Appendix, pp. 169, 177. Tony Blair repeated the message on many occasions, e.g. address to the Congress of the Party of European Socialists, Milan, 1–2 March 1999, *Corriera della Sera*, 3 March 1999, remarks at the World Economic Forum in Davos, January 2000, (comment in *The Independent*, 31 January 2000).

[125] Official version of Lisbon strategy at <http://europa.eu/scadplus/glossary/lisbon_strategy_en.htm>, still accessible from the Wayback Machine Web archive: <http://wayback.archive.org>; *The Economist*, 1 April 2000.

Elsewhere, Irwin Stelzer, American columnist on the London *Sunday Times*, and reportedly a close collaborator of Rupert Murdoch's News International empire, constantly upbraided the British governments for their lack of true free-market zeal, while Thomas Friedman of the *New York Times*, in his best-selling *The Lexus and the Olive Tree* of 1999, could be found lecturing certain of his foreign readers in these terms:

> As long as the Japanese and West Europeans stick with their rigid, protected welfare systems, which by making capitalism less destructive also make it less creative and enriching, they won't be a challenge to America. But the farther ahead America gets in this age of globalization, the more I expect these countries will seek to mirror and mimic America. This inevitable adjustment will be enormously painful, but they will be forced to do it in order to maintain anything like their current standards of living.[126]

And yet in the 2000 US election campaign, both the Presidential candidates seemed anxious to demonstrate that the US had no intention of imposing its ways on anyone. The Republican George W. Bush said:

> …our nation stands alone right now in the world in terms of power, and that's why we have to be humble. And yet project strength in a way that promotes freedom. So I don't think they [the outside world] ought to look at us in any other way than what we are. We're a freedom-loving nation and if we're an arrogant nation they'll view us that way, but if we're a humble nation they'll respect us.

His opponent, Al Gore, said, 'I agree with that…there is some resentment of U.S. power. So I think that the idea of humility is an important one.'[127]

Europe all split-up

The apparent success of the American model of modernity in the 1990s greatly exacerbated the long-standing and deep divisions among the Europeans on the meaning of the transatlantic inspiration in all its forms: divisions within the EU, between all the nations within it and without it, inside the nations themselves. It even brought out a new split: between the Western group and those societies released from the grip of the Soviet empire, since it remained true that, in spite of many disappointments,

---

[126] Stelzer example in *Sunday Times*, 13 April 2003; Friedman, *Lexus*, 304; although Friedman was unaware of the evolutions in European welfare systems that happened in this era, he had no illusions over the many high-risk features embedded in the American model; ibid. 32–3, 106, 161, 216–17, 241, 305, *passim*.

[127] Second Presidential Debate, 11 October 2000, at <http://www.debates.org/index.php?page=october-11-2000-debate-transcript>.

generally speaking the Eastern group was still far more likely at the end of the decade to admire American ways of doing and being than its Western counterparts.[128] As for the organized integration process, its social impact would be very slow indeed, said the sociologist Colin Crouch in 1994:

> 'Europe' does not confront individual national and sub-national cultures with a need to merge their characteristics, as America did to its immigrants. Rather it is a conditional coming together of a variety of such cultures. As a social force in its own right this is very weak indeed.[129]

On the strategic front, what the Europeans wanted from the formal Atlantic relationship was what they had so earnestly sought in so many different ways ever since 1916: not domination but hegemony *on their terms.* In other words they worked for the mobilization of as much or as little US power as they retained desirable, in order to ensure the realization of the security goals that they defined—singly or now together, via the EU—on their own behalf.[130] Europe's unmatched capacity to involve the United States in its conflicts in this way stretched back to the Great War era and was amply confirmed by the wars in the former Yugoslavia, the worst possible precedent for any notion of European independence in foreign and security policy.[131] Even the smallest dispute seemed to contain this potential, a reality clearly open to manipulation and requiring the most strenuous efforts on the part of America's governments to explain to their domestic constituencies. Wishing no longer to control or to reform the Old World by the late 1990s, official America was still unable to wean the West Europeans from this form of dependence, 'and its consequent, and psychologically inevitable, resentment of Washington', as the Paris-based American William Pfaff saw it.[132]

On economic matters, European commentators encountered difficulties in deciding where the balance of connection and independence should lie. In its New Year editorial for the year 2000, the *Financial Times* said:

---

[128] On the West–East split, Crouch, 'Continental Drift', 1; for Bulgaria, Dina Iordanova, 'Political Resentment versus Cultural Submission: The Duality of U.S. Representations in Bulgarian Media', in Yahya R. Kamalpour (ed.), *Images of the U.S. Around the World* (Albany, 1999), 71–86.

[129] Crouch, 'Continental Drift', 2.

[130] For an American impression of this behaviour, Henry Kissinger, 'A Role for the Atlantic Alliance Today', *The Washington Post/Guardian Weekly* (8 March 1992).

[131] Cf. Eichler, 'Role of Identity', 260.

[132] Pfaff, 'Western Europe Missed Its Chance to Take Charge', *International Herald Tribune* (5 December 1995); sense of American contempt for European flounderings in this area summed up in John L. Harper, 'American Visions of Europe after 1989', in Tod Lindberg (ed.), *Beyond Paradise and Power: Europe, America and the Future of a Troubled Partnership* (London, 2005), 31–2.

Critics reject the notion that there is anything to be learned from this transitory US success. The strength of the expansion, they say, is down to nothing more than speculative over-excess, built on unstable Internet hype. It will, they predict, end as all such periods have ended, in a spectacular crash that will undermine once and for all the notion that the so-called US model amounts to more than casino capitalism.

But on reflection—and after considering the failure of so many hopes placed not long before in Japan—the paper decided that America's job-creating powers, its embrace of new technology, and above all the flexibility of its capital markets, gave the United States the benefit of the doubt.[133]

Among conservative leaders in Europe, the contemporary American business model, with all its hi-tech companies and methods, generally found great rhetorical favour. Prime Minister Aznar of Spain and his industry minister organized a meeting in Madrid to boost awareness of the latest technology gap with the US, and the Finnish EU commissioner responsible for information technology spoke there in order to stimulate 'a wake-up and a shake-up' at the European level. In Italy, said another commentator, only 26 per cent of employees habitually used a computer. The EU average was 40, while in the US the figure was 68. All this was part of the process leading to the Lisbon Agenda of March 2000. The chief executive of Europe's largest media conglomerate, Bertelsmann AG, was quoted as saying that culture wars were a thing of the past, that 95 per cent of online content was in English, and that his company had already embraced this reality. He concluded:

The Internet has a lot to do with democracy, so it's no surprise the biggest gains were made so far in the United States. But there is a new kind of competition out there in this global economy. Europe needs to respond to this challenge by becoming fully engaged, not intimidated.[134]

Although one meteoric entrepreneur in France—Jean-Marie Messier of the Vivendi group—tried this route, things generally did not look this way in Messier's native land.[135] In the course of 1999 the French

---

[133] 'The US example', *Financial Times*, 4 January 2000; among the critics few were as prescient as Ronald Dore: *Stock Market Capitalism*, pp. v, 6, 219, 225.

[134] *International Herald Tribune*, 17 January 2000; Italian figures in *La Stampa*, 13 February 2000.

[135] After merging with the major French film company Pathé in 1999, and the leading television channel Canal+ in 2000, Vivendi acquired a Hollywood studio, Universal, the MP3.com technology company, and the Houghton Mifflin publishing house. But the company lost over $23 billion in 2002, and its colourful chairman, Messier, who had once declared that his rise spelled 'the end of French exceptionalism', was forced to resign; details at <http://www.ketupa.net/vivendi.htm>.

government, with its conservative President, Chirac, and socialist Prime Minister, Jospin, launched a concerted campaign to challenge what it perceived as the renewed 'global unilateralism' of American action in the world. Statements, declarations of principle, initiatives in Europe and at the UN all added up to what the *International Herald Tribune*'s leading commentator called 'an attempt to limit American power and to convince other countries that they should work together to contain it'. Hubert Védrine, the Foreign Minister, was quoted as saying that 'the predominant weight of the United States and the absence for the moment of a counter-weight' was 'the major fact of the global world today', a fact that 'leads [the US] to hegemony, and the idea it has of its mission is unilateralism. And that's inadmissible.' Védrine brought the notion of *hyperpuissance* (hyper-power) to the confrontation, explaining it this way:

> The United States has assets not yet at the disposal of any other power: political influence, the supremacy of the dollar, control of the communications networks, 'dream factories', new technology. Add these up—the Pentagon, Boeing, Coca-Cola, Microsoft, Hollywood, Internet, CNN, the English language—the situation is virtually unprecedented.[136]

The Minister proposed a five-step method to counter all this, and the President soon followed with a seven-point statement of principles. France appears to have been the only nation to have openly stated that the launch of the Euro in 1999 was part of a long-nurtured strategy to enable Europe to 'escape from the domination of the dollar', as Lionel Jospin put it.[137]

While elite opinion on America was fairly united in these years, the wider French public was divided, liking Americans but not feeling close to them, 'sympathetic' to the United States in 41 per cent of those interviewed in 2000, 'antipathetic' in 10 per cent of cases, and neither one nor the other in 48 per cent of the rest. On foreign policy, 92 per cent of the French agreed in 1995 with the word 'domineering' when applied to US behaviour, compared with 91 per cent of Italians, 83 per cent of the British, and 68 per cent of Germans. While the consensus that rejected the American model of society and economy was very strong—reaching 80 per cent—a majority 'have consistently said since 1998 that they hold a favourable opinion of American music, television programs and films', said the survey commentator and historian Richard Kuisel. 'It was the

---

[136] Cit. in Richard Kuisel, 'What Do the French Think of Us? The Deteriorating Image of the United States, 2000–2004', in *French Politics, Culture and Society* (Fall 2004), 91–119; cit. at p. 110; Védrine explained his views in detail in a book-length interview with Dominique Moïsi: *Les cartes de la France à l'heure de la mondialisation* (Paris, 2000); 'hyperpuissance' notion at p. 9.

[137] *International Herald Tribune*, 3 February 1999; Jospin quoted in J. Lloyd, 'I vow to thee, my superstate', in *New Statesman*, 22 January 1999.

1990s that ushered in the current darker disposition of the French towards America', wrote Kuisel in 2004.[138]

Polls conducted by the CSA Opinion organization in late 1998, and including Germany, Spain, Italy, and Britain, as well as France, confirmed this impression, speaking of 'deep reservations' over many aspects of the functioning of America's presence in the world and society. A summary of the findings reported that:

> The Italians seemed to appreciate America the most, but they still showed profound concern about the American model. From 57 per cent to 60 per cent said America's democracy and economy were worth admiring. But 56 to 62 per cent said Italians should not look to America for inspiration on their way of life or their culture.[139]

A detailed survey of US performance across the board by the economist Nicola Cacace explained why Italians might feel this way. Summing up much opinion in Europe (and elsewhere), Cacace listed, alongside the well-known successes of the US economy, its dark sides: the growth of inequality and job insecurity, the use of illegal immigrants, the low level of workers' protection, the scarcity of welfare provision in many key areas of life, the vast increase in the prison population and the use of the death penalty, the consequences of the unique freedom to possess guns.[140] But Italian opinion was, if anything, even more divided than most in Europe on the merits or otherwise of the American inspiration, and the controversial rise to power of the media tycoon Silvio Berlusconi during the 1990s brought a quite different vision of the relevance to his nation's future of American life, television products, and foreign policies.[141]

* * * * *

'It is both a glorious and a frightening time', wrote the authoritative London observers Giddens and Hutton in 2000: 'The optimists and the pessimists can write with equal fervor.... There may be fundamentalist forces, ranging from some fundamentalist Arabs to right-wing European nationalist parties, contesting globalisation, but the system is so powerful and the opportunities so great for those who play the game, that resistance will be episodic and weak.'[142] While few could agree on the extent to which globalization had been designed and managed around the interests

---

[138] R. Kuisel, 'The Gallic Rooster Crows Again: The Paradox of French Anti-Americanism', *French Politics, Culture and Society* (Fall 2001), 1–16; Kuisel, 'What Do the French Think of Us?', 93–101.

[139] *International Herald Tribune*, 10 April 2000.

[140] N. Cacace, 'Tutto il bene e il male dell'America', *Repubblica Affari e Finanza* (20 March 2000).

[141] Cf. Ellwood, 'Containing Modernity', 268–72.

[142] Giddens and Hutton (eds), *Global Capitalism*, 213–15.

of the remaining superpower, there was a widespread sensation that, as in the crisis times of World Wars I and II, the Americans were in a position to exert undue, even decisive, influence on questions that mattered more to Europeans than to the citizens or interests of the United States. This conviction reappeared forcefully during the 1990s, and most often independently of conscious US will or purpose. Some societies, like the British, seemed to adjust without difficulty to this reality. Others resented it, many (and the Europe Union itself) were divided on the effort necessary to come to terms with it. Nowhere were the consequent difficulties more evident than in the post-Cold War debates about collective identity that sprang up inside every European nation, large or small, western or eastern, affluent or needy as the century and the millennium came finally to an end.

11

Epilogue: The End of the 'American Century'?

THE DOUBLE TRAUMA: FROM 9/11 TO IRAQ

The post-Cold War age of 'soft power', if such it had been, came to a brutal end in its American version on the morning of the September 11 2001. Whatever the possible motives of the al-Qaeda terrorists who struck America and the West on that day, official responses in Washington to their blows could not have been 'harder'. With the subsequent military campaigns against Afghanistan, and then Iraq 18 months later, no one could have the slightest doubt about what the difference between 'hard' and 'soft' power meant to the administration in charge under George W. Bush. The agonizing political saga that connected the attacks of the September 11 2001 to the American-led invasion of Iraq in spring 2003 brought many to ask whether 'the West' could still be said to exist, in its contemporary, globalized sense.[1]

The earliest response of the West Europeans after 9/11 had been a vast outpouring of sympathy for the United States. The President's poll ratings were transformed. French, German, and Spanish opinion leaders competed to show solidarity with what remained, they said, the world's greatest symbol of hope for the persecuted and the dispossessed. Elizabeth Pond reports: 'The German embassy in Washington established a charity to aid 9/11 victims and survivors, expecting to attract some tens of thousands of dollars—and was immediately inundated with $42 million in donations.'[2] But this extraordinary wave of emotion soon crashed against

---

[1] E.g. David Marquand, 'Goodbye, The West', *Prospect* (August 2004); Dominique Moïsi, 'Re-Inventing the West', *Foreign Affairs* (November–December 2003).

[2] E. Pond, *Friendly Fire: The Near-Death of the Transatlantic Alliance* (Pittsburgh, 2004), 10–11; Spanish response in Fernando Escalante-Gonzalbo and Mauricio Tenorio-Trillo, '*Nuestro Once de Septiembre*: The Kingdom of the Comma', in David Farber (ed.), *What They Think of US: International Perceptions of the United States since 9/11* (Princeton, 2007), 134; but this response was very short lived, and reactions in the Spanish-speaking world generally much more ambivalent: ibid. 124–33.

the hard rocks of attitudes among Bush and his closest collaborators seeking much more than justice, or even vengeance, against the terrorists.

'The danger of American democracy is that it always endeavours to expand a majority into unanimity', said Robert Mead in the late 1960s, 'thus the constant drive to uniformity and consolidation.'[3] After 9/11, the means used by Washington to create the unison at home were to insist on the Iraq–al-Qaeda connection, and the danger that tyrants like Saddam Hussein would either use 'weapons of mass destruction' (WMD) on enemies such as Israel, or willingly supply terrorist allies with them.[4] This political project worked brilliantly in America. While there was much unrest at the highest levels of the military and in the foreign policy community, the Press fell in behind the President's lead. Congress remained largely quiescent. The advertising industry mobilized right away, as did Hollywood.[5]

Abroad, the project's effects were just the opposite. When it became clear in the course of 2002 that the Bush team was determined on a full-scale, regime-changing invasion of Iraq as the central project of its global 'war on terror', support and sympathy for everything done up to then turned into dismay. Many other nations recoiled before the domineering and truculent version of the land of the free that now rose up in anger, and which appeared to have mass support. Bush and company literally demanded that the world take sides—'either with us or with the terrorists'—and escalated the rhetoric of militancy and national supremacy to levels never before heard in Washington, even in the darkest days after Pearl Harbour. The Anglo-American historian Tony Judt summed up:

---

[3] Mead, *Atlantic Legacy*, 210–11; cf. Stanley Hoffmann, 'Sheriff and Missionary', in Andrew J. Bacevich (ed.), *The Imperial Tense Prospects and Problems of American Empire* (Chicago, 2003), 175. These were obvious echoes of famous pages in de Tocqueville's *Democracy in America* of 1835/1840: Part 2, ch. 7, 'On the Omnipotence of the Majority in the United States and its Effects', see also ibid. 212–14, 'On what efforts democracy is capable', and pp. 217–20, 'The manner in which American democracy conducts external affairs of state'.

[4] Among the most elaborate public expositions of this line of thinking was the one offered by Secretary of State Colin Powell to the UN Security Council on 5 February 2003; critical comment in Lloyd C. Gardner, 'Present at the Culmination: The Empire of Righteousness', in Gardner and Young (eds), *New American Empire*, 12.

[5] On political project, Gardner, 'Present at the Culmination', 12; on military disquiet, Thomas E. Ricks, *Fiasco: The American Military Adventure in Iraq* (London, 2007), 66–76, 81–4, *Financial Times*, 1–2 March 2003; on press, Ricks, *Fiasco*, 55–6, 93–4; on Congress, ibid. 85–90; on advertising, Nancy Snow, *The Arrogance of American Power: What U.S. Leaders Are Doing Wrong and Why It's Our Duty to Dissent* (Lanham, Md., 2007), 119–21; on Hollywood, articles in *International Herald Tribune*, 9 October, 16 October, 8 November 2001 (this last reports a meeting between film industry executives and a senior White House adviser). The most impressive cinema product to come out of this situation was probably Steven Spielberg's *War of the Worlds* of 2005, based on the H. G. Wells novel of 1898, as seen, and regularly revisited by the US media in times of crisis; cf. Prologue, p. 13.

The cold war is over, runs the unilateralist creed of the Bush administration and its supporters, and the dust has cleared. We know who we are, and we know what we want. Foreign policy is about national interests. National interests are served by the exercise of power. Power is about arms and the will to use them, and we have both.[6]

Faced with such a challenge, radical and bitter dissension appeared among America's allies, and inside their publics. In official policy, each of the key European nations fell back instinctively on positions that reflected its most basic impulses in defence and security, as filtered through a variety of post-Cold War identity debates in which a real or imaginary version of America had often played a key role.[7] European public opinion meanwhile showed every variety of love–hate, support, acquiescence, and dissent, and registered them all in anxious polling exercises. When Italians were asked by one such survey, ten days after the attacks, whether Italy should take part in armed action against any country harbouring the terrorists, 47 per cent agreed. But 36 per cent said 'no', while a further 8.5 per cent insisted on complete neutrality. Fully 15 per cent of those interviewed felt that the US should bear part of the responsibility for the attacks, 'because too strongly aligned with Israel against the Islamic world.'[8] Francis Fukuyama wrote: 'an enormous gap has opened up between in American and European perceptions about the world, and the sense of shared values is increasingly frayed... "Europe" has become a place-holder for global attitudes critical of American foreign policy.'[9]

[6] T. Judt, 'Its Own Worst Enemy', *The New York Review of Books* (15 August 2002), 12; cf. Anatol Lieven, 'The Push for War', *London Review of Books* (3 October 2002).

[7] On Britain, Ellwood, 'American Myth, American Model, and the Quest for a British Modernity', in Moore and Vaudagna (eds), *American Century in Europe*; on Italy, Ellwood, 'Containing Modernity'; on Germany, Stefan (ed.), *Americanization and Anti-Americanism*; on France, Philip H. Gordon and Sophie Meunier, *The French Challenge: Adapting to Globalization* (Washington DC, 2001); on variations in 'threat perception', Michael Cox, 'From the Cold War to the War on Terror: Old Threats, New Threats, and the Future of the Transatlantic Relationship', in Geir Lundestad (ed.), *Just Another Major Crisis? The United States and Europe since 2000* (Oxford, 2008), 65–8.

[8] Cit. in Massimo Teodori, *Maledetti americani. Destra, sinistra e cattolici: Storia del pregiudizio antimericano* (Milan, 2002), 9; citing other polls, Luciano Violante reported that 71% opposed any American armed action against a country hosting terrorist bases, and 51% cited US foreign policy (in general) as a factor in the attacks, Violante, *Un mondo assimetrico: Europa, Stati Uniti Islam* (Torino, 2003), 145–7; Europe-wide poll evidence discussed in Federico Romero, 'The Twilight of American Cultural Hegemony: A Historical Perspective on Western Europe's Distancing from America', in Farber (ed.), *What They Think of US*, 165–7.

[9] Philip H. Gordon and Jeremy Shapiro, *Allies at War: America, Europe, and the Crisis over Iraq* (New York, 2004), ch. 5; F. Fukuyama, 'Does the West Still Exist?', in Le Gloannec and Smolar (eds), *Entre Kant et Kosovo*, 32; Romero, 'Twilight of American Cultural Hegemony', 157, 167–72.

But it was at the moral level that many European commentators, and the Vatican, chose to express their worries over the American government's behaviour in the months and years around the invasion of Iraq, not least because Bush himself claimed without hesitation that his crusade against Saddam Hussein was divinely inspired.[10] To European sceptics a range of contrasting visions seemed to be emerging from the Bush challenge, fundamentally different interpretations of the meaning of the West's Enlightenment heritage at the level of moral values. Dominique Moïsi and Alain Minc, the French political commentators, Ian Buruma, the Dutch–Asian writer, Peter Schneider, the senior German novelist, and Javier Solana, the Spanish ex-Secretary General of NATO, subsequently the head of EU foreign policy, all expressed the same sentiments in articles published after February 2003, which saw massive anti-war demonstrations across Europe, as well as in many other regions of the world.[11]

In the wake of the February demonstrations, Jürgen Habermass and Jacques Derrida, the Continent's most prominent philosophers, signed a joint manifesto calling for the strengthening of a 'core' Europe, 'defined above all by its secular Enlightenment, and social-democratic traditions', and they 'sought to build a common European identity upon those traditions'. Their unprecedented joint intervention set off another round of wide-scale discussion, including American as well as European voices, carried on largely in German-speaking publications.[12]

Javier Solana talked of a 'moral certainty of religious America [that] is hard to replicate in secular Europe'. Minc mentioned the philosophical differences on the links between religion and the State, on abortion and the death penalty, on the purposes of politics and war as a crusade. But it was Schneider who best articulated what appeared to be at stake:

[10] Cf. Ivo H. Daalder, 'The End of Atlanticism', *Survival* (Summer 2003), 158–9; Pond, *Friendly Fire*, 53; John B. Judis, 'The Author of Liberty: Religion and U.S. Foreign Policy', *Dissent* (Fall 2005); full contextualization in James Carroll, 'Messiah Nation: Religion and the American Idea', in Kurt Almqvist and Alexander Linklater (eds), *On the Idea of America: Perspectives from the Engelsberg Seminar 2009* (Stockholm, 2010); Vatican positions visible at <http://catholicism.about.com/od/thechurchintheworld/f/popes_on_iraq.htm>.

[11] Moïsi, 'Re-Inventing the West', Minc in *Corriere della Sera*, 5 November 2004; Buruma in *Financial Times*, 10 December 2004; Schneider in *International Herald Tribune*, 7 April 2004; Solana in *Financial Times*, 8 January 2003; survey of protests in *Guardian Weekly*, 20–26 February 2003.

[12] The manifesto and the contributions to the subsequent debate were gathered together in Daniel Levy, Max Pensky, and John Torpey (eds), *Old Europe, New Europe, Core Europe: Transatlantic Relations after the Iraq War* (London, 2005); cits from Editors' Introduction, p. xi. Not all the authors expressed anti-war positions. In his magisterial survey, *Postwar*, Tony Judt claims that these debates went 'virtually un-noticed' at the key political levels, another confirmation, in his view, of the decline of the influence of intellectuals over the decades; *Postwar*, 786–7.

Europeans think that Americans are on their way to betraying some of the elementary tenets of the Enlightenment, ... [the notion for instance] ... that human judgments and decisions are fallible by their very nature. In its language of power the Bush administration has created the opposite impression, establishing a new principle in which [Americans] are 'first among unequals'. [Meanwhile] Washington accuses Europe of shirking its international responsibilities, and thus its own human rights inheritance.[13]

Minc—like Jürgen Habermass and Jacques Derrida—suggested that a transatlantic divorce should take place, preferably painless, which meant 'no' to anti-Americanism, 'yes' to realizing there were important security and economic interests all shared, but different values of reference. Never was there a greater need for a commonly recognized 'European individual', he suggested. The entire episode, said Habermass and Derrida, had thrown into painful relief the lack of clearly expressed common European values and ideas of legitimacy—not to mention common foreign policies—without which every effort at offering alternatives to whatever the hegemon set in motion would run into the sand.[14]

Soft power's moment of crisis

In the course of the year 2004, the Iraq invasion turned into a major strategic and political disaster. At the same time revelations started to spill out of torture by American soldiers of Iraqi detainees, of the functioning of the Guantanamo detention centre in Cuba, where inmates suspected of terrorist links could be held beyond the law, of 'extraordinary rendition' by which other suspects could be secretly sent to torture centres abroad, and of the deeply anti-liberal workings of the internal measures to defend US territory introduced by the Bush team in the name of 'homeland security'. Everywhere supporters and opponents of the war debated the extent of the damage to America's standing, prestige, and influence in the world, and in Europe in particular. At the simplest level, was not the US government once more—as in Vietnam—guilty of violating the very ideals it claimed to be fighting for?[15]

[13] Sceptical view of this line in Ian Buruma, 'Continental Drift', *Financial Times* (10 December 2004).
[14] J. Habermass and J. Derrida, 'February 15, Or, What Binds Europeans Together: Plea for a Common Foreign Policy, Beginning in Core Europe', in Levy, Pensky, and Torpey (eds), *Old Europe, New Europe, Core Europe*, 7–8; critique of their analysis by the British historian Harold James, ibid. 59–63; Cf. T. Garton Ash, *Free World: Why a Crisis of the West Reveals the Opportunity of our Time* (London, 2005); Tony Judt, 'Europe versus America', *New York Review of Books* (10 February 2005).
[15] Cf. Gardner, 'Present at the Culmination'; Manuel Castells, *The Information Age: Economy, Society and Culture, ii: The Power of Identity* (2nd edn, Oxford, 2004), 353–5; on crisis in US public diplomacy at this point, Cull, *Cold War*, 484; cf. Anne-Marie Slaughter,

This was the context that led Joseph Nye to produce the fullest elaboration of his thought on 'soft power', and to publicize it in a wide variety of articles and interviews. Nye's effort was part of a long-maturing spread of awareness in the governing classes of the West—and presumably elsewhere—that the very nature of 'power' in the world was changing, becoming more diffuse, multifaceted, and contradictory. The great corporations possessed it, but so did non-governmental organizations and religious faiths. International and supranational organizations could deploy it, but so could lobbies and pressure groups, terrorists and organized crime. All these private agencies had taken advantage of the endless expansion of the Internet to set up transnational networks of action and influence, conditioning the official choices of traditional states in ever more apparent fashion. If the world was in the middle of an unstoppable information revolution, then obviously information was a currency of power. The whole movement on climate change was only the most controversial example of what was happening generally.[16]

Emerging nations and economies—especially those of India and China—were also impinging on conventional ideas and balances of power in radical fashion. Would they become strategic challengers or just economic competitors?[17] Would they be the first since America to transform the history of their national success into a recipe for others, after Germany and Japan had failed to do so? Then there was the European Union, actively engaged in expanding, in taking care of its recent east European acquisitions and planning a new constitutional treaty for itself. Who could deny that much of its growth and attraction functioned through mechanisms—norms of democracy and governance, of markets and law, of development and welfare—that were taking it away from American models of 'civilization', and which to Nye and others handsomely confirmed their 'soft power' thesis in another setting?[18]

The Idea That Is America: Keeping Faith with Our Values in a Dangerous World (New York, 2007), pp. xii–xiii (the author, Dean of the Woodrow Wilson School of International Affairs at Princeton, would become head of the Policy Planning unit at the State Department under the Obama administration).

[16] Nye Jr, *Soft Power: The Means to Success in World Politics* (New York, 2004), chs 1, 2; cf. Castells, *Information Age*, vol. ii, ch. 5; Richard Haass, 'The Age of Nonpolarity: What Will Follow U.S. Dominance', *Foreign Affairs* (May/June 2008).

[17] A view from Washington in Fareed Zakaria, *The Post-American World* (New York, 2008), chs 4–5, from Singapore in Mahbubani, *New Asia Hemisphere*. Both books requested that the West, and the US in particular, stop being so fearful and give way gracefully to a world becoming multipolar strategically, economically, and culturally, a world that in any case acknowledged the irreplaceable heritage of Western ideals and innovations.

[18] On the EU as an alternative social model, Romero, 'Twilight of American Cultural Hegemony', 167–71; on EU mechanisms of attraction, Nye Jr, 'Soft Power and European-

In the face of all this, the soft power situation of the United States post-Iraq looked seriously damaged, at the very least precarious. Nye reported:

In the run-up to the Iraq war, polls showed that the United States lost an average of 30 points of support in most European countries. Levels of support were even lower in Islamic countries. After the war, majorities of the people held an unfavourable image of the United States in nearly two-thirds of 19 countries surveyed. Most of those who held negative views said they blamed the policies of the Bush administration rather than America in general.[19]

Then came this declaration: 'Opposition to American policies is not the same as general opposition to the United States.' What other representative of a free nation had ever felt the need to make this point in a foreign policy analysis? It was on the basis of doubt about this question that a significant evolution in the American polling industry took place in the these years, all sooner or later asking for those interviewed to state whether they were in favour or against an abstract entity called 'the United States'.[20] The fact that the American society, presided over by the government of the 'United States', presented in these years the image of a land divided by bitter partisan conflict on a wide variety of political, ethical, and economic questions, did nothing to deter the pollsters, who apparently thought it normal to ask foreigners whether they 'approved of the American people'.[21]

Nye acknowledged that societies might not always be as free as Americans imagined to reconfigure their identities using impulses and inspirations from outside, since some were much more resilient culturally than others, and so possessed the resources to create their own syntheses. But what Nye could not do was imagine a situation where cultural interaction

American Affairs', in Thomas L. Ilgen (ed.), *Hard Power, Soft Power and the Future of Transatlantic Relations* (Aldershot, 2006), 30–3; Carl Bildt, 'Europe Must Keep Its "Soft Power"', *Financial Times* (31 May 2005); Bildt was former Prime Minister of Sweden and UN envoy to the Balkans; on the Indian and Chinese versions—and their limits—Nye Jr, *Soft Power*, 88–9.

[19] Nye Jr, *Soft Power*, 35; cf. Pond, *Friendly Fire*, 53.

[20] Cf. Pew Research Center, Pew Global Attitudes Project, <http://www.people-press. org>; and the annual *Transatlantic Trends*, of the German Marshall Fund of the United States, <http://trends.gmfus.org /?s=transatlantic+trends>.

[21] On US public opinion, Steven Kull, 'Can the Circle Be Unbroken? Public Opinion and the Transatlantic Rupture', in Lundestad (ed.), *Just Another Major Crisis?*. Samuel Huntington dedicated one of his last books to America's own identity problems: *Who Are We? The Challenges to America's National Identity* (New York, 2004). Nye refers to the history of attitudes to things American including 'the American people'; *Soft Power*, 35–7. Pew poll on 'Am Character' cit. in Romero, 'Twilight of American Cultural Hegemony', p. 175, n. 29.

of all sorts between the US and the rest did not somehow, sooner or later produce 'an outcome' favourable to the specific foreign policies of his nation. In all his discourse there was always and everywhere the instrumental strain: 'The ultimate proof is in the outcomes, whether we get the outcomes we want or don't.'[22] A British analyst pointed to the underlying problem. The emphasis by people like Nye on the charismatic nature of so many American cultural products and icons, as judged by their apparent success around the world, said David Campbell, 'always invoked them as though they were state-controlled resources'. But they were nothing of the kind; they were the products of that society in the most diffuse sense, and its creative industries in particular, with all their talent for absorbing and reconfiguring the inventions of the world then relaunching them for a global market.[23]

BUSINESS AS USUAL: MONEY, PEOPLE, CREATIVITY AFTER IRAQ

Normality reasserts itself

We can now see that, until the great financial crisis of the end of the decade, the traditional sources of America's force as an economic and cultural inspiration abroad continued to exert their influence largely untouched by the upheavals of Iraq. On the front of economic growth, the US led the way up a curve of expansion that the others mimicked exactly—except the high-flyers China and India—until they all fell off the cliff in identical fashion in the banking upheaval of 2007–9.[24] Down to this moment of revelation, basic economic trends between the US and Europe remained fairly clear and consistent. Europeans continued to increase their direct investment in the US across the decade: $1.63 billion were invested in 2008, an increase of 61 per cent over 2001. Exports to

---

[22] Interview with Nye in *Guernica: A Magazine of Art and Politics*, October 2008, p. 7. Nye gave as an example of a 'soft power' failure the inability of the US to persuade the Turkish Parliament to allow passage of an infantry division at the start of the Iraq war: 'the United States had lost so much soft power and had become so unattractive in Turkey.' I am grateful to Martina Cropano for bringing this interview to my attention.

[23] Campbell, 'Contradictions of a Lone Superpower', 234; further elaboration of Nye approach in Matthew Fraser, *Weapons of Mass Distraction: Soft Power and American Empire* (New York, 2003).

[24] Graph comparing real GPD growth rates, 1991–2009, in US, GB, France, Germany, Japan, in *Financial Times*, 3 December 2009; the trend of close intertwining of the growth curves went back at least to 1960, cf. Fig. 2.1 in Antonio M. Chiesi, 'The Economic Sphere', in Alberto Martinelli (ed.), *Transatlantic Divide: Comparing American and European Society* (Oxford, 2007), 32.

the US rose consistently over the years, by almost 75 per cent. In contrast imports from the US to Europe expanded more slowly, growing by 61 per cent. China overtook the US as the biggest source of imports into the EU countries in 2006.[25]

Other trends confirmed the strictly temporary effects of the Iraq upheaval. Tourists going in both directions dipped after 2001, but had recovered their level of that year as soon as 2004. In 2001 over 9.1 million west European tourists had travelled to the US, plus another 385,000 originating in eastern Europe. In the same year over 11.4 million Americans visited Europe. By 2008 the figures showed almost 12.8 million Europeans travelling to the US, compared to over 11.2 American visitors to Europe. The falling dollar and the financial crisis were depressing transatlantic flows by that time. The dollar had started the decade at $0.95 to the Euro. By the end of it $1.43 were needed to buy €1.[26] Around 130,000–140,000 Europeans emigrated to the US each year on average (the only significant drop, as for all regions, was in 2003), a number dominated in the US statistics by Russians. They supplied well over a third of the total, followed at some distance by the British.[27]

The hegemony of the conventional expressions of American cultural power went largely unchallenged in spite of all the talk of 'anti-Americanism'. Hollywood's long reign in Europe persisted: this was still the region providing the industry with the largest share of its overseas revenues. But the fact that the US still attracted roughly two-thirds of all cinema admissions, and provided around half of all television fiction, provoked far less controversy than in previous eras. This was because of evolution in the modalities of film and television consumption in the age of the Internet, and the rise of an ever greater number of alternatives in local markets everywhere. Los Angeles and the studio system had become simply one big 'node' in a worldwide network of production and distribution, said Rob Kroes.[28] But long decades of exposure to the film challenge from Hollywood had also helped Europe's ways of making cinema to arrive at

---

[25] On investment, US Bureau of Economic Analysis, <http://www.bea.gov/international/index.htm>; on trade, OECD Statistical Extract, <http://stats.oecd.org>.

[26] Tourism figures from US Office of Tourism Industries, Department of Commerce, Bureau of Economic Analysis (accessed June 2009); exchange rates from *The Economist*.

[27] US Department of Homeland Security, *2008 Yearbook of Immigration Statistics* (Washington DC, 2009), 10.

[28] Figs on market share from European Audiovisual Observatory, *The Place of Third Country Film and Audiovisual Works in European Markets*, July 2008, at: <http://www.obs.coe.int/online_publication/reports/thirdcountry_av_works.pdf.en>; analysis in Pardo, *Europe–Hollywood Coopetition*, ch. 2; cf. Wagnleitner, 'The Empire of Fun: Pop Culture and Geopolitical Aesthetics', in Almqvist and Linklater (eds), *On the Idea of America*, 88; Kroes, 'Worlds Apart? The United States, Europe and the Cultural Ties that Bind Them', in Lundestad (ed.), *Just Another Major Crisis?*, 225.

least at a set of conventions and practices shared between them whether they realized it or not. The leading historian and critic Thomas Elsaesser talked in 2005 of 'a common heritage of story types and myths, of deep structures and feeling, genres of symbolic action and narrative trajectories that create recognizably European protagonists and destinies'.[29]

Over the Atlantic a complex but stable dialectic of cooperation and competition had emerged in the cinema world. 'Europe needs Hollywood's production and distribution machinery as well as its business expertise', wrote the Spanish specialist Alejandro Pardo in 2007. 'At the same time, Hollywood needs European money and creativity, apart from a significant share of the European market.'[30] Meanwhile classical European film-makers continued to defend their heritage in classical fashion. A veteran such as Gillo Pontecorvo in Rome said in 2004 that he was still struggling to create 'a cinematic space for Latin films...to better resist the hegemony of American cinema...and defend our cultural identity'. French film and television specialists argued over how consciously to create alternatives to Hollywood, in the name of 'cultural diversity', a creative industry equivalent of their nation's official belief in multipolarism in the world.[31]

Hollywood was not the only American legend to have acquired heritage status in the Old World by this time. Among the most highly visible of the traditional brands, McDonald's went from strength to strength in Europe, its leading region in the world. Profits increased every year in the decade, and easily outstripped net returns in the US. Germany led the way with 1,361 restaurants at the end of 2009. Britain was next with 1,250. In France the company franchise included 1,134 restaurants, while in Italy the figure was 392.[32] In spite of efforts to intensify its connections to local traditions, controversy continued to accompany the Big Mac's progress. In Britain there was surprise when the company was authorized by the government to award nationally recognized training qualifications. In France a small shock wave was felt when McDonald's penetrated the sanctuary of the nation's most celebrated museum and gallery, the Louvre. (Starbuck's had already arrived.) In a comment, the Director of the Uffizi gallery in Florence was quoted as saying that

---

[29] T. Elsaesser, 'European Cinema: Conditions of Impossibility?', in Elsaesser, *European Cinema: Face to Face with Hollywood* (Amsterdam, 2005), 24–5.

[30] Pardo, *Europe–Hollywood Coopetition*, 109–10.

[31] Pontecorvo interview in *International Herald Tribune*, 17 March 2004. The occasion was the news that the Pentagon had shown Pontecorvo's legendary film, *The Battle of Algiers* of 1965, to a group of experts pondering the situation in Iraq; sample of French film debate in Paris (ed.), *Quelle diversité face à Hollywood*.

[32] Results for 2009 and comments in Financial Times, 22 January 2010; franchise figures (with some variations in dates) at: <http://en.wikipedia.org/wiki/List_of_countries_with_McDonald's_franchises>.

cafeterias in museums were inevitable, but he would be offering Tuscan delicacies in his own establishment. This statement was likely to be welcomed in both the key centres of power in Rome. In a move without precedent, the founder of the McDonald's chain in Italy was recruited by the Minister of Culture in the new Berlusconi government of 2008. His job was to bring his commercial skills to rejuvenate the appeal of the country's museums and great archaeological sites. Meanwhile the Vatican condemned the products of the McDonald's brand and all such as un-Christian and un-Catholic.[33]

But Italy and its food culture showed how clear could be the difference between creating *alternatives* to the mass-cultural propositions of the American hegemon, and striking *antagonistic* postures to it. In contrast with France there would be no aggressive, militant counter-attack to the spread of McDonald's famous hamburger chain which, as elsewhere, was systematically modifying its menus to accommodate local tastes. Instead, the year 1998 saw the hugely successful launch in Turin of the nation's first fair of traditional gastronomy invented and sponsored by *Slow Food*. At its 2008 edition, 180,000 people attended.[34] By the end of the decade the original Piemontese *Slow Food* cooperative had blossomed into a vast association of producers, shops, fairs, seminars, publications, websites, and devoted consumers, with ramifications around the world. Its founder, Carlo Petrini, had become a sort of national hero, courted by politicians and a pillar of national environmental and gastronomic identity.[35]

California again

Yet the most clamorous cultural novelties of the decade all came in digital form, and here California triumphed once more. Silicon Valley had kept

[33] On British case, *Financial Times*, 28 January 2008; on Louvre and Uffizi, *Corriere della Sera*, 6 October 2009; on Italy, *Wall Street Journal Europe*, 16–18 January 2009, interview with Mario Resca, Commercial Counselor to the Ministry of Culture, in *La Stampa*, 18 April 2009; Resca recounted the difficult story of the founding of McDonald's in Italy in M. Resca and Rinaldo Gianola, *McDonald's: Una storia italiana* (Milan, 1998); on theologian's condemnation, *La Repubblica*, 9 November 2000.

[34] *International Herald Tribune*, 23 February 1999; the fair was the 'Salone del Gusto', Lingotto Fiere, Turin, 5–9 November, 1998; on the year 2000 edition, *The Times*, 27 October 2000; 2008 figures supplied by Press Office, Slow Food.

[35] On origins of the Slow Food project, Geoff Andrews, *The Slow Food Story: Politics and Pleasure* (London, 2008). Italian food culture could also count on another strong point: its weight in the world coffee market. Not only was Starbucks' kept out of Italy, major brands went on the offensive in the US and Europe, opening coffee shops and selling a variety of coffee-related products. The Bologna brand *Segafredo* was the most explicit in relating this effort to the exaltation of a vision of national identity.

its utopian promise: that the Internet would develop as an interactive medium like no other. The chief executive of Google, the fast-expanding search engine company, said at the end of 2006: 'the internet is helping to satisfy our most fundamental human needs—our desire for knowledge, communication and a sense of belonging.'[36] Europeans and the world noted the continuing flow of novelties—from YouTube to eBay and Amazon, from Wikipedia to Facebook, LinkedIn, Flickr, Twitter, and so on—which kept the United States in the forefront of innovation in that marketplace where technology met the dreams of popular culture, where fantasies turned into the real thing. Apple's iPod, a 2001 novelty, had been sold to 225 million people by the end of the decade. The social-networking site Facebook, started in 2004, had over 500 million sub-scribers worldwide by 2010.[37] Only Skype, invented by two young Scandinavians, and Nokia in mobile phones, from Finland, could match the world reach and prestige of these innovations. Not by chance they came from areas of Europe that had consistently outspent the rest in re-search and development as a proportion of GDP.[38]

Although the Europeans still dreamed of inventing their own Silicon Valleys, and British figures such as Tony Blair and David Cameron made devotional pilgrimages there, they were always told that they didn't un-derstand. Besides the extraordinary richness and depth of the links be-tween the inventors and their universities, time and 'the immigrant's drive—all that pent-up need and hunger...', were the key ingredients, said a local hero. The immigrants were often European. According to the head of a Brussels-based think tank set up to promote the Lisbon Agenda, over 400,000 scientists had moved from the Old World to the New in the years around the turn of the millennium, and she deplored the trend.[39]

The most controversial of Silicon Valley's brands invented by immi-grants turned out to be the biggest: Google itself, the brainchild of the Russian-born Serghei Brin and the American computer scientist Larry Page. Born in 1998 in the utopian and egalitarian spirit that California had inherited from the 1960s, and which as seen in Chapter 10, coloured

---

[36] *The Economist: The World in 2007*, 124

[37] Cf. David Nye, 'Imagining: Americanization in Context', paper delivered at the con-ference on 'Appropriating America, Making Europe', European Science Foundation (Am-sterdam, January 2009).

[38] Skype was sold to the American eBay in 2005 for $2.6 billion; other European inter-net successes listed in *Financial Times*, 5 May 2008.

[39] On European efforts to copy Silicon Valley, *Financial Times*, 3 October 2006, 16 July 2008; quote in *Sunday Times*, 12 November 2006; on brain drain, Ann Mettler in *Finan-cial Times*, 14 July 2004; Ms Mettler was head of the Lisbon Council: <http://www.lisbon-council.net/about-us/vision.html>; see below.

the nature of the Internet itself (as well as brand names), Google was an extraordinary enterprise. A booster said: 'They went from zero to twenty billion dollars in revenues in four hundred weeks!' All their numbers were fabulous. Their launch on the stock exchange in 2004 capitalized the company at $23 billion. By the end of the decade searches on Google amounted to about 3 billion per day. In 2008, the company's revenues exceeded $20 billion, and its stock market valuation was $174 billion, promising that it would soon overtake the world's biggest media players: Time Warner, the Walt Disney Company, and Rupert Murdoch's News International. In 2006 it spent $1.65 billion, purchasing YouTube, and continually expanded its services: Google Earth, Google Scholar, Google Health, Google News, Gmail, Chrome (a web browser), and so on, to a total of about 150 at the end of 2009. But the most controversial service of all was always going to be Google Print for Libraries, later known as Google Book Search.[40]

Alarm bells over Google's activities started ringing in Europe in the middle of the decade. Soon they would be heard in other parts of the world too, including America itself. The first signal was a swingeing attack by the head of the French National Library, Jean-Noël Jeanneney, on the threat of linguistic and cultural hegemony—as he saw it—implied by Google's 2004 plan to digitize the English-language contents of a series of major world libraries, up to 15 million volumes, and make them available in truncated form via Google Book Search.[41] In Paris and Brussels the Director's call was quickly answered. By the end of the decade a wide variety of initiatives was under way to create a European digital library. The EU Commissioner for Telecoms and Media, Ms Reding, in a major speech of July 2009, declared that she was in favour of all this, and suggested ways to end 'the present, rather ideological debate about "Google books"'. But she also made very clear that unless Europe harmonized its copyright and other related rules in this area, the Union's members would lose out: 'digitisation and the development of attractive content offers will not take place in Europe, but on the other side of the Atlantic.'[42]

[40] Cit. in Ken Auletta, 'Searching for Trouble', *The New Yorker* (12 October 2009), 56.

[41] Jeanneney went on to publish a book-length explanation of his preoccupations: *Google and the Myth of Universal Knowledge: A View from Europe* (Chicago, 2007).

[42] On Quaero, Babelot, and Delos, *Corriere della Sera*, 23 January 2006; Viviane Reding, 'Digital Europe—Europe's Fast Track to Recovery', The Ludwig Erhard Lecture 2009, Lisbon Council, Brussels, 9 July 2009, at <http://www.lisboncouncil.net/lecture-series/ludwig-erhard.html>.

AMERICA'S ECLIPSE YEARS:
THE DOWNWARD SPIRAL TO 2008

But in spite of Silicon Valley's glittering successes, and the continuing force of Hollywood, by the end of the first decade of the new millennium their home state of California was in the deepest financial and political trouble. And the outlook in the American nation's capitals of politics, money, and opinion on the east coast was not much better. After they had strenuously rejected the multipolar idea in both the Clinton and the Bush eras, much poignant reflection rose up among the elites on the extraordinary fall from grace that, in the course of the few short years from 2001 to 2008, had struck down America's self-perception, authority in the world, and status as the prime source of models of modernity for the rest of the West. 'You could argue that the first decade of the of the 21st century was the last decade of the American century,' said David Rothkopf, a former Clinton administration official and ex-triumphalist of American cultural imperialism, at the end of 2009, 'we are now entering the multipolar century.'[43]

Echoing the poet W. H. Auden's characterization of the 1930s, Thomas Frank in the conservative *Wall Street Journal* talked of 'a low, dishonest decade', dominated by a 'preposterous populism... [and] our failure to see through the ruse, to understand how our country was being disfigured'. The nation's citizens were said to be 'pondering the unthinkable: Could our leaders really have pushed us into an unnecessary war? Is the republic really dividing into an immensely wealthy class of Wall Street bonus winners and everybody else?'[44]

Over at the liberal *New York Times* in the same days, a team of writers was supplying a thumbnail sketch of each of the decade's years. The novelist Richard Ford evoked the 'vivid consequences' of the bizarre election process that had handed the White House to George W. Bush in the year 2000:

> ... two wars we're still fighting, plus the black hole of off-the-books spending to finance them; the whole financial collapse that either is or isn't over yet; an even deeper cynicism about governance than normally typifies Americans. A general degrading of both our constitutional underpinnings and our public-spiritedness about ourselves.[45]

The only foreigner invited to contribute to the *New York Times* series was a European, the Irish writer Colum McCann. He struck a quite different

[43] Cit. in *Financial Times*, 30 December 2009; cf. Chapter 10, p. 449.
[44] *Wall Street Journal*, 23 December 2009.
[45] *New York Times*, 27 December 2009.

note. McCann explained that out of guilt and doubt he had hidden the dual American–Irish citizenship he had acquired in 2005, until, that is, November 4 2008. That evening, 'Barack Obama stepped onto the stage of a country maimed by war, cleaved by greed, riven by a collapsing economy...and I felt those old bricks falling away from me, the guilt, the doubt, the American stammer. Up and down [my] street, people shouted out of the windows of their cars. Strangers were hugging one another. It was the briefest of parties... [but] it confirmed for me so much of what I had wanted from the American experience, and so much of what I'd already received from her literature. It was as if politics had woken me from books, and I felt rooted and at home.'[46]

The Irish had already proved that their modern history and culture, and its reworking through what America had to offer, had given them a peculiarly intense relationship with the meaning of the United States in all its forms, not least because they felt convinced that America had exceptionally returned the favour, recognizing the authenticity of its Irish heritage.[47] For Bono, leader of the Dublin-originated pop group U2 and a self-appointed spokesperson for the moral conscience of the rich world, music had done for him what literature had done for Colum McCann. Shortly after Obama's nomination as winner of the Nobel Peace Prize for 2009, he wrote:

> In a dangerous, clangorous time, the idea of America rings like a bell (see King, M.L., Jnr., and Dylan, Bob). It hits a high note and sustains it without wearing on your nerves.... This was the melody line of the Marshall Plan and it's resonating again. Why? Because the world sees that America might just hold the keys to solving the three greatest threats we face on this planet: extreme poverty, extreme ideology and extreme climate change. The world senses that America with renewed global support might be better placed to defeat this axis of extremism with a new model of foreign policy.

Whatever the echoes set off by this declaration of faith, there could be no doubt that like Woodrow Wilson and Franklin Roosevelt, Obama's personality had leaped the oceans and sent hope soaring once more, this time not simply in Europe but around the world.[48] Just as posters of FDR could be found in the houses of illiterate peasants in southern Italy in the 1930s, so the face of Obama could be seen on billboards in remote

---

[46] Ibid.

[47] Cf. Diane Negra (ed.), *The Irish In Us: Irishness, Performativity and Popular Culture* (Durham, NC, 2006).

[48] By the start of 2010 three musicals on the life of Obama had been produced, in Nairobi, London, and Frankfurt; website of the latter, entitled *Hope*, at <http://www.hope-musical.com>; *Il Sole 24 Ore*, 17 January 2010.

Fig. 10. In 2008 European enthusiasm for Presidential candidate Barack Obama reached its high point in Berlin, where a crowd of 100,000 assembled to hear his words and confirm his charisma.

(Rex Features)

corners of Ethiopia in 2009. In Oslo meanwhile, the most liberal parts of the Western world were reopening a large moral credit in favour of the United States.[49]

In his speech accepting the Nobel Peace Prize, the new President, who had been elected first of all to right the wrongs causing pain in his native land, and certainly not to reform the world,[50] indeed provided a discourse of the highest moral tone. Feeling the weight of the expectations placed on him, he referred to the heritage of some of the Americans who had preceded him: Woodrow Wilson, George Marshall, Martin Luther King

---

[49] See Chapter 5, n. 42, Johns Hopkins graduate student Elberta Seybold reported seeing posters of Obama in southern Ethiopia at Easter 2009, in regions where very few spoke English or had access to television; Bono in *New York Times*, 18 October 2009. In *Friendly Fire: Losing Friends and Making Enemies in the Anti-American Century* (New York, 2006), Julia Sweig points out that as recently as 2005 the Peace Prize had been awarded to the UN-sponsored International Atomic Energy Agency, whose head, Mohamed El Baradei, had been harassed by US intelligence for his opposition to the Iraq war; *Friendly Fire*, p. x.

[50] Obama's election campaign book, *The Audacity of Hope: Thoughts on Reclaiming the American Dream* (New York, 2006), contains but one chapter on foreign policy, the penultimate out of nine.

Jr. Obama provided his own account of the war situation he had inherited and supplied his own formulations for attempting to deal with it. He spoke of justice and human rights, of just wars and the need for democracies to make sacrifices if they were to face up adequately to the threats—including armed attack—that would always accompany their way in the world. He paid tribute to the American legacy of institutions and projects, including the United Nations, the Declaration of Human Rights (of 1948), the Marshall Plan, and NATO, which had been put in place to help promote peace.

The continuities as well the contrasts with the doctrinal pronouncements of the George W. Bush era were evident to all. Obama insisted on a universalist vision of 'justice' as his key conception of America's role in the world; Bush had placed a messianic idea of 'freedom' at the centre of his action. Whatever the contrasts, both felt the need to supply an ideological justification and basis of legitimacy for their action, constructing a narrative comprehensible to all from familiar reference points in American history.[51] Obama was the most explicitly Wilsonian and Rooseveltian in his language, even evoking those of the Four Freedoms, which spoke of 'freedom from fear' and 'freedom from want'. Although one early, campaigning version of George W. Bush had invoked a need to respect the cultures of others, Obama went much further in recognizing the destabilizing effects of globalization, the 'cultural levelling of modernity', and the fears spreading on all sides among peoples who saw their particular identities threatened, whether they were racial, tribal, or religious.[52]

Yet in each of the testimonies left by these two Presidents, outwardly so dissimilar, was to be found once more the conviction that *economic development* was in some way the key to democratic stability and peace in the world, taking it for granted that this implied some form of western-style capitalism.[53] Bush's universe was a defiant, hierarchical one, with the US unchallenged and unchallengeable on top. Might truly was right. Obama's international disorder saw the US as still the leader of the pack, but also a power struggling in a crowded international scene, including the good,

---

[51] Precisely this was the limit of Obama's speech, said the Washington political economist David Calleo: Calleo, 'Obama's Dilemma: Enraged Opponents or Disappointed Followers', *Bologna Journal of International Affairs* (Spring 2010), 6; to supply a fresh basis for this moral narrative was the purpose of Slaughter, *Idea That Is America*.

[52] This line of argument was particularly developed in Obama's Cairo speech of June 2009; full text at <http://www.guardian.co.uk/world/2009/jun/04/barack-obama-keynote-speech-egypt>, 4 June 2009.

[53] Francis Fukuyama took this to indicate that his original bet that 'history is over' was still functioning, especially as the crisis had thrown up no radically alternative models. But now he saw the conviction as a dangerous form of complacency; F. Fukuyama, 'History Is Still Over', *Newsweek* (12 December 2009).

the bad, and the ugly, to maintain a semblance of decency that in the end could only be delivered by better functioning international institutions. (Conservative experts had warned the Europeans in the middle of the decade that they had better forget their fond dreams of a return to this sort of liberal American leadership.[54] Well, here it was again.) But both visions tackled explicitly the connection between economic progress and political—'democratic'—stability in ways that the world had become used to since the era of the New Deal, Bretton Woods, Truman's Point Four, and the Marshall Plan, and then the Third World development programmes of the era of the Cold War.[55] Bush said: 'Poverty does not make poor people into terrorists and murderers. Yet poverty, weak institutions, and corruption can make weak states vulnerable to terrorist networks and drug cartels within their borders.' The remedy was to extend 'free trade and free markets' so as to deliver 'the rewards of liberty' to anyone seeking them. This was where 'real freedom' could be found, 'the freedom for a person—or a nation—to make a living'.[56]

Obama was ready to acknowledge the benefits of globalization—'Commerce has stitched much of the world together. Billions have been lifted from poverty'—and insisted that security and development were interlinked. Using language that could have been adapted from the Truman Doctrine, he referred to 'the absence of hope' that 'can rot a society from within', promising that America and its allies would always be interested in these realities. But there was no question of placing them at the heart of a presumed 'war on terror' as Bush did. Terrorism for Obama was simply 'a tactic' whose danger had been multiplied by 'modern technology which allows a few small men with outsized rage to murder innocents on a horrific scale'. Instead, the drive of America to secure 'freedom from want' was a moral one: rights should include 'decent education' and 'a job that supports a family'. Where America's self-interest was concerned, the key question was no longer simply economic development as such, but climate change, since 'if we do nothing, we will face more drought, famine and mass displacement that will fuel more conflict for decades'.[57]

[54] Charles Kupchan, 'Atlantic Orders: The Fundamentals of Change', in Lundestad (ed.), *Just Another Major Crisis?*, 52.

[55] For a sceptical reading of this history, Michael E. Latham, *The Right Kind of Revolution: Modernization, Development and U.S. Foreign Policy from the Cold War to the Present* (Ithaca, 2011).

[56] Preface to *The National Security Strategy of the United States* (Washington DC, September 2002), and Section 6, p. 18. This part of the document provides a detailed explanation and plan of action of the first Bush White House in the economic sphere. The EU received no mention, except as one of a number of sources of trade disputes.

[57] Ibid. n. 8. The 2002 *National Security Strategy* document did mention environmental concerns, with a specific target for emissions reduction. On the limits and ambiguities of

Obama looked like a radically innovative figure on the world political scene, and in symbolic terms his arrival was a very great break with America's past, which only the gravity of the times could fully explain. But not even Obama's rhetorical gifts and promise could hide the devastating effect of the financial crisis, from 2007 onwards, on America's power and prestige in international life. The end of the so-called 'Washington consensus'—stabilize, privatize, liberalize, globalize—spelled disaster for the post-Cold War version of the American economic models of production and consumption, and following the impact of the post-war Iraq debacle on US military credibility, acted as a heavy blow at the foundation of the other key pillar of the nation's hegemony: its financial force.[58]

In 2008 the harsh light of catastrophe fell on the nation's 'chronic deficit-prone economy', and on the mechanisms that had propelled the 'Washington consensus' inside the country as well as beyond it: the weight of free-market ideology, the centrality of over-extended banks, the deliberately contrived undermining of the regulators, the vast reliance on personal credit, the appropriation of extraordinary amounts of wealth by tiny minorities of plutocrats, the short-termism, and the avarice.[59] Around the world prominent observers connected the various disasters together, and wondered if the West itself was losing its capacity to create governance and leadership for the globalized order. No wonder that *Time* magazine, surveying the inheritance of the first years of the new century in December 2009, called it 'the decade from hell'.[60]

Obama's commitments in the sphere of development, Mario Del Pero, 'Alla ricerca del primato (in parte) perduto: La politica estera di Barack Obama', in *Quaderni di Relazioni internazionali* (November 2009), 23.

[58] Cf. John Williamson, 'A Short History of the Washington Consensus', in Narcís Serra and Joseph E. Stiglitz (eds), *The Washington Consensus Reconsidered: Towards a New Global Governance* (Oxford, 2008). Here the inventor of the concept defends its original purpose as a set of tools for developing countries, and deplores the wider ideological meanings ascribed to it by others; defence of other meanings in Stiglitz, 'Is there a Post-Washington Consensus Consensus?', in Serra and Stiglitz (eds), *Washington Consensus Reconsidered*. In 2010 Stiglitz declared that both the policies and the ideology of the Consensus were dead: *Freefall: America, Free Markets and the Sinking of the World Economy* (New York, 2010), 296.

[59] On risks, Larry Elliott in *The Guardian Weekly*, 15–21 December 2006, Sarah Lyall in *International Herald Tribune*, 21 September 2007; cf. Edward Luce, 'The Continuing Power of the US Economy', in Almqvist and Linklater (eds), *On the Idea of America*, cit. at p. 208; Paul Mason, *Meltdown: The End of the Age of Greed* (London, 2009); Mason was a leading economic correspondent of the BBC.

[60] Singaporean criticism at Western governmental incompetence in John Kampfner, *Freedom for Sale: How We Made Money and Lost Our Liberty* (London, 2009), 29; Indian doubts in 'Soft Power: India', BBC World Service documentary, broadcast 29 May 2010; *Time*, 7 December 2009.

EUROPE: DEPENDENT OR INTERDEPENDENT?

The effects of multiple collapses in America's banks were immediately felt across the Old World, showing how tightly integrated the transatlantic financial system had become, and at the same time how varied in reality were the margins of sovereignty that each nation defended so vigorously in its imagination, and often in its politics.[61] Ulrich Beck, the eminent German sociologist, spoke in 2003 of 'transnational states [in Europe] being cosmopolitanized from within' and thought that the common experience of this process would pull them all together, uniting them in diversity. But Iraq and the financial crisis divided them in adversity, throwing into sharp relief those who still believed in the unifying prospect of the EU, a dwindling minority, and those who did not wish to be cosmopolitanized either from within or without.[62] The world was not flat, it was hierarchical: some nations were subjects of the crash, some objects of it. The division the French had long played up between 'Anglo-Saxon' capitalism and the rest was now plain for all to see. Even *The Economist* used the term.[63]

'Where there is domination, there is resistance to domination', said Beck's distinguished Spanish colleague Manuel Castells, referring to the ties binding the winners and the losers in the functioning of global markets.[64] But life was not so simple inside Europe, whose peoples could be both at the same time, since its societies included those firmly anchored in the 'Anglo-Saxon' orbit of political economy, and those whose relationships between state and market functioned differently, either by chance or by design.[65] Was this a reason why no one mentioned 'anti-Americanism' in the course of the great financial disaster, even as America's media and its foreign policy community openly acknowledged that the calamity had been set in motion by the workings of their nation's financial system,

---

[61] At the end of 2009 American banks owned a total of $1.2 trillion of European debt, a figure similar to the amount of US sub-prime residential mortgage debt existing in 2008; *New York Times*, 29 May 2010.

[62] Cf. Jean-Pisani Ferry, 'Why Europe struggles—and how it can recover', 11 January 2010, at <http://www.bruegel.org>; Ulrich Beck, 'Understanding the Real Europe', *Dissent* (Summer 2003).

[63] *The Economist*, 3 October 2009.

[64] Castells, *Information Age*, vol. ii, p. xvii.

[65] In autumn 2009 the Centro studi Sintesi di Mestre applied to Italy's provinces the criteria developed by the Heritage Foundation in Washington to measure the degree of 'economic freedom' prevailing in single nations. The results favoured small cities in the centre and north-east of the country, with Siena the absolute winner, supposedly 100 times more free than Naples, which scored zero. But the survey also pointed out that the more open the local economy, the more it had suffered in the recession; full summary in *Corriere della Sera*, 11 September 2009.

including its overwhelmingly ideological notion of what constituted a 'free market'?[66]

Another possible reason for the total lack of Iraq-era animosity towards the United States at this point was that so many societies were forced to acknowledge the function of America's inspirations in certain big choices they themselves had made about what to do with their money. In Britain, Holland, Germany, Belgium, Switzerland, and elsewhere, some local banks, large as well as small, had been unable to resist the lure of the American sub-prime mortgage market. Of the so-called 'toxic' mortgages created by American finance houses in these years, 40 per cent had been bought by European banks. (In Italy this had not happened, simply because—joked Berlusconi's Treasury Minister Tremonti—no one inside Italian banks spoke English.)[67] The British financial system, more than any other nation's, had applied Wall Street's models with relish across its own domestic scene, with the result that by 2008 the British people owed as much money in absolute terms to their banks as the Americans did to theirs. But the UK economy was only a fifth the size of the US version.[68]

The revenge of the local: containing the collapse with identity politics

In the context of such a drama, anguished reflections of the 'who-do-think-we-are?' variety, audible since the early 1990s, now took on a new urgency in Europe, and in a nation like Britain in particular. Notwithstanding the torment they caused, the Iraq confrontations of 2003 had not brought the post-Cold War era to an end in the Old World. One proof of this truth was the continuity of distressed, self-conscious identity debates in local settings everywhere: over values, ideals, boundaries, readings of the past, ideas of the future, reflections on the State and the market, the collective and the individual. By looking at all this through the lens of 'identity', such issues had become in a sense domesticated and rendered apparently more comprehensible. Sovereignty and hence a sense of control were reasserted by political classes everywhere, no matter how harshly the banking saga treated these illusions. The nation-state connection was revitalized by bringing the old romantic-national trend of the nineteenth

---

[66] E.g. *Time*, 1 February 2010, from liberal side, Paul Krugman in *New York Times*, 14 December 2009, from centre, Felix G. Rohatyn, *International Herald Tribune*, 16 December 2008, from conservative wing, interview with ex-Senator Phil Gramm, in *New York Times*, 17 November 2008; on ideological dimension of crisis, Mason, *Meltdown*, ch. 7.

[67] *La Stampa*, 30 Jan. 2009.

[68] On Europeans and 'toxic' mortgages, Joseph Stiglitz, talk at the Edinburgh Book Festival, 21 August 2010; on British indebtedness, *International Herald Tribune*, 21 September 2007.

century back to life in a variety of imaginary forms. The business of inventing traditions and rediscovering local idiosyncrasies worked harder than ever. In this way the real or perceived effects of 'globalization' might, hopefully, be contained and even defied. The persistence of identity debates in every corner of Europe (and perhaps elsewhere: Russia, Turkey, Israel, Japan, Canada, as well as the US itself) suggested that in a post-ideological age, this was the place where national political and cultural leaders would try to locate the biggest, most enduring political, economic, and social questions of the times.[69]

The new French government of 2007, led by Nicolas Sarkozy, included a Minister of National Identity; the President himself often returned to the theme, relaunching it officially in 2009. In Catalonia even the 9/11 drama was lived through the prism of the region's permanent identity battle with Madrid. In Italy city and regional governments in the Veneto, Piemonte, Lombardy, and Sicily included Identity Departments.[70] In London, Gordon Brown, the Labour Prime Minister, repeatedly returned to the theme of 'Britishness', and inspired a remarkable essay collection entitled *Being British: The Search for the Values that Bind the Nation*, published at the end of 2009.[71] Everywhere—except Germany—right-wing populist parties gained strength and momentum as they exploited the issue supplying the emotional energy for all the arguments: immigration, and the cultural, social, and economic tensions the immigrants allegedly brought with them, especially hard for societies to manage in times of financial crisis.[72]

And in so many cases the identity debates contained, wittingly or otherwise, specific American elements that functioned quite independently of anything the lone superpower might be saying or doing. In Britain the Labour governments of Tony Blair and Gordon Brown were trying to modernize their nation's state and its markets by way of a sort of top-down Americanization. American models could be seen everywhere as they imported laws, corporations, slogans, people, ideas. Unlike the French, however, they preferred not to talk about it. France meanwhile elected its first 'American-style' President, according to a former editor of *Le Monde*.

---

[69] Cf. Castells, *Information Age*, ii. 30–5.

[70] On French debate, Nicolas Sarkozy in *Le Monde*, 9 December 2009; critical commentary in *Nouvel observateur*, 10–16 December 2009; *Financial Times*, 8 December 2009; on Catalonia, Escalante-Gonzalbo and Tenorio-Trillo, 'Nuestro Once de Septiembre', p. 150, n. 21: on Italy, Francesco Remotti, *L'ossessione identitaria* (Rome, 2010), p. xv.

[71] Matthew D'Ancona (ed.), *Being British: The Search for the Values that Bind the Nation* (Edinburgh, 2009).

[72] For debate on British experience, articles by government ministers and religious leaders, ibid.; cf. Ellwood, 'Bemused by America, Terrified of Europe: The Politics of Identity in Britain from Blair to Cameron', *Bologna Journal of International Affairs* (Spring 2010).

Nicholas Sarkozy was a man who went out of his way to praise American things and rejected the Gaullist heritage of 'anti-Americanism'.[73]

Italy was dominated by a business tycoon who claimed he believed in everything coming out of America even before he knew what it was, though the US Ambassador himself complained publicly of how distant was everyday Italian practice from the way the US did business.[74] In Europe's far west, the nation that American rankers of such things had dubbed the most globalized of all at the start of the decade—Ireland— was, just before the crash, coming to terms with the unintended consequences of this distinction. A Dublin sociologist wrote, in self-conscious parody:

> The unquestioned orthodoxy of the West is not just the right, not just the need but the moral imperative of every individual to pursue life, liberty and happiness. This has become a truth that most people in the West hold to be self-evident. This belief in individualism is increasingly becoming the core value in Irish society. The Irish believe in themselves. They have become self-reliant, self-confident, self-assertive. They have also become self-indulgent. They look after number one.... But self-belief and self-indulgence may have also made the Irish more selfish. The Irish may have become rich, but there is not much evidence that Irish society has become more equal and caring.[75]

In Brussels meanwhile, the EU's technocrats were forced to recognize by 2010 the Union's failure to live up to its own 'Lisbon Agenda', launched in 2000 to bring the members as a whole up to the standards of commercial competitiveness seen to shine forth from the United States. Perhaps this was because the vast majority of Europe's citizens made clear that they did not wish Europe's economy to be more like that of the United States. When asked precisely that question in an FT/Harris poll of September 2007 (i.e. just before the financial crisis broke), in the UK and France up to 80 per cent said 'no'; 70 per cent said the same in Italy, approximately 55 per cent in Spain and Germany. Despite what their international media were telling them, even the vast majority of Americans apparently believed that Europe should not turn itself into a simulacrum of the US.[76]

[73] Jean-Marie Colombani, *Un Américain à Paris* (Paris, 2008).

[74] Details in Ellwood, 'The American Challenge Revisited: Soft Power Struggles in Contemporary Europe', in Almqvist and Linklater (eds), *On the Idea of America*, 103.

[75] Inglis, *Global Ireland*, 257.

[76] Official documentation on Lisbon Agenda at <http://ec.europa.eu/environment/eussd>; poll in *Financial Times*, 23 September 2007; at the time there were still strong believers in the American model: 30% in the UK and France, 36–7% in Italy, over 40% in Spain and Germany. For evolution of views after the crisis, *The Economist*, 22 July 2010. The article pointed out that even those nations that expressed the most heated anti-capitalist views, France and Spain, possessed world-conquering brands and companies.

And yet a late 2005 interview found Vaclav Havel, still the most philosophical of the EU's supporters, and at the same time a great friend of US politicians and policies, complaining that EU Europe was far too devoted to the 'idea of growth' that America embodied: 'growth for the sake of growth, the creation of profit at any price, development and prosperity, although unfortunately utterly one-dimensional.' Europe had given birth to modern technology and consumer civilization, said Havel, and forcefully exporting them 'set in motion the ambiguous momentum that today we call globalization'. EU Europe had now lost control of this trend; had been swallowed up by it. The great need was for a revival of that (postwar) 'tradition of responsibility for the world that [Europe's] culture once helped to articulate', that 'spiritual dimension' that meant 'regard for civic culture, for human rights, for economic justice, for non-renewable resources [and] for the environment in general'. Havel demanded from the Union's ongoing process of constitutional redefinition a short, easily readable document that would sum up the project's values and aims in language that anyone could understand. Even children learning at school should be able to grasp this simple paper, said Havel, just as American schoolchildren were brought to understand their own Constitution.[77]

A POST-AMERICAN EUROPE?

If there ever had been such a choice, at the end of the first decade of the new era there was no longer any question of the Europeans 'defining themselves against America', as Dominique Moisi had described the French condition in the 1990s, and Tony Judt after the turn of the millennium. While some European leading lights may at one time have allowed a certain hubris to spread in their ideas of the progress of the European project, within a very few years such voices had been stilled.[78] There were too many disappointments, obstacles, splits. The essential 'cosmopolitanism' of the European project, aiming at reconciliation, and moral as well as economic interdependence, seemed to be going backwards, not necessarily towards new conflicts, but towards apathy and re-provincialization. Everywhere the conviction seemed to be spreading that whatever 'Europe' gained, the single nations must perforce lose.[79]

[77] Interview of 30 November 2005, in Havel, *To the Castle and Back* (London, 2008), 306–7.
[78] Judt, *Postwar*, 788–91; poll evidence of European hubris discussed in Romero, 'Twilight of American Cultural Hegemony', 159–63; examples of elite self-satisfaction in Perry Anderson, *The New Old World* (London, 2009), 47–9.
[79] Beck, 'Understanding the Real Europe', 33–6; Judt, *Postwar*, 796–9; cf. Helmut Kaelble, 'Identification with Europe and the Politicization of the European Union since the

Through the financial crisis of 2007 onwards, the stages that produced the Copenhagen climate conference of December 2009, and the steps that completed the Lisbon treaty process, one bias was clear: the three biggest members of the Union—France, Germany, and Britain—would never allow the EU to acquire more political power in the world than they *imagined* that they themselves possessed as traditional, single nation states. There could be no 'overshadowing', as the Press put it.[80] This was but one reason why, by the end of the first decade of the new millennium, the identity crisis of the Union itself was so deep, aggravated too by those of most of its players, big and small, that even the creation of a credible European digital alternative to all-conquering Google looked well beyond its reach. Far from building the United States of Europe, the EU would be lucky to create the United Europe of States.

In this context, some transatlantic observers began to berate the leading European nations for giving up on the big global issues, for falling back once more on the American connection—especially in its Obama incarnation—when faced with the toughest problems of the world, instead of facing up to their collective responsibilities and carrying out their promises of a united and balanced partnership with the US. In a 2009 report the new European Council on Foreign Relations talked of 'infantilism' and 'fetishism'. This damning indictment lumped Britain in with the rest, and denounced them all for a general reluctance to contemplate any other option than their alliance with America, least of all any that might imply increased involvement with each other.[81]

These were voices from the narrow world of conventional foreign and security policy. They claimed their results came from a detailed 'power audit' of EU–US relations. But in their confusion of the EU with the 'Europeans', and with their narrow, strictly arms-and-money idea of 'power', they lost sight of much broader realities and challenges. These would help to maintain the ties binding the West's societies together whether they liked it or not, since everyone within them knew how many of the biggest tests were coming from beyond the sphere that the West once thought it controlled.

1980s', in Jeffrey T. Checkel and Peter J. Katzenstein (eds), *European Identity* (Cambridge, 2009), 206–9.

[80] Cf. Cécile Chambraud, 'Le règne du chacun pour soi', *Le Monde: Bilan Economie 2010* (Paris, 2011), 42–3; Tony Barber, 'The Soft-Power Broker', *E!Sharp* (January–February 2010); substance and illusion in the power of contemporary nation states discussed in Castells, *Information Age*, vol. ii, ch. 5.

[81] Jeremy Shapiro and Nick Whitney, *Towards a post-American Europe: A Power Audit of EU–US Relations*, European Council on Foreign Relations, London 2009, 39; at <http:// ecfr.3cdn.net/cdb1d0a4be418dc49c_2em6bg7a0.pdf>.

'The greatest historical phenomenon of this period is the rise of the emerging nations', said the former French Foreign Minister Hubert Védrine, in a long end-of-decade interview that brought the key trends of the era into sharp focus. 'this marks the end of the monopoly of the West's universalism, be it with a European or an American face, and so the relativisation of its leadership.' Even the basic idea of an 'international community', a Western conceit, made no more sense, especially after 9/11, the rise of China, and the financial crisis. The shift from the G-7 to the G-20 would be the crucial one, said Védrine, an evolution that opened up epoch-changing perspectives, since apart from China, Brazil, and India, at least 40 nations could be counted as 'emerging' in one way or another across the continents. In every phase of the G-20's development, China had become more prominent and more outspoken. Now it was a world-class actor for the first time in its history.[82]

Having invented the concept of 'hyper-power' for the US, Védrine felt that in terms of the range of its power assets, America still need fear no rivals, its influence could still be felt throughout the world as none other in history. China, he said, 'is very, very far from commanding the *soft power* of the US, if it ever will.' Russia possessed none. But in terms of a unipolar force domineering all and untouchable, there could be no doubt. America's era of leadership was effectively over, to be replaced by no one, unless the immensely talented Obama proved able to rise to the challenge. The European leaders of the day would supply no help. 'Amorphous, divided, jealous, they moan because Obama neglects them', instead of rising together to meet the splendid occasion he offered. They needed to understand that for Obama, Europe was 'neither a problem nor a solution'.[83] Meanwhile they seemed to think they could get away with becoming a greater Switzerland, all soft power and good intentions, meaning moralism, 'human rights-ism', and 'Europeanism'. They could not face up to the reappearance of a multipolar world, with old-fashioned power struggles bursting out all over.

The last best hope for the West as a whole, concluded Védrine, was to get together with the Arab nations, China, and Russia to deal with (not 'modernize' or 'democratize'), Afghanistan, and above all find a decent solution to the Israel–Palestine problem, including a Marshall Plan for all. Beyond these, the West must deal with the bubble tendencies of its financial system (especially in London and New York), and promote a general ecological mutation of its idea of growth. But the alternative was not

---

[82] 'La rédistribution de la puissance', Entretien avec Hubert Védrine, *Le Débat* (May–August 2010), 23–4, 28; for a Chinese perspective on these shifts, Mahbubani, *New Asia Hemisphere*, 222–6.
[83] Védrine, 'La rédistribution', 26; Mahbubani, *New Asia Hemisphere*, 227.

simply decline. 'If we become obsessed with rebuilding our economies just as they were without worrying about the rest, *c'est fichu.*'[84]

The business of America is creativity; the business of Europe is to be as European as possible in the circumstances

So much for the great torments: geopolitics, geo-economics, and geo-climate change. At the end of the decade, in the texture of everyday life, the creative novelties of the time that enthralled peoples everywhere still continued to flow most triumphantly from America's creative industries, no matter how intensely Europe, Asia, or other regions strove to compete.[85] Behind those based on the Internet was a conventional power play. In 2005 the State and Commerce Departments had made sure the US government would keep control of ICANN, the central Internet addressing system, and the majority of the giant computers keeping the Internet going remained in the US.[86] But the popular culture sensation of the era came once more from big-time Hollywood. Repeating his global success of 1998, *Titanic*, the Canadian-born film director James Cameron brought forth the first 3-D epic of the era, *Avatar*, and swept instantly into cinema history, becoming the greatest earner in film history after 41 days, as it played in 122 countries on approximately 17,000 screens.[87] Meanwhile Cameron's former wife, Kathyrn Bigelow, won Oscar glory with *The Hurt Locker*, a painful examination of life in an army bomb disposal unit in Iraq. As Umberto Eco once said, the ability of the US creative industries to transform *any* variety of human experience into a form of mass consumption truly distinguished them from the rest.[88]

Everywhere the others went on seeking space and mobilizing resources to create their alternatives. In March 2001, in a large-scale survey, the *Wall Street Journal Europe* had claimed that 'the Internet was now a key battleground in Europe's quest to defend its culture from U.S. influence and global homogenization'. Potentially the Net was a global melting pot, said the survey, and the temptation for Europeans—including the EU

---

[84] Védrine, 'La rédistribution', 31–2, 35, 36.

[85] This is the theme of Martel, *Mainstream*, a massive investigation of the force and function in the world of America's 'creative industries'.

[86] The joint letter sent by the Secretaries of State and Commerce to the Acting President of the EU, insisting that control over Internet infrastructure remain firmly in American hands, was reproduced by *The Register*, 2 December 2005; <http://www.theregister.co.uk/2005/12/02/rice_eu_letter>; on structure of Internet governance Wagnleitner, 'Empire of Fun', 90–1.

[87] Box Office Mojo, '"Avatar" Is New King of the World', 26 January 2010, at <http://boxofficemojo.com/news/?id=2657>.

[88] Interview in *Il Manifesto*, 14 April 1991.

and its commissioner for the information society—was, as so often alleged, to find their unity in opposing what crossed the Atlantic. But things were not so simple, said this report. Music, television, and information-users all had different priorities; website design always featured local styles; some e-projects had transnational and American connections, many did not. The global–local tension was evident within Europe itself, even within nations. A Paris consultant suggested that while rock music was popular in Spain, 'Madrid goes for hard rock with guitars and Barcelona is more futuristic with German techno influences'. The head of a London-based web-design firm suggested that each capital city possessed its own digital culture. The 'French touch' was associated with the music and style of F Communications, the company of renowned French DJ Laurent Garnier.[89]

In a digital universe where every form of familiar cultural boundary or hierarchy was dissolving, the EU had set up in 2001 a special Multilingual Digital Culture programme to amass and analyse information 'on what Europe looks like, sounds like, and feels like on-line'. The results of this project were eventually published in 2009. They showed, to no one's great surprise, that what 'digital culture surfers' were generally looking for in a site was 'content, innovation and "coolness"'.[90]

Even in Albania, a land where Internet users had passed from 2,500 in 2001 to 471,200 in 2009? If there was one corner of the Old World where the American inspiration and its European alternatives could still be seen meeting head-on at the end of the decade it was the Balkans, and Albania in particular. Incomes, imports and exports, urbanization, growth—and mobile phone use—had all exploded in the course of the previous decade in Albania, said a report in Turin's *La Stampa*. The returns of the emigrants were still key to the economy, but emigration was declining, some were even returning. All the contradictions of fast, barely controlled development were once more on display: the energy and the corruption, the sense of exhilaration and the waste, the extremes of private affluence and public squalor, the disorientation of every moral and cultural reference point. *La Stampa's* reporter Pierangelo Sapegno asked: Were *we* like this in the 1950s? In this Albania, identities were up for grabs. Did the country want to be a little bit of Switzerland or an offshore region of Italy? 'Full of yesterday and full of the future', without a credible present, would an Albanian path to modernity ever emerge? Skyscrapers, hypermarkets, disco-pubs, even universities, were sprouting like

[89] *Wall Street Journal Europe*, 26 March 2001; www.frcom.fr.
[90] Ibid. 26 March 2001; <http://www.mudicu.org/index.html>.

mushrooms, yet cows still wandered undisturbed on the autostrada, buildings shot up without any sort of regulation.[91] But as for *hope*, there was apparently nothing to match America's hold on Albanian imaginations. Not the sad, deluded version of Gianni Amelio's *L'America* of 1994, which depicted masses of desperate refugees fleeing on grossly overloaded old boats, believing that Italy was their USA. But an America of decent incomes, open for business to energetic individuals, recognizing that an Albanian was not by definition a low-grade manual worker—as the north and west Europeans all seemed to think— but a person who might have a degree, skills, intelligence, a will to work and to get on. 'Our America is here now!', proclaimed the *Stampa* article, which appeared following the announcement from Brussels that citizens of Albania (and Bosnia) might henceforth travel freely in the Schengen zone of Europe without requiring a visa. To become fully European, the story implied, Albanians were embracing America's myths, transforming their country and transcending themselves.[92]

Unhappy days

These were not the best of times either in America or in Europe. 'If the Cold War was won in 1989, it was lost again through the inability to project American power lastingly into one region, never mind all the others', wrote the Columbia-based German historian Volker Berghahn. 'The "Americanization of the world" thus seems to have finally reached its limits', Berghahn went on. 'The erstwhile hegemon can no longer assert itself single-handedly. It is dependent on other powers as partners and on economic exchange.'[93] The tragedy was 'that the US can't or won't realise this', added a BBC World Service programme dedicated to the rise of China and India as 'soft power' competitors to the West.[94] The Americans were no less harsh when they came to judge Europe's performance. The President of the Council on Foreign Relations, Richard Haass, told his transatlantic audience: 'The European project is foundering.' What with

---

[91] *La Stampa*, 30 May 2010.

[92] On the great significance of the visas issue for Albanian attitudes to 'Europe', Rando Devole, 'Eurovisa, l'Europa unita dei visti', at <http://www.balcanicaucaso.org/aree/Albania/Eurovisa-l-Europa-unita-dei-visti>. Other critical comments by Devole on Albania's recent evolution, ibid. I am grateful to Luisa Chiodi, direttrice dell'Osservatorio dei Balcani e del Caucaso, for this reference.

[93] Volker R. Berghahn, 'The Debate on "Americanization" Among Economic and Cultural Historians', *Cold War History* (February 2010), 121.

[94] BBC World Service, The Monday Documentary, 'Soft Power: China', 17 May 2010; this is also a key message of Mahbubani, *New Asia Hemisphere*, e.g. pp. 38–9, 44–50, 104, 125, 211–14, 237.

weak political leadership, structural economic and financial flaws, and a mental demilitarization, the Old World was looking older and smaller every day. As for its cultural presence, Europe was doomed to marginality and obscurity, said *Newsweek*, because of the obscure, haughty, self-referentiality of its output, and its inability to bring modern selling methods and communications technology to the business of conquering influence among the masses, in the world soft power 'war'.[95]

But whatever the currencies of power considered, the relative shrinking of their exchange value that struck both sides in the 2000s afflicted Europe more than the US. If Europe was neither a problem nor a solution for the Americans, as in Hubert Védrine's formulation, the same could never be said for the US in Europe's existence. The virulence of some American language on the behaviour of certain West European opinion during the Iraq crisis—rhetoric that by the end of the decade already looked extremely bizarre—reflected the fact that whatever they were saying, European views on the big questions of the day did matter at that time to American opinion at all levels. Who could possibly claim the same at the end of the decade?

As for models of modernity, the violence of the attacks on Obama's health care reforms as a vehicle of European-style socialism showed how little those American opinions knew or cared about the way things worked in practice in the wide variety of European health systems (and even less on how those systems had been restructured over recent years to make them more productive, cost-efficient, and 'customer' oriented). All this simply confirmed the Europeans in their basic faith in each society's carefully worked out balance between state and market, no matter how deeply shaken that connection was by the general financial crisis.[96] Even the Conservatives in Britain—the nation that under Labour governments had done most to bring US practices, norms, and even private companies into the 'modernization' of its hospitals and clinics—were forced to recognize that the National Health Service was a mass article of faith.[97]

---

[95] Haass in *Financial Times*, 13 May 2010; *Newsweek*, 4 June 2010 (this was a review of Martel's *Mainstream*); a similar attack aimed specifically at French culture by *Time* magazine in December 2007 had provoked indignant responses: Donald Morrison, 'The Death of French Culture', *Time*, European edition (3 December 2007); full-length version in Morrison, *Que rest-t-il de la culture française?* (Paris, 2008); responses by Antoine Compagnon in *Le Monde/Guardian Weekly*, 7 December 2007, Bernard-Henri Lévy, in *Corriere della Sera*, 10 December 2007.

[96] Proof that the gap between the US and Europe on social spending, crime, poverty, education, pollution, control, etc. was almost entirely fictitious did nothing to reduce the temperature of debates on these issues on either side of the Atlantic; figs in Peter Baldwin, 'America: A Reality Check', in Almqvist and Linklater (eds), *On the Idea of America*; full comparisons in Martinelli (ed.), *Transatlantic Divide*, critical discussion ibid. ch. 10.

[97] Ellwood, 'Bemused by America'.

Nations, generations, companies, and individuals were free to choose whether to follow a more 'American' or a more 'European' path to the future, or to invent some synthesis of their own: identity debates were in some respects places for reconciling these demands of globalization and sovereignty. But choose they must if they wished to stay in the race to the future, or, more specifically, to take part in the competition to define what might become the leading model of change. That was the soft power game, not as its inventor imagined it, a technique for somehow leveraging America's allure into a source of support for US foreign policy. Such a ploy would not help Barack Obama solve the problems of the credit crunch. But its legacy over the years, including the variety supplied by 'the empire of fun',[98] certainly helped explain why Europeans had found themselves reunited for one fleeting moment in November 2008—along with much of the rest of the world—in discovering how much faith they had invested over the years in American democracy's ability to reinvent itself, and so provide a source of positive, forward-looking expectation for peoples everywhere.

[98] Wagnleitner, 'Empire of Fun'.

Conclusion: America and the Politics of Change in Europe

The years depicted in these pages were western Europe's American century. To Americans this appeared obvious, if only because they felt that they had come to the rescue of that version of Western civilization that was their own roots, no less than three times in the course of those decades.[1] In contrast, Europeans, at first in the western half then in all the rest, saw wave after wave of innovation sweep over their societies throughout this era, an experience that was deeply entwined with the American modernizing challenge in all its varying forms.

Everywhere the impulse to develop answers to it appeared, even as the model itself bore so many signs of its European origins. France, the nation mostly consistently aware over the decades of what was at stake, produced in 2000 the notion of 'hyper-puissance', a forceful characterization of the ever-changing *combination* of military, economic, cultural, and ideological resources that the transatlantic superpower was able to mobilize in so many situations. That this projection happened in ways impossible to foretell or control, could evolve either wittingly or—most often—with a disconcerting insouciance for its own consistency and its effects on others, only made it all the more disturbing.[2]

In other parts of the world, the American style of obliviousness to unintended consequences could easily produce tragedy. Europe was lucky, seeing usually the finest, most creative, dynamic, and generous of America's energies at work, normally spared the angry impulses that appeared when adversity or adversaries reared their heads in America's media. In the end, for all the talk, only (western) Europe got a Marshall Plan, and was duly grateful for this temporary, conditional inclusion in American expansiveness. Among its many meanings, the Marshall Plan was also a tribute America paid to its European origins and heritage. But its main

---

[1] Ronald Steel, 'How Europe Became Atlantic: Walter Lippmann and the New Geography of the Atlantic Community', in Mariano (ed.), *Defining the Atlantic Community*, 15.

[2] French outlook well explained in speech by former Prime Minister Lionel Jospin at Harvard in 2003; reproduced in *French Politics, Culture and Society* (Summer 2004), 118–26; historical precedents involving Europe's impact and reception in the non-Western world in Curtin, *World and the West*, Part 2.

lesson, to be repeated by that nation's experts in a hundred different way down the years, was that Europe should be more like America (or as America imagined itself to be) in its ways of getting and spending, if its peoples wanted to get away from all the malignancies of the past, and enjoy all the liberating fruits of an ever-expanding material prosperity for an ever-expanding majority.

But the force of this American utopianism has never been taken too seriously elsewhere, and long before the Iraq war was often regarded with downright suspicion. Perhaps this was one reason why European integration never acquired a *missionary* intention, with a strong ideological bent, transforming its protagonists even as it revolutionized its beneficiaries. The old colonial nations, especially the 'winners' of the Second World War, were more interested in redefining their past in their own perceived present interests than in transcending it. Old World cynicism and opportunism versus New World ingenuousness and perfectionism once more? Although this trope continued to be played out in films and literature on occasion (most often by way of revivals[3]), at the heart of European endeavours to reconcile the American forms of modernity with their own notions of sovereignty and identity was always the urge to 'retain the best and re-invent the rest', as the saviour of an ancient brand name once put it. Historians call it 'defensive modernization', and know it's an old story.[4] It is the O'Faolain quest again, the search for that 'formula of life as between the old traditions and the new world rushing into us from every side', a kind of 'grailing', that favoured activity of the knights at Mark Twain's Court of King Arthur, as they hunted for the Holiest of holy vessels.[5]

In 2003, in the context of the Euro-American intellectual debate over the Iraq war, Susan Sontag told a German audience:

> In the end, the model for whatever understanding—conciliation—we might reach lies in thinking more about that venerable opposition, 'old' and

---

[3] In the cinema, *Easy Virtue* (Stephan Elliott, 2009; film version of Noel Coward's play of 1928), in literature, Nancy Mitford, *The Blessing*, set in the Paris of the late 1940s and the Marshall Plan (1951 edn repr., London, 2009). But Ted Sanger's *Un Américain en Picardie* (Paris, 2005), fiction from the head of *Newsweek*'s Paris bureau, provided an entirely contemporary, and ironical, play on the old theme. A manager sent by an American private equity firm to bring an old-established French hardware manufacturer up to contemporary standards of action and profitability meets entrenched, trade union-based opposition to his reforming ways, with much talk of Taylorism, republicanism, and Washington's imperialism, incomprehensible to the American cost-buster. In the end the intense encounter leaves neither side unchanged.

[4] Curtin, *World and the West*, 143, 153–4, 170–1 (Japanese version), 179, 183–4 (Ottoman case).

[5] The role of television in this effort, especially historical material, fictional or otherwise, is documented in many chapters in Bignell and Fickers (eds), *European Television History*.

'new'…the opposition of 'old' and 'new' is genuine, ineradicable, at the center of what we understand to be experience itself.…We are told we must choose—the old or the new. In fact, we must choose both. What is life if not a series of negotiations between the old and the new?

What made dealing with America difficult in this context, said Sontag, was its own very peculiar mix of the inherited and the invented:

> It is the genius of the United States, a profoundly conservative country in ways that Europeans find difficult to fathom, to have devised a form of conservative thinking that celebrates the new rather than the old.[6]

If anything, this was the genius of the local version of capitalist ideology, and of the willingness of the people of the United States to identify so closely with its market mechanisms, embracing their costs as well as their benefits. As Habermass and Derrida, the main European protagonists of the same Iraq debate, pointed out, the European concepts of citizenship, political and juridical, predated the arrival of full-blown American-style capitalism by a very considerable length of time, during which the evolution of class politics had rendered Europe's peoples at all levels particularly sensitive to '*the paradoxes of progress*'. So the search for that 'formula of life' as between tradition and modernity, mediated by highly developed conservative, liberal, and socialist political cultures, had come down in Europe to the consideration of two main alternatives:

> Do the benefits of a chimerical progress outweigh the losses that come with the disintegration of protective, traditional forms of life? [In other words] do the benefits that today's processes of 'creative destruction' promise for tomorrow outweigh the pain of modernity's losers?[7]

It was part of the attractiveness of the early Barack Obama to many Europeans that he could understand this question perfectly, as demonstrated by his Cairo and Accra speeches of 2009. Those events also supplied more evidence of how problems and contrasts first thrown up by modernizing history in the Atlantic framework gradually arrived on the world stage in the era of globalization.

What Obama acknowledged on that occasion and others was that you could indeed be modern without being Western, and that his United

[6] S. Sontag, 'Literature is Freedom', October 2003, in Levy, Pensky, and Torpey (eds), *Old Europe, New Europe, Core Europe*, 215, 217.

[7] J. Habermass and J. Derrida, 'February 15', 11 (emphasis in original). Of course there were plenty of Americans sensitive to the same dilemmas. With her career long over, the 1960s songwriter Ellie Greenwich was quoted at one point as saying: 'progress is wonderful, but boy, it can ruin some nice things…', *Guardian Weekly*, 13 November 2009.

States would respect that choice.[8] The recognition was also a way of acknowledging the success of the Chinese experiment in offering a solution to the conundrum of creative destruction, even as the great mass of Chinese citizens remained extremely—but not desperately—poor. The achievements of the new model China seemed to confirm one of the predictions of the Cold Warrior elements in the Marshall Plan: that if liberal capitalism failed to provide the masses with the benefits of technological progress, then the totalitarians would do so.[9] But European-style totalitarianism had been much more interested in race, war, and conquest—the Nazi–Fascist versions—or the forced industrialization of mother Russia—the Leninist–Stalinist version—to think seriously about the living the standards of its masses, though the Nazis and the Soviets were certainly aware of the problem.

In this context the success of the American model of economic citizenship looked all the more glorious. Its victories included the complete, pacific defeat of the Soviet competitor. As the Marshall Planners had promised, their version of competitive capitalism had indeed succeeded—and continued to succeed more effectively than any other challenger—in bringing the fruits of science and technology to the publics of the industrialized world. Europeans had already seen the sound motion picture and the Fordist system of production and consumption at work. After World War II, they too gradually achieved access to the motor car and cheap electricity. After the Cold War, low-cost air travel, the Internet, and the entire digital revolution were the supreme symbols of this triumph. The shadow of nuclear war that loomed so large over the post-World War II years dwindled in the light of so much wish-fulfilment. This sort of fear faded, and the menace of the Bomb was ever more carefully hidden.[10]

In the West a private, individualistic, hedonistic form of life took over, deeply secular and usually untroubled by worries over its dependence on cheap oil and limitless access to the physical resources of the planet.[11] It involved endless innovation and 'future shock', and a great deal of entertainment. What it did not provide was a satisfactory code of moral values strong enough to compensate for the downswings, the bubbles, the gaps between winners and losers which multiplied and expanded the more the

---

[8] For a glimpse of the Indian version of this search for balance, Deepak Lal, 'The View of America from India', in Almqvist and Linklater (eds), *On the Idea of America*.

[9] Cf. Mahbubani, *New Asia Hemisphere*, 131–50, which highlights the limits as well as the benefits of this process.

[10] Behind the scenes, nuclear weapons remained as present and potentially dangerous as ever; lecture by former US Defence Secretary Robert McNamara, 'The Folly of US and NATO Weapons Policies', Johns Hopkins University, SAIS Bologna Center, 20 April 2005.

[11] Cf. Wirsching, 'From Work to Consumption', 21, *passim*.

system was successful. As Joseph Schumpeter had predicted in 1942, many hated 'its utilitarianism and the wholesale destruction of Meanings [*sic*] incident to it'.[12] For these reasons, free market capitalism would never achieve in Europe the ideological status it conquered in America, not even among the capitalists. Entire areas of European life—and not just in southern societies—would demonstrate no faith whatsoever in the competitive miracles of markets, least of all as the central organizing principle of the 'good life'.

Even in the era when it was no longer plausible to distinguish between 'masses' and 'elites' in Europe, the old divisions persisted between those who resisted the push to submit hiring and firing to the laws of the market, and those who worried most over allowing consumer tastes to dictate production and consumption in the world of culture, whether it be fashion, movies, music, literature, food, software, lifestyles, language—'whatever'. But this was the key to the American understanding of culture as a source or currency of demotic power, producing over time a form of global hegemony that none could even dream of matching, and making 'America' its own best brand.[13] The result was to make nonsense of so many of the arguments about globalization, interdependence, and transnationalism, since they steadfastly refused to contemplate how unequal were the resources the various protagonists brought to the dynamics of cultural exchange.

If Hollywood controlled 60–70 per cent of the European (or any other) film market, while the foreigners had access to 5–6 per cent of the American audience, whatever the causes, that was a power relationship. Countless numbers of American books were translated into foreign languages; 3 per cent of titles appearing in the US were translations. That too produced a certain type of balance of power in world publishing.[14] At one point around the turn of the millennium an abbreviated edition of the *New York Times* appeared in 25 other countries. Among the foreigners, only the British could contemplate making serious efforts to penetrate the US media market. Hierarchical ratings of economies and their competitiveness, of the success of brands[15], of the number of those speaking Eng-

---

[12] Schumpeter, *Capitalism, Socialism*, 129.

[13] On the film industry's love of the word 'America' in the titles of its productions, Nigel Andrews, 'Why Hollywood loves the A-word', in *Financial Times*, 9 November 2007; on the rise of would-be competitors in many parts of the world, especially in light entertainment and current affairs television, Reese Schonfeld, 'The Global Battle for Cultural Domination', in Lawrence E. Harrison and Jerome Kagan (eds), *Developing Cultures: Essays on Cultural Change* (London, 2006). This is one of the key themes of Martel, *Mainstream*, Part 2.

[14] Pardo, *Europe–Hollywood Coopetition*, 36, Jeanneney, *Google*, 8.

[15] Typical brand rating lists at <http://www.interbrand.com>; cf. Marcel Danesi, *Brands* (London, 2006).

lish compared to other international languages, of the diffusion of TV shows, of the quality of universities, of the prestige of public intellectuals, of the desirability of life in cities and a hundred other monitored realities—all this added to a top-down conception of power in the world that by the turn of the millennium had taken on a life of its own, connected or not to the familiar pecking orders of guns and money.

It was the extreme flexibility of the cultural resource that as often as not gave the Americans the ability to invent new ways to project power according to circumstances, or original combinations of new and old ways. The Persian Gulf War of 1991 provides the classic example. In itself, the intervention represented the oldest form of power projection of all: the punitive military expedition. But by combining this with the invention of the myth and the reality of CNN, and its 24-hour news bulletins apparently straight from the front, the Americans not only demonstrated their tactical superiority to the enemy, but also to all their allies in the venture. In the metaphorical as well as in the literal senses, yet again, the media were the message.[16] The limits to the usefulness of this form of power in a military context were tested to destruction by the Iraq crusade, and the endless saga of the war in Afghanistan, but who knew how it might yet be reconfigured again in some new test of wills?

'West is West and East is East—where will Europe come to rest?' It was an old Cold War question harking back to Kipling, and it never received a satisfactory answer, not even when Germany played a full part in bringing the Cold War to a peaceful conclusion and so transcended itself.[17] In the new century, with a new 'East' arising, it appeared that the two world continents or regions on either side of the Atlantic was each going its own way. Europe's greatest aspirations appeared to be deeply conservative, to recover enough growth to maintain living and social standards at the levels the majority of its peoples had come to expect, as the new President of the European Council of Ministers allegedly said after his appointment at the end of 2009. 'Lolling in its splendid berth', as a former Brazilian President put it, the Old World so configured might at best begin to look like a greater Switzerland, enjoyed, perhaps respected, but inspiring no one outside its borders, irrelevant to the big trends emerging in the wider world. Its immense, silent achievements in reintegrating east and central Europe, and—perhaps—calming the Balkans, would go unrecognized. Americans by contrast, showed far more determination to rebuild their

---

[16] Cf. comments of French media historian Marc Ferro in *Guardian Weekly/Le Monde*, 10–11 February 1991.

[17] Cf. Anne-Marie Le Gloannec, *Berlin et le monde: Les timides audaces d'una nation réunifiée* (Paris, 2007).

nation's prestige, influence, and capacity to invent ways to project power abroad.[18]

Whether they would succeed or not only the future would tell. Perhaps the great wave of digital innovations of the 1990s–2000s resembled the last burst that often signals the grand finale of a firework show. But even if the American cultural empire did come to an end one day, not with a bang or a whimper, but with a Twitter™, the sound would surely be heard everywhere in Europe, and all around the world.

[18] On Europe's age of anxiety, Dominique Moïsi, *The Geopolitics of Emotion* (New York, 2009), 146–60, 204–6. The Clinton Global Initiative, launched by former President Bill Clinton, supported as appropriate by his wife, the Secretary of State in the Obama administration, represented a classic demonstration of the nation's urge to invent ways to project power in the world, once more reflecting the usual porousness of the public–private boundary as well as that between the virtual and the real in foreign policy making; site at <http://www.clintonglobalinitiative.org>.

Bibliography

For purposes of further reading and research, this comprehensive list of references is divided into three sections : Secondary sources (academic books and theses, articles), Contemporary Materials (political and economic tracts, novels, short stories, articles, pamphlets etc. produced for public purposes at the time of their appearance), Official and Semi-official sources.

SECONDARY SOURCES

Books and theses

Abate, Janet, *Inventing the Internet* (Cambridge, Mass., 1999)

Absalom, Roger (ed.), *Perugia Liberata: Documenti anglo-americani sull'occupazione alleata di Perugia (1944–1945)* (Florence, 2001)

Addison, Paul, *No Turning Back: The Peacetime Revolutions in Postwar Britain* (Oxford, 2010)

Allen, Donald C., *French Views of America in the 1930s* (New York, 1979)

Almqvist, Kurt and Kay Glans (eds), *The Swedish Success Story?* (Stockholm, 2004)

Anderson, Perry, *The New Old World* (London, 2009)

Anderson, Stuart B., *Race and Rapprochement: Anglo-Saxonism and Anglo-American Relations, 1895–1904* (East Brunswick, 1981)

Andrews, Geoff, *The Slow Food Story: Politics and Pleasure* (London 2008)

Appel Jr, A., *Nabokov's Dark Cinema* (New York, 1974)

Ardagh, John, *The New France* (London, 1977)

Arieli, Yehoshua and Nathan Rotenstriech (eds), *Totalitarian Democracy and After* (1984 edn repr., London, 2000)

Arkes, Hadley, *Bureaucracy, the Marshall Plan and the National Interest* (Princeton, 1972)

Arndt, H. W., *The Rise and Fall of Economic Growth: A Study in Contemporary Thought* (Melbourne, 1978)

Arndt, Richard T., *The First Resort of Kings: American Cultural Diplomacy in the Twentieth Century* (Washington DC, 2005)

Arviddson, Adam, *The Making of a Consumer Society: Marketing and Modernity in Contemporary Italy*, PhD thesis, European University Institute (Florence, 1999)

Ascherson, Neal, *Stone Voices: The Search for Scotland* (London, 2002)

Aughey, Arthur, *Nationalism, Devolution and the Challenge to the United Kingdom State* (London, 2001)

Bacevich, Andrew J., *American Empire: The Realities and Consequences of U.S. Diplomacy* (Cambridge, Mass., 2002)

Bader, William B., *Austria Between East and West, 1945–1955* (Stanford, 1966)

Baldini, Gianfranco and Marc Lazar (eds), *La Francia di Sarkozy* (Bologna, 2007)

Balfour, Sebastian, *The End of the Spanish Empire* (Oxford, 1997)

Barber, Benjamin R., *Jihad vs McWorld: How Globalism and Tribalism are Reshaping the World* (New York, 1996; 2nd edn, London, 2003)

Barclay, David E. and Elisabeth Glaser-Schmidt (eds), *Transatlantic Images and Perceptions: Germany and America since 1776* (Cambridge, 1997)

Barnett, Correlli, *The Audit of War: The Illusion and Reality of Britain as a Great Nation* (London, 1986)

Barr, Charles (ed.), *All Our Yesterdays: 90 Years of British Cinema* (London, 1986)

Basinger, Jeanine, *How Hollywood Spoke to Women 1930–1960* (Hanover, NH, 1993)

Baylis, John and Jon Roper (eds), *The United States and Europe: Beyond the Neo-Conservativce Divide?* (London, 2006)

Becker, Josef and Frans Knipping (eds), *Power in Europe? Great Britain, France, Italy and Germany in a Postwar World, 1945–1950* (Berlin and New York, 1986)

Bédarida, François, *A Social History of England, 1851–1990* (2nd edn, London, 1991)

Beevor, Anthony and Artemis Cooper, *Paris after the Liberation, 1944–49* (2nd edn of 2004 repr., London, 2007)

Ben-Ghiat, Ruth, *Fascist Modernities: Italy, 1922–1945* (Berkeley, 2001)

Benson, John, *The Rise of Consumer Society in Britain, 1880–1980* (London, 1994)

Berg, A. Scott, *Lindbergh* (New York, 1998)

Berghahn, Volker, *America and the Intellectual Cold Wars in Europe* (Princeton, 2001)

—— *The Americanisation of West German Industry, 1945–1973* (Leamington Spa, 1986)

Berman, Marshall, *All That is Solid Melts into Air: The Experience of Modernity* (2nd edn, New York, 1988)

Bernardi, Emanuele, *La riforma agraria in Italia e gli Stati Uniti: Guerra fredda, Piano Marshall e interventi per il Mezzogiorno negli anni del centrismo degasperiano* (Bologna, 2006)

Bessel, Richard and Dirk Schumann (eds), *Life after Death: Approaches to a Cultural and Social History of Europe During the 1940s and 1950s* (Cambridge, 2003)

Best, Gary Dean, *Harold Laski and American Liberalism* (New Brunswick, NJ, 2005)

Beynet, M., *L'image de l'Amérique dans la culture italienne de l'entre-deux guerres*, 3 vols (Aix-en-Provence, 1990)

Bignell, Jonathan and Andreas Fickers (eds), *A European Television History* (Oxford, 2008)

Bigsby, C. W. E. (ed.), *Superculture: American Popular Culture and Europe* (London, 1975)

Bischof, Günter, *Austria in the First Cold War, 1945–55: The Leverage of the Weak* (London, 1999)

—— and Anton Pelinka (eds), *Contemporary Austrian Studies*, v: *Austrian Historical Memory and National Identity* (New Brunswick, NJ, 1997), xii: *The Americanization/Westernization of Austria* (New Brunswick, NJ, 2004)

—— —— and Dieter Stiefel (eds), *Contemporary Austrian Studies*, viii: *The Marshall Plan in Austria* (New Brunswick, NJ, 2000)

———— and Erika Thurner (eds), *Contemporary Austrian Studies*, vi: *Women in Austria* (New Brunswick, NJ, 1998)

——— and Dieter Stiefel (eds), *Images of the Marshall Plan in Europe: Films, Photographs, Exhibits, Posters* (Innsbruck, 2009)

Black, Lawrence, *The Political Culture of the Left in Affluent Britain, 1951–64* (London, 2003)

Bloch-Lainé, Francois and Jean Bouvier, *La France restaurée, 1944–1954: Dialogue sur les choix d'une modernisation* (Paris, 1986)

Boel, Bent, *The European Productivity Agency and Transatlantic Relations, 1953–1961* (Copenhagen, 2003)

Bogdanor, Vernon and Robert Skidelsky, *The Age of Affluence, 1951–1964* (London, 1970)

Bonazzi, Tiziano (ed.), *Quale occidente, occidente perché* (Soveria Mannelli, 2005)

Borgwardt, Elizabeth, *A New Deal for the World: America's Vision for Human Rights* (Cambridge, Mass., 2005)

Bourdon, Jérôme, *Haute fédelité: Pouvoir et télévision, 1935–1994* (Paris, 1994)

Boyce, Robert W. D., *British Capitalism at the Crossroads, 1919–1932* (Cambridge, 1987)

——— *The Great Interwar Crisis and the Collapse of Globalization* (London, 2009)

Braudy, Leo, *The Frenzy of Renown* (New York, 1986)

Brinkley, Alan, *The Publisher: Henry Luce and His American Century* (New York, 2009)

Brinkley, Douglas and David R. Facey-Crowther (eds), *The Atlantic Charter* (London, 1994)

Brown, Callum G., *The Death of Christian Britain* (London, 2001)

Bullen, R. J. et al. (eds), *Ideas into Politics: Aspects of European History, 1880–1950* (Exeter, 1984)

Bullock, Alan, *Ernest Bevin: Foreign Secretary, 1945–1951* (New York, 1983)

Burk, Kathleen, *Old World, New World: The Story of Britain and America* (London, 2007)

Burnet, Alastair, *America 1843–1993: 150 Years of Reporting the American Connection* (London, 1993)

Burns, James MacGregor, *Roosevelt: The Soldier of Freedom* (New York, 1970)

Burns, Rob (ed.), *German Cultural Studies: An Introduction* (Oxford, 1995)

Burton, Alan and Loraine Porter (eds), *Crossing the Pond: Anglo-American Film Relations Before 1930* (Trowbridge, 2002)

Bushell, Anthony (ed.), *Austria 1945–1955: Studies in Political and Cultural Re-Emergence* (Cardiff, 1996)

Cain, P. J. and A. G. Hopkins, *British Imperialism: Crisis and Deconstruction, 1914–1990* (London, 1993)

Calder, Angus, *The People's War: Britain 1939–1945* (London, 1969)

Camporesi, Valeria, *Mass Culture and National Traditions: The BBC and American Broadcasting, 1922–1954* (Florence, 2000)

Campus, Mauro, *L'Italia, gli Stati Uniti e il piano Marshall, 1947–1951* (Rome, 2008)

Cannistraro, Philip V. and Brian R. Sullivan, *Il Duce's Other Woman: The Untold Story of Margherita Sarfatti, Benito Mussolini's Jewish Mistress, and How She Helped Him Come to Power* (New York, 1993)

Cardini, Antonio (ed.), *Il miracolo economico italiano (1958–1963)* (Bologna, 2006)

Carew, Anthony, *Labour under the Marshall Plan: The Politics of Productivity and the Marketing of Management Science* (Manchester, 1987)

Carlton, Eric, *Occupation: The Policies and Practices of Military Conquerors* (London, 1992)

Castells, Manuel, *The Information Age: Economy, Society and Culture*, ii: *The Power of Identity* (2nd edn, Oxford, 2004)

——— *The Internet Galaxy: Reflections on the Internet, Business, and Society* (Oxford, 2001)

Cavazza, Stefano and Emanuela Scarpellini (eds), *La rivoluzione dei consumi: Società di massa e benessere in Europa, 1945–2000* (Bologna, 2010)

Ceaser, James W., *Reconstructing America: The Symbol of America in Modern Thought* (New Haven, Conn., 1997)

Chapman, James, *Cinemas of the World: Film and Society from 1895 to the Present* (London, 2003)

Charmley, John, *Churchill's Grand Alliance: The Anglo-American Special Relationship, 1940–57* (New York, 1995)

Cohen, Stephen F., *Bukharin and the Bolshevik Revolution* (New York, 1973)

Conekin, Becky, Frank Mort, and Chris Waters (eds), *Moments of Modernity: Reconstructing Britain, 1945–1964* (London, 1999)

Conrad, Peter, *Imagining America* (London, 1980)

Coser, Lewis A., *Refugee Scholars in America: Their Impact and Their Experiences* (New Haven, Conn., 1984)

Costigliola, Frank, *Awkward Dominion: American Political, Economic, and Cultural Relations with Europe, 1919–1933* (Ithaca, 1984)

Cox, Michael (ed.), *E. H. Carr: A Critical Appraisal* (Basingstoke, 2004)

Craveri, Piero and Gaetano Quagliarello (eds), *L'Antiamericanismo in Italia e in Europa nel Secondo Dopoguerra* (Soveria Mannelli, 2004)

Croall, Jonathan, *Don't You Know There's a War On? The People's Voice, 1939–45* (London, 1989)

Cull, Nicholas J., *Selling War: The British Propaganda Campaign Against American Neutrality in World War II* (New York, 1995)

——— *The Cold War and the United States Information Agency: American Propaganda and Public Diplomacy, 1945–1989* (Cambridge, 2008)

Curtin, Philip D., *The World and the West: The European Challenge and the Overseas Response in the Age of Empire* (Cambridge, 2002)

Danesi, Marcel, *Brands* (London, 2006)

D'Attorre, Pier Paolo (ed.), *Nemici per la pelle: Sogno americano e mito sovietico nell'Italia contemporanea* (Milan, 1991)

Daunton, Martin and Matthew Hilton (eds), *The Politics of Consumption: Material Culture and Citizenship in Europe and America* (Oxford, 2001)

Davis, Franklin M., *Come as a Conqueror: The United States Army's Occupation of Germany, 1945–1949* (New York, 1967)

Davis, John A. (ed.), *Italy and America, 1943–44: Italian, American and Italian American Experiences of the Liberation of the Mezzogiorno* (Naples, 1997)

Dear, I. C. B. (ed.), *Oxford Companion to the Second World War* (Oxford, 1995)

DeConde, Alexander, *Half Bitter, Half Sweet: An Excursion into Italian–American History* (New York, 1971)

Diggins, John P., *Mussolini and Fascism: The View from America* (Princeton, 1972)

Di Leo, Rita, *Il primato Americano: Il punto di vista degli Stati uniti dopo la caduta del muro di Berlino* (Bologna, 2000)

Dimbleby, David and David Reynolds, *An Ocean Apart: The Relationship Between Britain and America in the Twentieth Century* (London, 1988)

Diner, Dan, *America in the Eyes of the Germans: An Essay on Anti-Americanism* (Princeton, 1996)

Divine, Robert A., *Second Chance: The Triumph of Internationalism in World War II* (New York, 1967)

Dizikes, John, *Britain, Roosevelt and the New Deal: British Opinion, 1932–1938* (New York, 1979)

Dobson, Alan P., *Peaceful Air Warfare: The United States, Britain and the Politics of International Aviation* (Oxford, 1991)

—— *The Politics of the Anglo-American Special Relationship, 1940–1987* (Brighton, 1988)

—— *United States Economic Statecraft for Survival, 1933–1991: Of Sanctions, Embargoes and Economic Warfare* (London, 2002)

Doherty, Gabriel and Dermot Keogh (eds), *De Valera's Ireland* (Cork, 2003)

Doherty, Thomas, *Pre-Code Hollywood: Sex, Immorality and Insurrection in American Cinema, 1930–1934* (New York, 1999)

Dolowitz, David, *Learning from America: Policy Transfer and the Development of the British Workfare State* (Brighton, 1998)

Donald, James, Anne Friedberg, and Laura Marcus (eds), *'Close Up' 1927–1933: Cinema and Modernism* (London, 1998)

Donohue, Kathleen M., *Freedom from Want: American Liberalism and the Idea of the Consumer* (Baltimore, 2003)

Dore, Ronald, *Stock Market Capitalism: Welfare Capitalism, Japan and Germany versus the Anglo-Saxons* (Oxford, 2000)

Dougherty, James J., *The Politics of Wartime Aid: American Economic Assistance to France and French Northwest Africa, 1940–1946* (Westport, Conn., 1978)

Draper, Theodore, *American Communism and Soviet Russia* (New York, 1960)

Duchen, Claire and Irene Bandhauer-Schöffmann (eds), *When the War Was Over: Women, War and Peace in Europe, 1940–1956* (London, 2000)

Duchêne, François, *Jean Monnet: The First Statesman of Interdependence* (New York, 1994)

Dukore, Bernard F. (ed.), *Bernard Shaw on Cinema* (Carbondale, Ill., 1997)

Dunning, J. H., *American Investment in British Manufacturing Industry* (London, 1958)

Duroselle, J. B., *France and the United States: From the Beginnings to the Present* (Chicago, 1978)

Eckes Jr, Alfred E. and Thomas W. Zeiler, *Globalization and the American Century* (Cambridge, 2003)

Ekbladh, David, *The Great American Mission: Modernization and the Creation of an American World Order* (Princeton, 2010)

Eksteins, Modris, *Rites of Spring: The Great War and the Birth of the Modern Age* (London, 1989)

Ellwood, D. W., *Italy 1943–1945: The Politics of Liberation* (Leicester, 1985)

—— *Rebuilding Europe: Western Europe, America and Postwar Reconstruction* (London, 1992)

—— (ed.), *The Marshall Plan Forty Years After: Lessons for the International System Today* (Bologna, 1989)

—— and R. Kroes (eds), *Hollywood in Europe: Experiences of a Cultural Hegemony* (Amsterdam, 1994)

Elsaesser, Thomas, *European Cinema: Face to Face with Hollywood* (Amsterdam, 2005)

Engerman, David C. et al. (eds), *Staging Growth: Modernization, Development and the Global Cold War* (Amherst, 2003)

Engwall C. and V. Zamagni (eds), *Management Education in Historical Perspective* (Manchester, 1998)

Epitropoulos, Mike-Frank G. and Victor Roudometof (eds), *American Culture in Europe: Interdisciplinary Perspectives* (Westport, Conn., 1998)

Ermarth, Michael (ed.), *America and the Shaping of German Society, 1945–1955* (Providence and Oxford, 1993)

Esposito, Chiarella, *America's Feeble Weapon: Funding the Marshall Plan in France and Italy, 1948–1950* (Westport, Conn., 1994)

Fauri, Francesca, *Il piano Marshall e l'Italia* (Bologna, 2010)

Fehrenbach, Heide, *Cinema in Democratizing Germany: Reconstructing National Identity after Hitler* (Chapel Hill, NC, 1995)

—— and Uta G. Poiger (eds), *Transactions, Transgressions, Transformations: American Culture in Western Europe and Japan* (New York, 2000)

Fender, Stephen (ed.), *American and European National Identities: Faces in the Mirror* (Keele, 1996)

Fleming, Donald and Bernard Bailyn (eds), *The Intellectual Migration: Europe and America, 1930–1960* (Cambridge, Mass., 1969)

Foley, Michael, *The British Presidency: Tony Blair and the Politics of Public Leadership* (Manchester, 2000)

Folly, Martin H., *The Palgrave Concise Historical Atlas of the Second World War* (London, 2004)

Footitt, Hilary, *War and Liberation in France: Living with the Liberators* (London, 2004)

—— and John Simmonds, *France 1943–45: The Politics of Liberation* (Leicester, 1987)

Fox, Daniel M., *The Discovery of Abundance: Simon N. Patten and the Transformation of Social Theory* (Ithaca, 1967)

Fraser, Matthew, *Weapons of Mass Distraction: Soft Power and American Empire* (New York, 2003)

Gamble, Andrew, *Between Europe and America: The Future of British Politics* (London, 2003)

Gardiner, Juliet, '*Over Here*': *The GIs in Wartime Britain* (London, 1992)

Gardner, Lloyd C., *Economic Aspects of New Deal Diplomacy* (Madison, 1964)

—— *Imperial America: American Foreign Policy since 1898* (New York, 1976)

—— *Safe for Democracy: The Anglo-American Response to Revolution, 1913–1923* (New York, 1984)

Gardner, Richard N., *Sterling–Dollar Diplomacy* (3rd edn, New York, 1996)

Garfield, Simon, *Our Hidden Lives: The Everyday Diaries of a Forgotten Britain, 1945–1948* (London, 2004)

Garrard, John, Vera Tolz, and Ralph White (eds), *European Democratization since 1800* (London, 2000)

Garraty, John A., *The Great Depression* (New York, 1986)

Gelernter, David, *1939: The Lost World of the Fair* (New York, 1995)

Gentile, Emilio, *Fascismo: Storia e interpretazione* (Bari, 2002)

—— et al. (eds), *Novecento italiano* (Rome, 2008)

Geppert, Dominik (ed.), *The Postwar Challenge: Cultural, Social and Political Change in Western Europe, 1945–58* (Oxford, 2003)

Geraghty, Christine, *British Cinema in the Fifties: Gendre, Genre and the 'New Look'* (London, 2000)

Gerlach, Murney, *British Liberalism and the United States: Political and Social Thought in the Late Victorian Age* (Basingstoke, 2000)

Giddens, Anthony, *The Consequences of Modernity* (Cambridge, 1990)

—— and Will Hutton (eds), *Global Capitalism* (New York, 2000)

Gienow-Hecht, Jessica C. E., *Transmission Impossible: American Journalism as Cultural Diplomacy in Postwar Germany, 1945–1955* (Baton Rouge, 1999)

—— and Frank Schumacher (eds), *Culture and International History* (New York, 2003)

Gildea, Robert, *Barriers and Borders: Europe 1800–1914* (2nd edn, London, 1996)

Gillingham, John, *European Integration, 1950–2003: Superstate or New Market Economy?* (Cambridge, 2003)

Gilman, Nils, *Mandarins of the Future: Modernization Theory in Cold War America* (Baltimore, 2003)

Gimbel, John, *A German Community under American Occupation: Marburg, 1945–52* (Stanford, 1961)

—— *The American Occupation of Germany: Politics and the Military, 1945–1949* (Stanford, 1968)

Ginsborg, Paul, *A History of Contemporary Italy: Society and Politics, 1943–1988* (London, 1990)

Giovacchino, Saverio, *Hollywood Modernism: Film and Politics in the Age of the New Deal* (Philadelphia, 2001)

Glancy, H. Mark, *When Hollywood Loved Britain: The Hollywood 'British' Film, 1939–45* (Manchester, 1999)

Glaser, Elisabeth and Hermann Wellenreuther (eds), *Bridging the Atlantic: The Question of American Exceptionalism in Perspective* (Washington DC and Cambridge, 2002)

Gobetti, Eric (ed.), *1943–1945: La lunga liberazione* (Milan, 2007)

Goedde, Petra, *GIs and Germans: Culture, Gender and Foreign Relations, 1945–1949* (New Haven, Conn., 2003)

Gordon, Philip H. and Sophie Meunier, *The French Challenge: Adapting to Globalization* (Washington DC, 2001)

Graham, Helen and Jo Labanyi (eds), *Spanish Cultural Studies: An Introduction* (Oxford, 1995)

Grazia, Victoria de, *How Fascism Ruled Women: Italy, 1922–1945* (Berkeley, 1992)

—— *Irresistible Empire: America's Advance through Twentieth-Century Europe* (Cambridge, Mass., 2005)

Grosser, Alfred, *Germany in Our Time: A Political History of the Postwar Years* (New York, 1971)

Groves, Annie, *The Grafton Girls* (London, 2007)

Gundle, Stephen, *Bellissima: Feminine Beauty and the Ideal of Italy* (New Haven, Conn., 2007)

—— *Between Hollywood and Moscow: The Italian Communists and the Challenge of Mass Culture, 1943–1991* (Durham, NC, 2000)

—— *Glamour: A History* (Oxford, 2008)

Halasz, Nicholas, *Roosevelt Through Foreign Eyes* (Princeton, 1961)

Hardyment, Christine, *From Mangle to Microwave: The Mechanization of Household Work* (Cambridge, 1988)

Harp, Stephen L., *Marketing Michelin: Advertising and Cultural Identity in Twentieth Century France* (Baltimore, 2002)

Harper, John L., *America and the Reconstruction of Italy, 1943–1948* (Cambridge, 1986)

—— *American Visions of Europe: Franklin D. Roosevelt, George F. Kennan and Dean G. Acheson* (Cambridge, 1994)

Haslam, Jonathan, *The Vices of Integrity: E. H. Carr, 1892–1982* (London, 1999)

Hay, James, *Popular Film Culture in Fascist Italy* (Bloomington, 1987)

Heald, Morrell, *Transatlantic Vistas: American Journalists in Europe, 1900–1940* (Kent, O., 1988)

Hearden, Patrick, *Architects of Globalism: Building a New World Order During World War II* (Fayetteville, Ark., 2002)

Hebdige, Dick, *Hiding the Light: On Images and Things* (London, 1988)

Heindel, Richard Heathcote, *The American Impact on Great Britain, 1898–1914* (1940 edn repr., New York, 1968)

Heller, Joseph, *Catch-22* (1962 edn repr., London, 1982)

Herf, Jeffrey, *Reactionary Modernism: Technology, culture and politics in Weimar and the Third Reich* (Cambridge, 1986)

Hewison, Robert, *Culture and Consensus: England, Art and Politics since 1940* (London, 1995)

Higson, Andrew, *Waving the Flag: Constructing a National Cinema in Britain* (Oxford, 1995)

—— and Richard Maltby (eds), *'Film Europe' and 'Film America': Cinema, Commerce, and Cultural Exchange 1920–1939* (Exeter, 1999)

Hilton, Sylvia L. and Steve J. S. Ickringill (eds), *European Perceptions of the Spanish–American War of 1898* (Bern, 1999)

Hirst, Paul and Graham Thomson, *Globalization in Question: The International Economy and the Possibilities of Governance* (2nd edn, Cambridge, 1999)

Hixson, Walter L., *Parting the Curtain: Propaganda, Culture and the Cold War, 1945–1961* (New York, 1998)

Hobsbawm, Eric J., *Age of Extremes: The Short Twentieth Century, 1914–1991* (London, 1994)

—— and Terence Ranger (eds), *The Invention of Tradition* (1984 edn repr., 2007)

Hoekman, B. M. and M. M. Kostecki, *The Political Economy of the World Trading System* (1995)

Hoffmann, Stanley, *Decline or Renewal? France since the 1930s* (New York, 1974)

—— *The European Sisyphus: Essays on Europe 1964–1994* (Boulder, Colo., 1995)

—— and Charles Maier (eds), *The Marshall Plan: A Retrospective* (Boulder, Colo., 1984)

Hogan, Michael J., *The Marshall Plan: America, Britain and the Reconstruction of Western Europe, 1947–1952* (Cambridge, 1987)

—— (ed.), *The Ambiguous Legacy: U.S. Foreign relations in the 'American Century'* (Cambridge, 1999)

Höhn, Maria, *GIs and Fräuleins: The German–American Encounter in 1950s West Germany* (Chapel Hill, NC, 2002)

Hollander, Paul, *Anti-Americanism: Critiques at Home and Abroad, 1965–1990* (New York, 1992)

Holroyd, Michael, *Bernard Shaw*, ii: *1898–1918* (London, 1991)

Hombach, Bodo, *The Politics of the New Centre* (London, 2000)

Hopkins, A. G. (ed.), *Global History: Interactions Between the Universal and the Local* (London, 2006)

—— (ed.), *Globalization in World History* (London, 2002)

Howard, Michael, *War and the Liberal Conscience* (London, 1978)

Hoyt, Edwin P., *The GI's War: American Soldiers in Europe During World War II* (New York, 2000)

Hughes, H. Stuart, *The Obstructed Path: French Social Thought in the Years of Desperation, 1930–1960* (New York, 1968)

Ilgen, Thomas L. (ed.), *Hard Power, Soft Power and the Future of Transatlantic Relations* (Aldershot, 2006)

Iriye, Akira, *Cultural Internationalism and World Order* (Baltimore, 1997)

—— *The Cambridge History of American Foreign Relations*, iii: *The Globalizing of America 1913–1945* (Cambridge, 1993)

Jackman, Jarrell and Carla Borden (eds), *The Muses Flee Hitler: Cultural Transfer and Adaptation* (Washington DC, 1983)

Jackson, Julian, *The Politics of Depression in France, 1932–1936* (Cambridge, 1985)

—— *The Popular Front in France: Defending Democracy, 1934–1938* (Cambridge, 1988)

Jäger, Lorenz, *Adorno: A Political Biography* (Oxford, 2004)

Jarausch, Konrad H., *After Hitler: Recivilizing Germans, 1945–1995* (Oxford, 2006)

Jarvie, Ian, *Hollywood's Overseas Campaign: The North Atlantic Movie Trade, 1920–1950* (Cambridge, 1992)

Jay Martin, *The Dialectical Imagination: A History of the Frankfurt School of Social Research, 1923–1950* (Boston, 1973)

Jeffreys-Jones, Rhodri (ed.), *Eagle Against Empire: American Opposition to European Imperialism, 1914–1982* (Aix-en-Provence, 1983)

Jennings, Charles, *Them and Us: The American Invasion of British High Society* (Stroud, 2007)

Joll, James, *Europe Since 1870: An International History* (London, 1976)

Jones, Howard, *'A New Kind of War': America's Global Strategy and the Truman Doctrine in Greece* (New York, 1989)

Jones, Maldwyn A., *The Limits of Liberty: American History, 1607–1980* (Oxford, 1983)

Judis, J. B., *Grand Illusion: Critics and Champions of the American Century* (New York, 1992)

Judt, Tony, *Postwar: A History of Europe since 1945* (London, 2005)

Kagan, Donald and Frederick W. Kagan, *While America Sleeps: Self-Delusion, Military Weakness and the Threat to Peace Today* (New York, 2000)

Kanigel, Robert, *The One Best Way: Frederick Winslow Taylor and the Enigma of Efficiency* (London, 1997)

Kaplan, Amy and Donald E. Pease (eds), *Cultures of United States Imperialism* (Durham, NC and London, 1993)

Kasson, Joy S., *Buffalo Bill's Wild West: Celebrity, Memory and Popular History* (New York, 2000)

Kater, Michael H., *Different Drummers: Jazz in the Culture of Nazi Germany* (Oxford, 1992)

Kazin, Michael and Joseph A. McCartin (eds) *Americanism: New Perspectives on the History of an Ideal* (Chapel Hill, NC, 2006)

Kedward, H. R. and Nancy Wood (eds), *The Liberation of France: Image and Event* (Oxford, 1995)

Kelly, Michael, *The Cultural and Intellectual Rebuilding of France after the Second World War* (London, 2004)

Kennan, George, *Russia and the West under Lenin and Stalin* (New York, 1960)

Kennedy, Paul, *The Rise and Fall of the Great Powers: Economic Change and Military Conflict, 1500 to 2000* (New York, 1987)

Kent, Donald Peterson, *The Refugee Intellectual: The Americanization of the Immigrants, 1933–1941* (New York, 1953)

Kershaw, Ian, *Hitler, 1889–1936: Hubris* (London, 1998)

Keyserlingk, Robert H., *Austria in World War II: An Anglo-American Dilemma* (Kingston and Montreal, 1988)

Kimball, Warren F., *The Juggler: Franklin Roosevelt as Wartime Statesman* (Princeton, 1991)

—— *The Most Unsordid Act: Lend-Lease, 1939–1945* (Baltimore, 1969)

—— (ed.), *America Unbound: World War II and the Making of a Superpower* (New York, 1992)

Kipping, Matthias and Ove Bjarnar (eds), *The Americanisation of European Business: The Marshall Plan and the Transfer of US Management Models* (London, 1998)

Kissinger, Henry A., *Diplomacy* (London, 1995)

Knoles, George Harmon, *The Jazz Age Revisited: British Criticism of American Civilization During the 1920s* (Stanford, 1955)

Koht, Haldvan, *The American Spirit in Europe: A Survey of Transatlantic Influences* (Oslo, 1949)

Koppes, Clayton R. and Gregory D. Black, *Hollywood Goes to War: How Politics, Profits and Propaganda Shaped World War II Movies* (Berkeley, 1987)

Kramnick, Isaac and Barry Sheerman, *Harold Laski: A Life on the Left* (London, 1993)

Kroes, Rob, *If You've Seen One You've Seen the Mall: Europeans and American Mass Culture* (Urbana and Chicago, 1996)

—— (ed.), *Nineteen Eighty-Four and the Apocalyptic Imagination in America* (Amsterdam, 1985)

—— et al. (eds), *Cultural Transmissions and Receptions: American Mass Culture in Europe* (Amsterdam, 1993)

Kruger, Barbara and Phil Marlani (eds), *Remaking History* (Seattle, 1989)

Krusen, William A., *Flying the Andes: The Story of Pan American Grace Airways and Commercial Aviation in Latin America* (Tampa, Fla., 1997)

Kuisel, Richard, *Capitalism and the State in Modern France* (Cambridge, 1981)

—— *Ernest Mercier, French Technocrat* (Berkeley, 1967)

—— *Seducing the French: The Dilemma of Americanization* (Berkeley, 1993)

Kynaston, David, *Austerity Britain, 1945–51* (London, 2008)

Labohm, Hans H. J. (ed.), *The Fiftieth Anniversary of the Marshall Plan in Retrospect and Prospect*, Report of the Seminar organized by the Clingendael Institute (The Hague, May 1997)

Lacorne, Denis, Jacques Rupnik, and Marie-France Toinet (eds), *L'Amérique dans les Têtes: Un Siècle de Fascinations et d'Aversions* (Paris, 1986)

Lacouture, Jean, *De Gaulle: The Rebel, 1890–1944* (London, 1990)

LaFeber, Walter, *Michael Jordan and the New Global Capitalism* (New York, 1999)

—— Richard Plenberg, and Nancy Woloch, *The American Century: A History of the United States Since the 1890s* (6th edn, Armonk, NY, 2008)

Lanaro, Silvio, *Storia dell'Italia repubblicana* (1992 edn repr., Padua, 2001)

Langer, William L. and S. Everett Gleason, *The Challenge to Isolation, 1937–1940* (New York, 1952)

Lasch, Christopher, *The True and Only Heaven: Progress and its Critics* (New York, 1991)

Latham, Michael E., *The Right Kind of Revolution: Modernization, Development and U.S. Foreign Policy from the Cold War to the Present* (Ithaca, 2011)

Le Gloannec, Anne-Marie, *Berlin et le monde: Les timides audaces d'una nation réunifiée* (Paris, 2007)

——and Aleksander Smolar (eds), *Entre Kant et Kosovo: Études offertes à Pierre Hassner* (Paris, 2003)

LeMahieu, D. L., *A Culture for Democracy: Mass Communication and the Cultivated Mind in Britain Between the Wars* (Oxford, 1988)

Leventhal, Fred M. and Roland Quinault (eds), *Anglo-American Attitudes: From Revolution to Partnership* (Aldershot, 2000)

Levy, Carl and Mark Roseman (eds), *Three Postwar Eras in Comparison: Western Europe 1918–1945–1989* (London, 2002)

Livy, Roger, *Rotary International in Great Britain and Ireland* (Plymouth, 1978)

Looseley, David L., *The Politics of Fun: Cultural Policy and Debate in Contemporary France* (Oxford, 1995)

Lord, Walter, *The Good Years: From 1900 to the First World War* (New York, 1960)

Louis, William Roger, *Imperialism at Bay: The United States and the Decolonization of the British Empire, 1941–1945* (Oxford, 1977)

Low, Rachel, *The History of the British Film, 1918–1929* (London, 1971)

Lundestad, Geir, *'Empire' by Integration: The United States and European Integration, 1945–1997* (Oxford, 1998)

Lyttelton, Adrian (ed.), *Liberal and Fascist Italy, 1900–1945* (Oxford, 2002)

McCarthy, Patrick, *Language, Politics and Writing* (London, 2002)

——(ed.), *Italy since 1945* (Oxford, 2000)

Macdonald, Ian, *Revolution in the Head: The Beatles' Records and the Sixties* (London, 1995)

McKenzie, Brian A., *Remaking France: Americanization, Public Diplomacy, and the Marshall Plan* (New York, 2005)

McKercher, B. J. C., *Anglo-American Relations in the 1920s: The Struggle for Supremacy* (London, 1991)

McKibbin, Ross, *Classes and Cultures: England 1918–1951* (Oxford, 1998)

McLuhan, Marshall, *Understanding Media: The Extensions of Man* (New York, 1964)

Macpherson, James M., *Battle Cry of Freedom: The Civil War Era* (New York, 1988)

Madison, James H. (ed.), *Wendell Willkie: Hoosier Internationalist* (Bloomington, 1992)

Maier, Charles S., *Recasting Bourgeois Europe* (Princeton, 1975)

Mamatey, Victor S., *The United States and East Central Europe 1914–1918: A Study in Wilsonian Diplomacy and Propaganda* (Princeton, 1957)

Mann, William J., *Edge of Midnight: The Life of John Schlesinger* (London, 2004)

Mariano, Marco (ed.), *Defining the Atlantic Community: Culture, Intellectuals and Policies in the Mid-Twentieth Century* (London, 2010)

Marie, Michel, *The French New Wave: An Artistic School* (Oxford, 2003)

Marjolin, Robert, *Architect of European Unity: Memoirs, 1911–1986* (London, 1989)

Marrison, Andrew (ed.), *Free Trade and its Reception, 1815–1960* (London, 1998)

Marsh, David, *Postwar British Politics in Perspective* (Cambridge, 1999)

Marshall, Jonathan, *To Have and To Have Not: Southeast Asian Raw Materials and the Origins of the Pacific War* (Berkeley, 1995)

Martel, Frédéric, *Mainstream: Enquête sur cette culture qui plaît à tout le monde* (Paris, 2010)

Martinelli, Alberto (ed.), *Transatlantic Divide: Comparing American and European Society* (Oxford, 2007)

Marwick, Arthur, *British Society since 1945* (3rd edn, London, 1996)

—— *The Sixties: Cultural Revolution in Britain, France, Italy and the United States, c.1958–c.1974* (Oxford, 1998)

Mastny, Vojtech, *The Cold War and Soviet Insecurity: The Stalin Years* (Oxford, 1996)

May, Ernest R., *Imperial Democracy: The Emergence of America as a Great Power* (New York, 1961)

May, Lary, *Screening Out the Past: The Birth of Mass Culture and the Motion Picture Industry* (Oxford, 1980)

—— *The Big Tomorrow: Hollywood and the Politics of the American Way* (Chicago, 2000)

Mazlish, Bruce et al. (eds), *The Paradox of a Global USA* (Stanford, 2007)

Mazower, Mark, *Dark Continent: Europe's Twentieth Century* (London, 1999)

Mead, Robert O., *Atlantic Legacy: Essays in American–European Cultural History* (New York, 1969)

Menges, Constantine C. (ed.), *The Marshall Plan From Those Who Made it Succeed* (Lanham, Md., 1999)

Merkl, Peter H. (ed.), *The Federal Republic at Forty* (New York, 1989)

Merkle, Judith A., *Management and Ideology: The Legacy of the International Scientific Management Movement* (Berkeley, 1980)

Merritt, Richard L., *Democracy Imposed: U.S. Occupation Policy and the German Public, 1945–1949* (New Haven, Conn., 1995)

Migone, Gian Giacomo, *Gli Stati Uniti e il fascismo: alle origini dell'egemonia americana in Italia* (Milan, 1980)

Miles, Peter and Malcolm Smith, *Cinema, Literature and Society: Elite and Mass Culture in Inter-War Britain* (London, 1987)

Miller, James Edward, *The United States and Italy, 1940–1950: The Politics and Diplomacy of Stabilization* (Chapel Hill, NC, 1986)

—— *The United States and the Making of Modern Greece: History and Power, 1950–1974* (Chapel Hill, NC, 2009)

Milward, Alan S., *The European Rescue of the Nation State* (2nd edn, London, 2000)

—— *The Reconstruction of Western Europe, 1945–1951* (London, 1984)

Minden, Michael and Holger Bachmann (eds), *Fritz Lang's Metropolis: Cinematic Visions of Technology and Fear* (New York, 2000)

Minnen, Cornelis A. van and John F. Sears (eds), *FDR and His Contemporaries: Foreign Perceptions of an American President* (New York, 1992)

Monod, David, *Settling Scores: German Music, Denazification, and the Americans, 1945–1953* (Chapel Hill, NC, 2005)

Moore, R. Laurence, *European Socialists and the American Promised Land* (New York, 1970)

——and Maurizio Vaudagna (eds), *The American Century in Europe* (Ithaca, 2003)

Morgan, Ted, *A Covert Life: Jay Lovestone, Communist, Anti-Communist and Spymaster* (New York, 1999)

Moser, John E., *Twisting the Lion's Tail: Anglophobia in the United States, 1921–1948* (London, 1999)

Müller, Jan-Werner, *Contesting Democracy: Political Ideas in Twentieth Century Europe* (New Haven, Conn., 2011)

Muscio, Giuliana, *Hollywood's New Deal* (Philadelphia, 1997)

Nacci, Michela, *La barbarie del comfort: Il modello di vita americano nella cultura francese del '900* (Milan, 1996)

——*L'antiamericanismo in Italia negli anni trenta* (Milan, 1989)

Negra, Diane (ed.), *The Irish In Us: Irishness, Performativity and Popular Culture* (Durham, NC, 2006)

Ninkovich, Frank, *Modernity and Power: A History of the Domino Theory in the Twentieth Century* (Chicago, 1994)

——*The United States and Imperialism* (Oxford, 2001)

Nolan, Mary, *Visions of Modernity: American Business and the Modernization of Germany* (New York, 1994)

Nord, Philip, *France's New Deal: From the Thirties to the Postwar Era* (Princeton, 2010)

Nowell-Smith, Geoffrey and S. Ricci (eds), *Hollywood and Europe: Economics, Culture, National Identity, 1945–95* (London, 1998)

Nye Jr, Joseph S., *Soft Power: The Means to Success in World Politics* (New York, 2004)

O'Connor, Brendan (ed.), *Anti-Americanism: History, Causes, Themes*, 4 vols (Oxford, 2007)

Offe, Claus, *Reflections on America: Tocqueville, Weber and Adorno in the United States* (Cambridge, 2005)

Oldenziel, Ruth and Karin Zachmann (eds), *Cold War Kitchen: Americanization, Technology, and European Users* (Cambridge, Mass., 2009)

Ory, Pascal, *L'avventure culturelle française, 1945–1989* (Paris, 1989)

Osgerby, Bill, *Youth in Britain since 1945* (Oxford, 1998)

Overy, R. J., *The Inter-War Crisis, 1919–1939* (London, 1994)

——*War and Economy in the Third Reich* (Oxford, 1994)

Panchisi, Roxanne, *Future Tense: The Culture of Anticipation in France Between the Wars* (Ithaca, 2009)

Pardo, Alejandro, *The Europe–Hollywood Coopetition: Cooperation and Competition in the Global Film Industry* (Pamplona, 2007)

Parks, J. D., *Culture, Conflict and Coexistence: American–Soviet Cultural Relations, 1917–1958* (Jefferson, NC, 1983)

Passerini, Luisa (ed.), *Across the Atlantic: Cultural Exchanges between Europe and the United States* (Brussels, 2000)

Pelling, Henry, *America and the British Left: From Bright to Bevan* (London, 1956)

Pells, Richard, *Not Like Us: How Europeans Have Loved, Hated and Transformed American Culture since World War II* (New York, 1997)

Perez Jr, Louis A., *The War of 1898* (Chapel Hill, NC, 1998)

Perkins, Bradford, *The Great Rapprochement: England and the United States, 1895–1914* (New York, 1968)

Pick, Hella, *Guilty Victim: Austria from the Holocaust to Haider* (London, 2000)

Pinelli, Federica and Marco Mariano, *Europa e Stati Uniti secondo il 'New York Times': La corrispondenza estera di Anne O'Hare McCormick, 1920–1954* (Turin, 2000)

Pisani, Sallie, *The CIA and the Marshall Plan* (Lawrence, Kan., 1991)

Poli, Emanuela, *Forza Italia: Strutture, leadership e radicamento territoriale* (Bologna, 2001)

Pommerin, Reiner (ed.), *The American Impact on Postwar Germany* (Providence and Oxford, 1995)

Popper, Karl, *Unended Quest: An Intellectual Autobiography* (London, 1976)

Porter, Bernard, *The Lion's Share: A Short History of British Imperialism, 1850–1970* (London, 1975)

Portes, Jacques, *De la scène à l'écran: Naissance de la culture de masse aux Etats-Unis* (Paris, 1997)

——*Fascinations and Misgivings: The United States in French Opinion, 1870–1914* (Cambridge, 2000)

Porzio, Maria, *Arrivano gli Alleati! Amori e violenze nell'Italia liberata* (Bari, 2011)

Prendergast, Mark, *For God, Country and Coca-Cola* (London, 1994)

Pringle, Henry F., *Theodore Roosevelt: A Biography* (New York, 1931)

Puttnam, David, *The Undeclared War: The Struggle for the Control of the World's Film Industry* (London, 1997)

Range, Willard, *Franklin D. Roosevelt's World Order* (Athens, Ga., 1959)

Reisman, David, *Crosland's Future: Opportunity and Outcome* (Basingstoke, 1997)

Reitzel, William, *The Mediterranean: Its Role in American Foreign Policy* (New York, 1948)

Reynolds, David, *From Munich to Pearl Harbour: Roosevelt's America and the Origins of the Second World War* (Chicago, 2001)

——*From World War to Cold War: Churchill, Roosevelt and the International History of the 1940s* (Oxford, 2006)

——*Rich Relations: The American Occupation of Britain, 1942–1945* (London, 1995)

——et al. (eds), *Allies at War: The Soviet, American and British Experience* (New York, 1994)

Richards, Jeffrey, *The Age of the Dream Palace: Cinema and Society in Britain 1930–1939* (2nd edn, London, 2009)

Richards, Jeffrey and Dorothy Sheridan (eds), *Mass Observation at the Movies* (London, 1987)

Rioux, J. P., *The Fourth Republic, 1944–1958* (Cambridge, 1987)

Ritzer, George, *The McDonaldization of Society* (Thousand Oaks, Calif., 1996)

Rodgers, Daniel T., *Atlantic Crossings: Social Politics in a Progressive Age* (Cambridge, Mass., 1998)

Roger, Philippe, *L'ennemi américain: Généalogie de l'anti-americanisme français* (Paris, 2002), *The American Enemy: The History of French Anti-Americanism*, English language edition (Chicago, 2005)

Romero, Federico, *Gli Stati Uniti e il sindacalismo europeo, 1944–1951* (Rome, 1989)

Rosenberg, Emily S., *Financial Missionaries to the World: The Politics and Culture of Dollar Diplomacy, 1900–1930* (Cambridge, Mass., 1999)

——*Spreading the American Dream: American Economic and Cultural Expansion, 1890–1945* (New York, 1982)

Rose, Norman, *The Cliveden Set: Portrait of an Exclusive Fraternity* (London, 2000)

Rose, Phyllis, *Jazz Cleopatra: Josephine Baker in Her Time* (London, 1991)

Rossides, Eugene T. (ed.), *The Truman Doctrine of Aid to Greece: A Fifty Year Retrospective* (New York and Washington DC, 1998)

Rossini, Daniela, *Il mito americano nell'Italia della Grande guerra* (Bari, 2000)

Rostow, Walt Whitman, *The World Economy: History and Prospect* (London, 1978)

Rowland, Benjamin M. (ed.), *Balance of Power or Hegemony: The Interwar Monetary System* (New York, 1976)

Rubin, Barry, *The Great Powers in the Middle East, 1941–1947* (London, 1980)

Rupert, Mark, *Producing Hegemony: The Politics of Mass Production and American Global Power* (Cambridge, 1995)

Ryall, Tom, *Britain and the American Cinema* (London, 2000)

Ryan, Deborah S., *The Daily Mail Ideal Home Exhibition: The Ideal Home Through the Twentieth Century* (London, 1997)

Rydell, Robert W., *All the World's a Fair: Visions of Empire at American International Expositions, 1876–1916* (Chicago, 1984)

——and Nancy Gwinn (eds), *Fair Representations: World's Fairs and the Modern World* (Amsterdam, 1994)

——and Rob Kroes, *Buffalo Bill in Bologna: The Americanization of the World, 1869–1922* (Chicago, 2005)

Santoro, Carlo Maria, *Diffidence and Ambition: The Intellectual Sources of U.S. Foreign Policy* (Boulder, Colo., 1992)

Saul, Norman E., *The United States and Russia, 1914–1921* (Kansas City, 2001)

Saunders, Thomas J., *Hollywood in Berlin: American Cinema and Weimar Germany* (Berkeley, 1994)

Savage, Jon, *Teenage: The Creation of Youth Culture* (London, 2007)

Scalfari, Eugenio, *L'autunno della Repubblica* (Milan, 1969)

Schain, Martin (ed.), *The Marshall Plan: Fifty Years After* (New York, 2001)

Schissler, Hanna (ed.), *The Miracle Years: A Cultural History of West Germany, 1949–1968* (Princeton, 2001)

Schmitt, Hans A. (ed.), *U.S. Occupation in Europe after World War II* (Lawrence, Kan., 1978)

Schmitz, David F. and Richard D. Challener (eds), *Appeasement in Europe: A Reassessment of U.S. Policies* (Westport, Conn., 1990)

Schröder, Hans-Jürgen (ed.), *Confrontation and Cooperation: Germany and the United States in the Era of World War I, 1900–1924* (Providence and Oxford, 1993)

Scoppola, Pietro, *La repubblica dei partiti: Profilo storico della democrazia in Italia, 1945–1990* (Bologna, 1991)

Scott-Smith, G. and H. Krabbendam (eds), *The Cultural Cold War in Western Europe, 1945–1960* (London, 2003)

Selling Democracy: Films of the Marshall Plan, 1947–1955, Berlin International Film Festival (Berlin, 2004)

Skard, Sigmund, *The American Myth and the European Mind: American Studies in Europe 1776–1960* (Philadelphia, 1961)

Skidelsky, Robert, *John Maynard Keynes*, ii: *The Economist as Saviour, 1920–1937* (London, 1992), iii: *Fighting for Freedom, 1937–1946* (London, 2000)

—— *Keynes* (Oxford, 1996)

Sklar, Robert, *Film: An International History of the Medium* (London, 1993)

Slater, David and Peter J. Taylor (eds), *The American Century: Consensus and Coercion in the Projection of American Power* (Oxford, 1999)

Smith, David C., *H. G. Wells: Desperately Mortal: A Biography* (New Haven, Conn., 1986)

Smith, Tony, *America's Mission: The United States and the Worldwide Struggle for Democracy in the Twentieth Century* (Princeton, 1994)

Snyder, David J., *United States Diplomacy in the New Netherlands, 1948–1958*, PhD thesis, Southern Illinois University (Carbondale, 2006)

Sorensen, Viebeke, *Social Democratic Government in Denmark under the Marshall Plan, 1947–1950*, PhD thesis, European University Institute (Florence, 1987)

Sorlin, Pierre, *Europe Cinemas, European Societies* (London, 1991)

Spagnolo, Carlo, *La stabilizzazione incompiuta: Il piano Marshall in Italia (1947–1952)* (Rome, 2001)

Stafford, David, *Endgame 1945: Victory, Retribution, Liberation* (London, 2007)

—— *Roosevelt and Churchill: Men of Secrets* (London, 2000)

Stearns, Peter N. (ed.), *Oxford Encyclopedia of the Modern World*, v (New York, 2008), s.v. 'Modernity', 'Modernization'

Stephan, Alexander, *Anti-Americanism in Contemporary Europe* (New York, 2004)

—— (ed.), *Americanization and Anti-Americanism: The German Encounter with American Culture after 1945* (New York, 2005)

—— (ed.), *The Americanization of Europe: Culture, Diplomacy and Anti-Americanism after 1945* (New York, 2006)

Stephanson, Anders, *Manifest Destiny: American Expansionism and the Empire of Right* (New York, 1995)

Stirk, P. M. R., *A History of European Integration since 1914* (London, 1994)

Stokes, Melvyn and Richard Maltby (eds), *Hollywood spectatorship: Changing perceptions of cinema audiences* (London, 2001)

Stoler, Mark A., *Allies and Adversaries: The Joint Chiefs of Staff, the Grand Alliance and U.S. Strategy in World War II* (Chapel Hill, NC, 2000)

Strange, Susan, *States and Markets* (2nd edn, London, 1994)

Strasser, Susan et al. (eds), *Getting and Spending: European and American Consumer Societies in the Twentieth Century* (Washington DC, 1998)

Strauss, David, *Menace in the West: The Rise of French Anti-Americanism* (Westport, Conn., 1978)

Susman, Warren, *Culture as History: The Transformation of American Society in the Twentieth Century* (Washington DC, 2003)

Sutton, Anthony C., *Western Technology and Soviet Economic Development*, i: *1917–1930* (Stanford, 1968), ii: *1930–1945* (Stanford, 1971)

Swett, Pamela E. et al. (eds), *Selling Modernity: Advertising in Twentieth-Century Germany* (Durham, NC, 2007)

Taylor, A. J. P., *Beaverbrook* (London, 1972)

—— *The Struggle for Mastery in Europe, 1848–1918* (1954 edn repr., Oxford, 1971)

Tent, James F., *Mission on the Rhine: Reeducation and Denazification in American-Occupied Germany* (Chicago, 1982)

Thompson, Kristin, *Exporting Entertainment: America in the World Film Market, 1907–1934* (London, 1985)

Thorne, Christopher, *Allies of a Kind: The United States, Britain and the War Against Japan, 1941–1945* (London, 1978)

—— *The Issue of War: States, Societies and the Far Eastern Conflict of 1941–1945* (London, 1985)

Touchard, Jean, *Le gaullisme* (Paris, 1978)

Traxler, David A., *1898* (New York, 1998)

Trumpbour, John, *Selling Hollywood to the World: U.S. and European Struggles for Mastery of the Global Film Industry, 1920–1950* (Cambridge, 2002)

Tulloch, H., *James Bryce's 'American Commonwealth': The Anglo-American Background* (London, 1988)

Ulff-Møller, Jens, *Hollywood's Film Wars with France: Film Trade Diplomacy and the Emergence of the French Film Quota Policy* (Rochester, 2001)

Valladão, Alfred G. A., *The Twenty-First Century will be American* (London, 1996)

Vann Woodward, C., *The Old World's New World* (New York, 1991)

Vasey, Ruth, *The World According to Hollywood, 1918–1939* (Exeter, 1997)

Vickers, Rhiannon, *Manipulating Hegemony: State Power, Labour and the Marshall Plan in Britain* (Basingstoke, 2000)

Vidal, Gore, *Hollywood* (London, 1989)

—— *Williwaw* (London, 1970)

Vivarelli, Roberto, *Il dopoguerra in Italia e l'avvento del Fascismo (1918–1922)* (Naples, 1967)

Wagnleitner, Reinhold, *Coca-Colonization and the Cold War: The Cultural Mission of the United States in Austria after the Second World War* (Chapel Hill, NC, 1994)

——and Elaine Tyler May (eds), '*Here, There and Everywhere*': *The Foreign Politics of American Popular Culture* (Hanover, NH and London, 2000)

Wall, Irwin, *The United States and the Making of Postwar France, 1945–1954* (Cambridge, 1991)

Watt, Donald Cameron, *How War Came: The Immediate Origins of the Second World War, 1938–1939* (New York, 1989)

——*Succeeding John Bull: America in Britain's Place, 1900–1975* (Cambridge, 1984)

——(ed.), *Personalities and Policies: Studies in the Formation of British Foreign Policy in the Twentieth Century* (London, 1965)

Weber, Eugen, *The Hollow Years: France in the 1930s* (New York, 1996)

Weidenfeld, Werner, *America and Europe: Is the Break Inevitable?* (Gütersloh, 1996)

Weight, Richard, *Patriots: National Identity in Britain, 1940–2000* (London, 2003)

Welky, David, *The Moguls and the Dictators: Hollywood and the Coming of World War II* (Baltimore, 2008)

West, Anthony, *H. G. Wells: Aspects of a Life* (London, 1984)

Wexler, Imanuel, *The Marshall Plan Revisited: The European Recovery Program in Economic Perspective* (Westport, Conn., 1983)

Whelan, Bernadette, *Ireland and the Marshall Plan, 1947–57* (Dublin, 2000)

Wiener, Joel H. and Mark Hampton (eds), *Anglo-American Media Interactions, 1850–2000* (London, 2007)

Wightman, Richard and T. J. Jackson Lears (eds), *The Culture of Consumption: Critical Essays in American History, 1880–1980* (New York, 1983)

Wilkins, Mira and Frank Ernest Hill, *American Business Abroad: Ford on Six Continents* (Detroit, 1964)

Willett, Ralph, *The Americanization of Germany, 1945–1949* (London, 1989)

Wills, Clair, *That Neutral Island: A Cultural History of Ireland During the Second World War* (London, 2007)

Wilson, Joan Hoff, *American Business and Foreign Policy, 1920–1933* (Lexington, 1971)

Woodford, Chris, *The Internet: A Historical Encyclopedia*, ii: *Issues* (Santa Barbara, 2005)

Woolner, David B. et al. (eds), *FDR's World: War, Peace and Legacies* (London, 2008)

Yonnet, Paul, *Jeux, Modes et Masses: La société française et le moderne, 1945–1985* (Paris, 1985)

Zamagni, Vera, *Dalla periferia al centro: La seconda rinascita economica dell'Italia, 1861–1990* (Bologna, 1990; 2nd edn, Bologna, 1993)

Zink, Harold, *The United States in Germany, 1945–1955* (Princeton, 1957)

Zunz, Olivier, *Why the American Century?* (Chicago, 1998)

Articles

Adas, Michael, 'Modernization Theory and the American Revival of the Scientific and Technological Standards of Social Achievement and Human Worth', in Engerman et al. (eds), *Staging Growth*

Allum, Percy, 'Italian Society Transformed', in McCarthy (ed.), *Italy since 1945*

—— 'The South and National Politics, 1945–50', in S. J. Woolf (ed.), *The Rebirth of Italy, 1943–50* (London, 1972)

Apeldoorn, E. Bastiaan van, 'The Political Economy of European Integration: Transantional Social Forces in the Making of Europe's Socio-Economic Order', in Richard Stubbs and Geoffrey R. D. Underhill (eds), *Political Economy and the Changing Global Order* (Don Mills, Ontario, 2000)

Armus, Seth D., 'The Eternal Enemy: Emmanuel Mounier's *Esprit* and French Anti-Americanism', *French Historical Studies* (Spring 2001)

Arnstein, Walter L., 'Queen Victoria and the United States', in Leventhal and Quinault (eds), *Anglo-American Attitudes*

Auletta, Ken, 'Searching for Trouble', *The New Yorker* (12 October 2009)

Bakker, Gerben, 'America's Master: The Decline and Fall of the European Film Industry in the United States (1907–1920)', in Passerini (ed.), *Across the Atlantic*

Balfour, Sebastian, 'The Loss of Empire, Regenerationism, and the Forging of a Myth of National Identity', in Graham and Labanyi (eds), *Spanish Cultural Studies*

Barbezat, Daniel, 'The Marshall Plan and the Origin of the OEEC', in OECD, *Explorations*

Barisione, Mauro, 'La campagna presidenziale e l'offerta simbolica del leader', in Baldini and Lazar (eds), *La Francia di Sarkozy*

Barzini Jr, Luigi, 'From Italy', in Joseph (ed.), *As Others See Us*

Bauer, Ingrid, 'Americanizing/Westernizing Austrian Women: Three Scenarios from the 1950s to the 1970s', in Bischof and Pelinka (eds), *Contemporary Austrian Studies*, vol. xii

—— '"Austria's Prestige Dragged into the Dirt"? The "GI-Brides" and Postwar Austrian Society (1945–1955)', in Bischof, Pelinka, and Thurner (eds), *Contemporary Austrian Studies*, vol. vi

—— '"The GI Bride": On the (De)Construction of an Austrian Postwar Stereotype', in Duchen and Bandhauer-Schöffmann (eds), *When the War Was Over*

Baxendale, John, '"I Had Seen a Lot of Englands": J. B. Priestley, Englishness and the People', *History Workshop Journal* (Spring 2001)

Becker, Ron, '"Hear-and-See" Radio in the World of Tomorrow: RCA and the Presentation of Television at the World's Fair, 1939–1940', *Historical Journal of Film, Radio and Television* (October 2001)

Bell, Peter, 'The Foreign Office and the 1939 Royal Visit to America: Courting the USA in an Era of Isolationism', *Journal of Contemporary History* (October 2002)

Belmonte, Thomas, 'The Contradictions of Italian–American identity: An Anthropologist's Personal View', in Pellegrino D'Acierno (ed.), *The Italian–American Heritage: A Companion to Literature and Arts* (New York, 1999)

Benson, George C. S., 'American Military Government in Austria, May 1945–February 1946', in Friedrich et al. (eds), *American Experiences*

——and Maurice Neufeld, 'American Military Government in Italy', in Friedrich et al. (eds), *American Experiences*

Berger, Stefan, 'The Attempt at Democratization under Weimar', in Garrard, Tolz, and White

Berghahn, Volker R., 'Philanthropy and Diplomacy in the "American Century"', in Hogan (ed.), *Ambiguous Legacy*

——'Recasting Bourgeois Germany', in Schissler (ed.), *Miracle Years*

——'The Debate on "Americanization" Among Economic and Cultural Historians', *Cold War History* (February 2010)

Bergmann, Peter, 'The Specter of *Amerikanisierung*, 1880–1940', in Epitropoulos and Roudometof (eds), *American Culture in Europe*

Betts, Paul, 'The New Fascination with Fascism: The Case of Nazi Modernism', *Journal of Contemporary History* (October 2002)

——and David Crowley, 'Introduction', *Journal of Contemporary History* (April 2005), Special Issue: 'Domestic Dreamworlds: Notions of Home in Post-1945 Europe'

Bischof, Günter, 'Austria—a Colony in the U.S. Postwar "Empire"?', in John G. Blair and Reinhold Wagnleitner (eds), *Empire: American Studies* (Tübingen, 1997)

——' "Conquering the Foreigner": The Marshall Plan and the Revival of Postwar Austrian Tourism', in Bischof, Pelinka, and Stiefel (eds), *Contemporary Austrian Studies*, vol. viii

——'Two Sides of the Coin: The Americanization of Austria and Austrian Anti-Americanism', in Stephan (ed.), *Americanization of Europe*

Bjork, Ulf Jonas, ' "It's Better to Steal the Idea": Swedish Television Copies Programs from America, 1957–1969', *Historical Journal of Film, Radio and Television* (June 2009)

Björkin, Mats, 'European Television Audiences: Localising the Viewers', in Bignell and Fickers (eds), *European Television History*

Black, Lawrence, 'Whose Finger on the Button? Cultural Control versus Free Choice, Labour and the Politics of TV in the 1950s and 1960s', paper delivered at the conference *Governing Television? Politics and TV in Europe, 1945–1975*, University of Bologna (Bologna, May 2004)

Blair, John G., 'First Steps toward Globalization: Nineteenth-Century Exports of American Entertainment Forms', in Wagnleitner and May (eds), *'Here, There and Everywhere'*

Blanck, Dag, 'Television, Education, and the Vietnam War: Sweden and the United States During the Postwar Era', in Stephan (ed.), *Americanization of Europe*

Bondebjerg, Ib et al., 'American Television: Point of Reference or European Nightmare?', in Bignell and Fickers (eds), *European Television History*

Bossuat, Gérard, 'The Modernisation of France: A New Economic and Social Order after the Second World War?', in Geppert (ed.), *Postwar Challenge*

Boulat, Régis, 'Jean Fourastié ou le prophète repenti', *Vingtième Siècle* (July–September 2006)

Bourdon, Jérôme, 'Self-Inflicted Imperialism as Early "Global Culture"? The Early Americanisation of European Televisions', unpublished ms

Braun, Emily, 'The Visual Arts: Modernism and Fascism', in Lyttelton (ed.), *Liberal and Fascist Italy*

Braunthal, Gerard, 'The Anglo-Saxon Model of Democracy in the West German Political Consciousness after World War II', *Archiv für Sozialgeschichte*, 18 (1978)

Breit, Peter K., 'Culture as Authority: American and German Transactions', in Pommerin (ed.), *American Impact*

Breitenborn, Uwe, '"Memphis Tennessee" in Borstendorf: Boundaries Set and Transcended in East German Television Entertainment', *Historical Journal of Film, Radio and Television* (August 2004)

Brizzi, Riccardo, 'La televisione in Italia e Francia tra storia dei consumi e storia politica', in Cavazza and Scarpellini (eds), *La rivoluzione dei consumi*

Brooke, Stephen, 'Atlantic Crossing? American Views of Capitalism and British Socialist Thought, 1932–1962', in *Twentieth Century British History*, 2/2 (1991)

Brunetta, Gian Piero, 'Cinecittà', in Victoria de Grazia and Sergio Luzzatto (eds), *Dizionario del Fascismo*, i (Torino, 2002)

—— 'Cinema', in Victoria de Grazia and Sergio Luzzatto (eds), *Dizionario del Fascismo*, i (Torino, 2002)

Bruti Liberati, Luigi, 'Witch-Hunts and Corriere della Sera: A Conservative Perception of American Political values in Cold War Italy: The 1950s', in Tobia (ed.), *Cold War History*, Special Issue, 'Europe Americanized?' (February 2011)

Buchsbaum, Jonathan, "'The *Exception Culturelle* is Dead." Long Live Cultural Diversity: French Cinema and the New Resistance', *Framework* (Spring, 2006)

Bukey, Evan B., 'Between Stalingrad and the Night of the Generals: Popular Opinion in the "Danube and Alpine Regions"', in William E. Wright (ed.), *Austria, 1938–1988: Anschluss and Fifty Years* (Riverside, Calif., 1995)

Bullivant, Keith and C. Jane Rice, 'Reconstruction and Integration: The Culture of West German Stabilization, 1945 to 1968', in Burns (ed.), *German Cultural Studies*

Bunzl, John, 'American Attitudes towards Austria and Austria-German relations since 1945', in David F. Good and Ruth Wodak (eds), *From World War to Waldheim: Culture and Politics in Austria and the United States* (New York, 1999)

Burk, Kathleen, 'Money and Power: America and Europe in the 20th Century', *History Today* (March 1993)

—— 'War and Anglo-American Financial Relations in the Twentieth Century', in Leventhal and Quinault (eds), *Anglo-American Attitudes*

Campbell, David, 'Contradictions of a Lone Superpower', in Slater and Taylor (eds), *American Century*

Camporesi, Valeria, ' "There are no kangaroos in Kent": The American "Model" and the Introduction of Commercial Television in Britain, 1940–1954', in Ellwood and Kroes (eds), *Hollywood in Europe*

Carroll, James, 'Messiah Nation: Religion and the American Idea', in Almqvist and Linklater (eds), *On the Idea of America*

Casanova, Pablo González, 'The Americanization of the World', in Slater and Taylor (eds), *American Century*

Castells, Manuel, 'Information Technology and Global Capitalism', in Giddens and Hutton (eds), *Global Capitalism*

Castillo, Greg, 'Domesticating the Cold War: Household Consumption as Propaganda in Marshall Plan Germany', in Betts and Crowley (eds), *Journal of Contemporary History* (April 2005), Special Issue: 'Domestic Dreamworlds: Notions of Home in Post-1945 Europe'

—— 'The American "Fat Kitchen" in Europe: Postwar Domestic Modernity and Marshall Plan Strategies of Enchantment', in Oldenziel and Zachmann (eds), *Cold War Kitchen*

Castronovo, Valerio, '1960: Il miracolo economico', in Gentile et al. (eds), *Novecento italiano*

Caughie, J., 'Broadcasting and Cinema: 1: Converging Histories', in Barr (ed.), *All Our Yesterdays*

Cavazza, Stefano, 'Dal consumo desiderato al consumo realizzato: L'avvento della società dei consumi nell'Italia postbellica', in Cavazza and Scarpellini (eds), *La rivoluzione dei consumi*

Cayrol, Roland, 'French Public Opinion and the Marshall Plan: The Communists and Others', in Schain (ed.), *Marshall Plan*

Chafer, Tony, 'African Perspectives: The Liberation of France and its Impact in French West Africa', in Kedward and Wood (eds), *Liberation of France*

Chaveau, Sophie, 'Il consumo di massa in Francia dopo il 1945', in Cavazza and Scalpellini (eds), *La rivoluzione dei consumi*

Chessel, Marie Emmanuel, 'From America to Europe: Educating Consumers', review essay, *Contemporary European History* (February 2002)

Chiesi, Antonio M., 'The Economic Sphere', in Martinelli (ed.), *Transatlantic Divide*

Church, R. A., 'The Effect of the American Export Invasion on the British Boot and Shoe Industry, 1885–1914', *Journal of Economic History* (June 1968)

Claeys, Gregory, 'Mass Culture and World Culture: On "Americanisation" and the Politics of Cultural Protectionism', *Diogenes*, 34/136 (1986)

Clavin, Patricia, 'Shaping the Lessons of History: Britain and the Rhetoric of American Trade Policy, 1930–1960', in Marrison (ed.), *Free Trade*

Cleveland, Harlan, 'The Marshall Plan: Reflections in Retrospect', in Labohm (ed.), *Fiftieth Anniversary*

Cleveland, Harold Van B., 'If There Had Been No Marshall Plan …', in Hoffmann and Maier (eds), *Marshall Plan*

—— 'The International Monetary System in the Interwar Period', in Rowland (ed.), *Balance of Power*

Cockburn, Alexander, 'The Two-Way Street', *The Guardian* (12 May 1995)

Colarizi, Simona, 'I partiti politici di fronte al cambiamento di costume', in Cardini (ed.), *Il miracolo economico italiano*

Cole, Wayne S., 'American Appeasement', in Schmitz and Challener (eds), *Appeasement in Europe*

Collins, Richard, 'Unity in Diversity? The European Single Market in Broadcasting and the Audiovisual, 1982–1992', *Journal of Common Market Studies* (March 1994)

Conway, Martin, 'The Rise and Fall of Western Europe's Democratic Age, 1945–1973', *Contemporary European History*, 13/1 (2004)

Crafts, N. F. R., 'The Golden Age of Economic Growth in Postwar Europe, 1950–1973', *Economic History Review* (August 1995)

Crapol, Edward P., 'From Anglophobia to Fragile Rapprochement: Anglo-American Relations in the Early Twentieth Century', in Schröder (ed.), *Confrontation and Cooperation*

Cristina Carbone, 'Staging the Kitchen Debate: How Splitnik Got Normalized in the United States', in Oldenziel and Zachmann (eds), *Cold War Kitchen*

Cromwell, William C., 'The Marshall Plan, Britain and the Cold War', *Review of International Studies* (October 1982)

Crouch, Colin, 'Continental Drift: Are European and American Societies Drifting Apart?', paper presented at the Europaeum Conference (Oxford, September 1994)

Cull, Nicholas J., 'Speeding the Strange Death of American Public Diplomacy: The George H. W. Bush Administration and the U.S. Information Agency', *Diplomatic History* (January 2010)

Cullather, Nick, 'Development? It's History', *Diplomatic History* (Fall 2000)

Danan, Martine, 'Hollywood's Hegemonic Strategies: Overcoming French Nationalism with the Advent of Sound', in Higson and Maltby (eds), *'Film Europe' and 'Film America'*

Daniels, P. W., 'Overseas Investment by US Service Enterprises', in Slater and Taylor (eds), *American Century*

D'Attore, Pier Paolo, 'Sogno americano e mito sovietico nell'Italia contemporanea', in D'Attorre (ed.), *Nemici per la pelle*

De Felice, Franco, 'Introduzione', in Antonio Gramsci, *Americanismo e Fordismo* (Turin, 1978)

Dehousse, Renaud, 'La Francia e l'Europa: Continuità o rottura?', in Baldini and Lazar (eds), *La Francia di Sarkozy*

Deschamps, Bénédicte, 'Salvemini e gli intellettuali fuorusciti francesi negli Stati Uniti (1940–1944): Un'incontro mancato', in Patrizia Audenino (ed.), *Il prezzo della libertà: Gaetano Salvemini in esilio* (Soveria Mannelli, 2009)

Dicken, Peter, 'Global Shift—the Role of United States Transnational Corporations', in Slater and Taylor (eds), *American Century*

Dickhaus, Monika, ' "It is only the provisional that lasts": The European Payments Union', in OECD, *Explorations*

Dixon, Bryony, 'Crossing the Pond: The Special Relationship between Britain and American Film before 1930', in Burton and Porter (eds), *Crossing the Pond*

Dobson, Alan P., 'FDR and the Struggle for a Postwar Civil Aviation Regime: Legacy or Loss?', in Woolner et al. (eds), *FDR's World*

Doran, Charles F., 'Globalization and Statecraft', *Saisphere* (2000)

Dore, Ronald, 'Dore on Huntington', *Prospect* (March 1997)

Duranton-Crabol, Anne-Marie, 'De l'anti-américanisme en France vers 1930: La réception des *Scènes de la vie future*', *Revue d'histoire moderne et contemporaine* (January–March 2001)

Edelstein, David M. and Ronald R. Krebs, 'Washington's Troubling Obsession with Public Diplomacy', *Survival* (Spring 2005)

Edwards, Owen Dudley, 'Orwell's View of America', in Kroes (ed.), *Nineteen Eighty-Four*

Eichengreen, Barry, 'The Market and the Marshall Plan', in Schain (ed.), *Marshall Plan*

Eichler, Maya, 'The Role of Identity in European–U.S. Relations', in Gustav E. Gustenau et al. (eds), *Europe–USA: Diverging Partners*, Austrian Institute of International Affairs (Baden-Baden, 2006)

Eisenberg, Carolyn, 'The Limits of Democracy: U.S. Policy and Rights of German Labor, 1945–1949', in Ermarth (ed.), *America and the Shaping of German Society*

Ellwood, D. W., 'America as a European Power: Four Dimensions of the Transatlantic Relationship: 1945 to the Late 1990s', in Levy and Roseman (eds), *Three Postwar Eras in Comparison*

—— 'American Myth, American Model, and the Quest for a British Modernity', in Moore and Vaudagna (eds), *American Century in Europe*

—— 'Bemused by America, Terrified of Europe: The Politics of Identity in Britain from Blair to Cameron', *Bologna Journal of International Affairs* (Spring 2010)

—— 'Containing Modernity, Domesticating America in Italy', in Stephan (ed.), *Americanization of Europe*

—— 'European Cinema's Satire of Americanization 1949 to 1959', in *Selling Democracy: Friendly Persuasion*, Berlin International Film Festival/German Historical Museum (Berlin, 2006)

—— 'Italian Modernisation and the Propaganda of the Marshall Plan', in Luciano Cheles and Luciano Sponza (eds), *The Art of Persuasion: Political Communication in Italy from 1945 to the 1990s* (Manchester, 2001)

—— ' "Showing the World What it Owed to Britain": Foreign policy and "cultural propaganda", 1935–45', in Nicholas Pronay and D. W. Spring (eds), *Propaganda, Politics and Film, 1918–45* (London, 1982)

—— 'The 1948 Elections in Italy: A Cold War Propaganda Battle', *Historical Journal of Film, Radio and Television*, 13/1 (1993)

—— 'The American Challenge and the Origins of the Politics of Growth', in M. L. Smith and P. M. R. Stirk (eds), *Making the New Europe: European Unity and the Second World War* (London, 1990)

—— 'The American Challenge Renewed: U.S. Cultural Power and Europe's Identity Debates', *The Brown Journal of World Affairs* (Winter/Spring 1997)

Ellwood, D. W., 'The American Challenge Revisited: Soft Power Struggles in Contemporary Europe', in Almqvist and Linklater (eds), *On the Idea of America*
—— 'The Limits of Americanisation and the Emergence of an Alternative Model: The Marshall Plan in Emilia-Romagna', in Kipping and Bjarnar (eds), *Americanisation of European Business*
—— '*Un americano a Roma*: A 1950s Satire of Americanization', *Modern Italy* (Autumn 1996)
—— 'What Winning Stories Teach: The Marshall Plan and Atlanticism as Enduring Narratives', in Mariano (ed.), *Defining the Atlantic Community*
Elsaesser, Thomas P., 'German Postwar Cinema and Hollywood', in Ellwood and Kroes (eds), *Hollywood in Europe*
—— 'Two Decades in Another Country: *Hollywood and the Cinéphiles*', in Bigsby (ed.), *Superculture*
Elteren, Mel van, 'American Life by Proxy: Dutch Youth and Sense of Place', in George McKay (ed.), *Yankee Go Home (and take me with U)* (Sheffield, 1997)
Embacher, Helga, 'Unwelcome in Austria: Returnees and Concentration Camp Survivors', in Duchen and Bandhauer-Schöffmann (eds), *When the War Was Over*
Ermarth, Michael, 'Cultural Protectionism in "Media Mediae": "Normal" Germany Confronts Post-Modern Americanization Over the Last Decade (1987–1997)', paper delivered at the Forlì conference, University of Bologna (Bologna, March 1997)
—— 'German Reunification as Self-Inflicted Americanization: Critical Views on the Course of Contemporary Development', in Wagnleitner and May (eds), *'Here, There and Everywhere'*
—— '*The German Talks Back*: Heinrich Hauser and German Attitudes toward Americanization after World War II', in Ermarth (ed.), *America and the Shaping of German Society*
—— '"Unconditional Americanization?" German Identity, Cultural Criticism, and the West-Option, 1945–1955', unpublished paper
Escalante-Gonzalbo, Fernando and Mauricio Tenorio-Trillo, '*Nuestro Once de Septiembre*: The Kingdom of the Comma', in Farber (ed.), *What They Think of US*
Evans, Martin, 'Algeria and the Liberation: Hope and Betrayal', in Kedward and Wood (eds), *Liberation of France*
Evans, Peter, 'Cifesa: Cinema and Authoritarian Aesthetics', in Graham and Labanyi (eds), *Spanish Cultural Studies*
Fainsod, Merle, 'The Development of American Military Government Policy during World War II', in Friedrich et al. (eds), *American Experiences*
Farmer, Richard, 'Exploiting a Universal Nostalgia for Steak and Onions: The Ministry of Information and the Promotion of *World of Plenty* (1943)', *Historical Journal of Film, Radio and Television* (June 2010)
Fasce, Fernando, 'Appunti sull'americanismo all'Ansaldo nel Novecento', *Archivi e imprese* (July–December 1993)
Fayette, Jacques, 'Il volontarismo politico di fronte al realism economico', in Baldini and Lazar (eds), *La Francia di Sarkozy*

Fehrenbach, Heide, 'Cinema, Spectatorship, and the Problem of Postwar German Identity', in Pommerin (ed.), *American Impact*

—— 'Persistent Myths of Americanization: German Reconstruction and the Renationalization of Postwar Cinema, 1945–1965', in Fehrenbach and Poiger (eds), *Transactions*

—— and Uta G. Poiger, 'Introduction: Americanization Reconsidered', in Fehrenbach and Poiger (eds), *Transactions*

Fickers, Andreas, 'Presenting the "Window on the World" to the World: Competing Narratives of the Presentation of Television at the World's Fairs in Paris (1937) and New York (1939)', *Historical Journal of Film, Radio and Television* (August 2008)

Fiebig-von Hase, Ragnhild, 'The United States and Germany in the World Arena, 1900–1917', in Schröder (ed.), *Confrontation and Cooperation*

Fluck, Winfried, 'The Americanization of Modern Culture', in Agata Preis-Smith and Piotr Skurowski (eds), *Cultural Policy or the Politics of Culture?* (Warsaw, 1999)

Fontana, Benedetto, 'Political Space and Hegemonic Power in Gramsci', *Journal of Power* (December 2010)

Footitt, Hilary, 'American Forces in France: Communist Representations of US Deployment', in Tobia (ed.), *Cold War History*, Special Issue, 'Europe Americanized?' (February 2011)

Fordham, Elizabeth, 'From Whitman to Wilson: French Attitudes toward America around the Time of the Great War', in Passerini (ed.), *Across the Atlantic*

Fountain, Nigel and Anjana Ahuja, 'The Tale of Haley the Comet', *The Guardian* (12 April 1994)

Frank, Robert, 'The French Dilemma: Modernization with Dependence or Independence and Decline', in Becker and Knipping (eds), *Power in Europe?*

Friebe, Holm, 'Branding Germany: Hans Domizlaff's *Marchentechnik* and Its Ideological Impact', in Swett et al. (eds), *Selling Modernity*

Friedman, Thomas L., 'A Manifesto for the Fast World', *New York Times* Magazine, Section 6 (28 March 1999)

Fulton, Richard D., 'Sensational War Reporting and the Quality Press in Late Victorian Britain and America', in Wiener and Hampton (eds), *Anglo-American Media Interactions*

Furlough, Ellen, 'Selling the American Way in Interwar France: Prixs Uniques and the Salons des Arts Menagers', *Journal of Social History*, 26 (1993)

Gagnon, Paul A., 'French Views of the Second American Revolution', *French Historical Studies* (Fall 1962)

Galloux-Fournier, Bernadette, 'Un regard sur l'Amérique: Voyageurs français aux Etats-Unis, 1919–1939', *Revue d'histoire moderne et contemporaine* (April–June 1990)

Gardner, Lloyd C., 'FDR and the "Colonial Question"', in Woolner et al. (eds), *FDR's World*

—— 'Present at the Culmination: The Empire of Righteousness', in Gardner and Young (eds), *New American Empire*

Gardner, Lloyd C. 'The Atlantic Charter: Idea and Reality, 1942–1945', in Brinkley and Facey-Crowther (eds), *Atlantic Charter*
—— 'The United States, the German Peril and a Revolutionary World: The Inconsistencies of World Order and National Self-Determination', in Schröder (ed.), *Confrontation and Cooperation*
—— and Warren F. Kimball, 'The United States: Democratic Diplomacy', in Reynolds et al. (eds), *Allies at War*
Garncarz, Joseph, 'Hollywood in Germany: The Role of American Films in Germany, 1925–1990', in Ellwood and Kroes (eds), *Hollywood in Europe*
—— 'Made in Germany: Multiple Language Versions and the Early German Sound Cinema', in Higson and Maltby (eds), *'Film Europe' and 'Film America'*
Gassert, Philipp, ' "Without Concessions to Marxist or Communist Thought": Fordism in Germany, 1923–1939', in Barclay and Glaser-Schmidt (eds), *Transatlantic Images*
Gatt-Rutter, John, 'Naples 1944: Liberation and Literature', in Davis (ed.), *Italy and America*
Gentile, Emilio, '1900: Inizio secolo', in Gentile et al. (eds), *Novecento italiano*
—— 'Impending Modernity: Fascism and the Ambivalent Image of the United States', *Journal of Contemporary History*, 28 (1993)
Geyer, Michael, 'America in Germany: Power and the Pursuit of Americanization', in Frank Trommler and Elliot Shore (eds), *German–American Encounter: Conflict and Cooperation between Two Cultures* (New York, 2001)
Gienow-Hecht, Jessica C. E., ' "How Good Are We?" Culture and the Cold War', in Scott-Smith and Krabbendam (eds), *Cultural Cold War*
Girvin, Brian, 'Ireland and the Marshall Plan: A Cargo Cult in the North Atlantic?', in OECD, *Explorations*
Göktürk, Deniz, 'How Modern Is It? Moving Images of America in Early German Cinema', in Ellwood and Kroes (eds), *Hollywood in Europe*
Grazia, Victoria de, 'Mass Culture and Sovereignty: The American Challenge to European Cinemas, 1920–1960', *Journal of Modern History* (March 1989)
—— 'The Arts of Purchase: How American Publicity Subverted the European Poster, 1920–1940', in Kruger and Marlani (eds), *Remaking History*
—— 'Visualizing the Marshall Plan: The Pleasures of American Consumer Democracy or the Pains of "the Greatest Structural Adjustment Program in History"?', in Bischof and Stiefel (eds), *Images of the Marshall Plan*
Gribaudi, Gabriella, 'Napoli 1943–45: La costruzione di un'epopea', in Davis (ed.), *Italy and America*
Gries, Rainer, ' "Serve Yourself!": The History and Theory of Self-Service in West and East Germany', in Swett et al. (eds), *Selling Modernity*
Guazzaloca, Giulia, 'Le principali culture politiche italiane di fronte al *boom* della televisione', in Cavazza and Scarpellini (eds), *La rivoluzione dei consumi*
Guéhenno, Jean-Marie, 'Américanisation du monde ou mondialisation de l'Amérique?', *Politique Étrangère*, 64/1 (1999)
—— 'The French Resistance', *Prospect* (June 1998)
Guerlain, Pierre, 'Pride and Prejudice in the Saga of Anti-Americanism', in Fender (ed.), *American and European National Identities*

Gundle, Stephen, 'Adriano Celentano and the Origins of Rock 'n' Roll in Italy', *Journal of Modern Italian Studies* (October 2006)

—— 'Il Duce's Cultural Cachet', *History Today* (October 2010)

Gurney, Peter, 'The Battle of the Consumer in Postwar Britain', *Journal of Modern History* (December 2005)

Hacker, Jonathan, 'The Cinema and the Home Front: *Yanks, Hope and Glory* and *Chicago Joe and the Show Girl*', *Twentieth Century British History*, 2/2 (1991)

Haefele, Mark H., 'Walt Rostow's Stages of Economic Growth: Ideas and Action', in Engerman et al. (eds), *Staging Growth*

Hajkowski, Thomas, '*Red on the Map*: Empire and Americanization at the BBC, 1942–1950', in Wiener and Hampton (eds), *Anglo-American Media Interactions*

Hammerton, Jenny, 'Screen-Struck: The Lure of Hollywood for British Women in the 1920's', in Burton and Porter (eds), *Crossing the Pond*

Hannigan, Robert E., 'Continentalism and *Mitteleuropa* as Points of Departure for a Comparison of American and German Foreign Relations in the Early Twentieth Century', in Schröder (ed.), *Confrontation and Cooperation*

Harrison, Michael M., 'La solution gaulliste', in Lacorne, Rupnik, and Toinet (eds), *L'Amérique dans les Têtes*

Harrison, Richard A., 'The United States and Great Britain: Presidential Diplomacy and Alternatives to Appeasement in the 1930s', in Schmitz and Challener (eds), *Appeasement in Europe*

Hart, Roger, 'Universals of Yesteryear: Hegel's Modernity in an Age of Globalization', in Hopkins (ed.), *Global History*

Healey, Timothy, 'William Clayton, Negotiating the Marshall Plan, and European Economic Integration', *Diplomatic History* (April 2011)

Heineman, Elizabeth, 'The Hour of the Woman: Memories of Germany's "Crisis Years" and West German National Identity', *American Historical Review* (April 1996)

Hendriks, Gerda Jansen, 'High Stakes in the East: Dutch Government Films on the Dutch East Indies/Indonesia 1940–1945', paper presented at the Iamhist Conference (Amsterdam, July 2007)

Henrikson, Alan K., 'FDR and the "World-Wide Arena"', in Woolner et al. (eds), *FDR's World*

Hickethier, Knut, 'Early TV: Imagining and Realising Television', in Bignell and Fickers (eds), *European Television History*

Higson, Andrew, 'Cultural Policy and Industrial Practice: Film Europe and the International Film Congresses of the 1920's', in Higson and Maltby (eds), *'Film Europe' and 'Film America'*

Hill, John S., 'American Efforts to Aid French Reconstruction between Lend-Lease and the Marshall Plan', *Journal of Modern History* (September 1992)

Hilton, Matthew, 'The Fable of the Sheep, or, Private Virtues, Public Vices: The Consumer Revolution of the Twentieth Century', *Past and Present* (August 2002)

Hopkins, A. G., 'The History of Globalization—and the Globalization of History?', in Hopkins (ed.), *Globalization in World History*

Howe, Anthony, 'Free Trade and the International Order: The Anglo-American Tradition, 1846–1946', in Leventhal and Quinault (eds), *Anglo-American Attitudes*

Howe, Irving, 'Orwell in America', in Kroes (ed.), *Nineteen Eighty-Four*

Hughes, Merritt Y., 'Civil Affairs in France', in Friedrich et al. (eds), *American Experiences*

Hugo, Markus M., ' "Uncle Sam I Cannot Stand, for Spain I have no Sympathy": An Analysis of Discourse about the Spanish–American War in Imperial Germany, 1898–1909', in Hilton and Ickringill (eds), *European Perceptions*

Hutchinson, William R., 'American Dreams and European Responses, from the 1840s to the 1920s', in Norbert Finzsch and Herman Wellenreuther (eds), *Visions of the Future in Germany and America* (Oxford, 2001)

Ickringill, Steve J. S., 'Silence and Celebration: Ulster, William McKinley and the Spanish–American War', in Hilton and Ickringill (eds), *European Perceptions*

Ikenberry, G. John, 'A World Economy Restored: Expert Consensus and the Anglo-American Postwar Settlement', *International Organization* (Winter 1992)

—— and Charles Kupchan, 'Socialization and Hegemonic Power', *International Organization*, 44/3 (1990)

Iordanova, Dina, 'Political Resentment versus Cultural Submission: The Duality of U.S. Representations in Bulgarian Media', in Yahya R. Kamalpour (ed.), *Images of the U.S. Around the World* (Albany, 1999)

Jarvie, Ian, 'Dollars and Ideology: Will Hays' Economic Foreign Policy 1922–1945', *Film History*, 2 (1988)

Jeancolas, Jean-Pierre, 'From the Blum–Byrnes Agreement to the GATT affair', in Nowell-Smith and Ricci (eds), *Hollywood and Europe*

Jensen, Leon Dalgas, 'Denmark', in Labohm (ed.), *Fiftieth Anniversary*

Johnston, R. J., 'The United States, the "Triumph of Democracy" and the "End of History" ', in Slater and Taylor (eds), *American Century*

Jones, Howard, 'One World: An American Perspective', in Madison (ed.), *Wendell Willkie*

Judd, Denis, 'Diamonds are Forever? Kipling's Imperialism', *History Today* (June 1997)

Junker, Detlef, 'Hitler's Perception of Franklin D. Roosevelt and the United States of America', in van Minnen and Sears (eds), *FDR and His Contemporaries*

—— 'The Continuity of Ambivalence: German Views of America, 1933–1945', in Barclay and Glaser-Schmidt (eds), *Transatlantic Images*

Kaelble, Helmut, 'Identification with Europe and the Politicization of the European Union since the 1980s', in Jeffrey T. Checkel and Peter J. Katzenstein (eds), *European Identity* (Cambridge, 2009)

Kaiser, W., 'The Great Derby Race: Strategies of Cultural Representation at Nineteenth-Century World Exhibitions', in Gienow-Hecht and Schumacher (eds), *Culture and International History*

Kaminsky, Anne, ' "True Advertising Means Promoting a Good Thing Through a Good Form": Advertising in the German Democratic Republic', in Swett et al. (eds), *Selling Modernity*

Kaspi, André, 'One World: A View from France', in Madison (ed.), *Wendell Willkie*

Kennedy, Liam, 'Spectres of Comparison: American Studies and the United States of the West', *Comparative American Studies* (June 2006)

Kennedy, Paul, 'British and German Reactions to the Rise of American Power', in Bullen et al. (eds), *Ideas into Politics*

Kersten, Albert E., 'The Dutch and the American Anti-Colonialist Tide, 1942–1945', in Jeffreys-Jones (ed.), *Eagle Against Empire*

Kimball, Warren, 'The Atlantic Charter: "With All Deliberate Speed"', in Brinkley and Facey-Crowther (eds), *Atlantic Charter*

—— 'The Sheriffs: FDR's Postwar World', in Woolner et al. (eds), *FDR's World*

—— 'U.S. Economic Strategy in World War II: Wartime Goals, Peacetime Plans', in Kimball (ed.), *America Unbound*

Knight, Robert, 'Narratives in Postwar Austrian Historiography', in Bushell (ed.), *Austria 1945–1955*

Kramer, Paul A., 'Empires, Exceptions and Anglo-Saxons: Race and Rule between the British and United States Empires, 1880–1910', *Journal of American History* (March 2002)

Kroes, Rob, 'Between Rejection and Reception: Hollywood in Holland', in Ellwood and Kroes (eds), *Hollywood in Europe*

—— 'Worlds Apart? The United States, Europe, and the Cultural Ties that Bind Them', in Lundestad (ed.), *Just Another Major Crisis?*

Krüger, Peter, 'Germany and the United States, 1914–1933: The Mutual Perception of Their Political Systems', in Barclay and Glaser-Schmidt (eds), *Transatlantic Images*

Kupchan, Charles A., 'Atlantic Orders: The Fundamentals of Change', in Lundestad (ed.), *Just Another Major Crisis?*

Kuttner, Robert, 'The Role of Governments in the Global Economy', in Giddens and Hutton (eds), *Global Capitalism*

Labanyi, Jo, 'Censorship or the Fear of Mass Culture', in Graham and Labanyi (eds), *Spanish Cultural Studies*

Lacey, Joanne, 'Seeing Through Happiness: Hollywood Musicals and the Construction of the American Dream in Liverpool in the 1950s', *Journal of Popular British Cinema*, 2 (1999)

LaFeber, Walter, 'FDR's Worldviews, 1941–1945', in Woolner et al. (eds), *FDR's World*

Lal, Deepak, 'The View of America from India', in Almqvist and Linklater (eds), *On the Idea of America*

Lamb, Stephen and Anthony Phelan, 'Weimar Culture: The Birth of Modernism', in Burns (ed.), *German Cultural Studies*

Langhamer, Claire, 'The Meanings of Home in Postwar Britain', in Betts and Crowley (eds), *Journal of Contemporary History* (April 2005), Special Issue: 'Domestic Dreamworlds: Notions of Home in Post-1945 Europe'

Lant, A. and I. Perez, 'The Red Velvet Seat', paper presented at the conference *Hollywood and its Spectators* (London, February 1998)

Latham, Robert, 'Cooperation and Community in Europe: What the Marshall Plan Proposed, NATO Disposed', in Schain (ed.), *Marshall Plan*

LeMahieu, D. L., 'America and the Representation of British History in Film and Television', in Leventhal and Quinault (eds), *Anglo-American Attitudes*

Leventhal, Fred M., 'Leslie Howard and Douglas Fairbanks, Jr: Promoting the Anglo-American Alliance in Wartime, 1939–43', in Wiener and Hampton (eds), *Anglo-American Media Interactions*

Levy, Marie-Françoise, 'Television, Family and Society in France, 1949–1968', *Historical Journal of Film, Radio and Television* (June 1998)

Lipset, Seymour Martin, 'The Americanization of the European Left', *Journal of Democracy* (April 2001)

Lucas, Jean-Michel, 'Exception culturelle *versus* diversité culturelle: D'un concept usé à une pratique impensabile', *Cosmopolitiques* (June 2007)

Maase, Kaspar, 'Establishing Cultural Democracy: Youth, "Americanization", and the Irresistible Rise of Popular Culture', in Schissler (ed.), *Miracle Years*

—— 'From Nightmare to Model? Why German Broadcasting Became Americanized', in Stephan (ed.), *Americanization and Anti-Americanism*

McGlade, Jacqueline, 'From Business Reform Programme to Production Drive: The Transformation of US Technical Assistance to Western Europe', in Kipping and Bjarnar (eds), *Americanisation of European Business*

McKercher, Brian, 'Churchill, the European Balance of Power and the USA', in R. A. C. Parker (ed.), *Winston Churchill: Studies in Statesmanship* (London, 1995)

McNeill, W. H., 'Afterword: World History and Globalization', in Hopkins (ed.), *Global History*

MacPhee, Graham, 'Empire—What Empire?', *History Today* (November 2008)

Maggi, Stefano, 'La 600 e il telefono: Una rivoluzione sociale', in Cardini (ed.), *Il miracolo economico italiano*

Maier, Charles S., ' "The Politics of Productivity": Foundation of American International Foreign Economic Policy after World War II', in Peter J. Katzenstein (ed.), *Between Power and Plenty: Foreign Economic Policies of Advanced Industrial States* (Madison, 1978)

—— 'The Two Postwar Eras and the Conditions for Stability in Twentieth Century Western Europe', *American Historical Review* (April 1981)

Malament, Barbara C., 'British Labour and Roosevelt's New Deal: The Response of the Left and the Unions', *Journal of British Studies* (Spring 1978)

Maltby, Richard, 'The Cinema and the League of Nations', in Higson and Maltby (eds), *'Film Europe' and 'Film America'*

—— and Ruth Vasey, 'The International Language Problem: European Reaction to Hollywood's Conversion to Sound', in Ellwood and Kroes (eds), *Hollywood in Europe*

—— ' "Temporary American Citizens": Cultural Anxieties and Industrial Strategies in the Americanisation of European Cinema', in Higson and Maltby (eds), *'Film Europe' and 'Film America'*

Marin, Séverine Antigone, ' "L'américanisation du monde"? Etude des peurs allemandes face au dangér américain, 1897–1907', paper presented at the Roubaix conference (September 2001)

Menand, Louis, 'The Promise of Freedom, the Friend of Authority', in Kazin and McCartin (eds), *Americanism*

Menduni, Enrico, 'La nascita della televisione in Italia', in Cardini (ed.), *Il miracolo economico italiano*

Merkel, Ina, 'Consumer Culture in the GDR, or How the Struggle for Anti-Modernity Was Lost on the Battleground of Consumer Culture', in Strasser et al. (eds), *Getting and Spending*

Michie, A., 'Scotland: Strategies of Centralisation', in Barr (ed.), *All Our Yesterdays*

Minganti, Franco, 'Jukebox Boys: Postwar Italian Music and the Culture of Covering', in Fehrenbach and Poiger (eds), *Transactions*

Miskell, Peter, 'Americanization and its Limits: United Artists in the British Market in the 1930s and 1940s', in Wiener and Hampton (eds), *Anglo-American Media Interactions*

Mitchell, Michael, 'Restoration or Renewal? Csokor, the Austrian PEN Club and the re-Establishment of Literary Life in Austria, 1945–55', in Bushell (ed.), *Austria 1945–1955*

Moe, Nelson, 'Naples '44/"Tammurriata Nera"', *Ladri di Bicicletta*', in Davis (ed.), *Italy and America*

Moore, R. Laurence, 'American Religion as Cultural Imperialism', in Moore and Vaudagna (eds), *American Century in Europe*

Möser, Kurt, 'World War I and the Creation of Desire for Automobiles in Germany', in Strasser et al. (eds), *Getting and Spending*

Ninkovich, Frank, 'Wilsonism, Pre-Wilsonian American Liberalism, and the Atlantic Community', in Mariano (ed.), *Defining the Atlantic Community*

Nye, David E., 'European Self-Representations at the New York World's Fair of 1939', in Kroes et al. (eds), *Cultural Transmissions*

—— 'Imagining: Americanization in Context', paper delivered at the conference on 'Appropriating America, Making Europe', European Science Foundation (Amsterdam, January 2009)

O'Malley, Tom, ' "Typically Anti-American"? The Labour Movement, America and Broadcasting in Britain, from Beveridge to Pilkington, 1949–62', in Weiner and Hampton (eds), *Anglo-American Media Interactions*

Orvell, Miles, 'Understanding Disneyland: American Mass Culture and the European Gaze', in Kroes et al. (eds), *Cultural Transmissions*

Ory, Pascal, 'Introduction to an Era of Doubt: Cultural Reflections of "French Power", around the Year 1948', in Becker and Knipping (eds), *Power in Europe?*

Patriarca, Silvana, 'Italian Neo-Patriotism: Debating National Identity in the 1990s', in *Modern Italy*, 6/1 (May 2001)

Patrick, Stewart, 'Embedded Liberalism in France? American Hegemony, the Monnet Plan and Postwar Multilateralism', in Schain (ed.), *Marshall Plan*

Paxton, Robert O., 'Collaborateurs et Resistants', in Lacorne, Rupnik, and Toinet (eds), *L'Amérique dans les Têtes*

Pelinka, Anton, 'Taboos and Self-deception: The Second Republic's Reconstruction of History', in Bischof and Pelinka (eds), *Contemporary Austrian Studies*, vol. v

Pells, Richard, 'American Culture Goes Global, or Does It?', *The Chronicle of Higher Education* (12 April 2002)

Pertile, Lino, 'Fascism and Literature', in David Forgacs (ed.), *Rethinking Italian Fascism: Capitalism, Populism and Culture* (London, 1986)

Pew Research Centre Publications, 'Obama's Favourite Theologian? A Short Course on Reinhold Niebuhr' (26 June 2009)

Pharo, Helge, 'Norway, the United States and the Marshall Plan, 1947–52', in OECD, *Explorations*

Poiger, Uta G., 'Rebels with a Cause? American Popular Culture, the 1956 Youth Riots, and New Conceptions of Masculinity in East and West Germany', in Pommerin (ed.), *American Impact*

Popkova, Ludmila N., 'Russian Press Coverage of American Intervention in the Spanish–Cuban War', in Hilton and Ickringill (eds), *European Perceptions*

Porter, Vincent, 'The Construction of an anti-Hollywood Film Aesthetic: The Film Criticism of Walter Mycroft', in Burton and Porter (eds), *Crossing the Pond*

Prowe, Diethelm, 'Democratization as Conservative Restabilization: The Impact of American Policy', in Jeffry M. Diefendorf et al. (eds), *American Policy and the Reconstruction of West Germany, 1945–1955* (Washington DC and Cambridge, 1993)

—— 'The "Miracle" of the Political-Culture Shift: Democratization Between Americanization and Conservative Reintegration', in Schissler (ed.), *Miracle Years*

Reid, Brian Holden, 'Tensions in the Supreme Command: Anti-Americanism in the British Army, 1939–45', in Reid and John White (eds), *American Studies: Essays in Honour of Marcus Cunliffe* (London, 1991)

Repp, Kevin, 'Marketing, Modernity, and "The German People's Soul": Advertising and its Enemies in Late Imperial Germany', in Swett et al. (eds), *Selling Modernity*

Reynolds, David, 'American Globalism: Mass, Motion and the Multiplier Effect', in Hopkins (ed.), *Globalization in World History*

Richards, David A., 'America Conquers Britain: Anglo-American Conflict in the Popular Media During the 1920s', *Journal of American Culture*, 3/1 (Spring 1980)

Roberts, Mary Louise, 'The Price of Discretion: Prostitution, Venereal Disease and the American Military in France, 1944–1946', *American Historical Review* (October 2010)

Rockett, Kevin, 'Protecting the Family and the Nation: The official censorship of American cinema in Ireland, 1923–1954', *Historical Journal of Film, Radio and Television*, 20/3 (2000)

—— 'Protecting the Nation: The Reception of American Cinema in Ireland 1923–1954', paper presented at the conference *Hollywood and its Spectators* (London, February 1998), published in Stokes and Maltby (eds), *Hollywood spectatorship*

Rodriguez, Laura, ' "El Desastre": Spain in Defeat, 1898', *History Today* (December 1998)

Roholl, Marja, 'Uncle Sam: An Example for All?', in Hans Loeber (ed.), *Dutch–American Relations, 1945–1969* (Asse, 1992)

Roll, Eric, 'The Marshall Plan as Anglo-American Response', in Hoffmann and Maier (eds), *Marshall Plan*

Romero, Federico, 'The Twilight of American Cultural Hegemony: A Historical Perspective on Western Europe's Distancing from America', in Farber (ed.), *What They Think of US*

Ross, Corey, 'Vision of Prosperity: The Americanization of Advertising in Interwar Germany', in Swett et al. (eds), *Selling Modernity*

Rossi, Barbara, 'Televisione: Le immagini del "miracolo"', in Cardini (ed.), *Il miracolo economico italiano*

Rossini, Daniela, 'The American Peril: Italian Catholics and the Spanish–American War, 1898', in Hilton and Ickringill (eds), *European Perceptions*

Rowland, Benjamin M., 'Preparing the American Ascendancy: The Transfer of Economic Power from Britain to the United States, 1933–1944', in Rowland (ed.), *Balance of Power*

Rubens, Lisa, 'Re-Presenting the Nation: The Golden Gate International Exhibition', in Rydell and Gwinn (eds), *Fair Representations*

Rupnik, Jacques, 'Anti-Americanism and the Modern: The image of the United States in French public opinion', in John Gaffney (ed.), *France and Modernisation* (Aldershot, 1988)

Saresella, Daniela, 'La scoperta cattolica dell'America', in Agostino Giovagnoli and Giorgio Del Zanna (eds), *Il mondo vista dall'Italia* (Milan, 2004)

Schad, Geoffrey D., 'Competing Forms of Globalization in the Middle East: From the Ottoman Empire to the Nation State, 1918–1967', in Hopkins (ed.), *Global History*

Schäfer, Axel R., 'The Study of Americanisation after German Reunification: Institutional Transfer, Popular Culture and the East', *Contemporary European History*, 12/1 (February 2003)

Schissler, Hanna, ' "Normalization" as Project: Some Thoughts on Gender Relations in West Germany during the 1950s', in Schissler (ed.), *Miracle Years*

Schmidt, Oliver, 'Small Atlantic World: U.S. Philanthropy and Expanding International Exchange of Scholars after 1945', in Gienow-Hecht and Schumacher (eds), *Culture and International History*

Schmitz, David F., ' "Speaking the Same Language": The U.S. Response to the Italo-Ethiopian War and the Origins of American Appeasement', in Schmitz and Challener (eds), *Appeasement in Europe*

Schonfeld, Reese, 'The Global Battle for Cultural Domination', in Lawrence E. Harrison and Jerome Kagan (eds), *Developing Cultures: Essays on Cultural Change* (London, 2006)

Schröder, Hans-Jürgen, 'The Economic Reconstruction of West Germany in the Context of International Relations, 1945–1949', in Schröder (ed.), *Confrontation and Cooperation*

Schuker, Stephen A., 'Origins of American Stabilization Policy in Europe: The Financial Dimension 1918–1924', in Schröder (ed.), *Confrontation and Cooperation*

Schutts, Jeff, ' "Die Erfrischende Pause": Marketing Coca-Cola in Hitler's Germany', in Swett et al. (eds), *Selling Modernity*

Scrivano, Paolo, 'Signs of Americanization in Italian Domestic Life: Italy's Postwar Conversion to Consumerism', in Betts and Crowley (eds), *Journal of Contemporary History* (April 2005), Special Issue: 'Domestic Dreamworlds: Notions of Home in Post-1945 Europe'

Seidel, Hans, 'Austria's Economic Policy and the Marshall Plan', in Bischof, Pelinka, and Stiefel (eds), *Contemporary Austrian Studies*, vol. viii

Sharp, Clifford, 'Cecil Rhodes', in H. J. Massingham and Hugh Massingham (eds), *The Great Victorians* (London, 1932)

Shaw, Gareth, L. Curth, and A. Alexander, 'Selling Self-Service and the Supermarket: The Americanisation of Food Retailing in Britain, 1945–1960', *Business History* (October 2004)

Short, K. R. M., 'Cinematic Support for the Anglo-American Détente', in P. M. Taylor (ed.), *Britain and the Cinema in the Second World War* (London, 1988)

Siefert, Marsha, 'Allies on Film: US–USSR Filmmakers and *The Battle of Russia*', in M. Siefert (ed.), *Extending the Borders of Russian History* (Budapest, 2003)

—— 'Image/Music/Voice: Song Dubbing in Hollywood Musicals', *Journal of Communication* (Spring 1995)

Slotkin, Richard, 'Buffalo Bill's "Wild West" and the Mythologization of the American Empire', in Kaplan and Pease (eds), *Cultures of United States Imperialism*

Slupetzky, Nicole, 'Austria and the Spanish–American War', in Hilton and Ickringill (eds), *European Perceptions*

Smith, Michael, 'European Integration and American Power: Reflex, Resistance and Reconfiguration', in Slater and Taylor (eds), *American Century*

Startt, James, 'James Bryce and the Promise of the American Press', in Wiener and Hampton (eds), *Anglo-American Media Interactions*

Stead, Peter, 'Hollywood's Message to the World: The British Response in the 1930s', *Historical Journal of Film, Radio and Television*, 1/1 (1981)

Steel, Ronald, 'How Europe Became Atlantic: Walter Lippmann and the New Geography of the Atlantic Community', in Mariano (ed.), *Defining the Atlantic Community*

Sternhell, Zeev, 'Aux sources de l'idéologie fasciste: La révolte socialiste contre le matérialisme', in Arieli and Rotenstreich (eds), *Totalitarian Democracy*

Stiglitz, Joseph E., 'Is there a Post-Washington Consensus Consensus?', in Serra and Stiglitz (eds), *Washington Consensus Reconsidered*

Swann, Paul, 'The Little State Department: Washington and Hollywood's Rhetoric of the Postwar Audience', in Ellwood and Kroes (eds), *Hollywood in Europe*

Temperley, Howard, 'The Affluent Society Revisited', in Cristina Giorcelli and Rob Kroes (eds), *Living with America, 1946–1996* (Amsterdam, 1997)

Thompson, Christopher S., 'Prologue to Conflict: de Gaulle and the United States, First Impressions Through 1940', in Robert O. Paxton and Nicholas Wahl (eds), *De Gaulle and the United States: A Centennial Reappraisal* (Oxford and Providence, 1994)

Thompson, Kristin, 'The Rise and Fall of Film Europe', in Higson and Maltby (eds), *'Film Europe' and 'Film America'*

Tierney, Dominic, 'Franklin Delano Roosevelt and Covert Aid to the Loyalists in the Spanish Civil War 1936–39', *Journal of Contemporary History* (July 2004)

Tiratsoo, Nick, 'Limits of Americanisation: The US Productivity Gospel in Britain', in Conekin, Mort, and Waters (eds), *Moments of Modernity*

Tobia, Simona, 'Advertising America: VOA and Italy', in Tobia (ed.), *Cold War History*, Special Issue, 'Europe Americanized?' (February 2011)

—— (ed.), *Cold War History*, Special Issue, 'Europe Americanized?' (February 2011)

Toinet, Marie-France, 'French Pique and *Piques Françaises*', *Annals* of the American Academy of Political Science (May 1988)

Tomlinson, Jim and Nick Tiratsoo, 'Americanisation Beyond the Mass Production Paradigm: The Case of British Industry', in Kipping and Bjarnar (eds), *Americanisation of European Business*

Trentmann, Frank, 'Bread, Milk and Democracy: Consumption and Citizenship in Twentieth-Century Britain', in Daunton and Hilton (eds), *Politics of Consumption*

Trommler, Frank, 'Inventing the Enemy: German–American Cultural Relations, 1900–1917', in Schröder (ed.), *Confrontation and Cooperation*

Ulff-Møller, Jens, 'Hollywood's "Foreign War": The Effect of National Commercial Policy on the Emergence of the American Film Hegemony in France, 1920–29', in Higson and Maltby (eds), *'Film Europe' and 'Film America'*

Varni, Angelo, 'La grande trasformazione', in Cardini (ed.), *Il miracolo economico italiano*

Vaudagna, Maurizio, 'Mussolini and FDR', in van Minnen and Sears (eds), *FDR and His Contemporaries*

—— 'Social Protection and the Promise of a Secure Future in Wartime Europe and America', in Mariano (ed.), *Defining the Atlantic Community*

Wagner, Peter, 'The Resistance that Modernity Constantly Provokes: Europe, America and Social Theory', *Thesis Eleven*, 58/1 (August 1999)

Wagnleitner, Reinhold, 'Jazz—The Classical Music of Globalization', in Wagnleitner (ed.), *Satchmo Meets Amadeus* (Innsbruck, 2006)

—— 'The Empire of the Fun, or Talkin' Soviet Union Blues: The Sound of Freedom and U.S. Cultural Hegemony in Europe', in Hogan (ed.), *Ambiguous Legacy*

—— 'The Empire of Fun: Pop Culture and Geopolitical Aesthetics', in Almqvist and Linklater (eds), *On the Idea of America*

Wagstaff, Christopher, 'Italian Cinema of the Resistance and Liberation', in Davis (ed.), *Italy and America*

Walker III, William O., 'Crucible for Peace: Herbert Hoover, Modernization and Economic Growth in Latin America', *Diplomatic History* (January 2006)

Wall, Irwin, 'The Marshall Plan and French Politics', in Schain (ed.), *Marshall Plan*

Wanrooij, Bruno P. F., 'Dollars and Decency; Italian Catholics and Hollywood', in Ellwood and Kroes (eds), *Hollywood in Europe*

—— 'Italian Society under Fascism', in Lyttelton (ed.), *Liberal and Fascist Italy*

Warner, Geoffrey, 'Franklin D. Roosevelt and the Postwar World', in David Dutton (ed.), *Statecraft and Diplomacy in the Twentieth Century* (Liverpool, 1995)

Warren, James C., 'American Aid to Britain and the Problem of Socialism, 1945–51', in Watt (ed.), *Personalities and Policies: Studies in the Formation of British Foreign Policy in the Twentieth Century* (London, 1965)

—— 'Origins of the "Greek Economic Miracle": The Truman Doctrine and Marshall Plan Development and Stabilization Programs', in Rossides (ed.), *Truman Doctrine of Aid to Greece*

—— 'Those Who Made the Stabilization Program a Success', in Menges (ed.), *Marshall Plan*

Watt, D. C., 'U.S. Globalism: The End of the Concert of Europe', in Kimball (ed.), *America Unbound*

Weinberg, Gerhard L., 'Franklin Delano Roosevelt and Adolf Hitler: A Contemporary Comparison Revisited', in Glaser and Wellenreuther (eds), *Bridging the Atlantic*

White, Steven F., 'Liberal Antipodes: Omodeo, Smith and the Struggle over Schooling, Naples and Salerno, 1944', in Davis (ed.), *Italy and America*

Whitfield, Stephen J., 'The American Century of Henry R. Luce', in Kazin and McCartin (eds), *Americanism*

Whitham, Charlie, 'Seeing the Wood and the Trees: The British Foreign Office and the Anglo-American Trade Agreement of 1938', *Twentieth Century British History*, 16/1 (2005)

Wildt, Michael, 'Continuities and Discontinuities of Consumer Mentality in West Germany in the 1950s', in Bessel and Schumann (eds), *Life after Death*

—— 'Plurality of Taste: Food and Consumption in West Germany during the 1950s', *History Workshop Journal*, 39/1 (1995)

Will, Wilfried van der, 'Culture and the Organization of National Socialist Ideology 1933–1945', in Burns (ed.), *German Cultural Studies*

Williams, Daniel G., ' "If we only had some of what they have": Ralph Ellison in Wales', *Comparative American Studies*, 4/1 (2006)

Williamson, James, 'British Socialism and the Marshall Plan', *History Today* (January 2008)

Williamson, John, 'A Short History of the Washington Consensus', in Serra and Stiglitz (eds), *Washington Consensus Reconsidered*

Winkler, Allan M., 'American Opposition to Imperialism During World War II', in Jeffreys-Jones (ed.), *Eagle Against Empire*

Winock, Michel, 'La guerre froide', in Lacorne, Rupnik, and Toinet (eds), *L'Amérique dans les Têtes*

Wirsching, Andreas, 'From Work to Consumption: Transatlantic Visions of Individuality in Modern Mass Society', *Contemporary European History* (February 2011)

Wittrock, Björn, 'Modernity: One, None or Many? European Origins and Modernity as a Global Condition' *Daedalus* (Winter 2000), 'Multiple Modernities'

Woller, Hans, 'Germany in Transition from Stalingrad (1943) to Currency Reform (1948)', in Ermarth (ed.), *America and the Shaping of German Society*

Woods, Randall B., 'FDR and the New Economic Order', in Woolner et al. (eds), *FDR's World*

Zachariou, Stelios, 'Struggle for Survival: American Aid and Greek Reconstruction', in Schain (ed.), *Marshall Plan*

Zachman, Jon B., 'The Legacy and Meaning of World's Fair Souvenirs', in Rydell and Gwinn (eds), *Fair Representations*

Zamagni, Vera, 'Evolution of the Economy', in McCarthy (ed.), *Italy since 1945*

—— 'The Italian "Economic Miracle" Revisited: New Markets and American Technology', in Ennio Di Nolfo (ed.), *Power in Europe? II* (Berlin, 1992)

CONTEMPORARY MATERIALS

Acheson, Dean, *Present at the Creation: My Years in the State Department* (New York, 1969)

Adams, Brooks, 'Reciprocity or the Alternative', *Atlantic Monthly* (August 1901)

—— *The Law of Civilization and Decay* (Boston, 1895)

Adorno, Theodor and Max Horkheimer, *Dialectic of Enlightenment* (Amsterdam, 1947)

Ajami, Fouad, 'The Falseness of Anti-Americanism', *Foreign Policy* (September–October 2003)

Allsop, Kenneth, *The Angry Decade* (1958 edn repr., Wendover, 1985)

Al-Marashi, Ibrahim and Abdul Hadi al-Khalili, 'Iraqis' Bleak View of the United States', in Farber (ed.), *What They Think of US*

Almqvist, Kurt and Alexander Linklater (eds), *On the Idea of America: Perspectives from the Engelsberg Seminar 2009* (Stockholm, 2010)

American Foreign Policy Council, *The Transatlantic Drift Debates* (Lanham, Md., 2006)

Andriessen, Frans, 'Europe at the Crossroads', April 1990, in Center for International Affairs (Harvard University), *Allies or Adversaries?*

Applebaum, Anne, 'In Search of Pro-Americanism', *Foreign Policy* (July/August 2005)

Armstrong, Hamilton Fish, 'Europe Revisited', *Foreign Affairs* (July 1947)

Arnold-Forster, W., *Charters of Peace: A Commentary on the Atlantic Charter and the Declarations of Moscow, Cairo and Teheran* (London, 1944)

Aron, Raymond, 'From France', in Joseph (ed.), *As Others See Us*

—— 'Old Nations, New Europe', *Daedalus*, Special Issue, 'A New Europe?' (Winter 1964)

Aron, Robert and Arnaud Dandieu, *Le cancer américain* (Paris, 1931)

Austin, Bertram and W. Francis Lloyd, *The Secret of High Wages* (London, 1926)

Baldwin, Peter, 'America: A Reality Check', in Almqvist and Linklater (eds), *On the Idea of America*

Barber, Tony, 'The Soft-Power Broker', *E!Sharp* (January–February 2010)

Barker, J. Ellis, *America's Secret: The Causes of Her Economic Success* (London, 1927)

Beauvoir, Simone de, *The Mandarins*, translation of Paris edition of 1954 (London, 1957)

Beck, Ulrich, 'Understanding the Real Europe', *Dissent* (Summer 2003)

Bell, Daniel, *The End of Ideology: On the Exhaustion of Political Ideas in the Fifties* (1960; rev. edn, Cambridge, Mass., 2000)

Benjamin, Walter, *The Work of Art in the Age of its Technical Reproducibility, and Other Writings*, ed. Michael W. Jennings et al. (Cambridge, Mass., 2008)

Berlin, Isaiah, 'Roosevelt Through European Eyes', *The Atlantic* (August 1955)

Bernanos, Georges, *La France contre les robots* (Paris, 1947)

Bildt, Carl, 'Europe Must Keep Its "Soft Power"', *Financial Times* (31 May 2005)

Birt, John, 'Holding on to Auntie', *Prospect* (February 1999)

Bissell Jr, Richard M., 'The Impact of Rearmament on the Free World Economy', *Foreign Affairs* (April 1951)

Blum, Léon, *For All Mankind* (London, 1946)

—— *L'histoire jugera* (Paris, 1945)

Bonn, M. J., *Prosperity: Myth and Reality in American Economic Life* (London, 1931)

—— *Wandering Scholar* (London, 1949)

Booker, Christopher, *The Neophiliacs* (London, 1970)

Boris, George, *La révolution Roosevelt* (Paris, 1934)

—— *Servir la République: Textes et temoignages* (Paris, 1963)

Bourdieu, Pierre, *Contre-feux: Propos pour servir à la résistance contre l'invasion néo-liberale* (Paris, 1998)

Bourget, P., *Outre-Mer (Notes sur l'Amérique)* (Paris, 1895)

Bové, José and François Dufour, *Le monde n'est pas une marchandise: Des paysans contre la malbouffe* (Paris, 2000)

Brogan, Denis W., 'From England', in Joseph (ed.), *As Others See Us*

Brooks, Sydney, 'Europe and America', *Atlantic Monthly* (November 1901)

Bryce, J., 'The Essential Unity of Britain and America', *Atlantic Monthly* (July 1898)

Bukharin, Nikolai, 'Imperialism and Communism', *Foreign Affairs* (July 1936)

—— *L'economia mondiale e l'imperialismo*, translation of 1916 edition (Rome, 1966)

—— *Selected Writings on the State and the Transition to Socialism*, ed. Richard B. Day (Armonk, New York, 1982)

Burns, John Horne, *The Gallery* (New York, 1947)

Burns, Nicholas, 'Talking to the World About Foreign Policy', *Harvard International Journal of Press/Politics* (Fall 1996)

Buruma, Ian, 'Continental Drift', *Financial Times* (10 December 2004)

Butler, David, *The British General Election of 1955* (London, 1956)

Cacace, Nicola, 'Tutto il bene e il male dell'America', *Repubblica Affari e Finanza* (20 March 2000)

Calkins, Earnest Elmo, 'If Big Business Came to France', *Atlantic Monthly* (April 1929)

Calleo, David P., 'Obama's Dilemma: Enraged Opponents or Disappointed Followers', *Bologna Journal of International Affairs* (Spring 2010)

Carlyle, Thomas C., *Latter-Day Pamphlets* (London, n.d.)

Carr, Edward Hallett, *Conditions of Peace* (London, 1942)

——*Nationalism and After* (London, 1945)

——*The Twenty Years' Crisis, 1919–1939* (1946 edn repr., London, 1974)

Castaneda, Jorgé, 'La revanche des pauvres', *Nouvel observateur* (6–12 February 1992)

Cather, Willa, *One of Ours* (1922 edn repr., New York, 1971)

Céline, Louis-Ferdinand, *Mea Culpa* (Paris, 1937)

Center for International Affairs (Harvard University), *Allies or Adversaries? U.S.– European Relations in the Paul-Henri Spaak Lectures, Harvard University, 1985–1992*

Chambraud, Cécile, 'Le règne du chacun pour soi', *Le Monde: Bilan Economie 2010* (Paris, 2011)

Churchill, Winston Spencer, *The Gathering Storm* (Boston, 1948)

Clark, Mark, *Calculated Risk* (New York, 1950)

Clay, Lucius D., *Decision in Germany* (New York, 1950)

Cobden, Richard, *England, Ireland and America* (6th edn, Edinburgh, 1836)

Colombani, Jean-Marie, *Un Américain à Paris* (Paris, 2008)

Colyer, W. T., *Americanism: A World Menace* (London, 1922)

Common Council of American Unity, *European Beliefs regarding the United States 1949* (New York, 1949)

Cox, Michael, 'From the Cold War to the War on Terror: Old Threats, New Threats, and the Future of the Transatlantic Relationship', in Lundestad (ed.), *Just Another Major Crisis?*

Creel, George, *How We Advertised America: The First Telling of the Amazing Story of the Committee on Public Information that Carried the Gospel of Americanism to Every Corner of the Globe* (New York, 1920)

Crosland, C. A. R., *The Future of Socialism*, abridged version for US market of original 1956 edition (Westport, Conn., 1957)

Crowther, Geoffrey, *The Economic Reconstruction of Europe* (Claremont, 1948)

Crowther, Samuel, *America Self-Contained* (New York, 1933)

Crozier, Michel, 'The Cultural Revolution: Notes on the Changes in the Intellectual Climate in France', *Daedalus*, Special Issue, 'A New Europe?' (Winter 1964)

Daalder, Ivo H., 'The End of Atlanticism', *Survival* (Summer 2003)

Dahrendorf, Ralf, 'Recent Changes in the Class Structure of European Societies', *Daedalus*, Special Issue, 'The New Europe?' (Winter 1964)

Daily Mail, *The Daily Mail Trade Union Mission to the United States* (n.p., n.d. [1926])

D'Ancona, Matthew (ed.), *Being British: The Search for the Values that Bind the Nation* (Edinburgh, 2009)

Dean, Vera Micheles, *Europe in Retreat* (New York, 1939)

Deaglio, Enrico, *Patria 1978–2008* (Milan, 2009)

Debré, Michel, *La Republique et son pouvoir* (Paris, 1950)

Del Pero, Mario, 'Alla ricerca del primato (in parte) perduto: La politica estera di Barack Obama', in *Quaderni di Relazioni internazionali* (November 2009)

Demolins, Edmond, *A Quoi tient la superiorité des Anglo Saxons?* (Paris, n.d. [*c.*1900])

Denison, E. F., *Why Growth Rates Differ* (Washington DC, 1967)

Denny, Ludwell, *America Conquers Britain: A Record of Economic War* (New York, 1930)

—— *We Fight for Oil* (New York, 1928)

Dickinson, G. Lowes, 'SOS—Europe to America', *Atlantic Monthly* (March 1921)

Djilas, Milovan, *Conversations with Stalin* (London, 1963)

Domenach, Jean-Marie, 'Le modèle américaine', *Esprit* (July–August 1960)

—— 'Le modèle américaine', II, *Esprit* (September 1960)

—— 'Le modèle américaine', III, *Esprit* (October 1960)

Dos Passos, John, *Tour of Duty* (Boston, 1946)

Dos Passos, John R., *The Anglo-Saxon Century and the Unification of the English-Speaking People* (New York, 1903)

Dounic, R., 'La Manie de la Modernité', *Revue des Deux Mondes* (1 March 1898)

Duhamel, Georges, *America the Menace: Scenes from the Life of the Future* (London, 1931)

—— *L'umanité et l'automate* (Paris, 1933)

Eddy, Sherwood, *The Challenge of Europe* (London, 1933)

Einaudi, Luigi, 'Un scritto inedito: Sul cosidetto fondo lire', ed. P. Ciocca and E. Tuccimei, in *Annali della Fondazione Luigi Einaudi*, xxv (1991)

Eliot, T. S., 'The Man of Letters and the Future of Europe', *Horizon* (December 1944)

Ellwood, D. W. (ed.), 'Il Rapporto Harmon (Rapporto di un gruppo di dirigenti dell'industria cinematografica americana, 1945)', *Mezzosecolo*, 3 (Turin, 1982)

Farber, David (ed.), *What They Think of US: International Perceptions of the United States since 9/11* (Princeton, 2007)

Farchy, Joëlle, *La fin de l'exception culturelle?* (Paris, 1999)

Feiler, Arthur, *America Seen Through German Eyes* (New York, 1928)

Feis, Herbert, *Seen from E.A: Three International Episodes* (New York, 1947)

Ferguson, Niall, *Colossus: The Price of America's Empire* (New York, 2004)

—— 'Full Marx', *Financial Times* (17 August 2002)

Ferrero, Léo, *Amérique, miroir grossissant de l'Europe* (Paris, 1939)

Filene, Edward A., 'Mass Production Makes a Better World', *Atlantic Monthly* (May 1929)

Fisher, Allan G. B., 'The Clash Between Progress and Security', *Harper's* (July 1944)

Ford, Henry, *My Life and Work* (London, 1922)

—— *Today and Tomorrow* (New York, 1926)

Fourastié, Jean, *La productivité* (Paris, 1952 and 1968)

—— *Le Grand espoir du XX siècle* (Paris, 1949 and 1958)

—— *Les trente glorieuses* (Paris, 1979 and 2004)

—— *Machinisme et bienêtre* (Paris, 1951 and 1962)

Fox, T. R., *The Super-Powers: The United States, Britain and the Soviet Union— Their Responsibility for Peace* (New York, 1944)

Frachon, Alain, 'L'image des Etats-Unis ne cesse de se dégrader en France', *Le Monde* (31 October 1996)

Frank, Waldo, *Our America* (New York, 1919)

Frederick, Christine, *Selling Mrs Consumer* (London, 1929)

Freedland, Jonathan, *Bring Home the Revolution: How Britain Can Live the American Dream* (London, 1998)

Friedman, Thomas L., 'Cut Out for Globalization and Feeling Quite Good', *International Herald Tribune* (10 February 1997)

—— *The Lexus and the Olive Tree* (New York, 1999)

Fukuyama, Francis, 'Does the West Still Exist?', in Le Gloannec and Smolar (eds), *Entre Kant et Kosovo*

—— 'History Is Still Over', *Newsweek* (12 December 2009)

Gallup, George H., *The Gallup Poll: Public Opinion, 1935–1971,* Vol. 1: *1935–1948* (New York, 1972)

Galbraith, John Kenneth, *A Life in Our Times: A Memoir* (London, 1981)

Gardner, Lloyd C. and Marilyn B. Young (eds), *The New American Empire: A 21st Century Teach-In on U.S. Foreign Policy* (New York, 2005)

Garton Ash, Timothy, 'Anti-Europeanism in America', *The New York Review of Books* (13 February 2003)

—— *Free World: Why a Crisis of the West Reveals the Opportunity of our Time* (London, 2005), published in New York as *Free World: America, Europe and the Surprising Future of the West*

Gasset, José Ortega y, *The Revolt of the Masses* (1932 edn repr., New York, 1957)

Gelb, Michael (ed.), *An American Engineer in Stalin's Russia: The Memoirs of Zara Witkin* (Berkeley, 1991)

Ginsborg, Paul, *Silvio Berlusconi: Television, Power and Patrimony* (London, 2004)

Giroud, Françoise, *La Nouvelle Vague: Portraits de la jeunesse* (Paris, 1958)

Gonzalez, Emiliano, 'Made in USA', *Cambio 16* (15 July 1996)

Gordon, Philip H. and Jeremy Shapiro, *Allies at War: America, Europe, and the Crisis over Iraq* (New York, 2004)

Gorham, Maurice, *Sound and Fury: Twenty-One Years in the BBC* (London, 1948)

Gramsci, Antonio, 'Americanism and Fordism', in David Forgacs (ed.), *A Gramsci Reader* (London, 1988)

—— *Antonio Gramsci: Selections from Political Writings (1921–1926)*, ed. tr. Quintin Hoare (London, 1978)

—— *Prison Notebooks*, ii, ed. tr. Joseph A. Buttigieg (New York, 1996)

—— *Selections from the Prison Notebooks of Antonio Gramsci*, ed. tr. Quintin Hoare and Geoffrey Nowell-Smith (New York, 1971)

Graves, Robert and Alan Hodge, *The Long Weekend: A Social History of Great Britain, 1918–1939* (1940 edn repr., London 1985)

Grierson, John, *Notes for English Producers* (n.d. [April–May 1927]), reproduced as appendix to I. C. Jarvie and Nicholas Pronay (eds), 'John Grierson: A Critical

Retrospective', special issue of *Historical Journal of Film, Radio and Television*, 9/3 (1989)

Gruber, Karl, *Between Life and Liberty: Austria in the Postwar World* (London, 1955)

Gunther, John, *Inside Europe* (London, 1936)

Haass, Richard, 'The Age of Nonpolarity: What Will Follow U.S. Dominance', *Foreign Affairs* (May/June 2008)

Habermass, Jürgen and Jacques Derrida, 'February 15, Or, What Binds Europeans Together: Plea for a Common Foreign Policy, Beginning in Core Europe', in Levy, Pensky, and Torpey (eds), *Old Europe, New Europe, Core Europe*

Hall, Stuart, 'The Supply of Demand', in Thompson (ed.), *Out of Apathy*

Hansen, Alvin, *America's Role in the World Economy* (New York, 1945)

Harley, John Eugene, *World-Wide Influences of the Cinema: A Study of Official Censorship and the International Cultural Aspects of Motion Pictures* (Los Angeles, 1940)

Harper, John L., 'American Visions of Europe after 1989', in Tod Lindberg (ed.), *Beyond Paradise and Power: Europe, America and the Future of a Troubled Partnership* (London, 2005)

Havel, Vaclav, *To the Castle and Back* (London, 2008)

Hayek, Friedrich A., *The Road to Serfdom* (London, 1944)

Heidegger, Martin, *The Question Concerning Technology and Other Essays* (New York, 1977)

Henderson, Hubert Douglas, *The Interwar Years: A Selection from the Writings of Hubert Douglas Henderson* (Oxford, 1955)

Hersey, John, *A Bell for Adano* (1944 edn repr., New York, 1977)

Hertsgaard, Mark, *The Eagle's Shadow: Why America Fascinates and Infuriates the World* (London, 2002)

Hitler, Adolf, *Hitler's Secret Book*, translation of unpublished 1928 text (New York, 1961)

—— *Mein Kampf* (1943 edn repr., London, 1992)

Hoffmann, Stanley, 'Sheriff and Missionary', in Andrew J. Bacevich (ed.), *The Imperial Tense Prospects and Problems of American Empire* (Chicago, 2003)

Hoffman, Paul G., *Peace Can be Won* (Garden City, NY, 1951)

Hoggart, Richard, *The Uses of Literacy* (London, 1957)

Hoover, Herbert, *The Memoirs of Herbert Hoover*, i: *Years of Adventure, 1874–1920* (New York, 1952), ii: *The Cabinet and the Presidency, 1920–1933* (New York, 1952), iii: *The Great Depression, 1929–1941* (New York, 1952)

Hopkins, Harry, *The New Look: A Social History of the Forties and Fifties in Britain* (London, 1963)

Howson, Susan and Donald Moggridge (eds), *The Wartime Diaries of Lionel Robbins and James Meade, 1943–45* (London, 1990)

Huizinga, J., *America: A Dutch Historian's Vision from Afar and Near* (New York, 1928)

Huntington, Samuel P., 'The Clash of Civilizations?' *Foreign Affairs* (Summer 1993)

—— 'The West: Unique, Not Universal', *Foreign Affairs* (November/December 1996)

—— *Who Are We? The Challenges to America's National Identity* (New York, 2004)

Hutton, Graham, *We Too Can Prosper* (London, 1953)

Hutton, Will, *The World We're In* (London, 2002)

Huxley, Aldous, *Brave New World* (1932 edn repr., London, 1994)

Ikenberry, John G., 'Unilateralism in US Foreign Policy: What Roles does America See for Europe?', in Lundestad (ed.), *Just Another Major Crisis?*

Inglis, Tom, *Global Ireland* (New York, 2008)

James, Henry, 'Daisy Miller', in Napier Wilt and John Lucas (eds), *Americans and Europe: Selected Tales of Henry James* (Boston, 1965)

Jeanne, René, 'La crise cinématographique', *Revue des Deux Mondes* (1 September 1933)

—— 'La France et le film parlant', *Revue des Deux Mondes* (1 June 1931)

—— 'L'invasion cinématographique américaine', *Revue des Deux Mondes* (15 February 1930)

Jeanneney, Jean-Noël, *Google and the Myth of Universal Knowledge: A View from Europe* (Chicago, 2007)

Johnston, Eric, *America Unlimited* (Garden City, NY, 1944)

Joseph, Franz M. (ed.), *As Others See Us: The United States through Foreign Eyes* (Princeton, 1959)

Judis, John B., 'The Author of Liberty: Religion and U.S. Foreign Policy', *Dissent* (Fall 2005)

Judt, Tony, 'Europe versus America', *New York Review of Books* (10 February 2005)

—— 'Its Own Worst Enemy', *The New York Review of Books* (15 August 2002)

Kagan, Robert, *Of Paradise and Power: America and Europe in the New World Order* (New York, 2003)

Kampfner, John, *Freedom for Sale: How We Made Money and Lost Our Liberty* (London, 2009)

Kennan, George F., *Memoirs 1925–1950* (Boston, 1967)

Keynes, John Maynard, *The Collected Writings of John Maynard Keynes*, ii: *The Economic Consequences of the Peace* (1919 edn repr., London, 1971), xviii: *Activities 1922–32: The End of Reparations* (London, 1978), xx: *Activities 1929–1931: Rethinking Employment and Unemployment Policies* (London, 1981), xxiv: *Activities 1944–46: The Transition to Peace* (London, 1979)

Kipling, Rudyard, *American Notes* (1st edn, 1891; 1899 edn repr., New York, 1974)

Kissinger, Henry, 'A Role for the Atlantic Alliance Today', *The Washington Post/ Guardian Weekly* (8 March 1992)

Koestler, Arthur, 'Land of Bread and Wine', *The Trail of the Dinosaur* (London, 1955)

Kohut, Andrew, *America Against the World* (Washington DC, 2008)

Kracauer, Siegfried, *From Caligari to Hitler: A Psychological History of the German Film* (1947 edn repr., Princeton, 1974)

Kracauer, Siegfried. *The Mass Ornament: Weimar Essays* (Cambridge, Mass., 1995)

Krastner, Joseph, 'What to do with the World's Air', *Transatlantic*, 3 (March 1944)

Kühn, Hans, 'The Mass Man: Hitler', *Atlantic Monthly* (April 1944)

Kuisel, Richard, 'The Gallic Rooster Crows Again: The Paradox of French Anti-Americanism', *French Politics, Culture and Society* (Fall 2001)

—— 'What Do the French Think of Us? The Deteriorating Image of the United States, 2000–2004', *French Politics, Culture and Society* (Fall 2004)

Kull, Steven, 'Can the Circle Be Unbroken? Public Opinion and the Transatlantic Rupture', in Lundestad (ed.), *Just Another Major Crisis?*

Lane, David, *Berlusconi's Shadow: Crime, Justice and the Pursuit of Power* (London, 2005)

Larned, J. N., 'England's Economic and Political Crisis', *Atlantic Monthly* (March 1898)

Larrabee, Eric, 'Transcripts of a Transatlantic Dialogue', *Daedalus*, Special Issue, 'A New Europe?' (Winter 1964)

Laski, Harold, *Reflections on the Revolution of Our Time* (London, 1943)

Laurent, Pierre, *L'impérialisme économique américain* (Paris, 1931)

Leavis, F. R., *Mass Civilisation and Minority Culture* (Cambridge, 1930)

Le Bon, Gustave, *The Crowd: A Study of the Popular Mind* (original French edn, Paris, 1892; London, 1896)

Le Cinéma dans l'Enseignement de l'Eglise (Vatican City, 1955)

Le Monde: Bilan Economie Atlas 2010 (Paris, 2010)

Lengyel, Emil, *The New Deal in Europe* (New York, 1934)

Lenin, V. I., *On the United States of America* (Moscow, 1967)

Leroy-Beaulieu, P., 'Les Etats-Unis Puissance coloniale', *Revue des Deux Mondes* (1 January 1902)

Levi, Carlo, *Christ Stopped at Eboli* (1st edn, Milan, 1945; 1947 edn repr., New York, 1976)

Levy, Daniel, Max Pensky, and John Torpey (eds), *Old Europe, New Europe, Core Europe: Transatlantic Relations after the Iraq War* (London, 2005)

Lewis, Norman, *Naples '44* (London, 1978)

Lieven, Anatol, 'The Push for War', *London Review of Books* (3 October 2002)

Lilienthal, David, *Democracy on the March* (New York, 1944)

Lindbergh, Charles A., *We* (New York, 1928)

Lippmann, Walter, 'Britain and America', *Foreign Affairs* (April 1935)

—— *Isolation and Alliances: An American Speaks to the British* (New York, 1952)

—— *The American Destiny* (New York, 1939)

—— *The Method of Freedom* (New York, 1934)

—— *U.S. War Aims* (London, 1944)

Lord, Kristin M., *Voices of America: U.S. Public Diplomacy for the 21st Century*, Brookings Institution (Washington DC, 2008)

Luce, Edward, 'The Continuing Power of the US Economy', in Almqvist and Linklater (eds), *On the Idea of America*

Lundberg, Isabel Cary, 'World Revolution, American Plan', *Harper's* (December 1948)

Lundestad, Geir (ed.), *Just Another Major Crisis? The United States and Europe since 2000* (Oxford, 2008)

McCormick, Thomas, 'American Hegemony and European Autonomy, 1989–2003: One Framework for Understanding the War in Iraq', in Gardner and Young (eds), *New American Empire*

MacInnes, Colin, *Absolute Beginners* (1959 edn repr., London, 1964)

McKenzie, F. A., *The American Invaders* (London, 1902)

McMillan, James and Bernard Harris, *The American Take-Over of Britain* (London, 1968)

McNamara, Robert, 'The Folly of US and NATO Weapons Policies', Johns Hopkins University, SAIS Bologna Center (20 April 2005)

McNeill, W. H., *The Greek Dilemma* (London, 1947)

—— *The Metamorphosis of Greece since World War II* (Oxford, 1978)

McReary, Edward A., *The Americanization of Europe* (Garden City, NY, 1964)

Mahbubani, Kishore, *The New Asia Hemisphere: The Irresistible Shift of Global Power to the East* (New York, 2008)

Malaparte, Curzio, *Il compagno di viaggio* (Milan, 2007)

—— *La pelle* (1st edn, Milan, 1949; Milan, 1991)

Mann, Thomas, 'How to Win the Peace', *Atlantic Monthly* (February 1942)

—— *Royal Highness* (1916 English edn repr., London 1997)

—— *The War and the Future*, Library of Congress (Washington DC, 13 October 1943)

Maritain, Jaques, 'America's Role in the New Europe', *The Commonweal* (February 26 1943)

Marquand, David, 'Goodbye, The West', *Prospect* (August 2004)

—— 'Keynes was wrong', *Prospect* (March 2001)

Mason, Paul, *Meltdown: The End of the Age of Greed* (London, 2009)

Matthiessen, F. O., *From the Heart of Europe* (New York, 1948)

Maynes, Charles William, 'The Perils of (and for) an Imperial America', *Foreign Policy* (Summer 1998)

Meunier, Sophie, 'French Cultural Policy and the American Mirror in the Sarkozy Era', *French Politics*, 6/1 (2008)

Miller, Frances P. and H. D. Hill, 'Europe as a Playground', *Atlantic Monthly* (August 1930)

—— 'Europe as a Market', *Atlantic Monthly* (September 1930)

Miller, Perry, 'The Reimportation of Ideas', in Russell et al., *Impact of America*

Mises, Ludwig von, *Selected Writings of Ludwig von Mises*, iii: *The Political Economy of International Reform and Reconstruction*, ed. Richard M. Ebeling (Indianapolis, 2000)

Mitford, Nancy, *The Blessing* (1951 edn repr., London, 2009)

Moïsi, Dominique, '9 novembre 1989–11 septembre 2001: L'âge de la mondialisation', in Le Gloannec and Smolar (eds), *Entre Kant et Kosovo*

—— 'America the Triumphant', *Financial Times* (9 February 1998)

—— 'Re-Inventing the West', *Foreign Affairs* (November–December 2003)

—— *The Geopolitics of Emotion* (New York, 2009)

—— 'The Trouble with France', *Foreign Affairs* (May/June 1998)

Monnet, Jean, *Memoirs* (London, 1978)

Moorehead, Alan, *Eclipse* (London, 1945)

—— 'The Wasteland of Europe', *The Listener* (6 April 1944)

Morrison, Donald, *Que rest-t-il de la culture française?* (Paris, 2008)

—— 'The Death of French Culture', *Time*, European edition (3 December 2007)

Mowrer, Edgar Ansel, 'The Fifth Europe', *Horizon* (March 1963)

—— *This American World*, with a preface by T. S. Eliot (London, 1928)

Muhlen, Norbert, 'America and American Occupation in German Eyes', *Annals of the American Academy of Political and Social Science* (September 1954)

Muirhead, J. F., *America the Land of Contrasts* (1902 edn repr., New York, 1970)

Mulgan, Geoff, 'Case of Mistaken Euro-identity', *Times Higher Education Supplement* (20 September 1996)

—— 'Gordon Brown: Intellectual', *Prospect* (July 2007)

Murphy, Robert, *Diplomat Among Warriors* (London, 1964)

National Peace Council, *The British Commonwealth and the United States in the Post-War World*, papers from a conference (London, November 1941)

Nevola, Gaspare, *Una patria per gli italiani? La questions nazionale oggi tra storia, cultura e politica* (Rome, 2003)

New Statesman and Nation, *Stalin–Wells Talk: The Verbatim Record and a Discussion* (London, 1934)

Nicholas, H. G., *Washington Despatches 1941–1945* (London 1981)

Nicolson , Harold., *Diaries and Letters*, ii (London, 1967)

—— *The Future of the English-Speaking World.* Text of speech of November 1948 (Glasgow, 1949)

—— *Peace-making 1919* (New York, 1923)

Niebuhr, Reinhold, 'The Awkward Imperialist', *Atlantic Monthly* (June 1930)

—— 'The Perils of American Power', *Atlantic Monthly* (June 1932)

—— *The Irony of American History* (1952 edn repr., New York, 2008)

Nye Jr, Joseph S., 'Soft Power and European-American Affairs', in Ilgen (ed.), *Hard Power, Soft Power*

—— 'Soft Power', *Foreign Policy* (Fall 1990)

—— *The Paradox of American Power: Why the World's Only Superpower Can't Go It Alone* (New York, 2002)

—— and William A. Owens, 'America's Information Edge', *Foreign Affairs* (March/April 1996)

Obama, Barack, *The Audacity of Hope: Thoughts on Reclaiming the American Dream* (New York, 2006)

Oberdorfer, Don, 'A Journalist to His Profession: "I Am Deeply Worried" ', *Harvard International Journal of Press/Politics* (Winter 1996)

O'Faolain, Sean, *An Irish Journey* (London, 1940)

Orwell, George, *Coming Up for Air* (1939 edn repr., Harmondsworth, 1980)

—— *Essays* (1984 edn repr., London, 2000)

—— *The Collected Essays, Journalism and Letters of George Orwell*, ii: *My Country Right or Left, 1940–1943* (Harmondsworth, 1970), iii: *As I Please, 1943–1945*

(Harmondsworth, 1970), iv: *In Front of Your Nose, 1945–1950* (1968 edn repr., Harmondsworth, 1980)

Owen, David, *The Hubris Syndrome: Bush, Blair and the Intoxication of Power* (London, 2007)

Palliser, Michael, 'Forty Years On: The Nature of United States Power and European Influence', in Center for International Affairs (Harvard University), *Allies or Adversaries?* (Cambridge, Mass., 2000)

Paris, Thomas (ed.), *Quelle diversité face à Hollywood*, special edition of *CinémAction* (2002)

Paxman, Jeremy, *The English: A Portrait of a People* (London, 1999)

Penrose, E. F., *Economic Planning for the Peace* (Princeton, 1953)

Perkins, Frances, 'Social Security Here and Abroad', *Foreign Affairs* (April 1935)

Pfaff, William, *Barbarian Sentiments: How the American Century Ends* (New York, 1989)

—— 'Sole Superpower Status Goes to America's Head', *International Herald Tribune* (18–19 January 1997)

—— 'Western Europe Missed Its Chance to Take Charge', *International Herald Tribune* (5 December 1995)

Pimlott, Ben (ed.), *The Second World War Diary of Hugh Dalton 1940–45* (London, 1986)

Pizzorno, Alessandro, 'The Individualistic Mobilization of Europe', *Daedalus*, Special Issue, 'A New Europe?' (Winter 1964)

Polanyi, Karl, *The Great Transformation* (1944 edn repr., New York, 1957)

Pomaret, Charles, *L'Amérique à la conquête de l'Europe* (Paris, 1931)

Pond, Elizabeth, *Friendly Fire: The Near-Death of the Transatlantic Alliance* (Pittsburgh, 2004)

Postan, Michael M., *An Economic History of Western Europe, 1945–1964* (London, 1967)

Potter, David M., *People of Plenty: Economic Abundance and the American Character* (Chicago, 1954)

Prefaces to Peace: A Symposium (New York, 1943)

Priestley, J. B., *English Journey* (1934 edn repr., London, 1984)

—— *Essays of Five Decades* (London, 1969)

—— *Let the People Sing* (London, 1940)

—— *Midnight on the Desert: A Chapter of Autobiography* (London, 1937)

—— *Three Men in New Suits* (1945 edn repr., London, 1984)

—— and J. Hawkes, *Journey Down the Rainbow* (London, 1955)

Quignard, Patrice, *L'occupation américaine* (Paris, 1994)

Ramirez, Fatima, 'Come te ODIO, AMOR', *Cambio 16* (15 July 1996)

Rauschning, Herman, *The Redemption of Democracy: The Coming Atlantic Empire* (New York, 1941)

Rea, Ermanno, *Mistero napoletano: Vita e passione di una comunista negli anni della guerra fredda* (Turin, 1995)

Remotti, Francesco, *L'ossessione identitaria* (Rome, 2010)

Resca, Mario and Rinaldo Gianola, *McDonald's: Una storia italiana* (Milan, 1998)

Ricks, Thomas E., *Fiasco: The American Military Adventure in Iraq* (London, 2007)

Ridgeway, George L., *Merchants of Peace* (1938 edn repr., Boston, 1959)

Robbins, Lord, *Autobiography of an Economist* (London, 1971)

Roger, Charles, 'A "New Deal" for Belgium', *Foreign Affairs* (July 1935)

Romano, Sergio, *Il rischio americano: L'america imperiale, l'Europa irrelevante* (Milan, 2003)

Romier, Lucien, 'La disgrace du capitalisme', *Revue des Deux Mondes* (1 June 1933)

—— *Who Will Be Master, Europe or America?* (London, 1929)

Rosenman, Samuel I., *Working with Roosevelt* (London, 1952)

Ross, Kristin, 'The French Declaration of Independence', in Andrew Ross and Kristin Ross (eds), *Anti-Americanism* (New York, 2004)

Rostow, Walt Whitman, *The Stages of Economic Growth: A Non-Communist Manifesto* (Cambridge, 1960)

Roth, Joseph, *Hotel Savoy*, translation of 1924 edition (London, 1986)

Rothkop, David, 'In Praise of Cultural Imperialism? Effects of Globalization on Culture', *Foreign Policy* (June 1997)

Rusconi, Gian Enrico, Thomas Schlemmer, and Hans Woller (eds), *Estraniazione strisciante tra Italia e Germania?* (Bologna, 2008)

Rushdie, Salman, 'Rethinking the War on American Culture', *New York Times* (5 March 1999)

Russell, Bertrand, 'Where Do We Go Now?', *The Listener* (11 January 1945)

—— and Dora Russell, *The Prospects of Industrial Civilisation* (London, 1923)

—— et al., *The Impact of America on European Culture* (Boston, 1951)

Sales, Raoul de Roussy de, *The Making of Tomorrow* (London, 1943)

Schumpeter, Joseph A., *Capitalism, Socialism and Democracy* (1st edn, New York, 1942; New York, 2008)

Schurz, Carl, 'The Anglo-American Friendship', *Atlantic Monthly* (October 1898)

Schwarz, Benjamin, 'Sheer Data', *Atlantic Monthly* (February 2002)

Schwarzschild, Leopold, *Primer of the Coming World* (London, 1944)

Scott, Bruce, *The Concept of Capitalism* (Berlin, 2009)

Serra, Narcìs and Joseph E. Stiglitz (eds), *The Washington Consensus Reconsidered: Towards a New Global Governance* (Oxford, 2008)

Servan-Schreiber, Jean-Jacques, *The American Challenge* (New York, 1969)

Shaw, George Bernard, 'A Little Talk on America' (London, October 1931)

—— *Captain Brassbound's Conversion* (London, 1899)

—— *The Applecart* (London, 1926)

—— *The Intelligent Woman's Guide to Socialism and Capitalism* (London, 1928)

Sheehan, Marion Turner (ed.), *The World at Home: Selections from the Writings of Anne O'Hare McCormick* (New York, 1956)

Siegfried, André, *America Comes of Age: A French Analysis* (New York, 1927)

—— 'Can Europe Use American Methods?', *Foreign Affairs* (July 1952)

—— *La crise de l'Europe* (Paris, 1935)

—— 'L'Europe devant la civilisation américaine', *Revue des Deux Mondes* (15 April 1930)

Silone, Ignazio, *Fontamara* (1st edn, Zurich, 1933; 1949 edn repr., Milan, 1988)

Slaughter, Anne-Marie, *The Idea That Is America: Keeping Faith with Our Values in a Dangerous World* (New York, 2007)

Sloan, Stanley R., 'Where are American–European Relations Heading? A View from the United States', in Lundestad (ed.), *Just Another Major Crisis?*

Smith, Howard K., *The State of Europe* (London, 1950)

Snow, Nancy, *The Arrogance of American Power: What U.S. Leaders Are Doing Wrong and Why It's Our Duty to Dissent* (Lanham, Md., 2007)

Soldati, Mario, *America, primo amore* (Florence, 1935)

Sontag, Susan, 'Literature is Freedom', October 2003, in Levy, Pensky, Torpey (eds), *Old Europe, New Europe, Core Europe*

Soroka, Stuart N., 'Media, Public Opinion and Foreign Policy', *Harvard International Journal of Press/Politics* (Winter 2003)

Southard, Frank A., *American Industry in Europe* (Boston, 1931)

Spoerri, William T., *The Old World and the New: A Synopsis of Current European Views on American Civilization* (Zurich, 1937)

Stanger, Ted, *Un américain en Picardie* (Paris, 2005)

Stead, W. T., 'The Americanisation of the World or the Trend of the Twentieth Century', *Review of Reviews* (London, 1902)

Steel-Maitland, Arthur, *The New America* (London, 1934)

Steel, Ronald, *End of Alliance* (New York, 1964)

Stefansson, Anders, 'America Degree Zero and the Obama Non-Doctrine', in Almqvist and Linklater (eds), *On the Idea of America*

Stettinius, Edward, *Roosevelt and the Russians: The Yalta Conference* (London, 1950)

Stiglitz, Joseph E., *Freefall: America, Free Markets and the Sinking of the World Economy* (New York, 2010)

Stille, Alexander, *The Sack of Rome* (New York, 2006)

Streit, Clarence, *Union Now* (New York, 1939)

Sweig, Julia E., *Friendly Fire: Losing Friends and Making Enemies in the Anti-American Century* (New York, 2006)

Tardieu, André, *Devant l'obstacle* (Paris, 1927)

Taylor, Robert, ' "Immature, immoral, vulgar, materialistic…": How Britons viewed Yanks in the 1940s', *New Statesman* (3 March 2003)

Teodori, Massimo, *Maledetti americani. Destra, sinistra e cattolici: Storia del pregiudizio antimericano* (Milan, 2002)

Thompson, Edward P. (ed.), *Out of Apathy* (London, 1960)

Thomson, David, E. Meyer, and A. Briggs, *Patterns of Peacemaking* (London, 1945)

Tocqueville, Alexis de, *Democracy in America*, tr. of 1835/1840 editions by Harvey C. Mansfield and Delba Winthrop (Chicago, 2000)

Touraine, Alain, 'Management and the Working Class in Western Europe', *Daedalus*, Special Issue, 'A New Europe?' (Winter 1964)

Toynbee, Polly, 'Who's Afraid of Global Culture?', in Giddens and Hutton (eds), *Global Capitalism*

Trollope, Anthony, *North America* (1862 edn repr., London, 1992)

Trotsky, L., *Europe and America: Two Speeches on Imperialism* (New York, 1971)

—— 'Nationalism and Economic Life', *Foreign Affairs* (April 1934)

Tuckerman, Henry T., *America and her Commentators, with a critical sketch of travel in the United States* (1864 edn repr., New York, 1961)

Tynan, Kenneth, 'British Cultural Fatigue', *Atlantic Monthly* (November 1955)

Utley, Garrick, 'The Shrinking of Foreign News: From Broadcast to Narrowcast', *Foreign Affairs* (March–April 1997)

Varga, Eugen, *The Great Crisis and its Political Consequences* (London, 1935)

Védrine, Hubert, 'La rédistribution de la puissance', Entretien avec Hubert Védrine, *Le Débat* (May–August 2010)

—— *Les cartes de la France à l'heure de la mondialisation* (Paris, 2000)

Veltroni, Walter, 'Vogliamo gli Stati Uniti d'Europa', *liMes*, 4 (1996)

Violante, Luciano, *Un mondo assimetrico: Europa, Stati Uniti. Islam* (Torino, 2003)

Walker, Martin, 'Flawed Vision of the New Imperial Rome', *Guardian Weekly* (27 January 1991)

Wallace, Henry, *The Century of the Common Man* (London, 1944)

Ward, Barbara, 'Journey to America', *Horizon* (April 1943)

Watt, D. C., *Britain Looks to Germany: British Opinion and Policy Towards Germany since 1945* (London, 1965)

Wedel, Janine R., 'Aid to Russia', *Foreign Policy in Focus* (September 1998)

Weidenfeld, W., *America and Europe: Is the Break Inevitable?* (Gütersloh, 1996)

Welk, William G., 'Fascist Economic Policy and the National Recovery Administration', *Foreign Affairs* (October 1933)

Welles, Sumner, *The World of the Four Freedoms* (New York, 1943)

—— *Time for Decision* (New York, 1944)

—— *We Need Not Fail* (Boston, 1948)

Wells, H. G., *Experiment in Autobiography*, ii: *1898–1918* (1934 edn repr., London, 1966)

—— *In the Fourth Year: Anticipations of a World Peace* (London, 1918)

—— *The Future in America* (1906 edn repr., London, 1987)

—— *The New America: The New World* (London, 1935)

—— *The New Machiavelli* (London, 1910)

—— *The Peace of the World* (London, n.d. [1915])

Wharton, Edith, *The Buccaneers* (1st edn, New York, 1938)

Whidden, Howard P., 'Birth of a Mass Market—Western Europe', *Harvard Business Review* (May–June 1955)

Whitnah, Donald R. and Florentine E. Whitnah, *Salzburg Under Siege: U.S. Occupation, 1945–1955* (Westport, Conn., 1991)

Williams, Frances, *The American Invasion* (London, 1962)

Willkie, Wendell, *One World* (New York, 1943)

Zakaria, Fareed, *The Post-American World* (New York, 2008)

OFFICIAL AND SEMI-OFFICIAL SOURCES

Anglo-American Council on Productivity, *Final Report of the Council* (London, September 1952)

Annual Economic Report of the President 2000 (Washington DC, 2000)

Blair, Tony and Gerhard Schroëder, 'The Third Way/Die Neue Mitte', reproduced in Bodo Hombach, *The Politics of the New Centre* (London, 2000), Appendix

Blum, Léon, *L'Oeuvre de Leon Blum* (Paris, 1958)

Brune, Lester H. (ed.), *Chronological History of U.S. Foreign Relations*, i (New York, 2003)

Churchill, Winston S., *The Second World War*, iv: *The Hinge of Fate* (London, 1951)

Clarke, Sir Richard, *Anglo-American Economic Collaboration in War and Peace, 1942–1949* (Oxford, 1982)

Clay, Lucius D., *Decision in Germany* (New York, 1950)

Council on Foreign Relations, *The Problem of Lend-Lease: Its, Nature, Implications and Settlement* (New York, April 1944)

Degras, Jane (ed.), *The Communist International, 1919–1943: Documents*, iii: *1929–1943* (London, 1965)

Di Nolfo, Ennio, *Vaticano e Stati Uniti, 1939–1952: Dalle carte di Myron C. Taylor* (Milan, 1978)

Donnison, F. S. V., *Civil Affairs and Military Government in North-West Europe, 1944–1946* (London, 1961)

Eden, Anthony, *Memoirs*, ii (London, 1965)

Erhard, Ludwig, *Prosperity through Competition* (London, 1958)

Friedrich, C. J. et al. (eds), *American Experiences in Military Government in World War II* (New York, 1948)

Gaulle, Charles de, *Discours et messages: Pendant la Guerre, Juin 1940–Janvier 1946* (Paris, 1946)

—— *The Complete War Memoirs of Charles de Gaulle* (New York, 1998)

Hill, Robert M. and Elizabeth Craig Hill, *In the Wake of War: Memoirs of an Alabama Military Government Officer in World War II Italy* (University, Ala., 1982)

Hull, Cordell, *The Memoirs of Cordell Hull*, 2 vols (New York, 1948)

International Chamber of Commerce, Europe–United States Committee, Monographs Presented for Discussion at the Washington Congress (n.p., 1931)

Ireland's Economy: Radio Eireann talks on Ireland's part in the Marshall Plan (Dublin, n.d. [March–April 1949])

Italian Communist Party (PCI), *Il Piano Marshall e i comunisti*, pamphlet in series entitled 'Problemi economici' (Rome, 1949)

Jospin, Lionel, remarks at Harvard in 2003; reproduced in *French Politics, Culture and Society* (Summer 2004)

Kirk, George, *The Middle East in the War*, Survey of International Affairs (Oxford, 1952)

Lipgens, Walter (ed.), *Documents on the History of European Integration*, iii (Berlin, 1988)

Mendès-France, Pierre, *Oeuvres complètes: II Une politique de l'économie, 1943–1954* (Paris, 1985)

Meyer, Christopher, *DC Confidential* (London, 2005)

Moynihan, M. (ed.) *Speeches and Statements by Eamon de Valera, 1917–1973* (Dublin, 1980)

Notter, Harley A., *Postwar Foreign Policy Preparation, 1939–1945* (Washington DC, 1949)

OECD, *Explorations in OEEC History*, ed. Richard T. Griffiths (Paris, 1997)

OEEC, 6th Report (Paris, 1955)

—— 7th report (Paris, 1956)

OEEC/EPA, *Series of Lectures on Economic Growth* (Paris, 1961)

Roosevelt, F. D., *The Public Papers and Addresses of Franklin D. Roosevelt*, ix: *1940 Volume, War—and Aid to Democracies* (New York, 1941), xiii: *1944–45 Volume, Victory and the Threshold of Peace* (New York, 1950)

Roosevelt, T. R., *A Compilation of the Messages and Papers of the Presidents*, xvii (Washington DC, Bureau of National Literature, n.d.)

—— *The Letters of Theodore Roosevelt*, ed. Elting E. Morison, iii, iv (Cambridge, Mass., 1951)

—— *The New Nationalism* (1910 edn repr., Englewood Cliffs, NJ, 1961)

—— *The Strenuous Life: Essays and Addresses* (New York, 1901)

—— *TR: An Autobiography* (1913 edn repr., New York, 1920)

Scottish Council (Development and Industry), Annual Reports 1950–1952, *Scotland* and *Survey of Economic Conditions in Scotland*

Seitz, Raymond, *Over Here* (London, 1998)

Stalin, Giuseppe, *Questioni del Leninismo* (Moscow, 1946)

Stettinius, Edward, *Lend-Lease Weapon for Victory* (New York, 1944)

UNESCO, *The Old World and the New: Their Cultural and Moral Relations, International Forums of San Paolo and Geneva, 1954* (1956)

United States Government, *American Foreign Policy: Current Documents 1989* (Washington DC, 1990)

—— *Foreign Relations of the United States, 1898* (Washington DC, 1901)

—— *Foreign Relations of the United States, 1918*, Supplement 1, Vol. 1 (Washington DC, 1933)

—— *Foreign Relations of the United States: The Conferences at Washington and Quebec, 1943* (Washington DC, 1979)

—— *Foreign Relations of the United States, 1944*, i (Washington DC, 1966)

—— *Foreign Relations of the United States, 1945*, ii (Washington DC, 1967)

—— *Instructions for American Servicemen in Britain 1942* (1942 edn repr., Oxford, 2004)

—— *National Security Strategy of the United States* (Washington DC, September 2002)

—— *Recent Economic Changes in the United States: Report of the Presidente's Conference Committee*, 2 vols (New York, 1929)

United States Government, Department of Homeland Security, *2008 Yearbook of Immigration Statistics* (Washington DC, 2009)

Volkswagen Chronicle, Historical Notes, Vol. 7 (Wolfsburg, 2003)

Wagnleitner, Reinhold (ed.), *Understanding Austria: The Political Reports and Analyses of Martin F. Herz* (Salzburg, 1984)

Wilson, Woodrow, 'The Ideals of America', *Atlantic Monthly* (December 1902)
—— *War and Peace: Presidential Messages, Addresses and Public Papers (1917–1924)*, ed. Ray Stannard Baker and William E. Dodd (New York, 1927)

FURTHER READING

Anholt, Simon, *Brand America. The Making, Unmaking and Remaking of the Greatest National Image of All Time*, (London, 2010)

Baldwin, Peter, *The Copyright Wars. Three Centuries of Trans-Atlantic Battle* (Princeton, 2014)

Berghahn, Volker, *American Big Business in Britain and Germany: A Comparative History of Two "Special Relationships" in the 20th Century* (Princeton, 2014)

Castillo, Greg, *Cold War on the Home Front: The Soft Power of Midcentury Design* (Minneapolis, 2010)

Conrad, Peter, *How the World Was Won. The Americanization of Everywhere* (London, 2014)

Delanty, Gerard, *Formations of European Modernity. A Historical and Political Sociology of Europe* (London, 2013)

Friedman, Max Paul, *Re-Thinking Anti-Americanism. The History of an Exceptional Concept in American Foreign Relations* (New York, 2012)

Glancy, Mark, *Hollywood and the Americanization of Britain. From the 1920s to the Present* (London, 2014)

Kooijman, Jaap, *Fabricating the Absolute Fake. America in Contemporary Pop Culture* (Amsterdam, 2008)

Logemann, Jan L., *Trams or Tailfins? Public and Private Prosperity in Postwar West Germany and the United States* (Chicago and London, 2012)

Migone, Gian Giacomo, *The United States and Fascist Italy. The Rise of American Finance in Europe*, (New York, 2015)

Ninkovich, Frank, *The Global Republic: America's Inadvertent Rise to World Power* (Chicago, 2014)

Nolan, Mary, *The Transatlantic Century. Europe and America, 1890–2010* (New York, 2012)

Oldenziel, Ruth and Karin Zachmann (eds), *Cold War Kitchen: Americanization, Technology and European Users* (Cambridge, MA, 2009)

Parmar, Inderjeet and Michael Cox, *Soft Power and US Foreign Policy. Theoretical, Historical and Contemporary Perspectives* (Abingdon, 2010)

Petersen, Klaus, Stewart, John, and Michael Kuur Sørensen (eds), *American Foundations and the European Welfare States* (Odense, 2013)

Reich, Simon and Richard Ned Lebow, *Goodbye Hegemony! Power and Influence in the Global System* (Princeton, 2014)

Roberts, Mary, *What Soldiers Do. Sex and the American GI in World War II France* (Chicago and London, 2013)

Schmelzer, Matthias, *The Hegemony of Growth: The OECD and the Making of the Economic Growth Paradigm* (Cambridge, 2016)

Tooze, Adam, *The Deluge: The Great War and the Remaking of Global Order 1916–1931* (London, 2014)

Wagner, Peter, *Modernity. Understanding the Present* (Cambridge, 2012)

Acknowledgements

This book was a life-time's project: a quarter of a century has gone by since it was first conceived. Originally commissioned by Sir William Deakin and Lord Bullock in the Oxford History of Modern Europe series, it was intended to stop in the early 1970s, when the post-Second World War era supposedly finished. But as the work proceeded, the end of the Cold War and the 1990s revealed a resurgent America, with a new taste for 'globalization' and a revitalized impulse to invent ways to project its power abroad. In Europe a 20th century pattern of three postwar experiences loomed into view, with America in all its forms at the heart of them. Clearly Europe's destiny and character could not and would not be separated from that of the USA.

To reflect on all this I began in 1989 to teach a course entitled 'America and the Politics of Modernization in Europe' at the Bologna Center of the Johns Hopkins University's School of Advanced International Studies. This was an institution dedicated to the study and practice of European-American relations that I first encountered in 1970 as a postgraduate student. But through the Center I also discovered Italy, its language, politics, and history—particularly in their highly distinctive Bolognese versions. There I developed a doctoral project on the politics of the Allied war in Italy, 1943–1945, which would bring me into contact with all the local memories of the World War II liberation process. The armies of sixteen nations had participated in the war in Italy, but like so many Italians, the locals only remembered the Americans, with their food and music, their cigarettes and films, their energy and optimistic attitudes about what was going to happen in the world when the war was over. It was a first discovery for me of what in the 1990s became theorised as the 'soft power' version of America's impact in Europe.

By the time I started teaching at the Johns Hopkins Bologna Center in 1979, a wave of distinguished historians and social scientists were working on themes such as 'Americanization', 'glocalization', 'the appropriation of America', 'anti-Americanism' etc. I became a friend and collaborator of some of the most important authors engaged in this exploration, the people listed in the Introduction. I took part in the research project run by Rob Kroes at the Netherlands Institute for Advanced Study in the Humanities and Social Sciences, in 1991–92 dedicated to 'the reception of American mass culture in Europe'.

Studies and conferences on this sort of topic flourished in the 1990s. Volumes of essays trickled out, such as the one edited by the late Alexander Stephan of Ohio State University, *The Americanization of Europe: Culture, Diplomacy and Anti-Americanism after 1945* (New York 2005). This book was the fruit of an important conference organised at the Rothermere America Institute of Oxford University in 2003. Thanks to the conference I discovered the resources of the small but extremely interesting library of the Institute. Chapter 6 of the text was produced thanks to a fellowship at the Institute in the spring of 2005, for which I remain very grateful.

The most fundamental support for the project came from the aforementioned Bologna Center of Johns Hopkins University, from my students and colleagues there, from its Directors—starting with Dr Stephen Low in 1989 down to the current office-holder, Prof. Kenneth Keller - and from its Academic Deans, particularly the late Patrick McCarthy and Erik Jones. This small but very lively community of study, teaching and dialogue, has supplied an indispensable framework for the entire project, and for this I will always be grateful. Its library became my library and the help of its key people crucial and indispensable. A special mention then for Gail Martin, the Library Director, her deputy John Williams, and Ludovica Barozzi.

The volume was written between Bologna, Turin and Edinburgh, starting in late 2001. It benefitted greatly from the extreme freedom of research and teaching that prevails in the School of Political Science of the University of Bologna, where I have taught for many years. But it also reflects the limits imposed by that version of the Italian system. With seven thesis examinations a year, plus six oral exam sessions involving at times scores of students, all set in the context of an academic year that in practice stretches from early September to late July, serious archival research is rarely possible. Sabbaticals are few and far between; one should never leave town.

The Introduction and/or the Conclusion have been read by many distinguished historians. It is a pleasure to pay special tribute to those who also read some of the chapters in between: John Harper, Mario Del Pero, James E.Miller, Geoffrey Warner, Stephen Gundle, Adrian Lyttelton, Tiziano Bonazzi, Anne Marie Le Gloannec, Susan Carruthers and Douglas Young. Professor Marilyn Young deserves a special word of thanks. A sojourn in the environs of the History Department of New York University, where she is Senior Professor, radically facilitated the construction of Chapter 10.Having read most of the other chapters too, her encouragement has been constant, her generosity of time and patience to myself and other colleagues in Europe proverbial.

A vast array of libraries supplied material for the book. Particular thanks go to the National Library of Scotland, Edinburgh University Library, the Bodleian Library of Oxford and that of Nuffield College. The library of the Luigi Einaudi Foundation in Turin also deserves recognition.

Oxford University Press has kept faith in this project over a stretch of time that is embarrassing to recall. Their confidence in it, and that of commissioning editors from Ivon Asquith down to Chris Wheeler, has been outstanding and a remarkable testimony to the commitment to learning, and the people who carry it on, which the Press demonstrates. The psychological support that OUP's belief in the book provided, even at times when evidence for it was extremely scarce, has been deeply appreciated. Latterly I have benefited greatly from the editorial support of Stephanie Ireland, who has seen the book all the way through the long production process and of Emma Barber, who took care of the final stages. Picture research was provided by Sheila Corr of *History Today* magazine. This effort, which turned out to be much trickier than expected, could not have been finished without Sheila's professionalism and dedication. Many thanks also to Jack Whitehead, for what must have been an arduous job of copy-editing.

Finally a special salute for my dear wife Stefana Levi of Turin, who has tirelessly followed the development of this text through all of its stages, including the most tormented (many chapters took a year or more to write). Her strength and patience have been remarkable, qualities tested at times to the limit but fortunately developed in a family with a very concrete intellectual tradition. An infinite embrace for her.

As ever, the responsibility for what precedes remains exclusively with the author of these words, not least because every attempt to shift it elsewhere has always failed miserably.

Bologna
February 2012

Index